iWork '09

THE MISSING MANUAL

The book that
should have been
in the box®

iWork '09

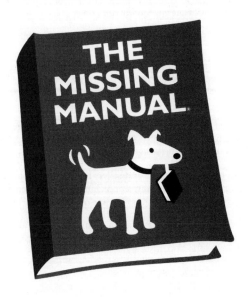

Josh Clark

POGUE PRESS™
O'REILLY®

Beijing • Cambridge • Farnham • Köln • Sebastopol • Taipei • Tokyo

iWork '09: The Missing Manual

by Josh Clark

Published by O'Reilly Media, Inc., 1005 Gravenstein Highway North, Sebastopol, CA 95472.

O'Reilly books may be purchased for educational, business, or sales promotional use. Online editions are also available for most titles (*safari.oreilly.com*). For more information, contact our corporate/institutional sales department: (800) 998-9938 or *corporate@oreilly.com*.

Printing History:

April 2009:   First Edition.

ISBN: 978-0-596-15758-6

[M]

Table of Contents

Part Three: Numbers '09

The Missing Credits

About the Author

Josh Clark is a writer, designer, and developer who helps creative people get clear of technical hassles to share their ideas with the world. When he's not writing about clever design and humane software, he's building it. Josh is the creator of Big Medium, friendly software that actually makes it fun to manage websites. In a previous life, Josh worked on a slew of national PBS programs at Boston's WGBH. He shared his three words of Russian with Mikhail Gorbachev, strolled the ranch with Nancy Reagan, and wrote trivia questions for a primetime game show. Now Josh makes words and spins code at his hypertext laboratory *www.globalmoxie.com* in Paris, France, where he lives with his wife Ellen. Josh welcomes your feedback at *jclark@globalmoxie.com* (but gently suggests steering requests for technical help to *www.apple.com/support*).

About the Creative Team

Jim Elferdink (author, previous edition) is the author of *AppleWorks 6: The Missing Manual* and *Office 2008 for Macintosh: The Missing Manual*. In former lifetimes he was a commercial photographer, carpenter, and cabinetmaker; currently he runs Macs for the Masses, a Macintosh consulting company in the redwoods of far northern California.

Peter Meyers (editor) is the managing editor of O'Reilly Media's Missing Manual series. He lives with his wife, daughter, and cats in New York City. Email: *meyers@oreilly.com*.

Dawn Frausto (copy editor/wrangler of copy editors and indexers) is assistant editor for the Missing Manual series. When not working, she plays soccer, beads, and causes trouble. Email: *dawn@oreilly.com*.

Nellie McKesson (production editor) lives in Brighton, Mass., where she makes t-shirts for her friends (*http://mattsaundersbynellie.etsy.com*) and plays music with her band Dr. & Mrs. Van Der Trampp (*http://myspace.com/drmrsvandertrampp*). Email: *nellie@oreilly.com*.

Nancy Reinhardt (copy editor) is a freelance copy editor living in the Midwest, who enjoys swimming, biking, and history. She is surrounded by electrical engineers and yet she is "...still fairly certain that given a cape, a wand, and nice tiara, she could save the world" (to quote Leigh Standley). Email:*reinhardt8@comcast.net*.

Carla Spoon (copy editor) is a freelance writer and copy editor. She works and feeds her tech gadget addiction from her home office in the shadow of Mount Rainier. Email: *carla_spoon@comcast.net*.

Ron Strauss (indexer) is a full-time freelance indexer specializing in IT. When not working, he moonlights as a concert violist and alternative medicine health consultant. Email: *rstrauss@mchsi.com*.

Mike Greenberg (technical reviewer) is a veteran Mac expert, and has been using the iWork suite since its first release back in 2005. He has been the technical reviewer for three iWork-related books (including this one). Mike has a degree in Visual Media from American University in Washington, DC, and lives in Santa Clara, California.

Christian Boyce (technical reviewer) is an Apple consultant with offices in Santa Monica, California and Round Rock, Texas.

Acknowledgments

When you're writing a book about iWork, it turns out that there's a lot more "we" than "i" involved, and I couldn't have done it without the help of many talented people. Special thanks to my friend and editor Peter Meyers whose contagious enthusiasm and keen attention to both style and substance kept this book (and its author) focused and friendly. The eagle eyes of technical editors Christian Boyce and Michael Greenberg saved me from myself time and again, spotting nitty-gritty errors and surfacing subtle features that would have otherwise gone unmentioned. This book is the first Missing Manual about iWork since *iWork '05: The Missing Manual* by Jim Elferdink. Many of Jim's words remain in this edition, for which I'm grateful, but I'm also indebted to Jim's good humor and plainspoken language, which inspired me to attempt the same in this edition. I'm also grateful to the many people who worked to get this book formatted, indexed, and printed: Thank you, Dawn Frausto, Nellie McKesson, Nancy Reinhardt, Carla Spoon, and Ron Strauss. Many thanks to Apple's Kirk Paulsen for giving up a few early-morning hours in Paris to explore the nooks, crannies, and deep dark secrets of iWork '09. Thanks also to Apple's Mark Elpers, Alan Hely, and Juriaan Bosman for their help along the way.

To show off iWork's stunning visual features, I relied on the equally stunning work of many photographers. Their names are listed in the Photo Credits section below, but I'd like to single out Jason Jerde, whose wryly dramatic photos of vintage action figures brought the Keynote slideshow examples to life. Most of the examples in this book follow the exploits of Up & Away, a general store for superheroes, which was inspired by the real-life Brooklyn Superhero Supply Co., whose racks of capes and canned light speed front the secret headquarters of 826NYC, a creative writing program for young people.

Thanks to the friends who fed, watered, and endured me through the writing of this book. Kristen, Rich, Colleen, Chris, Steve, and Rosy, thank you. Also, a big shout out to Global Moxie's customer community, who sent frequent messages of support and patiently waited for me to complete this project. Above all, I owe everything to Ellen, who weathered months of glassy stares and mad ramblings about spreadsheet functions and slideshow transitions. In return, she gave me far more support, encouragement, and affection than I possibly deserved.

—Josh

Photo Credits

Many photographers generously granted permission to use their photos in this book. Most share their work on the photo website Flickr and, where applicable, their Flickr accounts are listed in parentheses after their names. To see a photographer's recent photos online, browse to www.flickr.com/photos/NAME, replacing NAME with the photographer's account name (for example: *www.flickr.com/photos/joshclark*).

In addition to those taken by the author, the photos in this book are the work of: Carlos Afonso (otakubrasil); Bingo Jesus (bingojesus); Gustav Castañeda; Andrew Chipley (kenyaboy7); Margo Conner (margolove); Lee Cullivan (leecullivan); Eneas (eneas); Leo Getz (leogetz); James L. Gries (aye_shamus); Ran Yaniv Hartstein (ranh); Jason Jerde (tcmhitchhiker); Roger Lancefield (rlancefield); David Mathis of *eldavephoto.blogspot.com*; Peter McBreen; Stephen Monteiro (polarvoid); Brian Moore of *www.brianmooremedia.com*; Naitokz (naitokz); *www.FinancialAidPodcast.com* and *www.ChristopherSPenn.com*; Desmond Perrotto, San Francisco (champsf); Frederic Poirot (fredarmitage); Randy Robertson (randysonofrobert); Rafael Rubira, Jr. (rafaelrubira); ©2007 Kaz Shiozawa, *www.shiology.com*; Gerhard Singer (gerhard3); *www.zoomergear.com*; and Yonatan Zur (yonizur).

The Missing Manual Series

Missing Manuals are witty, superbly written guides to computer products that don't come with printed manuals (which is just about all of them). Each book features a handcrafted index; cross-references to specific pages (not just chapters); and RepKover, a detached-spine binding that lets the book lie perfectly flat without the assistance of weights or cinder blocks.

Recent and upcoming titles include:

Access 2007: The Missing Manual by Matthew MacDonald

AppleScript: The Missing Manual by Adam Goldstein

AppleWorks 6: The Missing Manual by Jim Elferdink and David Reynolds

CSS: The Missing Manual by David Sawyer McFarland

Creating Web Sites: The Missing Manual by Matthew MacDonald

David Pogue's Digital Photography: The Missing Manual by David Pogue

Dreamweaver 8: The Missing Manual by David Sawyer McFarland

Dreamweaver CS3: The Missing Manual by David Sawyer McFarland

Dreamweaver CS4: The Missing Manual by David Sawyer McFarland

eBay: The Missing Manual by Nancy Conner

Excel 2003: The Missing Manual by Matthew MacDonald

Excel 2007: The Missing Manual by Matthew MacDonald

Facebook: The Missing Manual by E.A. Vander Veer

FileMaker Pro 9: The Missing Manual by Geoff Coffey and Susan Prosser

FileMaker Pro 10: The Missing Manual by Geoff Coffey and Susan Prosser

Flash 8: The Missing Manual by E.A. Vander Veer

Flash CS3: The Missing Manual by E.A. Vander Veer and Chris Grover

Flash CS4: The Missing Manual by Chris Grover with E.A. Vander Veer

FrontPage 2003: The Missing Manual by Jessica Mantaro

Google Apps: The Missing Manual by Nancy Conner

The Internet: The Missing Manual by David Pogue and J.D. Biersdorfer

iMovie 6 & iDVD: The Missing Manual by David Pogue

iMovie '08 & iDVD: The Missing Manual by David Pogue

iMovie '09 & iDVD: The Missing Manual by David Pogue

iPhone: The Missing Manual by David Pogue

iPhoto '09: The Missing Manual by David Pogue and J.D. Biersdorfer

iPod: The Missing Manual, Seventh Edition by J.D. Biersdorfer

JavaScript: The Missing Manual by David Sawyer McFarland

Mac OS X: The Missing Manual, Tiger Edition by David Pogue

Mac OS X: The Missing Manual, Leopard Edition by David Pogue

Microsoft Project 2007: The Missing Manual by Bonnie Biafore

Office 2004 for Macintosh: The Missing Manual by Mark H. Walker and Franklin Tessler

Office 2007: The Missing Manual by Chris Grover, Matthew MacDonald, and E.A. Vander Veer

Office 2008 for Macintosh: The Missing Manual by Jim Elferdink

PCs: The Missing Manual by Andy Rathbone

Photoshop Elements 7: The Missing Manual by Barbara Brundage

Photoshop Elements 6 for Mac: The Missing Manual by Barbara Brundage

PowerPoint 2007: The Missing Manual by E.A. Vander Veer

QuickBase: The Missing Manual by Nancy Conner

QuickBooks 2008: The Missing Manual by Bonnie Biafore

Quicken 2008: The Missing Manual by Bonnie Biafore

QuickBooks 2009: The Missing Manual by Bonnie Biafore

Quicken 2009: The Missing Manual by Bonnie Biafore

Switching to the Mac: The Missing Manual, Tiger Edition by David Pogue and Adam Goldstein

Switching to the Mac: The Missing Manual, Leopard Edition by David Pogue

Wikipedia: The Missing Manual by John Broughton

Windows XP Home Edition: The Missing Manual, Second Edition by David Pogue

Windows XP Pro: The Missing Manual, Second Edition by David Pogue, Craig Zacker, and Linda Zacker

Windows Vista: The Missing Manual by David Pogue

Windows Vista for Starters: The Missing Manual by David Pogue

Word 2007: The Missing Manual by Chris Grover

Your Brain: The Missing Manual by Matthew MacDonald

Introduction

The words "productivity software" don't exactly make your skin tingle. Most of us use a word processor or spreadsheet program because we *have* to. It's how we get our day-to-day work done, pushing through the words and numbers that office, school, or household demands impose. What's to get excited about? Until recently, not much. For decades, word processors, spreadsheets, and presentation software have presented blandly efficient tools that solemnly transferred your work to page and screen. Bland gets the job done, it's true, but bland doesn't inspire. You and your ideas deserve an environment that's more stirring than that. Dreary work tools don't cut it.

An inspiring spreadsheet program? A rousing word processor? The concepts seem improbable—but as usual, Apple beats the odds. When the company unveiled its iWork collection of programs, Apple proved that doing serious work doesn't have to *feel* serious. The package includes Pages, Keynote, and Numbers: iWork's word processor, presentation software, and spreadsheet program, respectively. While familiar, all three are remarkably different than what came before.

All iWork programs put an unprecedented emphasis on the design and polish of your final documents, making it easy to create results that look not only professional, but actually stunning. It's like you've got an entire art department on the payroll—and in fact, that's not far from the truth. Pages, Keynote, and Numbers all come stacked high with prebuilt templates that you can put to use right away, letting the skill of Apple's talented designers shine through in your own work. Although the template concept isn't anything new in this category of software, the quality of design sets the bar at a whole new level.

But iWork is more than just a collection of paint-by-numbers templates. Pages, Keynote, and Numbers sport stylishly elegant interfaces whose airy flexibility give you plenty of room to work, rarely getting in your way. Apple designed the programs from the ground up to deliver high-impact visual documents, and all of them let you work with freestyle layouts that juggle photos and movies as well as they do words and numbers. The result: Pages turns the mild-mannered word processor into a graphic design program; Keynote's visual gymnastics make your Mac look like a Hollywood special effects studio (Al Gore even won an Oscar for *his* Keynote slideshow); and Numbers spreadsheets morph your gray columns and rows into dazzling multimedia reports.

When even your spreadsheets sparkle, it's hard not to feel energized about your work. This, of course, is Apple's strong suit. All the company's software is designed to help regular folks painlessly turn out sophisticated creations to rival the pros— from making music to editing movies to creating photo books. Apple has a certain magic for making powerful software approachable, and with iWork the results are so productive and satisfying that it becomes—and please, don't tell the boss— almost fun to get work done.

What You Can Do with iWork '09

You can use iWork to compose and design just about any kind of document. Although iWork's programs fall outside the traditional definitions of these categories, you use Pages for word processing, Keynote for making presentations, and Numbers for spreadsheets. Here's a brief tour of what awaits.

Pages: Word Processing Meets Graphic Design

When words are your game, Pages has you covered. As a *word processor,* Pages' most basic job is to make it easy to get words onto the screen and, once there, coax and refine them into irresistible prose for the printed page. Use Pages to write letters, pen the Great American Novel, draw up contracts, or write a term paper. The program gives you all the power-editing tools you're likely to need: spell checking, styles, footnotes, mail merge, change tracking, outlining, tables, and lots of other goodies.

But Pages has a whole separate career beyond word processing—the program moonlights as a graphic designer. Pages makes it almost embarrassingly easy to create gorgeous page layouts for glossy newsletters, catalogs, brochures, flyers, posters, greeting cards, you name it. Deck out any document with photos or graphics with drag-and-drop simplicity.

If you're blessed with a keen sense of style, you can use Pages' tools to build your own graphic designs from scratch; otherwise, lean on Pages' collection of more than 180 templates. Pick the design that you want to use and then drop in your own pictures and text, as easy as filling in the blanks. Just like that, *you're* the artsy designer (and you didn't even have to grow a goatee or buy a beret).

Keynote: Presentations with Gusto

Keynote is a *presentation program* for making slideshows, usually to accompany a talk or other live presentation. The program helps you build screens of text and graphics to illustrate important points as you roam the stage earning the awe and admiration of your audience. As you flip from slide to slide, Keynote shimmies and shakes with cinematic transitions, clever animations, and all the supporting razzle-dazzle that your presentation deserves.

More than just a pretty face, though, Keynote is also an elegantly simple program to use. There's an awful lot of complexity behind the scenes of the program's eye-popping effects, but Keynote modestly keeps the hard stuff to itself. For you, the presenter, the design process is always simple and straightforward. And like all iWork programs, Keynote gets you started with a big collection of themes that make your slides look great even when you don't use a single special effect. Whether subdued or noisy, your slideshow's design is always polished and consistent.

Numbers: Crunching Data with Style

Numbers is a *spreadsheet program,* tuned for organizing data and juggling numbers. The program has a special talent for math, of course—it eats balance sheets and financial models for breakfast. But like any spreadsheet program, Numbers can also put order to just about any kind of information. Use it for contact lists, team rosters, product inventories, invoices, or to-do lists. Once you've loaded up your data, Numbers can flip it every which way: sort it, filter it, categorize it, analyze it.

As usual with iWork programs, however, the thing that makes Numbers special is its remarkable talent for stylish design. Traditionally, formatting spreadsheets is an ugly, time-consuming process, and many people simply don't bother. With Numbers, however, it's easy—even addictive—to transform your data into a multimedia report by mixing your data tables with colorful charts, photos, and illustrations. The program's chart tools are especially dazzling, turning your stodgy figures into impressive infographics.

A Family Resemblance

From these descriptions, it might seem like the individual iWork programs do wildly different things, but it turns out that they're more similar than different. The resemblance starts with the interface, which iWork keeps clean and spare, avoiding a clutter of toolbars by relying on the incredibly useful Format Bar. All three programs feature this chameleon-like strip of menus and buttons, which changes its contents when you change the focus of your work, giving you a greatest-hits selection of commands that are most likely to be useful to you at any given moment. iWork also keeps things tidy by sweeping commands and controls into the Inspector window, a floating control panel of advanced settings.

iWork's integration goes much deeper than its toolbars. All three programs are on extremely friendly terms with the rest of the Apple software on your computer, a fact best illustrated by the super-handy Media Browser. This window, available in all three iWork programs, gives you an instant tunnel into your personal media ecosystem. Browse your iPhoto albums, iTunes playlists, or iMovie projects from Keynote, for example, to add pictures, music, or video to your slideshow with the click of a button. The programs similarly offer clever integration with Address Book, Mail, and iWeb.

While these niceties give similar *form* to Pages, Keynote, and Numbers, the programs have similar *functions,* too. Every iWork program works with the same raw materials—text, pictures, charts, shapes, tables, movies, sound—and offer the same icons and tools to manipulate them. Once you learn how to do it in one program, you know how to do it in all three: Page layout in Pages works like slide design in Keynote works like report layout in Numbers.

All iWork programs, in other words, have the same set of basic superpowers, but each program is more "super" at one particular aspect. Pages and Keynote both have the know-how to include spreadsheet tables, for example, but Numbers is designed for fast data entry and comfortable calculating. Likewise, both Keynote and Numbers can do page layout, but Pages makes it easier to create a design for the printed page. All of these similarities often make it feel more like you're using one program than three; for the newcomer, this has the happy benefit of making it easy to quickly get up to speed with all the programs at once.

In fact, the hardest part of using iWork may have nothing to do with using the programs themselves, but deciding which program is right for the job at hand, since they're all so versatile. And hey, speaking of which program to use…

How Does It Stack Up Against Microsoft Office?

Microsoft Office is, of course, the elephant in the room, the 800-pound gorilla, the lumbering wildebeest of the Serengeti. Word, PowerPoint, and Excel have dominated their respective fields for years as the business standards for word processing, presentation, and spreadsheet software. You'll find those programs in cubicles around the world. In most offices, you can't swing a senior VP without hitting a piece of Office software.

The question is whether that means *you* need it, too. Does iWork replace Microsoft Office? Your fearless author is bold enough to give you this clear and courageous answer: maybe, depending.

Of all the iWork programs, only Keynote surpasses its Microsoft counterpart in a feature-counting contest, beating PowerPoint in both tools and simplicity. Pages and Numbers simply can't match Word and Excel for their laundry lists of features. For the most part, though, iWork's "missing" capabilities are relatively esoteric power tools that most small businesses, educators, students, and home users won't miss. In exchange, you get an elegant, refined workspace that lets you churn out designed documents that would be a headache (and sometimes impossible) to create with Microsoft Office. However, if you're building a book index or need hyperlinked cross-references in a word processor, you'll miss Word. And if your spreadsheets tend to stray into tens of thousands of rows or rely on pivot tables or unusually sophisticated formula functions, then Numbers will disappoint you.

iWork's programs are still very young. Keynote was released in 2003, Pages in 2005, and Numbers in 2007—but even in that short span, all three have come a long way. The changes introduced by iWork '09 focus mainly on polish and power features, an indicator that the collection has already reached a certain level of maturity (they're a precocious set of programs). The feature gap between iWork and Microsoft Office continues to shrink.

But parity with Microsoft Office may not be Apple's goal. At heart, this suite of programs has a very different feel and approach. While iWork isn't the industrial-strength product that Microsoft Office is, it doesn't have Office's industrial flavor, either. Word and Excel offer a deep feature list, but that depth also contributes to a heavy interface and, often, a frustrating hunt for features that should be easy to find. By contrast, Pages and Numbers have a lighter, more flexible interface that's a pleasure to use. Along with superior attention to document design, this creative workspace is an overall advantage that you might appreciate more than any absent features. The bottom line: If you don't need those features, you won't miss them.

Whether or not *you* use Microsoft Office, it's crucial to be able to exchange files with people who do. The iWork programs can read and create Word, Excel, and PowerPoint files, and overall they do a good job at it. The book in your hands was written in Pages but exchanged back and forth between author and editors in Microsoft Word without a hitch.

There are occasional hitches, though, and this book details where you'll run into problems with your imports and exports (think macros, relatively esoteric Excel functions, and Office's inability to digest all of iWork's advanced visual stylings). In general, relatively simple files always make the transition from iWork to Office and back again no worse for wear. Go ahead and exchange files with your Microsoft-wielding colleagues with impunity.

What's New in iWork '09

iWork '09 introduces several new features that apply to all three programs:

- **iWork.com.** Apple's new Web-based service lets you share your Pages, Numbers, and Keynote documents online with invited guests. Although you can't edit the file online, you and your reviewers can browse and comment on it at iWork.com, which displays a pixel-perfect replica of your document right in your Web browser.

- **New themes and templates.** All three programs get a healthy update of new templates, giving you lots of slick new starter documents to work with.

- **New chart features.** iWork offers two new flavors of charts—two-axis charts and mixed charts—both of which let you display your data series in different styles (columns, areas, or lines) in the same chart. Error bars and trendlines are also available for the first time.

- **Enhanced Template Chooser and Theme Chooser.** You can now preview the contents of template files before you open them by skimming your cursor across each template's thumbnail image. The new choosers also remember the last template you used and let you open recent documents directly from the chooser window.

- **Font preview.** The Format Bar's font pop-up menu now lists each font in its own font face.

- **Password protection.** You can require a password to open any iWork file.

- **Connection lines.** Add flexible lines to point from one object to another.

- **Equation editing with MathType 6.** iWork doesn't have its own equation editor, but if you have the MathType program installed, you can now use it to add mathematical expressions to your iWork files.

- **Citations and bibliographies with EndNote X2.** EndNote is a program popular among researchers for creating a personal database of readings and sources. If you have the program installed, Pages can insert EndNote citations into your documents for footnotes and bibliographies.

- **Support for multitouch gestures.** Got a newish laptop with a multitouch trackpad? You can resize objects by "pinching" them on the trackpad, or rotate them by making a twisting motion.

New in Pages '09

- **Full-screen view.** Shut out distractions by drawing a virtual curtain behind your document window, handing your screen over to Pages for your exclusive attention.

- **Outline view.** Draft and browse your document by topic heading. Drag and drop headings to move entire sections of your document, or hide and reveal the text below.

- **Mail merge from Numbers.** Use the columns of any Numbers spreadsheet as a data source to print mass mailings or any bulk-generated document.

- **Live word counts.** The word count is always displayed at the bottom of the document window. (Pages used to show the count only in the Document Inspector.)

New in Keynote '09

- **Magic Move.** This new slide transition lets you gracefully animate an object from one slide to another while the rest fade away.

- **Text and Object transitions.** Instead of moving all of a slide's objects as a single unit, these new slide transitions animate every object individually, so you can make words from one slide morph into those on the next, for example.

- **New 3D chart effects.** New animations include the radial and crane effects, letting you fly, twist, and zoom into a chart. The Chart Colors window features new 3D textures and colors, too.

- **Keynote Remote.** Use your iPhone or iPod Touch to drive your slideshow.

New in Numbers '09

- **Over 90 new functions.** iWork now offers over 250 formula functions, including new Engineering and Duration categories.

- **Linked Numbers charts.** When you paste a Numbers chart into a Keynote or Pages document, iWork automatically creates a link to the original Numbers spreadsheet. When you update the Numbers data, you can refresh the chart in Keynote and Pages to slurp up the changes.

- **Table categories.** Group rows together based on shared column values to create table categories. Each category includes a summary row that lets you collapse, expand, or rearrange the categories and their included rows.

- **Freeze headers.** When the first row or column of your table scrolls off screen, the header labels stay behind, making it easy to keep track of which column is which.

- **Improved Formula Editor.** The Formula Editor now color-codes cell references and displays cells with their header names, making it easier to understand what formulas do at a glance. New keyboard shortcuts let you add cell references without using the mouse.

- **Improved Function Browser.** Every function gets a clear explanation, including copy-and-paste example cells. Adding a function from the Function Browser also inserts argument placeholders to help fill in your function variables.

- **New table cell formats.** Tables can now display numbers as durations (weeks, days, hours, and so on), numeral systems (binary or hexadecimal, for example), or your own custom format.

- **Formula List.** Display or print all the formulas in your spreadsheet.

- **Multiple header rows, header columns, and footer rows.** Go up to five cells deep.

File Format Follies

All three iWork '09 programs save their files in a new format that earlier versions don't understand. When you first go to save changes to a file created by a previous version of Pages, Keynote, or Numbers, iWork lets you know that the saved file will be readable only by iWork '09 and asks if you want to proceed. If you later change your mind, never fear: All the programs offer the option to save a copy as iWork '08. That option also comes in handy when you want to exchange files with lollygaggers who haven't yet updated to the latest and greatest. (Sorry, no options to save for versions earlier than iWork '08.)

Among other things, the big change in the new file format is that iWork no longer saves its files as *packages*. Under

the hood, a package is secretly a folder instead of a single file. This distinction, invisible to you as you browse your files, confused some programs and made it difficult to upload iWork '08 files to websites, for example. iWork '09 fixes that problem.

If you happen to fall into some category of extreme nerdery that gives you an irresistible urge to browse package contents, iWork lets you continue saving your files as packages. Each program has an option in its Preferences window to "Save new documents as packages". Turn that option on, and all freshly created files will get the pseudo-folder treatment. (If you have no idea what a package is, just leave that preference turned off.)

The Very Basics

You'll find very little jargon or nerdy terminology in this book. You will, however, encounter a few terms and concepts that you'll come across frequently in your computing life:

- **Clicking.** This book gives you three kinds of instructions that require you to use your computer's mouse or trackpad. To *click* means to point the arrow cursor at something on the screen and then—without moving the cursor at all—to press and release the clicker button on the mouse (or laptop trackpad). To *double-click*, of course, means to click twice in rapid succession, again without moving the cursor at all. And to *drag* means to move the cursor while holding the button continuously.

- **Keyboard shortcuts.** Every time you take your hand off the keyboard to move the mouse, you lose time and potentially disrupt your creative flow. That's why many experienced computer fans use keystroke combinations instead of menu commands wherever possible. ⌘-B, for example, is the keyboard shortcut for boldface type in iWork (and most other programs).

  When you see a shortcut like ⌘-S (which saves changes to the current document), it's telling you to hold down the ⌘ key, and, while it's down, type the letter S, and then release both keys.

- **Choice is good.** iWork frequently gives you several ways to trigger a particular command—a menu command, *or* by clicking a toolbar button, *or* by pressing a key combination, for example. Some people prefer the speed of keyboard shortcuts; others like the satisfaction of a visual command array available in menus or toolbars. This book lists all the alternatives, but by no means are you expected to memorize all of them.

About This Book

Despite the many improvements in software over the years, one feature has grown consistently worse: documentation. When you purchase most software programs these days, you don't get a single page of printed instructions. To learn about the hundreds of features in a program, you're expected to use online help, or download a manual from the company's website. (Apple offers PDF guides to all of the iWork programs; you can find them at *http://support.apple.com/manuals/#iwork*.)

But even if you're comfortable reading a help screen in one window as you try to work in another, something is still missing. At times, the terse electronic help screens assume you already understand the discussion at hand, and hurriedly skip over important topics that require an in-depth presentation. In addition, you don't always get an objective evaluation of the program's features. (Engineers often add technically sophisticated features to a program because they *can*, not because you need them.) You shouldn't have to waste time learning features that don't help you get your work done.

The purpose of this book, then, is to serve as the manual that should have been in the box. In this book's pages, you'll find step-by-step instructions for using every feature in Pages, Keynote, and Numbers. Because many features appear in all three programs, some features get in-depth treatment for one program but not another; when that's the case, the book always points you to the page where you'll find the full scoop. In addition, you'll always find clear evaluations of each feature to help you determine which ones are useful to you, as well as how and when to use them. Shortcuts and workarounds save you time and headaches, and you'll even unearth features that the online help doesn't mention.

Beyond just the mechanical aspects of using iWork, however, this book also gives you practical aesthetic advice about document design and presentation. Pages, Keynote, and Numbers give you amazing technical tools to create luxurious layouts—or shoot yourself in the foot. This book helps keep the lead out of your sneakers with simple, good-natured tips for planning and preparing your document layout, based on tried-and-true principles of graphic design. Similarly, the Keynote section offers tips for building a presentation that won't turn into a snoozefest, helping you use Keynote to add spark to your talk without turning your slideshow into a crutch.

Throughout this book, you'll find carefully constructed sample documents showing how to put iWork's tools to best effect and, hopefully, provide a hint of inspiration for your own work. Most of these documents follow the adventures of a company called Up & Away, Megaville's leading superhero outfitter, where no task is impossible and every cape fits perfectly. You, of course, are the hero of this particular story, and well before the end of this book you will have discovered your superpower: an unwavering ability to create spectacular documents.

iWork '09: The Missing Manual is designed to accommodate readers of every technical level. The primary discussions are written for advanced-beginner or intermediate computer users. But if you're a first-timer, special sidebar articles called "Up to Speed" provide the introductory information you need to understand the topic at hand. If you're an advanced user, on the other hand, keep your eye out for similar shaded boxes called Power Users' Clinics. They offer more technical tips, tricks, and shortcuts for the experienced computer fan.

About → These → Arrows

In this book, and throughout the Missing Manual series, you'll find sentences like this one: "Open the System Folder → Libraries → Fonts folder." That's shorthand for a much longer set of instructions that direct you to open three nested folders in sequence, like this: "On your hard drive, you'll find a folder called System. Open that. Inside the System folder window is a folder called Libraries. Open that. Inside *that* folder is yet another one called Fonts. Double-click to open it, too."

Similarly, this kind of arrow shorthand helps to simplify the business of choosing commands in menus. The instruction, "Choose Insert → Text Box" means, "Open the Insert Menu and then choose the Text Box command."

About MissingManuals.com

At *www.missingmanuals.com*, you'll find articles, tips, and updates to *iWork '09: The Missing Manual*. In fact, we invite and encourage you to submit such corrections and updates yourself. In an effort to keep this book as up to date and accurate as possible, each time we print more copies, we'll make any confirmed corrections you've suggested. We'll also note such changes on the website, so that you can mark important corrections into your own copy of the book, if you like. (Go to *http://missingmanuals.com/feedback*, choose the book's name from the pop-up menu, and then click Go to see the changes.)

Also on our Feedback page, you can get expert answers to questions that come to you while reading this book, write a book review, and find groups for folks who share your interest in iWork.

While you're there, sign up for our free email newsletter (click the "Sign Up for Our Newsletter" link in the left-hand column). You'll find out what's happening in Missing Manual land, meet the authors and editors, see bonus video and book excerpts, and so on.

We'd love to hear your suggestions for new books in the Missing Manual line. There's a place for that on missingmanuals.com, too. And while you're online, you can also register this book at *www.oreilly.com* (you can jump directly to the registration page by going here: *http://tinyurl.com/yo82k3*). Registering means we can send you updates about this book, and you'll be eligible for special offers like discounts on future editions of *iWork '09: The Missing Manual*.

Safari® Books Online

 When you see a Safari® Books Online icon on the cover of your favorite technology book, that means the book is available online through the O'Reilly Network Safari Bookshelf.

Safari offers a solution that's better than e-Books. It's a virtual library that lets you easily search thousands of top tech books, cut and paste code samples, download chapters, and find quick answers when you nee the most accurate, current information. Try it free at *http://mysafaribooksonline.com*.

Part One: Pages '09

1

Creating a Pages Document

Most of us think of a word processor as a glorified typewriter, a simple way to organize ideas and arguments for the printed page. You craft words into paragraphs, juggle them, refine them, and you're done. Tap, tap, tap. Print.

Pages goes a big step further, making it easy not only to *compose* your documents, but to *design* them, too. Whether you're publishing a glossy newsletter or just writing a thank-you note to Aunt Peg, Pages lets you grace your documents with the visual polish your words deserve.

This chapter takes you on a quick tour of your new word-processing digs, helping you find your way around Pages' well-appointed interface. You'll jump right into creating your own basic documents with some simple projects that highlight Pages' main features.

Two Programs in One

For all its emphasis on creating gorgeous documents, Pages recognizes that writing is a very different activity than page layout. Pages offers one mode for text-intensive projects, and another for creating more extravagant multimedia designs, as shown in Figure 1-1. This gives Pages an unusual but highly functional split personality: Pages is essentially two programs in one, and when you fire up a new document, you choose the one you prefer for the job at hand.

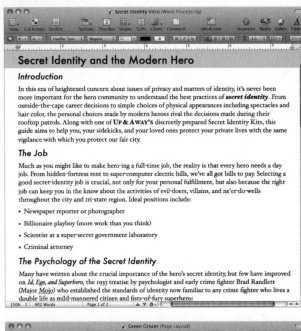

Figure 1-1:
Pages gives you two different modes to work in.

Top: Word-processing mode puts the focus on your words, for text-intensive projects.

Bottom: Page-layout mode lets you juggle complex designs, combining text and graphics into stunning results.

Meet Pages, the Word Processor

Pages' workhorse word processor puts your text in the spotlight, providing an uncluttered workspace where you can get your thoughts onscreen with a minimum of fuss. Pages doesn't reinvent the wheel here; if you've ever used a word processor before, this will feel familiar. Here the program gives you one big text area where you type a single, continuous chunk of text, adjusting font styles and formatting as you go. The word processor gives you plenty of options to augment your text with images, tables, and charts, but the emphasis remains on your words. From quick to-do lists to opus-length manuscripts, the text itself is the main (and often only) design element in these babies.

Pages supports your writing with a slew of helpful tools like spell checking, outlining, and change tracking, but Apple's word processor still does not have every last feature that you'll find over at the competition. If you've been a Microsoft Word power user in a past life, you may eventually notice some missing features like macros, index building, "word art," and so on. There's a silver lining here: What Pages might lose in skipping this kitchen-sink litany of features it gains back with a light, streamlined environment. As you get acquainted with Pages, you'll find that its slender diet of toolbars and other "window chrome" helps you stay focused on actually getting stuff done. This focus is where the Pages word processor shines.

But where Pages really departs from other programs is in its other half, the word processor's alter ego....

Meet Pages, the Page-Layout Program

Persuasion sometimes requires more than words, and Pages lets you deck out your work with photos, graphics, charts—even movies and music. In page-layout mode, you design your document one page at a time, using lots of smaller elements instead of editing a single monolithic block of text. You shuttle text boxes and graphics around the page, setting your design like a graphic artist pasting up a canvas in a less digital era. Sophisticated multipage projects like newsletters, catalogs, magazines, or brochures become a matter of drag and drop. Built-in image-editing tools make graphical single-page layouts like posters, flyers, or invitations a snap.

Choose Your Weapon

When you launch Pages, the program prompts you to choose either a word-processing template (see page 19) or a page-layout template (see page 26), and you're off. But you can't have it both ways. When you create a new file, you pick one format or the other, and you can't switch between the two modes. Once a word-processing document, always a word-processing document; ditto for page layout.

This isn't quite as Draconian as it sounds. Both document types are part of the same program, after all, and it turns out they share many of the same features. As you'll discover in the coming chapters, you can include page-layout elements in word-processing documents, and you can do word processing in page-layout documents. It's not all or nothing, but rather a matter of emphasis: Does your new document focus on developing a single work of text (word processing), or does it involve the page-by-page layout of several design elements (page layout). Table 1-1 offers some examples.

Table 1-1. *Pages document examples*

Word-processing documents	Page-layout documents
Letters	Flyers and posters
Research papers	Newsletters
Book chapters	Business cards
Résumés	Brochures
Invoices	Magazines
Screenplays	Catalogs
Contracts	Cards and invitations

Using Templates for Ready-to-Go Documents

Don't let all this talk about document design make you nervous. If you were out shopping for plaid pants the day they handed out aesthetic sensibility, it's OK. The style sense of Apple's professional designers is now ready to help. They've stocked the pantry to overflowing with a delicious array of over 180 *templates,* preformatted documents that can give you a tastefully elegant design right from the get-go.

As soon as you launch Pages, the program greets you with the Template Chooser (Figure 1-2), a document smorgasbord with a left-hand menu divided neatly into categories for both word-processing and page-layout documents. Here you can choose to start your creation from scratch with a blank page (choose a template from one of the Blank categories) or use one of the starter documents (choose any of the other templates).

To help you make your choice, the Template Chooser shows miniature previews, or *thumbnails,* of the design for each document template. Many of these templates, especially in the Page Layout category, contain several page design options, and you can quickly leaf through all of them by "skimming" your mouse pointer across the face of the template thumbnail. (Don't click the thumbnail; just point to it.) As you move your cursor, Pages flips through the template's layouts. Need a closer look before you can commit? Nudge the slider at the bottom of the Template Chooser to the right to make the thumbnails larger; move it to the left to make 'em smaller and fit more into the window at once. Double-click a thumbnail when you've made your choice, or click the thumbnail once to select it and then click Choose.

Pages responds by opening a new document window based on your chosen template and gives it the name "Untitled." In addition to offering you lots of design options, these templates are built to last. When you choose a template, Pages actually opens a carbon copy of the original; you're not editing the actual template itself. That way, you can work on your copy, safe in the knowledge that the blueprint is locked away—unmodified—ready for the next time you need it. (You *can* modify templates if you really need to, and you can create more templates of your own, too. For all the ins and outs of template creation and manipulation, see Chapter 10.)

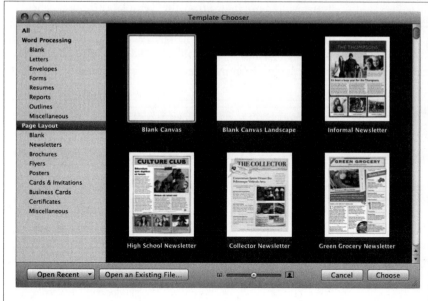

Figure 1-2:
To browse the available templates, click a category from the window's left pane, (choose "All" to view the entire collection). Use the scroll bar on the right side of the window to scan through previews of the templates in the selected category. Flip through a template's layouts by moving the pointer across its thumbnail image. To open an existing document instead of creating a new one, make a selection from the Open Recent pop-up menu, or click the Open an Existing File button (page 35).

Tip: Got buyer's remorse? If you're not crazy about your template choice after seeing it at full size, you can throw it back and start over by closing the window (click the red Close button in the upper-left corner of the document window) and opening a new document: Choose File → New or File → New from Template Chooser.

If you just want to shoot off a quick letter, shopping list, or note, choose the Word Processing category's Blank template and start typing away. Save, print, and you're done. But where's the fun in that? Apple's gone to the trouble of giving you a wide selection of carefully designed templates. The following sections explore how to put those templates to good use right away, making it fast and easy to create great-looking documents.

These quick-start introductions provide a high-level overview of Pages' key features to get you working right away, but don't fret: You'll get acquainted with the program's nuts and bolts in the following chapters.

Your First Word-Processing Document

Uh-oh, you've got an inventory problem at the warehouse, and an urgent order for one of your best customers is going to be late. Time to dash off an apologetic letter to break the bad news and smooth things over. At least Pages will help you to do it in style.

Launch Pages, and choose your template: From the Template Chooser, click the Letters category under Word Processing, and select your preferred template in the right pane. For this example, choose Modern Letter. Pages fills your new document window with the template design, including a few paragraphs of dummy text, ready to be replaced with your own mellifluous prose, as shown in Figure 1-3.

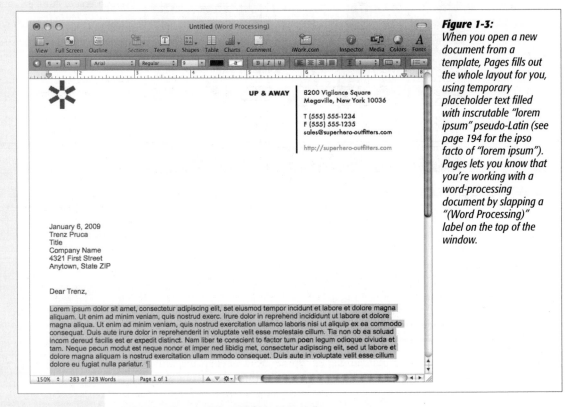

Figure 1-3:
When you open a new document from a template, Pages fills out the whole layout for you, using temporary placeholder text filled with inscrutable "lorem ipsum" pseudo-Latin (see page 194 for the ipso facto of "lorem ipsum"). Pages lets you know that you're working with a word-processing document by slapping a "(Word Processing)" label on the top of the window.

Integration with Address Book

Pages is even smart enough to go ahead and address the letter from you. This info comes straight from your Mac's Address Book program, where Pages looks up your contact info and plucks out your work address—assuming you've entered it. (Some of the other letter templates prefer your home address; this particular business template assumes you're at the office. See page 167 to find out how to swap your home and work info.)

Pages' letter templates include *merge fields,* smart placeholders for sender and recipient address info which—you guessed it—*merge* info from Address Book into your letter. Sure enough, you can use Address Book to grab your customer's contact info, too: Launch Address Book, find your customer, and drag the address card into your document as shown in Figure 1-4. Presto! The name, address, and even the salutation fill in automatically.

Tip: When you drag the address card, be sure to drag it sideways out of Address Book. If you drag up or down, you'll only highlight other address cards. Also, don't worry: Dragging a card out of Address Book doesn't remove it from your little black book; you're simply copying the card's info into your Pages document.

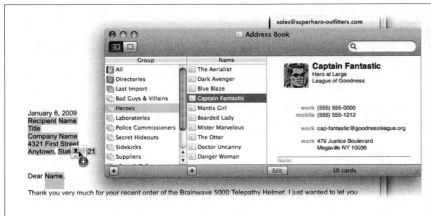

Figure 1-4:
Drop an address card into your document to update the address. In letter templates, there are two sets of merge fields—one for the recipient and one for the sender—and Pages usually plunks the new info into the recipient's fields. If you want to replace the sender's address instead, drag the card directly on top of a sender field. Pages highlights all the info that will be updated and, when you drop the address card, updates the info in one fell swoop.

If you don't have your dear customer in your address book—or if his address card doesn't include info for some of the Address Book fields in the document—you'll wind up with unfilled fields in your letter. You can just delete these stragglers, or replace them by clicking each one and typing them manually.

Tip: If you're going to the trouble of typing this info, though, you may as well do it directly in Address Book; by updating your customer's card now, you'll have instant access to his details for your next letter. Fill out your customer's address card with his latest info and then drag the card into the document to let Pages fill in the address for you.

This Address Book magic isn't limited to documents created from templates. You can add merge fields to your own custom documents and even use Address Book or a Numbers spreadsheet to automate mass mailings to large groups. For details, see page 165.

Note: Using Address Book to fill in addresses doesn't create an automatic link between your letter and your address book. If you update your customer's info in Address Book later, you'll need to come back to Pages and update your letter separately.

With your addresses taken care of, Pages frees you to focus on the main task: the letter to your customer.

How Does Pages Know Where I Live?

Way back when you first set up your computer, you gave your Mac a few nuggets of contact info, and it stowed those details in Address Book, your digital Rolodex. This program, which you can find in your Applications folder, organizes your contacts into address cards, and it gives special treatment to the card holding your own contact info so that Pages and other programs can fetch your details automatically.

Having your contact info at hand turns out to be a huge timesaver with Pages' letter templates, but also in programs like Safari, which uses your Address Book card to fill in web forms for you, for example. Save yourself a few thousand keystrokes and take a moment to make sure your contact details are up-to-date: Launch Address Book and choose Card → Go to My Card. If that's not the card you want to use, select a different card and choose Card → Make This My Card.

In Your Own Words

Pages' templates include *placeholder text* to show where you should type the body of your letter within the template's layout. Just click anywhere in the placeholder text and Pages highlights the entire text block. Start typing, and the block disappears to be replaced with your new text. You're off and running.

The next chapter digs into all the nitty-gritty options for editing and formatting text. For now, we'll keep it simple. If you've ever used a computer before, you already know how this works: Click to place the insertion point where you want to add or delete text. Type the text of your letter, and as you reach the end of each line, Pages automatically takes care of the line breaks for you—there's no need to press Return like you would on a typewriter (reserve the Return key for starting a new paragraph or adding a blank line).

When your text grows too long to fit on a single page, Pages automatically adds another page, jumping your text over to the next sheet automatically. Use the vertical scroll bar on the right side of the window to move up and down through the text, as you would in any computer program (for more on document navigation, see page 44).

Save and Print

When you're ready, save the document so you can come back later and continue working on it:

1. **Choose File → Save or press ⌘-S.**

   The Save dialog box appears (Figure 1-5).

2. **Type a title for the document in the Save As box.**

   This box is already highlighted, so you can just start typing. Click the Where pop-up menu and choose Documents (if it doesn't already say Documents) to store this Pages file in your Documents folder.

The Case of the Clever Cursor

As you use Pages, you'll see the cursor morph into new shapes as it moves around your document—don't let it throw you. For such a tiny thing, your mouse pointer is surprisingly intelligent, changing appearance in response to what's under it.

When there's no document open, the cursor maintains its traditional arrow-pointer shape. When it's positioned over something you've typed in Pages, however, the pointer changes into an *I-beam cursor*—so called due to its resemblance to the cross-section of a steel I-beam. The cursor is shaped this way so that you can precisely position it between two letters in a line of text. When you then click the mouse, the blinking *insertion point* jumps to that spot, so you can add or delete at that point.

When you start typing, the cursor *disappears*, leaving only the blinking insertion point. Pages makes the cursor invisible when you're actually typing so that it's not distracting.

IF you move the mouse a fraction of an inch, however, the cursor reappears. (This distinction between I-beam cursor and insertion point challenges beginners. Many folks feel compelled to carefully position the I-beam cursor *over* the insertion point before typing—a pointless effort.)

As soon as you move the I-beam cursor beyond a text-editing area, it resumes its arrow shape, ready to manipulate scroll bars, buttons, or menus.

In Pages, cursor transformation has yet another dimension: The arrow pointer sprouts a big green plus sign when dragging addresses, photos, music, or movies into your document, and takes on a variety of double-headed arrow shapes when manipulating objects.

As you get acquainted with Pages, pay attention to your clever cursor: It's giving you constant hints for what you can do with whatever you're pointing at.

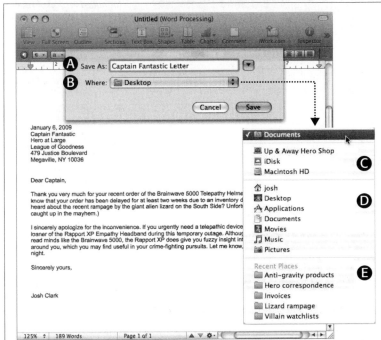

Figure 1-5:
The most important parts of the Save dialog box are (A) Save As, which is where you create the name for your document, and (B) Where, which indicates where your file will be saved. In its compact view, the Save dialog box shows only those two items. The Where pop-up menu lists (C) your computer's drives and disks, (D) your sidebar items, and (E) recently used folders. If you want to navigate elsewhere on your computer or network, click the downward-pointing triangle to the right of the Save As box, as shown in Figure 1-6.

3. **Click Save.**

The Save dialog box retracts, and Pages stores your document on your computer's hard drive. You can continue to work on your letter, periodically choosing File → Save (or, more quickly, ⌘-S) to update the saved file with any changes.

Tip: Save often! Pages doesn't offer an option to save your document automatically for you, so it's a good habit to save your document every few minutes, just in case. To find out how to make Pages create an additional backup of your document when you save, check out page 59.

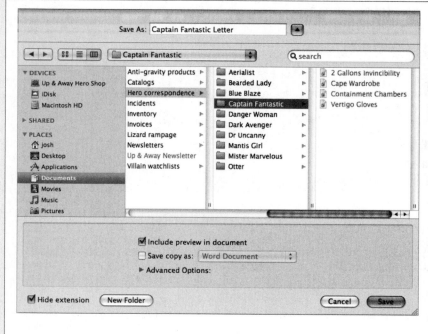

Figure 1-6:
The Save dialog box in its full glory gives you access to locations not listed in its compact version. You can navigate through your entire computer, your iDisk, or other computers on your network to find the perfect destination.

Turn on the "Include preview in document" option to let yourself and others browse a fully formatted version of your document directly from your desktop, using Mac OS X's Quick Look feature. Turn on the "Save copy as" option to save your document in Word or iWork '08 format (see page 326). The Advanced Options features let you reduce the file size of documents loaded with images and movies (see pages 240 and 248).

Print your document when you're ready to commit your correspondence to paper and send it on its way to your customer:

1. **Choose File → Print or press ⌘-P.**

   The Print dialog box appears.

2. **Type the number of copies you need in the Copies box.**

   If you just want one copy, no need to make any changes. If you don't see a Copies field in the Print dialog box, click the blue downward arrow next to the printer name to expand the window to its full view.

3. **Click Print.**

Your printer starts whirring and chirping and, in short order, delivers the hard copy.

Now that you're done writing your letter, you can close its document window. Click the red Close button in the upper-left corner of the window. If Pages asks if you want to save your changes, click Save. Your letter vanishes from the screen but remains safe on your hard drive, ready to be reopened if you ever want to review it.

Other Word-Processing Document Types

Back in the Template Chooser, you saw several document categories listed under Word Processing. In addition to letters, Pages offers you envelopes, forms, résumés, reports, and miscellaneous documents. A bit of casual browsing turns up many stationery templates with similar names, indicating that they belong to the same design "family." For instance, the example above used the Modern Letter template; Pages also offers Modern Envelope, Modern Résumé, Modern Outline, and Modern Business Card templates, all using styles that complement those in your letter. When you use templates from the same family for your various documents, Pages makes it easy for you to create visual consistency in your communications.

To make an envelope for your letter, for example, choose File → New from Template Chooser, and select Modern Envelope from the Envelopes category. The envelope opens in a new document window (Figure 1-7). Like your letter, it already sports your address as the sender. Using Address Book (page 20), just drag your customer's address card into the window, and you're ready to print.

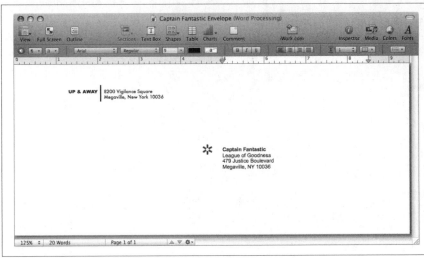

Figure 1-7:
Pages' envelope templates come preformatted to the correct size for business envelopes. Just add the address where you're sending your letter. Print it, and you're done.

Your First Page-Layout Document

Handy as it might be to have some prefab layouts for simple documents like letters and envelopes, Pages templates really shine in projects requiring more lavish layouts. The Newsletters category of page-layout templates, for example, offers a particularly rich collection of starter documents to create your own news bulletin.

Here's an example newsletter project to tackle: Up & Away is Megaville's leading outfitter for superheroes, providing essential gear (capes, utility belts, jet packs) and services (secret-identity counseling, sidekick placement, tights repair) to the city's crime fighters. The shop's quarterly newsletter features new items for sale as well as how-to articles and features about trends in the caped community. As editor, your superpower is newsletter design, and Pages is your secret weapon.

Launch Pages and, in the Template Chooser, click the Newsletters category under Page Layout; select your preferred template in the right pane. For this example, choose Extreme Newsletter; Pages fills your document window with a colorful full-page newsletter layout (Figure 1-8).

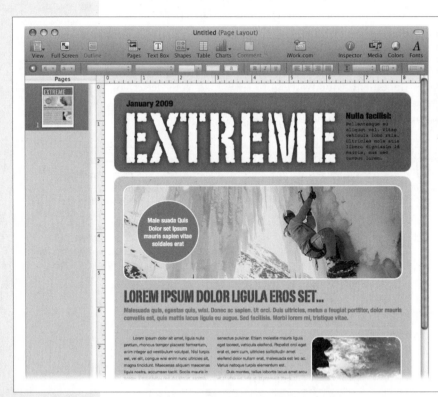

Figure 1-8:
Page-layout documents feature lots of design elements, including text boxes, photos, and fields of color—quite a departure from traditional word-processing documents with a single primary text area.

As with the letter template you saw earlier, your new document includes placeholder text waiting to be replaced with your own words. This time, though, the page also includes sample pictures, called *media placeholders,* which you can swap out with your own photos or graphics. Also, while your letter consisted of a single body of text which filled the document window, this page-layout document has several *text boxes,* individual snippets of text carefully placed around the page.

Working with Text Boxes

With word-processing documents like a letter, you always have a single primary area for prose—the window itself is one big text area and you simply click in the document window and type. With page-layout documents like a newsletter, however, there's no main text. Instead, the document is composed of a collection of design elements called *objects:* text, shapes, images, movies, and even sound. Each object is contained in its own little box which you can drag, resize, and layer inside the document. At the most basic level, working with a page-layout document is all about arranging these boxes into a balanced composition and filling them with words and pictures.

Chapters 6 and 7 explore the ins and outs of page layout and working with objects. For now, though, your newsletter template has given you a head start by providing a layout prestocked with objects. All that remains is to fill in your content.

Selecting and editing text

To edit any text on the page, just click it. Clicking once selects the containing text box, which lets you work with the entire text block at once, as shown in Figure 1-9. Clicking the text box a second time lets you type and edit the text inside. For text boxes containing a template's placeholder text, Pages highlights the entire text block when you click, and typing new text replaces the whole shebang. Give it a try:

1. **Give your newsletter a title.**

    Click the title, "EXTREME," to select it, and replace it with the name of your newsletter, *Up & Away*. Pages automatically displays your text in the same font and all-caps style. Whoops! It doesn't fit—time to make the text smaller: Click to place the insertion point inside the title and choose Edit → Select All to highlight the text. Keep tapping ⌘-- (that's ⌘-hyphen) to shrink the text until it fits.

2. **Replace the text above the title.**

    Click the text and type, *Outfitting Superheroes Since 1963*.

3. **Replace the right-column caption.**

    The text box to the right of the title contains a headline and caption text. Each section of text acts as separate placeholder text. Double-click the headline and type, *In this edition*. Now click the caption text and type in your own heroic text.

You get the idea. Just go through all the text boxes on the page and replace the template text with your own. With the text in place, you're ready to add some eye-popping imagery.

Note: If you run out of space in a text box but keep pouring in more words, Pages snips the overflow and shows you a + symbol at the bottom of the text box. That's the *clipping indicator,* which lets you know that there's more text waiting in the wings. You'll learn how to liberate this missing text on page 31.

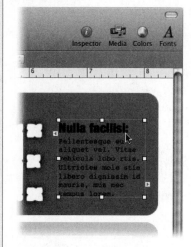

Figure 1-9:
Clicking once on a text box selects the entire text box, allowing you to drag it to a new location or resize it by grabbing one of the eight square handles on the box around the selection. Click again inside the text to edit it, and click anywhere outside the box to deselect it. For more about selecting and editing text boxes, see page 216.

Adding Pictures from iPhoto

Nearly all the page-layout templates contain placeholder images that you can replace with your own pictures (Figure 1-10).

Figure 1-10:
Media placeholders reveal themselves when you point to them, prompting you to replace them by dragging your own pictures into place. When you drop a new picture on top of the placeholder, Pages tugs and squeezes it into just the right size so that it still fits the layout. You can drag pictures onto the placeholder from your desktop or directly from your iPhoto collection via the Media Browser.

Say that you want to feature an article about the safety considerations of X-ray vision, and you've decided to add a photo of super goggles to the front page of your newsletter. You know that you already have the perfect picture in your iPhoto library, and happily, all the iWork programs make it easy to slurp pictures from iPhoto straight into your documents:

1. **Click the Media button on the toolbar.**

   Pages pops up the Media Browser, the window into your computer's collections of audio, photos, and movies, as shown in Figure 1-11.

Figure 1-11:
The Media Browser is a window into your computer's collections of audio, photos, and movies. The Photos tab gathers your personal photo collections from iPhoto, Photo Booth, and—if you have it—Aperture. In the top pane, click the arrow to the left of iPhoto to expand the display to show all your photo albums and events, and select the album to browse. You can also search the selected album by typing a word or phrase into the search field at the bottom of the Media Browser. The magnifying-glass pop-up menu lets you fine-tune your iPhoto collections search by using keywords, descriptions, and ratings.

2. **Choose your photo.**

   Select the thumbnail preview of the photo you want to use from the Media Browser.

3. **Drag the photo into your document window and drop it onto the placeholder image.**

   Pages replaces the placeholder image with your photo, automatically resizing it to fit the placeholder's dimensions.

Tip: If you don't like the first photo you choose, then try, try again. The image keeps its placeholder powers even after you add a new picture. Just drag another photo onto the placeholder, and Pages performs its placeholder squeezery again, formatting the new picture to fit the layout.

Coping with snipped images

When you exchange a placeholder image with your own picture, Pages pulls and squeezes the picture into the right size, hiding parts of the image that don't quite fit, as shown in Figure 1-12.

Figure 1-12:
Pages sliced off the top and bottom of the photo to fit the placeholder's horizontal layout.

Never fear, the missing bits of the photo aren't gone for good; they're just hidden by a *mask*. You use masks to crop pictures in iWork. Think of a mask as a cover with a window where part of the image peeks through. You can adjust the size of the mask's window and also slide or resize the picture under the mask to control the exact portion of the picture you want to show.

Time to unmask our masked man. Figure 1-13 shows how Pages' mask-editing features gives you your own X-ray vision to work with the hidden portion of the image. To edit the mask, click the photo once to reveal the Edit Mask controls and then click the Edit Mask button. Pages reveals the entire photo, with the hidden parts of the image dimmed and transparent so that you can see what's masked and what's not.

When you're done editing the mask, hit Return, or click anywhere outside of the image, and Pages shows you the final result. For complete details about adding, editing, and removing image masks, see page 230.

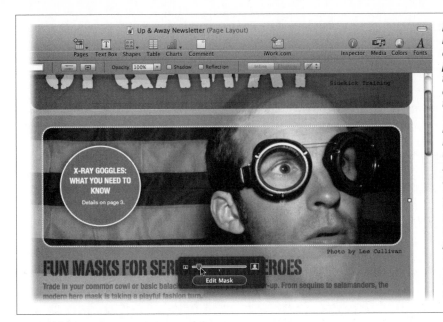

Figure 1-13:
*Editing a mask lets you
change which part of the
picture to reveal. Zoom
the image in or out by
dragging the slider above
the Edit Mask button.
When you point to the
image, the cursor turns
into a hand, which you
can use to drag the
image to a new position
behind the mask. (When
you're not in mask-
editing mode, dragging
the picture moves the
whole thing to a new
position on the canvas; if
that happens, choose Edit
→ Undo, click the Edit
Mask button, and
try again.)*

Adding Pages and New Layouts

After you've finished updating the first page of your newsletter with your own text
and photos, you're ready to add more pages. In word-processing documents, when
you hit the bottom of a page, Pages just gives you a new one and bumps you over
to the top of the fresh page automatically. Page-layout documents are a bit fussier:
You have to add new pages manually and give Pages some hints about how you
want to handle text that doesn't fit on the page.

To add a new page, click the Pages button in the toolbar, or choose Insert → Pages.
A pop-up menu appears, offering previews of all your template's *template pages,* its
prefab collection of page layouts (Figure 1-14). Choose the template page you want
to use for your new page.

Continuing text from a previous page

If your feature about the changing fashions in superhero cowls and masks is longer
than space allows on the first page, you can continue it in a new text box on
another page. Pages lets you know that your text box is bursting with copy by flipping on the *clipping indicator,* a "plus" sign at the bottom of the text box, which
tells you that the box contains more text than it can display. You can fix that by
linking your overstuffed text box to another text box, as shown in Figure 1-15.
Instead of unceremoniously lopping off the text, Pages flows the text into the second
text box. Here's how you do it:

1. **Click the first text box.**

   When you select a text box, blue arrows appear at the top left and bottom right
   of the box.

Figure 1-14:
The Pages pop-up menu displays all the preformatted layouts in your template, giving you lots of options to change up the look of each of your pages. Menu mavens can find the same options in the Insert → Pages submenu.

The Pages pop-up menu and submenu are available only in page-layout documents. (Word-processing documents offer a similar set of options, but the menu is labeled Sections instead of Pages.)

2. **Click the text box's lower-right arrow.**

   Pages shows a message prompting you to click the other text box you want to link *to*.

3. **Click the other text box (or press Escape to cancel).**

   Pages indicates that you've linked the two text boxes by connecting them with a line, as shown in Figure 1-15, bottom.

Note: You don't have to wait until a text box is full to link it to another one—you can string together your text boxes anytime you like. If you know in advance that you're going to need more space, you can go ahead and link up your layout beforehand. For more about linking text boxes, see page 218.

One page at a time

And so it goes: Keep adding pages, choosing the layouts that match your needs and filling them in with your photos of anti-gravity boots, ads for secret-fortress rentals, and your promotion for spray-on invisibility ("Now in fresh floral scents!").

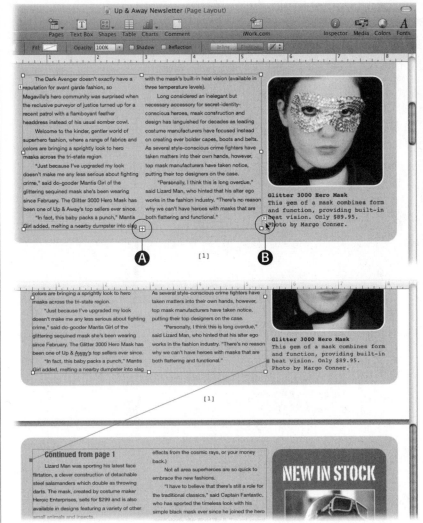

Figure 1-15:
Linking text boxes lets you jump your text from one place to another in your document.

Top: Pages displays the plus-sign clipping indicator (A) at the bottom of text boxes that contain more content than they can display. To flow the content into another text box, click the arrow in the lower right (B) and then click a second text box.

Bottom: After you select the second text box, Pages shows the connection by drawing a line between them. Text from the first text box now flows into the second. Pages updates the two text boxes automatically: When you add or delete text in the first page, the text at the bottom gets nudged back and forth across the page jump.

When you get to the back page, Pages thoughtfully provides a template page named "Mailer" for all its newsletter templates. Figure 1-16 shows an example. Save, print, staple, and voilà—you've created a pro-quality newsletter layout in just a few minutes.

Tip: Like the letter template you saw earlier, these Mailer pages also include merge fields, making it easy to do mass mailings from Address Book or a Numbers spreadsheet. See page 165 for more about Pages' mail merge features.

Figure 1-16:
The Mailer layout in the newsletter templates features content on the top half of the page and ample space for address info on the bottom half. After you print your newsletter, you can staple it in half, address it, and it's ready for the mailman.

In the Buff: The Blank Template

Templates are particularly useful for getting a jump on formal documents or complex layouts. But let's face it, not all documents require a fancy, elegant design. If you're dashing off a quick list, organizing your thoughts, crafting a short story, or building a fresh page layout from scratch, the best starting point is often a blank page.

Pages offers four blank templates—two for word-processing documents (Blank and Blank Landscape) and two more for page layout (Blank Canvas and Blank Canvas Landscape). Unlike the rest of the templates, you won't find any placeholder text or images in the blank templates. Pages gives you a *tabula rasa* without distractions. To use a blank template, choose one of these four options from the Template Chooser when you create a new document.

As you settle into a routine with Pages, the Blank word-processing template will likely become your go-to template, the fastest route to getting something down on paper. If you do fall into the habit of choosing Blank every time—or any other template for that matter—you'll inevitably grow impatient with the Template Chooser. Sure, it's only trying to help, but couldn't Pages just give you your favorite template when you want a new document? Yep, you just have to ask nicely.

Setting Your Default Template

Tell the Template Chooser to lay low in the Pages → Preferences window, where you can also anoint your preferred template. Going forward, when you create a new document, Pages will automatically give you a fresh document window with your chosen document type:

1. **Choose Pages → Preferences, and Pages displays the Preferences window.**

2. **Click the General button to display the General Preferences pane.**

3. **Next to "For New Documents," turn on the "Use template:" option.**

4. **Click the Choose button to display the Template Chooser, and select your preferred template.**

   Double-click the template's preview image, or click it once and then click the Choose button. The "For New Documents" setting updates to show the name of your new go-to template in the "Use template" option.

5. **Click the red Close button at the top left of the Preferences window to close it.**

This doesn't have to mean that you're giving up templates forever. You can call up the Template Chooser any time: Choose File → New from Template Chooser or press Shift-⌘-N.

Opening an Existing Document

After this flurry of creating and saving new documents, you've now got a tidy collection of Pages files on your hard drive. When you're ready to get at 'em again, follow any of these steps to open a file:

- In the Finder, double-click the Pages document, or drag it onto the Pages application icon.

- In Pages, choose File → Open, or press ⌘-O. Pages shows you the Open dialog box (Figure 1-17), which lets you browse your files and select the one you want to open.

- In the Template Chooser, click the Open an Existing File button, and Pages shows you the Open dialog box.

- If you're looking for the document you were working with 10 minutes ago, choose it from the File → Open Recent submenu (Figure 1-18), which gives you fast access to files you've whipped up lately. You can also choose the same options from the Template Chooser's Open Recent pop-up menu.

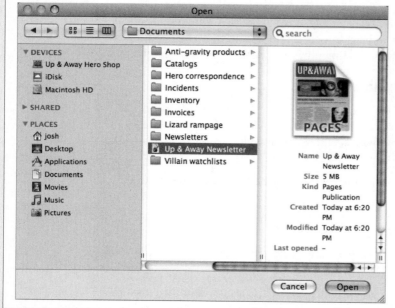

Figure 1-17:
The Open dialog box lets you browse your computer, iDisk, or any other computer on your network to find your file. Use the search box at the top right to hunt down the file if you've forgotten exactly where you stashed it, or use the pop-up menu at top center to jump to folders you've visited recently. Select the file that you want to open and then click the Open button.

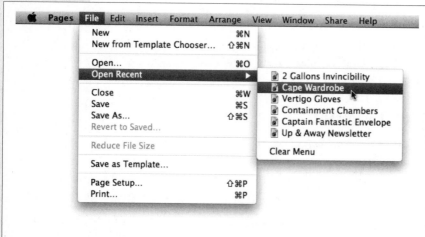

Figure 1-18:
The Open Recent submenu contains a listing of the Pages documents you've used most recently. Select the document you want, and Pages opens it for you in a new window. If others use your computer, and you prefer not to have them discover that you were editing a file inconveniently named "Secret Plan to Take Over the World," choose Clear Menu to make Pages forget your editing history.

Importing Files from Another Program

In the Open dialog box, Pages grays out any files that it doesn't know how to open, making it easy to see the ones that it can work with. Pages offers to open several types of files, not just Pages documents:

- Microsoft Word (.doc and .docx)

- Rich Text Format (.rtf and .rtfd)

- Plain text (.txt)

- AppleWorks 6 word processing (.cwk)

When Pages opens these other file types, it imports them into a brand new Pages document. That means that you're actually working with a *copy* rather than the original file. Save the document, and edit away. When you're done, if you want to save the file back to Microsoft Word or some other format, Pages lets you do that, too (see page 326).

When Pages opens a file from another program, it does its best to preserve the text and formatting of the original document. When opening Microsoft Word documents, for example, Pages knows how to manage Word's styles, lists, tables, charts, images, footnotes, change tracking, and more.

Tip: For most documents, Pages spins effortlessly through these file-format gymnastics, but you may occasionally find some minor display differences, particularly for very complex Microsoft Word documents. For ambitious layouts, it's a good idea to make a careful review of the document to make sure that all the formatting looks the way you want it.

The Document Warnings window

Pages doesn't stay quiet if it can't cope with parts of the imported document. When it thinks some elements might not have made the transfer as expected, it pops up a message to let you know. The Document Warnings window lists the problems and, in some cases, even lets you do something about it. If you import a document that includes fonts not installed on your computer, for example, you can select another font as shown in Figure 1-19.

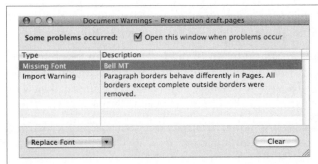

Figure 1-19:
The Document Warnings window details any problems that occur when you import a document from another program. If there's a missing font, you can choose an alternative: Click the warning and then click the Replace Font pop-up menu to choose a substitute. Turn off the "Open this window when problems occur" to hush the Document Warnings window; you can get it back by choosing View → Show Document Warnings.

Tip: If you need to let someone else know about these warnings, you can copy the message text and, for example, include it in an email message. Click a warning to select it (or choose Edit → Select All to highlight all of them), and choose Edit → Copy. You can then paste the copied text into your email missive. You'll learn more about copying and pasting on page 55.

Controlling the Document Window

Even though you've already created a few polished documents with the examples in this chapter, you might have noticed that you've barely touched the program's menus, toolbar buttons, or inspectors. As you've seen, the nuts-and-bolts editing of text and images takes place directly in the window's main work area with lots of typing and a bit of light mousework.

Over the next few chapters, as you get acquainted with Pages' more advanced formatting and layout tools, you'll set aside this mitts-off approach. Mastering the placement of the buttons and controls that light up your Pages dashboard is the next step to creating and editing great Pages documents. Fortunately, Apple's software designers have gone easy on you. Rather than cramming every possible tool and button into Pages' document window in a noisy clutter, they've pared the window down to the bone, opting for a Danish-modern starkness instead of the rococo of most word-processing programs.

In fact, when you first opened a new document (Figure 1-3), your first thought might have been, "Where is everything?" Don't panic, it's all there. Despite its minimalist design, Pages gives you easy access to the tools and features you're most likely to need by placing them at the top of the window, while keeping the ones you need less often—or for more esoteric tasks—hidden just below the surface. Figure 1-20 tours the highlights of your document-window cockpit.

You can choose to live with this minimalist window design, embellish it with more controls, or give the window a virtual makeover to express your own sense of style. All that's covered in the following pages.

Using the Toolbar

The toolbar graces the top of the document window with a set of colorful buttons for one-click access to common features, saving mileage on your mouse and strain on your menu memory. You'll learn more about each of these buttons in the coming chapters, but here's the condensed version for the standard button set:

- **View.** The first button is a pop-up menu (indicated by the tiny black triangle next to the icon) that lets you show and hide parts of your document window. You can slide out the Styles drawer (see page 95), reveal the thumbnail view or Search sidebar (see page 46), show the Comments pane (see page 133), or toggle the display of the Format Bar, rulers, invisible characters, or layout view.

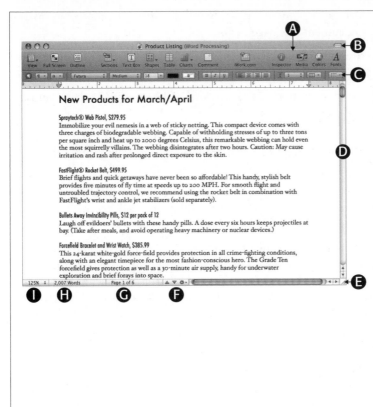

Figure 1-20:
The toolbar (A) is the most prominent component of your document dashboard, giving you one-click access to commonly used features. Use these buttons to change your document view, add design elements, make comments, share your work online, apply formatting, fetch photos, and access many more commands in the master toolbox known as the Inspector. Hide or show the toolbar by clicking the Hide/Show "Tic Tac" button (B). The oh-so-useful Format Bar (C) changes according to the active page element; when you're editing text, for example, it displays text-formatting options, as shown here.

The vertical scroll bar (D) lets you move up and down through your document. Resize the window by dragging the resize handle (E) in the lower-right corner. Jump a page at a time through your document by clicking the page up and down buttons (F). The page indicator (G) shows you what page you're on, and the word countometer (H) tracks your accumulated verbiage. In the lower-left corner, the View pop-up menu (I) lets you change the size of the page display on your screen.

- **Full Screen.** Click this button to make your document your sole focus of attention, tucking away all other windows and digital distractions behind a virtual curtain (see page 47).

- **Outline.** Switch in and out of outline view with this button. In outline mode, your document is stripped down to a skeleton view with topics and subtopics—ideal for big-picture organization of your ideas (see page 183). This option is available for word-processing documents, not page layout.

- **Sections.** This pop-up menu appears only on word-processing documents and lets you add new *sections* to give parts of your document their own formatting or layout rules. Many templates provide a choice of preformatted section layouts, and this pop-up shows thumbnail previews of each one (see page 149).

- **Pages.** This pop-up menu appears only on page-layout documents and lets you add new pages to your document with your choice of prefab layouts, or template pages, based on your current template (see page 149).

- **Text Box.** The Text Box button inserts a text box into your document (see page 216).

- **Shapes.** The Shapes pop-up menu lets you add lines, arrows, or geometric shapes to your document (see page 241).

- **Table.** This button inserts a table or mini-spreadsheet into your document (see page 280).

- **Charts.** Click this pop-up button to insert one of 19 varieties of charts into the page (see page 310).

- **Comment.** This button adds a note to your text, letting you annotate the document with comments, handy for collaboration and tag-team editing (see page 133).

- **iWork.com.** This button shares your document online at iWork.com, where you can collaborate with others to review and share feedback on any iWork document (see page 332).

- **Inspector.** This button summons or dismisses the *Inspector window,* the command center for formatting your document and all the elements it contains. The 10 inspectors inside this window contain controls for document and text formatting, chart and table construction, bookmark and hyperlink creation, and more. You'll learn more about the Inspector window throughout this book.

- **Media.** Click this button to show or hide the Media Browser, the shortcut to your entire collection of tunes, photos, and movies. For example, just drag a photo from the Media Browser to add a picture to your document (see page 228).

- **Colors.** These last two buttons actually access tools that are part of Mac OS X, though they're seamlessly integrated with Pages. The Color Picker appears when you click this button. Use this palette any time you need to change the color of text, objects, backgrounds, and so on (see page 265).

- **Fonts.** The Mac OS X Fonts window comes to the fore when you click this button, giving you control of your entire font collection. You can select fonts, adjust their size, view their appearance in a preview pane, add strikethrough or text shadow, and more (see page 62).

Customizing the toolbar

If you find it too distracting, you can banish the toolbar's banner of buttons by choosing View → Hide Toolbar, pressing ⌘-Option-T, or easiest of all, by pressing the "Tic Tac," button in the upper-right corner of the document window. You can call the toolbar back by repeating any of the three commands just listed—except this time the menu reads View → Show Toolbar.

Chances are, though, you'll probably want to keep the toolbar around while you're working on most documents. It's handy! Rather than hiding the toolbar, you might instead customize it to show only the buttons you want.

In that case, choose View → Customize Toolbar (or Control-click the toolbar and choose Customize Toolbar from the pop-up menu) and Pages displays its entire collection of buttons on a sheet that drops from the toolbar (Figure 1-21). Now you can drag buttons you don't want off the toolbar and see them vanish in a puff of smoke. Add to the toolbar by dragging individual items into place on the bar; the buttons already there politely shuffle aside to make room for the newcomer. Once the buttons are in the bar, you can drag them around to change their position.

Most of the toolbar buttons perform various commands you'd otherwise have to dig through the menus to find. But you'll find three items in the bottom row of buttons designed to help keep your newly customized toolbar organized: a separator line, a fixed space, and a flexible space.

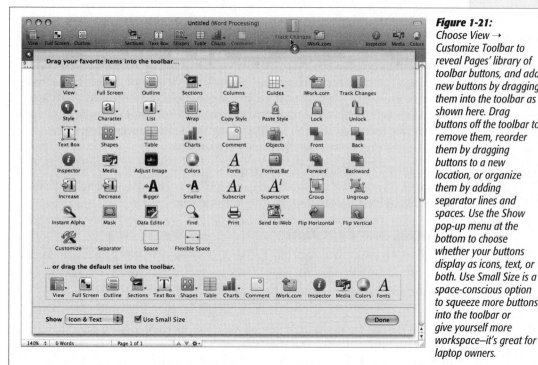

Figure 1-21:
*Choose View →
Customize Toolbar to
reveal Pages' library of
toolbar buttons, and add
new buttons by dragging
them into the toolbar as
shown here. Drag
buttons off the toolbar to
remove them, reorder
them by dragging
buttons to a new
location, or organize
them by adding
separator lines and
spaces. Use the Show
pop-up menu at the
bottom to choose
whether your buttons
display as icons, text, or
both. Use Small Size is a
space-conscious option
to squeeze more buttons
into the toolbar or
give yourself more
workspace—it's great for
laptop owners.*

If you're *really* crazy for customization, you can even add a Customize button to the toolbar so you can quickly summon the customization sheet when the spirit moves you to modify your button collection. If you add more buttons than can fit in the window—or if you make your window narrower—a double arrow appears at the end of the toolbar. Click it and a mini menu appears, presenting the button overflow in a list of tiny icons.

After a frenzy of toolbar transformation, if you decide you liked it better the way Apple shipped it from the factory, just drag the entire default set back up to the toolbar and Pages replaces your custom arrangement with the batch of basic buttons.

Shape Shifter: The Format Bar

The Format Bar is the toolbar's can-do sidekick, the narrow little strip of menus and buttons that rides along just below the toolbar. If you've used other word processors, you've used formatting toolbars for quick changes like italicizing a word or adding a list to your text, and the Format Bar works the same way here. The difference, though, is that other programs often make you add layer after layer of toolbars if you want to have one-click access to all your favorite features. That means giving up valuable onscreen real estate and burying your document under a cluttered mess of controls.

Pages cleans things up by giving you one and only one Format Bar, but Pages gives it chameleon-like qualities to shift its display depending on what you're doing. If you're typing inside a text box, the Format Bar shows options for formatting text to change the font, text alignment, line spacing, and so on. Click a photo, and options show up to let you adjust the image quality, add a drop shadow, or apply a mask. You get the idea: No matter what part of the document you're editing, the Format Bar keeps up with you, dispatching tools that are no longer relevant to make room for options you might actually want to use.

If even the toolbar's slim silhouette requires more space than you care to give up, you can send it packin' by choosing View → Hide Format Bar. Change your mind? Bring it back by choosing View → Show Format Bar.

Changing Your Page View

Pages always shows you your document just the way it will look on the printed page, complete with margins, page breaks, and the like. You can change the way it organizes your pages in the document window by choosing different options in the View pop-up menu in the bottom-left corner of the document window.

Choices include zooming in on the page or pulling back to get a big-picture view of your document design. The View pop-up menu offers options to shrink or magnify your document view anywhere from 25 to 400 percent. Just click the percentage you want to use. You can also press ⌘-> (that's ⌘-Shift-period) to tell Pages to enlarge the page to the next zoom level, or ⌘-< (⌘-Shift-comma) to zoom back out (these options are also available from the View → Zoom submenu). Zooming in and out doesn't affect the *actual* size of your document, only the way that Pages *previews* it for you onscreen. Think of it as holding up a sheet of paper for a close look or pushing it away; it doesn't change the size of the document, just how much detail you can see.

Note: In Pages' standard settings, new documents open at 125 percent magnification, a comfortable medium-sized view and about the size of your document when it prints. If you prefer a different size, choose Pages → Preferences: Click the General button and set the Default Zoom setting to your liking.

You'll find two other sets of options sandwiching the zoom percentages in the
View pop-up menu. At the top of the menu, you can choose *One Up* or *Two Up* to
tell Pages how many pages to show side-by-side in the document window
(Figure 1-22, circled). New documents always open as One Up (the normal view,
with only one page across in the window). Choose Two Up to show two pages side
by side, a useful view when you're designing a booklet or other document that you
plan to bind or fold into facing pages.

Figure 1-22:
*Top: The usual way to
view a Pages document
onscreen is in One Up
view. The pages appear
stacked on top of one
another, like a ribbon
stretching above and
below your monitor. Use
the scroll bar or the Page
Up and Down buttons to
move through the
document.*

*Bottom: When you
choose Two Up in the
View pop-up menu,
Pages presents your
document as if it were an
open book. This is the
best way to get the
overall feel of the spread
and make sure page
elements—headlines and
pictures, for example—
are in visual harmony
across both pages.*

At the bottom of the View pop-up, you'll find two automatic zoom settings that you can use as alternatives to the percentage settings. *Fit Width* adjusts the magnification so the page (or pair of pages, in Two Up mode) precisely fits the *width* of the document window—no matter how narrow or wide (don't you wish that your pants had this setting at Thanksgiving?). *Fit Page*, on the other hand, adjusts the magnification so that an entire single page—or two-page spread in Two Up mode—fits into your window. Turn on either of these settings and the magnification automatically changes as you adjust the window size with the window-resizing handle in the bottom-right corner of the window. You can also find these options in the View → Zoom menu.

Navigating Your Document

Scooting around a one-page letter doesn't present many challenges, but finding your way through a 200-page manifesto can be much tougher. Pages provides a number of tools for orienting yourself and moving quickly through your document. Just like most other computer programs, Pages documents sport scroll bars, and you can use the vertical scroll bar to move up and down through your document. Figure 1-23 shows you how things work.

You can also use OS X's little-known *Scroll to here* option. If you think of the vertical scroll bar as a diagram of your document, from the first page (at the top) to the last (at the bottom), you can Option-click anywhere on the scroll bar and the document jumps directly to that point. For example, Option-click three-quarters of the way down the scroll bar, and Pages jumps to a point three-quarters of the way through your document. Or click the page indicator to reveal the Go to Page field. Type the page you want to jump to, press Return, and Pages takes you there.

You can also move up or down an entire page at a time by clicking the upward- and downward-pointing arrows at the bottom of the window, next to the page indicator. You can even change the behavior of these handy little arrows to leap to something other than the next page. Click the gear-shaped Action menu next to the arrows and choose a different item (section, comment, footnote, specific text

Figure 1-23:
Fundamentals of scrolling: Click the up or down arrow buttons (A) in the bottom-right corner of the window to bring earlier or later parts of your document into view. The blue jellybean moves to show the relative position of your spot in the document. You can click the scroll bar above or below that jellybean to jump to the previous, or next, screenful (B). You can also drag the jellybean (C) straight to a different position in the document.

style, and so on). Instead of going to the next or previous page when you click the arrows, you'll now skip to the selected item. This is handy, for example, if you want to jump to the next heading or comment instead of the next page. You'll learn more about all of these different document items in the coming chapters.

True efficiency experts dismiss all this mousing around as so much wasted arm action when there are perfectly good navigation keys right on the keyboard. Table 1-2 reveals all.

Table 1-2. *Pages keyboard shortcuts*

Press this	To do this
Page Up (on laptops, fn-Up Arrow)	Scroll up a page
Page Down (on laptops, fn-Down Arrow)	Scroll down a page
Home (on laptops, fn-Left Arrow)	Jump to the beginning of the document
End (on laptops, fn-Right Arrow)	Jump to the end of the document
Left or right arrow	Move insertion point one character to the left or right
Up or down arrow	Move insertion point to the line above or below
Option-left arrow	Move insertion point to the beginning of the current or previous word

Table 1-2. *Pages keyboard shortcuts (continued)*

Press this	To do this
Option-right arrow	Move insertion point to the end of the current or next word
⌘-left or -right arrow	Move insertion point to the beginning or end of the line
⌘-up or -down arrow	Move insertion point to the beginning or end of the document
Option-up or -down arrow	Move insertion point to the beginning or end of the paragraph

You can also scroll by pressing the arrow keys: Hold down the up or down arrow key to move the insertion point up or down through your text. (When the insertion point reaches the edge of the screen, Pages scrolls a half screen, putting the insertion point back into the middle of the newly scrolled screen.)

Thumbnail view

Use Pages' thumbnail view to see a visual table of contents for your document, browsing your tome as a sequence of miniature pages. Thumbnail view is enabled for new page-layout documents but turned off when you open a new word-processing document. To turn it on or off, choose View → Page Thumbnails. The *Pages sidebar* opens along the left side of the window (Figure 1-24).

The Pages sidebar shows numbered thumbnail images of each page in your document—adding a scroll bar if there are too many to fit in the window. You'll find that thumbnail view makes it easy to find the page you're looking for in your document—especially if your document features colorful illustrations or distinctive page layouts. You can recognize the page you're after at a glance, since the thumbnails are actual images of the page—including headlines, columns of text, pictures, and so on.

To jump to a specific page, click its thumbnail. The page appears in the main viewing area, ready for editing, and the page's thumbnail highlights to indicate your place in the document. As you'll learn later, you can also use these thumbnails to rearrange or delete pages or entire sections of your document (see page 151).

Tip: Adjust the width of the Pages sidebar by dragging the resize handle in the lower-right corner of the sidebar. The thumbnails grow as you make the sidebar wider, a handy way to get a closer look at these page previews.

The Search sidebar

The *Search sidebar* is the brainy alternative to the Page sidebar's visual approach. It lets you build a smart table of contents on the fly, based on your own search keywords. This is handy when you want to see at a glance every one of your newsletter's

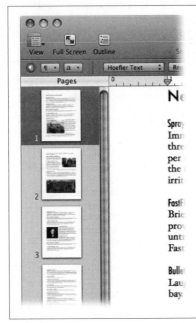

Figure 1-24:
In thumbnail view, the Pages sidebar shows your document's pages in miniature. Choose View → Page Thumbnails to show or hide the Pages sidebar, and click a thumbnail image to jump to the corresponding page in your document.

references to X-ray goggles, for example. Choose View → Search, and the Search sidebar appears at the left side of the document window in place of the thumbnail view (sorry, you can't have both panes open at once, it's an either-or situation).

Type a word or phrase in the search field—as you type, results materialize in the Search sidebar. By default, the search is not case-sensitive and also finds matches in the middle of words. That means that a search for "cap" matches "Caped" and "escape," as well as the word "cap" itself. You can change this behavior (and also revisit previous search terms) by clicking the magnifying-glass pop-up menu in the search field. Figure 1-25 shows the results.

Note: Pages also offers other, more advanced search tools in its *Find* and *Find & Replace* features (see page 108), but only the Search pane lets you browse all search results simultaneously in a single view.

Editing in Full-Screen View

The marvelous curse of your Mac is that it plays so many roles. It turns out that your work machine is also an engine for entertainment, communication, news, and—if you're not disciplined—rampant procrastination. When you're just trying to buckle down and actually do some work, your Mac's many tools and toys can be powerfully distracting. Pages' *full-screen view* helps you focus by making your document the one and only thing on your screen, hushing the siren calls of email, Web, and all the other goodies vying for your attention.

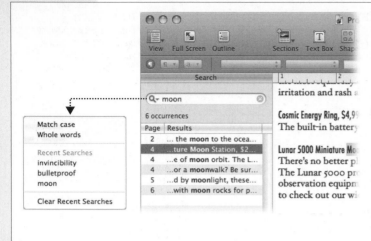

Figure 1-25:
Search results show the page numbers with matches for your search text, along with some nearby text to give you some context. When you click a search result, Pages takes you to that page in the main viewing area, with the matching word or phrase highlighted. Double-click the search result, and you can start editing the text right away; just type to replace the selected text.

The pop-up menu in the search field lets you fine-tune your search by choosing "Match case" or "Whole words" options. With "Match case" selected, Pages shows results only if they match the capitalization of your search text. With "Whole words" selected, results no longer show matches from the middle of a word. The pop-up menu also lets you jump to the results for a previous search term, and even clear your search history.

Click the Full Screen button on the toolbar or choose View → Enter Full Screen, and Pages banishes everything except for the document text. Even the menu bar, toolbar, and scroll bars disappear, leaving nothing but you and your words…along with a word and page count at the bottom of the screen (Figure 1-26). Type away without distraction.

If this stripped-down look makes you feel a bit naked, don't get nervous. Your scroll bars and menus haven't gone far; they're waiting quietly behind the scenes for you to call them into action:

- **Show the scroll bar** by moving the pointer to the right edge of your document; it disappears again when you move away.

- **Show the page thumbnails** by pushing the pointer to the very left edge of the screen.

- **Show the menu bar and Format Bar** by moving the pointer to the top of the screen. Choose View → Show Inspector to call up the Inspector window.

In full-screen view, the View pop-up menu moves to the far right of the Format Bar instead of its normal home at the bottom of the document window. There, you can adjust the zoom as usual—with all this screen space devoted only to your Pages document, you may want to choose a more magnified view. If the black screen background feels too somber, you can choose a new background color from the Background color well in the Format Bar.

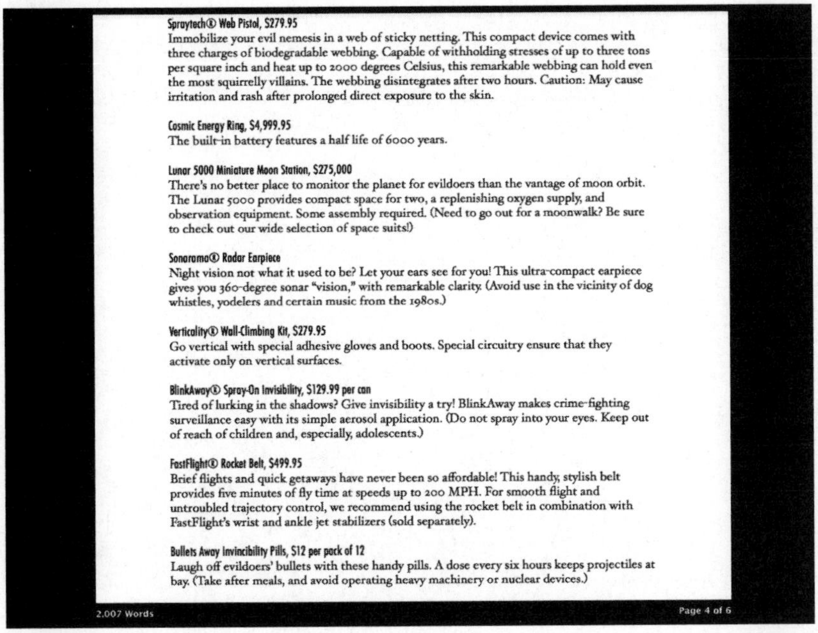

Spraytech® Web Pistol, $279.95
Immobilize your evil nemesis in a web of sticky netting. This compact device comes with three charges of biodegradable webbing. Capable of withholding stresses of up to three tons per square inch and heat up to 2000 degrees Celsius, this remarkable webbing can hold even the most squirrelly villains. The webbing disintegrates after two hours. Caution: May cause irritation and rash after prolonged direct exposure to the skin.

Cosmic Energy Ring, $4,999.95
The built-in battery features a half life of 6000 years.

Lunar 5000 Miniature Moon Station, $275,000
There's no better place to monitor the planet for evildoers than the vantage of moon orbit. The Lunar 5000 provides compact space for two, a replenishing oxygen supply, and observation equipment. Some assembly required. (Need to go out for a moonwalk? Be sure to check out our wide selection of space suits!)

Sonorama® Radar Earpiece
Night vision not what it used to be? Let your ears see for you! This ultra-compact earpiece gives you 360-degree sonar "vision," with remarkable clarity. (Avoid use in the vicinity of dog whistles, yodelers and certain music from the 1980s.)

Verticality® Wall-Climbing Kit, $279.95
Go vertical with special adhesive gloves and boots. Special circuitry ensure that they activate only on vertical surfaces.

BlinkAway® Spray-On Invisibility, $129.99 per can
Tired of lurking in the shadows? Give invisibility a try! BlinkAway makes crime-fighting surveillance easy with its simple aerosol application. (Do not spray into your eyes. Keep out of reach of children and, especially, adolescents.)

FastFlight® Rocket Belt, $499.95
Brief flights and quick getaways have never been so affordable! This handy, stylish belt provides five minutes of fly time at speeds up to 200 MPH. For smooth flight and untroubled trajectory control, we recommend using the rocket belt in combination with FastFlight's wrist and ankle jet stabilizers (sold separately).

Bullets Away Invincibility Pills, $12 per pack of 12
Laugh off evildoers' bullets with these handy pills. A dose every six hours keeps projectiles at bay. (Take after meals, and avoid operating heavy machinery or nuclear devices.)

2,007 Words

Page 4 of 6

Figure 1-26: *Pages' full-screen mode draws a curtain across your desktop, letting you focus exclusively on your document. The background dims to black, leaving only the document text, word count, and page count on the screen. To leave full-screen view, press Escape (Esc), click the Format Bar's Exit button, or choose View → Exit Full Screen.*

Tip: Full-screen mode is a handy way to review documents in meetings, too. Choose Fit Width from the View pop-up to make your document fill the entire screen—big enough for several people huddled around your Mac to see, or for an entire room when you're projecting onto a screen.

When you're done with full-screen view and want to return to the regular window view, press Escape, click the Format Bar's Exit button, or choose View → Exit Full Screen.

With this newfound ability for extraordinary focus, you're ready to start cranking out words. The next chapter gives you a leg up by exploring everything you need to know about adding, editing, and formatting text.

Editing Text in Pages

With Pages' flashy arsenal of design features, it's tempting to take the program's mild-mannered writing tools for granted. The page-layout features certainly set Pages apart from other word processing programs, but the gang at Apple haven't forgotten that, in the end, it's words that tell the story. Beneath the program's stylish veneer beats the heart of a full-featured word processor to help polish your prose to a high shine. Along the way, you can shape every aspect of your text's visual presentation, from the sublime (ah, subtle typography tweaks) to the ridiculous (shadowed text!). This chapter covers everything you need to know about editing and formatting your text in Pages.

Word Processor Text vs. Text Boxes

As you saw in the last chapter, Pages presents your text in one of two forms. It's helpful to think of them as rivers and islands. In word processing documents, the main text flows through your entire document in one continuous river of words, a fixed part of your document landscape. In page-layout documents, text instead shows up as little islands, independent *text boxes* that you can slide around the page freestyle. As you'll learn in Chapter 7, word-processing documents can actually contain both text types, letting you sprinkle text-box islands into your written river as callouts and sidebars (see page 225).

The important thing to remember is that no matter what form it might take in Pages, text is text. The same editing and formatting options are available to you whether you're working with the main text of a word processing document or a text box floating around your page-layout window. A text box is mobile, and word processor text isn't—other than that, editing text inside those elements works exactly the same way.

In fact, once you've mastered text editing in Pages, you've got it nailed in Keynote and Numbers, too. Both programs include text boxes, just like Pages. Although Pages gives you a few more text-formatting options than its iWork cousins, the essentials remain the same across all three programs, right down to the interface buttons and tools that you use to format your text.

Basic Text Editing in iWork

Pages, Keynote, and Numbers all follow the Mac's basic conventions for adding, editing, selecting, and moving text. If you're familiar with other Mac software, you'll feel right at home here. But even if you're a longtime Mac user, you might not be aware of all the handy shortcuts available for working with text. Here's the skinny.

Inserting Text

Inserting text or spaces in a document is the most basic editing task of all. Move the I-beam cursor to wherever you want to insert text, click the mouse, and then type. Pages nudges the words following your new text over to the right to make room for your new typing.

Note: In text boxes, you may need to click the text a second time before you get the I-beam cursor. Clicking a text box once selects the entire text box, which lets you move and resize it. Editing the text inside the box requires a second click. When you're done, click anywhere outside the box to deselect it. See page 216 for all the secrets about selecting and editing text boxes.

UP TO SPEED

Un-Typewriter Class

Even though most computer owners haven't touched a typewriter for years—if ever—many bad habits persist from that earlier technology. Here are a few of the more egregious examples of typewriter style that you're better off forgetting:

- Underlining: Although Pages makes it simple to format text with underlining, don't use this style for emphasis. Use **bold** or *italic*, which are much more stylish—and just as easy to apply. (Seriously, when's the last time you saw something underlined in a book or magazine article?)

- Spacing with the space bar: Use the space bar only for spacing between words. Never use the space bar for aligning successive lines of text; when printed, those spaces often cause your text to tumble out of

alignment. Instead, use Pages' tab feature, described on page 72 of this chapter, or use tables, described in Chapter 8.

- Special characters and accents are easy to produce correctly on a computer. Don't write resume if you mean résumé. Are you making copies or using the Xerox™? Don't put it off until mañana—take that vacation to Curaçao today! See ☞ page 82 to find out how to insert symbols, accents, and other special characters.

- Using two hyphens (--) to represent a dash is passé. What you want is an *em dash*—so called because it's the width of an uppercase M. Create it with the Shift-Option-hyphen key combination.

Deleting Text

More word processing basics: If you've just made a typo, press Delete to backspace and remove the offending characters. If you have to jump back only a few words to make a correction, you can *hold down* the Delete key and watch the letters disappear until you nip the mistake, then retype.

Tip: Delete whole words at a time by holding down the Option key while you delete. Option-Delete zaps the word to the left of the insertion point. You can *forward delete,* too, clipping the text to the *right* of the insertion point. If you use a desktop computer with a full keyboard, press the forward-delete key—that's the key with the "x" inside a right-facing arrow. Mac laptops don't have this key, but you can get the same effect by pressing Function-Delete (the Function key is labeled "fn").

If you find an error so far back in your typing that it'd be silly to delete all the words after it that are in fine shape, use the mouse to correct the mistake in one of two ways:

- **Click and then press Delete.** Position the *I-beam cursor* to the immediate right of the error you want to delete, click the mouse, and press Delete to remove the offending letters. Type your correction. Then click the I-beam cursor back to where you left off, and continue typing.

- **Highlight text and then retype.** If the error you want to delete is more than a few letters long, use the highlight-then-retype method. Start by dragging carefully from the beginning to the end (or from the end to the beginning) of the text to change. Sometimes this method means dragging perfectly horizontally, carefully staying on the same line; other times it means dragging diagonally from the beginning of a passage to the end. Either way, after you release the mouse, hit Delete to vaporize the highlighted text. Or you can just type your replacement text—anything you type instantly replaces whatever you've highlighted, no need to delete it first.

Note: Apparently iWork's designers think there are people out there who just have to do everything with the mouse. To honor the mouse-obsessed, they've included the Edit → Delete command. It does exactly the same thing to highlighted text as the Delete key but, y'know, with more effort.

Making a Selection

To edit text, you always follow a two-step process: First *select* the text and then retype (or use menu commands) to *change* it. You can select (or *highlight*) as little as a single character, or as much as the entire document:

- **Select a word or a passage.** Position your I-beam cursor at one end of your intended selection, drag to the other end, and then release the mouse button. Everything between those two points is selected, and you see the text highlighted.

- **Select an individual letter.** Drag across the letter.

You can deselect the text by clicking once, either inside or outside of the selection. (If you're determined to do it in the most roundabout way possible, you can also choose Edit → Deselect All.)

Using mass selection techniques

While selecting text with a drag of the mouse works just fine, your Mac offers several ways to speed up the process:

- **Select one word:** Double-click any part of the word.

- **Select several consecutive words:** Double-click anywhere on the first word—and on the second click, keep the mouse button pressed. Drag horizontally. As you go, Pages highlights the text in one-word chunks, which lets you be much sloppier (and faster) in your dragging effort.

- **Select a whole paragraph:** *Triple*-click anywhere in the paragraph. Triple-click and (on the third click) drag to select paragraph by paragraph.

- **Select a block of text:** Click to place the insertion point at one end of the block. Then, while pressing the Shift key, click the far end of the block you want to select, even if the far end is many pages away.

- **Select the entire document:** Choose Edit → Select All, or press ⌘-A. Use this technique when you want to make a global change, such as changing the font or the margins for the whole document. (Before you do this, though, check out Chapter 3 to find out how styles can help you make global changes in a more savvy fashion.)

Using keyboard selection techniques

Why interrupt your typing flow to use the mouse at all? Black belts in keyboard kung fu master every keyboard-based command shortcut and rarely use the mouse. No need to abandon the mouse completely, but learning keyboard shortcuts for common tasks saves time and preserves focus. When editing, for example, you can select text without letting your fingers stray from the keyboard.

Starting from the current location of the blinking insertion point, the Mac gives you a bunch of shortcuts to help select text, shown in Table 2-1.

Table 2-1. Mac text selection shortcuts

To select...	Use this shortcut
Next/previous character	Shift-right arrow or-left arrow
Next/previous word	Shift-Option-right arrow or -left arrow
To next/previous line	Shift-up arrow or -down arrow
To beginning/end of line	Shift-⌘-right arrow or -left arrow
To beginning/end of paragraph	Shift-Option-up arrow or -down arrow
To beginning/end of document	Shift-⌘-up arrow or -down arrow
Entire document	⌘-A

No matter which method you use to make a selection, your very next action applies to the text you've highlighted, whether you're typing new text or just changing its formatting. For example, when you choose a different font size, or style, Pages updates only the selected text.

Tip: Remember that anything you type *replaces* whatever text you've highlighted. This phenomenon can be useful when, for example, you want to replace one highlighted word in a sentence. On the other hand, this behavior can also be dangerous. If you've highlighted your entire document, for example, typing a single letter (or even pressing the Space bar) replaces all the text in your document. (Don't panic, though: The Edit → Undo command can save you. See page 58.)

Cutting, Copying, and Pasting

Back in the BC era—before computers—moving text around your paper document was a bona fide arts-and-crafts project: Cutting and pasting involved real scissors and real paste. Now, thanks to the Cut, Copy, and Paste commands, you're free to move text around as much as you like without ever getting your fingers sticky.

You'll find these three commands in the Edit menu, but do yourself a favor and avoid going through the menu. You'll repeat the Cut, Copy, and Paste routine over and over again, and your mouse would start racking up some serious frequent-flyer miles with all that travel. Save yourself the wrist fatigue and make it a habit to use the keyboard commands for these functions instead:

- ⌘-X *cuts,* or removes whatever text you've got highlighted. ("X" as in cross it out.) Your computer whisks the deleted material onto its invisible *Clipboard,* ready to be redeposited when you use the Paste command.

- ⌘-C *copies* the highlighted text—leaving the selection untouched, but cloning an exact copy onto the invisible Clipboard. ("C" as in *copy.*)

- ⌘-V *pastes* the cut or copied text back into your document at the location of the blinking insertion point or over any selected text. ("V" as in, *voilà, there it is!*) You can't use the letter P for Paste because it's assigned to the Print command. Besides, the V's right next to the C key, making all the editing keys—Undo, Cut, Copy, and Paste—a neat row on your keyboard. And the V looks like the caret mark proofreaders use to mean "insert."

Keep your Paste clean: Paste and Match Style

Normally when you copy text from one part of an iWork document and paste it into another, the text hangs onto its original text style—sometimes with unhappy results. For example, if you copy a few words out of an *italicized caption* and paste them into a **large, bold headline,** the result is a headline with a few small italic words. Yuck. To sidestep this problem, all three iWork programs offer a style-conscious pasting option: Choose Edit → "Paste and Match Style" (or press ⌘-Option-Shift-V), and the pasted words assume the style of the paragraph where they land. In the example just mentioned, the small italic words automatically take on the big, bold headline style when pasted into the headline.

Clipboard Crash Course

The Cut, Copy, and Paste commands rely on an invisible temporary storage platter called the Clipboard. It's not specific to iWork; it's built into the Mac operating system.

The Clipboard is a single-minded assistant: It can hold only one thing at a time. Hand it something else, and it immediately drops whatever it had been holding, forgetting it for good. The Clipboard then clutches this new item, ready for your command to paste, until you give it a new item or shut down the computer.

Put another way, whenever you cut or copy something, you obliterate whatever was already on the Clipboard. On the other hand, you can paste whatever's currently on the Clipboard an infinite number of times without wearing it out.

Because the Clipboard is part of the operating system, it's available in all programs, serving as a conduit to transfer information between them. Say that one of Up & Away's superhero customers sends you a glowing email about her new anti-gravity boots, and you'd like to stash it in a Pages document with quotes from happy patrons. Just copy the text in the email message, then switch to the Pages document and choose Edit → Paste.

Using Drag-and-Drop Editing

Drag-and-drop is a one-step alternative to the cut-and-paste two-step. Figure 2-1 shows the procedure.

Tip: The drag-and-drop method is most useful when you're dragging your selection a short distance. You can drag the selection to the top or bottom edge of the window to force Pages to scroll automatically, but even that technique can be clumsy. When you can't see both the point of origin and the destination for your change, you're better off sticking with the tried-and-true Cut (or Copy) and Paste.

You can also use the drag-and-drop technique to *copy* a selection: Hold down the Option key while dragging the text. When you release the mouse button, Pages drops a copy of the original passage into position, leaving the original McCoy untouched.

Tip: You can even drag a selection from one program and drop it into another—or onto your desktop. When you drag to the desktop, you create a *text clipping,* a standalone file that you can open and read or drag back into a document at any time.

Using Shortcut Menus

Along with an ever-shifting cast of commands, Cut, Copy, and Paste are also available via *shortcut menus,* or "contextual menus"—handy pop-ups that give you fast access to many common commands. Control-click just about anything on the screen to see its shortcut menu; different items appear in the menu depending on the context. The shortcut menu for a text selection is shown in Figure 2-2, for example, but the menu offers entirely different commands when you Control-click a picture or some other object in your document. If you ever get stumped about how to get something done with any text or design element in your document, bringing up the shortcut menu for the item can often point you in the right direction.

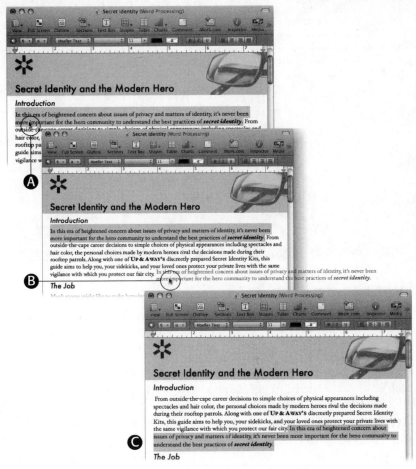

Figure 2-1:
Position your pointer over a chunk of highlighted text (A). Then drag that selection to another place in the document (B), and release the mouse to drop it at the insertion point that follows your cursor. The text you dragged appears in its new location at the insertion point (C). If you change your mind mid-drag, you can call the whole thing off by pressing the Escape key, and your selection zips back to its original home.

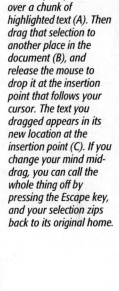

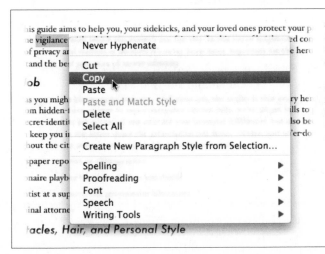

Figure 2-2:
Shortcut menus change and morph depending on the text or object you're pointing at. Control-click any element of your document (here the word, "vigilance"), and a pop-up menu appears, displaying a list of common commands for the selection. For text selections, shortcut menus include the Cut, Copy, and Paste commands, along with other commands and features explored in the coming chapters.

Undoing and Backing Up

All iWork programs offer a few special tools to save you from yourself—or from your cat walking across the keyboard just after you perform a Select All command.

When you have one of those "Oh no!" moments, always reach first for the Edit → Undo command (or press ⌘-Z), and Pages reverses your last action. Whether you just changed a word, deleted a page, or applied a new font color, ⌘-Z lets you take it back. (If you learn only one keyboard shortcut, you owe it to yourself to master ⌘-Z. You'll come back to this one over and over again.)

Note: The wording of the Edit → Undo command changes to reflect the kind of action that it's prepared to undo. For example, if you just dragged a paragraph into the wrong spot, the Edit menu says Undo Drop. You also see other possibilities like Undo Format, Undo Typing, Undo Cut, and so on.

The iWork programs all give you unlimited multiple Undos, which means that as you repeatedly press ⌘-Z, you throw the time machine into reverse and watch as it peels away the changes you've made to your document, one after another. Even if you've saved the document—which you should do frequently as you work, of course—you can still undo changes made before the save. But the time machine grinds to a halt when you *close* a document. Pages flushes all your changes out of its memory. The next time you open that document you have to start moving forward again—there's nothing to undo.

After you perform an Undo (and breathe a sigh of relief), the Edit menu features the *Redo* command—which you can use to *undo* the Undo. If you've just performed multiple Undos, you can now pop the time machine into forward and perform multiple Redos—until you end up right back where you started. On the keyboard, Redo is a Shift key away from Undo: Shift-⌘-Z.

If you've really made a mess of your document—you've muddled it thoroughly, and you're tired of pressing ⌘-Z over and over—you can leap back to the last saved version of your opus. Choose File → "Revert to Saved" to undo all the changes you've made since the last time you used the Save command. (Of course, doing so also discards any *good* work you've done in the meantime.) If you performed that Save *after* opening the document, you can then continue on with the Undo command until you've unraveled your tangled web back to where you want it.

Backing Up the Previous Version of a Document

Pages offers another insurance policy intended to give you one more layer of Undo, but the catch is that you have to activate this safety net *before* a crisis occurs.

Choose Pages → Preferences, click the General button, and turn on the checkbox for "Back up previous version when saving." From now on, Pages saves *two* copies of your documents. In addition to your normal document file, Pages creates another file in the same location and adds the words "Backup of" in front of the document name. Each time you save the document, Pages saves the *previously* saved version in the "Backup of" file. Save again, and the old "Backup of" file is replaced with the new previously saved version, and the older one disappears into digital oblivion. Only one version—the last saved version—is backed up.

In other words, you always have the two most recent versions of your document. If you find something wrong with the one you're working on, open the "Backup of" file to see the earlier version. If you like what you see, choose File → Save As, give the document a new name, perhaps, "My Bacon is Saved," and click Save.

Note: When you turn on this preference you're doubling the disk space required to store your Pages documents. Periodically take a look in your documents folders at the ever-growing list of "Backup of" files and toss out those you're no longer working on.

Changing Font Styles and Appearance

Now that you've mastered basic editing techniques, you've already got all the prose polishing know-how you need. But like any word processor, Pages lets you do much more than simply type and edit your words: You can change the way they look, too. Dress up your text with a new font, make it larger or smaller, mix in some color, or tweak the type style.

You can apply your font changes to as much or as little of your text as you like—from single characters to several words, paragraphs, entire pages, or the whole document. Just highlight the text to change and make your formatting changes. The Format Bar gives you fast access to the most common font-formatting requests, as shown in Figure 2-3. To change the font for your selection, for example, just click the *Font Family* pop-up menu and Pages lists all the available typefaces alphabetically from Arial to Zapfino, each one previewed in the typeface itself. Change the font size by picking a new size from the *Font Size* pop-up menu, or type a point size directly into the Format Bar.

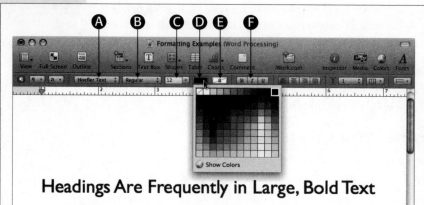

Figure 2-3:
*Format your text styles
directly from the Format
Bar. The Font Family
pop-up menu (A) selects
the typeface family for
your selection. The
Typeface pop-up (B)
selects the typeface font
style to use, as explained
in the box on page 64.*

*The Font Size pop-up
menu (C) lets you
change the font size from
a list of preset sizes. You
can edit and customize
this list from the Fonts
window's Action menu
(see page 61).*

*The Text Color pop-up
(D) offers a selection of
120 colors to tint your
text, or choose Show
Colors to launch the
Color Picker (see page
64). The Background
Color pop-up menu (E)
lets you choose a
background color for
your text. (If the text is
highlighted, the highlight
color will prevent you
from seeing the
background until you
deselect the text.)*

*The "B," "I," and "U"
buttons (F) make your
text bold, italic, and
underlined respectively
(and also remove that
formatting when you
click a second time).*

Tip: If you prefer a simple presentation without the font preview in the Font Family pop-up menu, you can turn it off in the Pages → Preferences window: Click the General button and turn off the "Show font preview in Format Bar font menu" option. You can also turn the feature off only for the current selection by holding down the Option key when you click the Font Family menu. Also, you can customize the list of font sizes list in the Fonts window: Click the toolbar's Fonts button and choose Edit Sizes from the Fonts window's gear-shaped Action menu. See page 265 for the details.

Be **bold** by clicking the Format Bar's "B" button, *italicize* with "I," and underline with "U." You can also get at these common font styles by pressing ⌘-B, ⌘-I, and ⌘-U respectively, or choose them from the Format → Font submenu, which also offers options for adding strikethrough or outline styles to your text.

Fonts, Families, and Faces

Most of us think of a font as a label for a particular lettering design. As it turns out, a font is more specifically a particular style (bold or italic, for instance) within a *typeface*. Although the words "font" and "typeface" are commonly used interchangeably, they actually have distinct meanings that are often important when you're choosing a font in iWork.

The combination of *typeface family* (Times, Helvetica, Courier, and so on) and *font* determines the actual text display. Times, for example, is a typeface family which consists of these fonts: Regular, Italic, Bold, and Bold Italic. In this case—and for most other typefaces, too—this family of fonts simply gives you bold and italic (or *oblique*) variations of the typeface. When you make text bold, for example, Pages takes note by updating the Format Bar's Typeface menu to "Bold." Likewise, making text italic updates the Typeface menu to "Italic," or sometimes "Oblique," letting you know that Pages has switched to a new typeface font behind the scenes. No need to give this a second thought—iWork automatically chooses the correct font for the bold/italic style you want.

Among these standard bold and italic variations, you'll always see a strong family resemblance. But ain't it the truth: In some families, siblings are remarkably different. Font styles for some typeface families go beyond simple bold or italic and very nearly stray off into entirely new typefaces altogether. While these font versions share similar features of shape and style, they squeeze, stretch, and strain into dramatically different forms, as the Futura typeface demonstrates in Figure 2-4.

As you choose your font, especially for big display fonts and headlines, it's worth peeking into the typeface pop-up menu to see what variations the typeface might have in store for you. You'll find some pleasant surprises.

Unfortunately, iWork plays it a little fast and loose with this typography lingo, labeling the two Format Bar pop-up menus as "Font Family" and "Typeface," when typography sticklers might insist on "typeface family" and "font." This is a practical compromise, though, since a typeface family is what most of us mean when we say, "font."

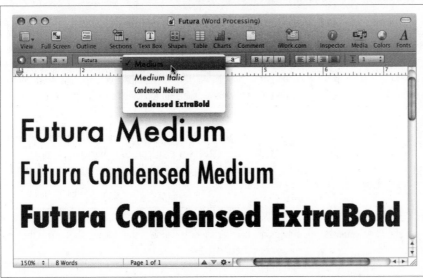

Figure 2-4:
The Futura typeface family includes Medium, Medium Italic, Condensed Medium, and Condensed ExtraBold font variations, all served up in the typeface pop-up menu, and offering dramatically different variations on Futura's letterforms.

Pages applies your formatting changes to the currently selected text, but if you don't have any text selected, the formatting is applied to the *entire word* where the blinking insertion point is located. This is handy if you want to italicize an entire word, for example: Just click anywhere inside the word and press the keystroke for italic (⌘-I). If the insertion point isn't inside a word, then Pages applies the formatting to *whatever you type next*. This lets you set the formatting as you type: Immediately before typing the word you want to italicize, for example, press ⌘-I, then type the word, which appears in italic—press the keystroke *again* to turn off italic and return to typing normal text.

The Fonts Window

The Format Bar will scratch most of your font-formatting itches, but when you need fine-tuned control over your fonts—or want to add zany effects—it's the Fonts window to the rescue. Click the toolbar's Fonts button or choose Format → Fonts → Show Fonts to open the Fonts window, shown in Figure 2-5. You can also open the Fonts window by pressing ⌘-T (for "Type").

The heart of the Fonts window is the display of columns that list your font collections (font groupings that came on your computer or that you've created), the font family (the typeface name—Helvetica or Times, for example), the typeface (the font style—plain, bold, italic, and so on), and the size. Select All Fonts under Collections to see every font available on your computer. Work your way through the columns from left to right to select a font, style, and size. When you choose a font, the Fonts window showcases the font in the window's Preview pane, at the same time updating the selected text in your document.

Although the Preview pane is quite possibly the Fonts window's best feature, it's closed when you open the Fonts window for the first time. You can correct that in the Fonts window's Action menu, the gear pop-up menu in the bottom-left corner. Choose Show Preview to reveal the Preview pane. As you select fonts, styles, and sizes you can now see exactly what they look like.

Tip: If you open the Preview pane to the entire height of the Fonts window, the font controls reduce into compact pop-up menus instead of the bevy of buttons and column listings that you see in Figure 2-5. You can likewise get the same effect by dragging the resize handle in the bottom-right corner of the Fonts window; when the window is small enough, the controls switch to the compact version. This is convenient when you want to keep the Fonts window around without giving up too much screen real estate.

The font effects toolbar. The Fonts window provides its own little special-effects laboratory, adding glitz to your text with effects including 3D shadows, colors, and custom strikethrough or underline styles. See Figure 2-5 for a rundown of all the options available in the effects toolbar.

Note: Oddly enough, the Fonts window's Preview pane doesn't give you much of a preview when it comes to effects. As you tickle the buttons on the effects toolbar, none of the changes show up in the window's Preview pane—only in your document's selected text.

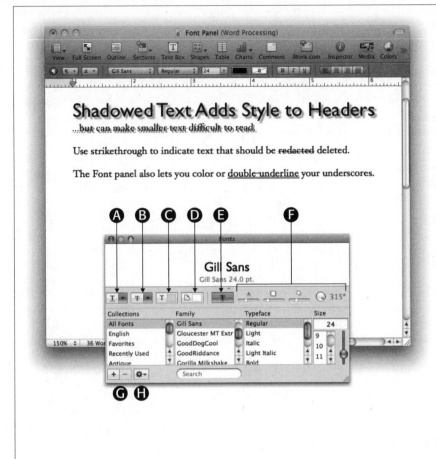

Figure 2-5:
Use the Fonts window to add special effects to your text. The Underline pop-up (A) lets you add single or double underlines and choose an underline color. The Strikethrough pop-up (B) applies a single or double line through your text, and lets you choose the line's color.

Click the Text Color button (C), and the Color Picker pops up to help you choose a text color (see page 265). A click of the misnamed Document Color button (D) also brings up the Color Picker, this time applying color to the background of the entire paragraph.

Click the Text Shadow button (E) to add drama to a headline–or make body text nearly unreadable. Four controls (F) adjust the shadow's opacity, blurriness, offset, and angle. Use the + and – buttons to create or remove font collections (G), and click the Action pop-up (H) to access yet more formatting options.

The Action menu. You can control the Fonts window's behavior and access some of its more esoteric font settings through the Action menu. Click the Action pop-up menu at the bottom of the Fonts window—it looks like a gear—to see these options.

- **Add to Favorites.** After you choose a font family, typeface, and size, use this command to add the font to a special collection called Favorites. Your Mac saves the font, style, and size in the Fonts window's Favorites and Recently Used collections. You can use these font collections in any program that uses OS X's Fonts window, such as Keynote, Numbers, and Mail.

- **Show/Hide Preview.** Toggle the display of the Preview pane on and off.

- **Hide/Show Effects.** Choose this command to hide the row of buttons for text special effects—underline, color, shadow, and so on.

- **Color.** The Color Picker appears when you choose this command, allowing you to choose a text color—useful if you choose to hide the color effects buttons, above. See page 265 for more about the Color Picker.

- **Characters.** Forget about trying to remember the convoluted keyboard combinations for the special symbols included in many fonts. This command brings up the *Characters window,* Mac OS X's built-in cheat sheet for selecting math and currency symbols, Greek letters, copyright signs, and so on. See page 82 for more info about the Characters window.

- **Typography.** Some fonts, such as Zapfino and Hoefler, have advanced typography features, which let you create different effects. The Typography window offers controls for these features, presenting different options depending on the font you've selected. This spins quickly into obscure realms like Unicode decomposition, Diacritics, Yiddish Digraphs, Diphthong ligatures, or Vietnamese Double Accents. (If such typographical exotica sound useful to you, a quick Google search turns up definitions for this lingo, which is, alas, beyond the scope of this book.)

- **Edit Sizes.** This command lets you show or hide the font size list and slider, and set a size range for the slider. You can also edit the list of sizes displayed, so, for example, if you often use a font size of 13.6 or 192 points, you can add those sizes to the list for easy access—and remove 9 if you never use it. And this is handy: As mentioned earlier, the changes you make here also show up in the Font Size pop-up menu in the Format Bar.

- **Manage Fonts.** Choose the final command in the Action menu to open Font Book, the heart of Mac OS X's font management system. In Font Book you can add or remove fonts, activate or disable fonts, search for duplicate fonts, and manage your font collections.

UP TO SPEED

Serve Up the Serifs

Serifs are the little points or lines at the ends of strokes that form certain typefaces—the "feet" at the bottom of H, I, or T, for example. They're remnants of the time before printing presses, when all type was inscribed by hand with a broad-tipped pen and ink. Over the past 500 years, type designers have retained serifs in these font designs—not out of a reverence for tradition, but because serifs make type more readable in print. Tests for readability have shown that serif-style typefaces like Garamond, Palatino, and Times are much easier to read in blocks of printed text than *sans serif* typefaces like Helvetica, Arial, or Verdana. Most books, including this one, use a serif font as the primary typeface, reserving sans serif fonts for headlines, titles, and little informative sidebar boxes like this one. Assuming that your documents are destined for print, do your readers a favor by following this convention, whether you're writing a letter, a newsletter, or a doctoral dissertation.

On the other hand, other studies show that *on computer screens,* sans serif fonts are more legible, particularly at smaller sizes. You can have it both ways: Set your body text in a serif font, but pamper your own eyeballs with a large Page View setting of 150 percent or more (see page 42).

Setting Colors and Character Spacing in the Text Inspector

The *Text Inspector* offers lots of additional options for formatting your text, but most of those sundries apply to paragraph and list formatting, which you'll learn about later in this chapter. For now, we'll take just a quick look at the Text Inspector's text controls for color and character spacing. To open the Text Inspector, click the Inspector button on the toolbar or choose View → Show Inspector and then click the Inspector window's Text button (the big "T"), as shown in Figure 2-6.

The Color Picker

The Text Inspector's Text tab includes the *Text Color* sample box, or *color well*. Clicking the color well calls up the Color Picker, the Mac OS X palette of millions of colors which you can use to paint your text. Choose a color, and Pages pours your selection into the Text Color well, applying the new color to your highlighted text at the same time. See page 265 for a full tour of the Color Picker's features.

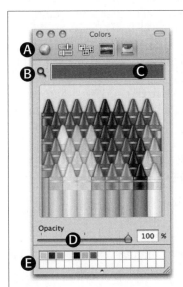
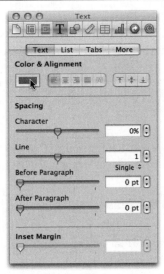

Figure 2-6:
The Text Inspector's Text tab offers control for character and paragraph spacing, alignment, and text color. Click the Text Color box to call up the Color Picker with its five top buttons offering different approaches to picking colors (A). Click the magnifying glass (B) to turn your cursor into a color sampling tool–click any color on the screen to load that color into the color swatch (C). Control the transparency of the color with the Opacity slider–or enter a percentage in the box (D). Store your favorite colors for later use by dragging them from the swatch into the little squares at the bottom of the window (E). If one row of favorites isn't enough, drag the dot at the bottom edge to expand the window.

Spread the word: Character Spacing

The Text tab also includes the *Character Spacing* slider which adjusts the amount of space between letters, known to typographers as *tracking*. You might want to use this control, for example, to expand or contract a headline to perfectly fit above a column. Used judiciously—just a few percent—the effect is nearly invisible, yet can make a big improvement to the appearance of your layout. Use it at higher or lower settings only if you're trying to attract attention.

Note: You can also use the Format → Font → Tracking menu to Tighten, Loosen or reset the character spacing (Use None). But because the Tighten/Loosen sub-submenu commands nudge the character spacing only one percent at a time, they're a maddeningly slow way to make changes; you're better off using the Text Inspector's Character Spacing slider.

Lifting your letters with Baseline Shift

Click the Text Inspector's More tab to get at one other text formatting control tucked in among the paragraph formatting controls: *Baseline Shift.* Use this setting to raise or lower the selected text relative to other text on the same line. Use the up arrow button or enter the number of points in the box to raise the text; use the down arrow button or enter a negative number to lower the text.

The Format → Font → Baseline menu holds commands for raising and lowering the baseline in one-point increments and for creating preset *superscripts* and *subscripts*—raised or lowered baselines and a smaller font size—which are useful for creating endnote reference numbers or chemical formulas. Those superscript and subscript commands will typically give you the effect you're after when you need a dash of mc^2 or a drink of H_2O. When you want to raise or lower the baseline without changing the font size, the Baseline submenu's Raise and Lower commands will work, but you'll find the Text Inspector's Baseline Shift control more flexible. With this control, you can make fractional-point adjustments to the baseline shift—just what you might need for precision character tweaking when you're mixing different fonts on the same line, or need to adjust a trademark ™ symbol, for example.

Note: If you raise or lower one or more characters' baselines, Pages increases the line spacing above or below that line, unless you set a fixed line spacing in Text Inspector → Text (see page 70).

The Format → Font Menu

As you've seen, you can use the Format → Font menu to access some of the same controls found in the Format Bar, the Fonts window, and the Text Inspector. This submenu adds a few new tricks, too:

- **Bigger/Smaller.** The Bigger and Smaller commands nudge the font size of the selected text up or down by one point. You can also use the keyboard shortcuts ⌘-+ for Bigger and ⌘-– for Smaller (that's ⌘-Minus).

- **Ligature.** The commands in this sub-submenu let you turn *ligatures* on or off for the selected text (see the box, "Ligatures: The Art of Linked Letters" on page 67). Choose Use Default to use the settings specified in the Fonts window's Typography window for the font you're using, or choose Use All to turn on all available ligatures for the selected text. (Note that these two commands have no effect if ligatures are turned off in the Document Inspector for the entire document.) Choose Use None to turn off ligatures for the selected text.

- **Capitalization.** Miscategorized as a set of font commands, this sub-submenu changes the case of the selected text, offering options for None, All Caps, Small Caps, and Title. "None" is the default state of affairs and displays your text just as you typed it. All Caps capitalizes EVERY LETTER of the selected text. Small Caps also makes every letter capital but observes your original capitalization by making CAPITAL LETTERS LARGER. Choose Title to capitalize The First Letter Of Every Word in the selection. These options don't actually change the text you originally typed—they change only the way the text is displayed. If you change text to All Caps and then back to None, for example, the text displays your original capitalization.

Tip: Consider adding the Bigger and Smaller buttons to your toolbar so you can quickly increase or decrease font size. If you write numbers in exponential notation or often use chemical symbols, you could likewise put the Subscript and Superscript toolbar buttons to good use. (See page 40 for more on customizing the toolbar.)

UP TO SPEED

Ligatures: The Art of Linked Letters

Ligatures are pairs of letters that share common components when printed next to each other. Scribes writing with pen and ink in the Middle Ages originally created ligatures to save space on the parchment and increase writing speed—just like when you cross two "t"s in a word at once when you write, "butter," for example. Believe it or not, the ampersand (&) is actually a stylized ligature for the letters *et*—Latin for *and*.

Typographers now create these special combination characters to improve the printed text's appearance. The most common ligatures are ff, fi, fl, ffi, and ffl. In most typefaces, ligatures provide very subtle typographic differences, but some typefaces have much more dramatic ligatures, as demonstrated by the Zapfino typeface, shown at right without ligatures (top) and with ligatures (bottom).

Formatting Paragraphs

All the text-styling you've seen so far can be applied to any selection—as little as a single character—but Pages offers another category of formatting options which apply to whole paragraphs at a time. These settings include line spacing, tabs, indentation, and paragraph background color. (Formatting lists with bullets and numbering is also a type of paragraph formatting, and you'll learn more about that later in this chapter; see page 84.)

Since these formatting styles apply to the entire paragraph, all you have to do is put your insertion point *anywhere* within the paragraph you want to change—no need to highlight the whole thing precisely from end to end. You can have a selection within the paragraph highlighted, or you can just click anywhere inside. To apply paragraph formatting to several paragraphs, you can select just a part of those paragraphs, grabbing the last few words of one paragraph and the first few of the next, for example. The point here: It's okay to be sloppy when it comes to selecting text for paragraph formatting. However you do it, when you make the change, Pages updates *all the text* in any paragraphs included in your selection.

When you press Return and start a new paragraph, that paragraph inherits the formatting of its predecessor. You can type merrily away, and your formatting will stay the same from paragraph to paragraph until you decide to make another change.

Aligning Your Text

You can use one of the most basic paragraph formatting options—*text alignment*—to enhance the overall appearance and readability of your document. Two of the four alignment styles look "normal" (left aligned and justified)—the other two (right aligned and centered) are better reserved for headings and other special occasions. To adjust paragraph alignment, click one of the four text-alignment buttons in the Format Bar, shown in Figure 2-7. (You'll also find these same buttons in the Text Inspector's Tabs pane, and the Format → Text menu also offers the four alignment options.)

Align left

Most people use the familiar, standard typewriter style for most text: *left aligned,* also called *flush left* or *ragged right.* It looks "normal" to most people. In fact, readability experts give the nod to left-aligned text for best readability because every line starts at the same point, words have uniform spacing, and hey, people are used to it. It doesn't distract. This style is typical for letters and manuscripts—in fact, for anything that you don't want to proclaim as "differently formatted."

Justified

Next on the readability scale is *justified,* a.k.a. *force justified* or *fully justified.* This style forces all lines to stretch themselves so that their ends line up neatly with both the left and right margins, making every line exactly the same width for a clean, well-ordered, and distinctly non-ragged appearance. You often see justified style used in magazines, newspapers, and books (including this one).

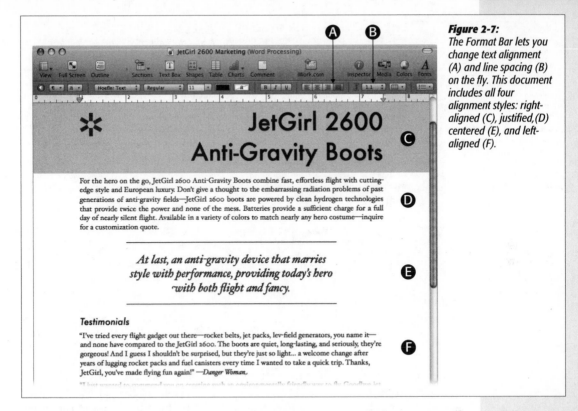

Figure 2-7:
The Format Bar lets you change text alignment (A) and line spacing (B) on the fly. This document includes all four alignment styles: right-aligned (C), justified,(D) centered (E), and left-aligned (F).

Pages teases lines all the way to the margin by varying the spacing between words. When the columns of text are wide enough and the words aren't too long, justification works well. But if the columns are too narrow, you can end up with an uneven look and huge gaps between words, as shown in the stretched text in Figure 2-8. Hyphenating long words helps reduce this problem.

Tip: The secret to successful justification is to make sure your text columns are wide enough. The recipe for minimum column width: Font size in points, divided by three, equals the minimum column width in inches. So for 12-point type, the narrowest column should be 12 ÷ 3 = 4".

Align right

Although difficult to read for more than a few lines, *right-aligned* text can be useful as a design flourish for headings and callouts. Also known as *flush right, ragged left, right justified,* or just weird, a paragraph formatted in this way demands attention. Remember, though, that readers have limited tolerance for such eccentricity. Like centered text (described next) and body piercing, the flush-right style can be effective when you use it selectively, but scary in excess.

Up & Away offers super-stretch abilities in a wide array of plasticity, giving the modern hero the long arm of the law—quite literally. Stretch your limbs and torso up to 100 meters, bend around complex obstacles, and step over tall buildings (leaping no longer required). Several new products from our plastics laboratory also offer low-viscosity plasticity, allowing you to "flow" under doors, through key holes and, generally, out of any tight spot.

Up & Away offers super-stretch abilities in a wide array of plasticity, giving the modern hero the long arm of the law—quite literally. Stretch your limbs and torso up to 100 meters, bend around complex obstacles, and step over tall buildings (leaping no longer required). Several new products from our plastics laboratory also offer low-viscosity plasticity, allowing you to "flow" under doors, through key holes and, generally, out of any tight spot.

Our plastics experts have also developed stretch-appropriate uniforms and battle costumes to allow your hero togs to keep up with you as stretch, melt, and squeeze. These unique, hypo-allergenic fabrics always spring back into shape—no more droopy tights or over-stretched sleeves. This new line of costumes is fully machine-washable, so you won't break the bank at the dry cleaner (or endure the usual prying questions costumes always invite at the cleaner.)

Figure 2-8:
Under the right conditions, justified text makes your page look especially tidy, but be on the lookout for the gaps of white space that tend to crop up in narrow columns (left). Typesetters call this effect rivers, as these gaps line up and seem to flow through your columns of text. The remedy: Be sure the columns aren't too narrow (right), and turn on automatic hyphenation (see page 147).

Centered

Give someone access to paragraph alignment controls, and it seems like they're magnetically drawn to *centered* text alignment. Centering can indeed bring an elegant and formal look to small amounts of text but please, use restraint. Like right-aligned text, this style is at the bottom of the heap for readability—every line begins and ends in a different spot creating a real tracking problem for the reader's eyeballs. If your document is longer than a few lines, think thrice about centering, and instead reserve it for headings and special display text.

Between the Lines: Line Spacing

Give your words some breathing room by opening up the space between lines, or go the other way to cram more words onto the page. Pages defaults to single-spaced lines but lets you set the *line spacing* anywhere from .01 to 10 lines, where one is standard single-spaced lines, two is double-spaced, and so on. Be careful setting this limbo stick too low, or your lines won't be able to clear it—the low, low, low .01 setting, for example, flattens your entire document into just a dense thicket of overlapping, illegible scribbles.

The Line Spacing pop-up in the Format Bar lets you set the spacing on the selected paragraph anywhere from .5 to two lines. For a wider set of options, open the Text Inspector and click the Text tab (Figure 2-6, shown previously) to adjust line spacing with the Line slider, the up and down arrows, or by typing a number into the Line field. Below the Line field is the pop-up menu for setting Single, Double, or Multiple spacing, plus three more settings allow for flexible line heights and spacing:

- **Single, Double, and Multiple.** When you select Single, Double, or Multiple spacing, Pages automatically adjusts the line spacing in proportion to the font size. In certain conditions, this means that some paragraphs could contain uneven line spacing: If one of your lines contains a word in a larger font or with a shifted baseline, the spacing around that line will also be larger.

- **Exactly.** This option gives you *fixed* line spacing, where every line is spaced at the same interval regardless of the font size. In truth, this setting doesn't really control line *spacing* but rather line *height*, the distance from one line's baseline to the next. Setting this to 12 points, for example, sets the height of each line to 12 points, rather than adding an *additional* 12 points between each line.

- **At Least.** As with Exactly, this setting applies to height rather than spacing. When you choose At Least, the line height adapts based on font size as it would with single-spaced text, but you guarantee a minimum height—all line heights will be *at least* the measurement set here. If you have one line set at a smaller font size than the value entered here, for example, then Pages bumps up the spacing for that line to meet this minimum height.

- **Between.** This setting lets you define the exact spacing *between* each line. Pages sets line heights as it would for single-spaced text, and then adds or subtracts the spacing set here. A value of zero points results in single line spacing. A negative value decreases line spacing, eventually overlapping the lines of text.

Spacing Your Paragraphs

Pages observes the usual keyboard physics when you press Return: The insertion point bumps down to the beginning of a new line. You can make your documents more reader-friendly by adding some white space between paragraphs to help break up a text-filled page. You *could* just press Return twice at the end of each paragraph, but instead Pages can take over this task, automatically inserting any amount of white space you desire between paragraphs. This isn't just a timesaving convenience or a matter of conservation ("Save the keystrokes!"); it gives you formatting flexibility, letting you set the spacing between paragraphs to be a bit more or a bit less than a full line break, for example.

Open the Text Inspector and click the Text tab (Figure 2-6, shown previously) to get at the paragraph spacing controls. Use the Before Paragraph slider to add space before the selected paragraph; use the After Paragraph slider to add space below it. Instead of using the sliders, you can also type a point measurement directly into the measurement box or use the up and down arrows.

Line breaks vs. paragraph breaks

Great, so you've added some paragraph spacing, and now you're flying through your document, trailing gorgeous plumes of white space behind every paragraph. But what if you just want a new line—a quick trip down to the next row of text, not a full-blown paragraph with its extra spacing? In that case, you need a *line break.* Until now, you might have thought that's what the Return key gives you, but as you've seen, pressing the Return key actually buys you a new paragraph, not just a new line. To get a simple line break, press Shift-Return. Pages bumps the insertion point down to the next line, but considers that you're still within the same paragraph—the same formatting rules apply, and you keep any automatic paragraph spacing at bay.

Setting Tabs

Back in the mechanical era of the typewriter, the most efficient way to create tables was to use *tabs,* short for tabulation. Instead of painstakingly tapping just the right number of spaces to line up every column, the typist set a mechanical lever at each column position, or *tab stop,* on the page. Pressing the Tab key zipped the typewriter carriage to the next stop, making column layout and paragraph indentation faster, easier, and more accurate.

Tabs are still with us, and they remain a handy way to make simple tables and line up columns on an invoice, résumé, or expense report. Just like its typewriter ancestors, Pages jumps the insertion point to the next tab stop every time you press the Tab key—until you reach the right margin, when pressing the Tab key zips the insertion point down to the first tab stop on the next line. This transition to the next line typically brings the last word of text along with it, too, so it makes for sloppy formatting; when adding tab stops to individual lines, you're usually better off pressing Return at the end of each line, a rare exception to the "don't treat it like a typewriter" rule.

Tip: For all but the most simple tables, you'll find Pages' built-in table tools to be much more powerful than the humble tab. These tables make it easy to make quick adjustments, add borders and shading, and even manage your math for you. For more on using tables, see Chapter 8.

As with other paragraph-formatting options, tab-stop settings apply to entire paragraphs at a time, and you can have different tab stops for individual paragraphs. Pages displays the tab stops for the selected paragraph(s) along the *horizontal ruler* just below the Format Bar, as shown in Figure 2-9. Choose View → Show Rulers or press ⌘-R to show the ruler—to hide it, choose View → Hide Rulers or press ⌘-R again. (Pages sets the standard ruler unit to inches; open Pages → Preferences and change the Ruler Units setting if you prefer centimeters, points, or picas.)

When you open a new document, the ruler is scrubbed clean, featuring no tab markers at all, which might lead you to believe that pressing the Tab key will have no effect. Au contraire: Until you create your own custom tab stops, Pages provides "invisible" stops every half inch—pressing tab jumps you ahead to the next half-inch tab stop. However, once you place any of your own tab stops, all the invisible tabs to the *left* of the custom tab evaporate; the ones to the right remain.

Note: If you prefer different spacing for these default tab stops, it's easy enough to change. Open the Text Inspector, click Tabs, and adjust the setting for Default Tabs. This changes the tab stops for the selected paragraph.

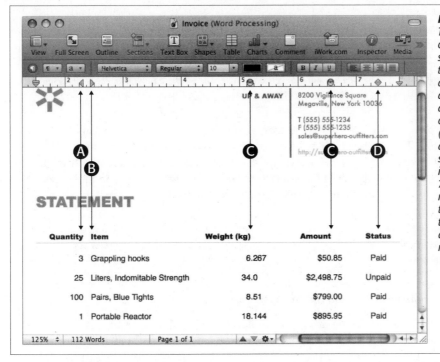

Figure 2-9:
This simple invoice contains all the tab styles: right-aligned for the quantity (A), left-aligned for the item (B), decimal for the weight and amount (C), and centered for the status (D). The ruler also displays the margin settings and the first-line indent marker (see page 75). Drag any of these markers back and forth to adjust their position in the selected paragraph, and drag a tab off the ruler to delete it.

Working with custom tab stops

Add a new tab to the selected paragraph by clicking anywhere along the ruler, and Pages adds a *left-aligned* tab stop at that location. Pages offers four tab styles, each represented on the ruler by a different icon and illustrated in Figure 2-9. Control-click a tab marker to choose a tab style. Or double-click the marker to change styles—keep double-clicking and Pages cycles through all the styles, in this order:

- **Left-aligned.** This is the "normal" type of tab, familiar to former typewriter users worldwide. When you tab to a left-aligned tab stop and start typing, the left end of the new text starts at this tab and continues to the right.

- **Center-aligned.** After tabbing to this tab stop, your subsequent typing remains centered under the tab. For example, you can make sure several lines in a column are centered above one another.

- **Right-aligned.** When you tab to a right-aligned tab stop, what you type next flows to the *left*; the right end of the text remains aligned with the tab stop.

- **Decimal or Aligned-On.** This kind of tab is the secret to keeping columns of numbers under control. When you press Tab and the insertion point lands under a decimal tab stop, it behaves like a right-aligned tab until you press the decimal point. That decimal point remains directly underneath the tab stop— and exactly under the decimal point in the line above—and now your typing flows to the *right* of the tab stop. In other words, a column of numbers aligns perfectly on the decimal point.

Tip: The decimal point doesn't have to be the symbol that aligns line after line beneath a decimal tab. Open the Text Inspector → Tabs pane to reveal the Decimal Tab Character setting. Type any character you like here, such as a comma, an asterisk, a percent sign, or even a letter. The first occurrence of this symbol serves as the balancing point between right and left-justified typing on this special kind of tab stop. For example, if you're aligning a column of version numbers for software programs, Pages aligns the version numbers on the first dot in "version 10.3.8".

To remove a tab stop, drag its marker off the ruler, and it disappears in a puff of smoke. To change a tab's position, drag its marker to the new location on the ruler. While you're dragging, Pages helpfully displays a vertical guideline through your document to help you line up the tab in your text—when you drop the marker at its new location, Pages automatically updates your tabbed text to reflect the change.

Tip: Tabs snap to the nearest ruler mark when you drag them; for more precise control hold the ⌘ key while dragging, or get more ruler marks by zooming in on the page with the Page View pop-up menu (see page 42).

Fine-tuning your tabs in the Text Inspector

In most cases, clicking around the ruler gives you all the control you'll need over your tabs. But the Text Inspector reserves an entire, er, tab for these settings, including a few options in the Tabs pane that are not available on the ruler, as shown in Figure 2-10. The Tab Stops field displays all your custom tab stops, listing each by their distance from the left edge of your document text.

Note: Stop rubbing your eyes, you're not seeing things: The values in the Tab Stops box don't match the tab stops' locations on the ruler. The ruler shows the distance from the edge of the *paper,* while the Tab Stops list shows the distances from the left edge of your *text*—in other words, the Tab Stops distances don't include the document margins.

To add a new tab stop from the Text Inspector, click the + sign at the bottom-left corner of the Inspector window. If this is the first custom tab stop for the paragraph, Pages adds the new tab stop at the same location as the first "invisible" tab stop (the default increment value shown in Default Tabs). If the paragraph already has custom tab stops, Pages adds the new tab stop after all your other tabs, separated by the default increment value—if Default Tabs is "0.5 in," and you already have a tab at "1 in," the new tab appears at "1.5 in."

To edit a tab stop's position from the Text Inspector, double-click it in the Tab Stops list, and type its new number. To change a tab's alignment style, select the tab in the Tab Stops list, and choose the new style from the Alignment radio buttons. To remove it, click the – (minus) button, or press the Delete key.

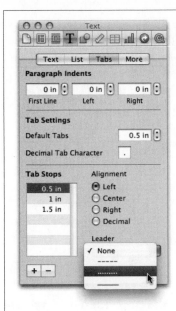

Figure 2-10:
The Text Inspector's Tabs pane offers the mathematically inclined an alternative to the ruler. Here you can set everything you can in the ruler: margins, first-line indent, and tabs. In addition, you can control the spacing for Default Tabs, select the Decimal Tab Character that provides the alignment point for that kind of tab, and control the presence of "leader lines" between tabs using the Leader pop-up menu.

At the bottom of this window is the Leader pop-up menu—the control for creating a *leader line* of dots, hyphens, or underlines between columns. When you add a leader to a tab, it leaves a streaming trail behind it, leading the eye to the next tab column across the page. Common uses of leader lines include menus, tables of contents, price lists, theater programs, and so on. The leader characters fill the space to the left of the tab to which the leader is assigned. The price list in Figure 2-11 shows the effect.

Note: Using leader lines isn't just the right way to do this particular job, it's the *easy* way. You might feel the urge to attempt this effect just by typing a line of periods, for example. Just say no. This will eventually backfire on you when you edit the text on either side of the periods, or change the font size of the document. You'll constantly find yourself trying to get things lined up again, cleaning up dots like some kind of existential Pac-Man game.

Indenting Text

Now that you've mastered the art of the tab, you might be tempted to start putting it to use by using tabs to indent the first line of your paragraphs. Resist. Although tabs were once the preferred way for generations of old-school typists to indent a line of text, Pages offers a more streamlined way to indent lines or paragraphs. Just like tab stops, you can change indentation by dragging the indentation controls on the ruler, or by working the sliders in the Text Inspector → Tabs pane.

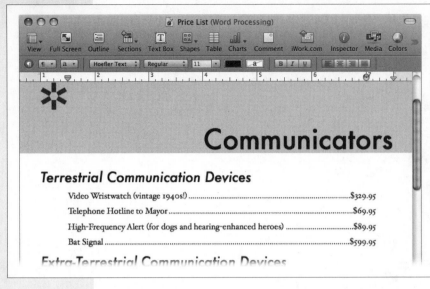

Figure 2-11:
*Don't duplicate this look
by pressing the period
key over and over again.
Instead, use leader lines
to lead the eye from one
column to the next; you
create them with the Tab
key. Add this option to a
tab in the Text Inspector's
Tabs pane: Click the tab
in the Tab Stops field,
and choose one of three
styles from the Leader
pop-up menu.*

The ruler displays the left and right boundaries of the current text as downward blue triangles, the left and right *indent markers* shown in Figure 2-12. To change the left or right indentation of the selected paragraph, drag the appropriate indent marker to the new location. Just like when you move a tab, Pages shows a vertical guideline while you drag to help you pinpoint the best location.

The left indent marker travels with a companion, the *first-line indent marker,* shown on the ruler as a horizontal bar. This marker controls where the first line of the paragraph begins. If you like to indent the first line of your paragraphs, you can use this control to have Pages handle that indentation automatically instead of using the Tab key (or worse, the space bar). For a traditional paragraph indentation, for example, drag the marker to the right of the left indent marker. You can also *outdent* the first line of text, also known as a *hanging indent,* by moving the marker to the left of the left indent marker, so that the first line of text hangs out into the left margin.

Tip: When you drag the left indent marker, the first-line indent marker moves, too. To move the left indent marker independently, hold down the Option key while you drag it.

As usual, the ruler gives you fast, visual access for making changes, but the Text Inspector gives you more precise controls over paragraph indentation. Open the Tabs pane in the Text Inspector (refer to Figure 2-10) and, under Paragraph Indents, make your adjustments to the First Line, Left, and Right settings. As with tabs, these settings reflect the distance from the edge of the document margins, not the edge of the paper.

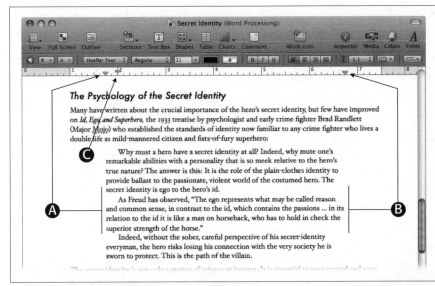

Figure 2-12:
The ruler's indent markers control the left (A) and right (B) boundaries of your text. You can give special treatment to the first line of your paragraphs with the first-line indent marker (C). Here, both the left and right margins of the quotation paragraphs are indented, and the first line is also set to indent.

DESIGN TIME

Em Space = Enough Space

If you indent the first line of your paragraphs, don't overdo it. In particular, avoid using the default half-inch tab stop as your first-line indent—the gaping size of the indentation gives your graceful prose a clumsy aesthetic.

If you care about such typographical niceties, you can make your pages look more professional with a much smaller

indent—one *em space*. So called because it is the width of an upper-case M, this typographically balanced indent measures only about .16 inch for 12-point type. To set the first-line indent, open the Text Inspector and click Tabs. Enter .16 or .2 inch in the first-line box and Pages applies this indent to selected or subsequent paragraphs.

Setting Paragraph Borders and Background Color

Judicious use of background color and borders can serve to highlight portions of your text, visually setting it apart from the main body of your document. You might put this trick to use, for example, for side notes like the "Em Space = Enough Space" box on this page, for contact information on a flyer, or an author bio at the bottom of an article.

Adding borders and rules

Pages lets you add lines around your text in two different styles, as *borders* and *rules*. A border is a box that surrounds the selected text, while a rule is a line that appears between paragraphs.

To add a box around one or more paragraphs, you add a *border*:

1. **Place the insertion point inside the paragraph to box, or highlight several paragraphs to draw the box around all of them.**

2. Open the Text Inspector → More tab, shown in Figure 2-13.

3. Choose a line style from the *Border & Rules* pop-up menu.

4. **Choose where you want the line to appear by clicking one of the border or rule buttons, labeled D in Figure 2-13.**

   In this example, you're adding a border around all four sides of the paragraph, so click the Border button, the far right button in the group.

Change the color of the border by clicking the color well to the right of the Border & Rules pop-up—Pages reveals the Color Picker to let you choose the color to use. Widen or narrow the border by adjusting the Line Width setting. The Offset field controls the amount of padding between the text and the border—increase the offset to give your text some breathing room, or decrease it to tighten the border.

Figure 2-13:
Add borders and rules to your text in the Text Inspector's More tab: The Border & Rules pop-up menu (A) selects the line style to use; The color well (B) selects the line color; The Line Width setting (C) controls the line thickness; the rule and border buttons (D) control the location of the border; and The Offset field (E) controls the padding between the line and the text.

To add a background color, turn on the Paragraph checkbox (F), and click the color well to choose the color from the Color Picker.

To add lines between paragraphs instead of a box around them, click one of the *rule buttons* to the left of the Border button (labeled D in Figure 2-13). These settings let you draw a rule above, below, or above *and* below the selected paragraphs. To remove all rules or borders from a paragraph, choose None from the Border & Rules pop-up.

Rules follow different, er, rules than borders. The border box always extends to the entire width of the column, plus a bit of offset, so that the box actually extends beyond the normal text column on both the left and right. Changing the left or right indentation of text inside a border box has no effect on the border—the box still extends for the whole width of the column, ignoring any paragraph indentation.

Rules, however, always observe paragraph indentation and stretch from the left indent to the right indent, giving you the same width as the text itself. Also, unlike borders, which you can apply to a set of paragraphs to draw a single box around all of them, rules stick to individual paragraphs only. If you highlight several paragraphs and click the top-line rule, for example, the rule shows up above *each* of the selected paragraphs, giving you a line between all your paragraphs. In this example, to add a line above only the top paragraph, you should instead select only that first paragraph, or use line breaks instead of paragraph breaks to split your text.

Paragraph background color

To add a splash of color behind the selected paragraph(s), go to the Text Inspector → More tab, and turn on the checkbox for Paragraph Fill. Choose a color by clicking the color well, and make a selection from the Color Picker.

Alas, if you try to add a border box *and* a background color to a paragraph, you'll find that the color doesn't quite make it wall-to-wall. The border box extends beyond the width of the text column, but the color does not, giving you uncolored stripes on either side. To create a shaded box, you'll get better results using a text box (see page 216 in Chapter 7).

Tip: When you use paragraph background colors, it's a good idea to fine-tune your paragraph spacing. Setting one half of the paragraph spacing before the paragraph and one half after results in the paragraph centered on the background color box.

Coping with Break-Ups

Carefully crafted words split asunder, paragraphs separated, headings introducing nothing at all, widows and orphans left behind—oh, the inhumanity! Who knew turning the page could be so violent? Most of the time, of course, page breaks are unremarkable, and your word processor does you a service by quietly and automatically continuing your text to a new page. Every so often, though, a page break conspires to split up a paragraph that should be kept whole (the caption for a picture or a sidebar box, for example). Other common page-break fractures: two paragraphs that should stick together (a heading and the text it introduces) or a single lonely line of text.

Them's the breaks, but don't despair. Pages gives you tools to prevent ugly break-ups.

Inserting a page break

Pages gives you explicit control over when to turn the page by letting you insert a page break. Choose Insert → Page Break, and Pages starts a new page at the insertion point. (Pages also offers section breaks, layout breaks, and column breaks, all described in Chapter 5.)

You can get a similar effect by specifying that a paragraph should always start on a new page. To do this, select a paragraph and, in the Text Inspector → More tab, turn on the "Paragraph starts on a new page" option.

Tip: In practice, you're usually better off inserting an actual page break than turning on the "Paragraph starts on a new page" setting. That's because a manual page break makes it more obvious why a new page is starting—the page break shows up as a formatting character when you select it or turn on invisible characters (see page 81), while the "Paragraph starts on a new page" option is hidden away in the Text Inspector. The exception, however, is when you want to create a recurring style—like a chapter heading—to always start a new page. You'll learn all about styles in Chapter 3, starting on page 93.

A manual page break is best used to separate different parts of your document—like chapters of a book or sections of a report—but it's a blunt instrument at best when it comes to fine-tuning page breaks for specific paragraphs. If text you want to keep together is getting split, then sure, you can fix that by forcing a page break before the paragraph, but at a price: When you make changes to the document down the road, your page break could slip to the middle of a page, leaving you with a gaping hole of white space. For situations like this, Pages instead lets you attach rules to paragraphs that control how they behave when a new page comes along.

Caring for widows and orphans

In typesetting lingo, *widows* and *orphans* are single lines of text isolated from the other lines of their paragraph by a page break. (A widow is a line that continues alone at the top of the next page, and an orphan is a line abandoned at the bottom of a page by the rest of its paragraph.) These dangling darlings are considered poor form in page design, and Pages prevents them by default with a no-line-left-behind policy, shifting page breaks as necessary to avoid chopping off a paragraph at its first or last line. Turn this option on or off for the selected paragraph in the Text Inspector → More tab, with the "Prevent widow & orphan lines" checkbox.

Keeping lines and paragraphs together

Preventing widows and orphans is all well and good, but what about keeping the whole family together? You can tell Pages that it should keep a paragraph whole by turning on the "Keep lines together" option in the Text Inspector → More tab. With that setting enabled, Pages will never split up the selected paragraph, instead starting a new page before the paragraph when necessary to keep its lines together.

You can similarly ask Pages to keep paragraphs together with the "Keep with following paragraph" option. As its name suggests, this setting prevents page breaks from separating the selected paragraph from the next one. This is especially useful to glue headings to the text they introduce, for example. (See "Herculean Headings" on page 100.)

Spaces, Invisibles, and Special Characters

So far, this chapter has reviewed how to format your text to make it more pleasing to the eye. But what about what the eye *can't* see? Don't look now, but your Pages document and your keyboard are both teeming with hidden symbols. Here's how to unleash these mysterious characters.

Viewing Invisibles

While you're crafting your words and paragraphs, you probably don't give much thought to the spaces between them, but they're not as empty as you might think. There's a whole universe of invisible characters living in that white space. Every time you press the space bar, the Tab key, or the Return key, for example, Pages adds a formatting character to your document. These formatting marks are called *invisibles* because, you guessed it, you can't normally see them, except for the space they leave behind. They're conspicuous by their absence.

Note: Joining these rather ordinary spacing characters are several other invisibles, which stand in for more complex formatting. These include page breaks, section breaks, column breaks, layout breaks, and anchor points which you'll learn about in the coming chapters.

As you format your document, it can be helpful to see the details of these spacing characters: Are those line breaks or paragraph breaks? Spaces or tabs? Is that an extra space between those two words?

The challenge with seeing invisibles is, of course, their invisibility. Many of these characters—specifically, all the "breaks," including paragraph breaks, line breaks, page breaks, and so on—show up when you highlight them as part of a selection. But spaces and tabs still remain invisible even under the highlight. To make all unseen characters drop their cloaking, you can instead choose View → Show Invisibles. Pages instantly peppers your document with arrows, dots, and paragraph marks for every behind-the-scenes element you've typed or inserted, as shown in Figure 2-14. Table 2-2 decodes these hieroglyphics.

Table 2-2. *Invisible characters*

Invisible character	Represents	To insert
•	Space	Space bar
⁑	Non-breaking space	Option-Space bar
→	Tab	Tab

Table 2-2. *Invisible characters (continued)*

Invisible character	Represents	To insert
¶	Paragraph break	Return
↵	Line break	Shift-Return
⬠	Page break	Insert → Page Break
⬚	Column break	Insert → Column Break
⊞	Layout break	Insert → Layout Break
⊟	Section break	Insert → Section Break
⸙	Anchor point (for inline objects with text wrapping)	Insert an inline object and turn on text wrapping.

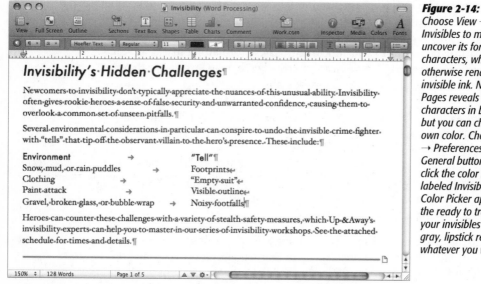

Figure 2-14:
Choose View → Show Invisibles to make Pages uncover its formatting characters, which are otherwise rendered in invisible ink. Normally Pages reveals these characters in baby blue, but you can choose your own color. Choose Pages → Preferences, click the General button, and then click the color swatch labeled Invisibles. The Color Picker appears, at the ready to transform your invisibles to gothic gray, lipstick red, or whatever you want.

Inserting Special Characters and Symbols

Other characters, while visible on your screen, can't be found on your keyboard and are certainly elusive, if not invisible. These include math symbols, accented letters, trademark and copyright symbols, arrows, and other "dingbat" shapes and symbols. Throw in the babel of every human language, and you have thousands and thousands of text characters from languages as disparate as Japanese, Chinese, Arabic, Hebrew, Greek, Farsi, you name it. Good luck tracking down all those characters on a standard keyboard.

Happily, the Mac OS X *Characters Window* has you covered. Here's how to insert just about any character you might desire:

1. **Place the insertion point where you want to add the special character.**

2. **Choose Edit → Special Characters to call up the Characters Window, shown in Figure 2-15.**

3. **Choose the type of characters you want to see from the View pop-up menu at the top left of the Characters window.**

   Choose Roman for common Western characters and symbols, or choose All for access to characters from just about every human language.

4. **Choose a category from the left column to see the characters that are available in each category.**

   In the Roman view, for example, categories include Accented Latin (for characters like ü or é), Math, Currency Symbols, and Miscellaneous, among several others.

   Double-click the character or symbol on the right that you want to insert into your document, or select the character and click Insert at the bottom of the window. Pages pops the character into your document at the insertion point. You can also drag the symbol directly into the document window and drop it into your text where you'd like it to appear.

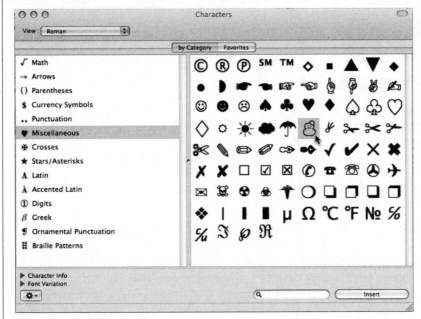

Figure 2-15:
The Mac OS X Characters window gives you access to thousands of symbols, accents, and special characters, including a whimsical collection of "dingbats." If you frequently use one or more special characters, you can mark it as a favorite so that it will always be available in the Characters window's "Favorites" tab: Select the character, click the gear pop-up at the bottom left of the Characters window, and choose "Add to Favorites."

The Missing Equation Editor

If you routinely work with equations featuring more Greek characters than a Euripides play, turning to the Character Palette for each and every character will quickly get your gammas and deltas in a twist. You need an equation editor. None of the iWork applications are themselves particular clever with sophisticated mathematical notation, but they're on good speaking terms with a program that is. Pages, Numbers, and Keynote all offer integration with MathType, a program specifically designed for editing equations. The program is available for purchase at *www.mathtype.com*.

If you have MathType 6 installed, you can use it from inside any iWork program to create a mathematical expression; iWork then takes a snapshot of it and inserts it into your document as an image. Here's how to do it:

1. Place the insertion point where you want the equation to appear.

2. Choose Insert → MathType Equation.

   This option is available only when MathType 6 is installed on your computer. When you choose it, MathType launches.

3. Type the equation you want, using MathType's tools.

   When you've finished typing your equation, choose File → "Close and Return to Pages" and then click Yes in the window that appears to save the equation.

4. Drag the equation to wherever you want it on the page.

After you've closed MathType 6, Pages treats the equation as an image object that you can reposition, resize, reorient, group, layer, or even mask (see page 2285 for all the details about working with images).

To make changes to your equation, double-click it to open MathType again. If you send a Pages file containing a MathType equation to folks who don't have MathType installed, it'll still show up in the document as an image object, but they won't be able to edit the equation.

Working with Lists

Our brains love a good list. We itemize, we rank, we categorize, we outline, we catalog (and apparently, some of us even list the ways we list). Different types of lists typically require different types of attention—you dash off shopping lists quickly, work through recipe instructions step by step, and painstakingly revise and reorder the outline for a research paper. Pages provides simple but flexible tools for managing all these types of lists, from quick and casual bullet lists to baroque *nested lists,* dense with topics and indented sub-sub-subtopics.

If Pages sees you making a list, it slips quietly into a special mode tuned for managing your list items. Pages calls this *automatic list detection,* which is fancy talk for, "I saw you start a paragraph with a number or a hyphen—I bet you're making a list." Pages recognizes that most of us make lists in the same way: one item per line, usually preceded with a number, an asterisk, or a hyphen (Figure 2-16). Specifically, Pages bumps you automatically into list mode when you do either of the following:

- Start a paragraph with a hyphen (–), asterisk (*), or bullet (•, Option-8), followed by a space, some text, and then the Return key.

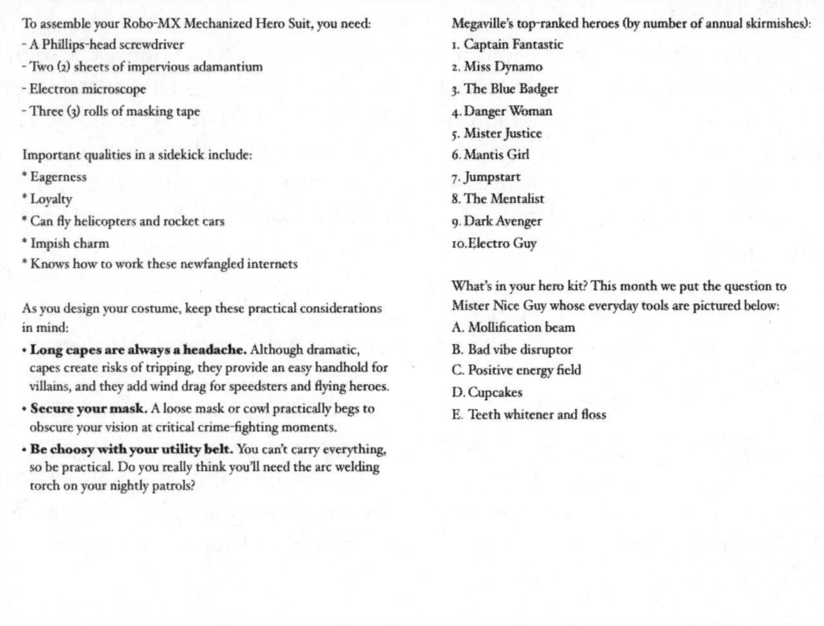

To assemble your Robo-MX Mechanized Hero Suit, you need:

- A Phillips-head screwdriver
- Two (2) sheets of impervious adamantium
- Electron microscope
- Three (3) rolls of masking tape

Important qualities in a sidekick include:

* Eagerness
* Loyalty
* Can fly helicopters and rocket cars
* Impish charm
* Knows how to work these newfangled internets

As you design your costume, keep these practical considerations in mind:

• **Long capes are always a headache.** Although dramatic, capes create risks of tripping, they provide an easy handhold for villains, and they add wind drag for speedsters and flying heroes.

• **Secure your mask.** A loose mask or cowl practically begs to obscure your vision at critical crime-fighting moments.

• **Be choosy with your utility belt.** You can't carry everything, so be practical. Do you really think you'll need the arc welding torch on your nightly patrols?

Megaville's top-ranked heroes (by number of annual skirmishes):

1. Captain Fantastic
2. Miss Dynamo
3. The Blue Badger
4. Danger Woman
5. Mister Justice
6. Mantis Girl
7. Jumpstart
8. The Mentalist
9. Dark Avenger
10. Electro Guy

What's in your hero kit? This month we put the question to Mister Nice Guy whose everyday tools are pictured below:

A. Mollification beam
B. Bad vibe disruptor
C. Positive energy field
D. Cupcakes
E. Teeth whitener and floss

Figure 2-16:
Pages quietly shifts into list mode when it sees you starting a list. Left: When your first list item starts with a hyphen, asterisk, or bullet, Pages starts a bulleted list.

Right: When your first list item starts with a number or letter, Pages starts a numbered list, automatically advancing the numbers or letters as you add new items.

If your items are longer than a single line, they wrap to the next line like any other paragraph, but the additional lines are indented to indicate that it's a continuation of the list item.

• Start a paragraph with a number or letter, followed by a period, a space, some text, and then the Return key.

After you press Return at the end of that first item, Pages gives you a new paragraph as usual, but this time the paragraph is preceded with another *bullet,* a label that marks each item in your list. If you used a hyphen, asterisk, or bullet to start your first list item, then Pages gives you that character as the bullet for the next line. This is called, naturally, a *bulleted list.* If you used a number or letter to start your first list item, Pages starts your next line with the next number or letter in the series—1 is followed by 2, A is followed by B. This is called a *numbered list.*

No need to do anything special—just keep listing away, pressing Return after each item, and Pages keeps giving you bullets on the next line. For numbered lists, Pages keeps advancing the number or letter—if you go back and add or delete an item earlier in your list, Pages renumbers your list on the fly.

Tip: Pressing Return always starts a new list item with its own bullet. If you want to add a second paragraph under an item without creating a new bullet or number, press Shift-Return to add a line break and Pages gives you a new line under the same list item.

When you're done with your list, press Return twice, and Pages releases you from list mode, returning you gracefully to normal text entry.

Note: If you're creating a list inside a table cell with the "Return key moves to next cell" option turned on in the Table Inspector, then you can't use the Return key to add new list items. Press Option-Return instead. For more about using tables, see Chapter 8.

Using List Styles

You don't have to rely on Pages' automatic list detection to start your list. Use the List Styles pop-up menu on the Format Bar to select a preformatted list style, and Pages changes your current paragraph to a list item in that style. You can use this technique to convert a run of paragraphs into a list—select all the paragraphs, and choose your list style. You can likewise change one type of list into another, morphing a bullet list into a numbered list or vice versa. Convert list items into plain old paragraphs by selecting them and choosing "None" from this menu.

Tip: If you prefer this manual manipulation of list styles over Pages' automatic list detection, you can turn the automatic feature off. Choose Pages → Preferences and click the Auto-Correction button. Turn off the "Automatically detect lists" option.

Pages offers four preformatted list styles: Bullet, Numbered, Harvard, and Legal, each list itself duly listed in Figure 2-17. You've already seen how Bullet and Numbered lists look—the Harvard and Legal styles are specialized numbered lists which offer special formatting options for labeling nested lists, described later in this chapter.

(A) *Membership in the Frequent Flyer Club includes:*
- Ten percent discount on all purchases of capes and cowls
- One free secret-identity makeover
- Priority seating for workshops and featured speakers (this month: Manta Ray on "Underwater Breathing Techniques")
- Free subscription to the Up & Away newsletter
- Special networking events and singles nights

(C) *History of the Frequent Flyer Club*
- I. "The Society of Costumed Adventurers," 1947-1971
  - A. Founding members
    - 1. Mister Incredible
    - 2. Miss Spontaneous
    - 3. Speed Lad
    - 4. Flame Girl
  - B. Club addresses
    - 1. 93 Excelsior Lane, 1947-1956
      - a) Destroyed in skirmish with Doctor Contagious
    - 2. 878 Invincible Avenue, 1958-1971
- II. The Seventies: "The Hideaway," 1971-1982
  - A. "A singles club for citizens of singular ability"
    - 1. Public reaction
    - 2. The feminist response
  - B. Heroes in Hollywood
  - C. Club address: 184 Boldness Boulevard, 1971-1982
- III. A new civic responsibility: "The Frequent Flyer Club," 1982-
  - A. Renewed liaisons with city hall and law enforcement
  - B. Charity efforts and fund drives
    - 1. The Captain Fantastic Telethon
    - 2. The Madame Uncanny Marathon and 5K
  - C. Club address: One Majestic Place (1999-)

(B) *To join the Frequent Flyer Club, please submit the following:*
1. Reference letters from two other heroes (sorry, no sidekicks)
2. Copy of certification by Mayor's Superhero Commission
3. Name of arch-nemesis
4. Rendering of your logo or emblem
5. Detailed list of your special abilities
6. Address and phone of your fortress or lair

(D) *Frequent Flyer Club bylaws*
1. Membership criteria
   1.1. All members must be superheroes ("Heroes").
      1.1.1. Heroes must be certified by a recognized authority, including the Mayor's Superhero Commission or the Presidential Bureau of Hero Affairs.
      1.1.2. For the purpose of membership, hero assistants ("Sidekicks") are not considered to be Heroes.
         1.1.2.1. A Sidekick is one who assists a Hero without having his own Hero franchise.
         1.1.2.2. The Sidekick category does not include teammates or fellow League members; the act of assisting another Hero does not automatically make a Hero a Sidekick.
   1.2. Former criminals ("Villains" or "Evildoers") may qualify for membership after at least three years of Crusading for the Cause of Good, in which no plots have been hatched to take over the city, nation, world, or galaxy.
2. Use of powers on club premises
   2.1. No powers allowed in the bar or lounge areas.
   2.2. Powers may not be used upon other members, except during specified events or conditions:
      2.2.1. to prevent another Member from breaking any of the bylaws included herein
      2.2.2. annual field day and family picnic

Figure 2-17:
Pages' templates provide four preset list styles to choose from. Although you can use any of these styles for either lists or outlines, two basic styles are ideal for simple lists: Bullet lists (A) place a small round bullet in front of each list item. Numbered lists (B) add an Arabic numeral—1, 2, 3—in front of each item, automatically updating the numbers as you add and delete items.

The other two styles are particularly well suited for outlines. Harvard lists (C) use Roman numerals for each main heading, then letters for subheadings, then Arabic numerals for sub-subheadings, and so on. Legal style (D) uses only Arabic numerals for labels, with each subtopic level adding a decimal point and another number to the label (3.2, 3.2.1, 3.2.1.1, and so on).

These prefab list styles cover most typical list scenarios, but the Text Inspector → List tab offers a range of options to gussy up your lists. You can change the bullet style, for example, to use any character you like or switch to one of Pages' 25 graphical alternatives—you can even import a bullet image of your own. For numbered lists, you can modify the numbering style to use various styles of Arabic or Roman numbers, or alphabetical characters.

To change the format of a list item, click anywhere in that list item, or select several list items by dragging the cursor over them to highlight them. Then go to the Text Inspector → List tab, choose a bullet or numbering style from the Bullets & Numbering pop-up menu, and Pages applies the new bullet style to your selected list items. The Bullets & Numbering menu gives you six choices, each with its own set of additional options (Figure 2-18):

- **No Bullets.** This list style can be useful when you want to create a multilevel, indented list with no bullets.

- **Text Bullets.** Choose this list style to use a text character for the bullet. Text characters include the standard "dot" type bullet as well as asterisks, stars, arrows, checkmarks, and so on. Click the Character pop-up menu to view some of the more common styles. These, however are just suggestions—you're free to type any character (or even several of them) into the box to use as a bullet. Fonts like Symbol, Wingdings, or Zapf Dingbats, for example, are nothing but signs and symbols that could be used for bullets, and many other fonts have extensive optional characters that you can see or select only via the Characters window (see page 82). To transfer a symbol from the Characters window to the Text Inspector, select the bullet in the Text Inspector and then double-click a symbol in the Characters window.

- **Image Bullets.** If the simple monochrome bullets available through the Text Bullet style seem a bit buttoned up, Pages provides 25 more informal, colorful bullets—chromium balls, hand-drawn checkboxes, pushpins, and more. Choose one from the scrolling window.

- **Custom Image.** For the chronic do-it-yourselfer, this bullet style lets you build your own bullet from just about any image file. Click the Choose button under the picture well and navigate to an image file on your Mac. You can use any file that QuickTime can read—and that's most graphics files. Large, high-resolution photograph files really slow things down, however. Since Pages displays the pictures at a very small size, you might want to make a copy of any large graphics files in a small, thumbnail size better suited for bullets.

Tip: The first time you choose a custom image for a document, you have to use the Choose button to select the image. After that, though, you can also drag and drop an image file from the Finder into the image well, usually a bit faster.

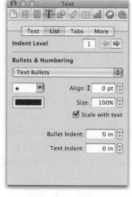

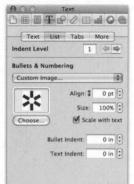
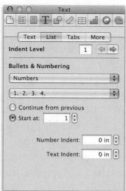
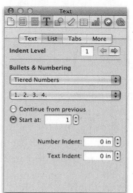
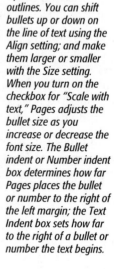

Figure 2-18:
Use the Text Inspector's List tab to adjust the bullets and numbering style for lists and outlines. You can shift bullets up or down on the line of text using the Align setting; and make them larger or smaller with the Size setting. When you turn on the checkbox for "Scale with text," Pages adjusts the bullet size as you increase or decrease the font size. The Bullet indent or Number indent box determines how far Pages places the bullet or number to the right of the left margin; the Text Indent box sets how far to the right of a bullet or number the text begins.

- **Numbers.** The first of the two numbered list styles lets you create lists with Arabic or Roman numerals or letters. Use the numbering style pop-up menu to choose how Pages displays the number or letter series.

- **Tiered Numbers.** A tiered number list is used in outline lists to number subtopics. A tiered-number list item adds its number label to the label of its "parent" item. If list item "3" has subtopics, for example, they would be numbered 3.1, 3.2, 3.3, and so on. At the top level of a list, which has no parent items, a tiered-number item looks just like a regular numbered item—1, 2, 3. (The Legal list style is a tiered-number list.)

The Text Bullet, Image Bullets, and Custom Image options offer settings to allow you to fine-tune the bullets' size, position, and indents. If you vary your font size and want the bullet to be sized larger for large fonts, for example, turn on the "Scale with text" option.

The Numbers and Tiered Numbers options meanwhile offer settings to adjust the starting number for your list, or whether the number series should instead continue from the previous list in your document.

Tip: If you need to interrupt a list with one or more paragraphs of regular text and then return to list numbering, choose None as your list style (or No Bullets in the Text Inspector) and type your plain-text interlude. When you're ready to return to the list, create a new list item as if you were starting a new list. Let Pages know that you're actually continuing your old list by opening the Text Inspector's List tab and turning on "Continue from previous." Pages makes the numbering adjustment, and you can continue your list where you left off.

Organizing and Nesting Your Lists

You've seen that Pages can help you create straight-up, single-level lists, but it can also manage lists with depth, turning simple lists into *nested lists* of topics and sub-topics. These are just regular lists whose items happen to contain other list items indented within.

You probably learned about nested lists way back in grade school, when your third-grade teacher taught you about outlines. You remember: You used Roman numerals and capital letters to summarize papers about Olympic curling, Egyptian mummies, koala bears, and the state flower. You can use Pages' nested lists to make this type of outline—Roman numerals and all—but depending on the job at hand, you might find Pages' *outline view* more useful. Unlike nested lists, outline view lets you switch between an outline and a regular word-processing document, letting you fill in each topic with your insights on mummies and state flowers. When you're building an outline in preparation for creating a longer text, outline view is the way to go (see page 183). When you're just after a simple indented list, or when you want to include an outline inside your regular text, a nested list is the right tool for the job.

You create a nested list just like you create an ordinary one, pressing Return after each list item to create another topic at the same level. Press the Tab key or ⌘-] (right-bracket) to indent, or demote, an item and turn it into a subtopic of the previous line. Pages lets you build nested lists up to nine *indent levels* deep.

Note: Pressing the Tab key anywhere inside a list item always indents it. If you instead want to use the Tab key to advance to the next tab stop, press Option-Tab.

Press Shift-Tab or ⌘-[(left bracket) to "outdent" the item, moving it to the left and back up the outline's hierarchy.

These keyboard shortcuts are, as usual, the most efficient way to manage the indent level of outline items. If you plan to do a lot of nesting, it pays to get used to using the Tab and Shift-Tab keys to weave in and out of your hierarchy. But Pages also offers several other methods for changing the indent level of a list item:

• **Drag-and-drop.** Grab a list item by its bullet or number, and drag to the right to indent, or to the left to outdent. A guide arrow appears as you drag to show you where the item will land when you drop it.

- **Text Inspector.** In the List tab, use the Indent Level field to adjust the level up or down.

- **Format menu.** Choose Format → Text → Increase List Indent Level or Decrease List Indent Level to move the selected item in and out.

- **Toolbar buttons.** You can customize the toolbar to add the Decrease and Increase buttons, which do exactly what you might guess they would to list items. To add the buttons, Control-click the toolbar and choose Customize Toolbar and then drag the Decrease and Increase buttons to the toolbar.

Moving list items

Did you catch that drag-and-drop option in the list above? It turns out that list items' bullets aren't just decorative—*they're handles.* Click any list item by its bullet, and Pages selects the entire item. Drag a bullet, and Pages moves the entire item to a new location, showing you a blue guideline and arrow where the item will wind up when you drop it (Figure 2-19). When you drag an item that contains a list of indented subtopics below it, Pages brings those items along with it, letting you move an entire branch of your list's "tree" to a new location. If you drag an item out of its current list and into a new location in the document, it starts its own new list.

Tip: You can select multiple list items by Command-clicking each item's bullet. With all of them selected, you can then indent or outdent all of them at once by pressing Tab or Shift-Tab. If the list items are all consecutive and at the same indent level, you can also drag all of them to a new location in your list.

Labeling nested lists

You can use any of Pages' list styles with nested lists, but Pages provides two styles in the Format Bar's List Styles menu that are particularly well suited. These styles label the items in your list with one of two classic notations and, like numbered lists, automatically update these notations as you make changes to your outline (Figure 2-17).

- **Harvard** is the outline style that your grade-school English teacher taught. Harvard style uses Roman numerals for each main heading, then letters for subheadings, then Arabic numerals for sub-subheadings, and so on. With this style, you can easily follow a hierarchy—at least for the first four or five levels. If you're creating outlines more complicated than that, you might prefer Legal style.

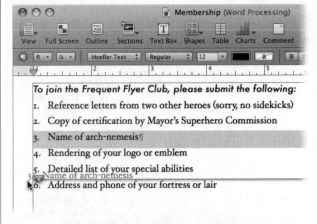

Figure 2-19:
Pages makes it easy to shuffle your list items with simple drag-and-drop. Grab an item by its handle and drag it to its new location.

Top: Pages displays a line while you drag to show you where the item will land in the list when you drop it.

Bottom: When you drag an item right or left, you indent or outdent it, promoting or demoting it in your outline hierarchy. Pages shows an arrow (circled) to show you exactly where the item will land when you drop it.

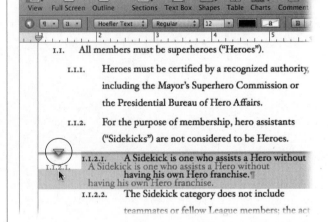

• **Legal** style uses only Arabic numerals for labels, with each subtopic level adding a decimal point and another number to the label (3.2, 3.2.1, 3.2.1.1, and so on). This tiered numbering style makes it much easier for you to keep things straight when your outlines become complicated. Lawyers, scientists, and government bureaucrats prefer this form because it handles complexity and detail so well.

To change a list to use one of these special styles (or any list style for that matter), highlight the list items to convert and choose your new style from the List Styles menu in the Format bar. You can also create your own custom outline notation by creating a new list style (see page 103). Figure 2-20 shows an example of how you can mix and match list styles with a nested list.

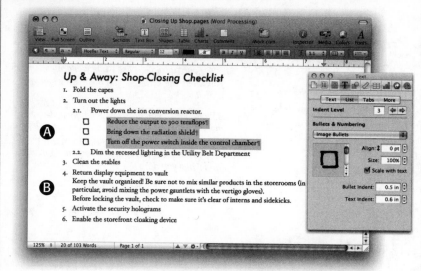

Figure 2-20:
You can create subtopics in a nested list that are styled differently than other items in order to, for example, provide checklists in the middle of a list (A), or to provide several paragraphs of description for a topic (B). To create the checklist, select the entries to modify, open the Text Inspector → List tab, and change the Bullets & Numbering pop-up menu to Image Bullets. To add descriptive paragraphs to any list item, press Shift-Return and type the paragraph. Press Return to continue with the list.

Creating and Using Styles

When you create a word processing document in Pages, you usually use a small assortment of formatting styles over and over again. In a short piece, formatting your titles or the occasional quote is no big deal; just highlight each and use the Format Bar to change its size, color, and so on.

But consider the longer document. What if your manuscript contains 200 headings, plus another 50 sidebar boxes and a slew of footnotes, captions, long quotations, and other heavily formatted elements? In such documents—this book, for example—manually formatting every heading, subheading, sidebar, and caption to make them all consistent would drive you nuts. Add to that the headache of accidentally pasting in fonts and styles from other documents or other portions of your text, and it's all too easy to spend more time toggling formatting buttons than actually writing.

Styles ease the pain. Here's the concept: You format a chunk of text exactly the way you want it—font, paragraph formatting, color, spacing, and so on—and then tell Pages to memorize all that formatting as a *style*. A style is a prepackaged bundle of formatting rules that you can apply with a click of the mouse; highlight some text, choose a saved style, and you're done. Repeat the process for all the styles you need: headings, sidebar styles, picture captions, whatever. You end up with a collection of custom-tailored styles for each of the repeating elements in your document. Figure 3-1 gives you a taste of how helpful styles can be.

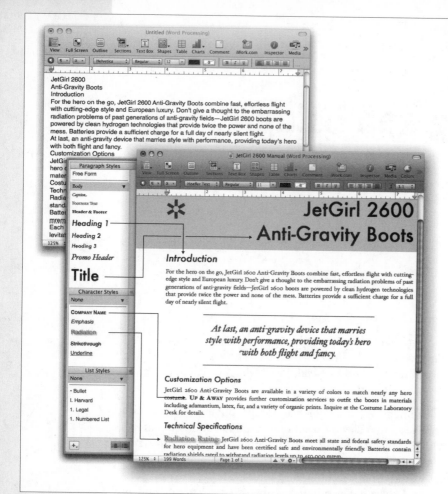

Figure 3-1:
With just a few clicks, you can transform plain text (top left) into a formatted document (bottom right) and be certain that your headlines, captions, and all the rest maintain their uniformity throughout the document. Pages applies the font, size, style, color, margins, and so on all at once, freeing you to concentrate on the words themselves.

Once you've created your styles (details start on page 98), you've done the hard part. Now, as you type along, you can choose styles as you need them. Since you're no longer formatting by hand, Pages guarantees consistent page elements throughout the document. As you go through your document during the editing process, if you happen to notice you accidentally styled, for example, a headline using the subhead style, you can fix the problem by applying the correct style with a single click. Select the text you want to update, click the headline style, and your errant heading automatically falls in line with the correct formatting.

Even better, if you later decide that you want to use a different font for all your headings, you can just update the style definition, and Pages updates every heading faster than you can say, "Helvetica bold"—no need to go back through each and every heading to change it manually.

When You Need Styles: Know the Warning Signs

Styles are more than just a handy tool—they're an essential part of good document hygiene. They keep your text clean, tidy, and consistent. If you've never used styles in your word processing—and most people haven't—it's time to start. Seriously: It's a bad habit to go to the Format Bar every time you want to italicize text or change the font. Break that habit and use styles instead.

If you're still not sure that styles are for you, you should at least get to know the warning signs. You know you need a style makeover when:

- The first thing you do when you open a document is go to the Format Bar to change the font or the text size.

- You frequently find yourself selecting the entire document to apply (or reapply) new formatting.

- You repeat the same formatting tasks over and over again when you add headings or other elements.

- You battle constantly with your fonts—you change the font of your text, for example, only to find that the old font pops back up when you type a new paragraph.

- You're always reformatting text pasted into your document to fix font and size differences.

- You want to use Pages' outline view to build an outline of your document (see page 183).

- You want to use Pages' built-in tools for automatically building a table of contents (see page 174).

If any of these symptoms sound familiar, styles are the remedy. In fact—surprise!—every time you use Pages, you're already using styles. Every Pages template, including the Blank templates, comes stocked with a prefab selection of styles, including the default font that Pages gives you when you open a new document from that template (see page 105).

Style Central: Meet the Styles Drawer

Pages stashes your document styles in the Styles Drawer, a special panel that glides in and out from the side of your document window. Click View → Show Styles Drawer to slide it out, or click the Styles Drawer button in the Format Bar—the one shaped like a paragraph symbol (see Figure 3-2). To tuck it away again, click View → Hide Styles Drawer, or click the Styles Drawer button again.

Note: The Styles Drawer typically makes its appearance at the left of the document window—but only if there's room. If you've got the window pressed up against the left edge of your screen, for example, the drawer shoots out of the window's right side instead.

Pages divides the Styles Drawer into three panes, one for each of Pages' three types of styles:

- **Paragraph styles.** These styles apply to entire paragraphs, letting you paint entire swaths of text with any combination of font, text, and paragraph formatting you might like. Use paragraph styles to shape the look of the major structural elements of your document: body text, headings, captions, footnotes, page headers and footers, and so on.

- **Character styles.** You apply these styles to text *inside* a paragraph, dressing up the underlying word-by-word style, or even the look of individual letters. Use character styles to emphasize a word, a sentence, or even a single character. These styles relate only to font and text formatting—typeface, size, color, and so on—and can't be used to set paragraph formatting like line spacing, alignment, borders, and the like. You'll typically use character styles for *emphasis*—you might create a "citation" style to italicize book titles, or an "our company" style to call out your company name in shadowed, electric-blue, 64-point text (you're tacky, but at least you're consistent).

- **List styles:** Pages uses list styles to help you build lists, formatting items with bullets or numbers depending on the style you choose. You could create one list style that uses a small red bullet, and another that uses a full-color image as the bullet—say, your logo. List styles apply to entire paragraphs.

Tip: The Styles Drawer always shows Paragraph styles, but you can show or hide the Character and List styles by clicking the buttons at the bottom of the drawer (Figure 3-2).

Applying Styles

You can apply styles by clicking them in the Styles Drawer, or by using the Paragraph Style, Character Style, or List Style pop-up menu buttons in the Format Bar. Both the drawer and the menus provide a preview of the font, color, and size of each style.

To apply a *character* style, highlight some text—for example drag across a word or two—and then click one of the character styles in the Styles Drawer. If there's no selection and the insertion point rests inside a word, Pages applies the selection to the entire word.

To apply a *paragraph* style, click anywhere inside an existing paragraph, and choose a style; Pages applies the style to the text of the *entire* paragraph no matter how much or little of its text you've selected. If you have a selection that includes text from multiple paragraphs, the style will be applied to all those paragraphs.

You apply *list* styles in the same way: Highlight the paragraphs to be included in the list and then choose a list style. If you're just beginning a list, choose your style first and then start typing the list.

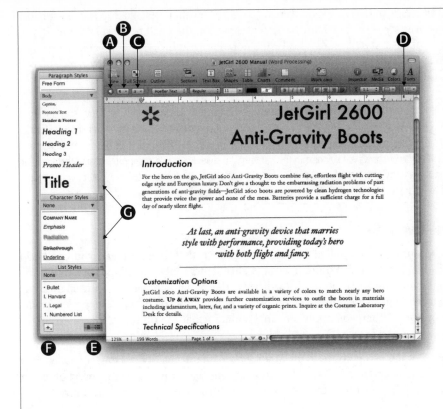

Figure 3-2:
Pull out the Styles Drawer to reveal your document's styles: Choose View → Show Styles Drawer, or click the Styles Drawer button (A) in the Format Bar. To apply a style, select some text and click the style you want from the Styles Drawer, or from the Format Bar's Paragraph Style (B), Character Style (C), or List Style (D) pop-up menu.

If you don't see the Character or List panes in the drawer (or you do and wish you didn't), click the Show/Hide buttons at the bottom-right corner of the drawer (E). Click the Add (+) button (F) and use its pop-up menu to create new styles from a selection.

If you've amassed more styles than can fit in one of the Styles Drawer's panes, a scroll bar appears. You can adjust the height of these panes by dragging the button marked with two horizontal lines (G) next to the Character and List styles headings. Adjust the width of the drawer by dragging its outside edge.

Note: If you apply the same type of style to an element you've already formatted—for example, paragraph style—Pages replaces the first style with the new one. In other words, one paragraph style replaces another paragraph style. You can, however, create *compound* styles using the three different style types (paragraph, character, and list). You could, for example, create a numbered list where each item is formatted with a different paragraph style, and individual words within the paragraphs are formatted with a character style.

To remove a paragraph style, replace it with another style or replace it with the Free Form style—the default basic text style for the current template. Or, if you just applied a style, choose Edit → Undo Paragraph Style to reverse your style change. Removing character styles or list styles works the same way—except you choose None in the Character and List panes of the Styles Drawer.

Tip: If you apply the same styles over and over again, save yourself some mousework by assigning those styles a *hot key*, a keyboard shortcut: Click the downward triangle next to the style, and choose Hot Key from the pop-up menu. Select the Function key to use for your keyboard shortcut (F1, for example), and the Styles Drawer shows the key next to the name of the style. From that point on, pressing that Function key applies the style to the selected text in the current document. (If you're using a laptop, you may also need to hold down the fn key when you press the Function key.)

Style Overrides

Just because you've applied a style to some text, that doesn't mean you can't add additional formatting. You're free to go ahead and apply italic, bold, or other *character* formatting to some of the words in the paragraph; or you can change the paragraph alignment, line spacing, background color, or other *paragraph* formatting options. When you apply any additional formatting on top of a style, you create a style *override*.

Pages uses the arrow to the right of a style's name in the Styles Drawer to alert you that you've added a style override to the current selection. When the insertion point is inside a snippet with an override, the arrow turns from its normal gray to red.

If you have second thoughts about the changes you make in an override, you can return a paragraph to its basic style. Place your insertion point within the paragraph to select it, click the red arrow next to its style name in the Styles Drawer and choose Revert to Defined Style from the pop-up menu (or just double-click the style name). Pages removes the overrides, including any character styles, and returns *all text* in the paragraph to its original underlying style.

Creating Styles by Example

Whether you're modifying an existing style or building a new one from scratch, Pages lets you "create by example"—in other words, you format the text in the document the way you want it to look and then tell Pages to memorize that formatting as a new style.

Modifying Existing Paragraph and List Styles

Paragraph and list styles both apply their formatting to entire paragraphs, and modifying either type of style involves the same process. The following steps use a paragraph style for the example, but you can use the same process to change a list style, too. To begin modifying a style, choose a paragraph in your document you'd like to see formatted with your new style, or just type a new paragraph so you have some text to work with.

1. **Place your insertion point in the paragraph and choose View → Show Styles Drawer, or click the Styles Drawer button in the Format Bar.**

   Pages presents the document's styles collection.

2. **Click the style that's closest to the one you want to create, and Pages formats the selected paragraph in your chosen style.**

3. **Make all your modifications to the paragraph, tweaking the font, size, color, indentation, spacing, tabs, you name it.**

   You can use any of the character and paragraph formatting options described in Chapter 2 (pages 59–81). Mold the paragraph to your whim.

4. **Click the arrow to the right of the current paragraph style in the Styles Drawer. The arrow is red, indicating you've applied style overrides.**

   The pop-up menu offers two ways to handle the new style you've created.

   Choose Redefine Style from Selection, and Pages updates the original style you began with, stacking your modifications on top. When you choose this command, Pages also applies your freshly modified style to *all occurrences* of that style in the document so that they all match the formatting of your current text selection. In other words, you should redefine the style only if you have no more use for the old style.

   Instead of updating the existing style, you can choose Create New Paragraph Style from Selection to create a brand new style based on your current text selection, without making any changes to the original style (or choose Create New List Style from Paragraph if that's what you're up to). Pages asks you to give the new style a name. If the "Apply this new style on creation" checkbox is turned on, Pages assigns the new style to the paragraph you've been modifying (usually what you want); turn off the checkbox and the paragraph retains its original style, with the style overrides you've added. Click OK and the new style appears in the Styles Drawer.

Creating New Paragraph and List Styles

The process for creating brand new styles from scratch is nearly identical to the one described above. Select a paragraph, and apply all your formatting modifications. When you're satisfied with the result, click the + button at the bottom of the Styles Drawer. You can also Control-click the formatted text and choose Create New Paragraph Style from Selection.

Note: The + button defaults to creating a new paragraph style—when you give the + button a simple click, Pages gives you a new paragraph style. To get a new list style or character style, hold down the + button and make your choice from the pop-up menu, choosing "Create New Character Style from Selection", for example.

Type a name for the new style and decide whether or not to apply it to the current paragraph by turning the checkbox for "Apply this new style on creation" on or off. Click OK, and Pages adds the new style to the Styles Drawer, now at your service to use anywhere in your document.

DESIGN TIME

Herculean Headings

Paragraph styles are especially useful for formatting text headings—and not just for the usual font size and color differences. You can save yourself some time—and pain around the temples—by giving your heading styles some special paragraph formatting that take note of a heading's typical status as the start of a new section of your text. When you define paragraph styles for your headings, consider putting these options to good use (all are in the Text Inspector → More tab unless otherwise noted):

- **Following paragraph style.** By default, Pages sticks with the same paragraph style when you click Return, so that a new paragraph has the same formatting as the one before it. But headings are almost always followed by a *different* style, the body text for your document. This setting saves you an extra click by automatically switching to your chosen style when you press Return after your heading.

- **Keep lines together.** Page breaks should never carve up your headings. This setting guarantees that multiline headings stick together.

- **Keep with following paragraph.** Don't let your headings charge straight into the bottom of a page—this setting ensures that headings are always on the same page with the text they introduce.

- **Paragraph starts on new page.** Use this setting to automatically create a new page when kicking off major new sections. If you turn this option on for a "Chapter Title" style, for example, Pages always gives you a new page before every chapter heading.

- **Paragraph spacing.** Open up some space before and/or after a heading to separate it visually from the surrounding text and mark the leap into a new section. You can handle this with the Before Paragraph and After Paragraph settings in the Text Inspector → Text tab.

Modifying Existing Character Styles

Character styles let you format text inside a paragraph, supplementing the current paragraph style with additional text formatting to emphasize a word or phrase. Like paragraph styles above, you can define character styles by taking a "snapshot" of a selection and all its text attributes, or you can cherry-pick the relevant formatting.

For example, say that you're creating a "Citation" style from a portion of text that just happens to be red italicized Courier, but you're really only interested in making Pages remember the italic for your new style—you don't want it to apply the red color and Courier font to every citation. In that case, you can tell Pages to ignore the color and font of the selection when it defines the style, so that the Citation style applies only the italic as the formatting, leaving the text with its original typeface and color. Here's how it works:

1. **Choose View → Show Styles Drawer, or click the Styles Drawer button in the Format Bar.**

   If the Character Styles pane isn't visible, click the Show Character Styles button at the bottom-right of the Styles Drawer to reveal it.

2. **Select some words in a paragraph, or type some new text and select it.**

3. **Click the character style closest to the style you want to create.**

4. **Apply all the character formatting attributes that you want to the selected text: font, size, color, bold, italic, strikethrough, and so on.**

   You can apply any of the formatting described in "Changing Font Styles and Appearance" starting on page 59 in Chapter 2. As you apply the first of these style overrides to your selected characters, the arrow next to the style's name in the Styles Drawer turns red.

5. **Click the red arrow and choose Create New Character Style from Selection to create a brand-new style. (Skip down to Step 8 if you want to choose Redefine Style From Selection.)**

   Pages displays the New Character Style dialog box.

6. **Give your new style a name, and then click the flippy triangle labeled "Include all character attributes" to reveal the checklist of attributes for this style (Figure 3-3).**

   When it opens, every checkbox is turned on, which would define the style as an exact snapshot of your current selection—applying the new style will paint text with the exact same font, color, size, everything. If only certain aspects of the formatting are relevant to this style, you can turn off some of them—apply all the character formatting except font color, for example, or only the italic text.

7. **Choose whether or not to apply this new style to the selected text using the checkbox at the bottom of the window, and then click OK.**

   Pages memorizes all this character formatting information and your style's new name shows up in the Character Styles pane of the Styles Drawer.

8. **Or choose Redefine Style from Selection in Step 5, to incorporate all your new formatting into the style you began with.**

   Choose to redefine the style only if you don't need any of the original style's formatting in your document—Pages transforms any existing instances of that style into your freshly defined style.

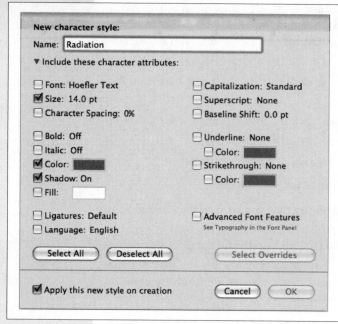

Figure 3-3:
The "New character style" sheet appears when you select Create New Character Style from Selection via the Add (+) button in the Styles Drawer, or the downward-pointing triangle next to a character style's name.

Click the flippy triangle next to "Include these character attributes" to reveal the on/off switches for the various character formatting attributes you're about to include in your new style. Turn off the checkboxes for any attributes you don't want to include. Use the Select All or Deselect All buttons to make your checking and unchecking task simpler. Click the Select Overrides button to see only the attributes you've modified—leave those items' checkboxes turned on if you want your style to affect only those items when you apply the style.

Creating New Character Styles

To create your own character style from scratch, select some text and make your character formatting modifications, just like in the previous example. When you're happy with the result, click the Add (+) button at the bottom of the Styles Drawer and, from the pop-up menu, choose Create New Character Style from Selection.

Continue on with steps 6 and 7 from the previous section, to complete the character style creation process.

Finding and Copying Styles

When you're working on a long document, just *finding* every occurrence of a style can be a challenge. Imagine you want to replace one style with another—for example, replacing a headline style with a new larger headline style and then using the existing headline style for your subheadings. In this case you wouldn't want to modify the existing style because you need to keep it to use in different places. Instead, Pages can find and highlight all the occurrences of a given style in your document—and then, with one click, you can apply a different style to those occurrences.

To do so, choose View → Show Styles Drawer and click the downward-pointing arrow next to the name of the style you want to replace. (Those arrows don't appear until you point to the style name.) From the pop-up menu, choose "Select All Uses of [style name]". Pages highlights all the occurrences of this style in your text. Click the name of any other style in the Styles Drawer, and Pages does the formatting switcheroo.

Custom Outlines with List Styles

Never one to follow conventions? If you're into outlines, you don't have to stick to Pages' built-in Harvard or Legal styles for nested lists—you can create your own outlaw outline style. Who knows, future generations of English teachers might end up teaching Chuck's outline notation.

The easiest way to create a custom outline style is to create a temporary list, style it the way you want, and then save it as a new list style. This dummy list should contain just one top-level item, which should contain a single second-level list item, which should contain a single third-level list item, and so on. Here's the drill:

1. Create a new top-level list item by choosing a list style from the Format Bar's List Styles menu.

2. Open the Text Inspector → List tab, and choose the bullet style for this indent level.

   Numbers and tiered numbers are the two most common categories for outlines, but you can also use text bullets, image bullets, or custom image bullets for the various levels of the outline. Or mix-and-match all the above—Pages lets your outline setup be as creative or as bizarre as you wish.

3. Press Return to create another list item, and press Tab to indent it to the next subtopic level.

4. Repeat steps 2 and 3 until you've defined the notation for all the subtopic levels you care to define.

5. Highlight all the list items that you've prepared with your custom bullet formatting.

   It's important to highlight *all* indent levels of your prototype outline. When you save the style, Pages takes note only of the styles in the highlighted indent levels.

6. Click the red arrow next to the highlighted style in the Styles Drawer.

The New List Style window appears. Name your freshly modified style, leave the checkbox turned on for "Apply this new style on creation," and then click OK.

Pages adds your new list style, making it available in both the Styles Drawer and the List Styles pop-up menu in the Format Bar.

Pages also gives you the option, in step 6 above, to choose Redefine Style From Selection. When you choose this option, Pages updates the original style with your changes and applies this new formatting *everywhere* you used that style in the document.

If you instead prefer to hop to individual instances of a style one by one, you can do that using the upward and downward arrows at the bottom of the document window. First choose the style you want to find from the neighboring gear-shaped Action pop-up menu, then click the downward arrow to jump to the next occurrence of the style; click the upward arrow to go to the previous occurrence.

Copying Styles

You don't necessarily have to have a style saved in the Styles Drawer in order to reuse style formatting in your text. You can also copy and paste paragraph and character formatting styles using commands in the Format menu. Unlike the normal copy-and-paste maneuver, copying a style doesn't copy the text of your selection, only its underlying formatting. To copy a paragraph style, place your insertion point anywhere within the paragraph and choose Format → Copy Paragraph Style; to copy a character style, select some formatted text and choose Format → Copy Character Style. Then place your insertion point in another paragraph or select some text you wish to style and choose Format → Paste Paragraph Style (or Format → Paste Character Style). Shazam! The text takes on the formatting of the pasted style, while the words themselves remains unchanged. This technique copies not only the style, but also any style *overrides* (page 98) that you've applied to the paragraph or character.

Better yet, you can copy and paste styles *between documents*. In other words you can pick and choose styles from any of your Pages documents and paste them into another document. Not only does this technique reformat the selected text in the document, but Pages adds the pasted style to the Styles Drawer, making it available for formatting any other parts of the document.

Tip: Consider adding the Copy Style and Paste Style buttons to the toolbar if you find yourself frequently copying and pasting paragraph styles. (Although the buttons don't indicate it, they copy and paste only paragraph styles—not character styles.)

Importing Styles from Another Document

When you have several styles to copy from another document, the copy/paste technique gets to be a ton of work. Consider instead importing some or all those styles in one fell swoop, making it easy to give related documents a similar look and feel.

1. **Choose Format → Import Styles to import styles into your document.**

   The Open dialog box appears.

2. **Navigate to the Pages document containing the styles you want to import, and double-click its title (or select the title and click Open).**

   Pages displays a window listing all the styles in the document, as shown in Figure 3-4.

3. **Use the scroll bar to view all the styles. Press ⌘ while you click to select several styles. Or, to import all the styles, click Select All. Click OK, and Pages performs the import.**

   If you turn on the checkbox for "Replace duplicates," Pages replaces the styles in your document with those it's importing that have the same name. If you *don't* turn on the checkbox for Replace duplicates, then when Pages imports styles with the same name, it adds a number to the name of the imported style. For example, if you import a style named Headline into a document that already has a Headline style, Pages names the newly imported style Headline 2.

Warning: If you import styles with "Replace duplicates" turned on, not only does Pages replace those duplicate styles in the Styles Drawer, but it also reformats all occurrences of that style in the document. That's handy when that's what you're after, but if not, you've got an unpleasant surprise on your hands when you scroll down your document to discover your carefully formatted subheads have somehow morphed into a different style.

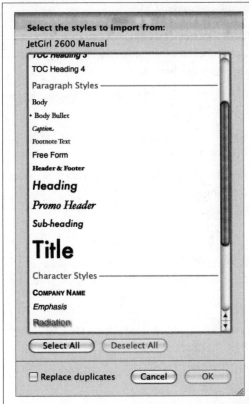

Figure 3-4:
Choose Format → Import Styles and select one of your Pages documents in order to import its styles into the current document. Pages displays this Import Styles dialog box from which you can pick and choose the styles you'd like to import—or just choose Select All to bring them all in. Be careful with the "Replace duplicates" checkbox. When it's turned on, Pages replaces same-named styles in your Styles Drawer and modifies the text in your document wherever you've used those styles.

Note: If you import a document created by Microsoft Word or AppleWorks, Pages imports the styles contained in those documents as well. They show up in the Styles Drawer alongside Pages' styles.

Changing the Default Font

All Pages' templates come with their own set of styles that define the document's default fonts and styles. The Blank templates for word processing and page layout both give you 12-point Helvetica as the default font. If your personal font fondness leans elsewhere, you can customize those built-in styles to use your own preferred font, as you've seen. But ugh, that means that you have to customize the styles *every time* you open a new document by manually redefining all the paragraph styles, or by importing styles from another document. No thanks.

With most word processors, you can just change a preference setting to choose your standard font—but Pages' emphasis on templates means that the default font rides along with each template, not in a global preference. That means that the easiest approach to getting your favorite font and styles at the outset of every new document is to create your own new template with your preferred font. Chapter 10 explores all the details of custom templates, but here's the quick and dirty:

1. **Create a new document from the Blank template.**

2. **Select your preferred typeface and font size.**

   Make any other formatting changes—tabs, indentation, line spacing, and so on—that you would like to have for your main body text.

3. **Choose View → Show Styles Drawer or click the Styles Drawer button in the Format Bar to slide out your styles.**

4. **In the Paragraph Styles pane, point to Free Form, click the downward arrow to the right, and select "Redefine Style from Selection".**

5. **Repeat step 4 for the Body style in the Paragraph Styles pane, and then update any of the other styles you'd like to customize.**

6. **Choose File → Save as Template.**

   Give the template a name and then click Save.

Your newly minted template appears in the Template Chooser window in the category "My Templates," ready to take the Blank template's place as your new starting point.

Tip: You can change this "My Templates" category name or add additional custom categories, but you have to dive deep into your hard drive to make those changes. You'll find all the details on page 360.

Typo-Busting Power Tools

The last chapter introduced you to Pages as the faithful transcriber of your words, an able assistant for capturing your ideas and juggling them into presentable shape. Like any good assistant, though, Pages does more than just take down your words—it catalogs them, quietly fixes errors, manages your drafts...and when asked, even offers its opinion about what you've written. Pages is reference librarian, proofreader, and project manager rolled into one.

Pages handles these roles by giving you a set of power tools to buzz through the jobs that support your writing: editing, sharing, and gathering feedback. The program's Find & Replace tool makes short work of sifting through long documents; the built-in dictionary, thesaurus, and encyclopedia help you catch errors or find the perfect word; Pages' in-house grammarian offers advice for sharpening your writing; and change tracking eases collaboration by keeping up with the edits and comments of multiple authors.

Together, this pit crew of support services adds up to a mean collection of typo busters, protecting you from careless mistakes while helping you find or solicit the right words to get your ideas across. This chapter explores them all.

Changing Your Mind: Find & Replace

Whether you're completing your 400-page novel or just polishing a three-page letter, you often have to change a word, a phrase, or even just a character that appears repeatedly throughout the text. For example, as newsletter editor for Up & Away, Megaville's leading outfitter for superheroes, you've been asked to write a book,

Fighting Crime with Super Powers: The Missing Manual. As you zoom into your final chapters, your editor asks you to make a few changes:

- You use Captain Fantastic as an example throughout the book, but the famously litigious hero threatened to sue to protect his action-figure and theme-park trademarks. Now you have to change all 273 mentions of Captain Fantastic to Mister Nice Guy, a lesser known but less lawyer-prone hero.

- The word "Kryptonite" is capitalized, who knew? Not you, unfortunately, and now you have to fix your many lowercase lapses.

- Your personal Kryptonite is spelling—throughout the book you've confused *heroin* (a drug) with *heroine* (a female hero), a slip certain to irritate your female following…and copy editors everywhere.

- Half your mentions of *Costumed Quarterly* magazine are in quotation marks, but you should instead italicize them with the *Emphasis* style, no quotes.

It's Find & Replace to the rescue! Hunting through hundreds of manuscript pages for these changes would require superhuman patience, but Find & Replace saves you the trouble, sifting through your document and making the changes in a split second.

Find

Find & Replace is really two commands rolled into one: *Find* and *Find & Replace.* Sometimes you just need to find a word or phrase in your document. For example, you might want to *find* the pages where you use the term, "rocket belt malfunctions":

1. **Choose Edit → Find → Find or press ⌘-F.**

   The Find & Replace window appears (Figure 4-1). Click Advanced to open the window to its full size. (You can sometimes use the Simple tab, but for most searches you'll appreciate the extra options available in the Advanced tab.)

2. **Enter the word or phrase you're looking for in the Find box:** *rocket belt malfunctions.*

   Turn off the checkbox for "Match case"—because you want to find both capitalized and non-capitalized occurrences of this phrase. In some cases, you'll also want to turn on the checkbox for "Whole words" to prevent the search from turning up words that merely include your search term (like caper or escaped when searching for "cape").

3. **Click Next (or press Return), and Pages jumps to the next spot in your document where you mention rocket belt malfunctions.**

   The Next button tells Pages to search forward from your current selection. When you turn on the "Search previous text (loop)" option, Pages automatically starts over at the beginning of the document when it hits the end. You can also search backward from your present location by clicking Previous.

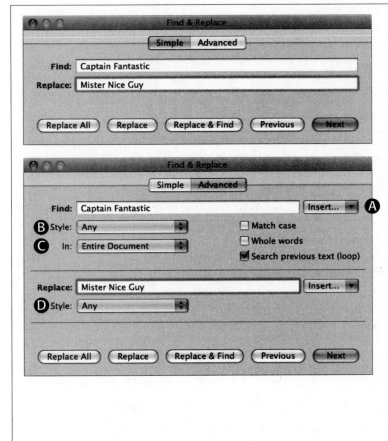

Figure 4-1:
The Find & Replace window in its Simple (top) and Advanced forms. The Insert pop-up menus (A) let you specify invisible formatting characters like tabs, line breaks, page breaks, and so on. The Style pop-up menu (B) allows you to limit your search to text in a specific text style—for example, Body Text or Caption. The In pop-up menu (C) lets you search in the Entire Document, including headers, footers, and footnotes; or just in the Main Text Body. In the Replace box, type whatever you want Pages to insert in place of whatever it finds. In the second Style pop-up menu (D) choose the style, if any, you want Pages to apply to the found text when it makes a replacement.

If you're certain about the terms you've set up for your Find & Replace, click Replace All and Pages makes the change and tells you how many occurrences it found. Click Replace to replace only the currently highlighted word; click Replace & Find to replace the current word and move on so you can evaluate the next occurrence. The Previous and Next buttons control the direction in which Pages searches through your document, and the "Search previous text (loop)" checkbox starts searching at the top of the document after the search reaches the end.

Tip: If you can't see the found word highlighted in your document, it could be hidden behind the Find & Replace window. To prevent this inconvenience, arrange the windows so the dialog box doesn't overlap your text before launching your search.

Work your way through your whole document by clicking Next repeatedly (or press ⌘-G), leaping from result to result in a single bound. In fact, you don't even need the Find & Replace window at this point—close the window and keep pressing ⌘-G to hop through the matches.

Tip: For simple searches like this, an alternative to the Find tool is the Search sidebar (page 46). Choose either View → Show Search or Edit → Find → Search, and type the text you're looking for in the Search box. Instead of taking you to each occurrence one by one, Pages lists all the results at once in the Search sidebar—like a table of contents. Unlike the Find tool, however, the Search sidebar doesn't let you specify searches for styles or invisible characters. More on that shortly.

Find & Replace

On its own, the Find tool is a nifty way to zip straight to specific portions of your document. But when you mix in Replace, things get interesting. Find & Replace can save you so much time and hassle that a better name might be Search & Rescue—it lets you motor through edits, telling Pages to automatically change matching words to some other text. You can review each of these changes before applying them, or you can just take the leap and tell Pages to go ahead and change all matches across the board.

Reviewing each change

Some changes require a yes-or-no decision from you. For example, you might want to review every occurrence of the words "heroin" and "heroine" to make sure you're using the right word for the specific context. When you find a mistake, you want to tell Pages to correct it; otherwise you want to leave the text untouched. Here's how:

1. Choose Edit → Find → Find or press ⌘-F to call up the Find & Replace window.

2. Enter the word you're looking for in the Find box: for example, *heroin.*

3. In the Replace box, enter the word that you *may* wish to use instead: *heroine.*

4. Click Next (or press Return), and Pages jumps to the first occurrence of "heroin" in your search text.

   Heroic woman or nefarious drug? After examining the word in context, click Next to leave it as is and jump to the next occurrence; or click Replace & Find to replace "heroin" with "heroine" and *then* move to the next occurrence. (This has the same effect as clicking the Replace button and then Next.)

Be aware that the *Replace* and *Replace & Find* buttons both do exactly what they say they do: They replace the current selection with the text in the Replace box. That's perfect when the text that you want to replace is already selected. But when you're just starting a search, that's probably not the case, and you'll get an unwanted result: Clicking Replace & Find adds the replacement word at your current insertion point before looking for the word you want to find. To avoid surprises, always begin a session by pressing the Next button before pressing either Replace button.

Tip: If you want to remove all occurrences of a word, leave the Replace box empty when you do your search. When you click Replace, Pages deletes the found text—replacing it with nothing at all.

Replace all automatically

Some circumstances don't require your review for every change. When you know that you definitely want to replace all instances of a word or phrase, the *Replace All* button is the answer. To capitalize every lowercase instance of "kryptonite" in your document, for example, type *kryptonite* in the Find box and *Kryptonite* in the Replace box, and click Replace All. Pages instantly processes all the Kryptonite in your document, without asking you to review each occurrence.

Note: When replacing all, be sure to turn on the "Search previous text (loop)" checkbox. Otherwise, Pages will make the replacements only in the text that comes *after* your current selection in the document.

Whole words vs. partial matches

When working with Replace All, it's particularly important to be clear about what you're replacing. Turn on the checkbox for "Whole words" when you want to change a specific word. This tells Pages not to confuse the word you're searching for with parts of other words. That way, when you want to change *Sue* to *Betty*, the words *issue* and *Suez* don't turn into *isBetty* and *Bettyz*.

Note: Searching for a word with the "Whole words" option turned on won't find the plural and possessive forms that may lurk in your document. To catch all these you really need to perform extra searches, one for the plural and one for the possessive—and perhaps one for the plural possessive.

Searching for spaces and invisible characters

Pages' search features don't limit you to "normal" words and characters—you can just as easily search for spaces, tabs, line breaks, and a range of other invisible characters (for more on "invisibles," see page 81). Say that you want to sweep out extra spaces from your document, replacing two or more spaces with a single space. In the Find box, type two spaces and then type one space in the Replace box. Make sure the "Search previous text (loop)" checkbox is turned on, and then click Replace All. Pages replaces all your double-spaces with one—but what if, in a spacebar-addled frenzy, you typed three or more spaces? Just click Replace All again to replace those extra spaces. Continue clicking Replace All until the indicator above that button says, "0 Found."

You can likewise nip spaces trailing at the end of paragraphs: In the Find box, type one space and then select Paragraph Break from the Insert pop-up menu next door (see Figure 4-2). In the Replace box, choose a Paragraph Break from the other Insert pop-up menu (no space this time). Click Replace All until you get the "0 found" message.

You can use the same technique to find and replace other invisible characters, too. For example, you might want to replace every layout break with a section break (more on what that means in Chapter 5).

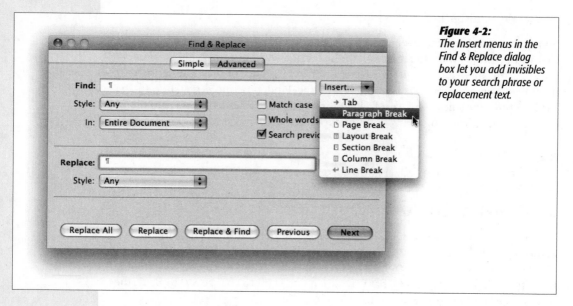

Figure 4-2:
The Insert menus in the Find & Replace dialog box let you add invisibles to your search phrase or replacement text.

Style-conscious searching

Find & Replace lets you target your search to text formatted in a certain style. For example, say that you want to add the "®" symbol to all instances of "Captain Fantastic," but only when the name appears in a heading: Enter *Captain Fantastic* in the Find box, and *Captain Fantastic*® in the Replace box. Then limit the search to headings by selecting the Heading 1 style from the Style pop-up menu under the Find box. Click Replace All, and Pages updates every occurrence of "Captain Fantastic" in the Heading style. (Of course, to take advantage of this feature, you actually have to use styles in the first place. Head back to Chapter 3 to review the details.)

You can likewise apply a style to found text. For example, if you want to replace every quoted mention of "Costumed Quarterly" with italicized text in the Emphasis style, Find & Replace can help: Enter "Costumed Quarterly" (with quotes) in the Find box and *Costumed Quarterly* (no quotes) in the Replace box. In the Style pop-up menu under the Replace box, choose Emphasis as shown in Figure 4-3. Click Replace All, and Pages removes the quotes and adds the style to every occurrence of "Costumed Quarterly."

Tip: You don't even have to be looking for specific text. If you just want to find every instance of a certain style, leave the Find box blank and choose the sought-after style from the Style menu under Find—choose Heading 2, for example. Click Next, and Pages takes you to the next subheading. Want to change all Heading 2 text to the Heading 1 style? Choose Heading in the Style menu under Replace. Be sure to leave the Replace box empty, and click Replace All. (Page 102 also describes another way to replace styles, using the options in the Styles Drawer.)

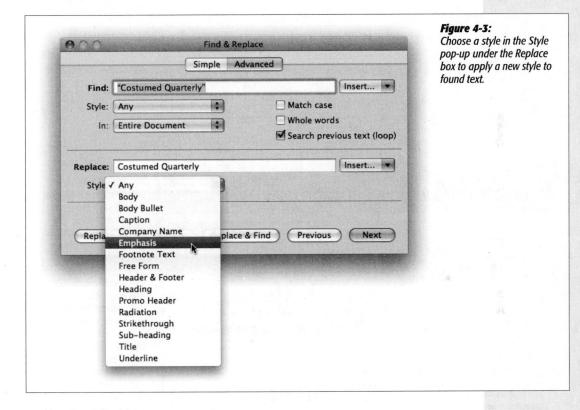

Figure 4-3:
Choose a style in the Style pop-up under the Replace box to apply a new style to found text.

Spell Checking

One of the most apreciated features of the modern word processor is its ability to corect embarassing misspellings. Pages can't save you from choosing the *wrong* word—it still can't tell a "heroine" from "heroin," or "there" from "their" from "they're"—but it can at least let you know when you've misspelled "appreciated," "correct," or "embarrassing."

Make a *spell check* the last stop before considering any document finished. Even if you're a spelling bee champ, typos eventually befall anyone who puts fingers to a keyboard. To catch these gaffes, Pages makes use of Mac OS X's systemwide spell checker—tapping the same dictionary used by other Apple programs like Mail, Keynote, Numbers, TextEdit, iPhoto, and so on.

Check Spelling As You Type

Unless you tell it otherwise, Pages quietly watches as you type and nudges you when it spots a problem. The moment that you type an unrecognized word, the program flags it with a red dashed underline and provides fast access to spelling suggestions—if you want them. This *Check Spelling as You Type* feature is turned on by default, but you can turn it on or off by choosing Edit → Spelling → "Check Spelling as You Type". When the feature is on, Pages shows a check mark next to that menu item.

When Pages adds a red underline to a suspicious spelling, Control-click the word. A shortcut menu appears, topped with the spell checker's guesses of correct spellings (Figure 4-4). Choose the word you're after, and Pages makes the correction.

Note: You can also tell Pages to automatically replace unknown words with the suggested spelling as you type, without waiting for you to approve the suggestion. See page 127 for details.

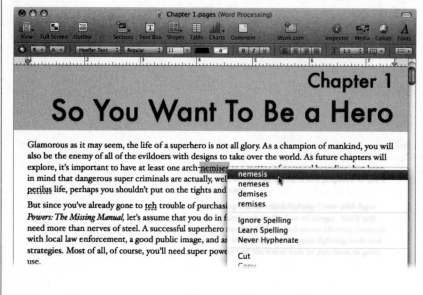

Figure 4-4:
The easiest way to correct misspellings is to Control-click the underlined words. The top of the pop-up menu presents Pages' best guesses of the correct spelling. Choose the one you want from the list, and Pages makes the substitution in your document. If the flagged word is actually correctly spelled—an unusual name, for example—choose Learn Spelling to add that word to the dictionary. If you don't want to add the word to the dictionary, yet want to accept it as correctly spelled for this document only, choose Ignore Spelling and Pages refrains from flagging it as misspelled for the rest of the document.

Just because Pages flags a word doesn't necessarily mean that it's misspelled—only that the spell checker doesn't recognize it. This is common, for example, with names, addresses, or specialized technical lingo not included in your Mac's dictionary. (This also happens with foreign words, but that's a special case—more on that in a moment.) You can teach the spell checker a new word by Control-clicking a red-underlined word and choosing Learn Spelling from the menu. The word is added to your Mac's dictionary and will stop getting flagged—not only by Pages but every other program that uses the Mac OS X spell checker.

Another choice in the pop-up menu is Ignore Spelling. Choose this setting when you don't want that word flagged in the current document, but you don't want it added to the dictionary either. For example, when your "Flying for Beginners" chapter makes several mentions of the SonicWing Z-10 and JetGirl anti-gravity boots, you might choose Ignore Spelling for "SonicWing" and "JetGirl." Pages will stay quiet about these brand names—as well as lowercase variations, "sonicwing" and "jetgirl"—for the rest of your editing session. New documents, however, will continue to catch those words as misspellings.

Note: Your Ignore Spelling commands last until you close the document. When you reopen the file later, Pages again flags your once-ignored words as unrecognized.

Once you've chosen to correct the word, Learn Spelling, or Ignore Spelling, Pages removes the red underline.

Whoops! You accidentally told the spell checker to learn the word, "superheroe," and now none of your programs spot the misspelling. Control-click the word and choose Unlearn Spelling from the shortcut menu. Ah, the red underline is back. Pages and all the other programs that use the Mac OS X spell checker immediately start flagging the word as a misspelling again. (This maneuver works only for words that you've added yourself—Mac OS X won't allow you to remove words from its standard dictionary.)

Tip: The "Unlearn Spelling" option was introduced in Mac OS X 10.5 "Leopard." If you're using Pages with version 10.4 ("Tiger"), you'll find the option to unlearn, or "forget," a word in the Spelling window (Edit → Spelling → Spelling). In the window's text field, type the word you want your Mac to forget, and click the Forget button.

Check Spelling in the Document or Selection

If red underlines derail your creative train of thought, you can turn them off. Choose Edit → Spelling → "Check Spelling as You Type" to remove the checkmark in front of that menu item. The red lines vanish and you can turn your attention back to your masterpiece. When you're ready to ask for the spell checker's help, you can ask it to take you through all the unknown words in your document one by one.

Place your insertion point where you'd like to begin spell checking—at the beginning of the document, for example—and press ⌘-; (semicolon) or choose Edit → Spelling → Check Spelling to tell Pages to highlight the first unrecognized word. Control-click the word to choose an alternative or tell Pages to learn or ignore the word. Press ⌘-; again to move on to the next misspelled word.

If all this Control-clicking is wearing you down, you can use the Spelling window to move through your document, showing you each unrecognized word and its suggested replacements simultaneously. Put your insertion point where you would like to start checking, and choose Edit → Spelling → Spelling (or press ⌘-:) to call up the Spelling window and highlight the next misspelled word. The Spelling window shows you the word and offers suggestions for changes, as shown in Figure 4-5.

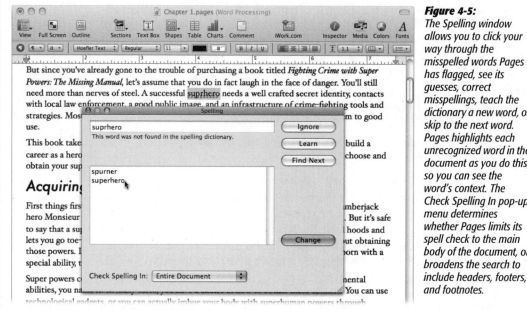

Figure 4-5:
The Spelling window allows you to click your way through the misspelled words Pages has flagged, see its guesses, correct misspellings, teach the dictionary a new word, or skip to the next word. Pages highlights each unrecognized word in the document as you do this, so you can see the word's context. The Check Spelling In pop-up menu determines whether Pages limits its spell check to the main body of the document, or broadens the search to include headers, footers, and footnotes.

Pages offers its recommendations with a list of suggested spellings. If you see the correct word, double-click it (or click once to select the word and then click Change)—Pages replaces it in the document and moves on to the next misspelling. The Ignore button skips this word for the rest of the document; the Learn button adds it to the dictionary. If you just want to skip over the word and move on to the next misspelling, click Find Next (or press ⌘-;).

If none of the displayed spelling alternatives is correct, or if none are provided, you can type the correct spelling yourself and click Change.

Using Foreign-Language Dictionaries

Your computer knows lots of languages and has a dictionary for each of them. Normally, the spell checker uses the dictionary that matches your Mac's system language setting. (If you change that setting in System Preferences → International → Language, you also change the language for your menus and dialog boxes.)

But say that you write multilingual documents, or perhaps you're known to sprinkle your prose with languages of the world to demonstrate your cosmopolitan credentials. When Pages spell-checks your document, it doesn't find those foreign-language words in your standard dictionary and incorrectly marks them as misspelled. Your chapter on global crime fighting is flummoxed by the mere mention of Frau Fantastische or Monsieur Magnifique. *Quelle horreur!*

You can sidestep this international crisis by telling Pages exactly what language you're using for certain words, paragraphs, or even the whole document. Use the Text Inspector's More tab for this, as shown in Figure 4-6. Now the dictionary for the selected foreign language governs spell checking for the specified portion of the document, while the rest of the document uses the standard language dictionary.

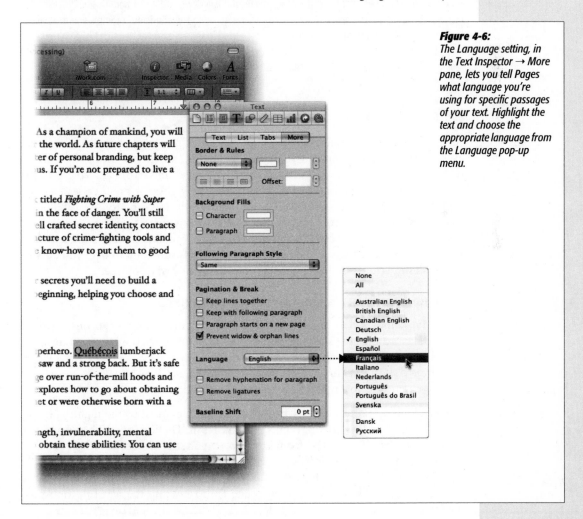

Figure 4-6:
The Language setting, in the Text Inspector → More pane, lets you tell Pages what language you're using for specific passages of your text. Highlight the text and choose the appropriate language from the Language pop-up menu.

If your *entire* document is in a different language than your standard dictionary, one approach is to use Select All (⌘-A) to highlight all your text and then choose the new language in the Text Inspector. This is OK for a quick fix, but as you continue working with your text, you might discover that the Language setting slips back into the standard language for new paragraphs or when you apply a style. That's because the language setting is actually cooked into the document's paragraph and character styles. For a more permanent solution, you should instead update the document's styles to use your preferred language by going through each style in the Styles drawer and updating its Language setting in the Text Inspector. For more on this, see page 98.

Note: If you frequently write documents in this second language, you might find it useful to save your restyled document as a template: Choose File → Save as Template, and Pages prompts you to save the file in your My Templates folder. Choose a name ("Fichier français," perhaps) and click Save. From now on, you'll find your new template in the Template Chooser in the My Templates category. For more on saving custom templates, see Chapter 10 (page 345).

Reference Tools

As helpful as the spell checker might be, you can't rely exclusively on it to catch every mistake. For example, if you type "lightening" when you mean "lightning," or "metal" when you mean "mettle," Pages won't spot the error, since these words are all in the dictionary and spelled correctly. Only you (or another reader) can spot correctly spelled but misused words. But we all might be forgiven the occasional lapse when we forget which version of a word is correct for the context: Do I use "affect" or "effect" here? "Your" or "you're"? "Compliment" or "complement"? Pages offers a set of tools in the Edit → Writing Tools submenu to help you answer those questions and also find lots more info about a word or phrase.

Look up Words in the Dictionary or Thesaurus

Your Mac comes with a full dictionary, complete with definitions, pronunciation, usage notes—the whole shebang. In fact, the Mac OS X Dictionary program gives you three volumes in one: *The New Oxford American Dictionary, The Oxford American Writers Thesaurus,* and the Apple Dictionary, which includes terms and definitions specific to Apple's software and products.

You can look up a word directly from your Pages document by highlighting it and then choosing Edit → Writing Tools → Look Up in Dictionary or Thesaurus" (or Control-click the word and, from the shortcut menu, choose Writing Tools → "Look Up in Dictionary or Thesaurus"). Pages launches the Dictionary program and flips you straight to the entry for your selected word in the dictionary, as shown in Figure 4-7. Click the appropriate tab to look up the word in the Apple dictionary or thesaurus—why settle for "bold" when you could say, "temerarious"?

Note: If your selection contains more than one word when you select "Look Up in Dictionary or Thesaurus," Dictionary uses the first word or phrase that it recognizes from the selected passage.

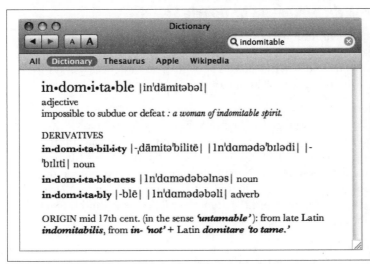

Figure 4-7:
Read up on a word's meaning in the dictionary—or look up synonyms and antonyms in the thesaurus to find just the right word. Go straight to the word you want by highlighting it in Pages and choosing Edit → Writing Tools → "Look Up in Dictionary or Thesaurus." Or type your word in the search box at the top right of the Dictionary window and press Return.

Your Mac knows an even niftier shortcut to the dictionary and thesaurus: Position your cursor over the word you want to define, hold down the Control and ⌘ keys, and tap the D key. A little window pops up with the definition of the word, as shown in Figure 4-8. The menu sticks around for as long as you continue to hold down the Control and ⌘ keys. You can even move your cursor from word to word, and Pages updates the definition to show you the meaning and pronunciation of the word under the cursor. When you're done, release the Control and ⌘ keys, and your cursor returns to normal duty. (You can use this trick in lots of Mac programs, not just iWork.)

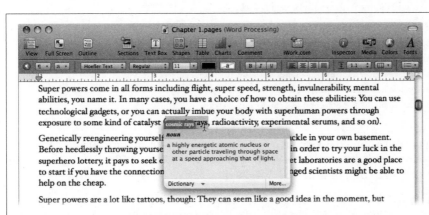

Figure 4-8:
The pop-up dictionary shows you the definition of the word under your cursor when you hold down the Control and ⌘ keys and then press D. To switch to the thesaurus or Apple dictionary, choose it from the Dictionary pop-up at the bottom left. To open the entry in the full Dictionary program, click More in the bottom right.

Note: When triggering this feature be careful not to click ⌘-Option-D by mistake—that hides the Dock! If your Dock floats away, bring it back by pressing ⌘-Option-D again.

Find It on the Web: Wikipedia or Google Search

Say that the simple definition of "cosmic rays" just doesn't cut it, and imagine that you're eager to soak up every detail about their origins in neutron stars and quasars. Hey, it could happen. And when it does, Pages gives you a few easy ways to find detailed information from the Web about any topic.

When you explored the Dictionary window, you might have spotted the Wikipedia tab in the Dictionary toolbar (this tab is available only in Mac OS X 10.5 or later). When you're connected to the Internet, clicking that tab calls up the encyclopedia entry for your word or phrase from *Wikipedia*, the Web's free volunteer encyclopedia. Just like looking up dictionary definitions, you can look up the encyclopedia entry for any term by highlighting it in your document and choosing Edit → Writing Tools → "Look Up in Dictionary or Thesaurus" and then clicking the Wikipedia tab, as shown in Figure 4-9.

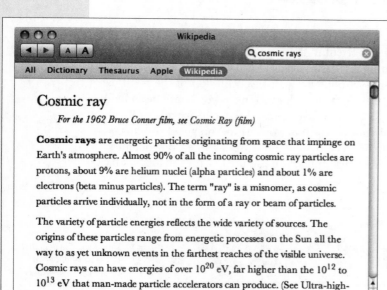

Figure 4-9:
The Dictionary program offers a Wikipedia tab, which lets you read the Wikipedia encyclopedia entry for any word or phrase.

If you prefer your Wikipedia in a browser window, you can instead select the term to look up, and choose Edit → Writing Tools → Search in Wikipedia. Pages opens the Wikipedia entry in your Web browser.

Pages offers a similar option to speed up a Google search. Highlight your search phrase and choose Edit → Writing Tools → Search in Google. Pages takes you straight to the Google search engine in your browser, displaying the results for your search term.

Find It on Your Computer: Spotlight Search

Sometimes, the answer lies within, or at least within your hard drive. Besides helping you pluck info from the Web, Pages can likewise help speed searches within your own computer. While writing a chapter on the practical benefits of telepathy for the modern hero, for example, it sure would be convenient to have that article you wrote for *Telepathy Review* about the new generation of precognition balms and lotions. If only you had the vaguest idea where you saved the file.

Happily, it doesn't take a mind reader to find your document. Mac OS X lets you search for files on your computer using *Spotlight,* the system's built-in search engine. Normally, you might launch a search by clicking the magnifying-glass icon at the top right of your screen, or by typing a word or phrase into the search box at the top right of any window in the Finder. But Pages gives you a slight head start by letting you launch a search from any text selection in your document. For example, to see if there's a found document in your future, highlight the phrase *precognition balms* in your document and choose Edit → Writing Tools → "Search in Spotlight". Pages launches a new Finder window listing all the files that contain those words.

For the Obsessive: Document Stats

When you're targeting your text to a certain word count or if you simply have a *Rain Man*-like fascination with numbers, Pages offers a wealth of statistics about your document. Under Pages' standard settings, the page and word counts are always displayed at the bottom of your document window, but you can also check a slew of other statistics on the growth of your bouncing baby book in the Info tab of the Document Inspector (Figure 4-10). Pages takes you directly there when you click the word count at the bottom-left corner of the Document Window, or when you choose Edit → Writing Tools → Show Statistics.

Tip: If you're distracted by the always-on display of your word count, turn it off in the Pages → Preferences window: Click the General button and turn off the "Show word count at window bottom" checkbox.

Word count and other statistics

While you're busy composing Great Thoughts, Pages constantly runs your numbers—lots of them. The Document Inspector counts just about everything in your document: words, pages, lines, paragraphs, sections, graphics, and individual characters. (If you need the character count with spaces omitted, Pages even throws that in, too.)

If you want the counts for just a specific passage of your document, just highlight the text to tally. The word count at the bottom right of the document window updates to show you how many words you've selected, along with the document's overall total ("5 of 4,387 Words"). With text selected, the Document Inspector similarly zeroes in on your selection: The Range pop-up menu automatically

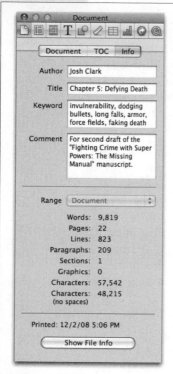

Figure 4-10:
The Document Inspector → Info tab displays statistics about your document. Fill in the author, title, keywords, and comments to help Spotlight find your file more easily. As you type, Pages updates the count of words, paragraphs, pages, and more. You can see these counts for any portion of your document by highlighting it; Pages automatically sets the Range pop-up menu to Selection and shows you the numbers for the selected text. Choose Document to go back to the full document stats.

switches to Selected, and the inspector shows you the counts for the highlighted text, with a slightly reduced number of categories: words, paragraphs, graphics, and characters. To go back to the figures for the full document, choose *Document* from the Range pop-up menu or click outside the selection to deselect the text (when there's no text selection, Document is the only option).

Author, title, comments, and keywords

The top of the Document Inspector → Info tab features four fields where you can describe your document: Author, Title, Keywords, and Comments. When you create a new document, these fields are always blank. You can leave them that way if you like, but filling them in makes it easier for Spotlight to find the document if you lose track of it later.

Note: Don't be confused by the Title field—it's not the same as the filename of your document. Changing the Title setting in the Document Inspector has no effect on what the document is named; it's just a description of the document for your own reference, and to help Spotlight find the file.

File size and dates

At the very bottom of the Document Inspector → Info tab, Pages displays the date the document was last printed (or "Never" if you haven't gotten around to it). Click the Show File Info button and Pages opens a new Finder window with detailed info about the document file, including its size, location, and the dates it was created and last modified. (This is the same window that you see if you select the file on your desktop and choose File → Get Info in the Finder.)

The Proofreader

Along with the spell checker, Pages gives you another eagle-eyed assistant to help you spot typos. The *Proofreader* combs through your text looking for errors in capitalization, punctuation, and writing style. Although prone to making occasional errors of its own, the Proofreader provides a valuable service by taking you through a careful review of your text, drawing attention to potential trouble spots.

First things first: The Proofreader is not a *grammar checker*. Other word processors like Microsoft Word include tools called grammar checkers which try to identify a variety of grammatical mistakes, like subject-verb disagreement ("I is grammatically challenged"), sentence fragments, and so on. Grammar checkers examine the structure of your sentence, try to understand what you're attempting to write, and then offer suggestions or corrections. As you might guess, however, programming a computer to offer advice on something as slippery as human language is a tough task, with unreliable results. Few grammar checkers do their job well, and it seems that Apple decided not to bother. The Proofreader doesn't really tackle the problem at all.

Instead, the Proofreader focuses on flagging simple typos and nudging you to reconsider jargon words or clichéd phrases. It's at its most useful spotting duplicated words ("I frequently have this this problem"), capitalization errors, and extra spaces around punctuation—all typical typing errors that can't be caught by the spell checker. For this category of typos, it's well worth running the Proofreader on the final draft of your work.

The Proofreader also offers writing advice, cautioning you against using clichés, long-winded phrases, flimsy words like "nice" or "actually," or informal constructions like starting a sentence with "and" or "but." These suggestions frequently stray into subjective realms of personal style and tone, and you should consider the Proofreader more of a source of possible alternatives than as the final authority. Whatever you do, don't blindly accept the Proofreader's suggested changes. As with Pages' spell checker, the Proofreader isn't particularly clever about context and may frequently offer vocabulary suggestions that aren't relevant to your specific use of a word (Figure 4-11). This means that accepting *all* the Proofreader's suggestions does more harm than good. That doesn't mean that you should avoid the Proofreader entirely—if nothing else, the Proofreader encourages you to review passages of your own writing and take a close look at your word choices, always a useful exercise as you're putting the final polish on your work.

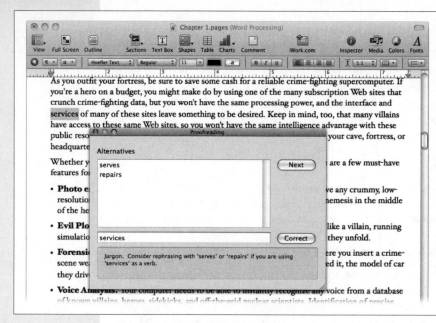

Figure 4-11:
The Proofreader can't always tell which meaning you intend when you use a word. Here, a sentence about online services prompts the Proofreader to flag the word "services" as jargon, incorrectly suggesting that you use "serves" or "repairs" instead. You can't argue with the Proofreader's good taste in counseling you not to use "services" as a verb, but the advice doesn't fit the context here.

Proofread Your Document

To launch the Proofreader's review of your document, place the insertion point where you would like to start the review—the beginning of your document perhaps—and choose Edit → Proofreading → Proofreader (or Control-click on the text and choose Proofreading → Proofreader from the shortcut menu). The Proofreader leaps ahead in your document, highlighting the first problem phrase it finds and opening the Proofreader window, as shown in Figure 4-12.

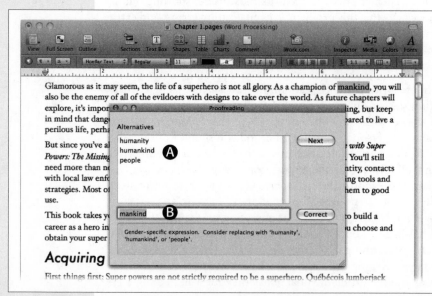

Figure 4-12:
The Proofreader window explains potential problems in your text and offers alternatives. To accept a suggestion, click the option you want from the Alternatives list (A)—your choice appears in the box below (B) and, when you click Correct, replaces the text in your document. You can also type your own alternative into the edit box and then click Correct.

To skip ahead to the next suggestion without making a change to the current selection, click Next. (If you click Correct without choosing or typing an alternative, the Proofreader also makes no change and takes you to the next selection.)

Proofread as You Type

Like the spell checker, the Proofreader can also review your text as you type, flagging problem phrases with a green underline the moment you type them (Figure 4-13). To turn this feature on, choose Edit → Proofreading → "Proofread as You Type". A checkmark appears next to the menu item to indicate that the feature is on, and Pages instantly marks any proofing problems it finds. Choose the command again to turn the feature off.

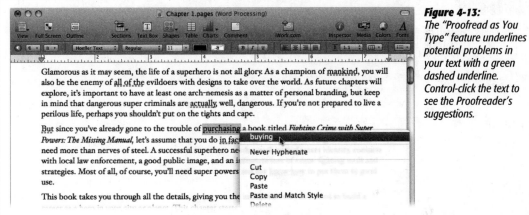

Figure 4-13:
The "Proofread as You Type" feature underlines potential problems in your text with a green dashed underline. Control-click the text to see the Proofreader's suggestions.

Like the spell checker, the Proofreader offers suggested changes in the shortcut menu for its flagged phrases; choose a suggestion to replace the flagged word or phrase. The shortcut menu, however, doesn't include the detailed explanation offered by the Proofreader window, contextual information that is often crucial to deciding whether to accept the change. Even with this weakness, "Proofread as You Type" is still practical for spotting simple typos, but it's less useful when the Proofreader has writerly advice like suggestions for different words. Rather than fill your document with inscrutable green squiggles, it's better just to leave this feature off and then ask the Proofreader to review the entire document as you're finishing the final draft.

Note: Pages provides a weak third proofing option via Edit → Proofreading → Proofread. This command jumps you to the next Proofreader problem in your document, but like "Proofread as You Type", doesn't provide the context that you get in the Proofreader window. You can safely ignore this command entirely, since it provides none of the advantages of using either the Proofreader window (more info) or "Proofread as You Type" (catch typos as you go).

Auto-Correction and Text Substitution

Pages offers one final automatic safety net to save you from fat-finger foibles on the keyboard. *Auto-correction* mends mistakes and applies simple formatting as you type, according to your preferences. For example, it can make sure quotation marks and apostrophes slant in the right direction, capitalize the first word of your sentences, replace "teh" with "the" on the fly, and so on. You give Pages its auto-correction marching orders from the Auto-Correction pane of the Preferences window, as shown in Figure 4-14.

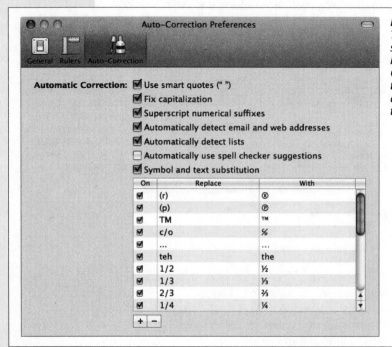

Figure 4-14:
To select your auto-correction settings, choose Pages → Preferences and click the Auto-Correction button. Here you can flip the switch on seven categories of auto-correction and add or remove text-substitution rules.

Pages offers you seven categories of auto-correction fixes, and you can turn any of them on or off from this preferences window:

- **Use smart quotes (" ")**. *Smart quotes* (or *curly quotes*) are curved quotation marks that indicate the beginning or end of a quotation. These brainy beauties offer more typographic elegance and meaning than the straight quotation mark of the typewriter era. With this option enabled, Pages automatically replaces regular up-and-down quotation marks and apostrophes with either an opening or closing mark depending on whether you're starting or ending a word. When you type a quote before starting a word, Pages gives you a left quotation mark; when you type a quote after a word, it gives you a right quotation mark.

Note: Smart quotes replacement doesn't always give you the correct result, especially for contractions where an apostrophe appears at the beginning of a word (*the roaring '20s* or *'nuff said*). In those cases, Pages points the quotation mark in the wrong direction, and you have to type the closing apostrophe manually: press Shift-Option-] or use the Characters window (see page 82).

- **Fix capitalization.** When you turn this option on, Pages always capitalizes the first word of your sentences—when you start a sentence with a lowercase word, it fixes it for you automatically.

- **Superscript numerical suffixes.** This option tells Pages to convert "1st" to "1st," "2nd" to "2nd," and so on.

- **Automatically detect email and web addresses.** With this setting enabled, Pages turns all email and web addresses into hyperlinks (see page 179).

- **Automatically detect lists.** This option tells Pages to switch to list-formatting duty when it looks like you're writing a list, turning a paragraph into a list item (see page 84).

- **Automatically use spell checker suggestions.** Turn this option on to let Pages go ahead and replace any unrecognized words with its suggested spelling. This works only when there's just one suggested alternative; Pages does nothing when it has multiple suggestions. This is somewhat risky, since Pages might replace a correctly spelled but unknown word with a completely different word. This feature works even when you don't have "Check Spelling as You Type" turned on (page 114); when you *do* have it turned on, the red underline indicates words that have more than one suggestion.

- **Symbol and text substitution.** This option lets you customize your own rules for substituting one set of text with another, and it's particularly handy for inserting frequently used symbols like © or ™ without memorizing the keyboard shortcuts or resorting to the Characters window. Below this checkbox, the Preferences window displays a table of replacements (Figure 4-14)—when you type any text shown in the Replace column followed by a space or a punctuation mark, Pages automatically substitutes the corresponding text from the With column. Add your own replacement rule by clicking the + button in the lower-left corner of the window. To remove a rule, select it and click the – button. You can also disable a rule temporarily by turning off its checkbox.

Tracking Changes

As you've seen, Pages provides a whole arsenal of tools to help spot, prevent, and correct errors in your text. In the end, though, these automated services can go only so far. No matter how cleverly programmed, a bucket-of-bolts wordbot is no substitute for the critical eye and creative mind of a living, breathing human editor. That's especially true when you move beyond mechanical considerations of spelling or typos and into more writerly concerns of style and substance.

Lightspeed Typing with Text Substitution

Although turned off when you first start using Pages, the *Symbol and text substitution* option in Auto-Correction Preferences is a hidden powerhouse of productivity. The pre-loaded list of corrections might make you think that this feature is useful only for doing subtle typographic corrections to turn (c) into © or 1/2 into ½. While those are handy enough, text substitution becomes really powerful when you tailor it for the words, phrases, or even paragraphs that you use all the time.

For example, as Chief Sidekick Officer of superhero outfitter Up & Away, you notice that you frequently start letters with the same sentence: "Thank you for your interest in Up & Away's sidekick placement services. We have a long tradition of finding the perfect match for solo heroes and aimless boy wonders. With our help you'll be part of a dynamic duo in no time." Whew, that's a mouthful, and it's tough to muster fresh enthusiasm to type that paragraph every day—better to let Pages do it for you instantly:

1. Choose Pages → Preferences, and click the Auto-Correction button.

2. Turn on the "Symbol and text substitution" check box.

3. Click the + button at the bottom left of the window to add a new text-substitution rule.

4. In the Replace column, enter some easy-to-remember shortcut text.

   It's a good idea to make this text a string of characters that you're unlikely to type normally—otherwise Pages might make your substitution when you don't want it. One strategy is to start your substitution with some punctuation, like a colon or period. For example, *:placement* might be a good shortcut for your sidekick-placement text.

5. In the With column, paste your long-form text—in this example, it's your sidekick intro paragraph.

Now whenever you type *:placement* followed by a space or punctuation, Pages expands it, automatically replacing that shortcut text with your timeworn intro.

Cleverly deployed text substitutions effectively turn you into the world's fastest typist for a range of frequent phrases:

- **Habitual typos.** Always typing "teh" instead of "the," or "becuase" instead of "because"? Add those to your text-substitution list, and Pages manages the correction automatically.

- **Web or email addresses.** If you often type the same email addresses or lengthy website URLs, you can save yourself time and errors by adding shortcuts. Now *:capfan* automatically gives you *cap-fantastic@goodnessleague.org*—and if you have the "Automatically detect email and web addresses" option turned on, the text gets turned into a hyperlink, too.

- **Phone numbers.** Like speed dial for your keyboard.

- **Product names or industry lingo.** If you're always forgetting the model number of the Entropy 3720MX Matter Disruptor, a quick shortcut for *:entropy* will save you time and, um, disruption.

- **Boilerplate text.** Most of us have text—like the sidekick-placement example—that we type or paste over and over again. Driving directions, company descriptions, personal introductions, and letter sign-offs are all good candidates for text substitution.

Even there, though, Pages can be helpful: When you're ready to solicit feedback from others, Pages plays traffic cop to keep the edit process flowing smoothly, monitoring every change made to your document.

With *change tracking,* Pages quietly catalogs every edit made to your document, letting you review all additions, deletions, and replacements before accepting revisions into the final draft. While this can be handy even when you're working on text by yourself, it becomes invaluable when you're collaborating with an editor, co-writing a document with others, or getting comments from your boss. Change tracking builds a paper trail of a document's edit history so that you and others can see exactly who changed what and when.

Note: Pages' change tracking works seamlessly with Microsoft Word. When you export a Pages document to Word format—or use Pages to open a Word document—Pages preserves the edit history. Word users can review your changes and vice versa.

Starting and Stopping Change Tracking

To turn on change tracking, choose Edit → Track Changes. Pages reveals the *Change Tracking toolbar* just below the Format Bar. Pages lists all edits and comments in the *Comments and Changes pane,* which you can reveal (or hide) by clicking the double arrow at the left side of the Change Tracking toolbar, or by choosing View → Show Comments and Changes Pane. The edits appear as a series of *change bubbles,* shown in Figure 4-15. When you click a change bubble, Pages highlights the corresponding text in your document.

If a page is chockablock with changes, the Comments and Changes pane may not be able to display all the change bubbles at once. When that's the case, arrows appear at the bottom of the pane to let you move up and down through the page's change notes.

To turn change tracking off, choose Edit → Turn Off Tracking. Be careful here: When you turn off change tracking, you not only stop tracking future changes, you also lose the current change history, too. Pages pauses to ask you if you really want to do this and, if so, lets you decide what to do with the current batch of edits, as shown in Figure 4-16.

A gentler way to shut down change tracking is to put it on *pause.* This puts change tracking temporarily on hold while maintaining the current edit history; Pages doesn't track any changes that you make in paused mode. To pause change tracking, click the Paused button in the Change Tracking toolbar. To resume, click the On button.

Note: When you make changes to tables, Pages adds a change bubble like any other change, but also adds a triangle-shaped indicator in the upper-right corner of the modified table cell, color-coded according to the editor who made the change. If multiple editors make changes to a cell, Pages colors the indicator gray. For more info about tables, see Chapter 8.

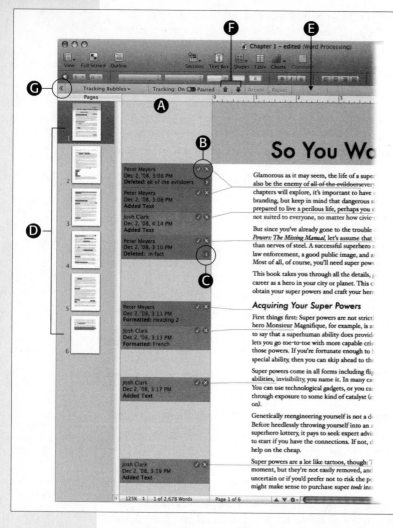

Figure 4-15:
When you turn on change tracking, Pages takes note of every edit in the Comments and Changes pane (A), where change bubbles list who changed what and when, with a line pointing to the edited text. Change bubbles offer buttons to accept/reject each edit (B); for deleted text, there's also a toggle button (C) to hide/show the original text. When the arrow points right, the deleted text is visible, when it points left, it's hidden.

Pages lists every editor's changes in a different color, making it easy to see who's responsible for every change at a glance. If thumbnail view is turned on (View → Show Page Thumbnails), Pages also highlights the edits in the Pages sidebar (D).

The Change Tracking toolbar (E) provides controls for navigating, viewing, and accepting or rejecting edits. Move back and forth through changes with the Previous/Next buttons (F). Hide and show the Comments and Changes pane with the arrow button at the left of the toolbar (G).

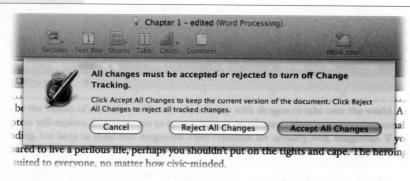

Figure 4-16:
When you turn off change tracking, Pages asks what it should do with the current set of changes. Clicking the Accept All Changes button keeps the current version as is. Clicking Reject All Changes throws out the edits and reverts to the original text. (If you change your mind, Edit → Undo brings it all back.)

Reviewing, Accepting, and Rejecting Changes

With change tracking on, you can step through every edit one at a time and decide whether you want to *accept* or *reject* each one. When you accept an edit, it becomes a permanent part of the text. When you reject it, Pages peels back the edit, reverting to the original unedited text. In both cases, Pages removes the change from the edit history. Think of accepting or rejecting changes like checking off items on your editorial to-do list; once you've reviewed a change and made your decision, Pages considers the edit closed and removes it from sight.

Use any of these methods to accept a change:

- Click the check-shaped Accept button in the edit's change bubble.

- Select the changed text (click its change bubble or place the insertion point inside the edited text) and then click the Accept button in the Change Tracking toolbar.

- Control-click the changed text and choose Accept Change from the shortcut menu.

Pages likewise gives you three ways to reject a change:

- Click the X-shaped Reject button in the change bubble.

- Select the change and click the Reject button in the Change Tracking toolbar.

- Control-click the changed text and choose Reject Change from the shortcut menu.

To step through the changes one at a time, use the up and down arrows in the Change Tracking toolbar to jump to the previous or next change respectively.

If you're feeling impatient, you can accept or reject all edits at once from the gear-shaped Action menu at the right side of the Change Tracking toolbar: Choose Accept All Changes or Reject All Changes. If you prefer to accept or reject changes from just a portion of the document, highlight the text and choose the Action menu's Accept Selected Changes or Reject Selected Changes command.

Controlling the Markup Display

As handy as change tracking can be, all this markup sometimes makes your document too busy to let you focus on your work. When your text is thick with edits, it becomes heavy with dense patches of multi-colored text, a forest of lines, a crowded Comments and Changes pane, and a confusing hash of strikethrough text. If you find yourself squinting just to follow the plot, you can tell Pages to make some cosmetic adjustments.

Showing and hiding changes

The View Markup pop-up menu in the Change Tracking toolbar offers three options for dialing the markup detail up or down in the text itself:

- **View Markup.** Pages displays both added and deleted text, color-coded by author, see Figure 4-15. Deleted text is crossed out, with the *strikethrough* style.

- **View Markup Without Deletions.** Pages displays only new text, hiding deletions, although a small triangle icon indicates where deleted text used to be.

- **View Final.** When you choose this option, Pages stops showing edits in the various author colors, returning your text to its usual (and presumably calmer) color scheme. Deleted text is hidden, although its presence is still noted by a triangle icon. The end result is that you see your document as it would look if you accepted all changes.

You can also pop a few change bubbles to make the Comments and Changes pane less crowded. Control the view in the Tracking Bubbles pop-up menu in the Change Tracking toolbar:

- **Show all.** Pages piles all the change bubbles into the Comments and Changes pane.

- **Show only for selection.** When you have lots of changes on a page, they can't all fit in visible view in the Comments and Changes pane. This option lets you narrow the display to changes made only in the currently highlighted text.

- **Hide all.** Choosing this option removes all change bubbles, leaving the comment bubbles behind (see page 133 for more about comments).

- **Show formatting bubbles.** When you change fonts, line spacing, or any other formatting, Pages normally includes the change with the rest of the change bubbles. Choosing this option turns that display on or off (a checkbox indicates when it's on).

Note: Pages doesn't track *all* formatting changes, particularly when it comes to tables. Changes that involve adding, removing, or moving table rows or columns aren't tracked. In addition, changes to a cell's borders, merging and splitting cells, and autofilling aren't tracked.

Finally, you can also hide the entire Comments and Changes pane, which also gets rid of the change bubbles and all their pointer lines, as shown in Figure 4-17. To hide this pane, click the arrow button at the left of the Change Tracking toolbar (and click it again to bring it back), or choose View → Hide Comments and Changes Pane.

Changing your color and name

If seeing your own text edits in a sickly green color is getting you down, you can choose a new author color. In the Change Tracking toolbar's gear-shaped Action

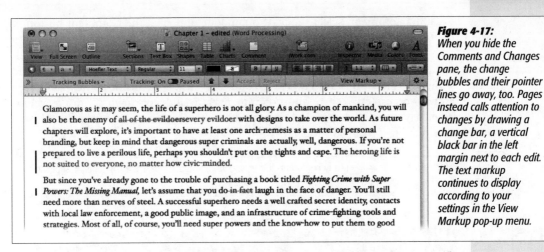

Figure 4-17:
When you hide the Comments and Changes pane, the change bubbles and their pointer lines go away, too. Pages instead calls attention to changes by drawing a change bar, a vertical black bar in the left margin next to each edit. The text markup continues to display according to your settings in the View Markup pop-up menu.

pop-up menu, choose Select Author Color and pick your new color. Alas, you can't choose colors for other authors, so you can't impose your creative color vision on others, but at least you have control over your own personal style.

While you're busy overhauling your personal branding, you can also choose your author handle. Unless you tell it otherwise, Pages labels your changes with your name from Address Book (see the box "How Does Pages Know Where I Live?" on page 22), but you can use any name you like. Go to Pages → Preferences and click the General button, or choose Preferences from the Action pop-up menu in the Change Tracking toolbar. Enter your preferred moniker in the Author field.

Changing the style of new and deleted text

Pages gives you a few minor options to change the look of new and deleted text. Go to Pages → Preferences and click the General button, or choose Preferences from the Action pop-up menu. At the bottom of the window, under Change Tracking, you'll find the Deleted Text and Inserted Text settings. The standard settings are Strikethrough for deleted text and None for new text, but you have your choice of Strikethrough, Underline, or None for either one.

Adding Comments

Besides keeping a record of changes to a document, Pages also lets you and other editors leave *comments* about the text. Comments are notes that never appear in the actual body of the text itself, but instead float in the Comments and Changes pane along with the change bubbles (if change tracking is turned off, Pages calls it simply the *Comments pane*). Like change bubbles, comments are tethered to a particular text selection, making them a useful way to ask questions, offer suggestions, or leave yourself a reminder about a particular passage. They're like Post-It notes that you slap on the document—temporary messages fixed to your text while also remaining separate from it. In fact, like Post-It notes, comments always appear on a yellow background in the Comments pane.

To add a comment, select the text to annotate and click the Comment button in the toolbar, or choose Insert → Comment. Pages opens the Comments pane and adds a comment bubble, drawing a line to the original text, now highlighted in yellow (Figure 4-18). Type your comment in the comment bubble, which grows and shrinks to fit your text. To edit a comment, just click inside its text and type away—you can edit other editors' comments as well as your own. To delete a comment, click the X-shaped Delete button in the comment, or delete the original annotated text from your document.

Tip: You can format the text in comments just as you would regular text, changing fonts or applying character, paragraph, or list styles as you wish.

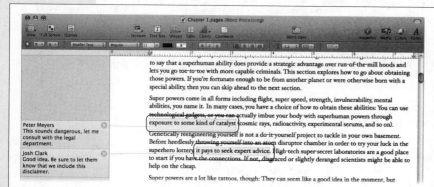

Figure 4-18:
Comments let you add notes and annotations to your text, a useful way to leave yourself research notes or reminders, or to gather suggestions as you pass a document around to a group for feedback. Every comment is anchored to a specific passage of the text (outlined here, to make it easier to see).

To hide the Comments pane, click View → Hide Comments. To show it, click View → Show Comments. This also shows and hides the change bubbles if change tracking is turned on (in which case, the menu calls it the Comments and Changes pane).

Tip: When you print your document with the Comments pane (or Comments and Changes pane) visible, the comments and edits show up in the printed document, too. That's terrific when you want a copy to edit on paper, but not so great when you're printing the upward job review of your boss. Before you print, choose whether to hide or show the Comments pane from the View menu or the toolbar's View pop-up button. See page 321 for more about printing your document.

Although comments share the same look and window location as change bubbles, they're not technically part of change tracking. You can leave comments when change tracking is turned off, for example. When you accept or reject all changes, comments remain intact.

Wiping the Change History

Before you email your business proposal to the client, it's probably best to clear out the comments making fun of the ridiculous shirt he wore to the meeting last Thursday. Ditto for the change tracking that shows that you arbitrarily doubled your fee five minutes before sending the proposal. You get the idea: After you've gathered and reviewed all the edits and finally rounded the corner into final-draft territory, save a "clean" copy of your document, with all changes accepted, change tracking turned off, and comments removed.

To do this, choose "Save a Copy as Final" from the gear-shaped Action menu in the Change Tracking toolbar. The Save dialog box appears, prompting you to choose a name and location for the clean copy. After you click Save, Pages saves the new file and returns you to your original document.

Note: You can get a similar effect by turning off change tracking in the document (click Stop Tracking in the toolbar or choose Edit → Turn Off Tracking) and accepting all changes. However, all comments remain behind with that method. The only way to remove all comments at once is to use the "Save a Copy as Final" command to create a separate, no-comment copy of your file. Thing is, this option is available only from the Change Tracking toolbar which itself is available only when change tracking is turned on. If you're trying to delete all comments with change tracking turned off, turn change tracking on and then choose "Save a Copy as Final" from the Change Tracking toolbar's Action pop-up.

Now your scrubbed and typo-free document is ready to be shared with the world. But before you do that…wouldn't your masterpiece look better with a table of contents, some numbered page footers, or perhaps a multicolumn layout? That's the stuff of document formatting, which just happens to be the subject of the next chapter.

Document Format and Organization

The last few chapters have focused on editing and formatting your prose, with an eye to refining the details of your document at the level of words, sentences, and paragraphs. This chapter takes the big-picture view, turning to the layout and organization of your entire document. That means nitty-gritty housekeeping tasks like setting page margins, headers, or footnotes, and it also involves the grander architectural work of building an outline, organizing content sections, or varying your layout rhythm with multiple columns.

As you'll see, most of Pages' document-management tools aim to help you with longer word-processing documents. Although some of these options, like mail merge, come in handy for short files or page-layout documents, most find their best use managing lengthy texts or complex documents that vary their layouts from section to section. These features benefit your readers, too, making it easy for you to help them navigate your text with tables of contents or, for onscreen browsing, with bookmarks and hyperlinks.

This chapter covers all those advanced organizational issues and more, but you'll ease in with some basic page formatting.

Document Formatting

The overall layout of an individual page—and the entire document—depends on what's known as *document formatting*. This high-level formatting determines the handling of things like your document's page margins, hyphenation, and footnotes.

To change document formatting, use the *Document Inspector* (Figure 5-1). Choose View → Show Inspector or click the toolbar's Inspector button to open the Inspector window. Click the first button (the blank-page icon) in the Inspector's toolbar to open the Document Inspector. The first of the three tabs—labeled Document— is where you'll find most of the action.

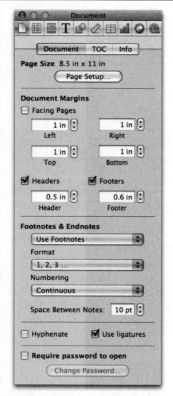

Figure 5-1:
The Document Inspector's Document tab lets you change the overall layout of your document–page size, margins, and footnote style. This is also where you'll find the master switches for auto-hyphenation, ligatures, and password protection.

Password-Protecting Your Document

Is your document top secret? Classified? For your eyes only? Whether you're working with state secrets or ordering your wife's birthday present, you can slap a padlock on your document by requiring a password to open it. Turn on the Document Inspector's "Require password to open" checkbox, and Pages prompts you to enter and verify the password for the file. You can also enter an optional password hint in case you forget that your password is the name of your kindergarten teacher. Click the key icon next to the password field to get some advice from the Password Assistant (Figure 5-2), which gives you feedback on the security of your password and offers suggestions for a new one.

Click Set Password when you're done, and a lock icon appears next to the title at the top of your document window to remind you that the file is now password-protected. Going forward, when you open the document, Pages asks you to enter the password first. If you enter the incorrect password three times in a row, Pages shows you the password hint (if you entered one).

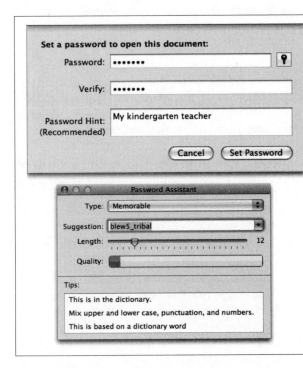

Figure 5-2:
Click the key next to the Password field to reveal the Password Assistant, which critiques your password and shows you an indicator of how difficult it might be to crack. The assistant also suggests secure passwords when you're fresh out of ideas: Choose the type of password to use in the Type pop-up menu ("memorable" is a good one, since it includes actual words that you're more likely to remember later). Then choose an option from the Suggestion pop-up menu, and Pages inserts it into the Password field.

If the name of your kindergarten teacher suddenly becomes common knowledge, you can change your password by clicking the Document Inspector's Change Password button. Enter the new password info and then click Change Password.

When the coast is clear and it's finally safe for the world to read your secret scribblings, you can remove the password by turning off the Document Inspector's "Require password to open" checkbox. Enter the password one last time to disable the protection, and then click OK.

Note: If you save a copy of the document as a Microsoft Word file or export it in any format other than Pages '09, the password won't apply to the new file. Likewise, if you upload a password-protected file to iWork.com (page 332), the online service won't ask your reviewers to provide the password when they view the document online. iWork.com also can't add online comments to the original Pages file for download when it's password protected. In any of these cases, Pages warns you about this and lets you cancel if you don't want to save or share an unprotected version of your document.

Page Setup

The Document Inspector's *Page Size* section indicates the paper size you'll use to print your document. Click the Page Setup button to conjure your Mac's standard Page Setup dialog box (also accessible via File—Page Setup) if you need to change the paper size to legal or tabloid size, for example. You can also change the *page orientation—portrait* (vertical) or *landscape* (horizontal)—and change the *scale* to print at a reduced (less than 100 percent) or magnified (more than 100 percent) size.

Adjusting Page Margins

The standard margins for Pages' Blank document templates are 1 inch all the way around the page. Use the up and down arrows in the Document Margins section of the Document Inspector to change the margins, or type a new value in the measurement fields for any of the four sides—Left, Right, Top, or Bottom.

Note: The top and bottom margins set the spacing between the edge of the paper and your body text. These margin settings don't affect headers or footers, which float *inside* the document margin that you set here. For example, if you set the top margin to 1 inch and the header margin to 0.5 inches, the header would start 0.5 inches from the edge of the paper, and the body text would start 1 inch from the edge of the paper. If the header runs long and extends beyond that 1-inch margin, it nudges the body text down so the text always appears below the header. You'll learn more about headers and footers in the next section.

The number you add to these fields must be in decimal form: .75 equals three quarters; fractions aren't accepted. And don't bother with entering the "in" for inches—Pages assumes you're using its current unit of measurement.

Tip: You can set the units used for measurements throughout the program by choosing Pages → Preferences and changing the Ruler Units setting in the Rulers pane.

Facing pages

If you're making a document with book-style formatting—that is, printed on both sides of the page and fastened with a binding—turn on *Facing Pages*. When this checkbox is turned on, the margin settings for "Left" and "Right" change to read "Inside" and "Outside". Now you can create an extra-wide margin on the inside for the *gutter,* the space between the binding and the text, or create an extra-wide margin on the outside where your readers can make notes.

Note: When you turn on Facing Pages, the program assumes you'd like to view them as facing pages onscreen and automatically changes the page view to "two up" (see page 42). If you'd rather not view it that way—or if you can't spare the screen space—use the View pop-up menu in the bottom-left corner of the document window to change it back to "one up".

Working with Headers and Footers

Use headers and footers to display information about your document at the top or bottom of the page. You can use these repeating strips to hold anything you want: a logo or other image, a date, a legal warning or copyright notice, or even an ad (see Figure 5-3).

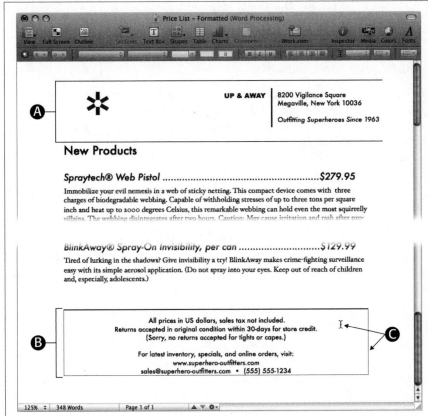

Figure 5-3:
Headers and footers can give your document design consistency from page to page. For example, a header (A) repeated on your product list can display your logo and address, while the footer (B) repeats ordering information on every page. (See page 228 for details about adding images to your document.)

When you hover the cursor over the header or footer, Pages reveals its borders (C). Just click inside them to edit it. As you enter text into a header or footer, Pages expands it–up to a maximum size of almost half a page.

Glance down at the bottom of this book's pages for another example of a footer. Here, headers and footers are different on right and left pages; both include page numbers, but left pages display the book title while right pages display the chapter title. You can also include headers and footers in much shorter documents to include your letterhead or return address, the date or time you created the document, the name of the computer file, and so on.

Headers and footers are always turned on in new documents, but you can get rid of them (or bring them back again) in the Document Inspector by turning the Headers and Footers checkboxes on or off. Be careful: *This setting affects every page of the document.* When you turn off headers or footers, you also delete the text they contain; turning them back on gives you only an empty field to start fresh.

The Document Inspector also lets you change the margins for headers and footers. Use the up and down arrows or enter a new value to adjust the space between the edge of the paper and the start of the header or footer.

Adding a header or footer

To add a header or footer to any Pages document, make sure that headers and footers are turned on in the Document Inspector, then choose View → Show Layout. Pages reveals ghostlike outlines around the header and footer. Click inside the outline, and then enter and format your text just as you would in the body of the document—use all the usual character and paragraph formatting tools, including styles, background colors, and so on.

Strictly speaking, you don't actually have to choose Show Layout to enter header and footer text—it simply reveals the header or footer outline to give you a target to aim for. You can instead just click in the header area, for example, and start typing. When you hover the cursor over a header or footer, Pages shows its outline to let you know where to click.

Tip: To add a page number to your header or footer, choose Insert → Auto Page Numbers. You'll learn more about this and other auto-formatted text on page 161.

Headers and footers aren't just for text. You can add photos or artwork—a logo perhaps—or use Pages' Shapes (Chapter 7), Table, or Chart (Chapter 8) tools to add those items. Any of these objects behave the same in a header or footer as they do in the body of the page.

As mentioned earlier, whatever you add to a header or footer shows up on *every* page of your document, unless you specifically tell Pages otherwise. To change the layout or content of headers or footers in different parts of the document, or to have headers and footers appear in only part of the document, you first have to break the document into sections using section breaks. You might do this to use one header for your introduction and table of contents, for example, and a different header for the main text of your document. You'll learn about section breaks and how to customize individual sections of your document later in this chapter (see page 149). In the meantime, there are a couple of exceptions that let you vary your header and footer *without* using section breaks. You'll find these options in the Layout Inspector → Section tab (Figure 5-4).

First page is different

You can give the first page of your document a different set of headers and footers. You might do this to create a letterhead with your name, address, and logo on the first page but not on subsequent pages, for example; or to make sure your report's title page doesn't display any headers or footers. Open the Layout Inspector, click the Section tab and then turn on the Configuration checkbox for "First page is different." Pages clears out the header and footer on the first page; go ahead and add your first-page text to those fields, or leave them blank if that's your game.

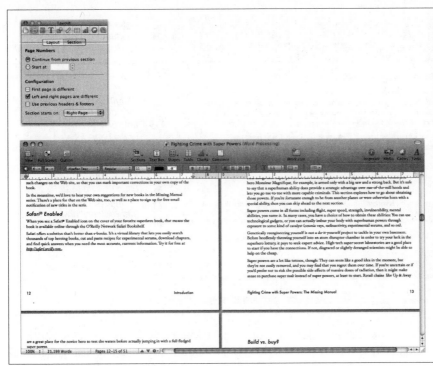

Figure 5-4:

Top: The Layout Inspector → Section tab has options in its Configuration settings that let you use different headers and footers on the first page of your document (or, more specifically, the first page of the current section) or on left and right pages, a method commonly used in books.

Bottom: Here, the footers on left pages show the chapter name, and the footers on right pages show the book title.

Left and right pages are different

Pages can create different right and left headers or footers—similar to those used in this book—if you turn on the checkbox for "Left and right pages are different." Technically, this setting really means "odd and even pages are different," since Pages gives you a different header or footer on every other page, whether or not you print the pages double-sided or have the Facing Pages option turned on.

The Fine Print: Footnotes and Endnotes

If you're the scholarly type or have a fetish for fine print, you can use *footnotes* or *endnotes* (collectively known simply as *notes)* to cite your sources or add a comment to your text. Pages inserts a superscript number or symbol—the *reference mark*—into your text, and then adds the actual note text to the bottom of the same page, just above the page footer (for footnotes) or to the end of the section or document (for endnotes). Figure 5-5 shows a footnote.

Adding notes

To add a note to your document, place the insertion point where you want the reference mark to appear and then choose Insert → Footnote (or Insert → Endnote or Insert → Section Endnote if you've told the Document Inspector to use one of the two endnote formats instead; see the next section). Pages adds the reference mark to your text and zips you down to the note's *note field,* a text box where you can

---

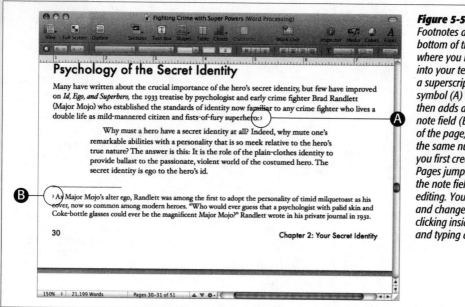

Figure 5-5:
Footnotes appear at the bottom of the same page where you insert the note into your text. Pages inserts a superscript number or symbol (A) into the text and then adds a corresponding note field (B) to the bottom of the page, labeled with the same number. When you first create the footnote, Pages jumps you directly to the note field to start editing. You can go back and change it anytime by clicking inside the note field and typing away.

type your note. Pages styles footnotes and endnotes with the built-in Footnote Text paragraph style, but you can format the text however you like, using the usual text-formatting tools or by choosing a new style from the Styles drawer (for more about styles, see Chapter 3).

After you're done typing your note, you can use the scroll bar to find your way back to the original point in your text, or even better, just double-click the note's reference mark to jump directly back. It works the other way, too: Double-click the mark in your text to leap straight down to the note field.

To delete a note, simply delete its reference mark in the body of your text. To move a note to a new location, cut (⌘-X) the reference mark and paste it (⌘-V) into its new home. As you add, move, or delete notes, Pages automatically renumbers your notes so that they're all kept ordered and tidy. For footnotes, Pages also does the necessary content contortions to keep the notes on the same page as the text to which they refer.

Note: You can add notes only to word-processing documents. If you want to add footnotes or endnotes to a page-layout document, you have to do it manually. Use Format → Font → Baseline → Superscript to format your reference mark in the text, and create a new text box to hold your notes (see page 216 for details about text boxes).

Setting your display preferences for notes

The Document Inspector → Document tab serves up the settings for displaying notes in your document. The *Footnotes & Endnotes* pop-up menu offers three options:

- **Use Footnotes.** Choose this option to display footnotes at the bottom of the same page where you insert a note.

- **Use Section Endnotes.** This setting tells Pages to hold your notes until the end of each section of your document (for chapter endnotes, for example). Pages adds the endnotes to the last page of the section. For more about sections, see page 147.

- **Use Document Endnotes.** Choose this option to show notes only at the very end of the document. Pages inserts a section break at the end of the document to create a new page for the endnotes. You can add your own additional text to this endnotes page—a header or introductory text, for example. If you prefer not to have the endnotes in their own page or section, delete the section break. (For documents with just one section, the result in that case is essentially the same as section endnotes.)

Pages provides three numbering styles for notes: Arabic (1, 2, 3), Roman (i, ii, iii), or Symbol (*, †, ‡, §). Choose the style you prefer from the *Format* pop-up menu.

Note: The symbol numbering format uses only the four characters shown above. After you run through those symbols, Pages starts over at the beginning but doubles the characters in the reference mark (** or ††), then triples them, and so on. You should use this numbering format only when you have a small number of notes, or when you restart their numbering on every page.

Although these three predefined numbering styles reflect standard numbering conventions, don't feel straitjacketed—you can use any reference mark you want. Option-click the Insert menu and the Footnote command switches to Custom Footnote (or Custom Endnote or Custom Section Endnote, depending on the type of note you've chosen in the Footnotes & Endnotes pop-up). A dialog box prompts you to enter a custom mark. Type the character you want to use and then click OK.

The Document Inspector's *Numbering* pop-up menu controls how Pages numbers your footnotes. Choose "Continuous numbers" to number all footnotes from the beginning of the document to the end. "Restarts on Each Page" begins the number sequence over again on each new page that contains footnotes. "Restarts for Each Section" restarts the numbering sequence after each section break (page 147 has more about sections).

The *Space Between Notes* setting lets you add or reduce the whitespace between each note. Click the up or down arrow to change the value, or type a new value directly into the field.

All of these settings apply to the entire document. This means that you can't mix and match endnotes and footnotes in the same document or switch numbering styles midway through your text. Changing any of these settings instantly converts all notes in your document to the new setting. To convert footnotes to endnotes, for example, choose Use Endnotes in the Document Inspector's Footnotes & Endnotes pop-up menu, and Pages shuffles all of your footnotes to the back of the document. Changing the Format or Numbering settings likewise renumbers all notes to match the new setting (except for any custom marks you've added, which continue to use the specified characters).

POWER USERS' CLINIC

Citations and Bibliographies with EndNote

For students, researchers, and academics, writing projects are typically chock-full of citations and bibliographic references—so much so that most scholars create elaborate systems to track and manage the articles and books they reference in their work. EndNote is an especially popular program for creating a personal database of relevant readings, and Pages works hand-in-hand with EndNote X2 to insert citations into your document, automatically adding and updating a bibliography of referenced works along the way. To learn more about EndNote or buy the program, visit *www.endnote.com*.

If a citation is just a traffic ticket as far as you're concerned, move along. But if you have EndNote X2 installed on your Mac, Pages adds the EndNote Citation and EndNote Bibliography commands to the Insert menu. Before using them, though, be sure that you've assigned a default library in EndNote that the program should use when it opens. In EndNote, a *library* is a collection of references to books, articles, and other sources; Pages always uses the default library when it adds citations. To add and edit a citation:

1. Place the insertion point where you want the citation to appear in your document—a footnote, perhaps—and then choose Insert → EndNote Citation.

   EndNote automatically opens and displays its Find EndNote Citations window.

2. Type text into the Find Citation field and press Return to search EndNote for the citation to use.

3. Choose how the citation will appear in your Pages document from the Find EndNote Citations window controls.

   Enter a page range, if applicable, in the Citation Range field; use the Author or Year checkboxes to hide or display author and year info; and type text in the Prefix and Suffix fields that you want to appear before or after the citation. Turn on "In Bibliography only" to add the citation to the bibliography without including the citation text in the document.

4. Select a citation from the list and click Insert.

When you add a document's first citation, Pages automatically adds a bibliography to the end of the file, with the citation as its first entry. As you add more citations, Pages updates the bibliography with the new info. To change the citation format, choose Edit → EndNote Citations → Bibliography Format and pick a style.

To delete a citation in your document, select the citation and press Delete or double-click the bibliography, select the citation in the Manage Citations window, and then click the Delete (–) button. The bibliography updates automatically.

If you just want a bibliography without adding citations into the document text, you can add a bibliography by choosing Insert → EndNote Bibliography. Add and edit citations by double-clicking the bibliography or choosing Edit → EndNote Citations → Bibliography.

Tip: To change a custom mark back to using auto-numbered styles, Control-click the reference mark and choose Use Automatic Numbering from the shortcut menu. You can also do the reverse: Control-click a "regular" reference mark and choose Use Custom Mark from the shortcut menu.

Automatic Hyphenation

The Hyphenate checkbox at the bottom of the Document Inspector turns *automatic hyphenation* on or off for the entire document. This tells Pages to squeeze as much text as possible onto each line by hyphenating words and splitting them onto the next line. Pages' standard setting for hyphenation is "off" which is just as well because the feature is aggressive about splitting your words, even short ones, making your text more difficult to read. For typical word-processing documents with wide columns of text, hyphenation isn't really necessary. Where it becomes particularly useful, however, is for narrow columns with justified alignment which would otherwise create unsightly wrinkles and bulges of whitespace in your text (see page 69).

Turning on the Hyphenate checkbox enables automatic hyphenation for the entire document, but you can turn it off for individual paragraphs by using the "Remove hyphenation for paragraph" checkbox in Text Inspector → More. (However, if hyphenation is turned *off* for the document, you can't turn it on for individual paragraphs.)

If Pages hyphenates a word that you don't want to split, Control-click the word and then choose Never Hyphenate from the pop-up menu (Figure 5-6). Use this feature with caution, however: The "never" in Never Hyphenate really does mean never. Once you make this change, it applies to *all* Pages documents containing that word—*even ones you've already created and saved.* You can reverse the never-hyphenate rule by Control-clicking the word and choosing Allow Hyphenation. Here again, this setting is a global one that applies to all Pages documents, past and future.

Using Ligatures

Turn on the Use Ligatures checkbox to enable ligatures for the document (see page 67 for the lowdown on ligatures). Like hyphenation, this feature is document-wide, but you can turn ligatures off for individual paragraphs via the Text Inspector → More tab's "Remove ligatures" checkbox. Not all fonts contain ligatures, but fonts that do generally look better when you use these connected characters, which is why this setting is automatically turned on for new documents.

Organizing Your Document with Sections

In Pages, you use *sections* to mark physical divisions between your document's main content topics, in the same way that newspaper sections or book chapters create clear breaks in subject matter. In fact, sections are exactly how you'd go

Figure 5-6:
When Pages splits a word that you always want to remain whole, Control-click the word to reveal this shortcut menu, and then choose Never Hyphenate. Pages stops hyphenating the word in all documents.

about dividing chapters of a book in Pages—in your manuscript for *Fighting Crime with Super Powers: The Missing Manual,* for example. Starting a new section in Pages for each new chapter lets you make subtle formatting changes for each one. You can make sure that every chapter starts on the right-hand page of the book, for example, or change the page footer so that your reader knows that she's reading "Chapter 3: Defying Death" instead of "Chapter 6: Cape, Tights, and the Modern Wardrobe."

Specifically, you can use sections to change any of the following formatting elements from one part of your document to the next: headers, footers, page numbering, margins, column layout, and background image. (Hang in there, you'll learn about columns later in this chapter, and Chapter 7 covers background images on page 261.) Sections also create an invisible "glue" between each section's pages, letting you move, delete, or apply changes to the entire section at once. You can even take a snapshot of a section and all its content and reuse it later—a mini-template inside your document.

This all-for-one approach to working with a group of pages applies only to word-processing documents. Page-layout documents don't have sections—or put another way, *every* page in a page-layout document is its own standalone section, with its very own layout rules that have no bearing on the pages around it. Like sections in word-processing documents, the content and design of individual page-layout pages can also be saved and recycled as mini-templates.

New Sections or Separate Files?

When you create lengthy, complex word processing documents—books, reports, dissertations, and so on—you may find it convenient to break them up into chapters, one per file. For example, a book with 10 chapters would be composed of 10 separate files. Once that's done, you can format each file differently to reflect the kinds of information it contains, while using styles to keep the overall appearance similar. Backup bonus: You don't put all your eggs in one basket this way—if one of your files goes south, you don't lose your entire manuscript.

There are also good arguments, however, for keeping your entire manuscript in one file. For example, you can use the *Find* or *Find & Replace* commands to search your entire manuscript at once; and making style changes across the entire document is a one-step process. Using Pages' sections feature, you can break up your document into individual sections. Pages can divide a document into as many sections as you like, each with distinct formatting.

So what's the right solution? It's really a matter of taste, but it's generally a good idea to split documents into separate files under these conditions:

Very long documents. Finding your way through hundreds of pages of text can become a slog. Dividing documents of more than, say, 100 pages into smaller files makes maintenance and editing easier.

Many authors. When different people are writing different sections of your text, give each author his own file for his portion of the text.

Rolling editorial process. If you want to send chapters of your book to your editor as you finish them, splitting them into separate files means that your editor can make revisions to that file while you forge ahead with the rest.

Under most other conditions, it's better to keep your document in one file, even when you have a complex collection of layout elements. For example, you might write a business report that contains an introductory narrative; a section with lots of facts and figures, tables and footnotes, set in two columns; another section featuring customer endorsements with photographs set in three columns; and the concluding narrative. For this type of job, divide (into sections) and conquer!

Adding Sections

You can insert a section break anywhere in a word-processing document: Choose Insert → Section Break, and Pages adds the break and moves the following text to the next page. Section breaks are like page breaks on steroids, giving you not only a new page but also a new set of display rules that you can customize for the new section of text. The new section starts life as a clone of the previous section, with the exact same layout, headers, footers, and so on.

If you're working from a word-processing template with a selection of built-in sections, like those in the Template Chooser's Reports and Miscellaneous categories, you can also start a new section by choosing from the Insert → Sections submenu, or by clicking the Sections pop-up button in the toolbar, as shown in Figure 5-7. Pages inserts a new section based on the selected section template, with all its settings and content. For page-layout documents, it works the same way but for individual pages: Choose a single-page "section" from Insert → Pages or click the Pages button in the toolbar. You'll learn more about all this in "Capturing and Reusing Sections" on page 159.

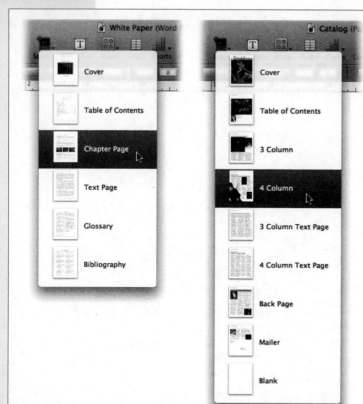

Figure 5-7:
Left: Some word-processing templates have built-in section templates, providing starter content that you can add to your document as a new section. At left, the White Paper template offers six section templates; to insert one, click the Sections button in the toolbar, or choose from Insert → Sections.

Right: In page-layout documents, you can do the same thing by choosing a page layout from the toolbar's Pages button, or choose from Insert → Pages. Here, the Program template offers nine page designs.

Once you have your new section in place, you can start customizing its layout and formatting. Use the Layout Inspector to modify these settings. Open the Inspector by choosing View → Show Inspector or click the toolbar's Inspector button. Click the second button (a page icon with two columns) to switch to the Layout Inspector, which includes tabs for Layout and Section. This tour starts with the Section tab, which you saw back in Figure 5-4.

Tip: If you find yourself frequently switching between Inspectors—or between two panes, like the Layout and Section tabs here—save yourself a few extra clicks by opening a second (or third or fourth) Inspector window: Choose View → New Inspector, or Option-click one of the icons at the top of the Inspector window.

Page numbering

The Layout Inspector → Section tab includes settings to specify how you want to handle page numbering in the new section. Put your insertion point anywhere in the text of the section and choose one of the options. "Continue from previous section" tells Pages to keep rolling with the same page numbering. If the previous section ended on page 14, for example, your new section keeps on truckin' with page 15. If you instead prefer to start at a different number, choose "Start at" and enter the page number where you want the section to begin counting.

You can do this for the first section of a document, too, or even if you don't have any section breaks at all. If you want to start numbering the first page of your document at a specific number, for example, choose "Start at" and enter the number for the document's first page. This is useful when you're writing a book and have your chapters in separate files: You can tell Pages that the first page of Chapter 4 starts on page 136.

Customizing headers and footers

It's often helpful to change the header or footer from one section to the next. When you're designing the Up & Away mail-order catalog, for example, you might have a different header for each category of products, so your customers can flip easily from "Bulletproofing" to "Utility Belts" to "Secret Identity Kits." Or you might number your book's preface with italic Roman numerals in the footer but switch to "regular" numbers with Chapter 1.

To customize the headers and footers for a section, place the insertion point within the section and go to the Layout Inspector → Section tab and turn off the checkbox for "Use previous headers and footers". Now, as you modify the contents of the header and footer, your changes affect only this section.

Page 142 describes the "First page is different" and "Left and right pages are different" settings in the context of a single-section document. For documents with multiple sections, turning these checkboxes on or off affects the headers for the current section only. Turning on the "First page is different" option, for example, means that the first page of the *section* is different than the rest of the pages in the section.

Setting the start page

Sections always start on a new page, but when you're working on a bound document, you might prefer to have your sections start on the left or right page. The "Section starts on" pop-up menu in the Layout Inspector → Section tab lets you take sides: Choose Right Page to start the current section on a right (odd-numbered) page, or choose Left Page to start on a left (even-numbered) page. If you don't care, choose Any Page. When you choose the right- or left-page option, Pages adds blank pages to your document whenever it's necessary to nudge a section over to the correct starting page.

Rearranging and Deleting Sections

Pages makes it easy to shuffle your sections, letting you move its entire group of pages en masse to a new location—or even delete them all—in the Pages sidebar. Choose View → Page Thumbnails to display the sidebar, which shows off your document in cute little page-by-page snapshots. In a word-processing document, clicking any page highlights its entire section in a yellow border (Figure 5-8).

With the selection highlighted, you can move its pages to a new spot in your document by dragging it to a new location in the Pages sidebar. If, for example, you decide it makes sense to move your "Surviving Long Falls" chapter *before* the "Learning to Fly for New Heroes" chapter, just drag and drop. The other sections nudge aside to make room as you drag.

Note: Page-layout documents don't have sections, but you can still use the same trick to move individual pages around your document. Here again, the individual pages of page-layout documents act like sections unto themselves.

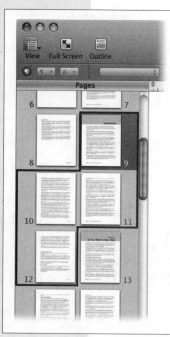

Figure 5-8:
When you click any word-processing page in the Pages sidebar, the entire section lights up with a yellow border (left). Drag any of the pages to move the whole section to a new spot. While you drag, the section condenses to a single thumbnail page in the Pages sidebar, with a numbered icon showing how many pages it contains (right). When you drop the section in its new location, it expands back to its original set of thumbnails.

You can also select multiple neighboring sections to move them all at once. To do that, hold down the Shift key and then select the first and last sections you want. Another way to select multiple sections is by dragging: Click to the left or right of a page thumbnail, and then drag up or down to select as many sections as you need.

Tip: If you prefer to *copy* a section to a new spot instead of moving it, hold down the Option key while you drag it. Pages deposits a pristine copy of the original section in the new location, leaving the original pages untouched.

You can cut, copy, and paste sections in the Pages sidebar, too:

1. **In the Pages sidebar, click the section to move and choose Edit → Copy or Edit → Cut. (You can also Control-click the section and choose Copy or Cut.)**

2. Click any page thumbnail in the section that should *precede* the copied or cut section.

3. Choose Edit → Paste and Pages pastes the section immediately after the high-lighted section.

Tip: To create a quick copy of a section, select it in the Pages sidebar and choose Edit → Duplicate. Pages inserts the new section immediately after the original.

If you press Delete (or choose Edit → Delete Pages) with one or more sections highlighted in the Pages sidebar, the program deletes *all the pages* in the section—but not before checking to make sure you really want to, as shown in Figure 5-9.

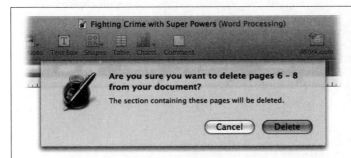

Figure 5-9:
Pages lets you delete a section and all of its content directly from the Pages sidebar. When you highlight a section and delete it, Pages warns you that you're about to delete a range of pages. Click Cancel to bail out, or Delete to go ahead.

Layouts and Multiple Columns

Layouts control the number of text columns in a section and let you vary the section's margins. In word-processing documents, every section has its own layout (in fact, as you'll soon see, they can even have several of them); changing the layout settings from section to section lets you have one column of text in the first section, three in the next, and so on. In page-layout documents, every text box has its own layout, allowing you to set a different number of columns in each one.

Adding columns to a document can dramatically improve readability by making it easier to track from one line to the next. A narrow text column means less distance for your eyes to sweep back across the page to find the beginning of the next line. By dividing the text into narrower columns, those poor eyeballs don't have to zig and zag quite so far. The wider the page and the smaller the type, the more you need columns to reduce line length. (For exhibit A, check out any newspaper.)

Tip: Readability studies show that a comfortable reading width is 50 to 80 characters per line. With words averaging between five and ten letters, that means that your columns should ideally allow for approximately 8 to 12 words per line.

Adding columns

Pages makes creating columns effortless. Put your insertion point anywhere in the *layout* that you want to format (a section or text box), and click the Columns pop-up menu in the Format Bar. Then choose one, two, three, or four columns from the pop-up menu, as shown in Figure 5-10.

Note: If you haven't added any section or layout breaks to your word-processing document, the change applies to the entire text.

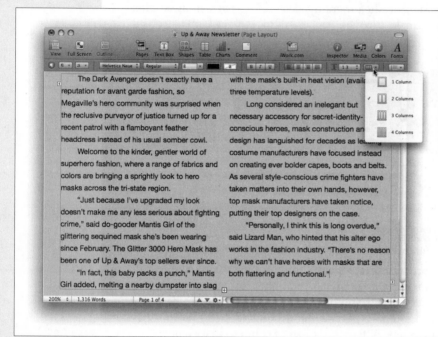

Figure 5-10:
The Columns pop-up menu in the Format Bar lets you slice your text into multiple columns, up to four across. Choose the number of columns you want, and Pages instantly stripes your document's text into evenly spaced columns.

But what if you'd like more than four columns, want your columns to be of varying widths, or need to add more space between them? The Layout Inspector → Layout tab has you covered.

Adjusting the number of columns

Open the Layout Inspector for more precise control of your columns. Choose View → Show Inspector or click the Inspector button in the toolbar to summon the Inspector window. Then click the second button in the Inspector's toolbar to switch to the Layout Inspector, and then choose the Layout tab (Figure 5-11).

Enter a number in the Columns box or use its up and down arrow buttons to set the number of columns. Pages creates that many equal-width columns on your page. Pages lets you create up to 10 columns, but the maximum for each document depends on the document's page size and orientation. For example, Pages will create up to eight columns on a standard letter-size sheet—but the maximum you'd actually want to use if someone's going to read those columns is more like four.

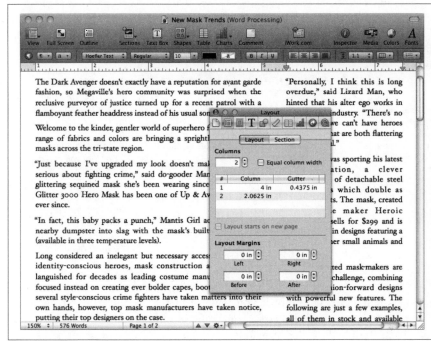

Figure 5-11:
The Layout Inspector provides precise control over the number and size of your columns and gutters (the space between columns).

As you'll learn, you can add additional layouts to a section, each with its own column and margin rules. You use the remaining controls in the Layout Inspector to start a new layout on a fresh page, or increase left and right margins for the layout—indenting the sides by this amount from the document margins—or to add space above or below a layout to keep it from bumping into its neighbor.

Adjusting column width

The easiest way to change the width of columns and *gutters* (the margins between columns) is directly on the page, using the ruler:

1. **Choose View → Show Rulers to display the ruler.**

2. **Place your insertion point within the layout containing the columns you want to adjust.**

   When a layout includes columns, the ruler sprouts gray areas to indicate the gutters (Figure 5-12). At the left and right edges of the gutters are column indicators, each with a tiny four-dot "grip."

3. **In the ruler, drag one of the column-indicator grips to move the corresponding column margin and change its width.**

   You don't have to click *exactly* on those tiny grips—Pages spares you that test of precision mousework and gives you some wiggle room, letting you click anywhere in the gutter to grab the closest grip. When you click, be prepared to see your cursor vanish. As soon as you click and begin to drag, a vertical guideline replaces the arrow cursor, to help you visualize the column border—even when the column contains no text.

Note: Working with columns and layouts is much easier if you can see the invisible margin guidelines (that is, the outlines of columns and page margins). Choose View → Show Layout (or press ⌘-Shift-L) to turn them on.

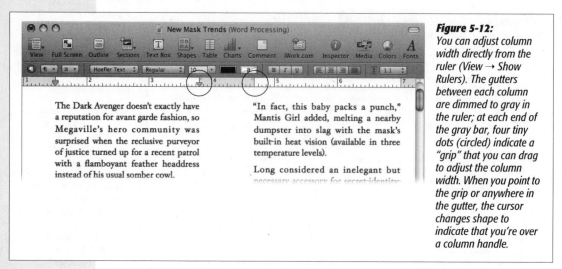

Figure 5-12:
You can adjust column width directly from the ruler (View → Show Rulers). The gutters between each column are dimmed to gray in the ruler; at each end of the gray bar, four tiny dots (circled) indicate a "grip" that you can drag to adjust the column width. When you point to the grip or anywhere in the gutter, the cursor changes shape to indicate that you're over a column handle.

Alternatively, the Layout Inspector lets you set column and gutter widths numerically. You might find this useful if you have to match a column width to some existing artwork, for example. First, turn off the checkbox for "Equal column width". Then double-click the measurement for the column you want to change and type a new measurement. Press the Tab key or click one of the other column or gutter widths, and Pages adjusts the column in your document. When you change the width of a column this way, Pages keeps the overall page width the same—it adjusts the other columns to compensate for your change (the gutters stay the same size).

Column breaks

Use a *column break* to end one column's text and force the text to continue at the top of the next column, as shown in Figure 5-13. To create a column break, place the insertion point where you want the column to end, and then choose Insert → Column Break. Pages moves the insertion point and any text below it to the top of the next column.

To remove a column break, choose View → Show Invisibles. Select the column break icon (circled in Figure 5-13) and press Delete. You can also Control-click the icon and then choose Delete.

Without column breaks, columns continue all the way down to the bottom of the page before starting another column; adding a break is the only way to jump over to the next column before reaching the bottom. Column breaks are a good way to

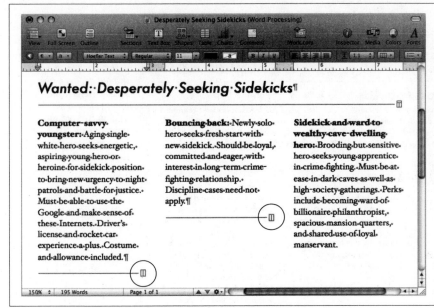

provide white space at the bottom of a page or layout, or to even out columns when the last column doesn't quite reach the bottom of the page. You can also use column breaks to prevent *"almost" orphans* and *"almost" widows*—two lines of a paragraph left behind at the bottom or top of a column.

Note: In a single-column layout—a normal page, that is—a column break functions like a page break, sending the insertion point and any following text to the top of the next page.

Layout breaks

As you've seen, every section has its own layout to control its column design—but you don't have to stop at just one layout per section. You can have multiple layouts in a single section of your document—or even on a single page—letting you change the number of columns for different portions of your text. For example, you could add additional layouts to a section in order to have two columns at the top of a page, three columns in the middle, and one column at the bottom, as shown in Figure 5-14.

Although you could get a new layout by adding a new section, adding a layout *within* a section lets you maintain the section's other settings and avoid adding a page break, which always comes with a new section.

To add a new layout, you insert a *layout break* at the point where you'd like to switch to a different column setup, whether it's changing the number of columns, their width, or their margins. (If you don't insert any layout breaks or section breaks, your whole document is one layout—in other words, the arrangement of columns is the same throughout.)

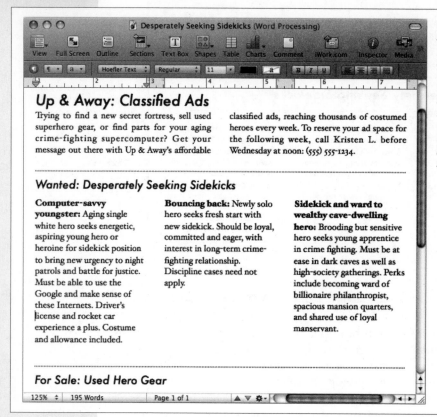

Figure 5-14:
Adding layout breaks to your document lets you switch your column design on the same page without adding a new section. Here, layout breaks allow one-column, two-column, and three-column text to live in harmony on the same sheet.

To add a layout break, choose Insert → Layout Break. Pages creates the invisible layout break at the insertion point. Move the insertion point above or below the layout break, and then adjust the number of columns via the Columns pop-up menu in the Format Bar, or use the Layout Inspector → Layout tab.

You can make a layout break start a new page by placing the insertion point in the text after the layout break and then turning on the Layout Inspector's checkbox for "Layout starts on new page."

You can also adjust the margins around a layout in order to set off the layout from the rest of the document. In the Layout Inspector → Layout tab, enter measurements in the Left or Right Layout Margins boxes to add that amount to the document's margins for this layout (these boxes are labeled Inside and Outside for documents with the Facing Pages option turned on). Enter measurements in the Before or After boxes to insert space before or after this layout to add some elbow room between the layout and its neighbors.

Note: If you add a section break within a layout, you actually split the layout in two; the first half of the original layout stays in the old section, and the second half is bumped into a brand-new layout with the same settings, located in the new section. If you make an adjustment to the first section's layout—change the number of columns, for example—it doesn't affect the second half in the new section's layout, since they're now independent of each other.

Capturing and Reusing Sections

Recycling is good for more than the environment; it speeds your document design, too. Pages lets you *capture* a snapshot of some or all of the pages in a section so you can reuse those pages in your document later—with all the original section's content, formatting, section settings, column layout...everything. (In page-layout documents, which don't have sections, you can still do this, but only for individual pages.) Think of these page snapshots as mini-templates; in the same way that you can use document templates to give you a head start on building your overall document, you can use these captured pages to save time and lend consistency to individual sections in your document.

Reusing sections becomes especially useful when you need to duplicate the layout or formatting in several places in a document. Say that you're assembling a member directory for the Up & Away Frequent Flyer Club. Every member gets his or her own page with a headshot, biography, summary of recent exploits, and so on. All of these pages use the same layout and formatting, so instead of formatting each one manually, you can save time by capturing one of them as a section and reusing it as a model for every new member page you create. Here's how to do that in a word-processing document:

1. **Separate your sample page(s) from the rest of your document with section breaks.**

   If the pages you want to capture aren't already in their own section, add section breaks before and after the desired pages: Place your insertion point at the very start of the first page you want to capture and choose Insert → Section Break; then place the insertion point at the end of the last page and insert another section break.

2. **Place the insertion point inside the section you want to capture, or select the section in the Pages sidebar.**

3. **Choose Format → Advanced → Capture Pages, or Control-click one of the section's page thumbnails in the Pages sidebar and choose Capture Pages.**

   Pages displays a dialog box that prompts you to name the set of captured pages and indicate how many pages you want to use, as shown in Figure 5-15. Click OK and Pages captures the selected pages.

Note: Unlike word-processing documents, page-layout documents let you capture only one page at a time. To do that, select the page and then jump straight to Step 3 above.

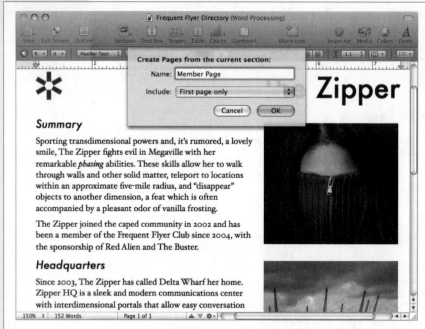

Figure 5-15:
Capture a section to reuse it later by clicking inside the section and choosing Format → Advanced → Capture Pages…. Choose a name for your captured pages and select the number of pages to grab. For sections with more than one page, you can choose to capture the first one, two, or three pages, or go ahead and grab them all.

Here, Pages captures a one-page section with a logo, two photos, and text. Reusing this section will insert a perfect clone of this page with all of its formatting and content intact.

Your freshly captured section now appears with a thumbnail preview in the Insert → Sections submenu as well as the Sections pop-up button in the toolbar. (For page-layout documents, it's Insert → Pages or the Pages pop-up button.) When you're ready to add a new page using this preformatted selection—you've inducted a new member into the club, for example—place the insertion point where you want the new page to appear and then choose the section from either of those menus. Pages inserts a copy of the original section into your document, and you're ready to update it with your new member's info.

To edit the list of captured pages in your document, choose Format → Advanced → Manage Pages. Pages unfurls a dialog box listing all the captured pages (including those automatically included with your chosen template), as shown in Figure 5-16.

Auto-Entry: Formatted Text Fields

Need to slug in repeating informational tidbits—things like page number, date, and so on—that show stats about your document? Pages offers four flavors of special auto-entry text called *formatted text fields,* which you add to your document as precocious placeholders. Pages automatically fills in the blank with the relevant info. These four types of formatted text fields are:

- **Page Number.** The number of the current page, useful to add to your document's header or footer.

- **Page Count.** The total number of pages in the document.

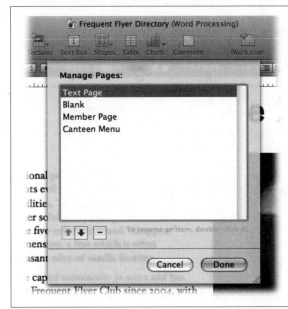

Figure 5-16:
Choose Format → Advanced → Manage Pages to rename or delete any of your captured sections or pages. To rename one, double-click its name in the Manage Pages list and type a new name. To delete an entry, select it in the list and click the – button. (This doesn't affect any text in your document; it simply removes the item from the Sections or Pages menu, so it's no longer available to add in the future.)

- **Date and Time.** The current date and/or time, formatted the way you like. You can tell Pages to refresh this timestamp every time you open the document, set it to a specific date, or leave it as-is from the moment you inserted the field.

- **Filename.** The filename and, optionally, its location on your hard drive.

The following sections explain each of these options in detail.

Page Numbers and Page Counts

What is hands down the most popular form of automatic text entry, usually found in headers and footers? The *page number*. Pages lets you insert the current page number anywhere you like in the document. But the program makes it especially easy to add and format page numbers for the header and footer, using the Auto Page Numbers dialog box, shown in Figure 5-17.

Choose Insert → Auto Page Numbers, and the dialog box slides down, prompting you to choose where and how you'd like the page number to appear. After you make your selections and click Insert, Pages adds the page number to your header or footer according to your instructions. Along the way, it also updates the settings in the Layout Inspector → Section tab to reflect your settings, turning on the "First page is different" and "Left and right pages are different" settings if necessary. If you change your mind about these settings, you can adjust them by again choosing Insert → Auto Page Numbers, or by changing them directly in the Layout Inspector → Section tab.

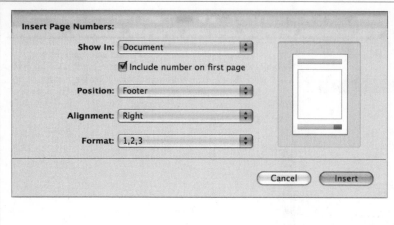

Figure 5-17:
Choose Insert → Auto Page Numbers, and Pages reveals the Auto Page Numbers dialog box. Here you can choose whether you want to apply the change to the entire document or just the current section, and whether to include the page number on the first page. Then choose where you want it to appear (header or footer), how to align it on the page, and what number style to use.

As you make your changes, Pages displays a preview in the dialog box to show where the number will appear. Click Insert, and Pages updates your headers or footers to include the page number.

Tip: To remove a page number from the header or footer, select it in the document text and then press Delete. Pages removes the page number from all pages of the current section (or the entire document if you have only one section).

You can't tell just by looking at the page number on the screen, but behind the scenes Pages has created an automatically updating page-number calculator—not just an ordinary typed number. So if you add a few pages to the beginning of your document, for instance, the page number on each page changes to reflect the page's new position.

This clever little digit is a *Page Number field*. Auto Page Numbers is the easiest way to quickly add a Page Number field to your header or footer, with its fast access to common formatting options, but you can also add the page number manually to any part of your document: Place the insertion point where you want to add the current page's number and then choose Insert → Page Number. When you first insert the page number, Pages formats it as an Arabic numeral (1, 2, 3). If you prefer a different style, Control-click the number to choose a different numbering format from any of these options:

- Arabic numerals (1, 2, 3)

- Lowercase alphabet (a, b, c)

- Uppercase alphabet (A, B, C)

- Lowercase Roman numerals (i, ii, iii, iv)

- Uppercase Roman numerals (I, II, III, IV)

Note: If you use one of the alphabet options and have more than 26 pages, Pages starts doubling up the letters for the second run through the alphabet; for example, aa, bb, cc, and so on.

As described on page 151, you can start your page-numbering sequence at a number other than 1 if, say, this document is the third chapter of a larger work. Open the Layout Inspector, click the Section tab, click the "Start at" button, and then enter a starting number in the box. You can also create more than one series of page numbers in the same document in order to, for example, number your 10-page preface using Roman numerals. To create more than one page-numbering sequence, first you have to divide the document into sections (see page 147).

Note: When you insert a Page Number or Page Count field into your document, it looks just like any other number you type into the document. Even if you choose to show invisibles (View → Show Invisibles), Pages gives you no indication that these numbers are actually formatted text fields. If you highlight the number and type another number to replace it, you've deleted a formatted text field and replaced it with a regular ol' number character. The only way to tell for sure whether a number is a formatted text field is to Control-click it. If it's a Page Number or Page Count text field, the top of the pop-up menu that appears lists the number display options. If it's a regular number character, the pop-up menu begins with Cut, Copy, and Paste.

Adding a page count

Add a *Page Count field* to your text by choosing Insert → Page Count. Combine this with the page number when you want your header to say, for example, Page 4 of 72. The Page Count text field, in other words, reports the total number of pages in your document…kind of.

More specifically, the page count is *the page number of the last page* in the current run of page numbers. Most documents start at page one and never reset their page numbers; in those cases, the page count is indeed the number of pages in the document—the same as the page number of the last page in your document. However, if you add a new section to your document that resets the page number (with the "Start at" option in the Layout Inspector → Section tab), then the page count gets reset, too.

Say that your document consists of a 10-page section (with pages numbered 1 to 10) followed by a five-page section which resets the page to 1 so that its pages are numbered 1 to 5. Even though you have 15 total pages in your document, Page Count fields in the first section show "10," and Page Count fields in the second section show "5"—when the second section resets the page number, it resets the page count for that section, too. Or say you have a 10-page document and you've set the page number to start at 5 so that your pages are numbered from 5 to 14. The document's Page Count fields display "14," the number of the last page, instead of the physical number of pages.

Inserting the Date and Time

When you choose Insert → Date & Time, Pages adds a *Date and Time* field, which at first lives up to only the first half of its name—the field shows today's date in this format: Saturday, December 6, 2009.

You'll quickly discover that you can't edit a Date & Time text field; it appears in your document as a solid, unbreakable block of text that resists your efforts to click inside it. Instead, to change the format or content of the field, double-click the field or Control-click it and choose Edit Date & Time. Either way, a little window zooms out from the text that lets you edit the display format, set the date and time to display, or make the field update automatically, as shown in Figure 5-18.

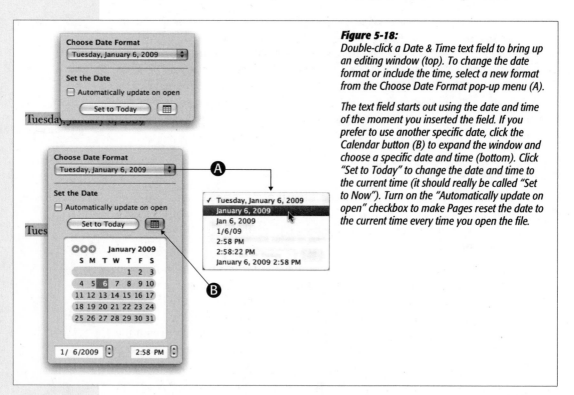

Figure 5-18:
Double-click a Date & Time text field to bring up an editing window (top). To change the date format or include the time, select a new format from the Choose Date Format pop-up menu (A).

The text field starts out using the date and time of the moment you inserted the field. If you prefer to use another specific date, click the Calendar button (B) to expand the window and choose a specific date and time (bottom). Click "Set to Today" to change the date and time to the current time (it should really be called "Set to Now"). Turn on the "Automatically update on open" checkbox to make Pages reset the date to the current time every time you open the file.

The "Automatically update on open" option tells Pages to refresh the text field to the current date and time each time you open the document. You might choose this option to create a daily press release or a fax cover sheet so that the day and time of those documents is always current, for example. This is a great choice for such one-shot throwaway items—but no good at all for record-keeping like invoices, letters, or journal entries (because the dates never stay put). Keep that checkbox turned off to create fixed dates and times that record the moment you insert them—and stay that way. You can also update the field manually to the current date and time: Control-click the date and choose Update Date & Time Now.

When you're done making changes in the editing window, you're ready to send it away. But like a late-night guest or a chatty officemate, the window doesn't always know when to leave. There's no Close button or other obvious way to get rid of it. The secret (and you can use this tip for the guest and officemate, too) is to ignore it: Click anywhere outside of the editing window to make it disappear.

Note: Pages plucks its date and time formats from your Mac OS X preferences. If you prefer to use a 24-hour clock for the time or want to format the date differently, choose → System preferences → International, and then click the Formats tab to change those settings.

Displaying the Filename

Let your document introduce itself by teaching it to say its own name. Choose Insert → Filename, and Pages adds the filename at the insertion point. In Pages's standard settings, the filename always appears with the *.pages* extension: *Sidekick Wanted.pages*, for example. If you prefer not to include the extension, double-click the filename and turn off the "Always show filename extension" option. Double-clicking also lets you choose whether to include the exact location of the file on your hard drive: Turn on the "Show directory" path option. (Like the Date & Time editing window, you close this window by clicking anywhere outside of it.)

Mail Merge with Address Book or Numbers

A close cousin of the formatted text field puts Pages on intimate terms with your little black book: *Merge fields* channel contact info from your Mac's Address Book program or a Numbers spreadsheet, letting Pages automatically add names and addresses to letters, invoices, and envelopes—or label fax cover sheets with a recipient's name and fax number. This process of updating your document text with outside contact info is often called a *mail merge*.

Merge fields are especially handy in document templates. For example, when you open a template for a letter or invoice, Pages automatically enters your return address. Adding the recipient's address is as easy as dropping her Address Book card into the page. Similarly, if you have a form letter to send to lots of people at once, you can automate your mass mailing by dragging the card for an Address Book group into the window, or by pointing Pages to a Numbers spreadsheet with all the contact info. Pages creates or prints a fresh version of the file for each person in the group, using their own individual contact info. Nice.

Note: Pages can also do a mail merge from *virtual address card* (or *vCard*) files, a commonly used file format for exchanging contact info, typically by email. Unfortunately, you can't do a mail merge from other sources beyond Address Book, vCards, or Numbers. If your mailing list is locked in a database or some other format, you'll first need to import that data into one of the three supported formats (hint: Numbers can import Excel and CSV files [comma-separated values]).

Using Merge Fields in Templates

As you saw back in Chapter 1, many of Pages' built-in templates already sport their own set of merge fields. All of the templates in the Template Chooser's Letters category, for instance, use merge fields for both the destination address and the return address. Pages refers to the return-address info as *sender fields,* reserving the name *merge field* for the destination address.

You typically put *sender fields* to work in return addresses, signature lines, and so on. Until you tell it otherwise, Pages assumes that you're the sender. The moment you create a new document from a template with sender fields, Pages automatically fills them in with your contact info (see the box on page 22). That still leaves the merge fields unfilled, and until you fill them with real info, they just display dummy placeholder text, as shown in Figure 5-19.

To add recipient info, drag your correspondent's Address Book card into your text. Address Book, which you can find in your Mac's Applications folder, organizes your contacts into address cards. Launch Address Book, find your pen pal, and drag her card into your document. You can drop the card anywhere in the window, and Pages automatically fills all merge fields with info from the card. The exception is when you drop a card directly on top of any of the sender fields—doing so replaces the sender fields instead of the recipient's merge fields. (When you drag a card from Address Book, be sure to drag it *sideways* out of the Address Book window; dragging up or down instead selects multiple cards.)

Note: To use contact info from a vCard instead of Address Book, locate the vCard file in the Finder and drag it into your document window, just like you would with an Address Book card.

Whether you're replacing the sender or recipient fields, dragging an Address Book card into your document replaces *all* fields of that type. In other words, you can have only one set of sender info and one set of recipient info—Pages can automatically juggle the info for only two people per document: the sender and recipient. That said, you can change those people as often as you like. If you want to send the same letter to two different people, for example, you can drag the second person's card into your letter after you print the letter to the first, and Pages makes the appropriate updates.

If you use an Address Book card that doesn't have info available for one or more merge fields in your document, Pages leaves those fields untouched in the text. For example, if you have a "job title" field in your letter template but your nephew Bobby hasn't yet acquired one, the dummy text for the job-title field sticks around when you drop Bobby's card into your document. Tidy up by clicking on the unfilled field and pressing Delete or typing some replacement text.

Note: Deleting or replacing a merge field removes that field from the document, and dragging new address cards into your text will no longer import that contact info. If you want to save a version of the file with all the original merge fields, choose File → Save As and save the file with deleted fields under a new name.

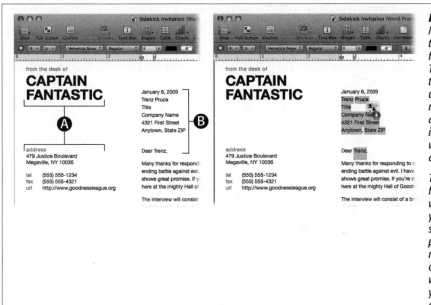

Figure 5-19:
Many of Pages' built-in templates use merge fields and sender fields. The San Francisco Letter template, for example, uses sender fields for the return address (A) and automatically fills them in with your address when you create a new document.

The template uses merge fields for the address where you're sending your letter (B), a new sidekick candidate, perhaps. Drag the recruit's Address Book card into the document window (right). When you drop the card, Pages automatically fills in the address.

Home vs. work addresses

Most working folk have separate addresses, phone numbers, and email addresses for work and home, and Address Book lets you add fields for both (as well as the mysterious "other" category to stow info for anything from summer homes to bat caves). Pages' merge fields are correspondingly specific: Address, phone, and email info are all either *work, home,* or *other.* Pages' built-in templates vary on which type of info they use—business-like templates tend to use work contact info, and more casual templates try to reach you at home.

If the template shows the wrong address—home when you want work, or vice versa—you can switch to a different address category by changing the *target* for the field: Select the merge field in your document and then open the Layout Inspector's Merge pane (Figure 5-24). You'll see your selected field highlighted in the Inspector's list of merge fields; click its Target Name column and choose the field's work or home counterpart. Pages updates the text to show the new address info; going forward, when you add a new Address Book card to the document, Pages uses the new field.

Managing Mass Mailings with Address Book Groups

If you want to send the same letter to a bunch of different people, finding and dragging each and every contact from the Address Book gets old fast: Find, drag, print…find, drag, print…find, drag, print…repeat 300 times. Oy.

Happily, Pages gives you a shortcut for this, letting you merge contact info for lots of recipients at once using *groups,* your own custom categories from Address Book (see Figure 5-20). There are two methods for doing this:

- Launch Address Book and drag your group of pen pals into your Pages document.

- Choose Edit → Mail Merge.

Note: You can also select several individual Address Book cards or vCards and drag them all at once into Pages to get the same result. To select multiple cards in Address Book, ⌘-click each contact.

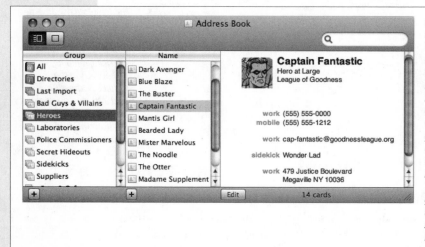

Figure 5-20:
Groups are collections of contacts in Address Book that you can use to automate mass mailings in Pages. To add a group, launch Address Book and click the + button under the Group list. Click the All group and drag contacts onto your new group in the Group list (contacts can belong to multiple groups). To remove a contact from a group, select the group in the Group list, and then select the contact to remove from the Name list and press Delete.

When you start the mail merge from the Edit menu, you're asked whether you want to merge from Address Book or a Numbers document (shown later in Figure 5-22); choose Address Book and the group to use for the merge. When you start the merge by dragging an Address Book group, Pages displays a much smaller dialog box (Figure 5-21). Either way, tell Pages how to process the results:

- **Merge to.** Choose New Document or "Send to Printer" from the pop-up menu. *New Document* creates a new file containing mail-merged copies of your letter for every contact from the Address Book group. Every copy is separated by a section break (page 149), which lets you restart page numbers for each copy or include each person's name in the header or footer, for example. *Send to Printer* likewise generates a personalized copy for every contact but sends the result directly to the printer instead of creating a new document.

Tip: If your merged document has facing pages, double-sided printing could cause one document to print on the other side of a previous document. To avoid this, place the insertion point into the first section of your document, and choose "Section starts on right page" in the Layout Inspector → Section pane before doing your mail merge.

- **Substitute closest match.** Turn on this checkbox to tell Pages to do its best to fill in missing fields, falling back on the work address if the home address is missing, for example.

Note: This automatic substitution is terrific if your contacts have a mix of work and home addresses, but it can cause problems if there's an incomplete address. For example, say that your document uses home Address Book fields, but you're missing the Zip code in one contact's home address. In that case, when the "substitute closest match" checkbox is turned on, Pages uses the contact's home address info but substitutes the work Zip code, giving you a useless hybrid address. Whenever possible, make sure that your Address Book info is accurate and complete.

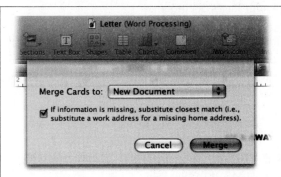

Figure 5-21:
When you start a mail merge for a group of contacts, Pages asks you how it should manage the processing.

Click Merge and Pages churns through your contacts to build the final, merged document. If you're dealing with even a few hundred contacts, this can take a few minutes. Give yourself plenty of time if you're generating a merged document from a contact list of thousands. (Unfortunately, if you change your mind in the middle of a merge, there's no way to cancel it midway through; you just have to sit it out.)

Pages handles mass mailings to groups slightly differently than when it updates a document with a single contact: If a contact in the group doesn't have any info for an Address Book field, Pages removes that field from the merged document—no need to check all 500 letters to make sure no dummy text slipped in. (When you do this with an individual card, by contrast, Pages leaves the field's dummy text in place.)

Merging Data from a Numbers Spreadsheet

It's not always convenient to use Address Book for merging data—you probably don't keep your entire newsletter mailing list in your personal address book, for example. When you keep a particular list of contacts elsewhere, Pages has you covered by letting you use a Numbers spreadsheet as your data source.

For that matter, you're not even obliged to use contact info at all; you can merge *any* kind of data from a Numbers spreadsheet. If you're hosting Megaville's Annual Sidekick Awards, for example, you could print a certificate for each eager

---

young hero by merging the certificate design in Pages with a spreadsheet containing sidekicks' names, ages, vital statistics, and award categories (ah, the coveted "Holy Enthusiastic Exclamations!" prize). Or you could send letters to award-show sponsors, automatically inserting the amount they donated last year and suggesting a figure for this year. You get the idea: By using a Numbers spreadsheet, you can include data fields that simply don't exist in Address Book.

You'll find out how to add your own custom merge fields to handle this kind of freewheeling data in the next section. For now, let's keep it simple and focus on using a Numbers spreadsheet to import contact info like you would from Address Book. (You'll find complete details about working with Numbers starting in Chapter 17.) This section assumes you've got a spreadsheet in place and lets you know how to weave its data into your Pages document.

Note: You can use Numbers data only to fill in merge fields for recipients—it has no effect on sender fields.

Before you do the merge, you have to do some minor housekeeping to make sure the spreadsheet is nice and tidy for Pages. Specifically:

- Your data should be in just one table; if the spreadsheet has more than one table, Pages will ask you to choose a table to use.

- The table has to have a header row (see page 634), and all columns that you want to import must have a label in their header cell.

- Each row of data should represent a contact or other item to merge, and the table has to have at least one data row. Every row, in other words, will result in a new copy of the document.

Note: If you try to merge using a table without a labeled header row or without any data rows, Pages complains, "Please select a Numbers document that has one or more named header columns and one or more rows of data." Don't let the reference to "header columns" throw you; your table doesn't need a header column, it needs a header *row* with at least one of its cells filled in. It would be handy if Pages treated the first row of data as a header row when you don't explicitly have one, but that's not the case; give the table a header row in Numbers' Format Bar or Table Inspector (page 635).

When you have your Numbers document ready and saved, choose Edit → Mail Merge, and Pages rolls out the Mail Merge dialog box (Figure 5-22). Choose Numbers Document, and then choose your spreadsheet from the window that appears.

Pages uses the column labels from the Numbers header row to figure out how to import the data. When a label is the same as the name of an Address Book merge field (First Name, Last Name, Work Email, and so on), Pages automatically "maps" that column to the merge field of the same name. When you do the merge, Pages uses that column's data to replace that particular merge field.

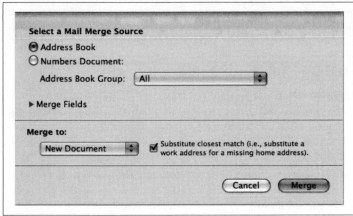

Figure 5-22:
When you choose Edit → Mail Merge,
Pages prompts you to choose a source for
your mail-merge contact info. Choose
Numbers Document and Pages displays
the Open dialog box for you to select the
Numbers spreadsheet you want to import.

If Pages can't find matches for all the merge fields in your document it asks for help, prompting you to select a *target* for each field, the Numbers column to use during the merge, as shown in Figure 5-23. If Pages doesn't ask for help matching spreadsheet columns, that means it has already matched up your data. Click the Merge Fields flippy triangle to review the fields and targets to make sure everything matches up as you expect. Remember: Fields are the placeholders inside your Pages document; targets are the columns in your Numbers spreadsheet.

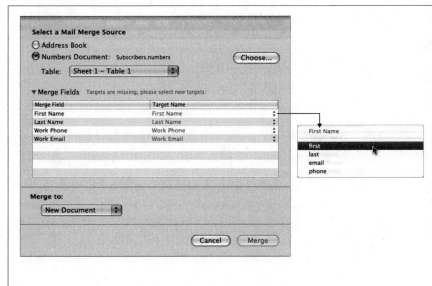

Figure 5-23:
When Pages can't sort out how to match up the merge fields in your document to your Numbers spreadsheet, it asks you to identify the targets (spreadsheet columns) to use for each field. The unknown targets are marked in red; click each one to select the matching spreadsheet column. If you don't see all the columns you expected, make sure that you have the correct table selected in the Table pop-up menu and that you've labeled all the columns in the table's header row in Numbers.

In the Merge To pop-up menu, choose New Document or "Send to Printer", just as described above for doing Address Book merges, and then click Merge. Pages plucks the data out of your Numbers spreadsheet and runs the mail merge.

Note: Pages cares only about the *data* in the spreadsheet, not how its text is formatted. When Pages runs the merge, it ignores whatever font, color, and text styles you used in Numbers.

Adding Merge Fields to Your Own Documents

So far you've seen how to use merge fields that are already included in Pages' built-in templates. But you can also add these fields to your own documents to merge contact info into any document. In addition to the usual address and phone info, Address Book can hold info including birthdays, notes, nicknames, spouse names, website addresses, and plenty more. Pages lets you add merge fields for any of these tidbits, allowing you to insert just about any type of info about your contacts that you might dream up. And if you're working with a Numbers spreadsheet, you can add fields that slurp in the values of any spreadsheet column.

Tip: The standard configuration of Address Book gives you traditional contact-info options like name, address, phone, and email. But there are several additional options available. To show one of these fields in Address Book, choose Card → Add Field and make your selection.

To get started, choose your *merge source,* the place where you're storing the info you'll use in the mail merge. You do this in the Link Inspector → Merge pane, shown in Figure 5-24. Pages always starts you off using Address Book, but you can choose a Numbers spreadsheet by clicking the Choose button and finding the file you want to use. Choosing the source determines the merge fields you can add to the document. When you select Address Book, you can add any of its contact fields; when you choose a Numbers spreadsheet, you can use any of its columns as merge fields (as long as the columns are labeled in the header row as described in the last section).

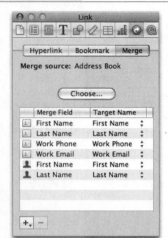

Figure 5-24:
The Layout Inspector's Merge tab displays the merge source that Pages will use to fetch data for your mail merge. Click Choose to select an Address Book group or a Numbers spreadsheet file. Below, the inspector lists the document's merge fields in the order they appear in your text—Sender fields are marked with a head-and-shoulders icon, and merge fields are marked with an address-card icon.

You can change the target, or data source, of a field by clicking its target name and then choosing from the pop-up menu. Delete a field by selecting it and pressing Delete or clicking the – button at the bottom left; you can also delete the merge field in your text. Add a new merge field or sender field by clicking the + button and choosing from the pop-up menu (or choose Merge Field or Sender Field from the Insert menu).

To add a merge or sender field, place the insertion point where you want the text to appear, and then choose the info to insert from the Insert → Merge Field submenu or the Insert → Sender Field submenu. Sender fields always draw from the Address Book, no matter what you choose as your merge source, and the Sender Field submenu accordingly presents seven categories of Address Book fields: Name, Address, Phone, Email, Instant Message, Related Name, and Other.

When Address Book is the merge source, the Insert → Merge Field submenu shows the same set of options. When a Numbers spreadsheet is the merge source, on the other hand, the Insert → Merge Field submenu lists the columns in your spreadsheet table. Make your selection and Pages adds the merge field to your document, updating the list of merge fields in the Layout Inspector → Merge pane, too.

In your text, Pages always fills merge fields and sender fields with dummy text, a placeholder that it replaces with the actual data when you do the merge. This is the *field label,* and it always starts out as the name of the field you chose from the Insert → Merge Field or Sender Field submenu. When you add a merge field for "First Name," for example, the text "First Name" appears in your document. If you prefer to use a custom label—*4321 First Street* instead of *Work Address,* for example—you can do that with some help from the Layout Inspector. Here's how:

1. **Type** *4321 First Street* **into your text where you would like the merge field to appear.**

2. **Highlight the** *4321 First Street* **text.**

3. **Open the Link Inspector → Merge tab.**

4. **Click the + button in the inspector's lower-left corner, and then choose Add Merge Field or Add Sender Field from the pop-up menu.**

   Pages adds the new field to the Inspector's list of merge fields and turns *4321 First Street* into a merge field or sender field, according to your selection.

5. **Choose the target to use as the data source for this field.**

   When you add a new field, Pages automatically assigns it to the first target in your data source (First Name if you're using Address Book, or the first column of your spreadsheet if you're using a Numbers file). If that's not what you want, choose a new target in the Link Inspector: Click the field's target name in the list of merge fields and then select the target from the pop-up menu.

You can't edit a merge field's field label after you add it. If you want to make a change, you have to delete the merge field and then add it all over again by following the steps listed above. To delete a merge field or sender field, select it in your text and press Delete, or select it in the Link Inspector and press Delete or the – button in the lower-left corner.

The Directory Dilemma

While working on the members' directory for the Up & Away Frequent Flyer Club, you decide that you want to add a compact address directory at the back of the book. After all, it would sure make it easy to look up the addresses of members' hidden fortresses (or lairs, aeries, caves, secret headquarters—whatever). You've already got all that info in Address Book, but the question is how to get it into Pages without retyping it.

Because Pages can cope with only two Address Book cards per document (the sender and recipient), you might think that it's not possible to create a document with more than two auto-generated addresses. That's technically true, but a bit of fancy mail-merge gymnastics can coax any group of addresses out of Address Book and into your Pages document:

1. Create a new document consisting only of merge fields for the info you want to include.

   Use Insert → Merge Field to add each snippet of contact info you want to include. As you go, format the text the way you want it to appear in your directory. For example, the entire final document might look like this:

   First name Last name
   Work Street
   Work City, Work State Work Zip

2. In Address Book, create a new group containing all your members.

   At the bottom of Address Book's Group column, click the + button and type the name of your new group. Next, click the All group, and then drag each member into the new group.

3. Drag the card for your new Address Book group into your Pages document.

   Pages asks you how you'd like to merge the document. Choose New Document in the "Merge to" field, and Pages creates a brand new document, with each member's address on its own page, separated by a section break.

4. Choose Edit → Find → Find, and Pages displays the Find & Replace dialog box. Click the Advanced tab.

5. Replace section breaks with one or two paragraph breaks.

   Add a section break to the Find box by choosing Section Break from the top Insert pop-up menu. In the Replace box, add one or two paragraph breaks (whatever you want to use to separate each address listing) by choosing Paragraph Break from the bottom Insert pop-up menu. Then click Replace All.

Thanks to this heroic effort, you now have an equally heroic list of addresses, each formatted exactly as you specified in the original, single set of address fields. Save the file, or copy and paste the directory listing into another document.

Adding a Table of Contents

With a little advance planning as you design your word-processing document, Pages can automatically generate a *table of contents* for you with one click. The secret is to format all your headings and subheadings using *styles*. In fact, that's the only way to do it—to let Pages build a table of contents, you have to consistently use styles to identify the headings in your document. If you're not yet converted to the church of styles, it's high time to become a believer: See page 93.

Note: You can't include a table of contents in a page-layout document. The feature is available only for word-processing documents.

Before adding a table of contents to your book, for example, make sure you've applied paragraph styles to your chapter titles, headings, and subheadings throughout the manuscript. You might use the Title, Heading 1, and Heading 2 styles that come with Pages' Blank templates, for example, or you could use your own custom styles—perhaps Chapter Title, Section, and Subsection. It doesn't matter what styles you use, as long as you're consistent in the way you use them.

With your heading styles to guide the way, Pages can now rocket through the document, noting those headings and their page numbers, and assembling them all into a tidy list. Here's how to set it up:

1. **Open the Document Inspector and click the TOC tab.**

   Pages displays a list of every paragraph style used in the document (Figure 5-25).

2. **Turn on the checkbox to the left of each style you want to include in the table of contents.**

   In your book, you'll certainly want to include every chapter title in your table of contents. If you used the Title style for your chapter titles, for example, turn on the Title checkbox. Follow the same steps for any other styles you want to include—Heading 1 and Heading 2, perhaps. If you also want page numbers listed in the table of contents for that type of heading, turn on the checkbox in the "#'s" column. You might want to include page numbers for main headings for each chapter, for example, but list subheadings without page numbers.

3. **Place the insertion point where you want Pages to insert the table of contents, and then choose Insert → "Table of Contents".**

   You may want to add a page break or section break after the table of contents to separate it from the rest of your document.

Tip: Several of Pages' word-processing templates come with a Table of Contents layout in the toolbar's Sections menu. If that's the case for your current document, click the Sections button and then choose "Table of Contents" instead of using Insert → "Table of Contents".

The table of contents can look ahead only—it catalogs the headings that follow it, which means that you have to add the table of contents *before* any text you want to include. Also, it stops listing headings when it runs into another table of contents. This way, you can have several tables of contents, each pertaining only to the section of the document that follows. However, that also means that the only way to create a table of contents that covers the entire document is to have only one and to place it at the very beginning.

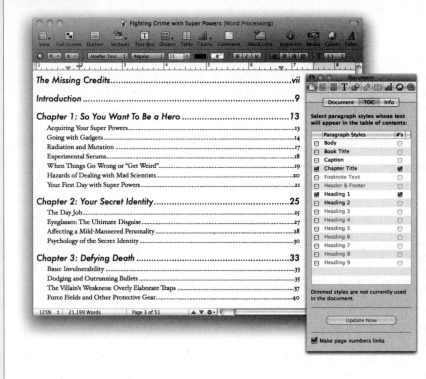

Figure 5-25:
The Document Inspector → TOC tab lets you select the paragraph styles you want to include in the table of contents. Turn on the left checkboxes of the styles to include, and turn on the right checkbox to include page numbers for those styles. Styles not used in the document are grayed out, but you can still add them as table-of-contents candidates in case you later use those styles.

Click the Update Now button to refresh the document's table(s) of contents, updating them with the latest page numbers and heading text. Turn on the "Make page numbers links" to have Pages automatically add hyperlinks to the page numbers so that you can click them to jump to that page (see page 179 for more about hyperlinks).

Note: All of this means that putting a table of contents at the end of the document won't get you far—it'll always be empty. Pages adds a note to the table of contents to warn you that that's the case.

As you edit your document, Pages busily keeps track of page number changes for your headings, automatically updating the table of contents with the latest numbers. But it's not quite so clever when it comes to changes to the headings themselves. New headings, text edits, and rearranged sections don't immediately show up in the table of contents. To trigger an update, click the Update Now button in the Document Inspector's → TOC tab, or click anywhere in the table of contents. (If the button is grayed out, that means there's nothing to change; move along, nothing to see here.)

Note: Pages also updates tables of contents every time you save the document.

Modifying a Table of Contents

Pages gives you some special styles, called *table of contents styles* or *TOC styles,* to fine-tune the way it displays your table of contents. TOC styles let you tell Pages to indent headings below chapters, for example, or add a dotted leader line between headings and their page number. You can edit these styles with the usual range of paragraph, character, and list formatting, giving you broad control over the *look* of your table of contents—but you can't edit its *text.* The table of contents is actually a special breed of formatted text field, and so defies your attempts to edit its contents. The only way to change its text is to change the original heading buried in your document text.

Since you can't directly edit the text inside a table of contents, that means that you can't add or remove words, or format text by selecting a word and changing its font size, for instance. You can't style individual words at all—changes you apply to TOC styles apply to the entire entry for every line that uses that style. The exception is page numbers; you *can* change a page number's style so that it has a different character style or font size than the rest of the line, for example.

Here's how to set the formatting of your table of contents with TOC styles:

1. **In the table of contents, click an entry whose style you'd like to modify—one of the entries styled with the Chapter Title style in your text, say.**

   Pages highlights *all* the headings in the table of contents that use that style. You can't highlight an individual entry in the table of contents (unless it's the only entry using that style).

2. **Choose View → Show Styles Drawer or click the Styles Drawer button in the Format Bar.**

   Pages reveals the secret Table of Contents panel in the Styles Drawer—visible only when you've selected part of a table of contents. The highlighted TOC style in the drawer matches the highlighted text in the table of contents (Figure 5-26).

3. **Click a different TOC style in the Styles Drawer to switch all entries with the selected style—the Chapter Title entries in this example—to the new TOC style.**

   This is an effective way to change the visual "level" of table of contents entries with the Chapter Title style, calling them out with large italicized text, for example.

4. **Make additional formatting changes using the usual set of tools.**

   Change the style's character and paragraph formatting using the Format Bar, the Fonts window, or the Text Inspector. Use the ruler to adjust tabs and margins.

   You can also use styles: Click the Character and Lists styles buttons at the bottom right of the Styles Drawer to expose those two panes. Click a character style to add it to your selected table of contents style, or click the Bullet list style to add a bullet in front of each table of contents entry.

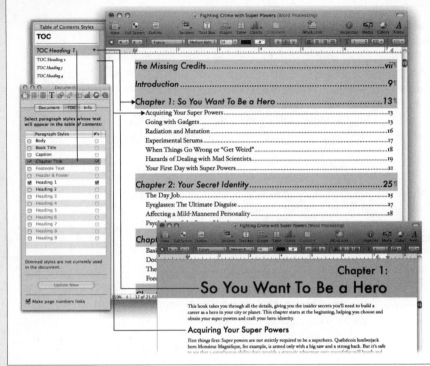

Figure 5-26:
Pages creates its table of contents from the styled headings you've used in your document and chosen in the Document Inspector's TOC tab. If you select an item in the table of contents, Pages highlights all items derived from the same paragraph style (here, Chapter Title) and displays the Table of Contents Styles panel in the Styles Drawer. You can modify table of contents text only by modifying the TOC styles.

5. **Adjust the tab settings for the TOC style to change the placement and display of page numbers.**

    If your selected style—Chapter Title, in this example—is set to display page numbers, Pages inserts a tab between the text title and the page number. You can use the ruler and the Text Inspector → Tabs pane to change the way Pages formats the number. For example, you might add or delete *leader lines*—the string of dots or dashes that leads your eyes from the text on the left to the page number on the right. In the Text Inspector, highlight the tab in the Tab Stop column, and then, from the Leader pop-up menu, choose a line style.

6. **Save the style changes by clicking the red arrow to the right of the style name, or click the + button at the bottom of the Styles Drawer.**

    Choose Create New TOC Style from Selection, and then give your style a name. Leave the checkbox turned on for "Apply this new style on creation" so that Pages applies the new style to the selected entries. (Or, if you're sure you won't need to use the original style ever again in this document, change it to the new style by clicking the arrow to the right of the style name and choosing Redefine Style from Selection.)

Tip: Before you save your style changes, if your modifications didn't turn out quite the way you'd hoped, double-click the style name in the Styles Drawer to revert to the original style, deleting all your style overrides and changing the red arrow to black. Then you can take another crack at your style changes.

Hyperlinks and Bookmarks

While a table of contents is the most traditional method for helping readers find their way around your text, the advent of the Web has rapidly made another type of navigation familiar to all: *hyperlinks* (or *links* for short). Just as they do in Web pages, hyperlinks in Pages documents let you hop, skip, and jump to new content by clicking on a linked word or phrase. If your document is destined for onscreen viewing—as a PDF document distributed on the Web, for example—hyperlinks are an efficient way to move around your document, browse web pages, or send email messages. Pages offers four types of links:

- **Bookmark links.** Click a bookmark hyperlink to move to another part of the current document. Whether the destination is on the same page or at the far end of a 200-page novel, Pages jumps to that location. Bookmarks are great for cross-references. Readers of your "Secret Identities" chapter, for example, would benefit from the option to leap directly to "Appendix C: Mild-Mannered Conversation" when you mention it as a resource.

- **Pages document.** Clicking a document link opens another specified Pages file.

- **Web link.** Clicking a web link launches your web browser and goes straight to the specified page.

- **Email Message link.** When you click an email link, Pages launches your email program with a preaddressed email message. This is handy to speed communications like product orders, requests for more info, or letters to elected officials.

Note: All of these links continue to work when you export your document to a new document type. Whether you save your work as a PDF file or a Microsoft Word document, your links keep on linking in their new environment.

Adding Bookmark Links

Adding bookmark links is a two-step process: first create the *bookmark* (the destination for your link), and then create the hyperlink that jumps to that bookmark (see Figure 5-27).

First, place the insertion point or select some text in your document where you want the bookmark. (You can only bookmark text—not an object, a text box, or text inside a text box.) Then choose Insert → Bookmark or open the Link Inspector, click the Bookmark tab, and click the + button). Either way, Pages adds the bookmark to the Link Inspector.

Tip: When in doubt, select an entire word or phrase when you add a bookmark. When you click a link that jumps to that bookmark, Pages pulses the bookmark text in yellow to call attention to it. Selecting the right text ensures that you're showing the reader not only where they've jumped but why.

Then select the text to use for a hyperlink, and choose Insert → Hyperlink → Bookmark. Pages opens the Link Inspector's Hyperlink tab with the "Enable as a hyperlink" checkbox turned on, the Link To pop-up menu set to Bookmark, and the Display field showing your selected text. Choose the bookmark you previously added from the list in the Name pop-up menu. (You can also define a hyperlink by selecting the text you want to use for the hyperlink, opening the Link Inspector → Hyperlink tab, and turning on the "Enable as a hyperlink" checkbox. Then choose Bookmark in the Link To pop-up menu.)

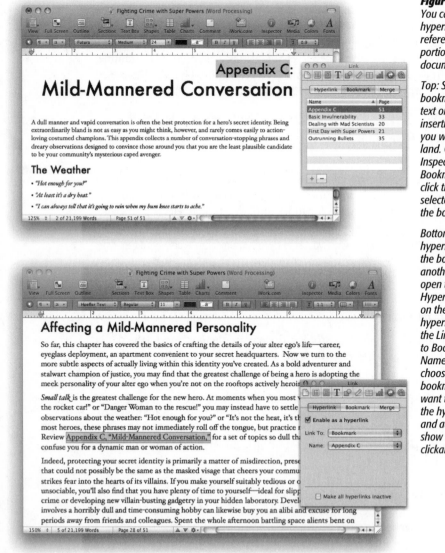

Figure 5-27:
You can make bookmark hyperlinks for cross-references to other portions of the document.

Top: Start by defining the bookmark. Select some text or just place the insertion point where you want the link to land. Open the Link Inspector, click the Bookmark tab, and then click the + button. Your selected text appears in the bookmark list.

Bottom: Next, define the hyperlink that points to the bookmark. Select another chunk of text, open the Link Inspector's Hyperlink tab, and turn on the "Enable as a hyperlink" checkbox. Set the Link To pop-up menu to Bookmark, and, in the Name pop-up menu, choose the name of the bookmark to which you want to link. Pages turns the hyperlink text blue and adds an underline to show that it's a clickable link.

Now when you click your hyperlink text, Pages jumps to the part of the document containing the bookmarked text, flashing the insertion point or highlighting the bookmarked text.

Note: Editing text you've defined as a hyperlink is tricky because Pages wants to jump to the bookmark, web page, or email message any time you click a hyperlink. To get around this, open the Link Inspector → Hyperlink tab and turn on the checkbox for "Make all hyperlinks inactive." Then you can edit hyperlink text as you would any text. When you finish editing, simply turn off the checkbox to reactivate the hypertext.

Pages' standard behavior is to underline hyperlinks and color them blue, making them easy to spot. Bookmarks are a bit trickier to find: To make them visible, choose View → Show Invisibles, and Pages displays a blue rectangle around both bookmark and hyperlink text. To remove a bookmark, go to the Link Inspector → Bookmark tab, highlight the bookmark in the list, and then press Delete or click the – button.

To change a hyperlink back into regular text, select all or part of the hyperlink text and turn off the "Enable as a hyperlink" checkbox in the Link Inspector → Hyperlink tab.

Linking to Another Pages Document

If hopping around the same document seems too parochial, document links let you get out and explore your hard drive's neighborhood, linking to other Pages documents on your computer—even to a specific bookmark in that file. To add a document link:

1. Select the text you want to link to another Pages document.

2. Choose Insert → Hyperlink → Pages Document, or turn on the "Enable as a hyperlink" checkbox in the Link Inspector → Hyperlink tab and choose Pages Document from the Link To pop-up menu.

3. In the Link Inspector, click the Choose button.

4. Select the target Pages document and then click Open.

5. To link to a specific bookmark in the Pages document, choose a bookmark from the Bookmark pop-up menu.

Adding Web Page Links

No document needs to be an island, and you can add a link from your file to anywhere out on the Web. In fact, Pages does this for you anytime you type a web address that starts with *www*, automatically converting the address into a clickable hyperlink. You can also add a web link to any other text by following these steps:

1. Select the text you want to link.

2. **Choose Insert → Hyperlink → Webpage, or turn on the "Enable as a hyperlink" checkbox in the Link Inspector → Hyperlink tab and choose Webpage from the Link To pop-up menu.**

   Pages opens the Link Inspector to its Hyperlink tab configured for this link. Enter the *URL*—the web address—and your web link is complete (see Figure 5-28).

Note: URL, which stands for Uniform Resource Locator, is just a high-falutin' term for web page address like *http://www.missingmanuals.com*. When you enter the address in the Link Inspector, you can begin your typing with *www*—Pages is smart enough to fill in the *http://* part when you're done.

If you'd rather not have Pages automatically link up all your web addresses, you can turn that feature off by going to Pages → Preferences. In the Auto-Correction pane, turn off the "Automatically detect email and web addresses" option.

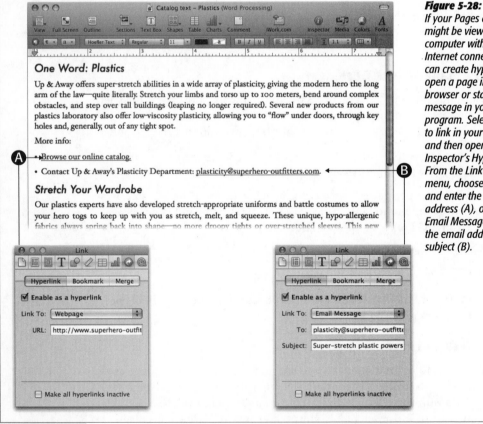

Figure 5-28:
If your Pages document might be viewed on a computer with an Internet connection, you can create hyperlinks to open a page in your web browser or start a new message in your email program. Select the text to link in your document and then open the Link Inspector's Hyperlink tab. From the Link To pop-up menu, choose Webpage and enter the web address (A), or choose Email Message and enter the email address and subject (B).

Adding Email Message Links

You can add email links to your document to make it easy for readers to contact you or to follow a call to action, encouraging the citizenry to contact their elected officials, for example. Select the text for an email message link—for example, "Tell Mayor McNiff you support the costumed community." Then choose Insert → Hyperlink → Email Message, or turn on the "Enable as a hyperlink" checkbox in the Link Inspector → Hyperlink tab and, from the Link To pop-up menu, choose Email Message.

In the Link Inspector, complete the email message setup by entering a subject for the message and an email address for the recipient (see Figure 5-28). Pages adds a link to your document text; clicking it opens a preaddressed message in your email program, ready to accept your eager prose.

Note: As with web addresses, Pages normally converts email addresses in your text into hyperlinks, too. You can stop this feature by turning off the "Automatically detect email and web addresses" option in the Auto-Correction pane of the Pages → Preferences window.

Organizing Text with Outlines

As you start writing, it usually helps to have some vague notion of what you want to say. That's where an outline comes in handy. Especially when embarking on a long piece of writing—a term paper, a book chapter, a project proposal—many of us attack the blank page by sketching out the topics we plan to address. The whole point of an outline, of course, is to eventually fill it in, to transform it from a simple laundry list of topic headings into a prose masterpiece. Pages' *outline view* helps you make this transition, letting you create a list of topics and subtopics and then gradually fill in the details, paragraph by paragraph, with your final text.

The outline view helps you not only structure long documents but manage them, too, letting you drag and drop topics to rearrange whole sections of text, or "collapse" topics to temporarily hide their content so you can focus on other areas of your document.

Note: Outline view is available only in word-processing documents, not for page layout.

Getting Started: Outline Templates

The Template Chooser's Outlines category offers six word-processing templates to help you get acquainted with outline view (Figure 5-29). Three of these templates—Harvard Outline, Basic Outline, and Research Outline—are formatted to give you the best results when your final document will itself be an outline. If that's your goal, these templates will suit you fine, although in that case, you could just as well use a regular template and nested lists (page 89) to create and style your outline. The finished result will be essentially the same, although as you'll see, outline view gives you more features to rearrange and view your outline.

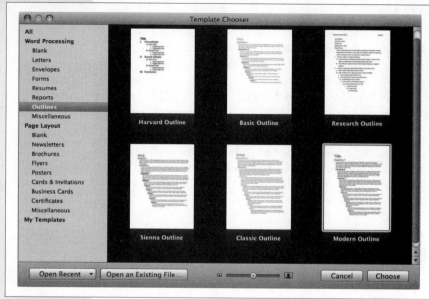

Figure 5-29:
The Template Chooser's Outlines category gets you started with outline view by giving you six sample outlines. The first three give you the best results when your overall mission is to create, and end up with, an outline. The last three are better when you plan to start with an outline and gradually turn it into a complete text.

Outline view gets much more interesting and useful when you use it as the basis on which to structure and develop a larger body of writing. In that case, the outline is a way station, not a goal in itself. You develop a skeleton of topics and then fill it in to create your final document, even switching back and forth between regular and outline view as you go. In that context, the previously mentioned templates may actually confuse more than help. Instead, choose one of the other three templates: Sienna Outline, Classic Outline, or Modern Outline.

To get started, choose File → "New from Template Chooser", and then click the Word Processing → Outlines category. Double-click Modern Outline, for example, and Pages opens a new document based on that outline template, with outline view turned on (Figure 5-30). You can tell you're in outline view because the toolbar's Outline button is highlighted in blue, and every paragraph has a blue diamond or dash to its left: Topic and subtopic headings get a blue diamond, and body text gets a dash.

In most other Pages templates, the placeholder text is carefully located to show you exactly where your text will go—just click, type to replace, and you're done. The outline templates, however, aren't especially useful as model documents in this sense. Like the Modern Outline template shown in Figure 5-30, most of these starter outlines include just a single set of nested headings and body text, which probably isn't what you have in mind for your final document. These templates are, however, great for helping you get the hang of working with the outline view. Once you've got it down, you can just delete all of the template's sample text and then build your outline from scratch. You'll still benefit from the text styles of the template, if not the organization of its placeholder text. First, though, let's take a look around.

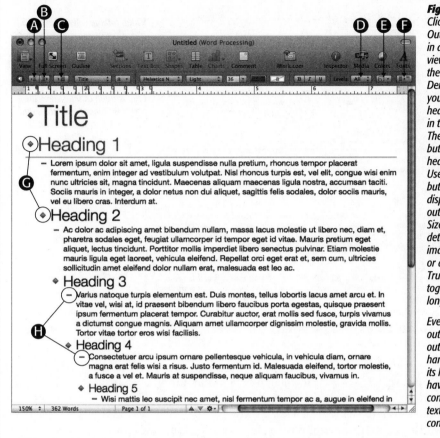

Figure 5-30:
Click the toolbar's Outline button to switch in and out of outline view. On the Format Bar, the Promote (A) and Demote (B) buttons let you move a topic heading higher or lower in the outline hierarchy. The Convert To Body button (C) turns a text heading into body text. Use the Levels pop-up button (D) to limit the displayed depth of outline topics. The Image Size pop-up button (E) determines whether images appear full-size or as thumbnails. The Truncate button (F) toggles the display of long text to just one line.

Every paragraph in outline view has an outline control, a blue handle that appears to its left. Topic headings have diamond-shaped controls (G) and body text has a dash-shaped control (H).

As you get started with outlining, the most important thing to know is that outline view is just that—one *view* of your document that happens to put a particular emphasis on topic headings. Turn outline view on and off by clicking the Outline button in the toolbar, or by choosing View → Show/Hide Document Outline. Figure 5-31 shows what the Modern Outline template looks like when outline view is turned off. The document suddenly looks like an ordinary word-processing document: The topic headings become regular text headings, and the indentation goes away. Click the Outline button again and the text snaps back to its outline form. See where this is going? You can develop the structure of your document—or even write the whole thing—in outline view, and then switch to the regular view to print or distribute the final version.

One thing that stays constant between these views is the font styles. The body text is the same size and style, and the topic headings maintain their varied looks, too. That's because the outline's topic headings all use *heading* paragraph styles, and body text uses the Body paragraph style. Pages uses this style information to switch fluidly between outline view and regular view. When you switch out of outline

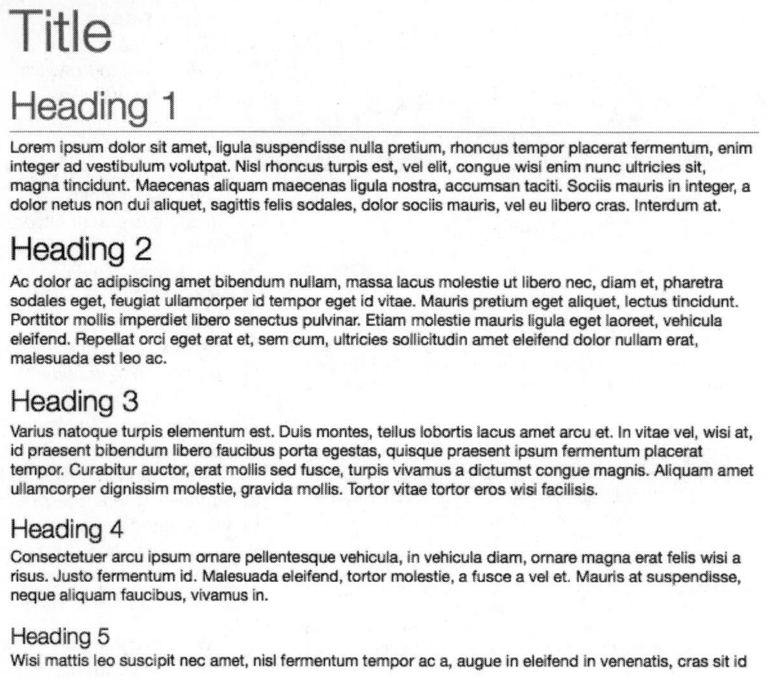

Title

Heading 1

Lorem ipsum dolor sit amet, ligula suspendisse nulla pretium, rhoncus tempor placerat fermentum, enim integer ad vestibulum volutpat. Nisl rhoncus turpis est, vel elit, congue wisi enim nunc ultricies sit, magna tincidunt. Maecenas aliquam maecenas ligula nostra, accumsan taciti. Sociis mauris in integer, a dolor netus non dui aliquet, sagittis felis sodales, dolor sociis mauris, vel eu libero cras. Interdum at.

Heading 2

Ac dolor ac adipiscing amet bibendum nullam, massa lacus molestie ut libero nec, diam et, pharetra sodales eget, feugiat ullamcorper id tempor eget id vitae. Mauris pretium eget aliquet, lectus tincidunt. Porttitor mollis imperdiet libero senectus pulvinar. Etiam molestie mauris ligula eget laoreet, vehicula eleifend. Repellat orci eget erat et, sem cum, ultricies sollicitudin amet eleifend dolor nullam erat, malesuada est leo ac.

Heading 3

Varius natoque turpis elementum est. Duis montes, tellus lobortis lacus amet arcu et. In vitae vel, wisi at, id praesent bibendum libero faucibus porta egestas, quisque praesent ipsum fermentum placerat tempor. Curabitur auctor, erat mollis sed fusce, turpis vivamus a dictumst congue magnis. Aliquam amet ullamcorper dignissim molestie, gravida mollis. Tortor vitae tortor eros wisi facilisis.

Heading 4

Consectetuer arcu ipsum ornare pellentesque vehicula, in vehicula diam, ornare magna erat felis wisi a risus. Justo fermentum id. Malesuada eleifend, tortor molestie, a fusce a vel et. Mauris at suspendisse, neque aliquam faucibus, vivamus in.

Heading 5

Wisi mattis leo suscipit nec amet, nisl fermentum tempor ac a, augue in eleifend in venenatis, cras sit id

Figure 5-31:
When outline view is turned off, as shown here, the outline goes back to being regular text. Although the font styles for the body text and each topic heading remain the same as they were in outline view, the text is no longer indented, and the outline controls disappear.

view, your outline topics become headings in the text, and when you return to outline view, they go back to their role as outline topics. That means that you can work in outline view to develop the overall structure of your document and then switch back to the regular view to work on the main text in a more comfortable word-processing environment. Here again, clean and consistent use of styles makes your work easier.

Working with outline topic headings

Open the Styles Drawer (page 95) of any outline template and you'll see that Pages has a complete set of numbered heading styles: Heading 1, Heading 2, Heading 3, and so on, each corresponding to an indent level of your outline. Top-level outline topics use the Heading 1 style; the next level uses Heading 2, and the level below that uses Heading 3. Pages has nine heading styles to accommodate nine indent levels, the deepest outlines can go. In outline view, if you change a paragraph to any of these heading styles, Pages moves it automatically to its corresponding "depth" in the outline.

But there's a much easier way to move topics and text around your outline: Drag and drop. Simply grab an outline topic by its diamond-shaped control and move it to a new spot in the text. Just like when you move a nested-list item by dragging its bullet point, Pages moves all the topic's indented text along with it to the new location, displaying a blue guideline and arrow to show you exactly where the text will land when you drop it.

Drag a topic to the left to promote it to a higher level in the outline's hierarchy (turning a Heading 2 into a Heading 1, for example); move it right to demote it. You can also use the Promote and Demote buttons in the Format Bar (Figure 5-30), or press Tab to indent and Shift-Tab to outdent—just like working with lists. Pages automatically updates the heading style of the moved topic and any of its subtopics to reflect the new location; a newly promoted top-level topic, for example, gets the Heading 1 paragraph style.

Tip: Because outline view uses the Tab key to indent (demote) topic headings, you can't use it for actual tab stops. Instead, press Option-Tab.

Working with body text in an outline

A traditional outline typically consists only of topic headings with subtopics indented below. In Pages' outline view, however, you can also indent body text below any heading. Body text is the full-sentence descriptive text that will evolve to become the prose paragraphs for your final document. Normally, you'll develop your topic outline first and then start to flesh out the skeleton by adding paragraphs of body text below each topic.

To convert a heading paragraph into body text, click the Convert To Body button in the Format Bar (Figure 5-30, shown previously). Then type away as you normally would, adding as many paragraphs as you like.

Tip: When you click Convert To Body, the Styles Drawer updates to report that the paragraph style is Body. It turns out that changing paragraph styles is really all the Convert To Body button does. You can likewise change a topic to body text by using the Styles Drawer to change its paragraph style to Body—or any non-heading style, for that matter.

You can go the other way, too, changing body text into a topic heading. Just click the Promote or Demote button, or change the paragraph style to one of the numbered heading styles, and Pages changes the body text into a topic, moving it to the corresponding indent level.

While you're working on a lengthy chunk of body text, you might find it more comfortable to switch out of outline view and do your typing in regular word-processing mode. You won't have to contend with the indentation, so you'll have the full width of your document window to work with. That said, working in outline view does offer some advantages that can help you focus on the topic at hand.

Focusing and compressing your outline view

In outline view, you can "collapse" a topic to hide all of its subtopics and body text, instantly compressing the view of your document so you can focus on other areas. Double-click a topic's diamond control to hide all of its content; double-click again to bring it back (see Figure 5-32). You can squeeze entire chapters of your book into single lines, for example, while you work on the rest.

Tip: Collapsing a topic is also useful when you want to move a topic and all of its text to a new spot in the outline. Instead of moving an enormous selection, you can collapse the topic first, then drag the single line to a new spot and double-click the diamond control to expand the text again.

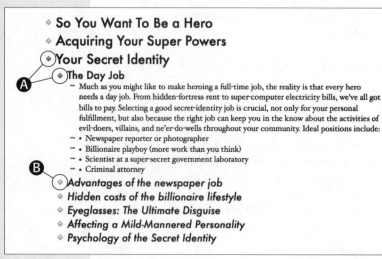

Figure 5-32:
Double-click a topic heading's diamond-shaped control to hide or reveal its contents. When a topic's contents are visible, its diamond is dark blue (A); when its contents are collapsed and hidden, the diamond is light blue (B).

You can also tell Pages to limit the outline view to topic headings only, hiding the body text. Choose a number from the Levels pop-up menu in the Format Bar (Figure 5-30), and Pages shows you only topic headings down to the selected depth. When you choose 3, for example, Pages shows you only the topic headings for the first three indent levels of your outline; it hides the body text and any deeper subtopics. If you want to see all topic headings but hide the body text, choose 9 from the Levels pop-up. To return to the full view, choose All.

You can compress the outline view even further by limiting the display of multi-line topics and paragraphs to the first line. Click the Truncate button in the Format Bar (see Figure 5-30) to temporarily hide the text; click it again to show the full text.

Building an Outline from Scratch

Now that you've got the hang of working with outline view, you're ready to build your own outline from a blank page. You can use one of the outline templates with its placeholder content deleted, or you can start with any word-processing document. Either way, turn on outline view by clicking the Outline button in the toolbar or by choosing View → Show Document Outline.

Note: When you switch to outline view in an existing word-processing document, Pages treats paragraphs as either topic headings or body text depending on their paragraph styles. Any paragraph using the built-in numbered heading styles (Heading 1, Heading 2, Heading 3, and so on) gets treated as a topic, and all other paragraphs get treated as body text.

Type your first topic heading, and Pages displays the topic in the Heading 1 style. (If you get body text instead of the Heading 1 style, press Shift-Tab, or choose Heading 1 from the Styles Drawer or the Format Bar's Paragraph Styles pop-up menu.) After typing your first topic, press Return and type your next topic heading. Pages creates a new topic at the same indent level. If that's not what you want, you can:

- **Indent** (demote) the topic by pressing Tab.

- **Outdent** (promote) the topic by pressing Shift-Tab.

- **Change the topic to body text** by clicking the Format Bar's Convert To Body button.

As you work through your topics, you can rearrange them any time by dragging a paragraph's diamond- or dash-shaped control to a new position in the document.

Automatic heading styles

One advantage of working with outline templates is that they have all nine levels of topic heading styles formatted and ready to go. Most other templates, however, start off with only Heading 1 and Heading 2 in the Styles Drawer. When that's the case, Pages automatically creates the new heading styles for you as you drill deeper into your outline, adding Heading 3, Heading 4, and so on, as you need them.

These new styles match the preceding heading style—Heading 3 starts out looking just like Header 2, for example. After Pages has added these heading styles to your document, you can customize them as you would any other paragraph style (see page 98). To automatically number your headings, add a list style (see page 96).

Note: You can't manually add your own numbered heading styles like Heading 3 and Heading 4 ahead of time; Pages reserves the names Heading 1 through Heading 9, and won't let you create new styles with those names. The only way to add these numbered heading styles is by first adding new subtopic levels to the heading, and Pages creates them for you as you drill deeper into your outline.

Adding pictures and other objects to your outline

You can add pictures, tables, shapes, and movies to your outline, just like you would to any other text, but with a few caveats. You'll learn all about adding these design elements in Chapter 7; if some of this jargon seems unfamiliar, skip ahead to see what it's all about.

First, what you can't do: Outline view doesn't let you add charts or floating objects to the document. In fact, these objects don't show up in outline view at all (never fear, they'll reappear as soon as you switch back to regular view).

Note: Oddly, while you can add inline text boxes in outline view, you can't *see* them. You have to exit outline view to work with text boxes as well as charts and floating objects.

In exchange, though, outline view gives you an extra trick for some inline objects—specifically, inline images, movies, and shapes. Along with all its tricks for compressing and collapsing your outline, Pages lets you make it even more compact by displaying any pictures, movies, or shapes as thumbnails. In the Format Bar, choose Thumbnail from the Image Size pop-up button (Figure 5-30, shown previously) and Pages temporarily shrinks these objects to miniatures. Choose Actual to bring them back to their full size. These settings change the way Pages displays these objects in outline view only; when you go back to regular view, the objects return to their normal size no matter how you set the Image Size option in outline view.

Note: When using this thumbnail option, you can move objects, but you can't otherwise edit them. Go to actual size or exit outline view to edit the objects.

Saving and printing outlines

When you save your document while in outline view, Pages returns you to the same view the next time you open the file, letting you get back to outlining right away. Not only does Pages have a good memory, it's good at sharing, too: No matter what view you're in when you save, if you save a copy as Microsoft Word (page 327), Pages makes sure your outline is compatible with Word's outline mode. Your Word-wrangling friends and coworkers can pick up your outline where you left off.

If you prefer to share your work on paper, you can print an outline like any other Pages file (the diamond and dash topic controls don't show up when you print). See page 321 for more about printing Pages documents.

Beyond Text: Laying Out Pages

Way back in Chapter 1, you heard lots of marveling about how Pages' graphic-design kung fu sets the program apart from other word processors. Since then, though, you've learned only about Pages' more traditional word-processing features—not a peep about graphic design. Patience, grasshopper. Now that you've got the basics in hand, you're ready to stretch your legs and move beyond text and into the stylish, colorful world of page layout.

Like most word processors, Pages lets you add images and free-floating text boxes to your documents. But the program's page-layout mode goes several steps beyond the typical offering, enabling you to do more than simply dress up your text. Pages gives you a full-blown set of layout tools in what amounts to a consumer-level version of heavyweight design software like Quark or InDesign. Whether you're making brochures, catalogs, newsletters, magazines, posters, or an elegant annual report, Pages helps you create documents designed for visual impact.

In page-layout documents, your creative focus shifts from words to the overall design. Your text becomes just one among many elements as you compose your pages into a symphony of images, tables, charts, shapes, and even sound and video. These design elements are known collectively as *objects* in Pages, Keynote, and Numbers, and in the next few chapters you'll dig into the details of working with these building blocks in your page layout.

If you've got all the design savvy of a platypus, don't be daunted. Although graphic design is a sophisticated field with infinite levels of nuance, the basic principles are uncomplicated. Even the most style-challenged novice can create a clean, clear design by following a few fundamental guidelines covered in the next several pages. And of course Pages' elegant collection of design tools makes it easy to pull it all together with grace and aplomb.

But first, a moment to breathe. Black-belt designers don't just jump in and start slinging design elements across the page. Great design always starts with a little prep work to plan your overall page composition and establish a few ground rules for your design. Doing this saves time and promotes visual consistency, especially when developing a design across several pages. This groundwork phase includes making decisions about fonts, colors, white space, column widths, and the overall visual structure of your pages. This chapter explores all those areas, helping you set the foundation for a great design.

Templates: The Key to Prefab Page Designs

First things first: If all this gentle encouragement isn't enough to convince you that you can create your own design from scratch—or if you're just feeling impatient—the templates bundled with Pages offer fast shortcuts to a polished and professional design. Apple's already done the design planning for you by selecting the fonts and color palette, and even providing choices of several additional page designs in many of the templates (Figure 6-1).

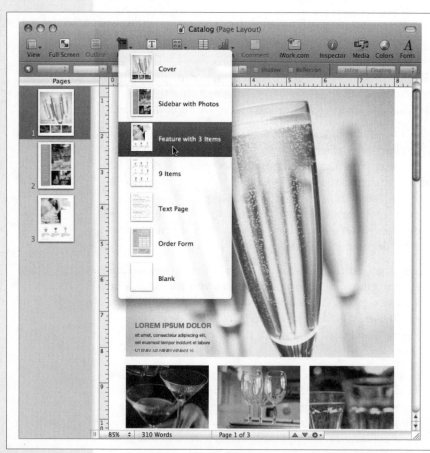

Figure 6-1:
Pages' built-in page-layout templates feature attractive designs, each with predefined text styles and several page layouts. Here, the Catalog template offers seven page types which you can add to your document from the toolbar's Pages pop-up button.

Chapter 1 gave you a quick-start tutorial for using a template to quickly drop your own text and images into a ready-to-go page design (see page 26). As you make your way through this chapter and the two that follow, you'll learn all the nuts and bolts that you'll need to work with the various objects included in the templates, or how to add your own objects to enhance the design and make it your own. First, though, a few quick pointers to help you get started with templates.

Working with Placeholder Text

Page-layout templates come prefilled with *placeholder text* to give you the complete visual picture of what your document will look like when it's done. Chances are, though, you don't want to send out your newsletter filled with text that reads "lorem ipsum dolor," so most of the job of working with templates is simply replacing this "Greek" text with your own words.

Page 216 gives you the lowdown on editing text boxes, but placeholder text puts a slight twist on the process. You can't *edit* placeholder text, you can only replace it. Click anywhere in the placeholder, and you select the entire clump of text at once. Just start typing, and your new text replaces the whole thing. With the placeholder out of the way, now you're back in the world of normal word processing. Often the templates include several placeholder text areas in a single text box, and you have to click and replace each one separately, as shown in Figure 6-2.

Note: If you add your text to a template by copying and pasting from another document, you undoubtedly want to choose Edit → "Paste and Match Style" (or press Option-Shift-⌘-V) to make your text match the template's style. See page 55 for more about this useful pasting option.

Working with Media Placeholders

Most photos in templates are also placeholders—*media placeholders,* like the three photos in Figure 6-2. Keep them if you like, or replace them with another picture of your choosing. Click the Media button in the toolbar to display the Media Browser, and then click the Photos tab and select a picture from your iPhoto, Photo Booth, or Aperture libraries. (Aperture is Apple's pro photo software and doesn't automatically come with your Mac like iPhoto and Photo Booth.) Drag any image out of the Media Browser and drop it on one of the placeholder pictures. Pages replaces the template's version with your new picture, resizing the image and applying the same borders, effects, and rotation as the placeholder image. Find out more about working with images on page 228.

Note: You can add placeholder text and images to your own documents—useful when you create templates for yourself or your colleagues. For details, see page 355.

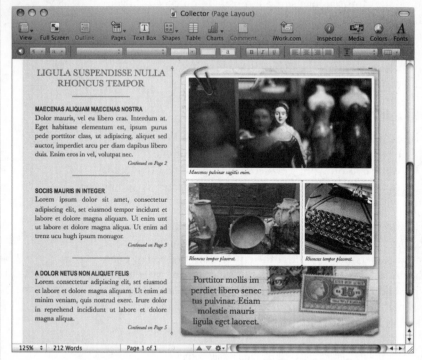

Figure 6-2:
Page-layout templates provide placeholder text and images to demonstrate how to use the template to best effect. Text boxes contain one or more placeholder text areas. In the Collector Newsletter template, the front page's primary text box, shown here on the left, has separate placeholders for the main heading, the subheadings, each chunk of body text, and the "continued on" text. Click anywhere inside any of these placeholders and start typing to replace it with your own prose.

The images at right are also placeholders. You can keep them as is, or replace them with your own picture by dragging and dropping images from the Media Browser onto the placeholders. Pages automatically sizes and formats your image to fit the layout.

Lorem Ipsum Dolor?

The text in this template—and in all Pages templates—is placeholder text, intended to be replaced by whatever text you wish to place there. Typesetters call this kind of placeholder "Greek text"—even though the standard filler is not Greek but is instead loosely derived from a 2000-year-old Latin treatise on ethics by Cicero, *de Finibus Bonorum et Malorum* (*The Extremes of Good and Evil*).

Designers use this dummy text when creating layouts so that (non-Latin) readers aren't distracted by the text's content—and instead pay attention to the page design. This practice goes back to the 1500s when it first appeared in a type specimen book—and it continues, using that same chunk of text, to this day.

Immovable Objects: Locked, Background, and Master Objects

An area that frequently puzzles newcomers when working with the prebuilt templates is when objects won't budge. You click and you click, but a shape, picture, or text box remains completely oblivious to your efforts to get its attention.

If the selection border appears around the image when you click it, but it's decorated with little X marks where the square selection handles normally are, this signals that the object is *locked*—fixed on the page and set to be uneditable. Many of the page-layout templates use shapes or images to add background colors or visual "containers" around other content, locking them so that you don't inadvertently sweep them to an off-kilter location on the page. In Figure 6-2, for example, the yellowed sheet of paper provides a background for the images on the right. But because the image is locked, you can't move it, delete it, or replace it. To unlock an object, click it, and choose Arrange → Unlock. For more on locking and unlocking objects, see page 263.

If you can't even select an image or other object to make its border appear, it's probably a *background object* or *master object,* which means that it's been added as a background element of one or more pages. To select and edit background or master objects, choose Arrange → Make Background Objects Selectable or Format → Advanced → Make Master Objects Selectable respectively. For more about working with background and master objects, see page 260.

Planning a Layout from Scratch

Templates are a nifty way to learn by example, giving you a designed document to dissect and examine to figure out how it hangs together. But there's still nothing like building your own layout from scratch to learn the principles and pitfalls of graphic design firsthand. The rest of this chapter gets you started on that process, taking you from blank page to lively layout. You'll finish the job in the next chapter as you learn the details of working with objects. Here's your assignment.

At long last, superhero outfitter Up & Away is launching its new real estate service, offering hidden-fortress sales and rental to heroes throughout the tri-state area. From stately manors to halls of justice to warehouse fixer-uppers, Up & Away aims to take the hassle out of finding your next secret headquarters. Likewise, Pages aims to take the hassle out of designing the catalog for your new service.

The catalog will be a magazine-style layout, with big splashy photos showcasing available properties along with their listing information. Brief articles scattered throughout will offer advice to heroic homebuyers, each accompanied by pictures and perhaps some charts or graphs showing local trends (sales of bat caves vs. arctic fortresses, for instance). You'll need several different page types—the cover, a few layouts to feature individual properties, and a couple of options for article pages.

In your enthusiasm for your new project, you might be tempted to launch right into Pages. Resist that urge. Take a few minutes to sketch some design options on paper. Even in a digital age, it's tough to beat pen and paper for working through visual ideas. Some great ideas started out as scrawls on a cocktail napkin or the back of an envelope—your page layout sketches are in good company. The goal here isn't to draw anything terribly refined. Instead, you're trying to capture some big-picture options for blocking out your pages and, along the way, identify the page elements that you want to use: Images, shapes, headlines, text, captions, and so on. Figure 6-3 shows some examples.

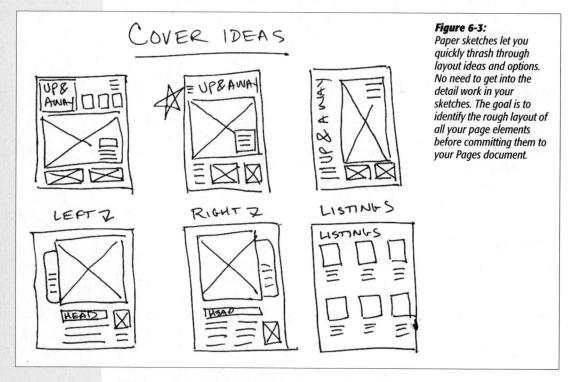

Figure 6-3:
Paper sketches let you quickly thrash through layout ideas and options. No need to get into the detail work in your sketches. The goal is to identify the rough layout of all your page elements before committing them to your Pages document.

More or Less, "Less Is More"

As you make your line-drawing sketches, focus on keeping the layout as simple and uncluttered as possible. A common mistake among novice designers is to use every option and nifty trick that the software offers, packing the design with a gaggle of graphics, lots of fonts, and every color in the spectrum. When you're trying to get noticed, this approach seems completely logical: To make noise, make a noisy design. The reality, though, is that noisy designs have less impact than more restrained, orderly visuals.

This doesn't necessarily mean that your goal should be to create a spare, minimalist design—only that you should avoid a busy layout by removing elements that add complexity without adding meaning. Architect Mies van der Rohe gave us the familiar phrase, "Less is more," but designer Milton Glaser later offered a more practical (if less elegant) version: "Just enough is more." As you make your sketches, keep asking yourself, "What can I take away? Does my logo really have to be *that* big?" Our brains naturally seek out order and rhythm—by creating a design with *just enough* information and imagery, you can get your message across efficiently without distracting your reader.

White space

Don't think that you have to fill every inch of the page. Designers consider *white space,* the unused portions of the page, to be a design element as important as the text and images it surrounds. Well deployed white space gives your design room to breathe and guides the eye to the page's important elements. When you open up space between text and image, or even within the line spacing of the text itself, you relax the design, making it easier to read and lending it an air of elegance. (Take a peek at any luxury ad campaign, and you'll see that it's chock-full of empty space.)

Alas, white space is not some magic pixie dust that you can sprinkle willy-nilly on your page. Poorly placed white space simply leaves scattershot gaps in the page, making your design appear incomplete. It takes practice to get it right. The main thing to remember is that in *most* design projects, your job is not to cram as much as possible onto the page—the goal is instead to make that information readable and clear. White space helps to do that.

Font restraint

Just because you have lots of fonts on your computer doesn't mean that you should use them all. And please, whatever you do, for the love of your reader, *don't use them all in the same document.*

Consistency is far more important in a well-designed layout than variety. Select just one or two fonts to use throughout your document, varying only their size or style for specific uses. For example, you might choose a sans-serif font for headings—like Helvetica, Futura, or Gill Sans—and choose a serif font—like Hoefler, Georgia, or Times—for your body text (see "Serve Up the Serifs" on page 64). You can then work with these fonts in varying forms to suit different roles. Make your headings and subheadings large and bold, for example, while you shrink and italicize your body text to turn it into a photo caption.

When you're ready to start working with your document in Pages, one of the first things you should do is set up its *styles.* Create a paragraph style for every type of text element you'll use in your pages: headings, subheadings, body text, captions, and so on. By using only the Styles Drawer to format your text, you'll ensure consistency throughout your document and also make it easy to apply changes across your entire design. For more about styles, see Chapter 3, starting on page 93.

Color palette

You're catching on: For the color palette, you guessed it, keep it simple. The palette is the primary collection of colors that you assemble in your design—whether in subdued balance or noisy contrast. When you choose your colors, the basic idea isn't that different than the ones you follow when you get dressed in the morning. Use no more than three or four colors for the text, backgrounds, and non-photo elements of your design. These colors should have visual harmony together, and it's a good idea to pick them immediately when you get started so that you're working from your full palette as you make the first strokes on your document's canvas.

DESIGN TIME

Color Me Inspired

When seeking inspiration for your color palette, one place to look is in your own photo collection, or in that remarkable photo gallery known as the Web. Plant and nature photos are an especially rich resource, with bright colors that Mother Nature manages to mix in imaginative and stunning combinations. With a little help from your Mac's Color Picker, you can swipe those colors for your own design. Here's how to build a color palette from a photo:

1. Create a new Pages document using the Blank Canvas template in the page-layout category.

2. Click the Media button in the toolbar to open the Media Browser to find a photo, or find a photo online using flickr.com or Google's image search. (Search for "purple flower," for example.)

3. Select a photo for color sampling, and drag it into your document window.

4. Click the Colors button to display the Color Picker.

5. Click the magnifying glass in the Color Picker to change your cursor into a magnifying glass. Click your new magnifying-glass cursor on a portion of the picture to capture its color, as shown in Figure 6-4.

6. Drag the color from the color well at the top of the window into one of the little boxes at the bottom for later use. For more details about choosing colors with the Color Picker (and then using them later), see page 265.

7. Repeat steps 5 and 6 to continue gathering your collection of colors.

Several sites on the Web are devoted entirely to color palettes, providing several ready-made combinations for your selection. When you're thinking about color, do a little window shopping at *www.colourlovers.com*, *www.colorcombos.com*, or *http://kuler.adobe.com*.

Collecting Your Materials

Behold the mighty hunter-gatherer, foraging the wilderness for sustenance. That's you, scavenging the vast savanna of your hard drive for the text and images to nourish your design. Thanks to your layout sketches, you even have a rough shopping list for your hunt, a visual inventory of the layout elements that you'll need to make your design work. Take this expedition seriously: By collecting the raw materials for your layout up front, you'll be able to focus on designing and assembling them without getting interrupted by errands to go out and search for more. (If you're building a house, in other words, you don't want to go to Home Depot every time you need a nail or a plank.)

Figure 6-4:
The OS X Color Picker lets you collect colors from anywhere on your screen. Click the magnifying-glass icon (A) to turn your cursor into a color-collecting magnifying glass (B). Click anywhere in the screen (even outside the Pages window) to capture a color in the Color Picker's color well (C). To save the color, drag it from the color well down to one of the boxes in the palette at the bottom of the Color Picker window (D). To remove a color from the palette, drag an empty box from the palette onto the color to zap.

Writing your text

Writing and design are two very different disciplines, and it's best not to tackle them both at the same time. Pages recognizes this with its two-format approach to document files, which gives you separate environments for word processing versus page layout. Embrace this distinction, and write your text ahead of time in one or more word-processing documents. You can of course use all of Pages' text-editing tools in page-layout documents, too, which lets you make any last-minute edits as you massage your layout. But the word processor is simply a friendlier place for spinning prose, and it makes the most sense to compose your initial drafts there without design distractions.

With your text in hand before you start your layout, you'll also have a better sense of exactly what you're designing in the first place. Images and even entire page layouts will suggest themselves more readily.

Assembling an album of working images

With a project like the Up & Away catalog, you're likely working with your own images or those provided by others within your organization (fortress realtors, for instance). In that case, you might already have all the pictures that you need in your iPhoto collection. But what if you don't have your own in-house images, or what if you need placeholder graphics while you wait for a few straggling realtors to send you their photos? In that case, the Web is chockablock with resources that you can use to source photos for your layout. See page 373 for pointers to sources of eye-grabbing photos.

Once you've collected your images onto your computer, pull them into iPhoto if you haven't already (or Aperture, Apple's pro photo software). As you'll learn, the Media Browser makes it easy to get fast, organized access to your iPhoto collection from any iWork program, and having your images in iPhoto is the most efficient way to work with them. To add photos to your iPhoto library, launch the iPhoto program, choose File → "Import to Library" and select the individual photo(s) to import—or select a directory to import all its photos in one dash. Click Import, and iPhoto hauls 'em in. You can also drag photos into the iPhoto window or drop them onto the iPhoto icon in the Dock.

Finally, create an album in iPhoto to hold the images for your project—"Fortress Sales & Rental," as suggested in Figure 6-5. Browse your iPhoto library to find all the graphic contenders for the document. Don't focus too much at this point on whittling down the selection—it's hard to predict what might work best in a layout before you start working with it, so it's better to have a broad set of options in your utility belt. When you have your working set of pictures in a single album, you'll be able to focus on just that group when you work with images in Pages.

***

Tip: Don't use iPhoto? Don't *want* to use iPhoto, at least not for this project? You can also add any Finder folder to the Media Browser. This lets you collect the graphics files for your project into one or more folders on your desktop but still enjoy all the benefits of the Media Browser. Just click the Photos tab in the Media Browser, and drag the folder icon from the Finder into the Media Browser's top pane. Folders that you add are displayed under a Folders category, and you can browse them just like iPhoto albums.

Figure 6-5:
Before launching into your design, gather a pool of working images into a single iPhoto album. To add an album in iPhoto, click the + button in the lower-left corner of the iPhoto window, and a new album appears in the left sidebar pane. As you browse your library, drag your photo picks onto the album. You can also select all the photos to include in the album and, when you click the + button, iPhoto automatically gets your new album started with the selected pictures.

Building a playlist of music and movies

If your layout is destined to be viewed onscreen, you can add sound and video to your document, too. If that's your plan, go ahead and gather the music and video that you'd like to use. Pages looks in your computer's Movies folder and iPhoto library to find video—organize your video files into a single directory inside the Movies directory, or add your movies to your project's iPhoto album. Similarly, for audio, Pages peeks into iTunes and the GarageBand folder in your computer's Music folder. Create a playlist for your project in iTunes, or organize your Garage-Band audio into a separate project folder.

Creating a Page-Layout Document

You've blocked out some rough layouts on paper, you've created an inventory of design elements, and you've gathered your raw materials. Hallelujah, you're finally ready to start building your design in Pages. Start by creating a new page-layout document: Go to File → "New from Template Chooser" and select a template to use. Since you're building a new document from scratch, the Blank Canvas page-layout template is a good place to start (you'll find it in the Blank category under Page Layout in the Template Chooser).

Fine-Tuning Your Document Settings

Before taking this baby out for a spin, check your cockpit controls. Run through some of the basics of document setup to ensure that your end product comes out the way you want. What paper size will you print on? Will it be a vertical (portrait) or horizontal (landscape) layout? Will the document be folded, printed on both sides of the sheet, or bound? Is it going to require page numbers, sections, or a table of contents? Keep these requirements in mind as you make adjustments using Page Setup, the Document Inspector, and the Layout Inspector before you begin entering text and inserting pictures.

If you plan to share your Pages document electronically with others who don't have Pages—by saving in Microsoft Word format and emailing, for example—you should be aware of some of the pitfalls you may encounter during the file translation process. See Chapter 9 to help prepare for the best possible transfer.

Page Layout vs. Word Processing

As you'll learn over the course of the next two chapters, your page-layout toolkit isn't limited only to page-layout documents. As you'll learn over the course of this chapter, you can add layout elements like images, shapes, text boxes, tables, and charts to word-processing documents, too. That said, when you're working on documents with a visual rather than textual emphasis, page-layout documents are typically the way to go. To reflect that, the next couple of chapters focus on page-layout documents—just keep in mind that you can use most of the techniques described here in your word-processing documents, too.

The big difference between the two file types is that page-layout documents consist solely of free-floating elements—there's no text built into the fabric of the document like there is in word-processing documents. Instead, you add text boxes, images, and other objects as you need them, on a page-by-page basis. Rather than following a constantly flowing river of text, the design of a page-layout document is built on an ad hoc collection of discrete elements, which you carefully arrange on the page canvas.

That's what's so cool: You can put anything anywhere you want on the page. But that's also the rub. When anything is possible, there are an infinite number of directions your design can take (not all of them good), making the blank page especially intimidating. Without a dash of discipline, your layout can devolve into a chaotic jumble of images and text scattered on the page. All designers benefit from a bit of structure. And so, before you start cajoling your design into place, it's a good idea to do one last stage of prep work.

Get on the Grid

It's not always obvious, but just about every professional layout is built on top of a very specific formal structure, a sturdy framework lurking under the surface of even the most complex and dizzying designs. For centuries, artists, printers, and designers have organized their compositions with *grids* composed of horizontal and vertical lines that invisibly slice the canvas into blocks, or *grid units*, that help the designer to align and size page elements, as shown in Figure 6-6.

The grid is like the foundation of a house, a carefully measured structure that gives stability to the overall design without ever being visible to the viewer. And like a building foundation, a grid itself is not especially exciting—it's a boxy structural device that can nonetheless support dazzling designs. Without a grid, you're just winging it: Images and text tend to float on the page unhinged from any internal order, and elements repeated from page to page pop up in positions that aren't in *exactly* the same place.

A grid keeps things clean, giving you guidelines to provide consistent placement and spacing throughout your document and to ensure well-proportioned elements within individual pages. Grids can help to organize any design, but they're particularly helpful in providing internal consistency to lengthy documents like books, magazines, newsletters...or the Up & Away catalog.

Figure 6-6 shows a pair of pages from the catalog, both of them organized with a six-column grid. For standard portrait pages like these, it's common to use five- or six-column grids, but that doesn't mean that you have to crowd your content into five or six narrow columns. Those columns are simply your building blocks, the lines of an invisible ruler that you use to line up your page elements. A six-column grid might contain only two text columns, for example. Both text columns could be three grid units wide, or one could be four and the other two. Or you could

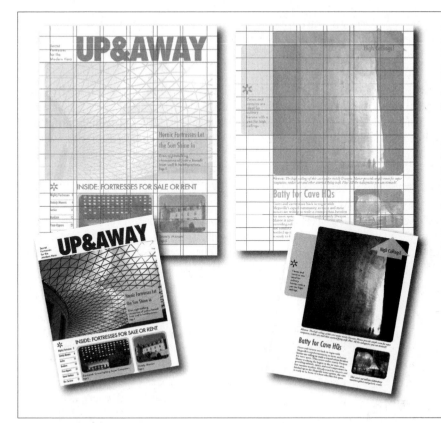

Figure 6-6:
A six-column grid organizes both of these catalog pages. But notice that these designs don't take the grid too literally—neither page has a six-column text layout, for example, and very few page elements actually fit inside a single grid unit. Instead, text and images extend into two, three, or even all six columns. All elements, however, align with lines of the grid, giving the design a proportional harmony not only within each page but between pages, too.

reserve one column entirely for white space. In other words, even though the grid itself is built of uniform blocks, the design elements that you build on top of it can be all different sizes.

Ideally, your design elements should all align to that grid, so that each cleanly fills a set of grid units. The key word here is *ideally*. Don't be a slave to the grid—it's only a guideline after all. As you work through your design, it's fine if a text column extends only halfway through a grid unit, and it's OK if your images jut into the margin or bleed to the edge of the paper. Leaving grid units unused is also a good way to open up some white space in your document. It's fair game, in other words, to bend the grid to your content's needs. However you use your grid, the important thing is to use it consistently. That's its role.

Using Alignment Guides

You build a grid in Pages using *alignment guides,* vertical and horizontal guidelines which you conjure from Pages' rulers and place anywhere on the page, like a virtual T-square. These lines aren't part of the document itself—they're visible only when you're editing, and they don't show up when you print. They're unique to every page of the document—every page has its own set of alignment guides that you can tweak and nudge without affecting guides on other pages.

Note: No need to build a grid each and every time you add a new page to your document. Using Pages' Capture Pages command, you can build your grid once and reuse it over and over again. More on that in a few pages.

You pluck vertical guides from the vertical ruler, and horizontal guides from the horizontal ruler (if you don't see them, choose View → Show Rulers). Click anywhere inside the ruler and drag the cursor into your document—your pointer now has a blue guideline in its craw, as shown in Figure 6-7. Drop the line wherever you want it in your document. To move an alignment guide, just drag it to its new location. To remove it entirely, drop it back into the ruler and the guide goes up in a puff of smoke.

Note: You can't create an alignment guide if the insertion point is inside text. To remove the insertion point, click outside of a text box, or (for word-processing documents) ⌘-click in the margin of the page. Also, word-processing documents do not display the vertical ruler under Pages' standard settings. To draw a vertical alignment guide in a word-processing document, go to Pages → Preferences, click the Rulers button, and turn on the "Enable vertical ruler in word processing documents" option.

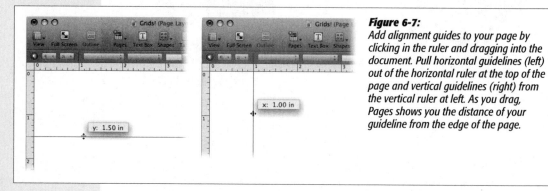

Figure 6-7:
Add alignment guides to your page by clicking in the ruler and dragging into the document. Pull horizontal guidelines (left) out of the horizontal ruler at the top of the page and vertical guidelines (right) from the vertical ruler at left. As you drag, Pages shows you the distance of your guideline from the edge of the page.

When you add or move objects, as you'll start to do in just a few short pages, the objects *snap* to these alignment guides, jumping over to line up automatically with these magnetic guides whenever you drag objects within a few pixels. This makes it effortless to keep things aligned, neatly avoiding the dreaded "one pixel off" syndrome.

Exactly *how* objects line up to the guides depends on your preference settings. In Pages' standard setup, objects *center* on alignment guides, snapping into position when an alignment guide goes through the exact middle of an object. In fact, Pages also goes ahead and snaps an object into position when it lines up with the center of another object on the page, or with the center of the page itself. This is handy when you're doing a very simple layout and you just want everything to be centered with the rest. But it's downright irritating when you're trying to line up objects with a grid—in that case, you want the *edges* to align with alignment guides, not the center.

Pages offers two preference settings to change the way that objects snap to alignment guides. Choose Pages → Preferences and click the Rulers button. Under Alignment Guides, you'll find two options:

- **Show guides at object center.** Turn this option on to make objects snap to position when they're centered on an alignment guide, on another object, or on the page itself.

- **Show guides at object edges.** Turn this option on to make objects snap to position when its edges line up with an alignment guide, with the edges of another object, with the page center, or with the page margin.

If you're building your own grid as described in the next section, turn off "Show guides at object center" and turn on "Show guides at object edges" for the best results. If you don't want your objects to snap to position at all, turn off both options. These preferences aren't specific to the individual document; when you change a setting, it affects *all* documents viewed in Pages.

To temporarily disable snapping to alignment guides, hold down the Command (⌘) key after you've started dragging an object (don't press Command when you actually click the object—you'll just deselect it—but only after you start dragging). This is handy if you want to place an image close to an alignment guide but not exactly on it. In that case, Pages would normally frustrate your effort to place the object, sucking it over to the alignment guide every time you get near. The ⌘-drag approach sidesteps the problem.

The Rulers pane of the Pages → Preferences window also lets you change the color of the guides to something other than Pages' standard blue. Click the Alignment Guides color well and choose a new color.

Tip: If you have lots of alignment guides, you'll occasionally find that they get in your way, or you might simply want to see what the design looks like without the guides. To hide them, choose View → Hide Rulers, and the guides disappear along with the rulers. Bring them back again with View → Show Rulers.

Building a Grid of Your Own

Like text columns, the columns of a graphic design grid are separated by *gutters,* the space between columns. Doing the math to figure out the spacing of these columns and gutters is a bit of a mind bender and then drawing the alignment guides onto the page at those intervals is a painstaking additional hassle. Fortunately, Pages' text-column features can save lots of time here, letting Pages do the column math and giving you column lines to trace. Here's how to quickly create a six-column grid in Pages:

1. **Choose View → Show Rulers, and choose View → Show Layout.**

2. **Drag vertical alignment guides from the vertical ruler to the left and right margins of your pages—say, half an inch from the edges of the page.**

3. **Click the Text Box button in the toolbar to add a text box to the page. You'll use this text box as a temporary positioning tool to create columns and then line up your alignment guides along those column outlines.**

Press ⌘-Return to select the text box so that its outline appears with eight handles on its sides and corners.

4. **Resize the text box so that its left and right edges align with the alignment guides you created in step 2.**

Drag the handle on the left side of the text box to line up with the left-margin guide, and then do the same for the right side and the right margin.

5. **Open the Layout Inspector and click the Layout tab, and add your columns.**

Set the Columns box to 6, and leave the "Equal column width" option turned on. In the Layout Inspector, double-click any of the gutter values for these columns. Enter 0.18 in, and press Return. (This seems like an odd number, but it works well for six-column layouts with pages that have a 0.5 in page margin. Just trust it.)

6. **Click outside the text box to deselect it.**

7. **Drag vertical alignment guides onto the lines traced out by the text box columns.**

In Layout mode, the column outlines are visible, as shown in Figure 6-8, showing you where to place your alignment guides.

8. **Delete the text box.**

Click outside the text box to deselect it, then click it once to select it. Press Delete.

9. **Drag horizontal alignment guides onto the page.**

Start at the top margin of your page—half an inch from the top edge, for example—and draw an alignment guide every inch down the page.

You now have a perfect six-column grid to help you lay out your page. If you prefer a five-column grid, you can follow the exact same steps but enter 5 in the Columns field in Step 5, and use *0.25 in* for the gutters.

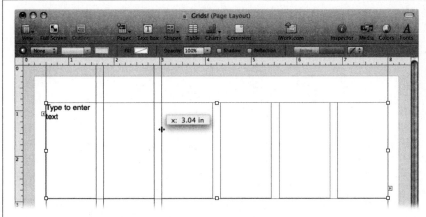

Figure 6-8:
Create your vertical alignment guides by tracing out the column borders of a multicolumn text box. Here, a six-column text box shows you where to draw the column and gutter lines.

Because alignment guides work on a page-by-page basis, your grid won't appear on other pages of the document. To make sure that you can easily reuse your grid on new pages, capture this blank grid page so that you can drop it into your document whenever you start a page that requires a grid. Choose Format → Advanced → Capture Pages, and give your page a name like "6-column grid." To add a new page with your grid, click the Pages toolbar button and choose your captured page. For more on capturing sections and pages, see page 159. It's also a good idea to save your blank grid page as a template: Choose File → "Save as Template" to add the grid to the Template Chooser. You'll learn more about creating custom templates in Chapter 10.

With your pristine gridiron in place, you are at last ready to start composing your first page. Let's get to it—those secret fortresses won't sell themselves, after all.

Objects Up Close: Adding, Modifying, and More

Pages, Keynote, and Numbers all let you plow a wide range of design elements into your documents—text boxes, pictures, movies, sounds, shapes, tables, and charts. As varied as these visual components might seem, they're much more alike than different. In iWork, all these elements are called *objects,* and you move, layer, and adjust them using the same basic techniques. It's like a pageant: Although each of these beauties has its own distinct talent, they all follow the same rules.

This chapter introduces you to most of iWork's objects (you'll get to know more about tables and charts in the next chapter) and then shows you all the graphical magic that you can unlock in all of them. From workaday actions like selecting and moving objects to spinning them in place or adding shadows, reflections, and borders, this chapter gives you the know-how to build sophisticated layouts with ease.

And here's the best part: Once you get the hang of working with objects in any single iWork program, you've got it down in the others, too. Designing a presentation slideshow in Keynote, for example, is very much like designing a page-layout document in Pages. You use the same tools in both programs to arrange your images, text, charts, and so on. This chapter introduces you to all of them, using the design of Up & Away's hidden fortress catalog as a working example.

Floating vs. Inline Objects

Objects are the building blocks of page-layout documents. Every object on the page is contained in its own invisible box, and you grab its box to resize, move, or shuffle it. At its most basic level, creating a page layout is about arranging these boxes to your liking—a text box here, an image over there, a table down below, a shape behind it all to add a splash of color. But objects aren't limited to flashy page-layout documents. They live happily in word-processing documents, too, where you can use them to illustrate your text with pictures, charts, text-box sidebars, and more.

Most objects in a page layout are free-floating elements that you nudge around the page independent of the others. But you can also *anchor* an object within a table or a specific part of your text so that an image, for example, always appears with the same paragraph or even acts like a word within a sentence. Pages manages this distinction with two categories of objects:

- **Floating objects** are placed on the page independent of the objects or text around them. When you add a floating object to your document, it stays in the same spot on the page even as you add new text or other objects around it. This term might seem counterintuitive, since "floating" often means drifting or on the move, but here it means fixed to a specific location. One way to think of it is that floating objects hover in place above the page. As your text moves and shifts on the page below, these objects *float* above the fray, their positions unperturbed by changes to text or objects elsewhere in the document. If you add your logo to the top left of your letterhead, for example, it stays on the top left even when you add text before or after it. More on how floating objects work in just a moment.

- **Inline objects** behave like a word or character in a line of text. If you add more text to your document prior to this kind of object, it gets pushed along with the text, always remaining tied to the words next to it. You'll find inline objects to be a good choice for text boxes containing a short quote that needs to stay connected to the surrounding text, for example, or images that you want to include in a table or to illustrate a particular paragraph (see Figure 7-1).

In general, all this means that inline objects tend to be more useful in word-processing documents, and floating objects are more useful in page-layout documents. That's because floating objects are ideal for placing objects in a precise location on the page (perfect for page layout), while inline objects let you tell Pages, "Keep this object lined up with this text no matter what" (ideal for word processing where text is always on the move).

Whether it's inline or floating, when you insert an object on a text-filled page you can determine how surrounding text *wraps* around it—flowing around the object to its left or right, or jumping down to continue below the object. For floating objects, you can choose not to have any text-wrapping at all, letting the text flow right over the object, or under it so that the object obscures the text. For more on wrapping, see page 252.

Since floating objects are distinct from the rest of the elements on the page, you can stack them in *layers*—just like you might arrange paper snapshots on a scrapbook page. One picture is on top, overlapping portions of other pictures beneath. Besides shifting the vertical or horizontal position of a floating object, you can also shift the *depth* of its layer, moving it in front of or behind other objects that it

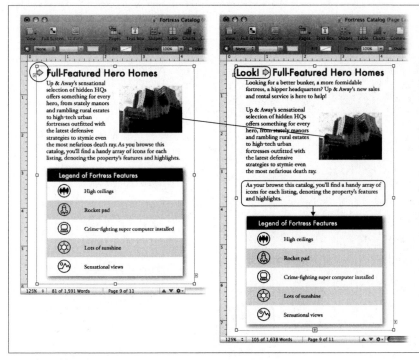

Figure 7-1:
These before-and-after views show a text box with several inline objects. As you edit the text, these objects move along with it, shifting position to stay lined up ("inline") with the text where they're anchored. The arrow shape in the headline behaves like a word within the text; the photo uses text wrapping (page 60) to keep it at the right side of the column; and the legend is an inline table which in turn contains its own inline images for the icons.

overlaps. (Inline objects always remain on the same layer as the text in which they're embedded.)

Unlike scrapbooking with paper snapshots, Pages also lets you adjust the *opacity* of each object, making it partly transparent so you can see through to the objects in layers below (see page 264).

After you place objects on the page, you can resize, rotate, and layer them on top of one another. You can add shadows, adjust their opacity, or group several objects together in order to reposition them simultaneously. For the full story on object manipulation, see "Working with Objects" on page 249 and "Modifying Object Styles" on page 252.

Floating Objects

Floating objects (Figure 7-2) give you precise control over exactly where you want an element to appear on the page. Drop a floating object into your layout, and it stays put, no matter how you might add or move other text and objects around it. This detailed control makes floating objects the tool of choice for page-layout documents, letting you arrange every picture and text box just where you want it. Pages prefers floating objects, too: When you use toolbar buttons or the Media Browser to add any object except for a chart or table to your document, Pages' standard behavior is to add it as a floating object. (Charts and tables are added as inline elements when the insertion point is inside text; otherwise, Pages sets them to be floating objects, too.)

Figure 7-2:
Every element of this page is a floating object. The photos, the shapes, the blocks of text—they're all individual "boxes" that you can slide around the page independent of the others. A reflection of the dome photo frames the page text, floating above it in three text boxes. A rounded rectangle shape peeks out from behind the photo to provide a background for the photo caption.

Even though the objects move independently, they still have an effect on one another. The main text, for example, wraps itself around the circular pull quote as well as the photos at bottom right. Those photos are set at a jaunty angle, overlapping each other and casting a shadow that gives them a 3D effect like actual paper snapshots (these particular shadows are secretly picture frames, as you'll discover on page 238).

To add a floating object, drag a picture, for example, from the Media Browser (or from a desktop folder) into your Pages document, drop it, and drag it into position. Go ahead, go nuts: Drag it anywhere on the page, wherever you want—that's the whole idea. The image is contained in a box with eight little squares called *selection handles* on its sides and corners. Drag any of the handles to resize the picture.

Note: If you have a recent Mac laptop with a multitouch trackpad, you can also resize objects by "pinching." With an object's selection handles visible, move your thumb and forefinger on the trackpad, opening and closing them to pinch or unpinch. As you do this, the object changes size. Rotate the object by twisting your thumb and forefinger on the trackpad like you're turning a dial.

You can also add floating objects by using the Insert menu. First ⌘-click the margin of the document, so that you no longer see a blinking insertion point, and from the Insert menu, choose Text Box, Shape, Table, or Chart. To insert an image or any other supported file, go to Insert → Choose, and Pages displays a file-choosing window that lets you select a file from your hard drive. Click Insert to finish the job. (Hang on, you'll get to the nuts and bolts of adding and editing all these various object types later in this chapter.)

Note: In page-layout documents, you're not strictly obliged to ⌘-click the margin of the document to get rid of the insertion point as described above; clicking any blank portion of the canvas will do. This trick *is* necessary, however, in word-processing documents, where that's the only way to deselect all objects on the page and remove the insertion point from the body text.

Inline Objects

While freewheeling floating objects have a place of their own, inline objects are stuck living with their parents. They always need to be inside another object—a text box, the main body of a word-processing document, or a table cell. Think of inline objects like another character or word in a sentence. Pages adds inline objects at the insertion point, just like a typed character, and they remain anchored to that portion of the text, adjusting location as you add and edit text around it.

Inline objects tend to be most useful in word-processing documents. There the focus is on content over presentation, and the precise location of specific elements on the page isn't as important as it is in page-layout documents. Inline objects make it easy to insert a picture or table into the overall flow of the text, letting your objects move fluidly in your document to stay with the words they illustrate.

To create an inline picture, for example, drag the picture into your Pages document from the Media Browser or desktop. As you drag across the page margin, notice the blue outline that appears around the edges of the page. (If you drop the picture at this point, it becomes a floating object.) Continue to drag into a column of text while holding the ⌘ key—the blue outline shifts to highlight that column, and the insertion point appears near the tip of your arrow cursor, visible through the shadowed thumbnail (Figure 7-3, bottom). Position the insertion point where you want the picture to appear in the line of text, and release the mouse button.

The picture appears at the chosen point in your text, sized just wide enough to fill the column if it's a large picture. Click the image to display its selection handles. Inline objects have only three active selection handles: the black ones on the bottom, right, and bottom-right corner. Drag any of the active handles to resize the image (the other handles don't do anything at all; you can't even grab them).

Tip: Can't see the new inline object you just added to a text box? It's almost certainly in there, but the text box is probably too small to show the whole picture or chart. Make the text box taller or narrower to reveal the missing object.

You can also add an inline object by first placing your insertion point at the spot you want it to appear, and choosing an object type from the Insert menu (or select Insert → Choose to add an image or other supported file from your hard drive).

Also, if you've copied an object to the clipboard, Pages pastes it as an inline object at the insertion point.

Note: Pages adds other file types that it can insert—picture and text clippings, web location files, and so on—as either floating or inline objects. Drag one of these files from the desktop and into the document to make it a floating object; ⌘-drag it into a column of text to make it inline.

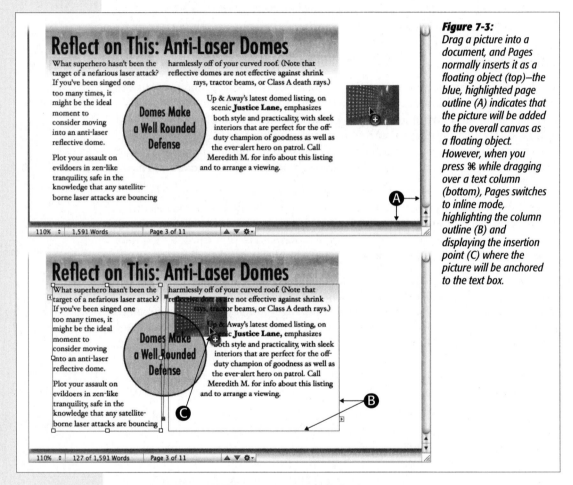

Figure 7-3:
Drag a picture into a document, and Pages normally inserts it as a floating object (top)—the blue, highlighted page outline (A) indicates that the picture will be added to the overall canvas as a floating object. However, when you press ⌘ while dragging over a text column (bottom), Pages switches to inline mode, highlighting the column outline (B) and displaying the insertion point (C) where the picture will be anchored to the text box.

Converting an Object's Layout Style

After you insert an object in your document, you can change it from an inline to a floating object, or vice versa. This switcheroo is particularly easy in word-processing documents, where it's a matter of flipping the switch on a single setting: Select the object so that you can see its selection handles, and the Format Bar morphs to show the object settings, as shown in Figure 7-4. Click either the Inline or Floating button in the Format Bar to select your preferred object style.

In word-processing documents, you can also make this change in the Wrap Inspector. Click the Inspector button in the toolbar or choose View → Show Inspector to reveal the Inspector window, and then click the third button from left to open the Wrap Inspector. Select the object, and choose either "Inline (moves with text)" or "Floating (doesn't move with text)". There's also a third option, "In background", which you'll learn about on page 260.

Note: The Format Bar does not display the Inline and Floating buttons when you select a table. To convert a table's layout style, you have to use the Wrap Inspector. For more about tables, see Chapter 8.

Figure 7-4:
When you select an object, like the photo pictured here, its object settings take over the Format Bar. In word processing documents, you can use these controls to change an object's layout style from floating to inline, or vice versa: Click the Inline or Floating button (A). Or choose an Object Placement option in the Wrap Inspector (B).

The Format Bar's Wrap button (C), as well as the remaining options in the Wrap Inspector, control how text should wrap around the object. To learn more about wrapping, see page 252.

When you select an inline object, like this image, Pages reveals its text anchor (D) to show you where it's tethered to the text.

Alas, these options are always grayed out for any objects inside text boxes and *all* objects in page-layout documents. If you've added an inline image to a text box, for example, Pages doesn't allow you to switch it to a floating image. In that case, the only way to change an object's style is to cut and paste it into a new context. To convert an inline object inside a text box to a floating object:

1. **Select the image so that you can see its selection handles.**

2. **Cut the image by pressing ⌘-X or choosing Edit → Cut.**

3. **Remove the insertion point by clicking a blank area of the page canvas or, for word-processing documents, ⌘-click in the margin of the document.**

4. **Paste the image by pressing ⌘-V or choosing Edit → Paste. Pages inserts the image as a floating object.**

To change a floating object to an inline object in a page-layout document, you have to fall back to a similar sleight of hand:

1. **Select and cut the object.**

2. **Double-click inside the text box where you want to insert the object, and place the insertion point where you want the object to appear.**

3. **Paste the image by pressing ⌘-V or choosing Edit → Paste. Pages inserts the image as a floating object.**

Adding Objects

With all that basic orientation out of the way, you're finally ready to start building your page by adding objects to the page canvas. This section provides a detailed guide to working with text boxes, images, shapes, movies, and sound (you'll find out about tables and charts in Chapter 8). The best way to learn about using this collection of objects is just to jump in and start working with them, which is what the next several pages are all about.

To let you get started with all this good stuff, this chapter holds the detailed descriptions of the shared actions, formatting, and styles that all objects have in common until later in the chapter. You'll get hints and pointers about those features in the next few pages, but if you prefer to learn those ins and outs first, feel free to jump ahead to "Working with Objects" on page 249 and "Modifying Object Styles" on page 264. Meanwhile, this section is all about actually designing content on the page, starting with your text.

Adding Text Boxes

In page-layout documents, if you want words, you need text boxes. Whether you're adding a headline to your design, inserting a lengthy article into your newsletter, or labeling an image with a caption, text boxes do the job. A text box is like a stripped-down mini word-processing document—a little window of words that you can edit with Pages' full set of text-formatting features. You can also use text boxes in word-processing documents to add sidebars or pull quotes to dress up your body text.

To add one of these essential elements, click the Text Box button in the toolbar. Pages creates a text box as a floating object, plunking it in the center of your screen with the placeholder text, "Type to enter text." Do just that: Start typing, and Pages replaces the placeholder text with your own words.

Note: You can also choose Insert → Text Box to add a text box. In a word-processing document, if you have the insertion point in the main body text, Pages inserts an inline text box. Otherwise, or if you're working with a page-layout document, Insert → Text Box gives you a floating text box. (Unlike other objects, text boxes can't be inline elements of another text box. In practical terms, that means that there's no such thing as an inline text box in page-layout documents, where text boxes must be floating objects.)

A text box can hold as much text as you can muster, but the volume of verbiage that it can actually display is limited by the text box's physical dimensions. If you type or paste more content into a text box than it has room to display, Pages adds the plus-shaped clipping indicator to the bottom of the text box, as shown in Figure 7-5 later in this chapter. You can resize the text box to make it large enough to display the hidden text—or, as you'll learn in a moment, you can direct Pages to display the overflow in another text box.

Here's the thing: While you're editing the contents of a text box, you can't resize the text box or move it to a new location on the page. To do that, click outside of the text box to deselect it, and then click the text box just once. Pages highlights the text box's boundary, sprinkling it with eight selection handles on the object's sides and corners. The appearance of those handles signals that you're editing the text box at the *object level*—think of it as editing the box instead of the text inside. You can now move its location, resize it, add a border around it, change its opacity, rotate it, and more. Drag the text box to wherever you want, and drag its selection handles to resize it. Click inside the text box again to start editing the text inside; now you're editing at the *text level* again.

Tip: Instead of doing the deselect/reselect hokey-pokey to switch from text editing to object editing, you can also press ⌘-Return when you're finished typing in the box. Pages sweeps away the insertion point, selects the text box, and displays its selection handles.

Be careful here: If you start typing while a text box is sporting its selection handles, your new text completely replaces the contents of the text box. A better, more foolproof way to start editing a text box is to double-click anywhere inside the box. You can format text inside a text box as you would any other text, applying styles, changing colors, adding shadows, and so on. When you're editing text, the Format Bar displays its usual collection of formatting options.

Note: There are a few things that you *can't* do in a text box. Text boxes can't include page breaks, section breaks, layout breaks, footnotes, or endnotes.

You can save yourself some moving-and-resizing time by directly drawing a new text box on the screen, specifying its exact location and dimensions from the get-go. Option-click the toolbar's Text Box button, and instead of giving you a text box immediately, Pages turns the cursor into a crosshair. Drag the pointer across the document window to create a text box in the size and location that you want. (You can also set the exact size and position of any object in the Metrics Inspector; see page 251.)

Tip: As layouts gather more and more text boxes, it becomes increasingly important to make sure that they all align neatly so that they don't descend into disorganized clutter. The trouble is that it can be difficult to see exactly where text boxes begin and end—their boundaries are normally invisible unless the box is selected. When you're lining up your text boxes on your grid, wouldn't it be nice to see those outlines light up? That's where *layout view* comes in. Layout view switches on the X-ray, letting you see the structural skeletons of your text boxes. Choose View → Show Layout to turn it on, and Pages shows you the outlines of all the text areas of your document, including headers, footers, columns, and the body text, in addition to your assortment of text boxes.

Linking text boxes

When you have more text than will fit in one text box, or otherwise want to jump text from one part of your document to another, Pages can link text boxes so the text flows from one to another. When the first text box fills up, its content continues into the second. Linked boxes behave as one virtual text box—if you add extra text to the first box, any displaced text flows into the next linked text box. You can chain several text boxes together in this manner, letting your copy flow from one box to another to another. You can have linked text boxes on the same page, or separated by many pages.

Note: You can link *floating* text boxes only. Inline text boxes don't share well with others.

To make a linked text box, create the first floating text box and type or paste text into it. Press ⌘-Return to select the text box at the object level (as opposed to its inner text), and Pages displays the selection handles, the link indicators, and (if the text box is full) the clipping indicator (Figure 7-5). Click the blue-arrow link indicator on the right side of the text box, and then click on the text box where you want to continue the text, or click in an empty portion of the document to automatically create a brand new text box.

Pages links the two text boxes, drawing a blue line from the lower-right link indicator of the first box to the upper-left link indicator of the second. If your first text box was overflowing—indicated by the + sign clipping indicator—the text automatically spills into the second text box. Reposition and resize the second box—and if you need to, click the blue link indicator on its right side to create another linked text box, and Pages continues your flow of text into a third box, as shown in Figure 7-5.

There are two other ways that you can create a link:

- Select a text box at the object level and choose Format → Text Box → Add Linked Text Box. Pages creates a brand new text box immediately below the original and flows the text from your selected box into the new one.

- If the text boxes you want to link already exist in the document, ⌘-click the pair (this works only for two text boxes at a time) and then choose Format → Text Box → Link Selected Text Boxes.

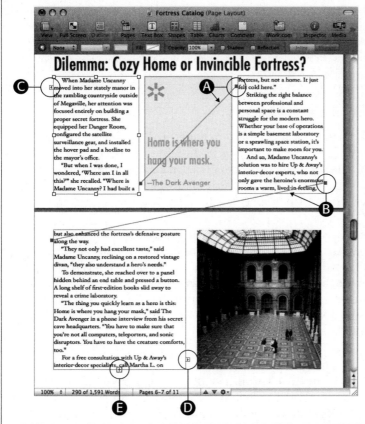

Figure 7-5:
Text boxes feature a few extra ornaments around their perimeter in addition to the usual resizing handles. The filled link indicators and connection lines show when a box is linked to a previous box (A) or a following text box (B). Open link indicators show that it's the first (C) or last (D) of the set. A clipping indicator (E) shows that there's more text than fits in the box.

When you click the left link indicator for the first box in a set (C), Pages adds a new first box before this one in the chain, shifting all the text so it begins in the new first box: After clicking the link indicator, click a text box to select it as the first box in the chain, or click anywhere in the page canvas to create a new text box at that location. Click a filled link indicator to insert another linked box in the middle of the series (here again, you click the text box to use or click in the page canvas to create a new text box). Pages reflows the text through the new box before continuing along to the boxes after it.

You can chain as many linked boxes as you like, in whatever location you want. The flow of the text has no bearing on the actual position of the text boxes in your document and vice versa. If you felt ornery, for example, you could flow text from page 3 to page 1 and then back over to page 5—aren't you the wild one.

Tip: To link to a text box on another page, use the scroll bar to browse to that page: Click the link indicator on the first text box, then scroll to the second text box, and click it. Don't use the Pages sidebar to navigate to the page, or that will break the link; you have to use the scroll bar to find the second text box.

Linked content behaves like a single block of text—you can select all the text in a series of linked text boxes to change font formatting or copy the text to another document, for example. To do so, place the insertion point in any of the text boxes and press ⌘-A (or choose Edit → Select All).

Tip: The connection lines between text boxes are displayed only when one of the linked boxes is selected. Even so, if your document starts to clutter up into a tangled web of connection lines, you can hide them by choosing Format → Text Box → Hide Connection Lines. Linked boxes are still indicated with solid blue link indicators, but Pages no longer points to where they lead. Bring the lines back by choosing Format → Text Box → Show Connection Lines.

Breaking the link between text boxes

Deleting a linked text box breaks the link, of course, but Pages still does its best to preserve the content and keep the text flowing. If you delete the first text box in a chain of links, for example, the text bumps down to the second text box and starts there; if you delete a text box in the middle of a chain, Pages heals the rift by linking up the preceding and following text boxes so that the "family" of text boxes stays together.

Note: When you choose Edit → Cut to *cut* one of the text boxes from a set of linked boxes, Pages follows the same behavior as it does when you delete, reflowing the content in the remaining linked box(es). But when you paste the text box back into your document, it no longer has its links—it still contains the same text as it did when you cut it, but now it's an orphan, unconnected to its former family. You can maintain the text box links only if you cut or copy the linked text boxes all at once: ⌘-click each of the text boxes in the set to select them, and then cut or copy them. When you paste them into the document, the text boxes appear with all their links intact.

Instead of deleting a text box, a less destructive way to break a link is to select the text box and choose Format → Text Box → "Break Connection into Text Box" (to sever the link from the previous text box) or Format → Text Box → "Break Connection out of Text Box" (to cut the connection with the following text box). This breaks the bond more completely than deleting the text box—Pages doesn't try to keep the text flowing to other text boxes in the chain. Instead, the text stops where you cut the link, and Pages once more shows the + clipping indicator if the text box no longer has room to display all its content.

Finally, you can also break a text-box link by dragging the link indicator from either text box. When you start dragging, the cursor turns into a puff of smoke. Let go of the mouse button, and the link disappears into said puff—text stops flowing between the text boxes.

Inserting a text box into a linked chain

Say that you have two linked text boxes in order to jump an article from one page to another. You've decided, though, that you first want to flow the text to another text box on the original page, so you need to add a new intermediary box between the two original text boxes. To do that, select the first text box and choose Format → Text Box → Insert Linked Text Box. Pages creates a brand new text box and inserts it into the flow of text between the originally linked boxes. This new text box intercepts the text that originally flowed to the second box, which is now the third text box in the chain.

Another way to insert a text box into the middle of an existing link is to click once on a loaded link indicator for one of the two linked boxes. Pages turns the pointer into a plus-bearing arrow, as shown in Figure 7-6, letting you click on an intermediary text box if it already exists or anywhere else in the document to create a new one.

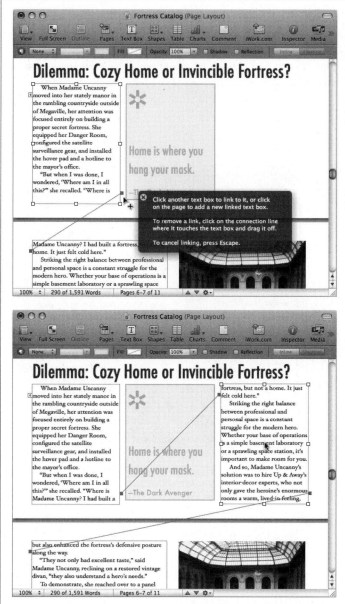

Figure 7-6:
To insert a new text box into the text flow of an existing text-box link, click the link indicator of one of the two linked boxes, and the cursor turns into a + sign (top). Click on an existing text box to link, or click anywhere else in the document to create a new box, and Pages flows the text through the new box (bottom).

Formatting text boxes

Think of text boxes as little documents within your document. And just like a word processing document, a text box can remain a modest construction of plain text, or you can dress it up and decorate it with a background color or image, borders, shadows, tables, charts, pictures, even columns.

The formatting of the text itself (its color, fonts, styles, alignment, and so on) is controlled with the usual formatting tools in the Format Bar, Fonts window, and Text Inspector. But text boxes give you additional formatting options at the object level, letting you apply styles to the entire text container. The Text Inspector contains two controls that control the position of text both inside and outside text boxes: the *Vertical Alignment* buttons and the *Inset Margin* field, shown in Figure 7-7.

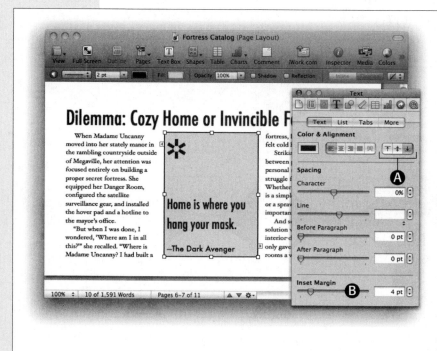

Figure 7-7:
The Text Inspector →
Text tab offers two text box-only formatting controls. The Vertical Alignment buttons (A) tell Pages to align the text with the top, bottom, or middle of the text box.

The Inset Margin field (B) controls the amount of padding between the boundary of the text box and its content. When you add a border to the text box, for example, it's useful to nudge the text back from the edge of the text box, as shown here in the bottom-aligned text box with the quotation. Drag the slider or enter a point value in the box to increase this interior margin, which affects all four sides equally.

Pages lets you control the way the surrounding text wraps around a text box, as you can with other objects. See page 252 for all the wrapping details.

You can add a solid color, a gradient (a fill color that gradually blends one color into another), or an image to the background of a text box; you can also choose to add a border, a shadow, a reflection, or adjust its opacity, as shown in Figure 7-8. The Format Bar and the Graphic Inspector are home to the controls for these functions, which also let you do the same things to other objects. Find all the details in "Modifying Object Styles" starting on page 264.

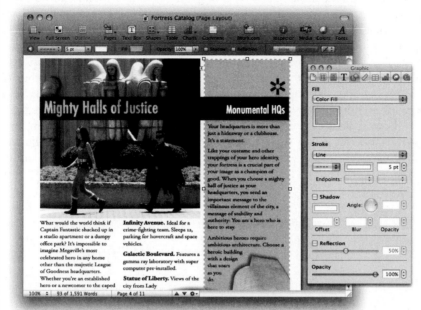

To style a text box, select the object (if you're editing the text inside the text box, press ⌘-Return to remove the insertion point). Click the Format Bar's Fill color well, and choose a color to add a background fill to the text box. Use the Stroke menu to add a line or border around the box. You can get some interesting border effects by choosing a color that matches the page background; in Figure 7-8, the sidebar's white dashed border gives it a postage-stamp border.

Turn on the Shadow checkbox in the Format Bar or Graphic Inspector to add a drop shadow to the text box, so it looks like it's floating above the page. (Be sure to add a fill color to the text box if you want the shadow to appear around the entire box instead of around individual letters.) The Opacity setting controls opacity for the entire text box: background, border, text, and inline graphics.

Combining text boxes with other objects

You can add other objects—images, shapes, tables, or charts—inside a text box as inline objects, as you saw back in Figure 7-1. This is convenient when you want to include a small image or shape inside a line of text as icons, for example, or to plant a table, chart, or picture next to a specific paragraph of text. Wherever the text box goes, its inline objects go with it; they live inside the text box. Place the insertion point in the text at the spot you want to insert the object, and choose the type of object from the Insert menu, or ⌘-drag a picture, movie, or song from the Media Browser.

Except for the examples listed above, though, it's far more useful and flexible to combine text boxes with *floating* objects rather than inline objects. Floating objects give you much more control over the layout of each individual object, making them your preferred tool for page-layout documents. With floating objects, however, you're actually creating one or more additional layered objects positioned *outside* of the text box, although they might overlap, one on top of the other. To add a floating object, ⌘-click the margin of the document so the insertion point disappears and then choose the type of object from the toolbar, Insert menu, or Media Browser. Resize the object and drag it so that it overlaps the text box. Open the Wrap Inspector, select the wrapping style for your new object, and adjust the Text Fit option if necessary (see page 254). The text in the text box wraps around your new object according to your settings, as shown in Figure 7-9.

Note: Pages doesn't let you nest an inline text box inside another text box, but you can still combine two floating text boxes to interesting effect, making the content of one text box wrap around another, overlapping text box to create a pull quote, for example.

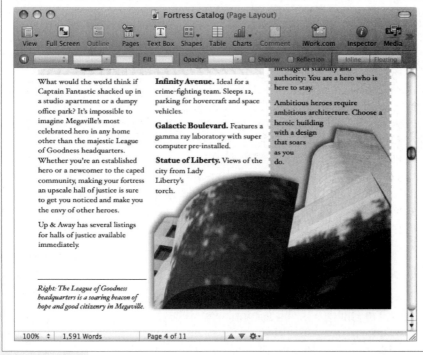

Figure 7-9:
Even though floating objects are positioned independent of other objects, they still have an effect on overlapping text boxes. Here, the image of the building elbows its way into the sidebar and main text, and the text wraps around it based on the Wrap Inspector settings for the image.

Although your new floating object affects the display of any overlapping text boxes, it's still a separate object, with its own life outside of the text box. The two move independently. If you want to make sure that the two objects always travel together as a unit, you can *group* the two objects. Command-click each of the objects to combine into a group, and choose Arrange → Group. Now if you move the text box, the object comes along for the ride and vice versa—the group behaves like one big object. (For more on grouping objects, see page 263.)

Note: When you group objects together, you can no longer resize them individually or change any of their display properties (background color, border, shadow, and so on). If you select an object group, the selection handles appear for the entire group—dragging them resizes *all objects* in the group. You can still edit the text within grouped text boxes (and shapes, too) by double-clicking the text and typing away, but other changes to individual elements are blocked until you *ungroup* them. To do so, select the grouped object, choose Arrange → Ungroup, and then make your changes. You can stick them back together again when you're done by selecting the objects and choosing Arrange → Group once more.

Pull quotes and sidebars

In page-layout documents, if you want to include text, text boxes are the main event. It doesn't matter whether you're creating long passages or a couple of brief callouts, you use text boxes for nearly everything (you can use shapes for text, too, as you'll learn on page 246). In word-processing documents, however, text boxes are most useful for highlighting or isolating some text from the main body text. *Sidebars* and *pull quotes* are two common examples, as shown in Figure 7-10.

Backgrounder: Fighting Crime in the Computer Age

As you outfit your fortress, be sure to save some cash for a reliable crime-fighting supercomputer. Whether you commission your own software or purchase it off the shelf, there are a few must-have features for every superhero:

- **Photo enhancement.** You should be able to simply say, "Enhance," and have any crummy, low-resolution picture instantly turn crystal clear to reveal the face of your arch nemesis in the middle of the heist.

- **Evil Plot Scenario Simulators.** Your computer needs to be able to think like a villain, running simulations and scenarios that will help you to predict evil plots even before they unfold.

- **Forensic Analysis.** Your computer should have one of those nifty slots where you insert a crime-scene weapon, strand of hair, or scrap of clothing, and it tells you who touched it, the model of car they drive, and their favorite boy band.

- **Voice Analysis.** Your computer needs to be able to instantly recognize any voice from a database of known villains, heroes, sidekicks, and off-the-grid nuclear scientists. Identification of precise address from background sounds is an added plus if you can get it.

A Your computer needs to be able to think like a villain.

Online Alternatives **B**

If you're a hero on a budget, you might make do by using one of the many subscription Web sites that crunch crime-fighting data, but you won't have the same processing power, and the interface and design of many of these sites leave something to be desired. Keep in mind, too, that many villains have access to these same Web sites, so you're not exactly giving yourself a strategic advantage by using these public resources as your source of underworld intelligence.

Figure 7-10:
Pull quotes or callouts (A) highlight an important point in the main text. Since they relate directly to part of the text, they need to be placed near the relevant text. Magazine articles often have pull quotes to add visual interest to the page by breaking up the columns of plain text.

Sidebars (B) hold a paragraph or several paragraphs that are related to, but not really part of, the flow of the main text. Sidebars can stand alone as a little chapter or chunk of information. This book, for example, uses sidebars to hold these kinds of digressions.

In a word-processing document, you can create a sidebar or pull quote as either a floating or inline text box, but one advantage to going with the inline style for a pull quote is that it will always appear next to the relevant text. If you make it a floating object, on the other hand, it remains in exactly the same position on the page, even if subsequent edits move the related text to a new location, or even to a different page entirely. Making a pull quote inline in a word-processing document means you don't have to manage it as you edit and craft the surrounding text.

Pull quotes and sidebars are close cousins that differ only in length and font style—a pull quote is typically brief text set in large type, while a sidebar is usually longer and set in the font size of the main text, or close to it. In any case, the process of creating them is essentially the same. Here's how to add an inline pull quote to your word-processing document:

1. **Create an inline text box in the body text.**

   Position the insertion point in the body text where you want the pull quote to appear, and choose Insert → Text Box. Or click the Text Box button in the toolbar, and Pages inserts a floating text box—press ⌘-Return to select the object, and click the Inline button in the Format Bar.

2. **Drag the box and position it, watching the insertion point as you drag. Drop it when you get the insertion point in the right spot.**

3. **Make the main text wrap around the pull quote by choosing a style from the Format Bar's Wrap pop-up.**

   You can also enable wrapping in the Wrap Inspector by turning on the checkbox for "Object causes wrap" and choosing one of the wrapping styles (see page 252 for more on wrapping text).

4. **In the Wrap Inspector, adjust the Extra Space setting by using the up and down arrow button to insert more or less white space around the text box.**

5. **Add a shadow around the text box to make it seem to float above the surrounding text.**

   Turn on the Shadow option in the Format Bar and—*blech*—Pages adds a shadow to the text itself, instead of around the border of the text box. To fix that, choose a background color from the Format Bar's Fill pop-up—white is just fine if you don't want it to be a different color than the page background.

Note: Pages can automatically create a text box from copied text, handy for pull quotes that repeat a portion of your main text. Copy the text for your pull quote, and ⌘-click the margin of the document so the insertion point disappears. Choose Edit → "Paste and Match Style," or press Option-⌘-Shift-V. Pages inserts a new floating text box containing your copied text. Resize or reposition the box, and reformat the text if you need to.

Shape objects make for attractive alternatives to text boxes for pull quotes and call-outs. Shapes give you the option to put your callout in a curvy container—a circle or rounded rectangle, perhaps—or a variety of other forms including stars and arrows. See page 241 to learn more about shapes.

WORKAROUND WORKSHOP

Tip o' the Cap

Grab a magazine or book and chances are good that its articles or chapters begin with an enormous capital letter. Large initial caps appear in many different styles, but most often you see the *raised cap,* in which the baseline of the initial letter matches that of the first line of text, with the letter rising up above the paragraph; or the *drop cap,* in which the top of the initial letter lines up with the top of the first line of text, with the rest of the letter dropping three or more lines below. Pages doesn't exactly make it easy to create either cap style—you can create a raised cap with some crafty adjustment of line spacing, and drop caps require an inline text box. Herewith, the details.

Creating a raised cap. You might try to create a large raised cap by increasing the first letter's font size, but that one large character results in wider line spacing beneath the first line. The page layout perfectionist has no choice but a somewhat convoluted workaround which, though time-consuming, works. It's a brittle solution, however, and breaks as soon as you edit the first line of the text. Consider this a technique to use only after you've completed editing your text.

1. Select the initial capital in the paragraph and increase its font size to three or four times the size of the body text. The large capital looks good, but the line spacing between the first line and the following line is much too wide.

2. Place the insertion point to the right of the last letter in the first line and press Return, adding a paragraph break and turning the first line into a separate paragraph. Pages adds a space at the beginning of the second line when you add the paragraph break. Remove the space so the second line begins flush with the rest of the paragraph.

3. Place the insertion point in your first-line paragraph and adjust the Text Inspector's Line slider to make the first-line spacing match the rest of the paragraph.

Creating a drop cap. Pages is much better at dealing with drop caps than with raised caps—once set up, a drop cap doesn't break as easily as a raised cap. Here's how to do it:

1. Place the insertion point at the beginning of the paragraph, choose Insert → Text Box, and Pages adds an inline text box to the paragraph. Type the letter for the drop cap in the text box, and set its font size to four times the size of the surrounding font.

2. Press ⌘-Return to select the text box at the object level, and resize the text box to fit the letter inside. In the Wrap Inspector, choose left-aligned text-wrapping, and set the Extra Space field to 0 pt. The text box should now hug the top left corner of the paragraph.

3. You're nearly there, but the drop cap isn't quite flush with the top of the paragraph's first line. In the Text Inspector → Text pane, set the pop-up menu below the Line Spacing field to "Exactly," and set the number to the same size as the drop cap's font size. For a 48-pt font, the line spacing should be exactly 48 pt, for example.

4. Adjust the font size and line spacing so that the drop cap is exactly three lines of type tall. (Three lines is a standard size; an odd number of lines looks best.) Drag the text box's bottom selection handle to adjust its height, allowing the text on the line below to fall into place under the drop cap.

Adding columns to text boxes

Just like the body text of a word-processing document, you can set text boxes to display content in multiple columns, which is handy for newsletter or magazine articles in a page-layout document, or wide multicolumn sidebars in word-processing documents. To set the column layout of a text box, double-click its text to place the insertion point inside the text box, and choose a column layout from the Format Bar's Column pop-up button. Or, to fine-tune your column settings, go to the Layout Inspector → Layout tab. See page 153 for more with working on columns.

Note: In text boxes, columns work the same way that they do in the body text of word-processing text except that, unlike word-processing sections, a text box can have just one column layout. No layout breaks here.

Adding Images

When visual impact is the goal, pictures often play a larger role in the design than the text itself. In page-layout projects like the Up & Away fortress catalog, for example, photos are the primary content, and text is reduced to a secondary role. Pages gives you a variety of tools to arrange and fine-tune your images as readily as you compose words in your text.

Meet the Media Browser

All the iWork programs provide fast access to your photos, movies, and audio by way of the Media Browser, a window into your personal media collections. You can access your photos, videos, and graphics stored in iPhoto, Photo Booth, or Aperture; your music, movies, and sound files stored in iTunes; the Garageband and other sound files stored in your Music folder; and the movies stored in your iMovie and iPhoto libraries or your Movies folder.

Click the Media button in the toolbar, or choose View → Show Media Browser to take a look at all the digital goodies stored on your Mac. The Media Browser appears (Figure 7-11). The tabs at the top of the window let you choose to browse audio, photos, or movies. The upper pane displays playlists, albums, or folders, and the lower pane displays songs, photos, or movies from the collection selected in the upper pane.

To add a picture to your document, click the Photos tab in the Media Browser, and browse through your collection. When you find the photo you want to use, drag its thumbnail from the Media Browser into your document window. Pages adds the picture as a floating object on your page. Drag the image to move it into position in your layout, or grab its selection handles to resize it. (With Pages' standard settings, resizing the image always keeps its original proportions. If you prefer to stretch or squeeze the image into new dimensions, turn off the "Constrain proportions" setting in the Metrics Inspector—see page 251 for more details.)

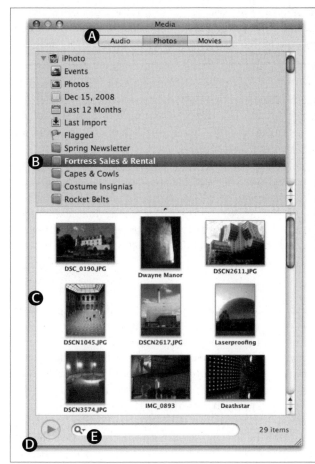

Figure 7-11:
Click the Media button in the toolbar to reveal the Media Browser, which opens a wormhole into your personal collection of photos, audio, and video. Use the tabs at the top of the window (A) to switch from one type of media to another and then, in the top pane (B), choose a playlist, iPhoto album, or Finder folder to browse your files in the bottom pane (C). Use the Play button (D) at the bottom left to preview audio and video selections.

The search box at the bottom of the window (E) lets you search for a photo, song, or movie. Type your search term and press Return, and the Media Browser plucks matches from the media collection selected in the top pane, sifting through names, descriptions, and keywords for matching files. When you locate the picture, song, or movie, drag it from the Media Browser into the document.

When you drag a picture from the media browser, Pages adds it to your page as a floating object. To add the image as an inline object to a text box or the body text of a word-processing document, ⌘-drag the image from the media browser into the text. For more on inline and floating objects, review the backstory on page 209.

Note: When you add a photo to a Pages document, Pages copies the picture—it becomes part of the document file. That means any changes that you might make to a picture in Pages don't affect the original picture from iPhoto or wherever it lives on your Mac. If you move that Pages document to another computer or email it to colleague, its images come along with it.

Choosing a file from your hard disk

The Media Browser is a quick and easy way to insert pictures in your document—but not the only way. Unless you specifically add desktop folders to the Media Browser, it displays only those pictures stored in iPhoto, Photo Booth, or Aperture.

If you don't use any of those programs, you can drag photos from other photo-organizing software—such as Lightroom or Photoshop's file browser—or directly from a Finder folder. Pages can handle a broad range of image formats, including JPEG, TIFF, GIF, PSD, PDF, PICT, EPS, and PDF.

You can also use Pages' menus to insert photos or other media. Choose Insert → Choose to call up a Finder-style dialog box giving you access to all the files on your computer, your iDisk, and on the network (if you're connected to one). Navigate to a picture, sound, or movie file and double-click it (or click once to select it, and then click Insert) to bring it into your document.

Tip: To include any folder from your hard drive in the Media Browser, click the tab where you'd like to display the folder (the Photos tab, for example), and drag the folder's icon from the Finder into the browser's top pane. These added folders are grouped under a Folders heading. To remove an added folder, click its name and press Delete (this doesn't delete the folder on your hard drive, it only removes it from the Media Browser.) To remove all folders at once, Control-click Folders and choose Remove Folders.

Cropping images with masks

When you add a picture to your document, Pages gives you the whole image to work with. But you don't always want the entire photo. You might need to trim the image to make it fit the document layout, or to excise a horrible ex-boyfriend. This is something that you could certainly do in a photo-editing program before adding it to Pages, but consider this common layout problem: You prepare a picture for your brochure, cropping it to just the right size before adding it to the layout. Later, when making the final adjustments to your design, you decide the picture needs to be a quarter inch taller and half an inch narrower. So you delete the picture, go back to your photo-editing program, open the original image again, recrop it, save the new cropped version, and reinsert it into your layout. Or, even worse, you go back to open the original picture and discover you saved only the cropped version. (This heartbreaking scenario can't happen if you use iPhoto, which always saves your original. Choose Photos → Revert to Original to get it back.)

Pages prevents all this shuffling back and forth to your photo program for cropping purposes. Instead, it lets you *mask* your photos right in your layout, cropping them by selecting the portion of the picture to display while hiding the rest of the picture from view. Just like a mask hides *part* of the face of your favorite superhero but lets the eyes peek through, a mask in iWork hides just part of the image with a hole punched through to reveal the portion to display in your final design. This hole is the *masking shape,* and you can adjust its size and position on the image.

Note: This book plays it a little fast and loose by using the word *crop* interchangeably with *mask*. Image impresarios will know, however, that cropping and masking are technically very different things. Cropping an image permanently removes a portion of an image, while masking merely hides it. Masking, in other words, creates the illusion of cropping without actually changing the original image–and that's how all iWork programs work. When this book refers to cropping an image, it's meant in the sense generally understood by regular folks–"show me only part of the image"–not the technical meaning of permanently removing a portion of the image, something iWork doesn't do.

The original picture always remains untouched when you add a mask—the only thing that changes is what portion shows through the masking shape. If you ever want to get the original image back, simply *unmask* the photo to reveal the entire image.

Here's how to crop an image with a mask:

1. **Insert a picture into your document.**

2. **Select the image and click the Mask button in the Format Bar, or choose Format → Mask.**

   Pages gives you a masking shape—a rectangle inside your selected picture—and displays a window with mask controls just below the image.

3. **Adjust the size of the masking shape with the selection handles to select which part of the image will peek through the mask.**

   As you adjust the size, Pages shows the dimensions of the mask (Figure 7-12). Press Shift as you drag to constrain the masks proportions. Rotate the mask by pressing ⌘ as you drag a selection handle.

4. **Drag the masking shape by its border to shift its position on your picture; or move the cursor over any other part of the picture and it turns into a hand that you can use to drag the picture under the mask.**

   When you drag the picture under the mask, this selects the picture instead of the mask window, and the selection handles appear around the image border. You can use these handles to resize the picture independent of the image mask—or resize the image by using the slider in the mask control. To return to editing the mask window, click the mask window's border (the cursor turns into a pointer when you point to the border).

5. **When you're happy with your cropping efforts, you can apply the mask in one of three ways: Press Return; click anywhere outside of the image; or click the Edit Mask button in the mask control.**

6. **If you need to recrop the picture, click the image once to select it, and the mask controls appear—click the Edit Mask button.**

   Just like in steps 3–5, click inside the image to change the image position or size under the mask, or click the mask window's border to move or resize the mask window. Resize, reposition, or rotate the mask, and then press Return to apply the mask to the picture again.

Figure 7-12:
Instead of cropping pictures before you import them into Pages, use a mask. Add the picture to your document and then click the Format Bar's Mask button (circled), or choose Format → Mask. Adjust the size of the mask to crop the picture (top); just like when you move or resize an object, alignment guides appear to show you when your mask lines up with other objects. Resize the image below the masking shape with the slider in the mask control that appears below the image you're masking.

Finish by pressing Return to hide the masked, or hidden, part of the picture (bottom). If you need to recrop the image, double-click the picture and readjust the mask.

7. If you need to completely unmask the picture, select it and choose Format → Unmask, or click the Mask button in the Format Bar. Pages displays the picture in its full glory once again.

Tip: You can make a mask larger than the picture to add white space around it. Using this method, you can create asymmetrical white space around a picture—something you can't achieve using the Extra Space control in the Wrap Inspector.

A masked picture effectively has two editing modes—one for adjusting the overall image, and one for adjusting the size and position of the mask:

- **Moving or resizing a masked image** works just like editing a regular image: Click it once to select it and then drag it to a new location or drag its selection handles to resize the image. When you resize it, the masking shape maintains its same shape, and the same portion of the image is shown, only at its new size.

- **Editing the mask size and position** works just like in step 6 above: Click the image once to reveal the mask controls.

Morphing pictures into new shapes with masks

Photos are rectangular. Sure, you can rotate them, or you can crop them with masks to change their proportions. But since the standard Pages mask are rectangular, too, you're still stuck with a four-cornered picture. If all this feels a little square, Pages lets you break the mold and reshape pictures into a variety of forms. The difference can be subtle, like adding *rounded corners* to an image, or you can make bold transformations like shaping your picture into a circle, star, quote bubble, or any shape you might imagine, as shown in Figure 7-13.

Figure 7-13:
Mask a picture with a shape to give your images a range of forms. Here, the same image has been masked with a rounded rectangle, an oval, a double arrow, a star, and a quote bubble. Mask a picture with the shape of your choice by selecting the image and choosing Format → "Mask with Shape".

It turns out this is just fancy cropping. Instead of using the standard rectangular masking shape, however, you apply a mask with a custom shape. Here's how:

1. **Insert a picture into your document.**

2. **Select the picture, and select a shape from the Format → "Mask with Shape" submenu.**

   To add rounded corners, for example, choose Rounded Rectangle, and to add a circle, choose Oval (this option does in fact add a circle, but you can then squish the shape of the mask into an oval). Whatever shape you choose, Pages displays the masking shape on your image, with the same familiar selection handles and mask controls that you saw with the standard rectangular mask.

3. **Drag, resize, rotate, and adjust the masking shape just as you would with the standard rectangle.**

4. **When you're done, click outside the image, and the image shows off its shapely new form.**

When you apply a mask with the Format → "Mask with Shape" submenu, you take the shape as is. When you choose Star, for example, Pages always gives you a five-pointed star, and Polygon always buys you a pentagon. What if you want more points in your star, more sides to your polygon, or a different shape entirely? You can use any shape you like by first creating a shape with Pages' shape tools (see page 241). After you've created the shape, position it on top of the picture as you'd like it to mask the image. Select both the shape and the picture by Shift-clicking or ⌘-clicking each of them, then choose Format → "Mask with Selected Shape", and Pages applies the mask, cropping the image into the form of the shape object. (If the shape contains any text, the text is deleted.) Or even easier: Add a shape to your document and drop a picture from the Media Browser on top of it. Numbers smooshes the two together as a shape-masked image object.

Note: To apply a shape as a mask, the mask and picture must have the same layout style: Both must be floating objects, or both must be inline objects in the same text.

When you choose Format → Unmask to unmask a picture masked with a shape, Pages reverts the image to its original form as usual, but also adds the masking shape to your document as a regular shape, which you can move, edit, and change as a normal object in the page. This is convenient, for example, if you want to edit the shape of your mask or make other customizations. You can unmask the image, edit the shape by adding points and curves, for instance, and then reapply the mask via Format → "Mask with Selected Shape".

Removing the background with "instant alpha"

Pages knows a nifty disappearing trick for your pictures which makes portions of them invisible. For example, you can remove the background of an image, or cut out the sky from a photo to draw more attention to the foreground and make text wrap around the pictured shape. Specifically, Pages makes certain colors in your picture see-through, approximating a process that graphics geeks call *alpha-channel transparency*. For a phrase about making images transparent, "alpha-channel transparency" is decidedly opaque, but Apple nevertheless embraced this technical lingo when it named this iWork feature *instant alpha*.

To give it a spin, select an image and choose Format → Instant Alpha. The cursor turns into a crosshair—click and drag the cursor in the area you want to remove, as shown in Figure 7-14. As you drag, Pages highlights the region that will be removed from the image, covering the affected portion in a purple fog. The farther you drag, the more image you select. Pages figures out which areas to select by choosing similar colors that touch the region that you're clicking. When you lift the mouse button, Pages dims the area to be removed. You can continue selecting additional areas by clicking and dragging there, too. When you're done, press Return or click outside the image. If you're not happy with the result, you can get the original image back by selecting the picture and choosing Format → Remove Instant Alpha.

Using instant alpha takes a bit of practice, and it works best in areas with solid colors and clear boundaries—clear blue skies or photos taken against a solid background. Pages has less success with complex patterns, so you'll likely run into some frustration cutting out busy backgrounds, for example. Often you can eventually get the effect you're looking for by keeping at it, working through the area you want to remove bit by bit.

Tip: Speaking of clear boundaries, normally instant alpha detects where your background color meets an edge and stops there, working its magic only on the field of color that touches your selection. If you hold down the Option key while you drag, you can select all occurrences of the chosen color anywhere in your image at once, even if they're not adjacent to the selection.

The Adjust Image window

Pages is hardly a full-fledged image editor—it's no Photoshop—but it does give you a selection of simple sliders that let you adjust picture appearance and quality. For simple tweaks, though, these settings can save you a roundtrip to a more sophisticated image editing program when you want to make a picture look just so. Pages houses these settings in the *Adjust Image window*.

To summon this control panel, select the picture to edit, and click the Adjust Image Window button in the format bar, or choose View → Show Adjust Image. Pages reveals a dark-tinted transparent window with a series of sliders, the Adjust Image window, shown in Figure 7-15.

The Adjust Image window gives you control over these features of your picture:

- **Brightness** makes the image lighter or darker.

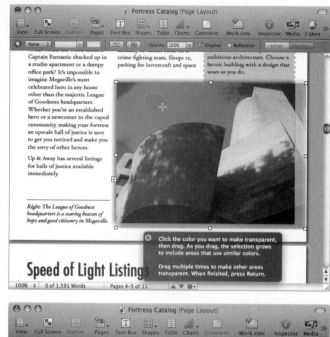

Figure 7-14:
Instant alpha gives the iWork programs their own green-screen special effects, letting you make certain colors and regions of a picture transparent. Select the image, choose Format → Instant Alpha, and drag the cursor in the area you want to hide (top). Press Return, and Pages makes the selected region invisible, letting the background shine through. You can also make the surrounding text flow through the parts of the image you removed and hug the contours of your image, as shown at the bottom. For details about this text-wrapping maneuver, see page 254.

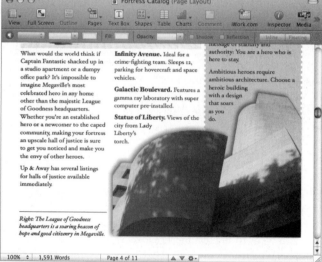

- **Contrast** controls the difference of the light and dark tones in the picture. Boosting contrast makes darks darker and lights lighter, which makes colors pop and tends to sharpen the edges of objects. Turning the contrast way up gives pictures a graphic, almost cartoony, effect that washes away subtle details. Turning it way down tends to make the image murky.

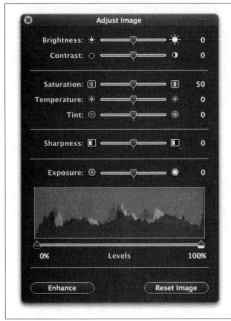

Figure 7-15:
The Adjust Image window lets you change the brightness, contrast, and a variety of color settings for a picture. Select an image, click the Adjust Image Window button, and nudge the knobs to your heart's content. Or let Pages do the fine-tuning for you automatically: Click the Enhance button in the lower-left corner, and Pages chooses levels for you. If your changes get away from you, and you want to bring back your original image, click the Reset Image button in the lower right.

- **Saturation** makes colors more or less intense.

- **Temperature** controls the amount of orange vs. blue tones in the picture, making the image seem "warmer" when you turn it up and "cooler" when you turn it down.

- **Tint** controls the amount of red vs. green tones in the picture.

- **Sharpness** makes the image more blurred or more sharp. Turning sharpness way down gives an image a Vaseline-on-the-lens softness.

- **Exposure** adjusts the picture's shadows and highlights.

- **Levels** changes the levels of light and dark tones. Just above the levels slider, the *histogram* charts the relative levels of shadows and highlights in the red, blue, and green tones of your image. The left side of the histogram shows the levels of the darker tones, and the right shows the lighter. As you adjust any of the picture settings, the histogram updates to reflect the changes, showing how much color information is in each range from darkest to lightest. The double slider of the levels setting lets you chop off the darkest and lightest tones in the image: Drag the left slider to eliminate darker tones, and drag the right slider to eliminate lighter tones. The result is a narrower range of color in your picture, which can sharpen highlights and shadows.

After making your changes, if you decide that the picture looked better before you started mucking around with it, click Reset Image to return to the original image.

Totally confused? If tinkering with image attributes isn't your idea of fun, you can just hand the whole thing over to Pages. Click the Enhance button, and Pages sets all the levels automatically, choosing settings that it thinks will show the picture to best effect. If you're using a completely undoctored photo—straight from your digital camera, for example—using the Enhance button is a quick and easy way to clean up your photo and give it some extra pop.

Frame it

Pages gives you several *"picture frames"* that you can use with your images to dress them up or give them a *trompe l'oeil* 3D effect, like an actual paper photograph on the page. These frames are a special category of *stroke,* a border that you can apply to objects in your document (see page 271). They're not limited to images—you can add a picture frame to any object except tables and charts. You browse and apply these frames directly from the Format Bar's Stroke pop-up menu, or you can use the Graphic Inspector:

1. **Select the picture.**

2. **Click the Inspector button in the toolbar, or choose View → Show Inspector. Click the Graphic button, the fifth from left, to open the Graphic Inspector.**

3. **Select Picture Frame from the Stroke pop-up menu.**

   Pages applies one of several available picture frames to the picture, and the Graphic Inspector shows a pop-up menu that lets you select different frame styles, as shown in Figure 7-16.

4. **Adjust the display setting(s) of your selected frame style.**

   Each frame style has one or more settings to adjust its size, scale, and/or color. The Size and Scale settings change the width of the picture frame, and color affects the color of the border where applicable.

If you change your mind, you can remove the picture frame by selecting the object and choosing None from the Stroke pop-up menu in the Graphic Inspector or the Format Bar.

Tip: Many of the picture frames are designed to make your picture look like a paper photograph. You can enhance this effect by adding a shadow (for picture frames that don't already have one) and setting the picture slightly askew, like a photo fixed to the page by human hands. Subtlety is a good goal here—just a slight angle and a light shadow give the best result. To rotate the picture (page 255), ⌘-click one of its selection handles and drag it. To add a shadow (page 273), turn on the Shadow checkbox in the Format Bar or the Graphic Inspector.

Reducing image file sizes

Don't skimp on great imagery. Pictures give your graphic design visual impact and draw readers into your work. But they do come at a cost, at least as far as your hard drive or Internet connection is concerned. As you pile high-resolution images into

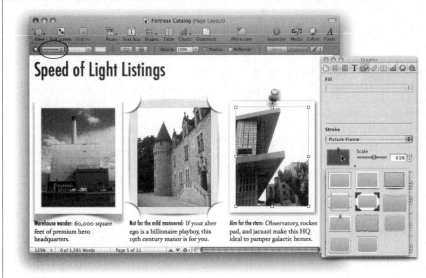

Figure 7-16:
These photos sport three different picture-frame styles. To add a frame, select the object, and choose Picture Frame from the Stroke pop-up menu in the Graphic Inspector. Pages offers a pop-up menu with several choices of frame styles, shown here. You can also choose any of these frames directly from the Format Bar's Stroke pop-up menu (circled). Make your choice, and Pages does the frame job. To remove a frame, select the object, and choose None from the Stroke pop-up menu or from the Format Bar's Stroke pop-up.

your Pages document, the file size inevitably grows—sometimes enormously. That's not necessarily a big deal if the document is going no farther than your own computer and printer, but if you plan to share the document by email or online (see Chapter 9), image-heavy documents become bandwidth busters. When your document gets too big to sling around online, Pages offers an option to trim the flab.

When you add a picture to your document, Pages normally holds a copy of the entire original image inside your document—at full size and full resolution. That can mean several megabytes per image. But are you really using every last one of those precious bits and bytes? Chances are, you've reduced the size of most of your pictures or masked them to crop out parts of the original. If you're happy with your image work, and don't need to go back to the original, you can tell Pages to throw out the clipped portions of your pictures. Pages keeps a smaller version of the picture, reducing your file's waistline along the way.

You can do this for individual images or all images in the document. To reduce the file size of a single picture, select the image and choose Format → Image → Reduce Image File Size (this command is grayed out when Pages can't reduce the file size further). To reduce the file size for all images, choose File → Reduce File Size. Either way, Pages asks if you really want to do it and provides a file-size savings estimate (Figure 7-17). If the file size of the image(s) can't be further reduced, Pages lets you know that the file is already at fighting weight.

Note: The document-wide Reduce File Size option also compresses audio and video in your document. For details, see page 248.

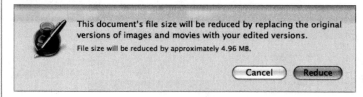

This document's file size will be reduced by replacing the original versions of images and movies with your edited versions.

File size will be reduced by approximately 4.96 MB.

Cancel   Reduce

Figure 7-17:
Tell Pages to reduce file sizes for an individual image (Format → Image → Reduce Image File Size) or for all images, movies, and sounds (File → Reduce File Size). Pages asks you to confirm the action and lets you know how much space you'll save. Click Reduce to continue.

Pages optimizes pictures for their current presentation in your document, but there's a downside to this. Your file no longer contains the original images, which means that cropped elements are gone for good, and trying to make the picture larger may give you grainy or blurry results. To avoid unpleasant surprises when you want to make changes, it's a good idea to save your file-reduction efforts until you've completed your design, or at least the current draft. If you do need to go back to the original, you've always got a fallback, though: The *real* original image remains untouched on your hard drive or iPhoto collection; you can simply go back and add the picture to the document again.

Also, keep in mind that this technique slims down the overall *resolution* of images too, optimizing them for onscreen display but reducing their printed quality. If you're looking for a gorgeous print, don't use this feature—or at least save a separate copy for printing.

Note: Some types of image files as well as images used in image fills (see page 269) may refuse to compress. Choose View → Show Document Warnings for details about any images that Pages could not shrink.

Including or excluding template images

Most of Pages' templates contain image-filled designs to help you create eye-popping documents. To save room, Pages normally doesn't package these template pictures inside the document file. For Apple-provided templates, that makes good sense—the template and its images are part of Pages, so they're already available on any Mac with iWork installed. When you send your Pages file to others, their Macs know where to find their own versions of these images.

This doesn't work so well, however, if you're using your own custom template (see Chapter 10). In that case, those template images won't be available on your friends' computers—unless they've installed those same templates, too—and some pictures will go missing when they open your document. That's when you need to tell Pages to copy template images into the document. You can do this only when you first save the document (or when you choose File → Save As to save it under a new name): At the bottom of the Save dialog box, click the Advanced Options flippy triangle, and turn on the "Copy template images into document" option (this option is grayed out if there are no template images).

Adding Shapes

Pages supplies a collection of lines, arrows, and geometric shapes that you can add to your document as objects. You can use shapes as graphic elements, to add fields of color behind portions of your page, or as containers for text. Figure 7-18 includes a pair of examples.

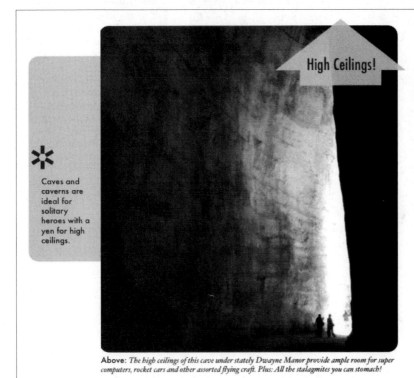

Caves and caverns are ideal for solitary heroes with a yen for high ceilings.

High Ceilings!

Figure 7-18:
In this layout from the Up & Away fortress catalog, a rounded rectangle shape peeks out from behind the image at left, providing a background container for the image caption. At the top right, an arrow shape draws attention to the cavern's high ceilings.

Above: *The high ceilings of this cave under stately Dwayne Manor provide ample room for super computers, rocket cars and other assorted flying craft. Plus: All the stalagmites you can stomach!*

To add a shape, click the Shapes pop-up button in the toolbar, and select an item from the menu, as shown in Figure 7-19. Pages plunks your new shape into the middle of the page as a floating object. Drag the shape to position it, and drag its selection handles to resize it, if you like. (If you prefer an inline object, place your insertion point where you want to add the shape, and select the shape to use from the Insert → Shape submenu.)

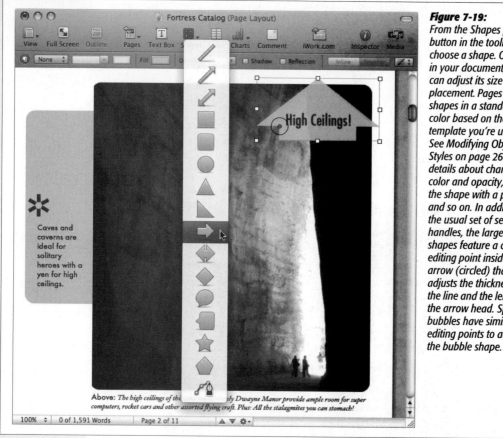

Figure 7-19:
From the Shapes pop-up button in the toolbar, choose a shape. Once it's in your document, you can adjust its size and placement. Pages creates shapes in a standard color based on the template you're using. See Modifying Object Styles on page 264 for details about changing color and opacity, filling the shape with a picture, and so on. In addition to the usual set of selection handles, the large arrow shapes feature a circular editing point inside the arrow (circled) that adjusts the thickness of the line and the length of the arrow head. Speech bubbles have similar editing points to adjust the bubble shape.

Tip: You can draw a shape directly in your document as a floating object. Hold down the Option key, click the Shapes button in the toolbar, select your shape from the pop-up menu, and then pick a shape from the submenu. Let go of the Option key. Your cursor changes to a crosshair shape. Drag starting at one corner of the object. Pages draws the shape and displays the shape's width and height measurements as you drag.

Hold the Shift key as you resize a shape to maintain its current proportions—this is especially helpful when you want to keep the shape as a perfect circle (for oval shapes), a square (for rectangle shapes), or an equilateral triangle. Hold the Option key as you drag to keep the shape centered on its current position. Hold both keys as you drag to *both* center and keep its same proportions.

Pages inserts the shape by using the default style of the template you're using. To change the color and border of the shape, select the shape and choose a style and color for the fill (page 265) or stroke (page 271) in the Graphic Inspector or in the pop-up menus in the Format Bar.

Tip: If you don't care for the template's standard shape color or border, you can change those settings: Style a shape the way you want it and then select the shape and choose Format → Advanced → Define Default Shape Style. Going forward, Pages uses your new shape style for any new shapes in this document. If you want to use this style for other new documents, you have to make a template document with your new shape style. See Chapter 10 (page 345) for details on how to create a template.

The line shapes

The first three shapes are variations on that paragon of straight-and-narrow: the line. You can choose a plain line, an arrow, or a double-headed arrow. After you insert a line in your document, it sports one selection handle at each end. Drag one of the handles to change the line's length or angle. Hold the Shift key while you drag to constrain the angle to exactly 45-degree increments.

Use the Stroke pop-up menus in the Format Bar or Graphic Inspector to adjust the line's thickness, color, and stroke (solid, dashed, dotted, or a variety of brush strokes). Use the Endpoints pop-up menus to choose various arrow and endpoint styles for the line, as shown in Figure 7-20. (The arrow and double arrow shapes in the menu are merely lines with preconfigured endpoints.)

Tip: Pages also offers another kind of line, a connection line, specially designed to connect two objects on the page. For more on connection lines, see page 257.

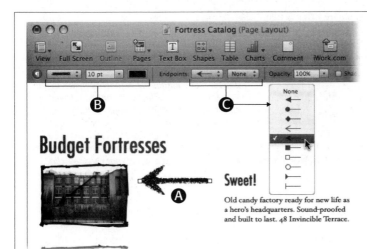

Figure 7-20:
Line shapes (A) have just two selection handles, which let you position its two end points. The style, size, and shape of the line is set in the stroke pop-up buttons in the Format Bar (B) or Graphic Inspector. The line shown here has an arrow as its left endpoint and nothing for its right endpoint. Select the shape of the endpoints from the Endpoints pop-up menus in the Format Bar (C) or Graphic Inspector. For a simple line, set the endpoints to None.

The geometric shapes

Basic geometric shapes are next in the Shapes lineup. Choose from a rectangle, rounded rectangle, oval (or circle), triangle, right triangle, or diamond. Pages inserts these shapes in their most regular forms: squares, circle, equilateral triangle, right isosceles triangle, and square diamond. Hold the Shift key while you drag a selection handle to preserve these proportions while you resize.

Tip: To change the curvy corners of rounded rectangles, select the shape and drag its circular control handle left or right to straighten or round the corners.

The arrow shapes

Pages provides two big fat arrow shapes—single or double-headed. Instead of being lines with arrow heads, like those produced by the line tool, these are shapes that can have an outline stroke and a color, gradient, or image fill just like the other geometric shapes. You can adjust the size of the arrow head and the width of the line by using the round *editing point* inside the arrow head, shown earlier in Figure 7-19.

The speech bubbles

Pages gives you two familiar comic-style speech bubbles—an oval with a point tumbling out of it, and the same thing with a rounded rectangle. Like the arrow shapes, the speech-bubble shapes give you extra, circular editing points to adjust its shape. This time, you get three editing points, which respectively control the length of the point, the width of the point, and the shape of the bubble.

Stars and polygons

If the regular geometric shapes seem too confining, Pages gives you options to add as many sides as you like to your shapes, with the polygon and star options. Stars let you vary the number and depth of their points, and polygons let you change the number of sides, as shown in Figure 7-21.

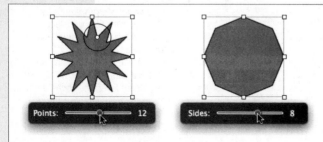

Figure 7-21:
When you select a star shape (left), Pages displays a slider that changes the number of points in the star, from 3 to 20. (The circle-shaped selection object lets you change the depth of the points to change the shape of the star.) Selecting a polygon shape (right) calls up a slider that changes the number of sides in the polygon, between 3 and 11. When you're done making your changes, click outside the shape.

Drawing custom shapes

All the built-in shapes are familiar, uniform silhouettes. If you're after something a bit more unusual, you can forego the predrawn selection and instead draw your own shape. To do it, you plot out your shape point by point, and Pages follows along, playing "Connect the Dots."

1. Click the Shapes button in the toolbar, and choose the Draw tool at the very bottom of the pop-up menu.

   The pointer turns into a pen shape. (You can also choose Insert → Shape → Draw with Pen.)

---

2. **Click anywhere in your document to create the first point.**

3. **Continue by clicking the second point, then the third point, and so on.**

   Pages draws a line from point to point, as shown in Figure 7-22. To create a curved point instead of a hard corner, click and drag the mouse to adjust the shape and angle of the curve. To delete a point you've just created, press Delete; pressing Delete again removes the previous point, and so on. If you don't get the shape exactly right the first time through, it's OK—you can go back and edit it later.

4. **Complete the shape by clicking the first point.**

   Until you complete a closed shape, Pages considers your creation to be a line. You can leave it as a line—keeping your rendering "open" so that there's no line between the first and last points—and even add endpoints. To stop drawing without completing the shape, press Escape (Esc), and Pages pulls you out of drawing mode, leaving your line as is.

Normally, when you add a shape, Pages fills it in for you with the document's standard shape color. It doesn't do that with custom shapes, however, instead setting the fill color to transparent so that background objects show through. To add a fill, choose from the Fill pop-up menu in the Format Bar, or make your selection in the Graphic Inspector.

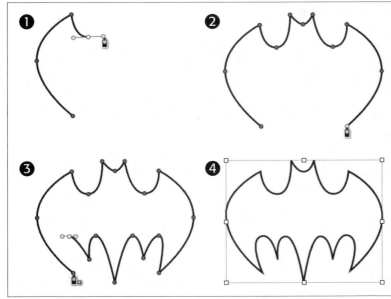

Figure 7-22:
Draw a custom shape point by point with the pen-shaped cursor. (1) To add a curved segment click and drag the pen, and two handles appear like wings on the point; drag them to adjust the shape and angle of the curve. (2) Continue drawing the points of the shape, and Pages connects the dots as you go. (3) When you're done, click the first point in the shape. (4) Pages pulls you out of drawing mode and selects the shape, showing the usual selection handles. To go back and edit the shape and its points, click the shape twice slowly.

Editing shapes point by point

Whether it's your own shape or a predrawn shape, you can nudge and cajole a shape object into a new form by adding, deleting, or reshaping its points. Before you can edit a shape, you have to tell Pages that you want permission to do so.

Select the shape and then choose Format → Shape → Make Editable. For custom shapes you've drawn yourself or predrawn shapes that you've previously edited, you can also click once in the shape to select it, then wait a beat before clicking a second time to show its points. (Double-clicking quickly instead puts the text-editing insertion point inside the shape, as you'll learn in a moment.)

When a shape is editable, red dots appear on the shape, marking its adjustment points. Drag the points to change its shape; you can move several points at once by Shift-clicking multiple points to select them before dragging. A selected point is white in the middle, while unselected points are solid red.

To add a new point, press the Option key and, when you point to the shape's border, the cursor turns into a pen shape with a little + sign; click to add a point in the border. To delete a point, click to select it, then press Delete.

Points can be corners or curves. When a curve is attached to a point, as is the case for several of the points in Figure 7-22, the line segments on either side curve through it. You can convert a corner point into a curved point and vice versa by double-clicking the point. To adjust a curved point, grab one of the control handles on either side of the point and drag it to adjust the length and angle of the curve. To adjust the length of both of the control handles together, press the Option key while you drag one of them—the other handle moves to mirror the change. To change the angle of one side of the point without changing the angle of the other side, hold down the ⌘ key while you drag the control handle.

When you're done editing the shape's points, deselect the shape or press Return.

Tip: To change all corner points in a shape into curved points, select the shape and choose Format → Shape → Smooth Path. To do the reverse and change all curved points into corner points, select the shape and choose Format → Shape → Sharpen Path. (In both cases you have to make the shape editable first by choosing choose Format → Shape → Make Editable.)

Text in shapes

Behind its mild-mannered facade, the humble shape has (nearly) all the powers of a text box. Add and format text in a shape just as you would a regular text box; you can even add the full array of inline objects to a shape. This makes shapes a playful alternative to text boxes for callouts and pull quotes—see page 225 for pointers on creating inline pull quotes.

To add text to a shape, double-click it and start typing. Enter your text, and format it as usual using the Styles Drawer, Format Bar, Text Inspector, or Fonts window. If you enter more text than will fit, a plus sign (+) clipping indicator appears at the bottom of the shape. To reveal the rest of the text, resize the shape by selecting it and dragging one of its selection handles. (Alas, unlike text boxes, you can't link text between shapes.)

Note: Just as you can't add an inline text box inside another text box, Pages doesn't let you have a text-bearing shape inside a text box either. You can still add inline shapes to a text box; you're just not allowed to put text inside them. As usual, floating objects give you more options here; the workaround is to add the shape as a floating object on top of the text box.

It's common to rotate or flip speech-bubble shapes and arrows to make them point at a specific location and better fit your layout (see page 255 for details about how to rotate objects). When you do this, though, the text makes the same transformation. When you flip a shape horizontally, for example, the text inside flips, too, as if you're reading in a mirror. Chances are, that's not what you wanted. After you've transformed the containing shape, you can tell Pages to reset the text back to its plain old horizontal, left-to-right orientation: Select the shape and choose Format → Shape → "Reset Text and Object Handles".

Adding Sound and Video

If you're just going to print out your documents, you don't need to add sounds and movies. But if you're designing documents for people to view onscreen, Pages helps you add features that let your viewers start and stop the playback of movies, narration, or music. For the best interactive environment, though, you're better off creating this kind of multimedia presentation in Keynote, which is better tuned for that kind of thing (see page 391). But hey, if you're still determined to put a video in your word-processor document, Pages lets you do it.

Adding sound or video works just like adding a picture. You can drag an audio or video clip from the Media Browser's Audio or Movies tab. When you drag a sound file into your document, it shows up as a loudspeaker icon. Double-click it to play; single-click to stop. Drag a movie into your page, and it looks like a still picture, showing the first frame of the movie. Here again, double-click to play; click to stop.

You can also drag sound or movie files directly from a folder into your document. Pages can work with any QuickTime or iTunes-supported file type, including MOV, MP3, MP4, AAC, AIFF, and others. Instead of dragging the file into your document, you can also select Insert → Choose, and Pages prompts you to select the file to add.

Tip: It's a good idea to choose Arrange → Lock when you're done editing a movie or sound, to prevent resizing or repositioning by your viewers as they click it to play or pause. This ban on changes includes you, too, though. To get back in there, choose Arrange → Unlock.

The QuickTime Inspector, shown in Figure 7-23, offers several options to control the playback of sound and movies in your document:

- **Start & Stop** sets where your clip begins and ends, letting you bracket a specific portion of the audio or video. Slide the left-side handle to the start time and the right-side handle to the end time.

- **Poster Frame** determines the image displayed for movies before you start playing them (and also when you print). Pages starts out using the very first frame of the movie, but you can change it to any other image in the movie by sliding the handle to the frame of your choice. This is useful if the first frame of your movie is black, or if another frame is more representative of the movie's subject. No matter which frame you select, when you double-click the movie in the document, Pages plays it from the beginning.

- **Repeat** tells Pages what to do with the audio or video when it reaches the end. Choose *None* to simply make the media stop playing; choose *Loop* to make it start again at the beginning; and choose *Loop Back and Forth* to make it start playing backwards when it hits the end, then forward when it hits the beginning, bouncing back and forth.

- **Volume** controls the volume level of playback.

- The **Controls** section gives you traditional playback controls to play, pause, fast-forward, rewind, or zip to the end. These are handy when the double-click-to-play and single-click-to-stop controls in the document itself aren't quite enough. (Alas, it's not possible to add these controls into the document itself; they're available only from the QuickTime Inspector.)

Figure 7-23:
The QuickTime Inspector controls the playback of audio and video in your document. Select the audio or video object, and click the Inspector button in the toolbar or choose View → Show Inspector. Click the very last button in the Inspector toolbar, the QuickTime button, to display the QuickTime Inspector.

Managing movie and sound file sizes

When you include music or movie files in a Pages document, the program normally doesn't include those files inside the actual document file. Instead, due to the large size of music or movie files, Pages *links* to those files on your hard disk.

If you need to be able to view the document on another computer, click the flippy triangle next to the Save field when you save the document. Turn on the checkbox labeled "Copy audio and movies into document" (this option is grayed out if you don't have any sound or video in the file). Turning on this checkbox ensures that all your media files are included in the Pages document—and it can also ensure that your Pages document file is going to be mighty big, possibly too big to email or even fit on a CD.

You can let a little air out of swelling multimedia files with the File → Reduce File Size command, described on page 239. When you do this, Pages removes any audio or video from before or after the start and stop points you set in the Quick-Time Inspector. After doing this, though, you can't get that clipped media back unless you add the original file again from scratch.

Working with Objects

As you've explored the ins and outs of adding pictures, text, shapes, audio, and video, you've no doubt noticed the similarities in how all these objects work. While the content of these object types may be very different, they share many of the same properties and behaviors as object-level building blocks that you stack, organize, and resize in your document. Whether an object contains a movie or a text passage, the methods you use to juggle it on the page, wrap text around it, poke it, and prod it are the same. This chapter has touched on many of those methods in passing, but now you'll dig into the details.

Selecting Objects

Select an object by clicking it once. The object's outline appears, fully loaded with selection handles—in objectland, this is the equivalent of standing at attention. The outline and selection handles also tell you whether the object is *floating* (eight open black squares), *inline* (three open black squares), a *group* (blue outline), *locked* on the page (eight gray X marks), or a *master object* (eight solid blue squares).

Here's the tricky bit: There's a difference between selecting the object—the box that contains the content—and the content itself. That means that most object types have two editing modes, one for editing its object-level characteristics (size, position, border, rotation, and so on) and another for editing the content within (text, image mask, table cells, and the like). When you've got an object selected at the content level, you can't change its properties at the object level: While you're editing the text inside a text box, for example, you can't change the text box's overall size or position. For newcomers, this can seem a bit frustrating: "I've got the text box selected, so why can't I move it?!"

The general rule is that you click an object once to select it at the object level and reveal its selection handles. Click it a second time to edit its content. Until you stop editing its content, you can't edit the overall object properties. Press ⌘-Return to exit content-editing mode for any object, and Pages instead selects it at the object level—the selection handles return. In other words, click to drill down into the content, and press ⌘-Return to come back out to the object level. Or you can simply click outside of the object to deselect it and then click it once to reselect it at the object level.

Tip: To select a shape that has no fill (for example, a transparent shape with only a border) you have to click its edge to select it.

To select several objects at once, hold down the Shift key as you click objects. In order to do this, all the objects must be floating, or all must be inline. You can also use Edit → Select All (⌘-A) to choose either all floating objects or all inline objects:

- To select *all floating objects* in the entire document, ⌘-click in the margin of the document to remove the insertion point. Press ⌘-A. Be careful here: You might expect this method to select objects only for the current page (especially when working with page-layout documents), but this selects every floating object in the entire document.

- To select *all the inline text and objects* in the body text or a text box, place the insertion point in the text area and press ⌘-A. The selection is limited only to text and objects in the text area where the insertion point is located.

In page-layout documents, you can also select several floating objects by dragging. Click the pointer outside of any objects and drag across the objects. When you release the mouse, Pages selects all the objects touched by your dragnet.

Moving Objects

As long as an object isn't locked (page 263) or fixed in the background (page 260), you can move it by clicking and dragging. You can drag floating objects anywhere in your document—or nudge them along one point at a time with your keyboard's arrow keys (bump them by ten points when you hold down the Shift key at the same time). Hold down the Shift key while you drag a floating object to limit its motion to a strictly vertical, horizontal, or 45-degree path.

Note: Under Pages' standard settings, a little yellow box pops up to show you the object's position in the document as you move it. You can change this by going to Pages → Preferences, clicking the General button, and then turning off the "Show size and position when moving objects" option.

Inline objects have a more limited range of motion. When you drag inline objects, you can only drop them into a line of text in the same text area. Watch the insertion point at the tip of your arrow cursor as you drag, and drop the object when your insertion point reaches the spot in the text where you want to move your object. If you want to move an inline object outside of its parent text, you have to convert it into a floating object first. Head back to page 214 for details.

If you're using alignment guides—and for careful page-layout work, you should—you may occasionally find that you want to position an object very close to, but not exactly on, a guideline. In this case, Pages' guideline magnetism thwarts your positioning efforts, snapping the object to the guideline against your wishes. Temporarily turn off this feature by pressing ⌘ while you drag, and you can position the object as you wish. For more about alignment guides, see page 203.

Hold down the Option key while you drag an object to make a copy instead of moving the original—the duplicate springs right out of the original, and you can drop it wherever you like in the document. You can also copy an object by selecting it and choosing Edit → Duplicate. If you have to move an object very far—to another page or to the other end of your document—select the object and choose Edit → Cut. Scroll to the point in your document where you want to insert the object, and then do one of two things: To insert it as an inline object, place the insertion point within the text and choose Edit → Paste. To insert it as a floating object, ⌘-click the margin of the document so that the insertion point disappears, choose Edit → Paste, and then drag the object into its final position. For more on copying objects (or just their styles), see page 275.

Resizing Objects

When you hover the pointer over one of an object's black-bordered selection handles, the cursor changes into a double-headed arrow, which means you can resize the object by dragging that handle. If the object is a picture or a movie, Pages locks its proportions to prevent you from stretching or squashing it while you resize. You're free to alter the proportions of other objects—like shapes and tables—while you drag their selection handles. To force Pages to preserve their proportions, hold down the Shift key while you resize. To resize the object so that the center of the object stays put, press the Option key as you drag.

If you *do* want to stretch a picture, open the Metrics Inspector and turn off the checkbox for "Constrain proportions", as shown in Figure 7-24. You can always click the Original Size button to easily return to square one if you don't care for the circus-mirror look you've created for your picture or movie.

Tip: If you're using a recent laptop with a multitouch trackpad, you can also resize an object by "pinching" it. Select the object so that its selection handles are visible, and pinch your thumb and forefinger together on the trackpad to shrink the object; open them to make the object larger.

The Metrics Inspector gives you detailed control over objects' measurements. If you want to give Pages the precise dimensions of an object instead of eyeballing it by dragging its selection handles, you can enter measurements in the Width and Height fields. This is handy, for example, when you need to match the dimensions of two or more pictures. Select two or more objects and enter width and/or height measurements. Presto: All your selected objects are now the same size. If "Constrain proportions" is turned on, you can control only one of the dimensions at a time; turn off that checkbox in order to enter both.

You can also use the Metrics Inspector to set an object's position on the page via the X and Y Position fields. X is the distance from the left edge of the object to the left edge of the page; Y is the distance from the top of the object to the top of the page (Figure 7-24).

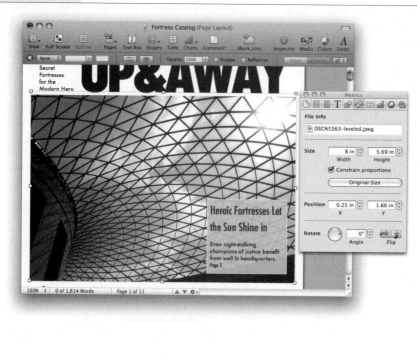

Figure 7-24:
*Measurement-oriented
object adjustments find a
home in the Metrics
Inspector. You can enter
size, position, and angle
measurements directly in
the inspector, or consult
it for information about
objects in your
document. Create mirror-
image objects with the
Flip buttons, return
pictures or movies to
their original size, and
turn on or off "Constrain
proportions"—which locks
an object's proportions
so you can't squeeze or
stretch it.*

*The File Info field
displays a picture, movie,
or sound's filename—
here, the filename of the
selected image. It also
provides a quick way to
copy these media files
out of a Pages document:
Just drag the file icon
from the File Info field
onto the desktop or into
a folder.*

When you're working with lines as floating objects, Pages changes the Metrics
Inspector's window to display the starting and ending coordinates of the line, letting you position a line by setting its X and Y coordinates. Pages assigns the Start
coordinates to the upper-left end point of the line when it first appears in the document, and the End coordinates to the lower-right end point. These coordinates
always apply to the same end of the line—even if you later rotate or flip it.

Wrapping Text Around Objects

When you use objects—whether inline or floating—on a page containing text, you
decide whether and how that text is going to flow, or *wrap,* around the object. Think
of your object as a stone lodged in the middle of your stream of words: As your text
flows past the object, how does it get around? Does the text flow to the right of the
object? To the left? Both? As your words pass by, do they hug the object's contours to
outline its shape? Or maybe the text doesn't flow around the object at all, instead
hopping over it to continue on the other side—or running directly below so that the
text is hidden by the object above. If you're not exactly sure how all this might look,
Figure 7-26 shows examples of several wrapping styles.

Pages gives you fine-tuned control over how text flows around any individual object by letting you choose text-wrapping settings for that object. You'll find these options in the Format Bar and the Wrap Inspector, as shown in Figure 7-25.

Figure 7-25:
To control the way text floats around an object, select the object and choose a wrap style from the Format Bar's Wrap pop-up button (A), or turn on the "Object causes wrap" option in the Wrap Inspector (B) and click the button for your desired wrap style.

Here, the floating circle shape is set to have text wrap around it on all sides, and its Text Fit setting is set to make text hug its shape, wrapping along its curve.

Wrapping works differently for inline vs. floating objects—even when you have wrapping turned off. Text wraps around a floating object only when the object is on top of the text in the layer stack; otherwise, the text just runs right over it (see page 260 for more about layering floating objects). In word-processing documents, a floating object is *always* on top of the body text, so the main text always wraps around it, unless you send the object to the background (see page 260) or turn wrapping off for the object. When wrapping is turned off, the object just sits on top of the text below, covering up the words that blithely run along underneath.

For an inline object, meanwhile, disabling its text wrapping makes the object sit in the text like an oversized word; text runs up to the object's edge and then continues along afterward on the same line. Inline wrapping styles differ from their floating-object cousins, but in many cases they can still produce wrapping results that are visually identical. Their vital distinction, of course, is that the object is tied to the text at the anchor point indicator and stays linked to that text, no matter how much you edit the text around it.

To turn on text wrapping, select the object, and choose a wrapping option from the Wrap pop-up menu in the Format Bar. You can also turn wrapping on with the Wrap Inspector: Click the Inspector button in the toolbar or choose View → Show Inspector and then click the Wrap button, the third from the left, to open the Wrap Inspector. Turn on the "Object causes wrap" option and click one of the wrap icons picturing the wrap style you want to use. Figure 7-26 shows a comparison of several wrapping styles.

Note: If your text won't wrap around a floating object no matter what settings you apply to it, try selecting the object and choosing Arrange → Bring to Front. Text wraps around floating objects only when the floating object is on top of the text in the layer stack. For more about layers, see page 260.

Use the controls at the bottom of the Wrap Inspector to set how tightly text wraps around an object. Use the up and down arrow buttons or enter a number in the Extra Space field to set the margin Pages creates between the object and the surrounding text.

On the Defensive: Escape Pods, Quick Getaways

The 60,000-square-foot structure on **Wharf Road** looks like a simple factory, or perhaps a warehouse. In fact, of course, this unassuming building is a state-of-the-art secret headquarters, and the towering "smokestack" is actually a launch tube for an escape pod, the latest must-have for the safety-conscious hero.

Defense is suddenly in vogue among the community's champions, and the

latest properties on the fortress market reflect this new emphasis, with getaway tunnels, invisibility fields, and interdimensional escape hatches among the features becoming standard in a new generation of secret headquarters.

"I think it's just recognition that even supers can't live forever," said Captain Fantastic, who recently invested in an emergency teleporter for his headquarters at the League of Goodness. "Protecting yourself doesn't mean that you lack pluck or derring-do. I call it good sense in a dangerous time."

A number of hero properties have upgraded their defenses to

take advantage of the new market trend. The domed fortress on **Stalwart Avenue,** available for sale through Up & Away, was recently retrofitted with laser-proofing and force fields (see the related story on page 3). And the recently abandoned **South Street** lair of The Buster has been outfitted with genetic recognition software and other devices to screen visitors.

The best offense is a good defense.

Figure 7-26:
You can determine exactly how text wraps around objects—or have your text ignore the objects completely and plow right over them—using the Wrap Inspector.

Here, the background asterisk image is below the text, so it causes no wrapping, and the text moves across unperturbed. The picture at the top left is set to allow text to wrap to the right, while text wraps to the left of the picture at bottom right, which also has the Text Fit setting turned on to allow text to hug the contours of the image. The pull quote is set to have text wrap on all sides, so its column-splitting position makes text flow around it on both the left and right.

The Text Fit buttons and the Alpha field apply to objects with non-rectangular shapes: rotated objects, shape objects, pictures masked with a shape, and images with transparent portions. When you click the right Text Fit button, the text hugs the contours of the shape, ignoring the transparent portion of the object and wrapping only when it runs into a visible region.

As you learned in the discussion of Pages' instant alpha tool on page 234, images can contain transparent regions called an *alpha channel*. The right-button option for Text Fit tells surrounding text to ignore the image's transparent regions and flow right through them. You can add this transparency in Pages by using the instant alpha tool, or you can do it in a separate image-editing program. (If you do it with an external image editor, the exact procedures for adding transparency vary according to program, and only some image formats like PNG, PSD, and PDF can include alpha channels.) If an image includes areas of partial transparency, the setting in the Alpha box chooses how transparent the region has to be in order to allow text to flow through.

Note: When you've added transparency, using Pages' instant alpha tool, text does wrap to the image's contours as described earlier, but it's a little bit buggy. Sometimes it doesn't work unless you set the Extra Space field to zero. If you're having trouble fitting text to the contours of your instant-alpha'd image, try zeroing out the Extra Space setting.

Rotating and Flipping Objects

Objects are normally upstanding citizens. When you add an object, Pages props it upright, its containing box aligned vertically and horizontally with the paper's edge. When all of this begins to feel a bit too conventional, you can tip objects askew by *rotating* them. Nudge an image ever so slightly, for example, to give it a jaunty, dynamic feel. Or you might spin a headline 90 degrees to run up the side of the page, flip an arrow shape to face the other way, or display the upside-down answer key to your newsletter's guess-their-secret-identity quiz.

To wrest your objects from the horizontal straight and narrow, press ⌘ while dragging any of an object's selection handles (Figure 7-27). When you drag the handle, Pages turns the arrow pointer into a curved, double-headed arrow, indicating its intent to spin the selected object. Drag a selection handle to swivel the object clockwise or counterclockwise. Press ⌘-Shift to rotate in 45-degree increments.

Note: Just because you tilt an object off its axis doesn't mean that it no longer fits your layout grid, described on page 202. Grid design doesn't require that objects stand straight up and down, only that you position and proportion your images according to the invisible grid organizing your layout.

Pages normally rotates an object around its center point. But press the Option key while you rotate, and Pages pivots the object around the selection handle opposite the one you're dragging. And yes, press ⌘-Option-Shift to pivot in 45-degree increments from the corner.

Tip: If you use a laptop with a multitouch trackpad, you can also rotate the object by putting your thumb and forefinger on the trackpad and twisting them like you're turning a knob. Hold down the Shift key while you do this to restrict the rotation to 45-degree increments.

The Metrics Inspector puts another spin on rotation. Select an object and use the Metrics Inspector's Rotate knob to twist it. You can also enter an angle measurement directly, or use the up and down arrows next to the Angle field to rotate in one-degree increments. The standard or right-side-up position is zero degrees. The angle increases as you rotate counterclockwise. Instead of spinning the Rotate

---

knob with your mouse, you can also just click the knob to move its angle indicator dot to that position. Unlike a compass where zero degrees occupies the top (North) position, Pages puts the zero degree indicator at the right (East) position to indicate horizontality.

Tip: The Metrics Inspector's Rotate knob is the only way to rotate two or more selected objects simultaneously, useful when you're trying to keep multiple objects equally off-kilter.

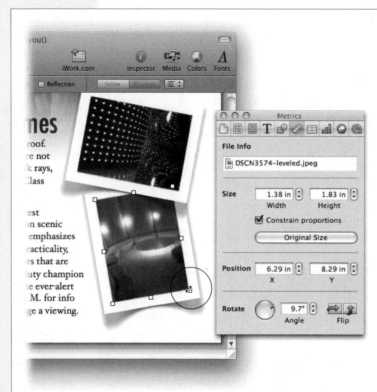

Figure 7-27:
When you hold ⌘ while dragging an object's selection handle, your cursor becomes a curved double-headed arrow (circled) and you can rotate the object directly. To make more precise rotation adjustments, open the Metrics Inspector and use the Rotate knob.

The final object controls you find in the Metrics Inspector are the two Flip buttons in the lower-right corner. You can flip a selected object horizontally or vertically with these buttons, turning the object into its mirror image. Or choose Arrange → Flip Horizontally or Flip Vertically to do the same thing.

Note: If you flip or rotate a shape containing text, you'll discover—whoops—the text is flipped, too, and possibly unreadable. Reset the text by choosing Format → Shape → "Reset Text and Object Handles". If you decide to keep it as is, though, the text remains editable. When you click to edit, Pages flips the text back to its normal orientation and, when you're done, sets it askew again.

Connecting Objects

A *connection line* is similar to a line shape—you can style it by adding endpoints and editing stroke settings in the Format Bar or Graphic Inspector—but a line shape lets you move its two endpoints anywhere you like. A connection line, meanwhile, is always leashed to the same two floating objects, its two ends permanently fixed to the two objects you choose when you insert the connection line. No matter how much you might move these objects around the page, the connection line stretches and compresses to keep the two objects linked up. Connection lines are useful for diagrams, flow charts, or anywhere it's useful to suggest a visual link between two objects.

Note: You can't draw connection lines between inline objects, only floating objects. Also, the two objects have to be on the same page; if you move a connected object to another page, Pages deletes the connection line without so much as a word.

To add a connection line, select two floating objects and choose Insert → Connection Line. Pages inserts an unadorned, straight line between the two objects. Click the connection line to select it, and Pages reveals three circular controls: a blue one on either end, and a white one in the center. Drag the white control to move the line, turning it into a bendy line; the line always passes through the white control, curving as necessary to keep the two objects connected (Figure 7-28). Similarly, if you move either of the two objects, the connection line stretches, shifts, and curves to keep the connection intact. The line starts out fastened directly to the two objects, but the blue controls let you add space between the endpoints and the objects. Drag them to adjust the gap; hold down the Option key while you drag to move both endpoints at once.

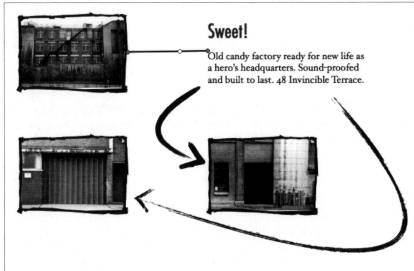

Figure 7-28:
These three photos are each connected to the caption text box with connection lines. When you first add a connection line, it looks like the simple line connecting the top left image. Add stroke styles and endpoints to your connection lines, and drag the white control in the middle of the line to change the line's position, making it curve through any point on the page, as shown here in the bottom two images. The blue controls at the line's endpoints let you control the space between the endpoint and the object.

Note: When you draw a connection line to one or more objects with instant-alpha transparency, the connection line goes right up to the edge of the visible area, just like wrapped text.

Once in place, you can change the stroke, endpoints, and color of the connection line in the Format Bar or Graphic Inspector, just as you would a regular line shape. To remove the connection line, select it and press Delete.

Note: Objects can have lots of connection lines, but they can only have one that points to any single given object. That is, two objects are allowed to have just one connection line connecting them.

Distributing and Aligning Objects

Sometimes being spaced out is a good thing. Say you have four objects and you want them evenly spaced across the page. You could certainly use a layout grid to do this, but for a quick-and-dirty project, you might not have troubled yourself to build one. Instead, Pages can handle the spacing and alignment for you automatically, using the Distribute Objects and Align Objects commands in the Arrange menu, as shown in Figure 7-29.

1. **Drag the objects into the approximate arrangement you want, placing the first and last objects precisely at the edges of the space where you want to arrange the group.**

2. **Hold the Shift key and click to select each of the objects to space and align.**

3. **When they're all selected, choose Arrange → Distribute Objects → Horizontally (or Vertically). Pages adjusts the objects, equalizing the space between them.**

4. **Choose Arrange → Align Objects, and choose one of the commands from the submenu.**

   Pages puts your objects in line. The Left, Center, and Right commands in the Align Objects submenu align the objects vertically along their left sides, vertical centerlines, or right sides. The Top, Middle, and Bottom commands align objects horizontally along their tops, horizontal centerlines, and bottom sides. Pages always aligns objects along the edge of the object group, in the chosen direction: When aligning left, the objects align along the left edge of the leftmost object in the selection; when aligning top, they line up with the top edge of the top object in the selection; and so on.

If you've lined up a group of objects vertically so they're directly above one another, and you choose Arrange → Distribute Objects → Horizontally, Pages moves the lower objects to the right, aligning the left edge of each object with the right edge of the object above it. Similarly, give the command to distribute objects vertically to a group of horizontally aligned objects, and Pages moves the right-hand objects downward, aligning the top of one object with the bottom of its neighbor to the left.

❶ Budget Fortresses & Fixer Uppers

❷ Budget Fortresses & Fixer Uppers

❸ Budget Fortresses & Fixer Uppers

Figure 7-29:
Your photos of budget fortresses are in a shambles, but you can get these fixer-uppers into shape by letting Pages align and space them for you automatically.

Step 1: Make sure that the left and right pictures are aligned to their respective margins.

Step 2: Choose Arrange → Align Objects → Top, and Pages hoists up the objects to line them up with the highest object in the selection.

Step 3: Choose Arrange → Distribute Objects → Horizontally to space the objects equally between the two end pictures.

Now they're perfectly aligned and spaced. You can drag the still-selected objects or use the arrow keys to jog the entire row up or down the page.

Tip: Contextual pop-up menus also give you access to object alignment and distribution commands. Select the objects, Control-click one of them, and, from the pop-up menu, choose the alignment or distribution command.

Arranging Objects

Much of this chapter has focused on how to format individual objects independent of the other objects around them. As you fill your layout with objects, however, they start to bump into each other, overlap, wrap around one another. As that happens, you have to start playing traffic cop, laying down the law for how objects relate to those around them.

Layering objects

Think of objects as cards scattered on your page. When one of these cards overlaps another, one of them necessarily lies on top of the other in *layers*—one card partially covers another, perhaps even obscuring it completely. Pages lets you shuffle the order of your object cards, the *layer stack*, so that you can control which object shows up on top. This is important not only for controlling whether one object covers another, but for text wrapping, too. Text wraps around a floating object only when that object appears on top of the text in the layer stack; otherwise the text just flows right over the object.

As you add objects to your document, Pages places them on the top layer; the new object covers up any portion of another object it overlaps. In word-processing documents the body-text layer is always the bottom layer (but you can slip objects below it by sending them to the background, as you'll see in a moment). You can move objects forward or backward through the layers by choosing Arrange → Bring Forward or Send Backward. Move a selected object all the way to the front or back of the pile by choosing Arrange → Bring to Front or Send to Back. Pages provides Front, Back, Forward, and Backward buttons that you can add to the toolbar to speed up the layer-adjusting process (see page 40). Better yet, Control-click a selected object (or right-click if you have a two-button mouse) and, from the pop-up menu, choose the layering command (Figure 7-30).

Sending objects to the background

In word-processing files, floating objects always hover above your document's body text, which always sits at the very bottom of the layer stack. That means that even using the Arrange → Send to Back command doesn't actually send an object to the page background; the main text always remains below your floating objects as the floor of your document. However, Pages does reserve a special layer, the document *background*, where you can slip objects to appear below everything else on the page, even the main body text. This is useful when you want to create a *watermark* effect, for example, adding an image, graphic, or even other text as a ghostly image behind your words. (You can get that phantom effect by turning down the object's opacity after you send it to the background; see page 275.)

Select an object, and choose Arrange → Send to Background or select the "In background" option in the Wrap Inspector. The object turns into a wallflower, slipping behind the scenes as everything else floats above. When you deselect the object, you'll find that you can no longer select it; under Pages' standard settings, background objects blend into the page fabric itself so that they don't get in the way when you work with text or other objects above them.

To work with a background object, you first have to choose Arrange → Make Background Objects Selectable or turn on the "Background objects are selectable" checkbox in the Wrap Inspector. Now you can select your background object, but Pages lets you know that it's special by turning the pointer white when you point

to it. To convert it back into a regular object, select it and choose Arrange → Bring Background Objects to Front, or choose the Inline or Floating option in the Wrap Inspector.

Note: Page-layout documents don't have this special background layer, since they don't have the body text to contend with. Instead, just send an object to the back with the Arrange → Send To Back command. You can fix it in place so that it's not selectable by locking the object (see page 263).

Repeating elements with master objects

When you're adding your watermark to a single page, sending it to the background layer is the way to go. But that's too much work if you want to repeat your logo in the background of every page of your 200-page prospectus. Pages can add an image—or any other object—to every page of a word-processing document by turning the image into a *master object,* making it a fixed part of every page of the current section. This is useful for adding a background element to all pages, but Pages doesn't limit master objects to the background. They can interact with your text and other objects on your page, too.

Note: Like background objects, master objects exist only in word-processing documents, not page-layout documents.

Master objects behave like headers and footers. They turn up again and again on every page, always in the same location and always with the same content. They even follow the same rules as headers, observing the "first page is different" and "left and right pages are different" settings in the Layout Inspector's Section tab (See page 142), so that you can put a different set of master objects on the first page of your section, for example. Unlike headers and footers, however, master objects can appear anywhere you might want to place them on the page; they're not limited to the top or bottom of the page.

To turn a regular object into a master object, select it and choose Format → Advanced → Move Object to Section Master. The selection handles disappear from the object, and you can no longer select or edit it—the object is now fixed in the layout, like wallpaper on your page, repeating on every page of the document (or the current section).

Unlike regular background objects, master objects continue to interact with normal objects. They keep their place in the layer stack, text wraps around them, and all other object settings apply as usual. Master objects are most commonly used for background images, however, and having your text wrap around your background image probably isn't what you had in mind. It turns out that a master object can also be a background image, too. Select the object and choose Arrange → Send to Background, as you would with any other object.

But wait, you *can't* select a master object. Like background objects, Pages defangs these objects by making them unselectable so they don't get in your way as you work through your document. To send a master object to the background, or make any other changes, choose Format → Advanced → Make Master Objects Selectable. Or just double-click the object and Pages will show you a dialog box offering to make it selectable for you. Either way, Pages adds a checkmark to the Make Master Objects Selectable menu item to indicate that the feature is on; choose the command again to uncheck it.

Tip: When an object is both a master object *and* a background object, you have to choose Arrange → Make Background Objects Selectable as well as the Make Master Objects Selectable command in order to edit it.

When master objects are selectable, you can edit, resize, or move them just like regular objects. (Pages lets you know that they're special by making the selection handles blue.) Changes made to master objects filter through every page of the document—likewise, if you delete the master object, it's removed from all pages.

You can transform a master object back into a regular floating object by selecting it and then choosing Format → Advanced → Move Object to Page. Pages exchanges the blue handles of a master object for the hollow black handles of a regular object—and now you can maneuver it like any other floating object. But there's a twist: When you change a master object back to a regular object by using the Move Object to Page command, Pages changes *every occurrence* of that master object in your document into regular floating objects, all of them selected. In other words, if you have a 20-page document featuring your logo as a master object on every page, choosing Move Object to Page creates 20 separate logo images, one for every page, all of them selected (press Delete to delete them all at once).

Tip: If you want to change an object's master status so it becomes a normal object on just one page of your document, select the master object, choose Edit → Cut, and then immediately choose Edit → Paste. Pages cuts the master object from your document, removing it from all pages, and then pastes it back in as a standard floating object.

Grouping objects

After going to the trouble of precisely positioning floating objects relative to one another, you'll often wish you could move, rotate, resize, or copy them as if they were a single object. Pages gives you the power to group objects in this way—and later, if you need to adjust them individually, ungroup them.

Hold down the Shift key as you click each object you want to include in the group to select them all (all objects must be on the same page). Choose Arrange → Group, and Pages replaces the individual selection rectangles with just one enclosing the whole group. Grouped objects feature a blue outline (Figure 7-31), instead of the usual gray outline that you see when you select an individual object. Pages treats grouped objects like a single entity. You can apply all the object manipulations and adjustments to a group that you can to a single object.

This all-for-one group approach means that you lose the ability to style or edit objects individually. The exception is editing text inside text boxes or shapes—you can continue to do that by double-clicking the text to edit. To make other changes to single objects within a group, you first have to disband your little club. Select an object group and choose Arrange → Ungroup to restore the objects' individuality so you can, for example, resize or delete one of the group members, or change its background fill or border stroke. Your group can stage a reunion tour at any time: Select them all and choose Arrange → Group to bring them together again.

Locking objects

You can lock a floating object to the page to ensure you don't accidentally shift it out of position as you work on your layout, an occupational hazard for pages well stocked with design elements. To lock an object, choose Arrange → Lock, and Pages nails it to the page, replacing its selection handles with X marks to indicate that it's off the market for editing (Figure 7-32). Although you can still select locked objects, you can't change them in any way until you unlock them.

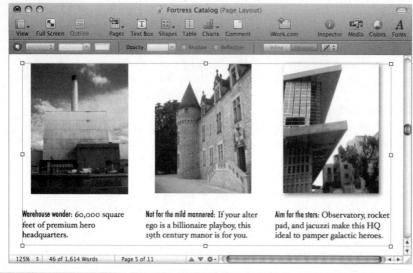

Figure 7-31:
When you click on any object in a group, Pages displays a blue selection rectangle around the entire group to indicate that they're now treated as a single unit. Dragging grouped objects moves all of them at once, and dragging the selection handles likewise resizes all objects in the group. (Like resizing objects individually, however, the text inside text boxes and shapes doesn't change size—only the overall dimensions of the enclosing object shape.)

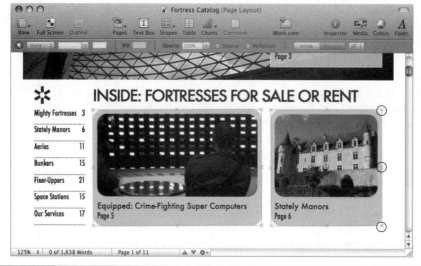

Figure 7-32:
Select an object, choose Arrange → Lock, and Pages fastens the object to the page to prevent you from shifting its position as you edit the document. If you select a locked object, it displays Xs instead of selection handles and resists your efforts to edit or delete it, as shown here on the two rounded rectangles. Choose Arrange → Unlock to make changes.

Unlock an object by selecting it and choosing Arrange → Unlock. Pages unchains your selection, and it's a normal object once again.

Modifying Object Styles

Besides arranging objects' size and placement on the page, you can also adjust the way each object looks by adjusting its various properties. Object properties include things like background color or image, line color and style, reflections, drop shadows, and object opacity. The Format Bar, Graphic Inspector, and Color Picker are your command centers for making these adjustments.

Tip: If your object-styling goes awry and you wind up with an object painted with garish colors and egregious effects, you can reset its styles by choosing Format → "Reapply Defaults to Selection". (The exact title of the command changes according to what's selected: Text Box, Shape, Image, and so on.) Pages reverts the object to the document's standard style, as defined by the template you used to create the document. See Chapter 10 (page 351) for details about setting default object properties.

Filling with Colors, Gradients, and Images

Pages provides the Graphic Inspector to control objects' colors—both their *fill* (interior color), and their *stroke* (outline color and border). The Graphic Inspector also lets you add a shadow or reflection to an object and adjust the object's opacity. Tools to adjust these settings also pop up in the Format Bar when you select an object.

You can add a fill color to any shape, text box, table cell, or chart element. Select one of these objects and choose a color from the Fill pop-up button in the Format Bar. Or, for literally millions of additional color options, choose Color Fill from the Graphic Inspector's Fill pop-up menu and then click the color well that appears beneath the pop-up to summon the Color Picker.

Choosing colors with the Color Picker

When you want to adjust the color of shapes, text, backgrounds, lines, or shadows, select the object and click one of the Inspectors' color wells to call the Color Picker to the fore. (You can also click the toolbar's Colors button, or choose View → Show Colors.)

The Color Picker is a part of Mac OS X, and comes into play in many different programs when you need to adjust colors. The Color Picker provides five different approaches to choosing colors through the buttons at the top of its window (Figure 7-33). But whether you choose the color wheel or the crayons for picking colors, the options in the rest of the window stay the same. Select a color, using any of the five Color Picker displays and see the color in the color box at the top of the window.

Slide the Opacity slider to the left to make the color more transparent (or enter an opacity percentage directly in the % box). As you adjust opacity, the color swatch takes on a diagonally split-screen appearance, with the reduced opacity color displayed on the bottom of the swatch. The upper part of the swatch box displays shades of gray—actually the mask that Pages applies to the selected color to reduce its opacity (or increase its transparency). In other words, if you set the opacity to zero, the upper part of the swatch shows pure black, masking out all the color and resulting in no color. Increase the opacity, and that black turns into lighter and lighter gray, letting more of the color show through, resulting in more opaque colors—until you reach 100 percent opacity.

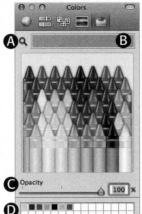

Figure 7-33:
The many faces of the Color Picker offer five different ways to choose colors. Switch between each one by clicking one of the buttons on the top row.

You can copy a color from anywhere on your screen in order to do things like match a text box color to a color in a picture. Click the magnifying glass (A) and Pages turns the arrow cursor into a magnifying glass. Drag the magnifying glass cursor over a color and click to load that color into the swatch (B). For an example, see "Color Me Inspired" on page 198.

Use the Opacity slider (C) to adjust the color's transparency, and drag from the swatch to one of the Text or Graphic Inspector's color wells to change the color of a text box or of a shape's fill, stroke, shadow, and so on. In order to use the exact same color somewhere else—even in another document or another program—drag from the swatch down to one of the palette squares (D), where you can save your color for future quick access.

Tip: When you use a transparent color for an object's background color, for example, text and objects behind it show through. You can get a similar effect by setting the object itself to be transparent—just adjust its opacity in the Format Bar or Graphic Inspector (see page 275). The difference, though, is that changing an object's opacity makes all its contents transparent, too (the text inside a text box, for example). Setting a transparent background color, allows the foreground content to remain completely opaque.

Instead of whipping up your own colors with the Color Picker, you can just find a color in any document or any object on your screen (even outside of Pages), and load it into the Color Picker's swatch. For this trick, click the magnifying glass icon next to the color swatch. Pages turns your cursor into a magnifying glass icon with a crosshair in the middle. The magnified view through this magnifying glass allows you to choose individual color pixels. Maneuver the magnifying glass over any part of your screen until the color you want appears as the central pixel in the crosshairs. Click the mouse to load that pixel's color into the Color Picker's swatch.

When you've captured a color you like, you can save it for future use as a favorite in the *color palette.* Whether it's a pure color or a reduced-opacity color, drag from the swatch down to one of the squares in the color palette at the bottom of the window. By saving your favorite colors in the color palette, you can use them in different parts of your document for different types of objects, text, or backgrounds. And since the Color Picker is a system-wide feature, you can use your colors in other documents or other programs.

This custom color-picking ability is especially helpful for maintaining a consistent look across several documents—like a brochure, business card, or stationery. The color palette's standard display is one line of boxes at the bottom of the Color Picker window, but if you need more, grab the little dot on the bottom edge of the window and drag it down to reveal more storage spots. You can also widen the Color Picker window to increase the palette—up to a maximum of 300 spots. Click a saved color in the palette to load it in the Color Picker's swatch, or drag it directly to an object.

Gradient fills

Instead of filling an object with a solid color, Pages can create a gradient fill, a fill color that gradually blends one color into another. From the Graphic Inspector's Fill pop-up menu, choose *Gradient Fill,* and Pages displays two color wells beneath the menu: one for the starting color and one for the ending color (Figure 7-34). Click the upper color well and choose a starting color with the Color Picker and then click the lower color well and choose an ending color.

You could choose, for example, red and yellow to create a gradient that transitions from red through all the shades of orange to yellow. That sunset color mix provides a somewhat garish example, though. It turns out that the most effective gradient is one you barely notice. A subtle color shift that maintains the same color but shifts just a few degrees of brightness often creates the illusion of a translucent inner glow that lends real elegance to an object. Using the Brightness slider next to the Color Picker's color wheel is an easy way to pick your second gradient color. For the best effect, give the slider only a little nudge. Reducing the opacity of one of the colors also lets you create a gradient that becomes gradually transparent (or just partially transparent) to give an object the appearance of fading into the background, for example.

A gradient starts at one side of an object and ends at the opposite side. Click the arrow buttons to set the gradient direction from top to bottom or left to right. Use the Angle knob or enter an angle directly in the Angle field to set any other gradient direction. Click the double-headed arrow to flip the gradient, swapping the starting and ending colors.

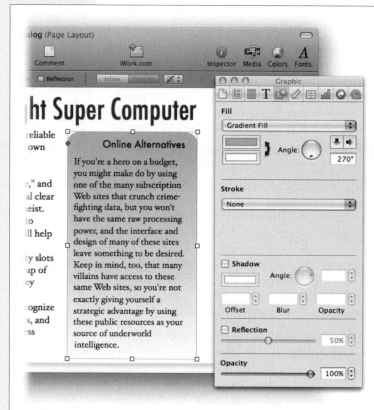

Figure 7-34:
From the Graphic Inspector's Fill pop-up menu, choose Gradient Fill to fill a shape or text box with a gradient that blends gradually from one color into another. Click each of the color wells to select a starting and ending color from the Color Picker, and then use the arrow buttons or the Angle knob to determine the gradient's direction. Here, a gradient in a sidebar shape blends to white, creating an elegant container for the sidebar text that gradually fades towards the bottom.

This Gradient Fill option is a good place to get acquainted with gradients, but Pages lets you in on several more gradient features when you choose *Advanced Gradient Fill* from the Graphic Inspector's Fill pop-up menu. These advanced options let you add more colors—instead of making a simple linear transition from one color to another, you can now step through an entire spectrum of colors. You can also change how sharply the gradient shifts from one color to another. Figure 7-35 shows you how it works.

Finally, the Advanced Gradient Fill option lets you choose a *radial gradient,* as opposed to the *linear gradients* you've seen so far. While linear gradients change the color from one side of the object to the other in a straight line, radial gradients change color from a central focal point that radiates outward in a circle. Change the center point of the radial gradient by dragging the object's *blend point,* the blue circle control that appears when you select the object.

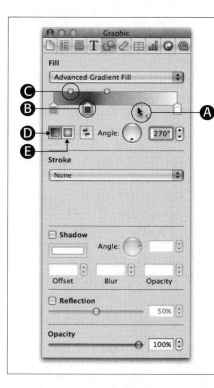

Figure 7-35:
The Advanced Gradient Fill option lets you add more colors to your gradient. Add a new color by hovering the pointer just under the gradient slider until it sprouts a + sign (A) and then click. Pages adds a new color control to the slider (B). Drag the color control to change the portion of the gradient where the new color takes hold. Slide the blend-point controls on top of the slider (C) to control how quickly or slowly the two adjacent colors blend.

Click a color control to choose a new color, or drag it off the gradient strip to remove it (Pages won't let you have fewer than two colors on the slider). Add a new color control for every color you want to include.

Switch the gradient style by clicking the Linear (D) or Radial (E) button. The double-arrow button flips the direction of the color gradient.

Filling with Images

Pages lets you use images instead of colors to fill objects. This is one technique for applying a background image to a text box or table cell, or to fill a shape with an image (although you might be better off using the Mask with Shape command for that; see page 233).

Select a shape or text box, for example, and, from the Graphic Inspector's Fill pop-up menu, choose Image Fill. Drag an image file from the finder, or a picture from the Media Browser, into the well below the pop-up menu—or click the Choose button and select an image file from your hard drive. (The first time you use Image Fill, Pages forces you to use the Choose method by displaying the file-choosing dialog box.) Pages adds the image to your selected object and scales it according to your choice in the Scale pop-up menu:

- **Scale to Fit.** Pages attempts to fit the entire image into the object when you choose this option. This method often results in some empty space within the object where its shape doesn't match the proportions of the image.

- **Scale to Fill.** Choose this option and Pages resizes the image just enough to completely fill the object's shape. Unlike "Scale to Fit," this option never leaves any blank space in the background but often means portions of the image are cropped. When you fill a horizontal shape with a vertical image, for example, the top and bottom of the vertical image aren't visible.

- **Stretch.** Pages stretches the image when you choose this option, distorting it a little or a lot as it transforms the image's proportions to conform to the object's shape.

- **Original Size.** Choose this menu item and Pages places the image into the object in its exact original size. If the image is large—like a high-resolution photograph—you see only a tiny portion of the picture. Pages crops into the center of a large original when you choose this option; you can't choose which part of the picture to display. If the original is smaller than the object you're filling, Pages places it in the center of the shape; you can't shift the position of a small image within the object.

- **Tile.** Choose this option and Pages fills the object with multiple copies of the image (like tiles on a countertop) only if the image is much smaller than the object. If the image is larger than the object, Pages cuts a section from the upper-right corner of the image and pastes it into the object at the original size. As you can see in Figure 7-36 (lower left), when this happens, you often end up with just a big splotch of fuzz—depending on what's in the upper-right corner of your image.

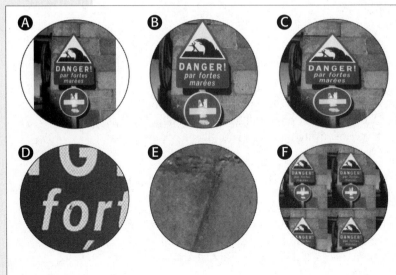

Figure 7-36:
You can fill a shape or text box with an image if you choose Image Fill from the Graphic Inspector's Fill pop-up menu. Choose the image you want, and then select one of the five fill variations from the Scale pop-up menu. The results are pictured here:

(A) Scale to Fit makes sure that as much of the image is visible as possible but often leaves empty space at the edges; (B) Scale to Fill sizes the image to fill the shape; (C) Stretch squeezes or stretches the image so that the entire image fits inside the shape, distorting the image if necessary; (D) Original Size centers the original image in the middle of the shape with no resizing; (E) Tile repeats the image at its actual size across the shape—if the image is larger than the shape, as it is here, you see only a portion of the image. When it's smaller than the shape (F), Tile displays several repetitions of the image.

Adding Tinted Image Fills

You can add a color tint to an image you use as an object fill to impart, for example, a rosy glow or a ghoulish green overcast to a picture or graphic. From the Graphic Inspector's Fill pop-up menu, choose Tinted Image Fill, select an image and a scaling method, and then click the color well (Figure 7-37). Pages displays the Color Picker, ready for you to choose your tint color. Select a color and adjust its opacity as Pages applies the filter to your image—it's like laying a transparent colored sheet over the picture. If you want to tint several objects with a matching filter, drag the swatch to the color palette to use later.

Tip: Use tinted image fills to fade an image without affecting the opacity of the image's container. For example, you might want to fade an image you're using as the background in a text box or table cell so that the text in the foreground reads more easily. Achieve this effect by using white for the image tint color and adjusting the Color Picker's Opacity slider to produce the desired image density.

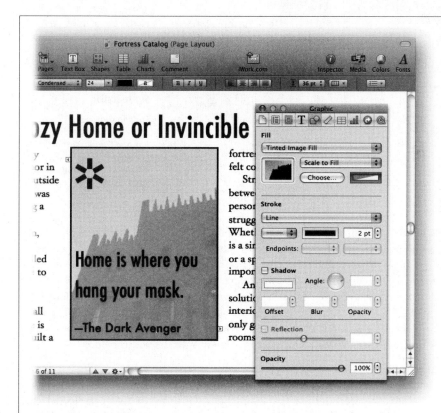

Figure 7-37:
You can use a tinted image fill to add a color overlay to the image fill for a shape or text box. From the Fill pop-up menu, select Tinted Image Fill and click the color well to choose a tint color. You can use a tinted image fill, for example, to reduce the density of a background image while keeping the shape's border and text at full opacity, as shown here. To do so, choose white as the tint color and reduce its opacity in the Color Picker.

Adjusting Line Styles

Pages uses lines (or *strokes*) as standard or optional components in most objects. Shapes have an outline, for example, table cells and chart elements have borders, and you can add borders to pictures or text boxes. You can even get fancy by replacing a simple border with a graphical picture frame. The Format Bar and the Graphic Inspector's Stroke section give you the controls for making all these line adjustments (Figure 7-38).

Note: You can apply line strokes to any object, but picture frames aren't available for tables or charts. On behalf of the Council on Good Design, thank you, Apple.

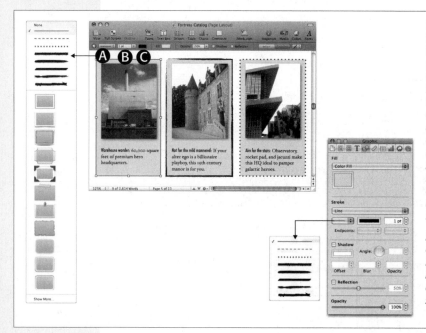

Figure 7-38:
Use the Format Bar to select the line style (A), line weight (B), and color (C) for an object's border, or stroke. Here, three rectangle shapes frame the pictures and captions, each with a different stroke. For all objects except tables and charts, the Line Style pop-up menu also includes picture frame options. These stroke options are also available in the Graphic Inspector's Stroke section.

For line shapes and connection lines, the Format Bar and Graphic Inspector both offer pop-up menus to choose arrow or endpoint styles for the lines.

Pages lets you choose to use a line or a picture frame as a stroke. This section focuses on adding lines; for details about picture frames, see page 238. To adjust an object's line style, select the object and choose from the Line Style pop-up menu in the Format Bar or open the Graphic Inspector and choose Line from the Stroke pop-up menu to reveal the Line Style pop-up. Either way, you can choose from among eight line styles. Click the Stroke color well to open the Color Picker and choose a stroke color. Set the line width or thickness by using the up and down arrow buttons or by typing a point measurement into the width field.

If you're formatting a connection line or one of the three line shapes—the plain line, arrow, or double-headed arrow—the Endpoints pop-up menus come into play. The arrow-style lines are just plain lines with one or two preselected endpoint options. Use these pop-up menus to choose from various arrow or endpoint styles for each end of the line. You'll find these pop-up menus in both the Format Bar and the Graphic Inspector, but only when you select a line.

To remove the stroke from an object altogether, choose None from the Format Bar's Line Style pop-up, or from the Graphic Inspector's Stroke pop-up.

Adding Shadows and Reflections

Drop shadows and reflections are perhaps the most popular design devices for enhancing a graphic's presence in a layout. Adding a *shadow* to a page element seems to lift it off the page, setting it apart from the rest of the page and subtly adding an extra dimension to your design. A *reflection* likewise adds an illusion of depth to the page by adding a dimmed mirror-image below the original object, as if you were looking at it across a wet or glossy surface. Figure 7-39 shows some examples.

Just don't overdo it. When you add special effects to every picture on the page, they're no longer special, are they? Good design is often more about restraint than showy effects: Use these effects judiciously or to call out just one or two elements on the page. Carefully choose the elements that you want to highlight and then add your effects with a light hand.

The mirrored contours of this domed fortress on scenic Justice Lane are both attractive and practical.

Figure 7-39:
Adding a shadow or reflection to an image creates the illusion of visual depth. A shadow makes the image look like it's floating above the page, while a mirror-image reflection makes the image seem inset, as if you saw it across a glossy floor.

Reflect on This: Anti-Laser Domes

What superhero hasn't been the target of a nefarious laser attack? If you've been singed one too many times, it might be the ideal moment to consider moving into an anti-laser reflective dome.

Plot your assault on evildoers in zen-like tranquility, safe in the knowledge that any satellite-borne laser attacks are bouncing harmlessly off of your curved roof. (Note that reflective domes are not effective against shrink rays, tractor beams, or Class A death rays.)

Domes Make a Well Rounded Defense

Up & Away's latest domed listing, on scenic **Justice Lane,** emphasizes both style and practicality, with sleek interiors that are perfect for the off-duty champion of goodness as well as the ever-alert hero on patrol. Call Meredith M. for info about this listing and to arrange a viewing.

Note: You can add reflections to images, text boxes, shapes, and movies—but not to tables or charts. If you add a drop shadow to a text box, you probably want to add a fill color (perhaps just white). Otherwise the text casts the shadow, not the text box. (You can also add text shadows by using the Fonts window, as described on page 62.) For movies, the reflection doesn't update as you play the movie, so you probably don't get the effect you're looking for.

Pages makes it easy to add these effects: Select the picture and turn on the Shadow or Reflection checkbox in the Format Bar. You can also apply these effects from the Graphic Inspector, where you find settings to fine-tune their display for each picture. The Reflection slider adjusts the opacity of the reflection. The Shadow controls (Figure 7-40) meanwhile offer several options:

- **Color.** Click the color well, and Pages displays the Color Picker to let you choose the color of the shadow.

- **Angle.** Dial the angle knob to the direction in which you want to cast the shadow—or enter a degree value from 0 to 360 in the Angle field to specify the exact angle of your virtual light.

- **Offset.** Change this value to set the distance of the shadow's outline from the picture. A setting of zero offset results in the kind of shadow you'd cast at high noon on the equator. The virtual light source is directly overhead, casting an equal shadow on all sides and rendering any angle setting moot. Increasing the offset shifts the shadow in the direction of the Angle setting, making the image appear to float higher off the page.

Figure 7-40:
Select an object and turn on the Shadow option in the Format Bar or in the Graphic Inspector. As shown here, you can get a variety of different effects by dialing the Graphic Inspector's Shadow settings up and down for subtle enhancements or bold transformations.

Tip: When you set the offset to zero, the shadow tool does double duty by giving you glow effects, too. To give a picture a red glow, for example, click the color well in the Graphic Inspector's Shadow settings and choose red from the Color Picker. Change the Offset setting to zero, and boost the Blur value to increase the size of the glow.

- **Blur.** Adjust the softness of the shadow with the Blur setting. A minimum setting of one point creates a hard-edged shadow with a very slightly soft edge. Higher numbers increase the virtual cloud cover, blurring the shadow and eventually producing an indistinct haze beneath the object.

- **Opacity.** Turning this setting up makes the shadow darker and bolder, and turning it down makes it more transparent. This opacity setting affects only the shadow. The Opacity slider at the bottom of the Graphic Inspector controls the opacity of the entire object, shadow included.

To remove a shadow or reflection, select the object and turn off the Shadow or Reflection checkbox in the Format Bar or Graphic Inspector.

Adjusting Opacity

When you add objects to a Pages document, they begin life opaque, completely obscuring anything underneath them. But Pages gives you the ability to reduce the opacity of any object—in other words, you can make it partially transparent. In addition to creating elegant translucent effects, you can also use this setting to wash out objects—handy for creating pale background images or de-emphasizing an object to direct the reader's attention to another, bolder page element.

To adjust opacity, select an object and choose a value from the Opacity pop-up menu in the Format Bar—or type a value directly into the field. You can also drag the Graphic Inspector's Opacity slider (Figure 7-41).

Note: Pages includes three opacity controls, all with separate functions. The Graphic Inspector's Opacity slider affects entire objects. You can use the Color Picker's Opacity slider to adjust opacity of an object's fill, a line or stroke, or the text color. The Graphic Inspector's Shadow section contains an opacity control strictly for shadows.

Copying Objects and Graphic Styles

When you design longer documents, you often need to repeat similar objects over and over again, like the pull quotes and sidebars in the Up & Away catalog. For consistency, it's important that these elements have the same color, shadow, border, text alignment, and so on. But ugh, who wants to repeat all those formatting steps every time you add a new pull quote? Pages offers a few features to help.

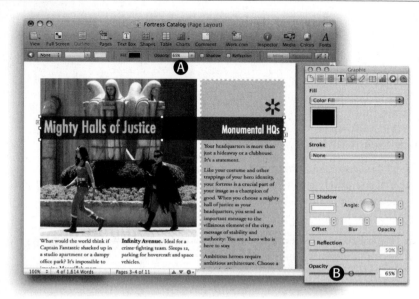

Figure 7-41:
Adjust an object's transparency by using the Opacity pop-up menu (A) in the Format Bar or the Opacity slider (B) in the Graphic Inspector. The "Mighty Halls of Justice" text box shown here has a black background with reduced opacity, creating a translucent layer for the headline.

When you want to create a new object, the easiest way to duplicate the look of another one is to clone the original and then edit the copy as necessary—copy another sidebar's text box, for example, and fill it in with your new text. Pages provides three ways to copy an object:

- **Copy and paste.** Select the object to copy and choose Edit → Copy. Click where you want the copy to appear, and choose Edit → Paste.

- **Option-drag.** Hold down the Option key and drag the original object, and Pages gives you a copy.

- **Duplicate.** The Edit menu gives you a command to copy floating objects. Select the object to copy and choose Edit → Duplicate. Pages clones the object and adds the copy on top of the original, slightly offset. (This method is available for floating objects only.)

Making a brand new copy of an object is all well and good when you want to add a *new* sidebar to your document. But what about when the object already exists and you just want to restyle it to match another sidebar? Pages lets you do this by copying one object's *graphic style*—all its object-level settings—to another object, quickly and effectively repainting the second object with the look of the first.

Select the object whose styles you want to copy and choose Format → Copy Graphic Style (or press Option-⌘-C). Then select the object to receive those styles, choose Format → Paste Graphic Style (or Option-⌘-V), and the object inherits all the settings of the original—stroke, fill, shadow, reflection, text wrap, and all the other object-level settings. Unlike the regular Paste command, Paste Graphic Style doesn't touch the actual content, just the object's style and formatting.

Note: In addition to object-level settings, using Paste Graphic Style on text boxes and shapes brings along all the font and text formatting of the original, too.

And with that last nifty trick, you've now got all the know-how you need to juggle and finesse your layout's words and pictures. But what about numbers? Pages gives you a sleek collection of tools to add tables, mini-spreadsheets, and charts in your document. These are objects, too, but they have enough going on to merit a chapter of their very own. Pull up a chair to learn about *tables,* all in the next chapter.

Building Tables and Charts

Numbers often spell out an idea even better than words can. When you're writing an annual report, for example, or charting Megaville's monthly ebb and flow of hero-villain skirmishes, the actual figures add up to much more than a lengthy written description. Pages might be a *word* processor, but it does a fine job at slinging numbers, too, giving you the tools to present data and other complex information clearly and efficiently.

Numbers? The ever-attentive reader might notice that this also happens to be the name of a certain spreadsheet program included in iWork. In fact, the way that Pages uses tables and charts to manage your data reveals a strong family resemblance to its math-minded cousin. As you'll learn when you dig into Numbers later in this book, tables are central to Numbers documents, where every table acts as its own standalone spreadsheet. In Pages (and Keynote, too), tables are lightweight versions of the full-featured tables in Numbers, and the same goes for charts. You can even copy and paste tables and charts between iWork programs, letting you share data between your spreadsheets, written documents, and slideshows.

Like the images, shapes, and text boxes explored in Chapter 7, tables and charts are objects, too—you can move, resize, and manipulate them like you can any other object. You'll learn all the advanced details of building tables and charts in the Numbers section of this book, but this chapter gets you started on the fundamentals as it takes you through Pages' table and chart features.

Making Tables

Tables are efficient containers for displaying a large amount of data, creating forms, or quickly formatting a page full of pictures. A table is a grid of information constructed from rows and columns that slice-n-dice the table into blocks called *cells.* Table cells have some special math know-how, as you'll see on page 303, but you can use them to organize just about any kind of info. Each cell can contain a chunk of text or numbers—or even other objects like pictures and shapes. Pages can dress up tables or individual cells with borders and color, or with image fills for backgrounds. You can create very simple plain-text tables—as you might otherwise do by simply using the Tab key to create basic columns—or something more elaborate, complete with color and pictures, that looks nothing like a table at first glance. Figure 8-1 shows a few examples.

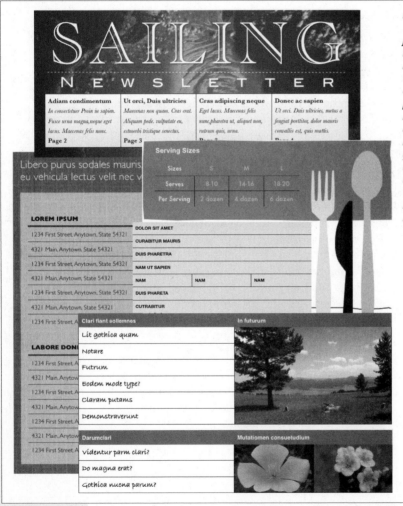

Figure 8-1:
You can make tables that are just columns of facts and figures, but with Pages' table-making abilities–combined with your imagination–it's easy to create forms, catalogs, photo layouts, and oodles more. The tables pictured here are examples from Pages' built-in templates, which are good places to start exploring table creation. Clockwise from the top: Sailing Newsletter, Catering Brochure, Catalog, Lab Notes, and Real Estate Newsletter.

You can add tables to a Pages document as either floating or inline objects, with one important distinction: Floating tables are limited to one page, while inline tables can span several pages. (Pop back to page 209 for a recap of the difference between floating and inline objects.)

How many cells can you put in a table? Though you'd be hard-pressed to think up a need for such a table, a table can be as small as one cell: one column wide by one row high. At the other extreme, you can make tables up to 65 columns wide. A floating table can fill an entire page with as many rows as you can squeeze in, while an inline table can stretch over many pages, columns, or linked text boxes, with a virtually unlimited number of rows—for a catalog product list, for example. Massive tables, however, can slow down Pages as it manages thousands of cells— especially when those cells contain arithmetic calculations, something you'll learn about on page 303. If you need a table that's more than a few pages long, consider breaking it up into two or more tables.

Inserting Inline Tables

You determine whether a table is floating or inline when you add it to a Pages document, just like with other objects. To add an inline table, place the insertion point in the text where you want the table to appear, and click the Table button in the toolbar, or choose Insert → Table. You can insert a table in any text column or text box (but not into another table).

Pages starts you off with a table of three columns and four rows, which occupies the entire width of a text column, as shown in Figure 8-2. Pages puts your insertion point in the table's first cell to let you start typing right away, and opens the Table Inspector so you can tailor the number of rows and columns or adjust the Column Width and Row Height to suit your needs. (The Table Inspector offers a bunch of other options, too, which you'll explore over the next several pages.)

Tip: You can also create a table by converting tab-separated text into an inline table. Select the text to convert, and choose Format → Table → Convert Text to Table. Pages makes every paragraph its own row, adding a column wherever you've typed Tab. You can also do the reverse, converting an inline table into tabbed text: Select the table at the table level or cell level (page 284), and choose Format → Table → Convert Table to Text.

Like other inline objects, inline tables of one page or less in height possess only three active selection handles: at the bottom side, right side, and bottom-right corner. Drag these handles to resize the table as you would any other object.

Note: Whenever an inline table extends onto another page or another column, all of its selection handles are inactive, faded to a dim ghostly blue. Turn to the Metrics Inspector and use the Size boxes to adjust the overall size of the table: Click the up and down arrow button or enter measurements directly into the Width and Height boxes, and then press Return. When a table occupies more than one page or column, the Metric Inspector's height measurement is the total from the top of the table on its first page or column to the bottom of the table on its last page or column, with one oddity: The measurement counts the size of header cells just once, even when they're repeated on subsequent pages or columns.

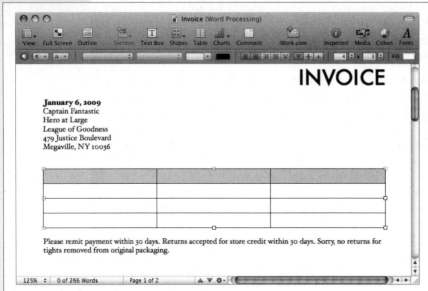

Figure 8-2:
When you add a new table, Pages always gives you a blank table with three columns and four rows—one of the rows is a shaded header row, intended to label your columns. For more about header rows and columns, see page 289.

Unless and until you specifically change the width of an inline table or any of its columns, the table always fills the width of the surrounding text. If you change the text margins, for example, the table automatically becomes narrower and wider to fit. This behavior changes, however, when you change the width of the table in the Metrics Inspector or of individual cells in the Table Inspector's Table pane. Narrowing the text column still narrows the table, but when you subsequently make the text column wider, the table width increases until the table reaches your specified width, at which point the table stops expanding.

Note: Pages doesn't allow you to wrap text around the sides of an inline table—it dims those options in the Wrap Inspector. That means that if you want to add a table inside the body text of your word-processing document, the surrounding text always hops over the table, ending just above and starting up again just below. You can't have a right-aligned inline table, for example, with text flowing around to the left. Text wrapping around floating tables, on the other hand, works as usual—Pages treats them like any other floating object. Need a refresher on the difference? See page 209.

Inserting Floating Tables

Add a floating table by ⌘-clicking in the margin of the document so the insertion point disappears, and then click the Table button in the toolbar or pick Insert → Table. Pages drops its standard table of three columns by four rows into the center of your screen and opens the Table Inspector so you can tailor the number and size of rows and columns to your needs, as shown in Figure 8-3. The size settings apply to every row and column when you select the whole table. Drag any of a floating table's eight selection handles to resize it.

Tip: You can change the size and look of the table Pages gives you if you prefer that your new tables not be three columns by four rows with a gray header row. To do so, follow these steps: When you insert the first table in your document, add or remove rows or columns, resize the table, and change backgrounds or borders. Then select the table and choose Format → Advanced → Define Default Table Style. Pages uses your new table style for any new tables in this document. If you want to use this table style for other new documents, you have to save your document as a template with your new table style. See Chapter 10 (page 345) for details on how to create a template.

Figure 8-3:
Pages drops a new floating table into your document and opens the Table Inspector so you can get right to work modifying it. Resize the table by dragging any of its selection handles (the empty white boxes), or by changing the number of rows and columns in the Format Bar (A) or the Table Inspector (B). The Format Bar's count of rows and columns includes the table's headers and footers, while the Table Inspector Body Rows and Body Columns fields do not. You'll learn more about table headers and footers on page 289.

The Table Inspector is chock-full of other options for formatting your table, too—many of them tucked away in the Edit Rows & Columns pop-up menu (C).

You can also insert floating tables using Pages' drawing technique—ostensibly to place a floating table in an exact size and location in your document, although this turns out to be not terribly useful. To draw a table in your document, Option-click the Table button in the toolbar, position the crosshair cursor where you want one corner of your table, and then drag to the opposite corner. Pages helpfully displays the table dimensions as you drag, adjusting the number of rows and columns to fit your selection size. Release the mouse to set down your table, and then use the Table Inspector's Table pane to adjust the number of rows and columns and all the other table settings to your liking. But here's the rub: Adding rows and columns (which you'll almost certainly want to do) adds to the size of your table, negating your carefully drawn size and making you wonder why this option even exists.

Tip: If you continue to hold the Option key as you drag to draw a table, Pages centers the table on the point where you begin dragging. Hold down the Shift key while you drag, and Pages performs its usual proportion constraint.

Dragging a floating table's selection handles is the easiest way to resize a table, but you can also use the Metrics Inspector to manually adjust table dimensions (the Metrics Inspector also gives you tools to position, rotate or flip your table, just like other objects). Use the up and down arrow buttons or enter width and height measurements in the Size boxes. You can also change the size of a table by resizing its columns and rows. For more on this, see page 298.

Note: When you make a floating table taller than the page itself, the rest of the table juts out beyond the bottom or top page margins—in digital limbo. You can get at these "invisible" rows or columns by dragging the table up or down the page, reducing the row heights, or deleting some rows.

Selecting Tables, Cells, and Text

When you work with tables, you can select and edit them at three different levels:

- **The table level.** When you click once on a table, Pages selects the entire table at the object level, revealing the eight selection handles at its borders. Font, style, and formatting changes at this level apply to all cells and text within—and of course you can apply all of the usual object formatting to the table, changing its size, position, rotation, shadow, and so on.

- **The cell level.** Clicking a second time within a table selects a specific cell, and Pages highlights it by adding a blue border around the cell's edges. From here, all changes apply only to the selected cell and the text within, and you can no longer move the table or edit its object-level settings. At the cell level, you can set the background and borders of individual cells, for example. Be careful here, though: Pages implicitly selects the full text of the selected cell—if you start typing as soon as you first select it, you'll replace *all* text in that cell. If that's not what you want to do, you should instead switch to editing the table at…

- **The text level.** This is where you actually edit the text within an individual cell. Click inside a selected cell and Pages places the insertion point into the cell, letting you make changes at that specific point in the text.

As described above, you just keep on clicking inside a table to continue drilling further down into its content from the table level to the cell level to the text level. To reverse direction, press ⌘-Return; pressing ⌘-Return while editing text inside a cell selects the entire cell, and pressing it again selects the entire table.

When you have a table selected at either the cell level or text level, you can move through the cells from left to right by pressing Tab, which selects the next cell. When you reach the last cell in a row, pressing Tab bumps you down to the first cell in the next row. If you're already at the last row of the table, Pages adds a new row and takes you down to its first cell. This is an easy way to grow your table organically, row by row, as you add new content.

Throw the cell-selecting machinery into reverse by pressing Shift-Tab, which moves through your cells from right to left. When you click Shift-Tab from the very first cell in the table, Pages teleports you down to the very last cell.

Tip: Since pressing the Tab key inside a table advances to the next cell, you can't use it to insert an actual tab into table text. Since you typically use the table itself to manage columns of text, it's rare that you'll need to add a tab in a cell, but when you do, you can do so by pressing Option-Tab.

You can also use the arrow keys to skip from cell to cell. When you have a cell selected at the cell level, you can use any of the arrow keys to move to the next cell in that direction. When you're editing a cell at the text level, the arrow keys move you around the text as usual. But when you reach either the beginning or end of the text, the arrow key hops you over to the next cell, selecting the whole thing at the cell level. As when you use the Tab or Shift-Tab keys, the right and left arrow keys bump you to the next or previous row when you hit the end of the line; the up and down keys move you to the previous or next column when you reach the start or end of a column.

Tip: When you turn on the Table Inspector's "Return key moves to next cell" checkbox for a table, pressing Return moves you to the cell below the current selection, and pressing Shift-Return moves you up to the previous cell. Under Pages' standard settings this option is turned off, and pressing Return creates a new paragraph in the cell. However, if you need to insert a paragraph or line break into a cell when this setting is turned on, hold down the Option key: Option-Return for a paragraph break and Shift-Option-Return for a line break.

You can select several cells at once in order to, for example, change their background color or delete all their content. Pages gives you a few ways to select groups of cells:

- Shift-click cells or drag the mouse across the cells to select a block of neighboring cells.

- ⌘-click individual cells anywhere in the table; unlike the Shift-click approach, the cells don't have to be adjacent to each other. You also use ⌘-click to deselect cells that you've already selected.

- To select an entire row or column, select a cell within the row or column, and choose the Select Row or Select Column command from any of these locations: the Table Inspector's Edit Rows & Columns pop-up menu; the cell's shortcut menu (Control-click the selected cell); or the Format → Table submenu.

- You can select multiple rows or columns by selecting cells in each of the rows or columns before using the Select Row or Select Column command.

Typing into Table Cells

A table is essentially a cluster of text boxes—adding and editing text in a table cell works the same as it does in a text box. When you first select a table at the cell level or tab into a new cell, Pages selects all of its text. Start typing to replace *all* the text in that cell, or click again to select the cell at the text level and place the insertion point where you want to add text to the cell. Then type away.

You edit text within a cell just as you would anywhere else in Pages: Click once to place the insertion point in a particular spot, double-click to select a word, triple-click to select a paragraph. Choose Edit → Copy to copy some selected text from a cell, and choose Edit → Paste and paste that text at the insertion point in the same cell, a different cell, or outside of the table. Format the text using any of the options available in the Format Bar, Text Inspector, Styles Drawer, or Fonts window (for the full overview, review Chapter 2 starting on page 59). Just like a text box, a table cell can also contain inline shapes, images, charts, movies, and sounds—but not text boxes or other tables. (Only floating tables can contain charts and shapes.)

Tip: Pages tries to help finish your thought when you type into a table cell. If the beginning of your typed text matches the value for a cell above in the same column, Pages suggests that value by auto-completing the text. To accept the value, press Tab or Return; if you don't like the suggestion, just keep typing. (If there's more than one matching value, you get a little drop-down list; just click to pick one.) To turn this feature off, go to the Pages → Preferences window, click the General button, and turn off the "Show auto-completion list in table columns" checkbox.

Text alignment inside table cells works the same as aligning text inside a text box. In addition to the usual horizontal alignment styles—left-aligned, centered, right-aligned, or justified—table cells also have an *automatic alignment* option. This setting changes the alignment based on the type of content within the cell: Text aligns left, and numbers align right, for example. To set the alignment, select the entire table or one or more individual cells, and choose any of the alignment options in the Format Bar or in the Text Inspector's Text tab, as shown in Figure 8-4. These alignment options also include vertical controls, letting you align text to the top, bottom, or middle of the cell.

Note: Vertical alignment applies to all text in the selected cell, but you can apply horizontal alignment on a paragraph-by-paragraph basis.

Control the distance between the text and the edge of the cell with the Text Inspector's Inset Margin slider. Tighten up the gap between the text and the cell edge by moving the slider to the left or entering a lower number in the Inset Margin measurement box. Pages applies the inset margin around all four sides of the cell.

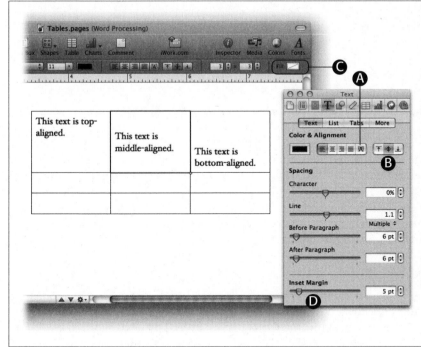

Figure 8-4:
Set the horizontal and vertical alignment for table cells from the Format Bar or the Text Inspector. In addition to the usual left, right, center, and justified options, table cells also have an auto-alignment option (A) to shift the text according to its content (left-aligned for text, right-aligned for numbers). Click one of the vertical alignment buttons (B) to stick the content to the top, bottom, or middle of the table cell.

Click the Fill color well (C) to set the background color for the selected cell(s). The Inset Margin slider (D) controls the amount of space between the text and the cell boundary.

This Inset Margin setting determines the outer boundaries of the text area for a cell, but you can further adjust a cell's text margins with the ruler. Choose View → Show Rulers to adjust right and left margins inward from the inset margin—as well as set first-line indents and tabs for the selected cell. You can use the rulers on only one cell at a time and only when you've selected the cell at the text level, so that the insertion point is visible or text is highlighted. See page 72 for more about changing margins and tabs with the rulers.

Automatically resizing table rows

As you add new text to a cell, Pages keeps up with you by expanding the height of the row so that it has enough room to display all of your text. Since Pages makes room in the row as you add more content, the rows below are nudged down, making the entire table grow. This table growth stops when an expanding inline table cell reaches the bottom of the page, column, or text box—a cell can't spread out onto another page, column, or linked text box.

If you prefer to have a row stay a fixed height no matter how much content you pour into it, turn off the "Automatically resize to fit content" checkbox in the Table Inspector → Table pane. With this checkbox turned off, Pages hides any overflow text and displays a clipping indicator (+) to alert you to the hidden text so you can trim the text or adjust its font size to fit. Use this option for tables that don't need to display much text, in order to maintain row regularity.

Tip: When Pages automatically resizes rows as you type, an inline table can expand to fill more than one page or column, and Pages automatically continues the table on the other side of the break. But in the case of a floating table, the expanding rows can end up pushing the lower rows of the table right off the bottom of the page, into digital oblivion. If this happens, you have to insert another table on the next page, and cut and paste the overflow rows into it.

When you add more text than can fit on one line of a cell, Pages normally wraps your text to a new line, just like it would in any text column. If you don't want it to do this, turn off the Wrap Text in Cell option in the Table Inspector's Format pane, and Pages limits the display to one line. If the cell next door is empty, the extra content spills over into that cell (the contents actually remain in the original cell, and that's where you click to edit the text, but the content is no longer penned in by its cell boundaries). If the neighboring cell has its own content, the text doesn't spill over and the display is clipped to the cell's width. The extra data is still there, just hidden. To show the whole thing, turn on the Wrap Text in Cell option again.

Moving cell content

You can move the contents of one cell, along with all its formatting, to another cell by cutting/copying and pasting, or by dragging. The trick is to first make sure that the cell is not in text-editing mode and that it's instead selected at the cell level: If the insertion point is visible in the cell, press ⌘-Return so that the blue border appears around the cell and the insertion point disappears. Now drag the cell's contents to another cell. As you drag, the cursor turns into a hand and a blue border appears around the cell in which Pages intends to drop your selection. When you release the mouse, the contents of the first cell appear in the second one, replacing any content that used to exist there, and Pages empties out the first cell. You can get the same result with cut and paste: Select the cell you want to move, press Edit → Cut to remove its contents, select the target cell, and press Edit → Paste.

If you want to *copy* a cell's content instead of moving it, follow the same drag-and-drop maneuver, but hold down the Option key while you drag. The pointer sprouts a green ball bearing a + sign, and Pages copies the contents of the first cell into the second, again replacing any content that might have been in the second cell. Copy and paste does the same thing: Choose Edit → Copy to copy the selected cell to the Clipboard, select the destination cell, and choose Edit → Paste.

Tip: If you want to strip a table of all of its formatting as well as its content—to remove its background color, for example—select it at the cell level and choose Edit → Clear All (also available from the cell's Control-click shortcut menu). Edit → Cut will also give you the same effect; both are more effective than pressing Delete, which removes only the text and no formatting.

Use these moving and copying techniques to create new tables, too. When you drag cells from a floating table and into any other part of the page canvas, it adds a new table using *copies* of those cells (the original content stays put in the original table).

You can do this with inline tables, too, but only to create other inline tables in the same text column; to create a floating table, hold down the Command (⌘) key while you drag.

Adding and Deleting Rows and Columns

If you set up your table with exactly the right number of rows and columns when you inserted it, congratulations! You can skip ahead to the next section. Usually, though, you'll find it necessary to adjust the number of rows and columns as you work on a table.

You can add more rows and columns to your table any time. To do so, select a cell and choose Format → Table → Add Row Above or Add Row Below to add a new row above or below your selected cell. Or choose Format → Table → Add Column Before or Add Column After to add a new column before or after your selected cell. When Pages adds a new row or column to a table with the Add Row or Column Before or After commands, it duplicates the cell backgrounds and other formatting from the selected row or column—but not the cell text. These commands (along with all the other table-related menu commands) are also available in the gear-shaped Action pop-up menu in the Table Inspector's Edit Rows & Columns area. You can also find these commands in the shortcut menu: Control-click anywhere in the table to invoke this timesaving feature.

Tip: Because adding rows and columns is so common when you're working inside a table, get to know the Option-arrow keyboard combinations to do this: Option-Up adds a row above the selected cell, and Option-down adds a row below; Option-left adds a column to the left of the selected cell, and Option-right adds a column to the right.

You can also add more rows to the bottom of the table or more columns to the right side by increasing the number of rows and columns in the Table Inspector's Rows and Columns boxes. Pages tacks on the new cells, duplicating the bottom row's or right column's background fill and other formatting. If you lower the numbers listed in the Table Inspector's Rows and Columns boxes, Pages similarly trims cells from the bottom or the right side of the table, unless those cells contain data—in that case, the Table Inspector won't let you reduce the setting any further.

Delete a row or column by selecting a cell within it, and choosing Format → Table → Delete Row or Delete Column. You can also delete multiple rows or columns by selecting two or more cells in neighboring rows or columns, and choosing the same commands, which now read Delete Rows or Delete Columns. As with the Add commands, these Delete commands are also available in the Table Inspector's Edit Rows & Columns pop-up as well as the Control-click shortcut menu.

Labeling tables with header rows, header columns, and footer rows

Tables typically sport labels on their rows or columns to advertise their contents, and Pages provides *header rows* and *header columns* to help you out with that—in fact, all newborn tables appear with a header row. A header row is the very first row in a table, and a header column is the leftmost column. You can format header rows and columns however you like, but Pages starts off by shading them to make them stand out from the rest of the table, which Pages calls *body rows* and *body columns.*

Table headers act just like the table body but with a few special perks. For one thing, header rows keep coming back. Just like page headers that appear on every page of a document, a table header row appears at the top of each page, linked text box, or text column when an inline table continues across a break, as shown in Figure 8-5. This helps your reader stay oriented after flipping the page or dragging her eyes up to a new column—the table's columns are always neatly labeled. You can edit the text inside a repeated header row, but doing so also updates every other instance of the row, in other pages or columns.

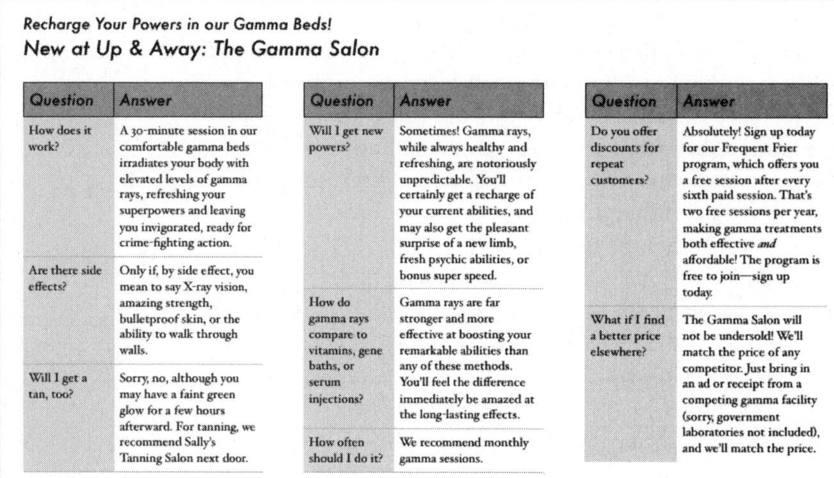

Recharge Your Powers in our Gamma Beds!

New at Up & Away: The Gamma Salon

Question	Answer
How does it work?	A 30-minute session in our comfortable gamma beds irradiates your body with elevated levels of gamma rays, refreshing your superpowers and leaving you invigorated, ready for crime-fighting action.
Are there side effects?	Only if, by side effect, you mean to say X-ray vision, amazing strength, bulletproof skin, or the ability to walk through walls.
Will I get a tan, too?	Sorry, no, although you may have a faint green glow for a few hours afterward. For tanning, we recommend Sally's Tanning Salon next door.

Question	Answer
Will I get new powers?	Sometimes! Gamma rays, while always healthy and refreshing, are notoriously unpredictable. You'll certainly get a recharge of your current abilities, and may also get the pleasant surprise of a new limb, fresh psychic abilities, or bonus super speed.
How do gamma rays compare to vitamins, gene baths, or serum injections?	Gamma rays are far stronger and more effective at boosting your remarkable abilities than any of these methods. You'll feel the difference immediately be amazed at the long-lasting effects.
How often should I do it?	We recommend monthly gamma sessions.

Question	Answer
Do you offer discounts for repeat customers?	Absolutely! Sign up today for our Frequent Frier program, which offers you a free session after every sixth paid session. That's two free sessions per year, making gamma treatments both effective *and* affordable! The program is free to join—sign up today.
What if I find a better price elsewhere?	The Gamma Salon will not be undersold! We'll match the price of any competitor. Just bring in an ad or receipt from a competing gamma facility (sorry, government laboratories not included), and we'll match the price.

Figure 8-5:
When a table crosses into a new page, column, or linked text box, the header row makes the leap, too, automatically relabeling the table in its new context. Here, a table of frequently asked questions spans three columns, repeating its header at the top of each one.

As you'll see when you learn about using formulas on page 304, header rows and columns are also clever with math, providing shortcuts to apply automatic calculations to their row or column. This is particularly handy with *footer rows,* which appear as the very last row in the table; they're frequently used to provide tallies for each of the table's columns. Header rows and columns also provide informal names for your rows and columns that you can use to identify individual cells with those names when you refer to them in formulas. You'll learn more about this in the section "Making Mini-Spreadsheets with Formulas" starting on page 303.

To add header rows, header columns, or footer rows, use the Headers & Footer pop-up buttons in the Table Inspector → Table pane, shown in Figure 8-6. Choose the number of rows or columns to display from the three pop-ups. To remove a table header or footer, reduce the number in the corresponding pop-up button—set it to *0* to remove all rows or columns of that type.

Note: The same options are available in the Format → Table submenu, which in turn contains the Header Rows, Header Columns, and Footer Rows submenus. Select the number of rows or columns to display for each type.

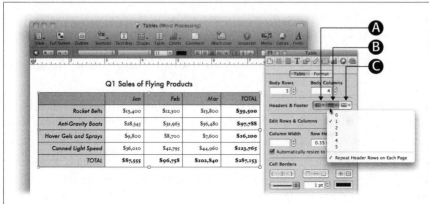

Figure 8-6:
The Headers & Footer pop-up buttons in the Table Inspector let you control the display of header columns (A), header rows (B), and footer rows (C). Here, the table has one header column and one header row. Pages lets you add up to five of each of these header/footer elements—pick the number by selecting from the appropriate pop-up button.

Most tables require no more than one footer row, header row, or header column, but multiples can be useful when you want some header or footer cells to be taller or wider than the rest by merging them (page 298) with their neighbors. If you don't want header rows to repeat and instead prefer to display a header row only once, at the very beginning of a table, turn off the "Repeat header rows on each page" option in the Header Rows pop-up button.

Although Pages creates row and column headers with a background fill to differentiate them from the rest of the table, you can remove that fill or replace it with another that better suits your table design. For more on changing the background color of cells, see page 295.

Setting the Data Type with Cell Format

Pages recognizes that the data in your table cells has more meaning than just a collection of typed letters and numbers—there are *kinds* of data. A monetary value is different than a plain number, and a date is different than regular text. To help yourself format, sort, and organize the various kinds of data you enter into your table, you can tell Pages exactly what type of data is in each cell and how you'd like Pages to display it. For example, you can format cells with monetary values to include a currency symbol ($, ¥, £, and so on), or you can tell it to display all dates in a consistent manner no matter how you enter them (1/6/09, Jan 6, 2009, and so on).

You do all this by setting the *cell format* in the Table Inspector's Format tab, shown in Figure 8-7. Select the cell(s) to format and then select one of these options from the Cell Format pop-up menu:

- **Automatic.** This free-form setting tells Pages to wing it, leaving it to its own devices to figure out what kind of data you're entering. It recognizes currency, numbers, text, dates, and percentages as you type them. When you select one or more cells with Automatic formatting that also have the same data type, the Table Inspector also shows preferences for displaying that data type—if all the cells happen to be dates, for example, picking Automatic shows you options for choosing the display format for date and time.

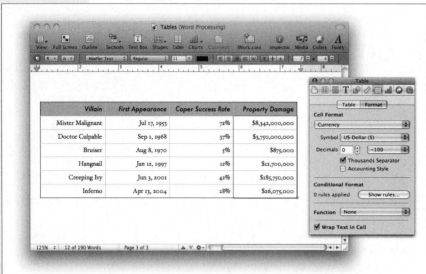

Figure 8-7:
Set the data type for table cells in the Cell Format pop-up menu of the Table Inspector's Format pane. In the table shown here, the Villain column is set to Text, the First Appearance column is set to Date and Time, Caper Success Rate is set to Percentage, and Property Damage is set to Currency. Because the Property Damage cells are selected, the Table Inspector shows the settings for the Currency format.

- **Number.** Choose this setting to deal with digits, and select from the number-specific options to fine-tune the display. Set the number of decimal points to include in the display, and Pages manages the rounding for you. When you want a cell to display a value rounded to the nearest integer, for example, set the

Decimals field to zero—if the cell's value is 1.264, Pages displays 1. This is only what's *displayed*. Pages remembers the real value behind the scenes, so if you later change the number of decimal points, Pages will update the display to 1.3 for one decimal, 1.26 for two decimals, 1.264 for three decimals, and so on. The Numbers settings also let you choose the format to use for negative numbers and whether to include a thousands separator (1,000,000 vs. 1000000).

- **Currency.** The Symbol pop-up menu determines the currency symbol to display—choose among 25 currencies, from the Australian dollar to the Polish zloty, and Pages automatically adds it to numbers entered in the selected cell(s). No need to type a $ sign before all of your values, in other words—just type the number and Pages adds the $ for you when you move to another cell. Turn on the "Accounting style" checkbox to display the currency symbol at the left side of the cell, with the number at the right.

- **Percentage.** This setting is also similar to Number and offers the exact same options. The difference is that decimal numbers are displayed as percentages. A cell with a value of 0.5, for example, is displayed as 50% and 10 is displayed as 1000%.

- **Date and Time.** This setting lets you display a date and time with a variety of different formats, no matter how you enter the date. You can enter the date as 12/6/09, for example, and depending on your settings, have it display as "Tuesday, December 6, 2009". Make your selections from the Date menu and Time menu, respectively. (To enter both a date and time, separate them with a space. For example: 12/6/09 10:00 am.)

- **Duration.** This format displays an amount of time (weeks, hours, seconds, and so on). Duration fields can display a variety of time units, but the standard setting is hours, minutes, and seconds (h, m, and s). For example, you can format the duration field to display one hour, three minutes, and 34 seconds as: 1:03:34. Use the Units slider to select the three time units to display (see Figure 8-8) and use the Format pop-up to tell Pages how you want to display your selected units.

- **Fraction.** Choose this option to display decimal numbers in their fractional equivalents—or at least their rough equivalents. Enter 0.25 into a fraction cell, for example, and Pages turns it into 1/4. When you choose Fraction, the Table Inspector offers up the Accuracy field, which lets you choose how detailed you'd like the fraction to be, from one digit (7/8) to two digits (23/24) to three digits (445/553). You can also choose to have the fractions displayed with a fixed denominator (halves, quarters, eights, sixteenths, and so on), and Pages rounds your number to the nearest fraction. As with rounding in Numbers, Decimals, and Percentages, this is just for display purposes—Pages always remembers the "real" value for you.

- **Numeral System.** Switch your cell to a whole different number system to count in base 2 (binary), base 16 (hexadecimal), or some other numeral system. If that sentence made no sense to you, don't worry—that almost certainly means that you don't need this particular cell format, which is generally reserved for hard-core math folks. Pick the base value of the system you want to use from the Base field, and choose the number of digits to display in the Places field. If you selected Base 2, 8, or 16, you can also choose an option for displaying negative values.

- **Scientific.** This option displays numbers in *scientific notation,* a numbering scheme that's particularly useful for very, very miniscule numbers or enormously large numbers. This setting lets you choose how many decimal places to display, and Pages rounds as necessary.

- **Text.** Just as its name suggests, this setting indicates that the cell contains regular text—numbers get no special treatment in text fields.

- **Custom.** If this flurry of formatting options still doesn't offer quite what you're looking for, Pages lets you build your own. See page 611 for details about creating a custom number format.

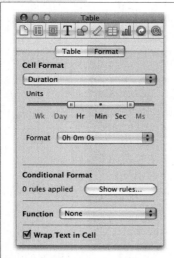

Figure 8-8:
When you choose the Duration cell format, Pages lets you pick the units to display as well as their format. The Units slider "brackets" the units to use. Here, it's set to display hours, minutes, and seconds. Move the slider all the way to the left to display weeks, days, and hours, or all the way to the right to display minutes, seconds, and milliseconds. You can stretch or squeeze the slider to display more or fewer units: Drag the left or right end of the slider to resize its width to cover the units you want to include.

Sorting Table Rows

Tables are designed to organize and communicate data—chances are, you want that data to appear in a certain order. If you have a table listing all the members of the Up & Away Frequent Flyer Club, for example, you might want to sort the list alphabetically by hero name, or chronologically by the date members joined, or in descending order by the number of times the hero has saved the planet from insidious evildoers.

You can do just that by choosing a column to use to reorder the table's rows. Select a cell in the column you want to use—the "Hero Name" column in our first example. In the Table Inspector's Table pane, choose Sort Ascending from the Edit Rows & Columns pop-up menu, and Pages reorders all of the rows alphabetically by hero name, A to Z. Choose Sort Descending, and Pages flips the order, Z to A, bumping Aardvark Man from his usual first slot in the club roster. Click a cell in a different column, and choose Sort Ascending or Sort Descending to reorder all of the rows based on the values in that column instead.

Tip: To reorder only some of the rows in the table, select a set of neighboring cells in the sort column. When you choose Sort Ascending or Sort Descending, Pages reorders only the rows included in the selected set.

Pages sorts your rows differently depending on the type of data in the sort column. As you might expect, text is sorted alphabetically, numbers are sorted numerically, and dates are sorted chronologically. When cells contain a mix of text and numbers, numbers come first in ascending sort order, followed by letters—the reverse is true in descending order. Rows with empty cells in the sort column are basically ignored, dismissed to the bottom of the table to bring up the rear behind the sorted rows. Header cells aren't sorted at all.

Tip: To get your data sorting the way you want, you may have to give Pages a nudge in the right direction. Dates, for example, don't sort chronologically until you set the column's cells to use the Date & Time data format in the Table Inspector's Format pane.

Formatting Tables

When the time comes to move beyond basic text tables, Pages is ready with a host of table formatting options. You can add a background color or image fill to the entire table or to individual cells; control whether and how Pages displays cell borders; adjust opacity, rotation, and so on.

Adding backgrounds

You can add background colors, gradients, or images to the entire table or to individual cells. Choose a fill style from either the Graphic Inspector's Fill pop-up menu—just like you would for a shape or text box—or from the Cell Background pop-up menu in the Table Inspector's Table menu. (Both menus represent exactly the same setting; they just happen to show up in two places with different names.) If you're adding a solid background color, you can also use the Fill pop-up menu in the Format Bar to select the color. For all the filling possibilities, see page 265.

Note: Unlike other objects, tables and cells don't get the advanced-gradient option for fill style.

To add a background color to the entire table, select it at the table level so that the object's selection handles appear, and then choose your fill style. To add a background to one or more cells, select them, and apply the fill style to the selected cells. If you add a background to the entire table *and* to individual cells, the cell background "wins" and appears on top of the table background. If you change your mind about the cell's color, set its fill to "None" or choose a transparent fill color, so that the table's background color shows through again. (If you try to "match" the cell to the table, you'll just have to do the whole thing all over when you later change the table's fill.)

You can also apply background colors to individual cells by drag and drop: Click the Colors button in the toolbar or choose View → Show Colors to display the Color Picker. Select a color, adjust its opacity, and drag from the swatch into the table. Pages displays the green + sign ball next to your arrow cursor as you drag, and outlines the table cell beneath it in blue, indicating its readiness to receive the color when you release the mouse button. See page 265 for a complete tour of the Color Picker.

When working with tables with many columns, you can increase readability by adding an *alternating row color* so that odd rows have one color and even rows have another. This creates a subtle visual distinction between each entry and helps readers scan more easily across individual rows of the table. To do this, turn on the Alternating Row Color checkbox in the Table Inspector's Table pane and choose a color by clicking the color well next door. You can use this feature in combination with any kind of cell background, but the alternating rows always use a solid color. For example, if you have the table set to display an Image Fill background and you add an alternating row color, odd rows display the image background, and even rows have the solid color of your choice—no image. (If you reduce the opacity of the alternating color in the Color Picker, however, you can allow a table's background image to show through, which has the same effect as a tinted image fill for the alternating rows.)

Note: If you want alternating backgrounds that use another fill style—a gradient fill, for example—you can do that, too, but you have to do it manually. Leave the Alternating Row Color setting turned off, and style one row the way you want your alternating background to look. With one or more of those cells selected, choose Format → Copy Table Style. Then go through every other row of your table and, for each of them, select all of its cells and choose Format → Paste Table Style (or press Option-⌘-V) to apply the formatting.

Formatting cell borders

New Pages tables feature a one-point, black border around every cell. That may be fine for a bare-bones, quick-and-dirty table, but a little time spent modifying your table borders can pay off with a more visually appealing and more readable table. You can change the color, opacity, and border thickness—or remove the border entirely for the whole table, individual cells, or even a single side of a cell.

Change the borders for the whole table at once by selecting the table at the table level so its selection handles are visible. In the Table Inspector → Table tab, choose a line style in the Cell Borders pop-up menu (or choose None to remove borders entirely). Set the border width by typing a number into the Width box and pressing Return or using its up and down arrow buttons. Pick the border color by clicking the color well and using the Color Picker.

If you think this sounds suspiciously like choosing stroke settings for other objects, you're exactly right. In fact, you can also use the Graphic Inspector's Stroke settings to change table borders—it's the same setting in a different place. You'll notice, though, that the Cell Borders section of the Table Inspector has a few additional buttons to help you choose specific borders. This lets you style some borders differently than others—adding a strong border to the four sides of the table, for example, while having a more subtle border between rows, as shown in Figure 8-9.

Note: Alas, tables don't get the full range of stroke styles as other objects. The brush strokes enjoyed by other objects, for example, are banished from the table's stroke options, leaving you a modest selection of solid, thin, dashed, or dotted lines.

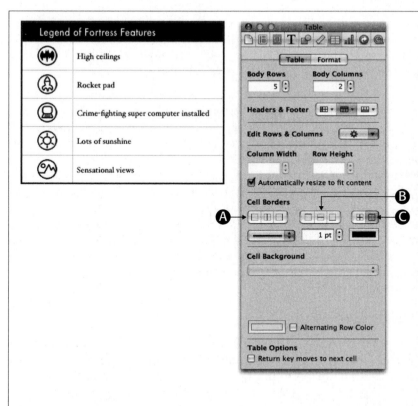

Figure 8-9:
The Table Inspector's Cell Borders section has buttons to help select certain borders within a table so that you can apply styles to those lines without affecting the rest.

The vertical border buttons (A) respectively select the left border, vertical borders between cells, and the right border. The horizontal border buttons (B) select the top border, horizontal borders between cells, and the bottom border. The last two buttons (C) select all interior borders between cells or the outer-boundary borders surrounding the selection. These selection buttons choose borders relative to the selection. If you have the entire table selected, for example, clicking the left-border button selects the left border of the entire first column of cells. If you have just one cell selected, Pages selects the left border of just that one cell.

You can also select individual border lines in order to adjust their stroke style. Click inside a table to select the whole table or a cell. Position your arrow cursor so the very tip of the arrow is on a cell border, and then click the mouse. Pages highlights the line in blue and changes the arrow cursor into the line-selecting cursor—a pair of lines with a pair of perpendicular, outward-facing arrows. Hold down the Shift key or ⌘ (they do the same thing in this case) while you click to select multiple lines.

To select the border of an individual cell, or *border segment,* select the entire border as described above, and then click again on the individual segment in that border—the selection changes to highlight just that one segment. To select (or deselect) additional segments, Shift-click or ⌘-click those individual cell borders.

Resizing cells, rows, and columns

If the regularity of your table's cells makes you feel a little square, loosen up by resizing individual cells or entire rows and columns by selecting and dragging the cell borders. Select a border line or cell side so that it's highlighted as described above, and then drag to reposition it. As you drag, Pages displays the line's x or y coordinates—the distance from the left or top edge of the page. You can drag only one line at a time.

Use the Table Inspector when you want to set the dimensions of rows and columns by manually adjusting their settings. In the Table pane, select one or more cells, enter the measurements in the Column Width and Row Height boxes, and then press Return—or use the up and down arrow buttons.

If you've made lots of sizing changes to your table's cells and things are starting to look a bit lopsided, Pages provides two commands that can tidy things up for you. Select a group of cells and choose Format → Table → Distribute Rows Evenly, and Pages adjusts the height of the selected cells so that they all match. Similarly, the Distribute Columns Evenly command tells Pages to adjust the selected cells to make their widths match. If you select the entire table and then use both of these commands, Pages makes every cell in the table the same size. If you have the Table Inspector's "Automatically resize to fit content" checkbox turned on, the Distribute Rows Evenly command adjusts the rows to match the height of the cell that contains the most text. If that checkbox is turned off, Pages keeps the dimensions of the entire table the same while equalizing the height of the rows. Pages tacks the + clipping indicator onto cells containing more text than can fit to show that they have some hidden text.

Splitting and merging cells

Pages can split individual cells into two, or merge two or more cells into one. For example, you could subdivide a large cell to break up its text or to add different background colors or images to the divided cells. Pages splits cells either horizontally or vertically into two equal halves. After they're split, you can adjust the new cell border to create cells of any proportion.

To slice horizontally across a cell or group of cells, select the cell(s) to split and choose Split into Rows from the Format → Table submenu, the Table Inspector's Edit Rows & Columns pop-up menu, or the table's shortcut menu (Control-click the table). Choose the Split Columns command to chop the cells vertically. This cellular division leaves your content intact: When you split a cell into rows, any text it contains stays in the top cell. If you split a cell into columns, its text stays in the left cell. The new cells you create possess the same background color or image as the original cell.

Instead of dividing cells, you can unite them—as long as the cells you're bringing together form a rectangle. You might find this ability useful in order to add a large photo in place of a group of text-free cells within a larger table, or to change an entire column of cells into one large cell to act as a divider between columns. Start by selecting two or more cells. Then choose Format → Table → Merge Cells—or use the same command from the Table Inspector's Edit Rows & Columns pop-up, or the table's shortcut menu. Alternatively, use the more direct method of selecting the cell border you wish to merge and pressing Delete. Pages tears down the wall and fuses the neighbor cells into one, using the background image or color from the upper, left, or upper-left cell of the group. If the cells contain text, Pages combines it in the new cell, separating text from cells in the same row with tabs and separating text from separate rows with paragraph breaks.

Restore merged cells to their gotta-be-me individual cells by deselecting Merge Cells in the Format → Table menu or in the shortcut menu. This doesn't "unmerge" the content inside, though; any content that had been merged from two separate cells remains together in the left or top cell of the freshly split group.

Setting graphic styles

Pages lets you style tables with the full range of graphic styles available to other objects. Use the Graphic Inspector to add a shadow to your table (page 273) or make it transparent by adjusting the Opacity setting (page 275). Resize the table without adding new rows or columns by dragging its selection handles or by using the Metrics Inspector (page 251), where you can also flip or resize floating tables (sorry, inline table, you're on a tight leash).

A subtle difference between tables and other objects is that you can apply opacity and shadow effects to individual cells as well as the entire table object. When you have a single cell selected at either the cell level or text level, for example, changing the opacity affects only that cell. With the whole table selected, meanwhile, the opacity setting applies to the entire object.

Note: If you add a shadow to an individual cell, Pages adds the shadow to the text within the cell, not to its overall outline.

To copy one table's formatting styles to another, select the first table and choose Format → Copy Table Style, then select the second table and choose Format → Paste Table Style.

Monitoring cell values with conditional formatting

You can light up a cell with colors of your choice when the cell meets certain criteria. This nifty visual alarm system is called *conditional formatting*. In a table of club members, for example, you could use this feature to highlight whose member fees are due this month. In a table of monthly sales, you could color-code sales numbers of individual associates according to different commission tiers.

To add conditional formatting to a table:

1. **Select the entire table or a selection of one or more cells.**

2. **In the Table Inspector's Format pane, click the Show Rules button.**

   The Conditional Formatting window appears, showing any rules already applied to the selected cells.

3. **Choose a condition from the pop-up menu shown in Figure 8-10, and provide any additional info to complete the condition.**

Note: The Between condition requires that you specify two test values. The condition is met if either of the numbers or any value in between them appears in the cell(s).

---

4. **Just below the rule you just created in Step 3, click the Edit button to choose the formatting to apply when a cell meets the conditions.**

5. **Select the Text Color, Font Style, and Fill Color to add to matching cells, and click Done.**

   The Font Style buttons let you choose any combination of bold, italic, underline, or strikethrough text. As you make your changes, Pages displays a preview of what the formatting will look like.

6. **To add another rule, click the + sign and repeat steps 3–5.**

   You can add as many rules as you like, setting a bright green color for a cell that matches one condition, for example, and dull red for a cell that matches another. To add a new rule, click the + sign next to the rule that comes immediately before where you'd like to insert the new rule. To remove a rule, click its − sign. If a cell matches more than one rule, the first rule in the list wins.

Note: There's no easy way to rearrange rules once you've added them. To change their order, you have to delete a rule and then add it again.

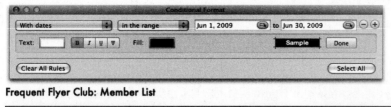

Frequent Flyer Club: Member List

Hero	Hero Since	Locker Number	Ability	Fees Due Date
Captain Fantastic	Feb 15, 1946	2	Super strength, speed, invulnerable	Jun 15, 2009
Madame Uncanny	Aug 17, 1989	136	Psychic powers	Jan 30, 2010
Dark Avenger	Jan 14, 1994	210	Phase through walls	Jun 30, 2009
Mantis Girl	May 13, 2002	12	Martial arts	Dec 3, 2009
Danger Woman	Sep 10, 1996	141	Super strength	Jul 15, 2009

Figure 8-10:
Conditional formatting lets you highlight cells that meet certain criteria. Here, the Fees Due Date column is set to highlight dates between June 1 and June 30. Choose a rule from the "Choose a Rule" pop-up menu (where "With dates" is selected here) and provide any additional info required to complete the condition. The menu is divided into three chunks: The top section applies tests to numeric values; the middle section is for text; and the bottom section is for dates.

Below the rule fields, Pages shows a preview of what the conditional formatting looks like. Click the Edit button to get the view shown here and make changes to the formatting. Select the Text Color, Font Style, and Fill Color to use for cells matching your criteria.

To stop using a specific rule, click its – button, and Pages removes the rule from the list. To stop using all rules for the selected cells, click the Clear All Rules button.

Tip: Your conditional formatting rule can use the value of another table cell as the test value. To do this, click the small blue circle in the value field, and a cell reference field pops up (this field looks a little bit like the Formula Editor). Add a cell reference by clicking a table cell or typing the reference directly, and then press Return. You'll learn all about cell references on page 301.

If you want to set the same rule on several cells at once, click the Show Rules button with all of the cells selected, and make your changes in the Conditional Formatting window. After you've set conditional formatting rules for a cell, you can go back and edit the rules anytime by selecting the cell and clicking the Show Rules button in the Table Inspector's Format pane. To find all the cells in a table that have the same conditional formatting rules as a particular cell, select the cell, open the Conditional Formatting window, click Select All, and Pages selects all cells with identical conditional formatting rules.

Autofilling Table Cells

Autofilling lets you use the content in one or more cells to automatically add values to neighboring cells. This is particularly handy when you want to add cells that increment dates or numbers from cell to cell—like a counter.

Every cell has a magical Fill handle that appears in its lower-right corner when you select the cell, as shown in Figure 8-11, circled. Drag the Fill handle over the cells you want to fill, and any data, cell format, formula, or background fill associated with the selected cell is pasted into those cells, replacing any previous values they might have contained.

You can also autofill several cells with the same value by selecting a range of neighboring cells and choosing Format → Table → Fill Right, replacing all of the cells with the leftmost value(s) in the selection. Similarly, choose Format → Table → Fill Down to fill the selected cells with the top value(s) in the selection.

Note: When you copy a formula into a new cell—whether by moving, pasting, or autofilling—Pages updates the formula's cell references to reflect the new location. You'll learn all about formulas in just a moment; for details, see Moving Formulas on page 309.

This alone is useful enough when you're setting up a table to copy cell formatting or initial cell values. But autofilling gets especially interesting when it fills values based on detected patterns, letting you increment or cycle through values as you drag the Fill handle into adjacent cells. To do this, select two or more cells before dragging. For example, if two selected cells contain 1 and 2, Pages adds the values 3 and 4 when you drag through the two adjacent cells. And if two selected cells contain 1 and 4, the values 7 and 10 are added when you drag through the adjacent two cells (values are incremented by 3). Likewise, if two selected cells contain A and B, Pages adds the values C, D, E, and so on when you drag the Fill handle into new cells.

This works with dates, too: Select just one date cell, and drag the Fill handle into neighboring cells to increment the date day by day. When you select two cells and drag the Fill handle, Pages increments the value by the interval between the two dates. If seven days separate the dates in the selected field, then Pages bumps each autofilled value up by a week. Pages knows lots of these combinations: If you type "January" into a cell you can autofill to get February, March, April, and so on (the same works with Jan, Feb, Mar, …). Use Monday to get Tuesday, Wednesday, and Thursday, or use Q1 to get Q2, Q3, and Q4. (Alas, Pages can't do just any list. It doesn't know about "Dasher" and "Dancer," or "Huey" and "Louie"—and it doesn't know about "Michael," which *necessarily* means that it has no idea who "Jermaine" or "Tito" are.)

If you choose more than two cells with an irregular interval (or cells with text values), autofilling simply repeats the pattern of the selected cells: If you select cells containing 1, 2, and 5, for example, dragging the Fill handle adds 1, then 2, then 5, then 1, then 2, then 5, and so on to the new cells.

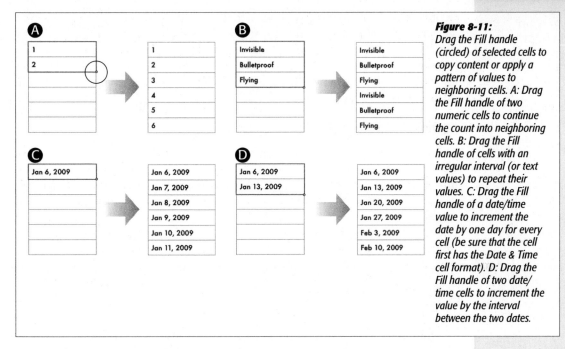

Figure 8-11:
Drag the Fill handle (circled) of selected cells to copy content or apply a pattern of values to neighboring cells. A: Drag the Fill handle of two numeric cells to continue the count into neighboring cells. B: Drag the Fill handle of cells with an irregular interval (or text values) to repeat their values. C: Drag the Fill handle of a date/time value to increment the date by one day for every cell (be sure that the cell first has the Date & Time cell format). D: Drag the Fill handle of two date/time cells to increment the value by the interval between the two dates.

Autofilling doesn't set up an ongoing relationship among cells in the group. After autofilling, you can change the cells independently of each other. If you prefer to link the cells' values so that they update when one of them changes, you probably want to use formulas instead, which brings us neatly to the next topic.

Making Mini-Spreadsheets with Formulas

You can use tables for lists of pretty much anything, but very often tables involve some kind of calculation. When your table lists items in an invoice, you have a total amount due. When tracking student grades for a class, you show the average grade for each student. A table of monthly sales figures by product might add up the total annual sales for each product, as well as the total monthly sales for all products. You get the idea.

You might have heard about this already, but it turns out that computers are good at math. No need to strain your brain adding columns or figuring averages—when you use tables to list your data, Pages can run the numbers for you. In iWork, tables are actually spreadsheets and vice versa—any calculations that you can do in a Numbers spreadsheet, you can also do in Pages tables. This means that your clever tables can update calculations on the fly as you add new data. You can even swap these mini-spreadsheets back and forth with Numbers.

When you add a calculated value to a cell, Pages doesn't simply run the numbers once and forget about it. It gives the cell a *formula,* a mathematical expression that tells Pages to do its arithmetic using other cells in your table. If you change a value of any of those cells, Pages automatically updates the formula's result. A formula, in other words, is a smart placeholder that's constantly updating its value as you add new data—formulas keep your tallies up to date so that you don't have to. You'll find out much more about working with formulas when you learn about Numbers (see Chapters 20 and 21)—you can use those techniques to build formulas in Pages, too. In the meantime, this section provides a quick intro to help you do basic math in Pages.

"Quick Formulas" for Common Calculations

Although Pages can perform incredible feats of mathematical gymnastics, most table arithmetic isn't exactly Einstein-level calculus. You usually just want to add up a row or column of values and display the total at the end. Pages' *quick formula* feature offers fast access to the most commonly used math operations, making it easy to run a calculation on a column or row. To apply a quick formula, select a cell or range of neighboring cells and choose from the Insert → Function menu or from the Function pop-up menu in the Table Inspector's Format pane. These menus offers six common calculations:

- **Sum** adds up the cells.

- **Average** calculates the mean value of the cells.

- **Minimum** displays the lowest value among the cells.

- **Maximum** displays the highest value among the cells.

- **Count** shows the number of numeric or date/time values in the cells (text values aren't included in the tally).

- **Product** multiplies all the cells.

When you choose a quick formula, Pages inserts the formula result into your table—but the exact cell where that formula lands and which values are tallied depends on the cells you've selected when you choose a formula. Read on.

Using header rows and columns with quick formulas

The easiest way to do a calculation on all the values in a row or column is to use its header cell. (Turn on the Header Row or Header Column option in the Table Inspector → Table pane to add a header row or column.) To add all the values of a column, for example, select the column's header cell and, in the Table Inspector's Format pane, choose Sum from the Function pop-up menu. Pages tallies the column and puts the total into the column's footer cell. If the table doesn't have a footer row, Pages adds one; if the table *does* have a footer row, Pages replaces any value in the column's footer cell with the formula tally.

Likewise, you can add the values of a row by selecting the row's cell in the header column and applying the Sum quick formula. Because there's no such thing as a "footer column," however, Pages puts the result into the last column of the table if that cell is empty. If there's already a value in that last column cell, the table adds a new column to hold the result.

Note: If you later reapply a quick formula to the header column for a row, Pages isn't quite clever enough to recall that it already added a formula for that row. Instead of updating the previous formula, it keeps adding new columns. If you choose Sum multiple times on a header column cell, for example, it will continue to add new columns summing up the row. Columns don't have this problem, thanks to the special footer row; reapplying a quick formula to the header row for a column always updates the same cell in the footer row, rather than adding new rows.

Using a range of cells with quick formula

If you just want to add up a few cells in a column or row instead of the whole she-bang, select a set of neighboring cells, and choose Sum from the quick formula window. Pages shows the result in the first cell after the selected cells. If there is no following cell or if it already has a value, Pages adds a new column or row to display your tally (unless the next cell is a footer cell—in that case, the footer cell's value is replaced with the new formula).

Adding a quick formula to a single cell

When you add a quick formula to a single cell outside a header row or column, Pages looks around at neighboring cells to find values to work with and inserts the result into the selected cell. When Pages is trying to figure out which cells to use, it runs through its checks in this order:

1. Is the cell a footer cell or in the bottom row? If so, Pages applies the formula to the entire column.

2. Are there values to the left of the selected cell? If yes, Pages tallies the columns to the left of the cell.

3. Are there values above the selected cell? If yes, Pages runs its calculation on the rows above the cell.

Note: Unless the cell is a footer cell, you can't replace a manually typed value with a quick formula. If a cell has a non-formula value in it, you have to delete that value before you can add your quick formula.

Removing a formula

You remove a formula just as you would any other value: Select the cell and press the Delete key.

The Formula Editor

Quick formulas are handy for running common calculations involving a range of neighboring cells, like an entire row or column. For most Pages tables, these pre-fab formulas will likely provide everything you need. Every so often, though, you might want to do something a little bit different—add cells from different parts of the table, or multiply a dollar value in one cell by an exchange rate—if you have a yen for Japanese currency, for example. In that case, you need to add your own custom formula, and that's where the *Formula Editor* comes in. Chapter 20 in the Numbers section of this book covers all the nitty-gritty details of constructing formulas, but for now, here are the basics.

To open the Formula Editor for a cell and create a new formula, select the cell and type the equal sign (=); the Formula Editor appears over the selected cell, as shown in Figure 8-12. If the cell already has a formula, double-click the cell to bring up the Formula Editor. You can also conjure it up by choosing Insert → Function → Formula Editor or choose Formula Editor from the Table Inspector → Format pane's Function pop-up.

Tip: If the Formula Editor gets in your way, you can move it by hovering the cursor over its left side until the cursor turns into a hand, then drag the editor to a new spot.

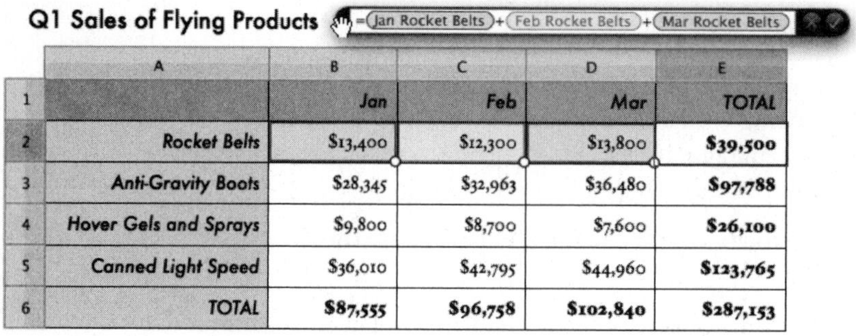

Q1 Sales of Flying Products =(Jan Rocket Belts)+(Feb Rocket Belts)+(Mar Rocket Belts)

	A	B	C	D	E
1		Jan	Feb	Mar	TOTAL
2	Rocket Belts	$13,400	$12,300	$13,800	**$39,500**
3	Anti-Gravity Boots	$28,345	$32,963	$36,480	**$97,788**
4	Hover Gels and Sprays	$9,800	$8,700	$7,600	**$26,100**
5	Canned Light Speed	$36,010	$42,795	$44,960	**$123,765**
6	TOTAL	**$87,555**	**$96,758**	**$102,840**	**$287,153**

Figure 8-12:
The Formula Editor appears when you select a cell and type the equal sign (=) to create a new formula, or when you double-click a cell containing a formula. To use the value of another table cell in your calculation, just click the cell and the Formula Editor inserts a cell reference into the formula. A cell reference is a coordinate that combines the name of the column with the name of the row. Here, the formula is adding the Jan, Feb, and Mar columns of the Rocket Belts row.

Starting a cell value with the equal sign (=) signals to Pages that you're adding a formula instead of literal text. If you don't start a formula with an equal sign, the cell will just display whatever you type. If you type *=2+2* into the Formula Editor, for example, the cell displays *4*—but when you omit the equal sign and type simply *2+2*, the cell stops doing math for you and simply displays *2+2*.

Just like your math teacher told you in grade school, you do arithmetic with *operators*, a fancy word for the plus, minus, multiplication, and division symbols, as shown in Table 8-1.

Table 8-1. *Arithmetic operators*

To do this	Operator	Example
Add two values	+	2+2
Subtract one value from another	–	5–3
Multiply two values	*	10*10
Divide one value by another	/	20/5

To use the value of another table cell in your calculation, just click the cell and the Formula Editor inserts a *cell reference* into the formula. (You can tell that you're about to add a cell reference because the cursor turns into a white cross with a *fx* function symbol when you hover over other cells.) Cell references are coordinates that identify the location of the cell in your table, a combination of the column name and the row name. When you've labeled your table with header rows and columns, Pages uses those labels as the column and row names, as shown previously in Figure 8-12. If you haven't named your rows and columns in this way, you can use their letter and number labels instead. When the Formula Editor is active, lettered and numbered labels pop up next to the rows and columns of your table. These are called *reference tabs,* and you can combine their letters and numbers to build a cell reference. Think Bingo: B2 refers to the cell in column B, row 2. In addition to clicking cells to add their references, you can also simply type their coordinates. To multiply B2 and C2, for example, the formula is: *=B2*C2.*

Doing math on cells that hold numeric values works as you would expect, but Pages chokes on formulas that do math on cells with text values. You can, however, do math on dates. A formula that adds one to a date, for example, displays the date for the following day; a formula that subtracts seven from a date displays the date for the week before. Subtract one date from another to get a duration value (page 293).

In addition to familiar arithmetic, formulas can also include *functions,* predefined shortcuts that do calculations on the cells or values that you give to them. For example, use the SUM function to add several cells: *=SUM(A1,B3,C5)* adds up the values of the three cells. Similarly, *=AVERAGE(D1,D2,D3,D4)* gives you the average value of those four cells. Pages gives you more than 250 functions to do a wide range of mathematical or financial operations, manipulate strings of text, get the current date and time, and much more.

Although you can type functions directly into the Formula Editor, you can also add them by selecting the cell and then choosing Insert → Function → Show Function Browser. The Function Browser gives you access to the entire library of functions, as shown in Figure 8-13. For more info about using functions, see Chapter 21.

When using functions, it's frequently useful to refer to a range of cells or to an entire column or row. When editing a formula, you can add a reference to a set of consecutive cells by dragging across the cells you want to add. Pages inserts a reference in the form of *B1:B5,* for example, which indicates rows one through five in

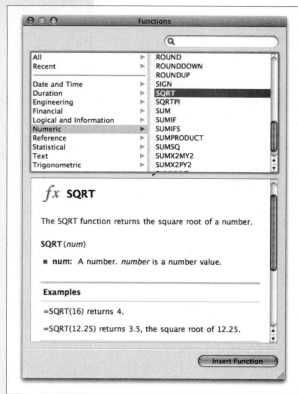

Figure 8-13:
The Function Browser lets you flip through all of Pages' formula functions. To call it up, select a cell and choose Insert → Function → Show Function Browser (you can also choose this option while you're working in the Formula Editor). Select a category in the left pane to narrow the selection of functions in the right pane. Click a function name to select it and display a description and examples in the Help pane below. Double-click the function name, or click Insert, to add the function to the cell and open the Formula Editor.

the B column (you can also type this reference directly). If you then want to add those cells using the SUM function, the formula is: *=SUM(B1:B5).*

Tip: Because adding a range of cells is such a common activity, the Formula Editor offers a shortcut: Type the equal sign (=) to start your formula, and then drag across the cells you want to add up. When you release the mouse, Pages updates the formula to include the SUM function.

To refer to *all* the body cells in a column or row (excluding the header cells), click the column's reference tab (the lettered or numbered label sticking out of the table). You can also type the reference by using the column letter (C or C:C) or row number (2:2). For example, *=SUM(B)* or *=SUM(B:B)* adds all the values in column B, and *=SUM(2:2)* adds all the values in row 2. Just be careful that your range doesn't include the cell where you're adding the formula—formulas can't include their own cell's value, and Pages will show an error icon in the cell. Putting formulas in a footer row is a good way to help avoid this problem, since row and column references ignore header and footer cells.

Note: In the example above, *=SUM(2)* always displays "2", since the function treats "2" as an actual value instead of a row reference. Always use the 2:2 format when you want a row reference, or use the value of the row's header cell instead ("Rocket Belts" in Figure 8-12, for example).

Coping with formula errors

When a formula in a table cell is incomplete, contains invalid cell references, or is otherwise incorrect, Pages displays a red triangle icon in the middle of the cell. Click the cell to see a description of the error message. To edit your formula and fix the error, double-click the problem cell to bring up the Formula Editor—just don't double-click on the error icon itself, or you'll simply toggle the error message.

Moving Formulas

You can copy a formula to another cell just as you would any other cell value. Select the cell at the cell level so that it's outlined in a blue highlight, and then drag the cell to another cell. You can also copy and paste cells, or copy them by autofilling cells (page 302). For complete details about moving cell content, flip back to page 288.

When you move a formula to a new cell, Pages does a little sleight of hand to adjust cell references for the new location. For example, if a formula in the footer row of column A adds up all the values in column A, moving that formula to column B changes the cell references to add up the values in column B. References to cells, columns, and rows change relative to the position of the new cell: If you move a formula down two rows, all of its column references move down two rows; if you move it right two columns, all column references shift two columns.

If you want to use the same cell reference in both formulas and avoid this cell-shuffling sidestep, you can use an *absolute cell reference*. You do this by adding a dollar sign ($) in front of the column and row identifiers in the cell reference. For example, if you want a formula to refer to cell B5 no matter where you copy it, use the Formula Editor to replace B5 with B5 in the formula. For more about absolute and relative cell references, see page 693.

Using Numbers Tables in Pages and Vice Versa

Now that you've got the hang of making spreadsheets inside your Pages documents, you might find yourself wishing that you could include these spreadsheets in, y'know, an actual spreadsheet program. Happily, Pages tables can also live happily inside Numbers documents. In fact, you can swap tables back and forth between all the iWork programs, building a spreadsheet table in Numbers and then pasting it into Keynote and Pages or vice versa.

To copy a table from one program to another, select the table and choose Edit → Copy. Switch to the document in the other program and choose Edit → Paste. The table appears in the second document, with its original data, appearance, and formatting intact, with a handful of caveats:

- Numbers allows formulas to reference cells in other tables, but Pages does not. When you copy a Numbers table into Pages, any formulas containing references to other tables are removed, replaced with their current calculated values.

- Comments added to the table in the original document don't make the leap to the new document.

- Rows or columns that were hidden in a Numbers spreadsheet remain hidden after being copied into Pages, until you choose Format → Table → Unhide All Rows or Unhide All Columns. (For details about hidden rows and columns in Numbers, see page 641.)

Creating Charts

Tables are an efficient way to store and organize a large amount of information in a highly readable format, but *charts* make your data dance. Charts turn numbers into graphic visuals which, when used well, highlight trends at a glance and communicate the message of your data far more efficiently than a table of raw figures. They're certainly less tedious than reading the straight prose: "In 2004, Up & Away's sales of vertigo gloves were $1.5 million a year; in 2006 they rose to $1.76 million, before dipping to $1.3 million in 2008."

Charts are graphical representations of lots of little bits of data—data that you organize in a table or spreadsheet. With your numbers in place, the stage is set for a modern miracle: From the stultifying columns of numbers, Pages helps you instantly create a gorgeous chart to reveal the hidden pattern behind the numbers. True, the most revealing charts are not always gorgeous, and gorgeous charts are not always revealing. Pages gives you the tools to build and dress your charts, and it's up to you to use them the right way (see "Beware of Chartjunk" starting on page 796).

In Pages, you can't build charts *directly* from tables, handy as that would be. But your table data is still just a quick two-step away from its chart metamorphosis. As you'll see, you create and edit a chart's data with the *Chart Data Editor,* which works like a very basic table of numbers—no formulas, no autofill, none of the other clever math-minded goodies you'll find in a regular Pages table. If you're making a simple chart with a small amount of data, it's quick and easy to enter your data directly into the editor. For larger data sets, however, or when you plan to update chart data frequently, it's much easier to work inside a table. In that case, a better option is to copy and paste the data directly from a table in Pages or Numbers, or from another spreadsheet program like Microsoft Excel. Copying cells into the Chart Data Editor is a quick maneuver that lets you import large amounts of data into a chart and start shaping its visuals right away.

In fact, for charting lots of data, the best plan is simply to do all of your chart work in Numbers, which is specifically tuned for working with data. When you paste a Numbers chart into your document, Pages cleverly maintains a link with the original Numbers spreadsheet and can automatically update the chart data anytime with the click of a button (page 315). That means you can adjust data over in your Numbers spreadsheet and then instantly pull the changes into your Pages chart, without having to touch Pages' clunky Chart Data Editor.

For all but the most simple charts, this integration with Numbers means that iWork's spreadsheet program should be your go-to factory for banging out charts and graphs, letting Pages present the final polished chart as the result. That's why this book reserves most of the detailed features of working with charts for the Numbers section, in Chapter 22. Consider this section an appetizer—an introduction to iWork's chart features and a primer for creating and managing charts in Pages using the Chart Data Editor.

Inserting Charts

Like other objects in Pages, charts are either inline or floating objects (see page 209 for details about these layout styles). To add an inline chart, place the insertion point in the text where you want the chart to appear, and select a chart type from the Charts pop-up button in the toolbar (Figure 8-14), or from the Insert → Chart submenu. For a description of all of the chart types, see page 763. When you select a chart type, a chart containing sample data appears in your document, and Pages simultaneously opens the Chart Inspector and the Chart Data Editor (Figure 8-15). Along with your chart, Pages also adds a separate object to your document: the chart's *legend,* the visual key that helps your reader decode your chart's lines, bars, and symbols.

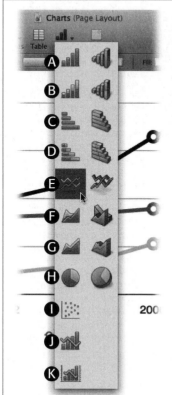

Figure 8-14:
Add an inline chart to your document by choosing a chart type from the Charts pop-up button. Pages offers 11 chart types, and eight of those come with 3D versions, too, giving you 19 display options for your data. In the Charts pop-up, Pages displays the 3D chart types to the right of their 2D counterparts.

The chart types include: (A) column chart, (B) stacked column chart, (C) bar chart, (D) stacked bar chart, (E) line chart, (F) area chart, (G) stacked area chart, (H) pie chart, (I) scatter chart, (J) mixed chart, and (K) two-axis chart.

You can insert an inline chart in any text column, text box, or shape. Resize it with one of the three active selection handles. An inline chart's legend appears as a separate inline object above the chart. Resize it separately with its one active selection handle.

To add a floating chart, ⌘-click the document's margin so the insertion point disappears, click the Charts button in the toolbar, and Pages deposits your chart into the center of the screen. Drag the floating chart to its spot on the page, and drag any of its eight selection handles to resize it. A floating chart's legend appears as a separate floating object you can resize or reposition anywhere on the page.

You can also draw a floating chart of just the right size in your document. Hold down the Option key when you choose a chart type from the toolbar's Charts button. The pointer turns into a crosshair cursor; position the crosshair where you want one corner of your chart to be, and drag to the opposite corner. As you drag, Pages shows you the resizing chart and displays its changing dimensions. Release the mouse, and Pages drops the chart into your document.

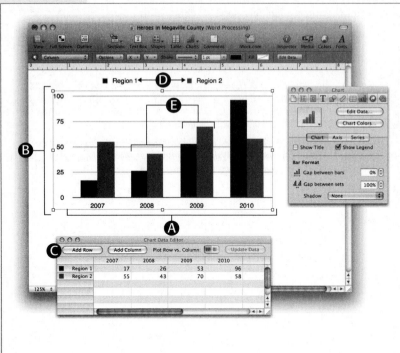

Figure 8-15:
New charts always come with sample data to help you get oriented. The standard chart, shown here, plots two data series, Region 1 vs. Region 2, over four years along the X-axis (A) with values represented along the Y-axis (B).

The numbers behind the chart reside in the Chart Data Editor (C), a table where each row represents one of the charts' regional data series. The Region 1 and Region 2 labels in each row also appear in the chart's legend (D), along with matching color keys to identify which column represents which data series. Each number in the table is a data point, represented by a column in the chart. The numbers from both data series for each year are a data set (E), represented by the paired columns in the chart.

Understanding data series and data sets

Before jumping into editing the data for your chart, you'll need to wrap your brain around some of the chart lingo iWork uses. In particular, it's important to understand how charts organize your data into *data series* and *data sets*. The simplest charts have a single data series, but Figure 8-15 compares two series back-to-back: The number of heroes in Region 1 vs. the number of heroes in Region 2. Each region's data tells its own story, called a data series, which provides just enough info that it could itself be its own chart (Figure 8-16 shows what these two data series would look like in separate charts, for example). But when you combine data series into a single chart, you create a visual comparison between the two stories, providing more context and insight than the two series tell separately.

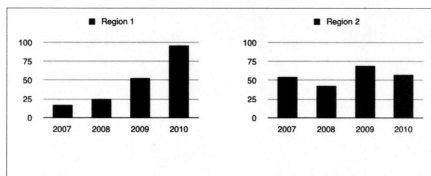

Figure 8-16:
Each data series is its own independent "story" that could just as easily be represented in its own chart. Here, the Region 1 and Region 2 data series are shown in separate charts, an approach that sacrifices the visual ease of comparing the two regions in a single chart.

Each data series consists of data values (or *data points*) plotted against the X- and Y-axes of the chart. (The X axis is the chart's horizontal measuring stick, and Y is the vertical.) Each of Pages' chart types draws these data points in different ways (as bars, columns, points on a line, and so on). In this heroes-by-region chart, each data point is a column and represents the number of heroes per year. The chart groups results by year, and each year represents a *data set*: 2007 is a data set, 2008 is a data set, and so on. A data set, in other words, is a collection of data points for all of the chart's data series.

In this example, the regions are data series, and the years are data sets. But Pages lets you flip this around, changing chart orientation so that the data is grouped by year instead of region. Clicking the "Plot Row vs. Column" button in the Chart Data Editor makes the change happen, as shown in Figure 8-17, where the years are now the data series, grouped into regional data sets. You have a choice of how you want to represent the rows and columns of your data, in other words: When rows are your data series, columns represent the data sets along the X-axis; when columns are your data series, rows represent the data sets. Either way, data values in most charts are always represented along the Y-axis (except bar charts, which show values along the X-axis).

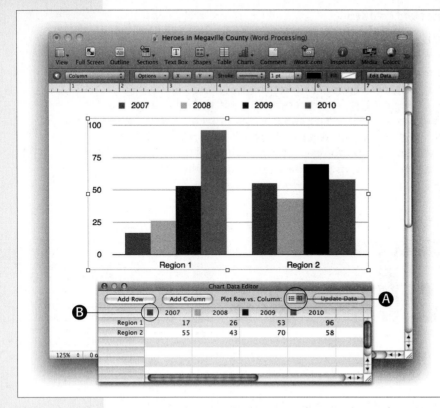

Figure 8-17:
Change chart orientation by clicking the "Plot Row vs. Column" button (A) in the Chart Data Editor: Click the left side of the button to use rows as the data series, or click the right to use columns. Here, the year columns are now the data series, grouped into data sets by region. The Chart Data Editor further marks the change by placing the square legend symbols (B) next to the years, showing that each year is a data series and denoting the color used in the chart for each one.

Entering Data in the Chart Data Editor

Pages helpfully opens the Chart Data Editor when you insert a new chart. In both Pages and Keynote, you use this lightweight table to add and arrange the data for your charts. You can get to the Chart Data Editor anytime by selecting the chart to edit and clicking the Edit Data button in the Format Bar or the Chart Inspector (or choose Show Data Editor from the Format → Chart menu or from a selected chart's Control-click shortcut menu). The Chart Data Editor appears, revealing the numbers illustrated by the chart (see Figure 8-15).

Note: From its name, you might think that the Edit Data button in the Chart Inspector always opens the Chart Data Editor. Instead, it's really a hide/display toggle switch. If you click Edit Data when the Chart Data Editor is open, it closes the editor; click it again, and it brings it back.

Enter your data directly into the Chart Data Editor. Click a data cell and type to replace its contents. Press Tab to move to the cell to the right, and press Shift-Tab to move to the left (sorry, arrow keys don't do the job here; when entering data, you have to tab). Double-click row and column labels to rename them; double-click blank row or column labels and type a name to create a new row or column— or press the Add row or Add Column buttons. (To see the new row or column, you may have to scroll, or expand the Chart Data Editor window by dragging the resize handle at the bottom-right corner.)

You can reorganize the Chart Data Editor's rows and columns by dragging a row or column label to a new position. To add new rows or columns between the existing ones, select a cell, and then click Add Row or Add Column. A new row appears above the selected cell, and a new column appears to the left of the selected cell. You can also Control-click an unselected cell and choose the Add Row Above or Add Column Before commands from the pop-up menu. If no cell is selected, Pages adds the new row or column at the bottom or right edge of the data editor's table.

To delete a row or column in the Chart Data Editor, click its label and press Delete; Shift-click to select several rows or columns, and then press Delete to obliterate them all.

Use the shortcut pop-up menu on an *unselected* cell to access all the commands for adding and deleting rows and columns. Control-click an unselected cell in the table to delete rows or columns; add a row above or a column to the left of the selected cell; or add a new row at the bottom or a new column at the right.

Copying spreadsheet or table data into your chart

If you already have your data in a Pages table or in a separate spreadsheet—in Numbers or Excel, for example—you can copy it right into the Chart Data Editor.

Select all the cells in the spreadsheet that you wish to chart, including the cells containing the column and row labels if you like, and then choose Edit → Copy. In the Chart Data Editor, select the top left data cell (below the header row), and then choose Edit → Paste, and Pages inserts the block of cells into the data table, and the chart changes instantly to reflect the new data.

Pages does its best to detect header rows or columns when you paste a selection into the Chart Data Editor, and it uses a simple rule to do this: If the first cell of either the top row or left column contains a letter, Pages treats the entire row or column as a header, as shown in Figure 8-18. When it identifies header rows or columns, Pages inserts those values into the Chart Data Editor's headers and places the remaining cells as data into the table.

If the pasted block of cells is smaller than the occupied cells in Pages' Chart Data Editor, the occupied cells outside of the pasted block remain in the table until you delete them. Select the columns and rows to delete by clicking their header cells, and press Delete.

As usual, copying and pasting is straight-forward, and it's not much trouble to add your data to a chart in this way. But if you keep your data in a spreadsheet, Pages offers a better way to keep your charts in sync—no paste required.

Using Charts from Numbers

They don't call it Numbers for nothin': The iWork spreadsheet is a natural at juggling data. When you're working with big data sets or find yourself updating a chart's data frequently, it's lots more pleasant to build and edit your chart data in Numbers. It's a matter of choosing the right tool for the job: Let Pages focus on

Giant Lizard	Huge Spider	Atomic Ant	Alien Robot
4	10	8	24
30	18	22	48
40	32	24	36
45	34	16	24

1940s	4	10	8	24
1950s	30	18	22	48
1960s	40	32	24	36
1970s	45	34	16	24

C

	Giant Lizard	Huge Spider	Atomic Ant	Alien Robot
1940s	4	10	8	24
1950s	30	18	22	48
1960s	40	32	24	36
1970s	45	34	16	24

D

4	10	8	24
30	18	22	48
40	32	24	36
45	34	16	24

Figure 8-18:
Pages uses the presence of alphabetical characters in the first row or column of pasted cells to detect header rows and columns:

A: The first row contains header text, so the Chart Data Editor would paste that row into its header row, while all remaining cells would go into the data table.

B: The first column contains header text (the "s" in each decade title), so the Chart Data Editor adds it as its header column, treating the remaining cells as data values.

C: The first row and first column both contain text, so they're both considered headers and inserted into the Chart Data Editor as the header row and column.

D: None of the cells contain letters, so they're all treated as data values, and Pages makes no changes to the chart's header row or column.

your words and page design, while Numbers manages your digits. Behind the scenes, iWork links your Pages chart to the Numbers spreadsheet; after you edit the data in Numbers, you can tell Pages to fetch the revised data and update your chart with the click of a button. Here's how it works:

1. **Create your chart in Numbers (see Chapter 22), and save the Numbers spreadsheet.**

   Note that Pages can't link to an untitled Numbers document. Be sure to save the spreadsheet before copying the chart.

2. **Select the chart in Numbers and choose Edit → Copy.**

3. **In Pages, open your Pages document and place the insertion point where you want the chart to appear.**

4. **Choose Edit → Paste to add the chart to your document.**

After you paste a Numbers chart into Pages, you can update its data as usual from the Chart Data Editor, but you can also go back to the source, refreshing the chart's data directly from the original Numbers spreadsheet. When you select the chart, Pages shows that it's linked to a Numbers spreadsheet with an arrow pointer immediately to the right of the chart (Figure 8-19).

Tip: Don't see the arrow pointer after you paste from Numbers? You probably didn't save the Numbers spreadsheet. Head back to Step 1 above, then save the spreadsheet and try again.

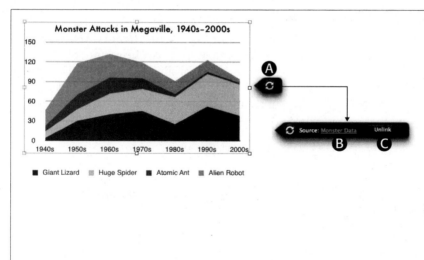

Figure 8-19:
When you select a chart pasted from Numbers, Pages displays a pointer arrow with a refresh button (A). Click the button to reload the latest data from the original Numbers spreadsheet.

Click the dot at the end of the arrow to expand it, revealing a link to the original Numbers file (B) and the Unlink button (C). Clicking the file link opens the spreadsheet in Numbers, letting you edit the source data. When you click Unlink, Keynote cuts the tie with Numbers, and the chart is no longer linked.

Now, instead of editing the Chart Data Editor, make your data changes to the original Numbers spreadsheet. After saving the spreadsheet with its new data, go back to Pages and click the chart's Refresh button to reload the data from the Numbers document. Pages fetches the data from your spreadsheet and replaces all of the data in Pages' Chart Data Editor for the chart. *Be careful here:* If you've made any changes to the chart in Pages, those changes are wiped out when you reload the data from Numbers.

The link to Numbers is only to the *data*—not to any chart formatting. Go ahead and change the look, colors, or even the type of chart in either Pages or Numbers, and your styling won't be affected when you update the chart. Another way to look at this is that Pages doesn't really link to the original *chart* in Numbers—it links to the *table* that feeds the Numbers chart. Formatting changes that you make to the chart on either side aren't affected by the linked data.

Tip: When you paste your chart from Numbers, choose Edit → Paste and Match Style to make the chart's formatting match the standard chart formatting and colors of your Pages document. If you choose simply Edit → Paste, the chart looks just like it does in the original Numbers spreadsheet.

Should you decide that you no longer want to link back to the original Numbers document, click the Unlink button in the expanded link arrow, and Pages severs the tie. Going forward, you'll edit the chart's data only in the Chart Data Editor.

Note: Sorry, there's no similar feature to link tables between Numbers and Pages—only charts.

Changing the Type of Chart

You can change the type of chart at any time by selecting the chart and choosing a new type from the Chart Type pop-up menu in the Chart Inspector or Format Bar (Figure 8-20). The Chart Type menu is also available from the chart's shortcut menu when the chart is selected. Not all charts use the chart data in exactly the same way, however, so as you flip through chart types, your data may not always make sense in its new context. Whenever possible, it's a good idea to select your chart type first, and then load up its data so that it's completely clear to you how Pages will put your data to use in the chart.

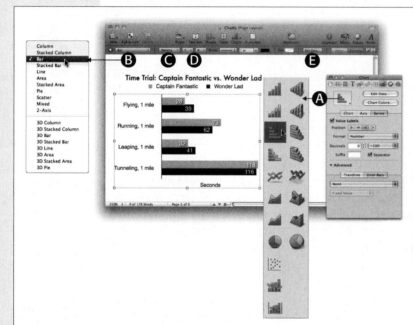

Figure 8-20:
Switch to a new chart type by selecting the chart to change and choosing from the Chart Type pop-up menu in the Chart Inspector (A) or the Format Bar's pop-up menu (B).

The Format Bar also gives you fast access to several other common chart-data settings: The Options pop-up menu (C) lets you hide or display the chart's title and legend; the Y and X pop-ups (D) control settings for the Y- and X-axis, including labels, tick marks, gridlines, and axis lines (see page 788); the Edit Data button (E) hides or reveals the Chart Data Editor.

Most chart types use chart data in the same format, and flipping back and forth between these styles will generally work as you expect. As described on page 313, these charts use either rows or columns as the data series and the other as data sets along the X-axis, for example. Pie charts and scatter charts, however, have a different view of the chart data than other chart types.

Pie charts illustrate only a single data set, and so they show the percentages for only the first row or column from the Chart Data Editor. If the Row button is selected in the editor's "Plot Row vs. Column" button so that each row is a data series, only the first column's data set is used; if the Column button is selected, the first row's data set is used. The rest of the table is ignored.

Scatter charts work an even bolder change on the data table when flipping between other chart types. The "Plot Row vs. Column" button is disabled, and the chart uses pairs of columns as data series, as shown in Figure 8-21. Row headings are removed from the data table, with each row now representing a set of value pairs: The first column is the X-axis value, and the second is the Y-axis value, giving the chart the coordinates to plot on the chart.

Note: Changing to a scatter chart from another type of chart reorganizes the data chart, removing row headers and half of the column headers to accommodate its format for two-column data series. That doesn't mean your original data has permanently gone missing, though; Pages tucks the original data table away, and if you choose to switch back to another type of chart, the header information returns to its original state.

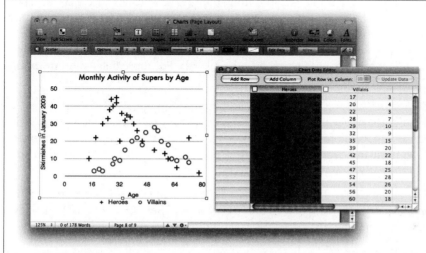

Figure 8-21:
A scatter chart organizes its data differently than other chart types. Every data series consists of two columns of values, and each row is a set of data points where the first column is the X-axis value, and the second is the Y-axis value. Here, the two-column data series are Heroes and Villains, where the first column for each represents the age of an individual hero or villain, and the second column represents his or her number of skirmishes.

Formatting Charts

Like any other object in a Pages document, you can resize, reposition, or rotate charts, adjust their opacity, wrap text around them, and so on—head back to page 249 for a general review of how to modify object styles. Beyond that, though, all the iWork programs provide a stuffed toolbox of options to modify the appearance of just about every element of your chart. You can make broad-stroke changes like painting graph bars with colors or textures, or subtle tweaks like refining the tick marks on the axis lines.

Chapter 22 goes into all the formatting possibilities in detail. That chapter focuses on Numbers charts, but the options and processes of styling charts are nearly exactly the same there as for Pages and Keynote. In all the iWork programs, you use the same settings in the Format Bar and the Chart and Graphic inspectors to make your changes. As you'll see, Numbers' Chart Inspector offers a handful of extra options that are specific to the way its charts interact with tables; other than that, though, everything works identically in all three programs. Here's a quick summary:

- **3D effects.** You can convert any chart except scatter, mixed, and two-axis charts into a three-dimensional model. To convert a chart into its 3D version, select it and choose one of the 3D chart types from the Chart Type pop-up button in the Format Bar or Chart Inspector. When you select a 3D chart, the Chart Inspector's Chart pane sprouts extra settings to let you change the chart's viewing angle, turn it three dimensionally in space, or add lighting effects and depth. See page 785 for more about working with 3D charts.

- **Chart text and labels.** Each of the tabs in the Chart Inspector offers options for labeling your chart. Add or remove the chart's title or legend by turning the Show Title and Show Legend options on or off in the Chart Inspector's Chart pane or in the Format Bar's Options pop-up. Add labels to the X- or Y-axis using the Choose Axis Options pop-up menus in the Chart Inspector's Axis pane or in the Format Bar. Label every data point by turning on the Value Labels checkbox in the Chart Inspector's Series pane. You can use all of Pages' usual text-formatting tools to style these labels. For more details about working with chart labels, see page 779.

- **Colors and textures.** Use the Fill setting in the Graphic Inspector or in the Format Bar to change the color of the chart's canvas or of an individual data series, just as you would for any other object. Or click the Chart Inspector's Chart Colors button to select from Pages' sleek collection of color and texture palettes. Flip to page 786 for the full-color version.

- **Slicing pie charts.** Pie charts are a completely different animal than the other charts and get a whole new Chart Inspector, too. See page 790 for the lowdown on formatting the labels, wedges, and rotation of your pie charts.

- **Formatting the other chart types.** Every chart type offers a slightly different choice of settings in the Chart Inspector: Control the spacing between column and bar charts in the Chart pane, or choose the symbols for marking data points in line, area, and scatter charts in the Series pane. See page 792 for details about these options.

- **Trendlines and error bars.** Pages can calculate trendlines and error bars for most 2D charts except for pie charts and, for trendlines, stacked charts. These options are available in the Chart Inspector's Series pane: Click the Advanced Options flippy triangle to reveal them, and skip ahead to page 794 for the whole story.

- **Axis and gridlines.** You can add gridlines, tick marks, or axis lines to any chart (except pie charts) using the Axis pane of the Chart Inspector, or the X and Y pop-up menus in the Format Bar. See page 788 to get your charts lined up.

These myriad formatting tools mean that you have a limitless set of possibilities for styling your charts—and in truth, playing with these charts becomes oddly addictive. Don't get carried away, though; your goal is to communicate your data, and simplicity and clarity should win out over showy effects. However you ultimately decide to format your information, though, the next step is to get it out there and share it with others. That's the focus of the next chapter.

Sharing Pages Documents

After you create a Pages document and carefully lay out, tweak, and polish it to perfection, your work is done—if you want to view it only onscreen, that is. More likely, you'll usually want to print a hard copy, or share it with others via email, the Web, CD, or fax. This chapter explores the next step in the life of a Pages document: delivering it from your computer into the hands, inboxes, and web browsers of your intended audience. Several new features in iWork '09 make online distribution of your masterpiece especially easy, particularly Apple's new iWork.com online service, which lets you share your document and gather feedback from invited reviewers in a sleek and simple web interface. You'll also learn about how to export files in several formats, ready for other programs like Microsoft Word or iWeb.

Printing Your Documents

For decades, pundits have declared the paperless office to be just around the corner—and now that we've waited long enough, it appears to be slowly coming true. After years of skyrocketing paper consumption, paper use in the U.S. has leveled off in the past several years and slowly begun to decline. A new generation of worker has become accustomed to reading and archiving documents on the computer instead of squirreling them away into file cabinets.

We're still a long way from going completely paperless, though, and printing will undoubtedly be one of your preferred methods for liberating Pages documents from your Mac. Printing Pages files is just like printing anything else on your computer—so if you have a handle on how printing works in other programs, feel free to skip this section.

Page Setup

Setting the Page Setup options should really be a part of the document setup you did at the beginning of the document (see Chapter 5 for details on how to format your document). But still, it's a good idea to double-check it now. Choose File → Page Setup to open the Page Setup dialog box (Figure 9-1), whose main purpose in life is to choose the paper size, orientation, and scaling adjustment (if any) for the document.

The first pop-up menu, labeled Settings, always says Page Attributes when you open the Page Setup dialog box. Leave it set that way, choose the name of your printer from the "Format for" pop-up menu, and, from the Paper Size pop-up menu, choose the paper size you want. The two Orientation buttons determine whether the paper size you just selected prints out *portrait* (the traditional vertical orientation) or *landscape* (tipped sideways for horizontal orientation). Most documents are portrait style, but if you're printing envelopes, brochures, or panoramas, choose landscape instead.

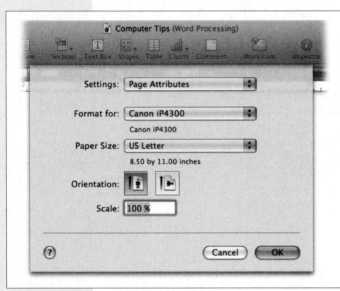

Figure 9-1:
Set the basic document format—the paper size and portrait or landscape orientation—in the Page Setup dialog box. The Paper Size options change for different kinds of printers. If you want to print the document at a reduced or enlarged size, set the Scale control to less than or more than 100 percent.

When you click OK to close the Page Setup dialog box, Pages takes you right back to your document, where you can continue to work on it or print it. Pages memorizes these Page Setup settings along with your document—once you've set it for a document, you don't need to return to Page Setup unless you need to change one of the settings.

Tip: The standard Page Setup settings that you get when you first start a new file depend on the template that you use to create the document. To save your own preferred settings for reuse in other documents, you have to save your document as a template, a topic covered in the next chapter.

The Print Window

Although you need to open Page Setup only once in the life of a document, you use the Print dialog box every time you need to print something. Press ⌘-P (or choose File → Print) to get started. The Print dialog box has a simple view that you can expand for access to several screens of options, as shown in Figure 9-2. If Pages gives you the simple view, click the downward-facing arrow next to the Printer pop-up menu to switch to the full dialog box. Going forward, Pages will remember to show you this expanded view when you go to print.

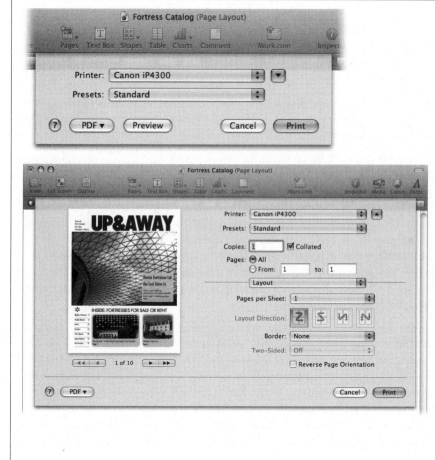

Figure 9-2:
The Print dialog box has a simple view (top) and an advanced view (bottom). To toggle modes, click the arrow button at the top right, next to the Printer pop-up menu. Go ahead and switch to the advanced view—this expanded dialog box has lots of useful options for formatting your printed document.

Use the Printer pop-up menu to select a printer if you have more than one hooked up to your Mac or network. (If you don't see the printer you want, choose Add Printer and follow the instructions.) In the Copies box, type the number of copies you want (this box is highlighted when you open the expanded Print dialog box, so just type the number of copies—no need to use the mouse). Choose a page range if you don't want to print the whole thing—use the preview controls on the left to browse the document to find the pages you want. Then press Return (or click Print) to send your document to the printer.

The expanded print dialog box gives up half of its real estate for a preview of your document. Use the forward/back buttons to flip through the pages to make sure that it looks like you expect, or to find page numbers if you want to print a limited range of pages.

Tip: If you have the Comments pane open to show comments and tracked changes, you'll see that the pane is visible in the page preview, too, signaling that Pages will print that column of comments along with the rest of your document and any change-tracking markup. If you don't want to print the Comments pane or tracked changes, choose View → Hide Comments before you open the Print dialog box. (This command is called Hide Comments and Changes Pane when change tracking is turned on.)

The right side of the dialog box shows the printing controls. The top portion of these settings lets you choose from a fixed set of options, while the options below change according to your selection of the pop-up menu, which always opens to Layout. The fixed set of options at the top right prompt you for these basic settings:

- **Printer.** Choose the printer where you want to send your document. If you don't see the printer you want, choose Add Printer from the pop-up menu and follow the instructions.

- **Presets.** Once you have your printing preferences just so, you can take a snapshot of them and save them as a *preset* for future use. If you frequently choose to print two pages per sheet, for example, you might save a preset named "Two Per Page" with that option selected. Choose Save As from the Presets pop-up menu, give your preset a name, and click OK. Your Mac adds them to the Presets menu so that you can access them again and again from any program. To use a saved preset, choose its name from the Presets pop-up. If you make subsequent changes to a preset, you can save them by choosing Save from the Presets pop-up menu—or choose Rename to give your preset a new name or Delete to remove it from the menu.

- **Copies.** Type in the number of copies you want and decide if you want them automatically collated. When you print several copies of a multipage document, turn on the Collated checkbox, and the printer prints the document all the way through before starting on the second copy—all that's left for you to do is staple the pages together. If you turn off the Collated checkbox, the printer prints five copies of page one followed by five copies of page two, and so on. (This option often results in faster printing, especially on laser printers, but of course it also means that you have to go back and organize the pages by hand.)

- **Pages.** Set the page range if you don't want to print the whole document. For example, if you just want to proofread the five pages of your pre-nup that cover household pets, then enter, say, *From 52 to 56*. If you leave one of the fields blank, your Mac assumes that means either beginning or end. In other words, to print the last half of a document enter, say, *From 12*, and leave the "to" box empty. Turn on the All button to return to printing all pages.

In the lower-left corner of the Print dialog box, the PDF pop-up button offers several options to save your document as a PDF file, which stands for Portable Document Format, a file that can be opened with the Preview program on your Mac or with the free Adobe Reader program on any computer. The Mac saves this file on your hard drive instead of printing it—you'll also find options to email or fax the PDF. too. Saving a document as PDF is handy because it lets you share the file with others, no matter what programs or fonts they have installed, and they can still see your complete, original layout and formatting.

Tip: When you create a PDF using the File → Export option instead of doing it here in the Print dialog box, you have a bit more control over the image resolution in the resulting PDF (see page 330).

The first option in the PDF button's pop-up menu is "Open PDF in Preview", a useful option if you're at all unsure about your document's margin settings or page layout options. Save yourself some time, expensive ink, and deforestation guilt by clicking this button to see exactly what the document's going to look like on the page. The Mac manages this advanced showing by displaying a PDF version of your document in your Mac's Preview program. If you like what you see, click the Print button at the bottom of the Preview window.

Tip: The short-form unexpanded version of the Print dialog box makes seeing this preview option even faster, giving you a separate Preview button to click. It gives you the same result as choosing "Open PDF in Preview" from the PDF button.

Below the page-range settings in the Print window, a pop-up menu lets you flip through a slew of other print options. The items in this menu and the controls they provide are different for different printers, but a few of the typical choices are the following:

- **Layout.** Choose how many of your document pages to print on each sheet of paper. One is standard, two lets you save paper, and four or more are best suited for a remake of *The Incredible Shrinking Man.*

- **Paper Handling.** If you're interested in double-sided printing (*duplexing*)—and your printer doesn't offer this feature—choose to print only odd or only even pages so you can flip them over and run them through a second time to print the back side. Depending on the way your printer shoots out its pages, the "Reverse page order" checkbox can make the stack of pages come out with page one on top—or not.

- **Print Settings.** Depending on the manufacturer of your inkjet printer, this panel may be called Quality & Media or something else. But whatever it's called, it's the place where you choose the type of paper you're printing on and the print quality you desire—or select grayscale printing to save color ink when you print a draft.

• **Summary.** This panel shows a text summary of all the print settings you've made in the Print dialog box.

When you're happy with the settings in the Print dialog box, click Print (or press Return) and your print job heads to the printer.

FREQUENTLY ASKED QUESTION

How Do I Fax My Document?

Once upon a time, when Internet dial-up ruled the earth, just about every Mac came standard with a built-in modem. Nowadays, modems are few and far between, but if you happen to have one in your computer, you can use it to fax documents.

Starting with OS X 10.3, the ability to send and receive faxes is built into the Mac operating system. You can fax any document you can print—including, of course, Pages documents. To fax a document, make sure your Mac is plugged into a telephone line, and choose File → Print. Click the PDF pop-up button at the bottom left of the Print window, choose Fax PDF, and the Fax dialog box appears. Type your recipient's fax number in the To box; fax to multiple recipients by separating their numbers with commas. Or click the little silhouette button to choose fax numbers from the Address Book.

Click the lower pop-up menu (that reads Fax Cover Page) to access other printing controls, a few of which are actually useful when faxing—in particular, check out Printer Features to downgrade the resolution for faster transmission.

When you're ready to send, press Return or click Fax to send your document on its way. Faxing happens very much in the background; it seems as if nothing's happening at all. However, your Mac has quietly activated the faxing monitor program called Internal Modem, which appears in the Dock. Click it to see a window showing the fax's progress and offering options to delete or hold the job for later.

Exporting Documents

As you learned way back on page 37, Pages does a great job at opening documents created by other word processors like Microsoft Word. Alas, Word and other programs don't return the favor—while Pages speaks Word, for example, Word doesn't understand Pages at all. If you want to share a Pages document with Windows users or anyone who doesn't have iWork, you need to *export* the file, telling Pages to save it as a different file type. Other occasions call for exporting, too—you might want to save your file as a PDF to share a read-only version that anyone can open, for example.

Pages gives you a shortcut to save a copy of your file as Microsoft Word right from the File → Save As window, as you'll soon see, but most export operations happen from Pages' Export dialog box. Choose Share → Export to reveal this expert translator (Figure 9-3). Here you can choose one of four formats to save: PDF, Microsoft Word, RTF, or Plain Text. Each of these formats varies in how "true" the result will be to your original document—PDF will be an exact read-only replica, for example, while plain text will keep only the content and strip out all your graphics and formatting. Your results will vary according to your specific content and the export format you choose, but in general, the fewer graphics, columns, tables, headers, footers, and footnotes involved, the more accurate your exported file will be. When Pages runs into problems, it lets you know about translation trouble by opening the Document Warnings window and giving you the details, as shown in Figure 9-4.

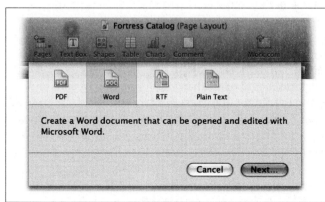

Figure 9-3:
Choose Share → Export, and Pages displays the Export dialog box. Click one of the four buttons at the top of the dialog box to select an export format: PDF, Word, RTF, or Plain Text.

Microsoft Word, RTF, or Plain Text formats are your best export options—in that order—when you want to let people edit the document. However, when you distribute a file that's intended only to be read, choose PDF for the most reliable results—the exported document will *always* be a precise match with the original, and PDF documents are readable from any computer.

Note: Exporting a password-protected Pages document to any of these formats will give you an unprotected copy of the file—no password required (although PDF documents let you add their own separate password). Pages warns you about this when you start the export and gives you a chance to cancel if you feel all naked and vulnerable without your password. See page 138 for details about password-protecting your document.

Exporting Microsoft Word

Microsoft Word (.doc) files can be opened and edited in Word on either Mac or Windows. Because the program is so widespread, pretty much every other word processor can open Word documents, too, making this file format the right choice just about anytime you need to share an editable version of your file with anyone who's not an iWork convert, even if they don't use Word themselves.

Pages also makes it especially easy to save a copy of your document as a Microsoft Word .doc file. Although you can do it via Share → Export as mentioned above, a slightly more convenient route is to go to File → Save As and, at the bottom of the Save window, turn on the "Save copy as" checkbox. Choose Word Document in the pop-up menu, click Save, and Pages saves a separate copy of your document, ready to be opened in Word.

Note: Pages does not export .docx files, only .doc files which provide compatibility with older versions of Word. The .docx file format refers to Office Open XML, which Microsoft adopted as Word's official file format starting with Microsoft Office 2007 for Windows and Microsoft Office 2008 for Mac. Pages can *read* .docx files but *writes* only .doc files. Never fear, this shouldn't make a difference to your Word-wielding comrades: All versions of Microsoft Word can read .doc files just fine.

Don't expect pixel-for-pixel perfection, however. Although Pages does a good job overall at maintaining your formatting and layout in Word, there are usually a few discrepancies (see Figure 9-4). In particular, text spacing differences often give the Word document a different number of pages than your original, and table and column layouts may show some variation, too. Text borders and rules (see page 77) often don't make the transition at all. You'll also find several graphic glitches: shadows in the Word version will be solid black; images with transparency (see page 234) may not display correctly.

Tip: Previous versions of Pages exported charts as plain, uneditable images in Word. Pages '09 remedies this so that charts are exported as MS Graph objects, which can be edited.

The good news is that exported Microsoft Word files maintain all comments and tracked changes from your Pages document—and Pages does the same for imported Word files. If you're doing some heavy collaboration on a document, flip change-tracking on, and you and your Word-wielding colleagues can track every change throughout the editing process.

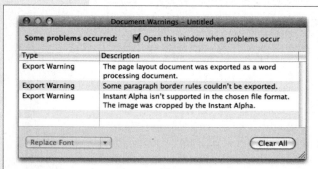

Figure 9-4:
When Pages has trouble translating any part of your document into the target file format, it lets you know about it in the Document Warnings window. Here, after exporting a page-layout document to Microsoft Word, Pages cautions that the exported file will be a word-processing document (as opposed to a page-layout one) and that some borders and instant alpha images may look a bit funky.

Exporting RTF

Microsoft invented the RTF (or Rich Text Format) file type as a go-between to help move documents among rival word processors and page-layout programs with the formatting—even graphics—intact. It's a simple format compared to Microsoft Word, so you'll run into more formatting gotchas than you would when exporting a Word file. But RTF is very close to universally accepted, even by very old word processors, making it a good choice when sending fairly simple word-processing files to a large group when you're not sure what program they use.

To export a RTF file, choose Share → Export, click RTF, and then click Next. Pages rolls out a Save dialog box for you to name the file and choose the destination to save it.

Parlez-Vous Times New Roman?

When Pages can't quite reproduce identical formatting in an exported document, the trouble almost always stems from basic feature differences between Pages and the target program. If Word doesn't support Pages' image transparency, for example, there's not much that you can do about it except to avoid that feature in your document.

One major area that *is* in your control, however, is choosing fonts you know other computers will understand. When you plan to export a Word or RTF document to share with Windows users, try to use fonts that come standard on Windows—otherwise, their word processor will substitute other fonts, throwing off the look and spacing of your document.

Here's a list of standard Windows fonts that are also common on Mac systems:

- Arial
- Arial Black
- Comic Sans
- Courier New
- Georgia
- Microsoft Sans Serif
- Palatino
- Symbol
- Tahoma
- Times New Roman
- Trebuchet MS
- Verdana
- Webdings
- Wingdings

This isn't an issue when you export a PDF file—PDF files send font information inside the file itself, so even when someone doesn't have the font installed on their computer, it still shows up just fine in the PDF.

Exporting Plain Text

Plain text is the most basic type of word-processing file. The good news is that any word processor, regardless of the computer it's running on, can open plain text files and edit the words inside. The bad news is that plain text files don't contain any formatting. Bold, italic, colors, font choices, text alignment, tables, graphs, graphics, backgrounds, and virtually all the other kinds of formatting that make a Pages document so attractive are lost in translation. For most purposes, since you're losing even rudimentary text formatting, plain text isn't worth much for creating documents that you exchange with colleagues, but it can be useful in a pinch if you need to save a text file like a HTML page.

To export a plain-text file, choose Share → Export, click Plain Text, and then click Next. Type a name for the file in the Save window, and choose the destination to save it.

Exporting PDF

Given the translation hiccups Pages occasionally encounters when exporting to Word or RTF formats—especially with complex documents—the only way to export a Pages document and be sure it's going to look *exactly* like you expect, is to use PDF (Portable Document Format). This type of file is designed to maintain the exact look of a document, no matter what computer it's viewed on. PDF files even include all the fonts inside the file so you don't have to worry about whether your readers have all the correct fonts installed.

PDF files are ideal for sharing on websites, since you can open them with most web browsers. You can also open PDF files with the Mac's Preview program or with the free Adobe Reader program that's available for all computer operating systems: Macintosh, Windows, Linux, Palm, PocketPC, you name it.

The downside is that PDF files are not editable without special software. When you send around a PDF file, consider it read-only—if you think others will need to edit the file, use one of the other formats instead.

As mentioned on page 325, you can save a PDF file from the Print dialog box, but using Share → Export gives you one advantage that the Print dialog box does not: When you choose PDF in the Export window, the Image Quality pop-up menu lets you choose from three levels of image quality which also affects your file size.

To export a PDF file, choose Share → Export and click the PDF button. Pages asks what image quality you'd like to use. Choose Best to keep the original image resolution (but also the highest file size). Choose Better to reduce the image resolution to 150 dpi (dots per inch), acceptable quality for inkjet printing, for example. For the lowest file size, choose Good, which reduces images to 72 dpi—a fine resolution for viewing your document onscreen, but not ideal for printing.

To add a password to the PDF, click the Security Options flippy triangle to reveal a set of options and fields, shown in Figure 9-5. (If your Pages document is password-protected, that password won't make it through to the PDF file, but you can choose a new one here.)

Click Next after you've selected your options. Choose a filename and location for your new PDF file, and click Export.

Saving as iWork '08

The final export format isn't advertised in the Share → Export window, but Pages also lets you save a copy of your file as Pages '08 to share with behind-the-times iWork enthusiasts. To do it, choose File → Save As, turn on the "Save copy as" checkbox, and choose iWork '08 from the neighboring pop-up menu. Choose a destination for the file, and click Save.

The hitch, of course, is that any features new to Pages '09 won't translate exactly to the older version's file. Specifically:

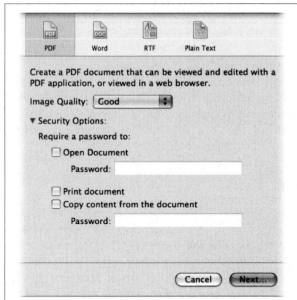

Figure 9-5:
When you export a PDF file, Pages lets you select the image quality of the included images and, optionally, passwords for opening, printing, or copying content. Click the Security Options flippy triangle to reveal the password options.

- If change tracking is turned on when you save, changes to tables and floating objects are accepted in the saved copy (Pages '08 can't track those types of changes).

- Merge fields tied to a Numbers document turn into plain text (Pages '08 doesn't support mail merge from a Numbers document, only Address Book).

- Pages '08 doesn't have outline view.

- Password protection is dropped (Pages '08 doesn't have that security feature).

Emailing Your Document

Now that you know how to export a document, what are you going to do with it? Chances are, you're getting ready to email it to someone. In that case, Pages gives you a shortcut to export your document and add it automatically to a new email message. Choose a file format (Pages, PDF, or Word) from the Share → Send via Mail submenu, and Pages packs up your file, launches the Mail program, and opens a new message window with your document already attached. All that's left is to address the message, dash off a note, and click Send.

When you send the file via PDF, Pages normally uses the "Good" image-quality setting described on page 330, which gives you the smallest file size, handy for shipping it out via email. However, if you previously exported the file as a PDF with a different quality setting, then Pages sends the PDF using that setting instead. The same goes for passwords: Pages normally sends a PDF with no password protection, but if you previously exported a password-protected PDF, then Pages requires the same password in the emailed version, too.

Tip: If you're emailing an image-heavy document, you may have a long wait on your hands to send it out through email. Before sending it along, try shrinking it down by choosing File → Reduce File Size (see page 238 for details).

As convenient as it can be to fire off a document via email, though, it's not always the most efficient way to distribute a document to lots of people—especially when it comes to catching the comments and suggestions that you receive in return. For that, other methods of online distribution can be more effective, and Apple introduced a new service alongside iWork '09 that promises to do just that....

Sharing on iWork.com

On the very day that Apple released iWork '09, the company announced the birth of a bouncing baby website to mark iWork's latest generation: iWork.com is an online hub designed to help share your iWork documents with coworkers, friends, family, or anyone you care to invite. As this book went to press, iWork.com was still taking its first steps, available only as a free "beta" preview, complete with the inevitable glitches that accompany a new site in its testing phase. Even at this early stage, though, iWork.com is a precocious little helper, and the service shows promise. The following overview reflects the state of iWork.com during its first weeks. The service has very likely evolved since these words were written, but the fundamental concepts almost certainly remain the same. (The free price of the iWork. com beta probably has not, however. When Apple announced iWork.com, they also announced that the service would eventually be a paid service.)

Here's the scoop. iWork.com provides an online space to share your Pages, Keynote, and Numbers documents privately with people you select. Think of it as an alternative for the email merry-go-round with which we're all too familiar: You email a document to a group for feedback, and they respond by emailing their comments to you, or even to the entire group, attaching their own edited document for good measure. A flurry of electronic mail ensues, and you're stuck trying to sort out who changed what and where. iWork.com sidesteps the mail storm by providing a centralized place for the group to review the document and share comments.

Here's how it works: You load a document to the service directly from Pages, Keynote, or Numbers and then send invitations to the people you'd like to share with. This specially invited group can read, download, or comment on the document right in their web browsers. The iWork.com website is remarkably good at recreating the exact look of your document, no download required. No matter how complex your page-layout confection might become, iWork.com always displays a pixel-perfect replica within the website itself. It doesn't matter what software your team may (or may not) have installed—Mac or Windows, iWork or Microsoft Office, or none of the above. As long as your reviewers have a web browser and an Internet connection, they can see your document just as you designed it, with all the fonts, photos, charts, and flaming logos you could muster. When you choose to allow comments, your group can leave virtual sticky notes right on the page to ask questions or offer suggestions.

What you and your team *can't* do, however, is edit the document—at least not inside the browser. iWork.com isn't an online word processor; it's simply a place to distribute the document and share feedback. You and your invited guests *can* download the document and edit it offline, though: When you publish the file to iWork.com, you can choose to allow your guests to download the file in any of several formats. A Pages document, for example, may be downloaded as a Microsoft Word, PDF, or Pages file. When you download the document, it includes all the comments added at iWork.com; in Pages, they show up in the Comments pane like regular Pages comments (page 133).

Note: Apple recommends that Windows users access iWork.com with the Safari or Firefox browser, warning that Internet Explorer yields a slow experience. iWork.com does work with Internet Explorer, it's just a bit sluggish. Windows users can download these alternative browsers at *www.apple.com/safari/ download* and *www.mozilla.com/firefox.*

Sending Your Document to iWork.com

To share your Pages document at iWork.com, open the document, and click the toolbar's iWork.com button, or choose Share → Share via iWork.com. If you've done this before, you may already be signed into iWork.com; if not, Pages asks you for your Apple ID and password (Figure 9-6).

Sign In to share documents via iWork.com Public Beta

To create an Apple Account, click Create New Account.

(Create New Account)

If you have an Apple Account (from the iTunes store or MobileMe, for example), enter your Apple ID and password.

Apple ID:

[   ]   Example: steve@me.com

Password:

[   ]   (Forgot Password?)

☑ Remember this password in my keychain

(Cancel)   (Sign In)

Figure 9-6:
Provide your Apple ID and password to sign into iWork.com. If you've ever made a purchase at the iTunes Store or the Apple Online Store, or if you use Apple's MobileMe service, it's the same account—enter your ID and password and click Sign In. If you don't recall your password, click "Forgot Password?" and Apple will arrange a reminder. If you don't yet have an Apple ID, click Create New Account, and Pages opens your web browser to a page where you can sign up.

Chances are, you've already got an Apple ID. If you've ever made a purchase through one of Apple's services—the iTunes Store, the Apple Online Store, MobileMe, or iPhoto's print products, to name a few—you created an Apple account along the way. iWork.com uses this same account to identify you when you sign in. If you don't have an account yet, it's easy to create one. Click the Create New Account button in the sign-in screen, or visit *myinfo.apple.com* to create an Apple ID.

After you sign in, Pages unfurls the iWork.com invitation window (Figure 9-7), where you add the people you'd like to review your document. Pages taps into Address Book's archive of names and addresses, so that typing a name into the To box works just like addressing an email message in Mail. Start typing a name, and Pages offers options as you type, completing the name and email address for you. If someone is new to your email universe, just type their email address into the To field. You can invite as many people as you like, but you have to invite at least one person (even if it's only yourself), or Pages won't let you upload the document. It's determined to teach you to share.

Note: Pages sends your iWork.com invitations using Apple's Mail program. If you don't use Mail, or if you haven't yet set up your email account, you'll need to launch Mail and set up at least one email account in order for the iWork programs to send out iWork.com invites.

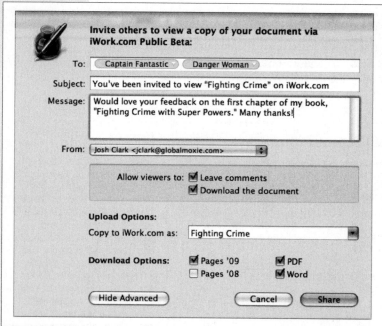

Figure 9-7:
Pages asks who you want to invite to review your document at iWork.com. Type their names in the To box, and Pages fetches their email addresses from Address Book. Enter the Subject and Message to send along with the invitation to view your file. Choose whether you'd like your reviewers to be able to comment and download the document. If you allow people to download, you can select which types of files to provide by clicking the Show Advanced button.

The Subject and Message boxes determine the text of the invitation message your group of reviewers will receive after you load the file. Pages suggests an email subject, but you can use any title you'd like.

iWork.com lets your group add comments and download the file, options that are both turned on when you first start your invitation. If you uncheck "Leave comments" or "Download the document," your reviewers will be little more than window shoppers—they'll be able to review your document online, but they won't be able to take it with them or leave any notes. If you do allow downloads, you can choose which types of documents to offer. Pages' standard settings offer the file in Pages,

Word, and PDF formats. Click the Show Advanced button to change any of these or to add Pages '08 as an option. These advanced settings also include the filename to use at iWork.com; type a new name in the box, or select a previously uploaded filename from the pop-up menu. (Choosing a previously uploaded filename replaces the original on iWork.com; see page 339 for more details.)

Click Share to start loading the file to iWork.com. Pages shows you its progress along with an estimate of time remaining. You can't work on the document that you're sharing while Pages sends the file, although you can work on other files. Most documents take only a few seconds to load, but files with lots of pictures or video can get hefty, and in that case, this upload process can take a while. If that's the case, this might be a good time to grab a cup of coffee—or maybe make a whole pot.

When Pages finishes uploading the file, it announces that the document is ready for action at iWork.com and offers to take you there. Click the View Document Now button to go. (If you decide to go later, you can do so any time by reviewing your list of shared documents—see page 340—or check your email, and you'll find a link to the iWork.com document page waiting for you.)

Your invited guests have meanwhile received emails letting them know that you've added a document for their review at iWork.com. These emails include special web links that not only take your reviewers to the document but also identify who they are. Instead of signing into iWork.com with an account name and password, in other words, your reviewers access the page exclusively through this invitation link. No one can see your document without one of these special links.

Note: Your viewers never need to enter a password to access your document on iWork.com, even when you publish a password-protected file. For that matter, when you download copies of the document from iWork.com in Microsoft Office, iWork '08, or PDF formats, the password protection is removed there, too. However, password protection is retained in copies that are downloaded in iWork '09 format. In general, it's a good idea just to go ahead and remove password protection from the document before uploading, since the password offers very little protection at iWork.com but does prevent iWork.com from adding online comments to the document (see page 337).

Viewing the Document on iWork.com

When you open your Pages file on iWork.com, it looks just like it did when you designed it, with all the fonts and layout in place, as shown in Figure 9-8. On the left is the document itself, and on the right is information about the document, including its owner, the grandly titled *document publisher*. This is the person who loaded the file, the host of the party with the right to invite guests (the *viewers*), kick them out, and clean up the mess they might make.

Note: If change tracking (page 127) is turned on when you send your Pages file to iWork.com, the change-tracking markup is visible in your shared document, too. Likewise, the document shows the same outline mode (page 183). Before you share your Pages document, set these views to be exactly how you'd like your reviewers to see them.

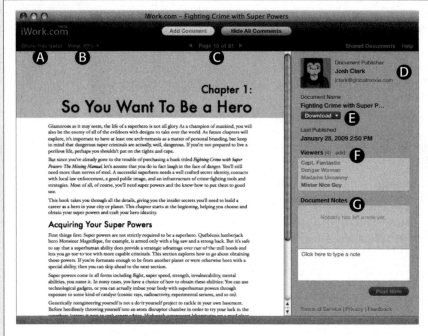

Figure 9-8:
iWork.com displays your Pages document exactly as you designed it. Move from page to page by clicking the navigation buttons at the top of the screen (C). You can also show the file's page thumbnails by clicking Show Navigator (A), which adds the Navigator pane at the left of the screen, just like in Pages itself, letting you click thumbnails to move through the document. Adjust the size of the document display by clicking the View pop-up menu (B).

The document publisher is shown at the top right (D), above the Download menu (E), the list of authorized viewers (F), and the Document Notes panel (G).

The document opens to its first page. From there, you navigate from page to page by clicking the navigation buttons at the top of the screen. Adjust the size of the display by choosing a new size from the View pop-up menu, which works just like the View menu in Pages (page 42). The standard View setting is "Fit Width," so that you can make the text larger or smaller by resizing the window.

You can also use the Navigator pane to jump from page to page. If the Navigator isn't visible when you first open the document, click Show Navigator in the top left, and iWork.com opens it for you at the left side of the screen. Just like the Pages sidebar in Pages, click a thumbnail to jump to that page.

Note: You can even view the document on an iPhone or iPod Touch, but iWork.com gives you a different view on these devices, displaying only the document view. Instead of clicking the navigation buttons or using the Navigator, you scroll through the pages in one long view. You can't add comments or notes on iPhone or iPod; you can only view documents.

Adding and Viewing Comments

Comments show up in iWork.com as yellow sticky notes, an effective visual means for your group to pool questions and suggestions. If your Pages document already included comments when you sent it to iWork.com, those comments show up in iWork.com, and you and your viewers can add new ones, too. Comments also happen to be the only way that iWork.com lets you make changes to the actual document itself. When you later download the document from iWork.com in Pages '09 format, the new comments are included; you can review them in Pages' Comments pane.

Warning: If the document was password-protected when you uploaded it, iWork.com adds no new comments to the document file. Also, comments are not added when you download in a Microsoft Office, PDF, or iWork '08 format.

Slap a sticky note on the document by selecting the text where you'd like to add a comment, and click the Add Comment button. A yellow comment bubble appears; type your comment and click Post. To reply to a comment, click the Reply button in the comment bubble, type your snappy rejoinder, and click Post (Figure 9-9). You can also add comments to an inline image, a table, or a table cell.

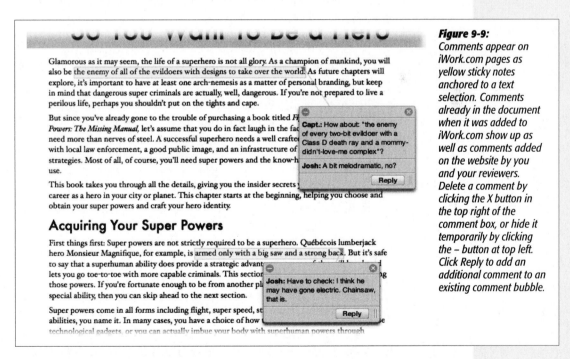

Figure 9-9:
Comments appear on iWork.com pages as yellow sticky notes anchored to a text selection. Comments already in the document when it was added to iWork.com show up as well as comments added on the website by you and your reviewers. Delete a comment by clicking the X button in the top right of the comment box, or hide it temporarily by clicking the – button at top left. Click Reply to add an additional comment to an existing comment bubble.

The document publisher can delete any comment by clicking the X button at the top right of the comment. Guests, or viewers, can delete only their own comments. If you wrote the comment, or if you're the document publisher, you can drag the Post-It anywhere on the page—iWork.com keeps it tethered to its text with a yellow line to maintain the comment's context. If it's not your comment, and you're not the document publisher, you can drag the comment aside temporarily, but it snaps back into place after you release the mouse.

If the sticky notes are flying fast and furious, and you're having trouble reading the actual text, click the Hide Comments button at the top of the screen to hide them all. To hide just one comment bubble, click the – button at the top left of the bubble. When you hide comments, their commented text remains highlighted in yellow, with a yellow triangle, the *comment indicator,* at the right of the highlighted text. Move the pointer over the comment indicator to show its comment; click the indicator to permanently show it (and click again to hide it once more).

Even when comments are hidden, you can use the Navigator pane to scan quickly for comments. Pages with sticky notes are marked with a triangle in the top right corner of their thumbnails. Click the thumbnail to jump to that page and see its comments.

Adding Notes to iWork.com

Comments are useful for adding detailed notes or questions about specific parts of the text, but they're not ideal for adding big-picture commentary about the document as a whole. That's where *notes* come in. The iWork.com Document Notes panel gives you and your viewers a scratch pad for sharing overall comments, to-dos, and progress reports. Notes are listed chronologically, first to last, as shown in Figure 9-10. The first note is the message included by the document publisher announcing the document's availability on iWork.com.

To add a note, click in the white area at the bottom of the Document Notes panel, type your message, and click Post Note. Although you can't delete other reviewer's notes, you can delete any note you wrote yourself: Point to the note and an X button appears at the top right; click this button to permanently remove the note. If you're the document publisher, you can remove anyone's note, or delete them all by clicking the "clear all" link above the Document Notes panel.

Unlike comments, notes are not included in the document when you download a copy from iWork.com. They're for discussion on iWork.com only.

Downloading the Document

To download a full, editable copy of your Pages file, click the Download button, and iWork.com rolls out a pop-up menu of available formats, along with the file size of each (Figure 9-11). Make your selection, and your browser downloads the file to your computer.

When you choose the Pages '09 format, the downloaded file includes all the comments added on iWork.com (but not the notes). The other formats don't include these comments, and Microsoft Office and iWork '08 files may also look slightly different than the original, as described earlier in the discussion of exporting documents (page 328).

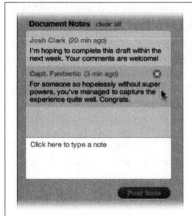

Figure 9-10:
The Document Notes panel hosts discussion for the overall document. Add a note by typing in the white box at the bottom of the panel. To delete your own note, point to the note and iWork.com reveals an X button; click to permanently remove the note from the page.

Figure 9-11:
Click the Download button to choose a file format to download. For Pages, the standard set is Pages '09, Word, and PDF, but you can mix and match formats when you first load the document to iWork.com.

Republishing a Document

When you or your viewers download a copy of the file from iWork.com, it can be edited as usual. But since those changes are made offline, they don't have any effect on the online version at iWork.com. The only way to update the content of the published file is for the document publisher to *republish* it, loading a revised copy to iWork.com.

This process takes you through the same steps as loading a new document to iWork.com. Open the update document in Pages, and choose Share → Share via iWork.com, and the iWork.com invitation window appears.

When you've previously uploaded the same document (or another document with the same name), Pages recalls the guest list, and fills in the To field for you. Make any changes to this collection of viewers, and edit the Subject and Message text. Pages' standard behavior is to load the file to iWork under a new name, adding a version number to the original title. "Fighting Crime with Super Powers" becomes "Fighting Crime with Super Powers-1"—subsequent uploads bump the number up to 2, 3, 4, and so on. This actually creates a whole new document page in iWork.com, so you can keep multiple versions in your library of shared documents.

If you don't want to keep the previous version on iWork.com, and want to replace it outright, click the Show Advanced button in the invitation window. The "Copy to iWork.com as" setting controls the iWork.com filename. Change it to the original filename (or choose it from the pop-up menu). When you send a document with the same name as another file in your iWork.com collection, Pages warns you that you're going to replace an existing file. If you go ahead, iWork.com replaces the original file with the new one. The notes from the original file are kept in the Document Notes pane, but the content and comments are replaced with the new file.

Click Share to send the document to iWork.com. When Pages is done with the upload, it sends new email invitations to your selected group of viewers with new URLs for viewing the document.

Reviewing your Shared Documents

To browse your growing iWork.com library, choose Share → Show Shared Documents (if this option is grayed out, choose Share → Sign In and then try again). This menu item also doubles as a comment indicator, showing you how many documents have new comments since your last visit. You can also click the Shared Documents link at the top right of the iWork.com window in your web browser, or by visiting *http://publish.iwork.com* (no www) in your web browser and providing your Apple ID and password.

Your browser takes you to the Shared Documents screen at the iWork.com website (Figure 9-12), listing all the Pages, Keynote, and Numbers documents you've loaded. If iWork.com asks you to sign in before you get to this page, enter your Apple ID and password.

The Shared Documents screen shows you the status of all your documents, as well as the amount of storage space you've used in your account. From here, you can:

- **Go to a file's document screen.** Click the name of the file to view.

- **Download a document.** Click the downward arrow for the file.

- **Delete a document.** Click the Delete link to permanently remove the file from iWork.com

The Shared Documents page shows only the documents that you've published yourself, and it's visible only to you. This screen does not show documents published by others but which you've been invited to review. Those *viewer links* are available only from the invitation email viewers receive when the document is first published. If you misplace your viewer link, contact the document publisher and ask her to send it to you again. Document publishers can look up viewer links from the document screen's Viewers pane, which is the topic of the next section.

Managing Viewers

When you first send a document to iWork.com, you choose the folks to invite to your document-viewing party, but you're not locked into this guest list. The document publisher can add or remove viewers anytime.

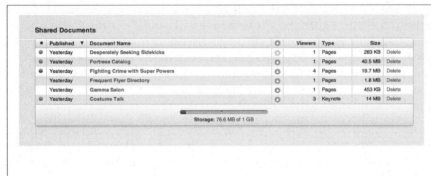

Figure 9-12:
The Shared Documents page lists the files you've published on iWork.com. The indicators in the left column are blue for files with new comments. Click the downward arrow to download the file in iWork '09 format, complete with any comments added at iWork.com. To change the order files are displayed, click one of the column headings.

To add a viewer, click the "add" link above the Viewer pane. The viewer list is replaced by a form for you to add the name and email address of the new viewer (Figure 9-13). Type the info, click Add, and iWork.com updates the Viewer list and displays the viewer link for you to send to the latest member of your posse. Since iWork.com doesn't send invitations to viewers added from the document screen, this bit is important: Copy the web address, and paste it into an email message to your new guest, letting her know that she should visit that web page to view the document.

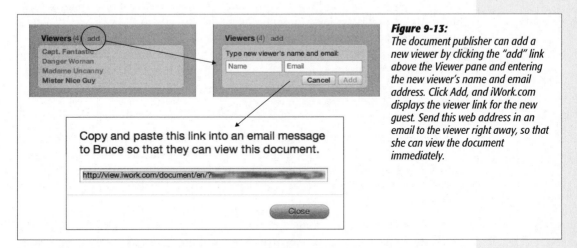

Figure 9-13:
The document publisher can add a new viewer by clicking the "add" link above the Viewer pane and entering the new viewer's name and email address. Click Add, and iWork.com displays the viewer link for the new guest. Send this web address in an email to the viewer right away, so that she can view the document immediately.

Don't send the same address out to more than one person. Every viewer has her own unique web address that lets her into the document page and identifies who she is when she adds a comment or note to the page. If you or your guest share the viewer link with someone else, that person will also be able to view the shared document, leaving notes and comments under the name of the original viewer.

The link, in other words, plays the same role that a user name and password play on many other sites—giving access to the site and confirming the identity of the visitor. All of this likewise means that you should discourage visitors from forwarding invitation emails to others. To keep everyone's roles straight, everyone should use their very own link, and publishers should invite new people only by adding new people as described above (or by including them in the invite when the document is first loaded to iWork.com).

If someone misplaces his viewer link, the document publisher can look it up and send a reminder: Move the cursor over the name of your forgetful guest in the Viewer pane, and a downward arrow appears. Click it, and choose Show Viewer's Link. A window appears with the web address. Copy it into an email message, and send it as a reminder to your visitor.

To revoke a viewer's visiting privileges to a document, click the downward facing arrow next to her name in the Viewer pane, and choose Remove Viewer. A confirmation message asks if you really want to do it and, after you agree, the viewer's name is removed from the Viewer pane, and they can no longer visit the page. Any comments they've already added to the page remain behind, however.

Publishing Online with iWeb

iWork.com is a convenient way to share a document with an invited group. But when you're ready to share your creation with the masses, it's time to graduate from a private website to the public Web. To help you fast-track your Pages documents to the net, Pages lets you send documents directly to iWeb, Apple's friendly software for creating personal websites, blogs, and podcasts. If you use iWeb to create and maintain your site, this makes for an easy way to add a document download to your page.

Note: This feature requires iWeb '08 or later.

From the Share → "Send to iWeb" submenu, choose a file format to use on your site—either PDF or File. PDF is pretty much always the way to go here, unless you're positive that all your site's visitors use Pages. (Both options save a separate copy of the file, and any subsequent changes that you make won't appear on the iWeb site.)

As soon as you make that selection, iWeb launches. If you haven't yet set up a site in iWeb, it asks you to select a template to use and creates a site. If you've already got multiple sites, iWeb asks you which site you want to edit. A brand new page opens with a thumbnail image of your document. Use iWeb to bring the web page up to date with any text and images you'd like to add to introduce or describe your document. When you publish the page to your site, visitors can click the thumbnail image in their browsers to download the document.

Visitors who subscribe to your site's podcast via iTunes will also automatically download the document into iTunes, if you saved it as PDF. File this under "strange but true": While it might seem odd to crack iTunes to catch up on your reading, iTunes is savvy not only about sound and video in podcast feeds but PDFs, too. Include a PDF on your iWeb site, and it lands in your subscribers' collection of podcast feeds. So in iTunes and other feed readers, your podcast doubles as a PDF distribution service.

Tip: For more details about using iWeb to build web pages, launch iWeb and choose Help → iWeb Help, or visit *www.apple.com/ilife/tutorials*.

Streamline Your Projects: Creating Templates

You've undoubtedly used—and come to appreciate—Pages' timesaving templates. They range from very simple, like Classic Letter, to the complex, multipage layouts of the various newsletters. But whether plain or intricate, they all share the same purpose: to get you started on a document quickly, with a large part of the formatting already in place—so you can concentrate on the content instead of the layout. This chapter shows you how to make your own templates so you can add them to Pages' Template Chooser, the design roster you learned about way back on page 18.

Template-Building Basics

Don't let templates fool you—they're really just plain old Pages documents. In fact, every template begins its life as a regular Pages file with text, pictures, tables, anything you want. After you get the file just the way you want it, choose File → Save as Template, give the template a name, and click Save. From now on, when you open the Template Chooser, you find your new template, along with any others you've created, in the My Templates category (Figure 10-1).

When you choose your template to create a brand new document, Pages opens a fresh, untitled file that looks exactly like your template document looked when you saved it. Not only do you get all the template's text, pictures, charts, and so on, even the window itself is in the same state. The Styles Drawer, rulers, alignment guides, invisibles—all are visible or hidden just as they were when you saved the template.

Figure 10-1:
Pages typically stows your custom templates in the My Templates category of the Template Chooser, just below the standard Word Processing and Page Layout categories. See page 360 for details on how to organize your templates into additional categories.

Most of Pages' built-in templates enjoy sophisticated designs stocked with sample content (and yours certainly can, too). But templates don't have to include any content at all. You might not think of the templates in the Template Chooser's Blank categories as "real" templates, but that's exactly what they are. While they don't carry any content or layout elements, they do come loaded with text styles and a slew of settings that define the look of text and objects as you work on your document. In fact, creating blank templates like these is the best way to save your preferred settings for fonts, page margins, page numbering headers and footers, you name it. Prep an empty file with all your favorite settings and styles and then save it as a template. When you choose the template from the Template Chooser, you get a blank untitled document with the text and object settings as you like them.

Creating and choosing these background settings for your template is very nearly as important as setting up its layout and placeholder text. Specifically, every template—actually every Pages document—contains an array of formatting attributes that instruct Pages how to display each and every element of your documents. When designing a template, you can choose to leave these attributes in their standard, or *default,* state, or you can modify any or all of them to create your own defaults:

- **Placeholder text and graphics.** Sample text and pictures that can be replaced with a click of the mouse.

- **Document formatting.** The paper size and orientation (vertical or horizontal), page margins, footnote or endnote preferences, table of contents styles, and page numbering settings.

- **Text styles.** The Styles Drawer's collection of paragraph, character, list, and table of contents styles. (Setting the styles for the Free Form and Body paragraph styles determines your document's default text style.)

- **Headers and footers.** Text or graphics to appear at the top or bottom of all pages, including page numbers if you like.

- **Text boxes, shapes, and connection lines.** Set the standard text style, fill, border, shadow, and so on used for new objects.

- **Tables.** Configure the number of rows and columns, as well as the text style and object settings for new tables.

- **Charts.** Choose the colors and formatting for every individual type of chart.

- **Pictures and movies.** Configure shadows, reflections, opacity, and outlines applied to new graphics.

- **Background images.** Graphics, watermarks, and other master objects that appear on every page.

- **Additional pages.** A collection of page and section snapshots that you can optionally drop into your document via the toolbar's Pages or Sections button.

- **Alignment guides.** The grid of guidelines to use to line up objects on your pages.

Modifying an Existing Template

Just as you can use Pages' built-in templates as a starting point for your documents, you can also use them as a springboard for your own custom templates, too. Say that you're a fan of the Business Letter template's basic layout, but you want to update it with your company's logo, change the font, and add a few other tweaks (Figure 10-2). To do that, you create a new document from the template, make your changes, and then save it as a new template:

1. **Create a new document from the template to modify.**

   Choose File → New from Template Chooser, and open the Business Letter template.

2. **Change the logo.**

   Drop your company logo into the placeholder at the top of the page and adjust its size and placement.

3. **Move the logo, company name, and address from the master layer and back into the mix of "normal" objects. Doing this prevents them from showing up on subsequent pages if your letter runs over one page.**

   Select the logo, and then Shift-click the company name and return address. The solid blue selection handles around the logo and text boxes indicate their master object status. Choose Format → Advanced → Move Objects to Page. (For more about master objects, see page 261.)

4. **Update the company name and return address if necessary.**

The template uses sender fields to automatically fill in the work address from your card in the Address Book program (see page 22). To change it to use your home address, for example, open the Link Inspector's Merge tab. In the list of merge fields, click the Target Name of each work-address field and change it to its home alternative (Work Street becomes Home Street, Work City becomes Home City, and so on). Or, if you don't want the template to pluck the return address from Address Book at all, replace the sender fields in your document by typing whatever text you want to appear.

Note: Pages does not automatically change the displayed data as you update the targets for your sender fields and merge fields. To refresh the display, drag an Address Book card onto one of the changed fields.

5. **Redefine text styles.**

Open the Styles Drawer (choose View → Show Styles Drawer or click the Styles Drawer button in the Format Bar). Select the body text of the letter, and make adjustments to make the text look the way you want, a new font for example. When you're done, click the red triangle next to Body in the Styles Drawer, and choose "Redefine Style from Selection" to update the style.

Repeat the process for all the styles in the template, clicking on each snippet of text you'd like to change and then redefining its underlying style in the Styles Drawer. See page 93 for more about using styles.

6. **Lock objects.**

Lock down the static parts of the letterhead to protect them from modification. Select the small logo and then Shift-click the company name and the return address text boxes. With those three items selected, choose Arrange → Lock (or send them to the background by choosing Arrange → Send Objects to Background).

7. **Add a background image.**

To add a bit more style to this letterhead, insert your logo again as a floating object to use as a background. In the Format Bar's Wrap pop-up menu, choose None so that text doesn't wrap around the image as you position it (see page 252 for more about text wrapping). Increase the logo's size and adjust its position; turn down its opacity with the Format Bar's Opacity field to wash it out. When you've got it just right, choose Arrange → Send Objects to Background (flip back to page 260 for a refresher on background objects).

8. **Tidy up the window, and select the placeholder text.**

A template saves not only the document's contents, but also the state of all your window accessories (rulers, Styles Drawer, Format Bar, alignment guides, and so on). Arrange these items the way that you want them when you first open a new document. That includes the insertion point, too: Click the main placeholder text to highlight it, and Pages will preselect that text when you open the document.

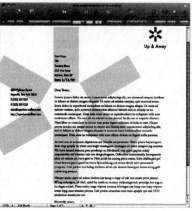

Figure 10-2:
You can use one of Pages' templates as a foundation to build your own—adding, removing, or changing any of its elements before saving it as a template. Starting with the Business Letter template (left), you can add your own logo, add a background image, change fonts, and more (right).

9. **Save the new template.**

   Choose File → Save as Template, give the new letterhead template a name, and save it in the My Templates folder.

After you save the template, the letterhead document you've been working on remains onscreen. You can save it as a regular document if you like (and Pages will ask if you want to do just that when you go to close its window). When you do that, you basically have two versions of the file—one is a regular document and the other is a template available from the Template Chooser. Forget about the regular document for now: You can get a fresh, untitled copy of the file anytime by creating a new document. Take your new template out for a spin: Open the Template Chooser, click My Templates, and then double-click your new template. Your letterhead opens with the text of the letter selected, ready for you to begin typing immediately.

Note: Only the Templates you save in the My Templates folder (or in other folders inside [home folder] → Library → Application Support → iWork → Pages → Templates) show up in the Template Chooser. However, you can save templates anywhere on your hard drive, for example, in your Documents folder. Double-click those template files to launch Pages and open a brand new document based on the template.

Creating Templates from Scratch

If you're a real do-it-yourselfer, you can create templates from scratch, by starting with the Blank template and building up a sample document exactly the way you want it. Even though you're starting with the Blank template, it still contains a complete set of standard settings for all the document elements listed on page 346. You can accept these factory settings or change some or all of them for your custom template.

Start by opening a new document, using a blank template from either the Word Processing or Page Layout category in the Template Chooser, depending on the type of file you're building. This empty canvas will become the *model document* that you build to create a template. Choose File → Save right off the bat to save the file as a regular Pages document (don't choose Save as Template just yet), and give it a title. If you're making a template for Up & Away's new series of secret fortress catalogs, for example, you might call it, "Fortress catalog model." Then, as you work on it, periodically press ⌘-S to save your work. You'll save it as a template file only after you're done creating the model document.

Begin by choosing File → Page Setup and selecting the paper size and orientation. Then start defining all the styles and standard settings for the document's various elements: text styles, text box styles, shape styles, connection lines, table styles, chart styles, image styles, and movie styles.

Defining Text Styles

Choose View → Show Styles Drawer or click the Styles Drawer button in the Format Bar. In the Paragraph Styles pane, click the Body style and type some text into the document so you have something to work with. Modify the font and paragraph attributes, using the Text Inspector and the Fonts window to create your version of that style. Then click the red triangle next to the style name and, from the pop-up menu, choose Redefine Style from Selection (see Figure 10-3). Pages replaces the stock style with your own.

Work down the list, clicking the style name, modifying the text for each style, and saving the results with the "Redefine Style from Selection" command. Add new styles by choosing "Create New Paragraph Style from Selection" from the red triangle's pop-up menu, or by clicking the + button at the bottom of the Styles Drawer. Remove any unneeded styles by clicking the arrow to the right of the style and choosing Delete Style. You'll find all the details about creating and editing styles in Chapter 3, starting on page 93.

You can also set default styles for tables of contents, but first you need to get at 'em. Pages hides away its table of contents styles, or *TOC styles,* when you're not working directly with a table of contents. To get access to these styles, you first need to create a table of contents to work with: Add some temporary headings to your model document and then, at the very beginning of the document, add a table of contents by choosing Insert → Table of Contents. Open the Styles Drawer, and update your TOC styles just as you styled your regular text styles. When you're done, you can delete the table if you don't plan to keep it in the template; Pages will continue to remember the TOC styles. For more about working with tables of contents, see page 174.

Setting Document Formatting

Open the Document Inspector to set the standard document styles for files using your template. Click the Page Setup button if you want to change the page size or

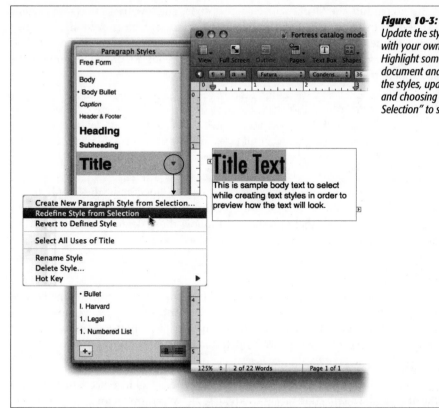

Figure 10-3:
Update the styles in the blank template with your own text preferences. Highlight some sample text in the document and step through each of the styles, updating the text formatting and choosing "Redefine Style from Selection" to store the changes.

choose either portrait (vertical) or landscape (horizontal) page orientation. Set the document margins, and choose your footnote/endnote preferences. If your documents might use a table of contents, click the Document Inspector's TOC tab and select the styles whose text should be included in the table.

In the Layout Inspector's Section pane, set your preferences for handling page numbering as well as page headers and footers. Turn on the "First page is different" option if you want to use different headers or footers on the front page than on other pages of your documents. Choose "Left and right pages are different" if you want to alternate headers or footers, for bound documents, for example.

For complete details about document formatting, see Chapter 5.

Defining Object Styles

Every type of object in Pages has a standard, or *default,* style that Pages uses when you add a new object. When you add a new shape to a document based on one of the Blank templates, for example, the shape is always green with a 1pt black border line. If your color taste wanders more toward burnt sienna, you can change the default for your document so that all new shapes use that color instead. You can similarly change the standard settings for every other type of Pages object—not just the color, but the stroke, opacity, text style, shadow, reflection—the whole range of object stylings. To do it, insert an object, adjust it to your liking, and then define it as the default style by choosing Format → Advanced → Define Default [Object] Style. Going forward, new objects added to your document will mimic the formatting of that object.

Note: When you redefine the default settings for an object type, all the other objects in the document update to reflect the change. When you set your burnt-sienna shape as the default, for example, all other shapes turn burnt-sienna, too, except for any that were explicitly set to use a different color. In other words, all shapes still using the old standard settings update to the new standard color.

When you set these default object styles in a regular document, they apply to the current document only. But when you save the document as a template, any new documents created from that template will follow those default object styles. The specific formatting options vary according to object type.

Text boxes

Add a floating text box to your document, and type some text into it. Use the Format Bar, Text Inspector, and Fonts window to set the font, style, color, alignment, column layout, paragraph spacing, and so on—or even better, simply select a paragraph style to use. (See page 59 for details on text formatting.)

When you're done editing and formatting the text, press ⌘-Return to select the text box. Now use the Format Bar or Graphic Inspector to set all its object attributes: the fill, stroke, shadow, reflection, and opacity. Use the Wrap Inspector to set the wrapping style (page 252). Don't bother adjusting the text box's size or rotation—Pages doesn't save these attributes in the template's default text box style.

When you're pleased with the appearance of the text and the text box, select the text box at the object level (if the insertion point is still inside the text, press ⌘-Return). Choose Format → Advanced → Define Default Text Box Style. Pages stashes away all the adjustments you've made for a standard text box. Give it a try by adding another text box. It should match your model text box in all respects, except it will contain only the standard "Type to enter text" content, as shown in Figure 10-4. Start typing and you see the text displayed in your chosen font. Now that you've defined the default text box style, you can delete these sample text boxes to get them out of the way.

Note: If the text box has multiple text formats or several styles, Pages pays attention only to the style of the very first character in the text box when you use the box to define the default style. Other styles are ignored.

Shapes

Since they can also contain text, shapes are very similar to text boxes. Insert a floating shape in the document and repeat the same steps you used for a text box to format the shape's text and object attributes. When you're happy with the effect,

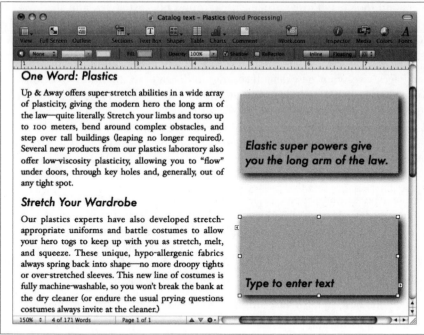

Figure 10-4:
*After you define default
text box styles, every new
text box that you add
matches the new
formatting. Here, a text
box for pull quotes (top)
was used to define
default styles. Adding a
new text box (bottom)
creates an object that
mimics the original's text
style, color, shadow, text
wrapping, and bottom
alignment.*

choose Format → Advanced → Define Default Shape Style to add this new style to the defaults. Insert another shape to test it out. Then you can delete the shapes to get them out of your hair.

Connection lines

Add two objects—two shapes, for example—to your document and choose Insert → Connection Line, and Pages yokes the two together. Select the line, and use the Format Bar or Graphic Inspector to choose its stroke style, weight, color, and end points—even add a shadow or reflection if you like. If you don't want your standard connection lines to fasten directly onto each object, drag the blue circular controls at each end point to add a gap between line and object.

Note: Dragging the white circular control in the center of the connection line turns the connection into a bendy line, but Pages ignores this when you set the default styles. Every new connection line always starts out as a straight line between its objects.

When you're done styling your connector, choose Format → Advanced → Define Default Connection Style.

Tables

Insert a table and then alter and adjust its many attributes until it meets your demanding standards. Click the toolbar's Table button to add a table to your document. Then format away, setting the number of rows and columns (including

---

headers and footers), border strokes, background fill, text styles, and shadows for the table. See Chapter 8 for the complete story on table construction. Select the table and choose Format → Advanced → Define Default Table Style when you've perfected your design.

When Pages saves your new default settings, it doesn't pay attention to settings for individual cells, only to settings that you apply at either the table level or to *all cells* of the header row, header column, or footer row. There's a similar all-or-nothing deal for table borders, too: You can style outer borders separately from inner borders, but all four outer borders should have the same style; likewise, all inner borders should have the same style. You'll get unpredictable results if you try to set the default table using a table with different borders for some cells.

Unlike text boxes and shapes, Pages takes note of the size of the table when you save it as the default table style. New tables match the default table's overall size as well as its number of rows and columns. You can't choose the size of individual columns or rows, however. When you add a new table, you always get columns of equal width and rows of equal height, although you can of course adjust individual tables to any dimensions you like after you've added them.

Test out your new style by inserting another table—and then clear the decks by deleting the tables to make room for…

Charts

Defining chart styles for your template is a bit different from other objects because there are 19 varieties of charts to choose from, including all the 3D charts. In theory, you're supposed to define the style for each of the 19 chart styles (or at least the ones that you plan to use in your documents for this template). Unfortunately, this feature works only partially as advertised. Here's how it's supposed to go: Insert a chart, adjust the chart's attributes (size, gridlines, tick marks, axis labels, text wrapping, and so on), and choose Format → Advanced → "Define Default Style for [chart type]". Up to this point everything works fine.

Now you're supposed to repeat the process for each of the other chart types. But as you select other chart types you find that most of the settings you just made for the first chart type apply to all chart types. Here's how it works in practice: Default colors for column, bar, and area charts also apply to their stacked counterparts (or vice versa), so default colors are always the same for both "regular" and stacked charts of each type. With that one exception, all the remaining default settings apply to *all* chart types. So if you set a chart with a certain number of gridlines for one chart type, the remaining chart types also get those same gridlines as their standard setting, no matter what settings you might have given it previously.

In practice, this means that you should use the "Define Default Style for [chart type]" command to set most default settings for all charts at once, and then change the chart's primary colors one at a time for each chart type. (You'll find complete details on formatting charts on page 784.)

Images

Insert an image on the page—from either the Media Browser or a folder on your hard drive. If you like, use the Format Bar or Graphic Inspector to add a stroke, reflection, shadow, or picture frame, or adjust the image's opacity. Set the text-wrapping style in the Format Bar or Wrap Inspector. You can't set a standard image size or rotation, and any image masks are likewise ignored. When you're done, choose Format → Advanced → Define Default Image Style.

Movies

Insert a movie on the page, and make any of the same adjustments that you would make to a picture—you have all the same formatting options. As with images, size and rotation are ignored for movies. When you're ready, choose Format → Advanced → Define Default Movie Style.

Changing your mind

As you build your document, you may change your mind about some of the default settings and text styles that you created at the outset; never fear, you're not locked in. Change your default settings for any object type whenever you like, and your changes filter through all the objects in the document. Likewise, you can always update your paragraph, character, and list styles at any time. For details on saving and modifying text styles, see page 98.

Making Placeholders

Now that you've defined the standard styles for every possible element that you can add to a document, you can begin formatting the model document with placeholder images and text. Approach your model document as if you were building a complete prototype of your final design—mock up the entire catalog, brochure, newsletter, letterhead, or whatever it is you're designing. If you've already published a full newsletter, for example, you can even use a previous edition as the basis of the model document for your newsletter template.

Or build the model from scratch by placing sample text and graphics, adding layout and section breaks, columns, headers and footers—all the elements you might include in your final newsletter, formatted just the way you want them. When you have all your design elements in place, you're ready to mark your sample text and graphics as *placeholders,* a special category of temporary content that's easily replaced when you use your custom template to create new documents.

Regular text and placeholder text

You can add two different kinds of text elements to a template: regular editable text and *placeholder text.* When you click regular text, you can place your insertion point within it and add or delete characters—nothing unusual about it. When you click placeholder text, however, Pages highlights the entire placeholder, which can be a word, a line, a paragraph, or several paragraphs—even the entire document. Then, when you type even one character, Pages replaces the whole thing.

Use regular text in a template for content that you don't plan to change from document to document, or which you might need to modify only occasionally. This choice is good for the salutation on a letter, or a story that's repeated in your newsletter every month with small changes, for example, "Congratulations to Employee of the Month Jennifer Ball of the Utility Belt Department! She's now automatically entered in our Employee of the Year competition and could be the lucky winner of a hydrogen-fueled jet pack!"

Use placeholder text when you just want to demonstrate how and where text should appear, but when you don't actually want to use the example text in the final document. Placeholders are just that—disposable text that fills in for the real text to be provided later. Because it's throwaway copy, you can use any text you want for a placeholder: copy some random text from another document, from a web page, or use so-called "Greek" text like you find in Apple's templates (see "Lorem Ipsum Dolor?" on page 194). If you're building a template that will be used by someone else, placeholder text is also a good place to add instructions for how to use the template.

Tip: There are plenty of sources of "Lorem ipsum" "Greek" text on the Internet. A good one is *www.lorem2.com*, where you can copy the text in your web browser and then paste it into Pages. Or, if you prefer placeholder text that's a bit less stuffy, try *www.malevole.com/mv/misc/text* which generates text using the lyrics of TV theme songs from the 1970s.

Placeholders begin life in your document as regular text. To convert regular text to placeholder text, choose View → Show Invisibles, and select a block of text (or even just a word or phrase) to turn into a placeholder—but don't select the final paragraph break if there is one. Choose Format → Advanced → Define as Placeholder Text (Figure 10-5).

Note: If you see a paragraph break at the end of your placeholder text, don't select it when you define the selection as placeholder text. If you *do* select that final paragraph break, you're telling Pages to replace the entire paragraph—including all its formatting. Then, when you type into your document to replace the text in the placeholder, your typing takes on the format of the *following* paragraph instead of the placeholder paragraph. (This is typically only an issue when you're adding a placeholder into an area of text where there's more than one paragraph.)

Once you've set text to be a placeholder, clicking anywhere in the text selects the whole block, ready to be replaced with "real" text. This means, though, that you can't make any changes to the placeholder text—any change you make will replace the whole thing. If you later need to modify placeholder text—perhaps you want to update template instructions you've included there—you first have to choose Format → Advanced → Enable Placeholder Text Authoring (which, in less geeky English, means Make Placeholder Text Editable). This turns off the click-to-select-all nature of *all* placeholder text in your document, and you can now make changes to any and all placeholders. When you're done editing, choose Format → Advanced → Disable Placeholder Text Authoring to return placeholders to their normal behavior.

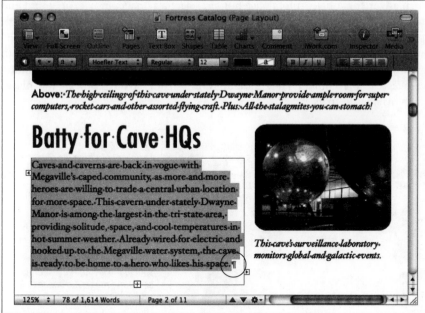

Figure 10-5:
After creating your model document, you can change blocks of text into placeholder text for your template. Choose View → Show Invisibles and select all the text except the final paragraph break (circled). Then choose Format → Advanced → "Define as Placeholder Text".

You can select a placeholder and press Delete to delete the entire thing. Or you can select it and choose the checked Format → Advanced → Define as Placeholder Text command to uncheck it and turn the placeholder back into plain old text.

Merge and sender fields

If your template includes addresses or other contact info that will change depending on who creates or receives the document, you can use merge fields to fill in addresses automatically. This is especially useful for letter templates, for example, which can address and sign letters for you when you open a new document. For details about adding merge fields, see the mail merge information starting on page 165.

Note: If your template uses a Numbers spreadsheet for its merge-field targets, documents created from your template will use the same spreadsheet.

Media placeholders for pictures, movies, and sound

Pages handles placeholders for your graphics, too. Use *media placeholders* for any pictures, movies, or audio you'll want to replace when you create a new document: property photos for listings in your secret-fortress catalog, pictures accompanying newsletter articles, a video interview with the employee of the year (and her new hydrogen-powered jet pack), and so on. You don't have to make every graphic a placeholder, though. Leave regular pictures in your document when you always want to use them in the finished document—background images, logos, a newsletter title graphic, or your author portrait, for example.

To turn any media object into a placeholder, select an image, movie, or sound and choose Format → Advanced → "Define as Media Placeholder". Now, when you drop a picture onto the placeholder, it replaces the placeholder graphic and inherits its picture frame, masking, size, rotation, shadow, reflection—everything about it (Figure 10-6). Likewise, when you drop a movie or sound onto the placeholder, it replaces the placeholder and fits snugly into your layout with all the placeholder's original settings.

Figure 10-6:
Drag a photo from the Media Browser onto a media placeholder, and the cursor sprouts a green plus sign (left). Release the mouse button to drop the photo, and Pages replaces the placeholder with your new image (right). The image fits neatly into the same spot in the layout—Pages rotates, sizes, and masks the image to fit, adding the same picture frame, shadow, and other formatting as the original placeholder image.

You can reposition, resize, rotate, and adjust any of a media placeholder's attributes. To remove the placeholder, select it and press Delete. Turn a media placeholder back into a regular object by using the same command again: Choose Format → Advanced → "Define as Media Placeholder" to remove the checkmark and return the selection to regular duty.

Building Multipage Templates

A template can be as many pages long as you need. For example, if you create a 12-page document and save it as a template, then creating a new document from the template starts you off with the same 12-page document. It may be more practical, however, to create a multipage document and divide it up into pages, or sets of pages, that you can choose to add to the document only when you need them. Many of the Apple templates are designed this way. They open up to a first page and then you can decide to add more pages to the document by choosing them from the Pages or Sections button in the toolbar, or from the Insert → Pages or Insert → Sections menu.

First create all the pages you want to offer in the template. For example, your real estate catalog for secret fortresses might contain a cover page, a featured-property page, a grid of property listings, an article page with a right sidebar, an article page with a left sidebar, and a back page. Once you have a multipage document with all these page types represented, you *capture* each of the pages or sections, adding them to the Insert → Pages menu (for page-layout documents) or the Insert → Sections menu (for word-processing documents).

In page-layout documents, you capture one page at a time. Click anywhere in the page to capture, choose Format → Advanced → Capture Pages, and give it a name. A thumbnail of the page is added to the Insert → Pages menu (Figure 10-7)—when you select the thumbnail, Pages deposits an exact copy of the page into your document, with all its images, text, alignment guides, and formatting.

Figure 10-7:
When you capture pages of a page-layout document, they appear in the toolbar's Pages pop-up button, shown here, as well as the Insert → Pages menu. This template's menu offers a variety of page types for the secret-fortress catalog. Choosing one inserts a copy of the page into your document.

In word-processing documents, however, you capture pages for an entire section at a time—so depending on the size of the section, that could mean that you're capturing many pages at once, or even the entire document. To make sure that you're capturing the specific portion of the document you want, add section breaks before and after the section to capture.

For complete details on capturing sections and pages, see page 159.

Tip: Considering all the work that goes into the creation of this master document—and since the next step involves deleting many of its pages for your final template—you might find it prudent at this point to save a copy of this document in its full-length form. Choose File → Save As, give this backup copy a unique name, and then click Save.

Congratulations, you've finished the creation part of making a template! Now there's just a little cleanup. Go ahead and delete all the pages you don't want to appear when you open this template. For example, you might delete all the pages except for the cover page of your fortress catalog. When you open the template, you'll have a single page to start working with, and you can add additional pages from the Pages menu (or Sections menu in the case of word-processing documents).

Fine-tune your document window to get it just how you want it. When you save your template, Pages takes a snapshot of your window so that it always opens the same way for new documents when you open the template. Decide whether you want to show or hide the Styles drawer, Format Bar, layout view, ruler, or invisibles in your new-document view. Place the insertion point where you want it when you open new documents, or ⌘-click the margin to have no selection at all.

The last step: Choose File → Save as Template, give your new template a name, choose a destination folder to save it (usually My Templates), and then click Save.

Organizing Templates

If your innocent penchant for creating your own templates turns into a raging addiction, you'll need to create new categories in the Template Chooser to hold them, or delete templates you no longer need. Pages doesn't offer "New Folder" or "Delete Template" commands in the Template Chooser; you have to manually make new folders and trash templates directly in the Finder.

Pages separates all the templates you've created on your own from Apple's assortment of stock templates. When you save your templates in the standard location suggested by Pages, you find them in the My Templates folder by following the path: [home folder] → Library → Application Support → iWork → Pages → Templates → My Templates. Drag any templates you no longer need from the My Templates folder to the trash.

To add a new category to the Template Chooser, create a new folder next to My Templates in the Templates folder. Name it for your new category, drag templates from the My Templates folder into it, or choose it when saving new templates. To rename the My Templates category, change the name of its folder here.

Sharing, Exchanging, and Buying Templates

You can share templates with other Pages fans and let them take advantage of your hard work (and creative brilliance) by sending a template as an email attachment, burning it on a CD, copying it to a USB flash drive, and so on.

But first you have to find the template file you want to share. One way is to dig deep into your hard drive to find Pages' template storage vault and make a copy of one of your templates. They're in [home folder] → Library → Application Support → iWork → Pages → Templates → My Templates.

A much easier way, however, doesn't involve any hard-drive excavation at all. Open the Template Chooser and create a new document from the template you want to share. As soon as it opens, choose File → Save as Template. You have to rename the template, and then choose an easy-to-find destination—say, your desktop—and click Save. You've created an exact clone of the template which you can now easily share with others.

Tip: Templates can be a bit hefty in the file-size department. If you want to email a template, compress it first. Control-click the template icon and, from the pop-up menu, choose "Create Archive of [filename]". Your Mac creates a compressed .zip archive of the file.

Templates Online

If you've created a fabulous template, consider sharing it with the world by submitting it to *www.iworkcommunity.com* or *http://iworktemplates.blogspot.com*. These websites offer an ever-expanding collection of templates created by Pages aficionados around the world—all free for the downloading. If you don't mind spending a little coin, you can also buy templates: Bundles of professionally designed Pages templates are available for sale online from commercial design outfits including *www.jumsoft.com*, *www.stocklayouts.com*, and *www.oneeyedgoldfish.com*.

Part Two: Keynote '09

2

Planning and Giving Great Presentations

Right from their invention, slideshows have been a mixed blessing. Old-timers will recall painfully long evenings enduring carrousels of family vacation slides, inflicted on unwitting guests by an enthusiastic host. As a kid, you might've been subjected to educational filmstrips about igneous rock or isosceles triangles. Slide projectors, filmstrips, overhead transparencies—ever since we figured out how to project images, we've used these projections to try to connect with audiences, with uneven results. Since the mid-1990s, those technologies have given way to the computer slideshow, which all too often drown audiences in numbing bullet points and clunky clip art.

It doesn't have to be that way. On the contrary, well-designed slideshows can bring a presentation to life, helping a speaker engage and educate her audience with stimulating visuals. Keynote can help you do just that.

Keynote is a *presentation program* for making slideshows, usually to accompany a talk or other live presentation. In fact, the program was originally designed specifically for Apple founder Steve Jobs (Figure 11-1), a design stickler who's legendary for his entertaining and effective presentations. Like its Microsoft counterpart PowerPoint, Keynote lets you build screens of text and graphics to illustrate important points. Keynote does Microsoft one better, though, with an emphasis on polished visuals and a light, streamlined interface that never gets in your way. With its cinematic transitions and stunning effects, Keynote makes your slides sparkle (literally, as you'll discover in Chapter 14).

For all its razzle dazzle, though, Keynote is still only a tool. All the special effects in the world can't save dull material that's not relevant to your audience (vacation slides, igneous rock). And too many special effects—or too much text or poorly chosen images—can bury your message or confuse your audience. This chapter is designed to help you avoid those pitfalls by walking you through the process of crafting your presentation's message and, along the way, finding the best way to sharpen its points in your slideshow.

If you're an award-winning member of the dinner-speech circuit and you're interested only in the mechanical details of learning Keynote, feel free to skip ahead to the last section of this chapter to read about presentation hardware, and then mosey along to Chapter 12 to learn the ins and outs of Keynote. But if you're like most mortals—sometimes you give great presentations; sometimes you bomb—or if you've never given a presentation at all, this chapter's loaded with advice that can help you plan, prepare for, and deliver your pitch. Along the way, you might just pick up some fresh ideas about the proper role of a slideshow in your talks.

Figure 11-1:
Apple founder Steve Jobs uses Keynote for the elegant, understated slides that accompany his crowd-pleasing presentations.

Planning the Presentation

Before you even boot up your computer, it's worth spending some time identifying your audience and the goal of your presentation (convince Mom and Dad to let me go away to camp; convince Junior that camp would be good for him—whatever). To succeed, your presentation has to hit the audience where they live, where they work, in the way they think, and in the way they believe—or, as a wise man once said, "You scratch 'em where they itch." Once you've identified *what* you want to say, there's the equally important work of figuring out *how* to say it. The best presentations combine style and substance in ways that naturally complement each other without distraction.

The Goals of Your Presentation

There's nothing worse than being on the receiving end of an aimless talk. Begin by really thinking through what you want your presentation to accomplish. In other words, what do you want your audience to walk away with? Here are some examples:

- Gain knowledge or skills.

- Understand a new concept.

- Be inspired or moved.

- Change their behavior.

- Change their belief system.

- Take action.

- Buy something.

- Donate to your organization or invest in your company.

- Become involved in a process or a cause.

- Get media coverage for your business or organization.

Know Your Audience

Put yourself in their shoes and figure out how you can make your presentation interesting and relevant to them. Sometimes you'll know exactly who you're talking to: the members of your project team, the Board of Directors, or your fellow Rotary members. In these cases, you've probably already got a pretty good idea of who these people are, what interests them, what their group culture is like, and what the norms are for typical presentations.

At other times, the audience may be much more of an unknown quantity: the attendees at a conference you've never been to before, reporters at a press conference, a brand-new client, or the circuit court judge. In that case, make an effort to learn about your audience to give yourself a better chance of really connecting with them. This doesn't mean you have to try to *become* one of them—in fact, you can often be more effective if you show your audience something different than what they're used to—but it does mean you have to understand what engages them. You might be the one in the spotlight, but the audience is the whole reason that you're there. Don't lose sight of them as you prepare your talk.

Tailor the presentation to the audience

With your presentation goal and target audience clearly in mind, you can tailor what you're going to say to this particular group. Ask yourself these questions:

- Do they use colloquial language or jargon?

- How might their culture—corporate, regional, ethnic, class, or generational—affect how you communicate with them?

- What kinds of presentations are they accustomed to watching?

- What would this audience consider appropriate dress for a presenter?

- What would make this topic important to this audience?

- Does this audience prefer nitty-gritty details or high-level concepts?

Tip: Try to have a few conversations with potential audience members or other people who've presented to this group previously and ask for advice on how to make your presentation successful.

Speech vs. performance

As you ponder your audience and how you plan to connect with them, it might gradually dawn on you that you're preparing for a *performance.* Up until now, you might've thought you were just planning a lecture or a speech, a one-way dissertation of your ideas where you funnel words into your audience's passive ears. But now that you've started thinking about how to engage your audience, they're suddenly not so passive after all, are they? The best presentations draw the crowd into the narrative, turning bystanding listeners into active participants who are curious, involved, and implicated in the topic.

You're telling your audience a story, in other words—a story about *your* ideas and experiences, sure, but also one where your audience members are primary characters with something at stake. That's why they're showing up, after all; for one reason or another, your topic is personally important to each of them. It doesn't matter whether you're doing a book report, trying to sell widgets to Supermega Corp., or describing prenatal mortality statistics in West Africa; the best talks boil down to good storytelling.

Most of all, keep in mind that when you tell your story, you'll actually be speaking—*talking out loud* to living, breathing human beings. We call that conversation. Many of us think of a speech as a prepared text, read out loud from a podium, but that's neither a performance nor a conversation. Reading a speech doesn't have the same impact as storytelling. As you plan your talk, resist treating it like a paper. Don't write out each and every word like it's aimed for publication. That's writing, which is very different from speaking.

Instead, plan your talk from the get-go as a spoken presentation. Think about it as if you were having a conversation with just one member of your audience. How would you talk to him over lunch? What would you say to convince him of your ideas? You might speak casually or you might speak formally, but chances are the words you'd use are very different than the ones you'd use if you were writing an article or paper on the topic. Your tone, pacing, and even the topics you address might be different when you talk through your subject instead of approaching it as a written project.

That doesn't mean you shouldn't prepare or have written notes when you present. Just keep in mind that your final presentation isn't a text, it's a talk. As you prepare it, your job is to turn your content into a performance.

DESIGN TIME

Slideshow Simplicity

You and your audience probably have a set of expectations about what a presentation slideshow looks like. You might take it for granted, for example, that every slide has to be sprinkled with bullet points, perhaps decorated with an occasional graph or photo. One way to get your audience's attention, however, is to shake up those expectations with a different visual presentation. Two alternative approaches take a "less is more" route:

The Takahashi Method: Big text as image

Do you even need pictures in your slideshow? Individual words have connotations as strong as any image and, writ large, can have bold visual impact. Programmer Masayoshi Takahashi actually earned national coverage in Japan when he went against the prevailing business culture that values incredibly dense text in presentation slideshows. While Takahashi likewise uses only text in his presentations, his is big—huge text with ten characters or fewer on the screen at a time (Figure 11-2). Every slide represents a single idea, communicated in a brief, enormous title.

Although the Takahashi Method foregoes images, it remains vital and visual, with an unrelenting focus on the content itself. Every slide headlines what the speaker is saying with stark simplicity. Behind the scenes, while you prepare your presentation, this method also keeps you focused on the message, encouraging you to choose precise, topic-focused words to organize your talk—without the distraction of looking for pictures.

The Abstract Pointillist: Vague is in vogue

Technologist Chris Heathcote threw text overboard altogether when he created The Abstract Pointillist PowerPoint Toolkit, a collection of presentation slides that consist only of abstract shapes. As you speak, your slides cycle through a set of shapes that convey…nothing at all (see Figure 11-3). Equal parts slideshow template and tongue-in-cheek art piece, the Abstract Pointillist toolkit even comes with Heathcote's three-point manifesto: "1) Presentations are about ideas, not text; 2) Reading from slides is a heinous crime; 3) People cannot cope without some kind of visual stimulation."

Figure 11-2:
The Takahashi Method relies on text-only slides consisting of enormous text, providing stark visual headlines for your talk. These slides from Takahashi's Japanese presentation read, from left to right, "Huge Characters," "History," and "Easy to See."

The Slideshow's Role in Your Presentation

If your talk is a performance, your slideshow is the stage dressing—an important, even critical element, but not the main event. Don't fall into the trap of thinking the Keynote presentation is the star of the show. You and your audience are the stars, and Keynote, your handouts, and your sharp new suit play only supporting

---

 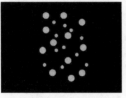 

Figure 11-3:
The Abstract Pointillist relies on simplicity (and a healthy dose of irony) by stocking slideshows with abstract shapes that vaguely resemble charts. This approach uses visuals but keeps the focus on the speaker and her ideas.

roles. Be careful not to let those materials upstage your message, the whole reason you worked up the nerve to stand up and speak in the first place.

Your slides should be as simple and uncluttered as possible. Think of slides as illustrations for your talk, images that complement your words *without repeating them.* It's a common rookie mistake to crowd slides with text-laden bullet points and then read those items out loud. Don't let your slides deliver all your content; that's supposed to be your role in this fandango. Instead, rely on your slides to highlight key points or get across visual information that's tough to communicate in words—photos, charts, tables, the design of your new tattoo.

Tip: If you're tempted to include bullet points in your slides to give yourself cues about what to say, consider putting those points into the presenter notes instead (see page 406). No need to share your speaking notes with the audience; reserve your slides for info that *enhances* your words rather than duplicating them.

Also keep in mind that while slides are ideal for expressing big-picture ideas, they're not great vehicles for detailed information. Have sympathy for your audience members who are north of 35 years old—it's difficult for aging eyeballs to read dense thickets of projected text. Even more importantly, when you ask your audience to take in lots of visual detail, it shifts their attention away from you. Reading your slide or making sense of a complex diagram necessarily means shutting you out for a few seconds. Don't set yourself up to compete with your slides.

What you say, what you show, and what you give as handouts should all be distinctly different, while of course supporting your overall message. Tailor the content of each of these elements to its particular medium, while reserving the most central points for you to express in your own words. In fact, it's fine to show nothing at all during portions of your presentation. Displaying a blank slide puts the focus back on you (you can also make the screen go dark with the presenter display's Black button; see page 507). With no distractions, it's all about the chemistry between you and your audience.

Note: If you're interested in learning more about how to give a great presentation and are looking for a book-length treatment of it, check out Garr Reynold's eminently readable and highly inspiring *Presentation Zen* (New Riders).

Building the Presentation

With your goal and audience identified and the relative roles of speaker and slide-show clear in your mind, you're ready to crack Keynote. You'll find all the details about using Keynote starting in the next chapter; the focus of this section is on the overall process of developing your talk and building the slideshow as you go.

Outline Your Talk

Just as every museum masterpiece starts as a sketch, every jaw-dropping presentation starts as an unadorned outline, a rough pass at capturing the main themes of the talk. At this stage, think in terms of big-picture topics—don't worry about how to say it or how (or even whether) to picture it in your slides. Just capture as many of your ideas as possible to give yourself the raw material that you'll transform into your presentation. Start with the high points—one per slide as shown in Figure 11-4—and then gradually fill in bullet points or additional slides to flesh out the details of your talk.

And guess what: It turns out that underneath all its fancy trimmings, a Keynote slideshow is actually an outline in disguise. That's how your audience experiences it, too. Every slide represents a topic, often with bullet points or other text for sub-topics. Groups of slides cluster together naturally to form "chapters" of your talk. As you'll learn in Chapter 12, Keynote even has an outline view that makes it easy to organize slides by topic (see page 414 for details). While you're massaging your talk into shape, it's easy to rearrange your outline by shuffling the slides into a new order. All of this makes Keynote just the right tool for organizing the ideas for your presentation.

"But what about the nifty outline feature in Pages?" the devoted Pages fan will wonder. You might be tempted to write your talk in Pages; this book has already spilled lots of ink detailing what a great writing environment it is. But here's the thing: Composing your talk in presentation software keeps your focus on the presentation. As you've already read, speaking is different—very different—than writing. Organizing your ideas as slides prevents your talk from sliding into thesis-paper territory.

Working through an outline in slides also encourages you to start thinking about illustrating your ideas, and about which words will best complement those graphics. You'll begin to hear your speaking voice in your head and start to get a feel for how to deliver your words and where your slides can help: "This is a lot of info to take in, and I should pause here to let it sink in…I'm going on and on here, maybe I should break this part up with a question for the audience…This stretch is a bit dreary and could stand some visual fun in the slides…This part is too dense, maybe I should spin this off into a separate handout."

Here are a few tried-and-true pointers to keep in mind as you build your outline:

• Know your subject thoroughly, but don't feel you have to say *everything* you know.

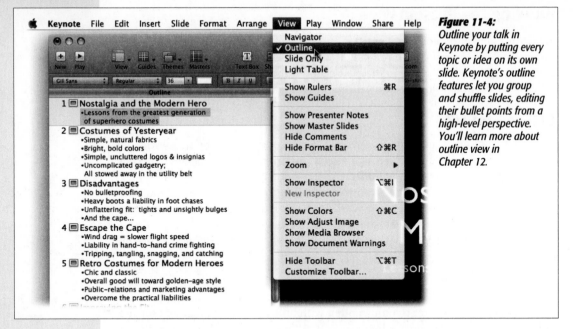

Figure 11-4:
Outline your talk in Keynote by putting every topic or idea on its own slide. Keynote's outline features let you group and shuffle slides, editing their bullet points from a high-level perspective. You'll learn more about outline view in Chapter 12.

- The structure of your talk may be obvious to you, but the audience won't see it right away. Help them out by sandwiching your presentation with an overview and then a review: Tell them what you're going to tell them, then tell it to them, and then tell them what you told them. It sounds simplistic, but it keeps your audience oriented and underscores your key points.

- Don't feel like you're obliged to *start* with this summary. Beware the pitfalls of sounding like you're reading a table of contents. Consider prefacing this "tell them" approach with a kickoff routine that's disarming and often captivating: Begin, without even introducing yourself, with a story. Today's presentation audiences are so used to hearing talks that start, "My name is Jane McGillicuty and I'm here today to talk to you about…" that a speaker who launches headlong into a yarn can often find himself rewarded with rapt listeners.

- Find opportunities for audience participation. Get a show of hands. Present a problem or question to the audience, and pause to let it sink in. Or ask audience members to discuss the question with their neighbors for a minute.

- Don't be too serious. The best way to educate is to entertain.

- Vary the pace of the presentation—especially if it's a long one—by using other visual aids, special guests, demonstrations, and so on.

- Keep the audience involved by staying focused on *their* goals, needs, and aspirations. Aim to elicit emotional responses that trigger new questions, thoughts, and perspectives for your audience.

- Include a periodic review or quiz of material covered so far to help listeners start to use and process the new information you've taught them.

Tip: While you work through your outline, specific phrases and detailed ideas will likely come to you. While these elements of your talk's "script" don't belong in the slides that you'll show to your audience, you can still capture them in Keynote. For quick ideas, add a comment to your slide (page 461), or jot down more detailed thoughts in the Presenter Notes pane (page 406).

Once you pile your main topics into Keynote slides, keep passing through the slideshow, refining and building upon your ideas, putting them in just the right order. As you go, polish the text on your slides and identify the photos, charts, and illustrations that you'll need. When you're done, you'll have a complete skeleton of your talk, along with a to-do list (in slide form) of the graphics and illustrations you need to flesh out your slides.

Find Great Images

Photos and graphics can go have a big influence on the mood of your talk, lending drama or humor to your presentation while also giving your audience visual "hooks" to help them remember your main points. Like all the iWork programs, Keynote makes it easy to grab pictures from iPhoto or other nooks and crannies of your Mac. But if you're not the world's greatest photographer or don't have a collection of pictures for the topic at hand, the Internet is a great resource for picture-hungry presenters.

Copyright and Creative Commons

Be respectful of the talented folks who created the pictures you find on the Web. Just because you stumble across a photo online doesn't necessarily mean you can use it free and clear in your presentation or project. Every photo belongs to its photographer, and you should get his or her permission before you use the picture, as well as the okay of anyone pictured in photos. It's common courtesy, but it's also more than that: It's the law.

Happily, many photographers have donated their work to the public, sharing their photos under *Creative Commons licenses,* which allow free use of images under specific conditions. These conditions vary according to the work and might, for example, limit use to non-commercial projects, or simply require a photo credit. When in doubt, check with the photographer.

Free online resources

There's a slew of community sites where photographers share their work. Here are a handful of the best:

- Flickr (*www.flickr.com*). The mother of all photo community sites, Flickr hosts over 3 *billion* photos from a huge community of photographers, both amateur and professional. Many (but not all!) of these photographers share their pictures under Creative Commons licenses.

- MorgueFile (*www.morguefile.com*). MorgueFile is a library of free, high-resolution photos for both commercial and personal projects. All images are free and may be used without additional permission from or credit for the photographer.

- Stock.xchng (*www.sxc.hu*). This site hosts over 350,000 photos by more than 30,000 photographers, all offering their works free of charge.

- Wikimedia Commons (*commons.wikimedia.org*). Operated by the same folks who run Wikipedia, the Wikimedia Commons contains over 3 million photos, videos, and sound files—all in the public domain or licensed for free use.

Commercial stock-photo houses

If there's a downside to the sprawling amateur photography sites mentioned above, it's that they're sprawling and amateur. While they're full of remarkable photos, it can sometimes take time to find them. Commercial stock-photo companies save you time by featuring carefully selected catalogs from professional photographers. Getty Images (*www.gettyimages.com*), Jupiter Images (*www.jupiterimages.com*), and Corbis (*www.corbis.com*) are the big, big players in the field. But there are lots of smaller stock-photo houses with correspondingly smaller fees and, often, quirkier collections. These include *www.veer.com*, *www.crestock.com*, *www.dreamstime.com*, and *www.istockphoto.com*.

Organize your materials

As you identify the pictures (and videos and sounds) that you plan to use in your slideshow, gather them into an album or playlist in iPhoto, iTunes, iMovie, or GarageBand. Keynote's Media Browser makes it easy to grab photos from anywhere in those programs, but you'll make your work even easier by gathering all of your slideshow's elements into a single place, as shown in Figure 11-5. See page 199 for some pointers.

Note: For GarageBand files, the Media Browser looks only in the GarageBand folder in your Music directory. GarageBand files saved elsewhere don't show up in the Media Browser.

Design Your Keynote Slideshow

You've got your slideshow skeleton; now it's time to put some meat on its bones. Your job as you give your presentation is to communicate information clearly, simply, and interestingly. That's especially true for your slides. Constantly remind yourself that the slideshow isn't the talk, and it doesn't have to include each and every point you'll make. Your slides should illustrate and accompany selected points in your talk, each carefully chosen for the best visual impact. Keep your slideshow focused on supporting those specific ideas, and be ruthless about cutting off-topic visuals and unnecessary text.

In that spirit, choose an uncluttered design theme with as few graphic decorations as possible. Every element on your slides competes for your audience's attention.

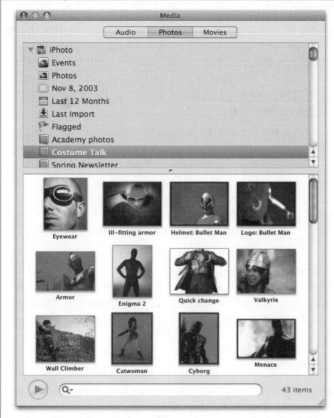

Figure 11-5:
Gather photos and images that you might use in your slideshow into an album in iPhoto to make them easy to find with the Media Browser, shown here. Similarly, collect music into iTunes playlists and movies into their own folder inside your Mac's Movies folder.

The simpler your design theme, the better it will showcase your content. Ask yourself: Do you really need a logo on every slide? Would the slide be easier to read with fewer colors? Does a floral theme really match up with a talk about Australian football?

Use as many slides as you need—and not one more. It's possible you could give an hour-long talk with just five slides. Some slides may be up for several minutes each, while others may be onscreen for only a few seconds. You almost certainly don't need as many slides as you started with in your outline. That doesn't mean that you're going to say less in your talk, only that you don't necessarily need a slide for each and every point. Look for opportunities to consolidate slides or to move their points into your speaker notes.

Throughout the design process, the most important thing to remember is that your slides are for your audience, not for you. Every slide should be designed to help your listeners understand or remember a key point. Build your slideshow to enlighten your audience, not to remind you what to say. (Keep your notes to the side.)

Your talk is not bullet points

One of the great things about Keynote is how well suited it is for outlining presentations. That's great for planning your talk. But that detailed outline shouldn't make it all the way through to your final slides. Your goal is to give your audience a full-blown story, not an outline. The reason that you've been asked to speak is because you're the expert and have ideas to share; don't sell those ideas short by reducing them to bullet points on a slide.

That doesn't mean you shouldn't have slides with text or that you can't headline topics in your slides. Slides are great for introducing topics but they do a poor job of summarizing them. Instead of packing slides with bullet points that compress each of your ideas into outline-style bullets, you'll have better visual and narrative impact with a single headline that introduces the overall topic. Add a strong visual—a chart, a photograph—and then speak about the topic instead of trying to express it through bullet points. A picture is worth a thousand bullets, as Figure 11-6 shows.

If you can't resist including bullet points, don't crowd too many onto a single slide. Use a larger font than you think you need, and then bump it up yet another size. If you have several bullet points on a slide, build them in one at a time as you discuss each one. Don't give your audience too much to read, or that's just what they'll do—scan your slides instead of listen to their amazing speaker.

It's about ideas, not special effects

Keynote's animations and transitions are incredibly fun—they look amazing, even hypnotizing. Keynote can make your slides shimmer, twist, spin, shatter, or dance. But remember: All good things in good measure. These features should *serve* the presentation, not distract from it. Along with restraint, consistency is important: Use just a small handful of effects to develop a visual language that subtly communicates what's happening in your presentation. For example, you might use a fade transition for all your slides, except between topic-changing "chapters" of your talk, where you use the cube transition.

Whatever you do, don't let yourself get lost down a rabbit hole chasing the perfect effect for that one slide. If you find yourself spending an hour getting that animation just so, step back and ask yourself if it's really worth it. A two-second animation won't make or break your presentation. If you're convinced that you need that effect just to make your point interesting, then maybe the point isn't especially strong; instead of spending more time on the effect, this might be an opportunity to trim and tighten your presentation.

Need handouts?

You don't have to squeeze everything into your talk *or* your slides. In fact, some things are better left out. In particular, data-rich tables and detailed charts are tough to communicate in your slides. Computer screens, especially projected ones, have low resolutions—they can show only a limited amount of info compared to the details you can get across on paper.

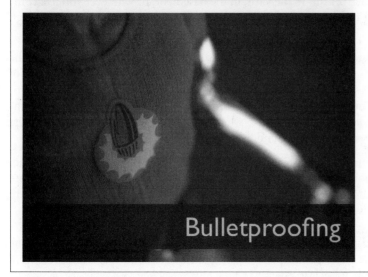

Figure 11-6:
*Filling your slides with bullet points (left)
tends to oversimplify your ideas and
encourages your audience to read ahead
without listening to you. Resist the urge to
bullet, and instead consider high-impact
visuals and brief headlines that
introduce topics.*

This is where handouts come in. Consider whether some of your material might be better shifted off the screen and onto good old-fashioned wood pulp. If so, fire up Pages and create a page-layout document for your audience to take home with them, or hand out detailed data or charts printed from a Numbers spreadsheet. You can also send people home with printed versions of one or more of your slides; Chapter 15 has details about printing Keynote slideshows.

Practice

You know what you want to say, and you've got your slides assembled. Great! But does the thing actually hang together? The only way to know for sure is to try it out. Stand up in your office, fire up your slideshow, and give your presentation. Out loud. To no one. Straight through, from start to finish. Again and again; rinse and repeat.

First and most obviously, practicing your presentation makes you better at it. You not only want to learn the content of your talk, you want to *absorb* it, make it second nature. Going over your talk ad infinitum eventually transforms the logic of your presentation into a reflex. If you're a nervous public speaker, that down-deep knowledge of your talk will give you confidence.

Just as important, practicing your talk—saying it out loud—also uncovers what works and what doesn't. Are there spots where things get dull? (If *you're* bored, do you really think your audience is going to feel any different?) Where do you need better transitions? Do you repeat yourself? Does that fourth slide really match up with what you're saying? Practicing the presentation helps you edit it.

The first run-through

This one's important, and it's not going to be pretty. But grit your teeth and go. As soon as you have your rough draft together, give your entire presentation out loud, alone in your office (or out in the yard, in the basement, or wherever you feel comfortable blurting out your talk). Don't stop to make changes, just barrel through the whole thing.

At this point, your talk is probably, um, not so great. But take comfort: This is the absolute worst it's going to be—it's onward and upward from here. You'll learn a lot from the first run-through. You'll discover that your talk sounds a lot different coming out of your mouth than it did in your head. You'll identify awkward transitions and areas where you're not really sure what you want to say. There will be useless slides that don't serve your point, and there will be others that need beefing up.

Take notes on all of this and jump right into editing your presentation. Be bold. Don't be shy about cutting out slides and, especially, reducing their text. Where can you use photos, graphics, or charts instead of words? This is the stage where you're likely to make the biggest changes to your talk and slides.

Tip: While you're practicing your presentation, make a contingency plan. Identify parts you could simplify, gloss over, or cut out completely if your guest speaker rambles on for 10 minutes instead of three; if audience questions take longer than expected; or if you have to send someone to find the janitor when you turn on your projector and trip a circuit breaker.

Don't stop practicing

Keep on going, rehearsing your talk out loud to yourself. As you gradually get comfortable with the material, your storytelling will feel more natural, your use of the slides easier. Keep trimming, editing, and refining as you go.

Get out a stopwatch or use the presenter display (page 498) to track how long it takes to give your speech, and then factor in the time you need to spend on introductory comments and the question-and-answer period. Make any adjustments you need to remain comfortably within your allotted time.

Tip: If you've got the stomach for it, you can even "watch" yourself give your presentation: Keynote's voice-over feature lets you say your talk out loud and then play it back synced with the changing slides. See page 412 for more about recording voice-overs.

Finally, find some guinea pigs. Practice giving your presentation to a coworker, an indulgent spouse, or an attentive dog, and listen carefully to any feedback (from the humans, at least). Watch yourself in the mirror or shoot a video of yourself as you practice. Pay special attention to your gestures, expressions, and body language. Be yourself, but remember you are essentially on stage—even if your audience is composed of only two people. And to reach an audience, you need to project not only your voice, but your movements and gestures as well. Practice all of these things.

Backup

Now that you've planned, produced, and practiced your presentation, don't take any chances with it. Before you head to the conference room or Carnegie Hall to give your talk, back up your Keynote file and any of your supporting materials: scripts, handouts, and so on. Burn them onto a CD or copy them to a portable flash drive, an external hard drive, or another computer on your network. You may also want to email your presentation to a web-accessible email account or send it to iWork.com (see page 528); that way you can download it in a pinch. There's nothing special about making these kinds of backups—it should be standard operating procedure for all your important files.

But you also need another kind of backup for your presentation. If you're taking your presentation on your laptop to plug it into a video projector, you should think about what you'll do if the laptop conks out when you get there—and then have a backup plan. Prepare copies of your presentation on CD in Keynote, PowerPoint, and even QuickTime format so you can borrow a computer and still present your slides (see page 518 for information on exporting to the PowerPoint format). Always bring a printout of your slides and speaker notes. You may not be able to show the audience your charts and graphs, but you'll still be able to make it through your speech, using a whiteboard or flip chart to create quick illustrations, if necessary.

Delivering the Presentation

Your moment has arrived—the Big Day. You've polished your presentation to a high shine, and you're ready to roll. Giving a successful talk, though, involves more than just standing up and holding forth. From handling the on-the-ground logistics of the event space to helping your audience find out more about your topic the next day, you've got several responsibilities to make your talk a hit.

Handle the Preliminaries

If you're responsible for the whole event, you'll need to consider a handful of ancillary tasks that aren't part of your presentation, yet have a huge impact on how your audience experiences your talk:

- Know how to unlock the doors, adjust the lights, and control the temperature. If you have to dim the lights to see the screen, make sure there's a light projecting on wherever you're speaking so your audience can see you.

- If you have control over the way the room is set up, place the podium at center stage and your screen off to the side. Remember: The slides are for speaker support—what you're saying is the main attraction.

- Set up and test the equipment, or coordinate with the tech support people who'll be running the lights and the public address system. Try everything well ahead of time so you can solve any problems before the audience arrives.

- Set up tables or set out information packets or programs.

- Make sure there are clear, prominently posted signs to help attendees find the room so they know they've come to the right place. Meet people as they come in to welcome them and help them get oriented.

- If your audio person needs to manage inputs—say, from your laptop's sound output to your microphone—print a slide list for her (see page 515) with all the audio cues clearly indicated. For example, she might need to fade out the "walk in" music and turn on your microphone input; or she may need to turn up the sound from your computer's audio during part of the presentation, while at the same time turning off your mic.

Set the Mood

Rig the environment to your advantage by putting your audience in a good mood. First things first: Feed their addiction by serving coffee. Caffeine makes people cheerful and, if all goes well, unlikely to nod off in the middle of your talk.

Give people name tags—big name tags—to encourage them to introduce themselves and chit-chat while they're waiting and drinking all of that coffee. Play upbeat music as they arrive, and play it loud so they have to speak up to hear each other. Loud music, loud conversation, and a crowded room all combine to feed the energy level, to create an event.

When it's time to start and your audience is seated, don't launch right into your program. First welcome them, introduce yourself, and tell them what presentation they're attending so they know they're in the right room. Make sure everyone has a seat and a program. Explain how you'd like to handle questions from the audience—whether they should shout them out at any time, save them until the end, line up at a microphone, or whatever.

Prep Your Mac

Well before you give your talk, make sure your presentation computer is ready to go. Assuming you're using Keynote and a MacBook laptop for your slideshow, review the display settings (page 495) and check that your slideshow projects on the screen as expected.

Make sure you've got power and that your power cord is plugged in so you don't run out of juice midway through. Your Mac won't go to sleep while Keynote is playing your slideshow, but if you plan to leave Keynote, you can prevent your Mac from drifting off to sleep by updating your system preferences. Here's how:

1. Choose → System Preferences.

2. In the Hardware category, click the Energy Saver button.

3. Click the Sleep tab and set the slider under "Put the computer to sleep when it is inactive for" to Never.

A free program aptly named Caffeine can also help keep your computer awake (*www.lightheadsw.com*). It adds an icon to your Mac's menu bar; click to prevent your Mac from going to sleep, dimming the screen, or starting a screensaver; click again to return to normal behavior.

If you're using Keynote Remote to control your slideshow from your iPhone or iPod Touch, it can take a while to connect it to your computer. Be sure to do that in advance (see page 507).

Finally, put up your title slide before the audience comes in so they don't see your messy desktop or the Keynote editing environment. (If you use the timer in Keynote's presenter display, it won't start counting until you launch past that first slide.)

Explaining these seemingly simple things to your audience increases their comfort level, lowers their defenses, makes them feel like they're part of the group—all of which will make them happier, more receptive listeners.

Give the Presentation

The time has finally come to give your talk. Try to open with a bang—catch your audience's attention and tell them how this presentation is going to be valuable to them, and what they're going to take away from it.

At this point, throw them a question to see how they relate to your topic—both for your own benefit and theirs. Ask for a show of hands: "If your super power could be flying or invisibility, how many of you would choose flying? Invisibility?" "How many of you are already familiar with using Keynote for presentations?" "How many of you are parents of seventh or eighth graders?"

Choose your questions so all the audience members see themselves as part of one or another of these groups. The responses will give you a better idea of the makeup of the audience—and they help everyone feel like they belong as they identify with others who respond similarly.

Now that your audience members have told you something about themselves, tell them something about you, like why you're especially qualified to speak on this topic.

Try to transition smoothly from the introduction to the meat of your presentation. After all your preparation, planning, and practice, the talk should be a piece of cake. Actually, it should be fun! You've got great information, you know it inside out, and you've tailored it to this particular group of people. Relax and enjoy the process of sharing.

Nerves: Don't throw up

Feeling nervous? It's okay—a touch of anxiety is a good sign, a demonstration of how invested you are in this thing. If you've lost a little sleep over your talk, it just means that you care.

Relax. If you're not relaxed, fake it. You might feel like a jittery mess inside, so this might seem hard to believe, but it's true: No one else can tell that you're having a meltdown inside. The audience doesn't see your nerves anywhere near as much as you feel them. They won't know unless you tell them so. Don't mention your nerves, and just stride into your talk.

Even more important, realize that your audience is not your enemy. They're rooting for you. They came to your talk because they believe in you and expect to learn from you—after all, you're the expert. Your audience arrived trusting your authority, and you should, too.

If you find the size of the audience overwhelming, don't think of them as a giant crowd. Focus on just one face in the audience, and talk to that person, one on one. Don't be creepy, though; rest on that person for a few seconds and then coast along to your next conversation partner. If you lose your train of thought, it's OK to pause for a few seconds. These brief breaks are not only OK, they even help to punctuate and add rhythm to your talk. Give yourself and your audience a chance to catch up, and then move on.

Talk to them

Remember all that hullabaloo at the beginning of this chapter about how your presentation is a performance and a conversation? This is it. You've practiced and you know the material; all that remains is to say it out loud. Take in your listeners from all parts of the room, and look them in the eyes, speaking naturally. Use your notes if you need them, but don't recite from a script (and please, please, please don't read from your slides).

You care enough about your topic that you've spent hours on this talk. Let your audience see that enthusiasm—it's contagious. Unlock your energy by escaping the podium and roaming the stage. Stay focused on your audience and keep them in your sights—don't stare at your laptop or look back at your screen. By now you know your own slides, so you don't need to consult them. Concentrate instead on your words, on connecting with that sea of eager faces.

Review

Wrap up your presentation with a review. This is when you tell them what you told them. Let them know what you hope they've gained from this presentation and what you expect them to do with it: buy your product, sign up for a time-share, host a foreign-exchange student, or whatever.

Make any other concluding statements, put up a slide with your contact info, and let them know where you'll be after the presentation in case they have more questions. Finally, thank them for coming and for their attention, and take a bow as the audience goes wild with applause.

The Day After

You've completed your presentation. You think you did a pretty good job: the audience applauded, no rotten fruit or vegetables hit the stage, and several people told you, "Swell job." Congrats! You've just armed your audience with lots of new knowledge and, hopefully, enthusiasm for your ideas.

Now that the talk is over, be sure to take advantage of this opportunity by giving your new friends a way to learn more and spread the word about what you had to say. If you or your organization have a blog or website, your fans will likely stop by after your talk. Be sure that your site provides an easy way to contact you or, even better, to leave feedback. Post a blog entry about your talk, and let attendees leave their comments. Consider posting your slideshow online, even if you don't have your own site; a variety of services let you share and distribute slide presentations. Check out *www.slideshare.com*, for example, or see page 531 for details about uploading your slideshow to YouTube.

Most of all, be sure to gather as much feedback as possible. If your audience filled out feedback forms about your presentation, review them as soon after your talk as you can. Audience feedback can tell you whether you succeeded in getting your message across, how useful the info was to the audience, and how you might improve the presentation—or similar presentations—next time.

Likewise, carefully review your own impressions of how the talk went. What worked and what didn't? Where did people laugh (and were they supposed to)? If you're giving your talk more than once, it'll naturally improve as you give it more often, but you can nudge things along by making edits right away, while your observations are fresh. There's nothing like a live audience to sharpen a presentation.

Presentation Setting and Gear

If you're lucky, you have complete control over every aspect of your presentation—including the choice of room, computer, projector, and all the other technical bits and pieces required. More often, though, you'll be stuck using others' equipment; plugging your laptop into a video projector at a conference; or just showing up with your presentation on a CD and running it on someone else's computer. When the equipment isn't your own, you have to be more flexible—and often improvise.

Get a Room

Environment matters, and *where* you speak affects not only your audience's experience that day but also the lasting image that they have of you going forward.

If you're in charge of choosing the venue, think classy. Hotels and conference centers might seem like the most natural choices, but before you go there, look around for less obvious options. Libraries, museums, and universities often have stunning lecture halls available on the cheap.

Wherever you wind up, do your best to find a room for your presentation that's exactly the right size. If you're not sure, err on the side of too small. If the room is too large, the place will feel empty, sapping energy from your show and giving the presentation a slack feeling. Given the choice, it's much better to pack 'em in, standing room only.

If you're presenting to more than 10 or 15 people, aim for a room with a high ceiling so there's plenty of room for a big screen hanging well above everyone's heads. Otherwise, you can't guarantee that everyone will have a clear view of your slides.

Finally, find out if your room comes with audio gear and a projector, if you need them. When you're speaking to more than a handful of people, you'll want speakers and a microphone to make sure they can hear all your perfectly selected pearls.

The Mighty Dongle

When you're giving a presentation from your own laptop, be sure that *someone* has the right *dongle,* the cable that connects your Mac to the projector (see Figure 11-7). There's nothing worse than discovering that your presentation is locked inside your computer with no way of getting onto the big screen. The dongle is your slideshow's only means of escape.

This can get confusing, because there are several possible combinations of plugs—you need just the right one to fit both your Mac and the projector. Even if you bring a dongle with you, in other words, there's no guarantee that it'll fit the projector. If you give talks frequently, your best protection is to buy and carry three types of dongles (about $30 each), one for each of these projector inputs:

- **S-video and composite video.** Apple offers a video adapter that combines outputs for both of these types; you'll also need a cable to connect the adapter to the projector.

- **VGA.** This is a particularly popular input for projectors specifically designed for computer presentations. Apple's VGA adapter connects directly to the projector.

- **DVI.** Apple's DVI adapter also goes straight into the projector. DVI connections generally give you better image quality than VGA.

Each of those dongles plugs into the projector. On the other end, though, you have to make sure that it fits your *laptop,* and that varies depending on what kind you're using. The 2009 editions of the MacBook, MacBook Pro, and MacBook Air laptops all require *Mini DisplayPort* dongles. Previous editions offered DVI or mini-DVI ports.

Of course, to most of us, all of these video inputs and outputs are just so much alphabet soup. If you're buying a dongle and none of this makes any sense, bring your Mac into your local Apple Store or electronics store so they can help you figure out what type of connector you need.

Figure 11-7:
Make sure you have the right dongle for the job. This crucial cable connects your Mac to the projector.

Projectors

Depending on the size of your audience, the type of room you're in, and the size of your budget, you can show your Keynote presentations right on your laptop, on an external monitor, or with a video projector. If you're presenting to a group of any size, though, a projector is almost always your best bet. The projector market is booming, fueled by the home-theater movement and by computerized presenters like you. Consequently, prices are falling and new models are coming out all the time, so there's a bewildering array of projectors to choose from. Prices start at about $400, but plan on at least $700 as a minimum price for a bright, high-resolution projector.

Tip: If you're not familiar with video projectors and you're considering dropping $1,000 or more on one, find a store where you can compare the models you're interested in under lighting conditions similar to the ones you'll use it in. Get a head start on your comparison shopping by visiting sites like *www. projectorcentral.com*, where you can read reviews and buyer guides, and post projector-related questions.

Choosing a projector

When you go shopping, it pays to know the lingo. There are two basic types of video projectors: *LCD* (liquid crystal display) and *DLP* (digital light processing). Most of the time, though, the projector type is less important than its key specifications. After you figure out your budget and how large and heavy a projector you're willing to carry around, consider these important criteria:

- **Resolution.** The *resolution* is the number of pixels the projector can display, and should match your computer's video output. Most projectors are designated XGA (1024×768 pixels), but you'll also find SVGA (800×600 pixels), 720p (1280×720 pixels), and SXGA (1280×1024 pixels). More pixels give you a sharper image and—surprise, surprise—cost more. All modern Mac laptops can output any of these resolutions, but some projectors go even higher; check your laptop's technical specs if you're going for lots of pixels to be sure your machine can handle it. If you plan to use your projector exclusively for Keynote presentations, you won't gain much from higher resolutions unless you happen to lean heavily on high-definition video and huge mega-pixel pictures. If that's the case, though, especially if you plan to show HDTV video, you'll definitely benefit from higher resolution (at least 720p). For pointers on choosing slide-show resolution, see page 396.

- **Brightness.** Just like slide or movie projectors, video projectors produce an image on the screen by projecting it with a very bright light. The intensity of that light is measured in *ANSI lumens*. Methods of measuring lumens vary from manufacturer to manufacturer, so consider these specifications ballpark figures only. Less than 1,000 lumens is fine when projecting on smaller screens in dark rooms, but it's too dim on larger screens or under brighter lighting conditions. 1,500 lumens is a good minimum for rooms with some light; kick it up to at least 2,000 lumens for rooms with bright light. For large rooms, though, you'll need to bump it up even more: Go for 3,000 lumens to be sure groups of up to 200 can read your slides.

- **Weight.** If you plan to carry your projector around to your presentations, you'll want a lightweight, portable one. These portables weigh in around three to eight pounds and are often smaller than most laptops.

Renting projectors

If you don't find yourself giving Keynote presentations at the drop of a hat, you may be better off renting a projector. When you rent, you can take advantage of the newest technology, get a projector that suits that particular presentation space, and let somebody else worry about repairs and expensive bulb replacement.

Look in the Yellow Pages under Audio-Visual Equipment to find a local outlet. And if you don't have a local AV house, you can rent equipment by mail (or at least, by UPS). If you're renting the room where you're doing your talk, the hotel or conference center probably has projectors, too, but usually at a premium price. It might be worth shopping around before you lock in.

Projection screens

An often-overlooked element of projection quality is the screen. A poor screen—or wall—can make even the best projector's image look terrible. There are as many different kinds of screens as there are projectors, starting at about $100 for rollup screens. Any screen is better than a wall—although you can get good results in a darkened room from a carefully prepared and painted wall. You might find that a wall is a reasonable option in a conference room, where walls are often smooth and painted pure, matte white.

Projection screens come in a wide range of surfaces, which provide varying amounts of *gain,* enhanced brightness attained by directing the light from the projector back to the audience instead of letting it scatter in all directions. High-gain screens have a lower viewing angle. In other words, they reflect more light to viewers closer to the centerline of the screen. A matte white screen—or a flat, white wall—provides the widest viewing angle and the least gain.

Remote Controls

The trouble with running a presentation from your laptop is that you have to run the presentation, well, from your laptop. Your computer tethers you to the podium, tying you to a fixed spot on the stage. Several remote-control options let you escape the lectern and roam the stage, flipping through your slides with a flick of your hand.

Keynote Remote for iPhone or iPod Touch

What's the price of freedom? Just 99 cents if you already own an iPhone or iPod Touch. For a buck, Apple's Keynote Remote program puts a miniature view of your slideshow's presenter display on your iPhone, as shown in Figure 11-8, complete with speaker notes or a preview of upcoming slides. You can click and swipe through your slides right from the touch screen. For details on setting up and using Keynote Remote, see page 507.

Note: Keynote Remote uses a WiFi network to make your iPhone or iPod talk to your computer; make sure your presentation room has a sturdy network signal, or you could wind up stranded mid-stage without a connection. The fail-safe fix for this is to set up your own wireless network on your Mac. You'll find all the details on page 508.

Figure 11-8:
Keynote Remote lets you run your slideshow from your iPhone or iPod Touch over a wireless network. You can consult your speaker notes, preview the next slide, check your running time, and of course flip from slide to slide.

Don't feel left out if you don't have an iPhone or iPod. Apple and other manufacturers also sell other remote-control devices—many of them simple clickers that are much smaller than an iPhone. Small size and simple operation means you can even run through your slides from your pocket.

The Apple Remote

Apple's slender wisp of a remote control (Figure 11-9) is marketed for controlling movies and music in Front Row, iTunes, or even iPods, but it works for Keynote presentations, too. These little wonders used to come with every MacBook laptop, but you now have to order them separately.

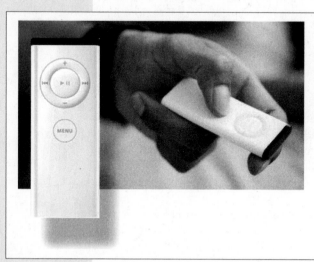

Figure 11-9:
Use the tiny Apple Remote to control your Keynote slideshow. As you might expect, pressing Play starts your slideshow, and the Fast-Forward and Rewind buttons move to the next and previous slides (holding them down takes you to the very first or last slide, respectively). You can also press the Menu button to open the slide switcher and skip directly to any slide.

Other Remote Controls

Most remote controls (although not the Apple Remote) use RF radio waves to communicate with a receiver plugged into your laptop's USB port. That means there's no need to point the remote at your laptop (as you would with a TV remote that communicates using infrared beams). But pointing still comes in handy: When you want to point something out on one of your slides, some remotes have a built-in laser pointer, so you don't have to fumble with more than one device.

Some remotes can also function as a mouse, or control your iTunes and DVD playback. However, when you're in the midst of the presentation, you may find that simpler is better—and the only buttons you really need are forward and backward. The winner of the simplicity competition is Satechi's RF Wireless Laser Pointer, sporting only forward and back buttons and a laser pointer (*www.satechi.com*). The popular Keyspan Presentation Remote (Figure 11-10) adds a mouse controller to the mix (*www.keyspan.com*).

Figure 11-10:
Plug this remote's receiver into your computer's USB port and you needn't be tied to your laptop to change slides. Whether you're seated at a table or mingling with your audience, a handheld remote lets you spend more time connecting with your audience— and less time connected to your computer.

Don't look now, but you might *already* own a remote control for your computer— albeit one with lots of buttons: your cell phone. Salling Clicker is software that lets you use certain phones to control your computer with a Bluetooth or WiFi connection. This $24 piece of software is all you need to turn your phone into a remote control for Keynote and many other programs. Learn more at *www.salling.com*.

But let's not get ahead of ourselves. Before you can start controlling your slideshow remotely, you have to have a slideshow in the first place. Turn the page, presenter-to-be, to find out how to start constructing presentations in Keynote.

Creating a
Keynote Slideshow

Slideshows have come a long way since the days of kerosene-powered magic lanterns, but the basic concept remains the same: Project an image with words or pictures on a screen for an audience's entertainment or edification. Whether you're an old-schooler clicking your slide carousel or a 21st-century citizen with a computer connected to a video projector, slideshows derive their power from their simplicity. By displaying a single static image one at a time, slideshows present information simply and clearly—and often with more impact than you could achieve with a moving picture.

Keynote lets you create very basic, simple slides—for example, just words on a plain background or a single picture—or carefully designed slides containing photographs, animation, or even movies and sound. Whether you opt for simple or fancy, the basic idea is the same: Pick a *theme,* a predesigned template that gives your slideshow a cohesive style or look; create the individual slides; and arrange them in the proper order.

This chapter takes you through the basics of all these steps, giving you an overview of all of Keynote's main features before diving into them in more detail in the following chapters.

Themes = Templates

If you've made your way through the Pages section or peeked ahead at Numbers, you already know that those programs come with a whole arsenal of killer design templates that you can adopt or adapt for your own documents. Keynote does the same but, in a gotta-be-me moment, refers to its templates as *themes* throughout.

Don't let the vocabulary shift throw you; whatever you choose to call them, themes work exactly the same way as templates in Pages and Numbers.

When you first launch Keynote, the Theme Chooser window greets you with a spread of Keynote's 44 built-in themes (Figure 12-1). Just like the Template Chooser in the other iWork programs, the Theme Chooser shows miniature previews of the available slide designs. Skim your cursor across the face of any of these thumbnail images to flip through an abbreviated selection of the slide layouts within, as well as previews of the theme's table and chart styles.

Figure 12-1:
The look and feel of your presentation depends on your choice of theme. Apple provides 44 themes with Keynote '09, and you can also create your own or purchase themes from third-party designers. Choose the size of your slides in the Slide Size pop-up menu, and double-click one of the themes to get started on your slideshow. Change the size of these previews by adjusting the size slider (A), or adjust the size of the overall window by dragging the resize handle in the lower-right corner (B).

To open an existing slideshow, choose from the Open Recent pop-up menu, or click the Open an Existing File button to flip the Theme Chooser over and choose a file from your computer.

Unlike templates in Pages and Numbers, Keynote's themes are not divided by category. The Theme Chooser gives you all of them at once in one big bucket, and this collection grows as you make your own themes or install themes that you buy or find online. That's a lot of slide designs to take in, but you can make it easier to scan the whole lot at once by making the previews smaller. At the bottom of the window, nudge the size slider to the left to fit more thumbnails into the window; pull the slider to the right to make these miniatures larger for a closer view.

When you find the theme you want, double-click it, or click once to select a theme and then press Return or click Choose. A new, untitled document window zooms out from the Theme Chooser, and you're on your way.

Tip: The next time you open the Theme Chooser, Keynote remembers your choice and helpfully selects it for you; just press Return to start a new project with the same theme. If you find yourself using that same theme all the time, you can tell Keynote to use it automatically for new documents instead of pestering you with the Theme Chooser every time. Choose Keynote → Preferences and click the General button. Next to For New Documents, click the "Use theme" button and make your selection from the Theme Chooser.

Your First Keynote Slideshow

As the head costume stylist for Up & Away, the leading outfitter for the super-heroes of Megaville, you've been invited to speak to students at the Excelsior School for Heroic Design. The plan is to give an introductory talk on the nostalgic designs of classic superhero costumes and how to update them for the new millennium—from cape pros and cons to basic bulletproofing. To build your slideshow, you'll turn to the newest tool in your utility belt, Keynote.

For this project, choose Gradient from the Theme Chooser—a simple theme for a look as bold, dramatic, and practical as your costumed clients. A new document window flies out at you, filled with the title slide for your presentation (Figure 12-2). You're ready to explore your workspace and start designing your slides.

Tip: Although you haven't done a thing yet, it's a great idea to save the project right at the start. Choose File → Save (or ⌘-S), name your presentation, select a destination folder, and click Save. Then periodically press ⌘-S as you work to save your changes on your hard drive, protecting you from possible power outages, software glitches, or creative tantrums.

Familiar Faces: The Toolbar, Format Bar, and Inspectors

One of the things that makes using iWork so comfortable is that all its programs share a similar look and feel. The strong family resemblance between Keynote and its siblings starts with the controls in the document window; if you've been tinkering with Pages in the preceding chapters, you'll feel right at home with your old friends the toolbar, Format Bar, and inspectors.

The toolbar

At the top of the window, Keynote's toolbar displays its standard collection of buttons. Toolbar buttons provide quick access to your most frequently used commands. Keynote's standard toolbar crowds no less than 22 icons into the top of your slideshow window, but helpfully organizes this bevy of buttons into six clusters. You'll learn more about each of these buttons in the coming chapters, but Table 12-1 gives a quick tour. You can hide and reveal the toolbar by clicking the "Tic Tac" button at the top right of the window.

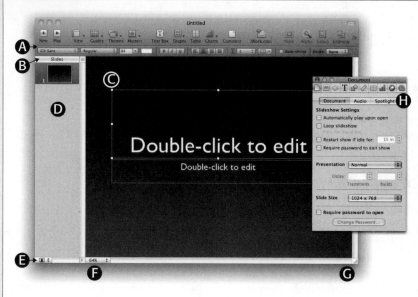

Figure 12-2:
Topped by the toolbar (A) and Format Bar (B), the Keynote window displays two panes when it first opens. The slide you're editing occupies center stage on the slide canvas (C). The slide navigator (D) displays thumbnail images of each slide in the presentation when in Navigator view, or displays an outline of your slides' text when in Outline view. Adjust thumbnail size in the slide navigator by choosing from the Thumbnail Size pop-up menu (E).

Adjust the slide canvas' display size by choosing from the Zoom pop-up (F)—when you're working on a small screen, choose Fit in Window. As with all Mac windows, resize the Keynote document window by dragging the resize handle (G). The Inspector window (H) is your command center, offering controls for every aspect of slideshow design. Click the buttons at the top of the Inspector to flip through the inspector control panels.

Decorate the toolbar just the way you want it: Add, delete, and rearrange the buttons to create a toolbar that reflects the way you like to work. Customizing the toolbar works just the same as it does in Pages, although many of the specific options and icons are different in Keynote. Control-click the toolbar, and choose Customize Toolbar to see all the choices, or chose View → Customize Toolbar (see page 40 for the details).

Tip: As a shortcut, you can ⌘-drag a button to a different location on the toolbar even without choosing Customize Toolbar mode. You'll also find a few other options when you Control-click a button (but not the toolbar itself).

Table 12-1. Keynote's Standard Toolbar Buttons

New Play	New inserts a new slide, and Play launches a full-screen slideshow starting with the current slide.
View Guides Themes Masters	View offers options for changing the document window display; Guides shows/hides alignment guides and gives access to their preferences; Themes lets you jump to a new design theme; and Masters lets you choose a new layout for the current slide.
Text Box Shapes Table Charts Comment	The object buttons respectively insert a new text box, shape, table, chart, or comment into your document.
iWork.com	The iWork.com button lets you share your slideshow online.
Mask Alpha Group Ungroup Front Back	The Mask button crops pictures, and Alpha lets you remove background colors; Group, Ungroup, Front, and Back help you arrange objects on the slide.
Inspector Media Colors Fonts	Inspector, Media, Colors, and Fonts respectively summon the Inspector, Media Browser, Color Picker, and Fonts window.

The Format Bar

The Format Bar rides shotgun with the toolbar, sandwiched between the toolbar buttons and the slide canvas. As in the other iWork programs, Keynote's Format Bar morphs its contents depending on what you select in the slide: Click a chart, and chart-specific commands pop up; pick a picture, and the Format Bar tailors its options for images. This little transformer stays on the move, adapting to your needs as you move through the design process. If you prefer to give up this convenience in favor of a few pixels of additional real estate, you can tuck the Format Bar away by choosing View → Hide Format Bar; get it back with View → Show Format Bar.

The inspectors

Keynote stows most of its advanced settings in the inspectors, floating control panels that give you detailed control as you work your way through your slides. Click the Inspector button in the toolbar to open the inspector window, and switch between inspectors by clicking the buttons at the top of the inspector window. (Point to a button to see its name when you're not sure what its icon represents.) From this floating command post, you get quick access to controls otherwise tucked away in the menu bar—along with a few that are unique to the inspector. You'll learn all about the inspectors and their many options in the coming pages and chapters.

Slide Size and Slide View

Before diving into your slides, decide just how much slide you want. The *slide size* determines the number of pixels in each screen of your presentation. You can choose the size from the Slide Size pop-up menu in the Theme Chooser (Figure 12-1) or in the Document Inspector (Figure 12-2).

Keynote's Slide Size menus offer several standard sizes, but which to choose? The right size depends on your projector's screen resolution; ideally, your slide size should match the resolution of the projector that you'll use. Projectors start around 800×600 (that's 800 pixels wide by 600 pixels wide), but the majority of modern projectors handle the 1024×768 (or XGA) resolution. If you're not sure what to use, either of those two options will serve you well.

But don't goose the slide size thinking that will let you fit more stuff on the screen. While that's technically true, keep in mind that the screen itself doesn't change its dimensions; increasing the slide size only packs more pixels into the same space. As you add more pixels, everything in the slide gets smaller on your projected screen, making it that much more difficult for your audience to see it. Using a very large slide size *does* increase the sharpness of the image on projectors that can handle it—just be sure to increase the size of your text and images to maintain the same proportion in your slides. (When you change the slide size in the Document Inspector, Keynote is clever enough to scale your text and images so that they retain their relative size on the slides.)

Whatever slide size you choose, it's a good idea to adjust the *slide view* of your Keynote window so that you can see the entire slide at once. Keynote opens the slide view of new slideshows at full size, or 100 percent. Trouble is, depending on your slide size, this may be more slide than you can fit into your window, particularly on smaller laptops. Save yourself some scrolling hassle by adjusting the Zoom pop-up menu in the lower-left corner of the slide canvas (Figure 12-2) so that you can see the slide's edges. You can choose Fit in Window so that the current slide always fills up the window. This option is also available from the View → Zoom submenu.

Adding Your Text

When you open a new slideshow, Keynote gets you started by giving you the *title slide* for your selected theme (officially, it's called the Title & Subtitle slide). The exact layout varies from theme to theme, but the title slide typically consists simply of a title and subtitle, usually with some simple decoration. You're not obliged to use this layout—you can rearrange it, add new elements, or choose an entirely new slide design from the theme's collection of master slides. More on all that in a bit. For now, go with what Keynote gives you, as shown in Figure 12-2.

Most new slides, including title slides, have *placeholders* that show where to add your text, pictures, or other objects to the layout. The placeholders for text aren't shy about telling you what to do—"Double-click to edit," they command. It really is that simple: Double-click the large title text, and type your title. Then double-click the placeholder text below, and type your subtitle. Presto! You've already finished your first slide: "Nostalgia and the Modern Hero: Rethinking superhero styles for the 21st century."

You can format text just like you format text in Pages, using the Format Bar, the Format menu, the Fonts window, and the Text Inspector. For more on working with Keynote's text boxes, see page 433. Don't worry about these finer formatting points just yet, though. You can make all those changes later. The easiest way to get started with a slideshow is to get the first pass of all your text into the document—enter it all at once and then organize it. Start designing your slides after you have all your ideas lined up.

You've already got the first slide in place; keep on going with the rest. Click the New button (+) in the toolbar, and Keynote gives you a fresh slide, this time with a slightly different layout—every theme has a standard slide that it uses after the title slide. This slide typically has two text boxes, one for the slide title and one for bullet-point text. Figure 12-3 shows examples of these two standard slide types in the Gradient theme.

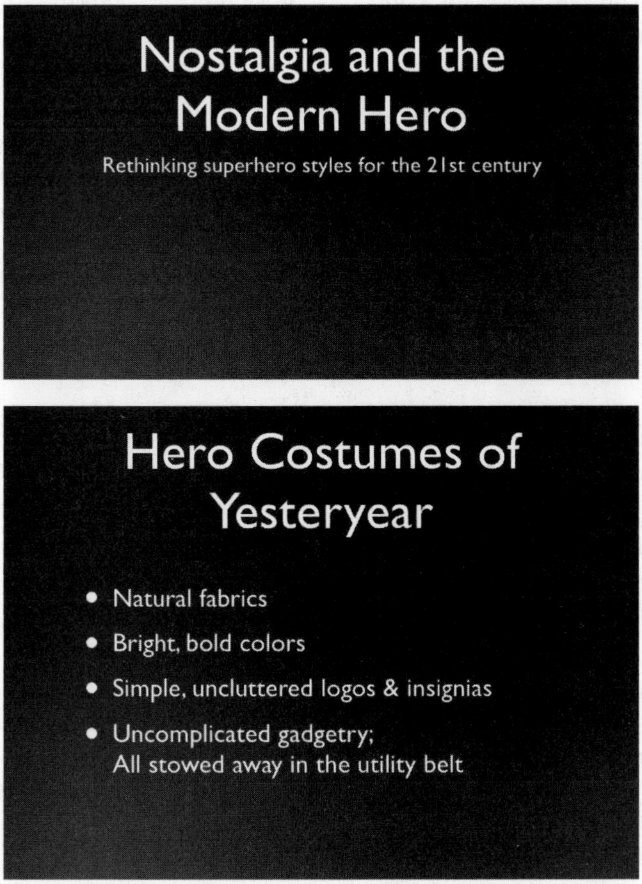

Figure 12-3:
Every theme has a Title & Subtitle slide (top), which Keynote gives you when you first open a new slideshow. Subsequent slides get a different layout (bottom), usually consisting of two text boxes for the title above and bullet points below. You can choose a different slide layout from the toolbar's Masters pop-up button.

When you add a new slide, Keynote also adds its thumbnail to the *slide navigator,* the left pane of your slideshow window. This gives you an easy way to navigate your slides—just click a slide's thumbnail to work on it in the slide canvas. For more on the slide navigator, see page 409.

Continue typing the rest of your text, clicking the toolbar's New (+) button to make a new slide for each topic or idea in your talk. If you're not certain about the order or hierarchy of bullet points, don't worry. Just enter all the text—it's easy to adjust the order of things later.

Now that you've got all your text into your slides, you could actually stop right there. You've got a complete slideshow covering all the points of your talk. But let's be honest: Visually, it's a bit dull. Your slideshow is text-only, and every slide uses the same humdrum layout. Time to spice things up a bit.

Changing the Slide Layout with Master Slides

Every theme comes with a collection of slide layouts called *master slides.* These prefab designs consist of some combination of title, body text, and picture. The title slide and standard content slide that you've already seen are both master slides, for example. You can switch up a slide's design anytime by choosing a new master slide from the Masters pop-up button in the toolbar.

Try it now with the second slide in your new deck. In the slide navigator at the left of the window, where Keynote shows a miniature lineup of all your slides, click the second slide. Keynote highlights the thumbnail slide in yellow, and calls it up in the slide canvas. Now choose a new master slide, as shown in Figure 12-4. When you select the "Title, Bullets & Photo" master slide, for example, Keynote adds a photo to the slide, keeping your slide's original title and text. That's a handy piece of magic that Keynote performs for you: Once you add title text to a slide, it sticks as the title text no matter what master slide layout you're using. The same goes for the body text. Change the master slide with impunity, choosing a new layout as many times as you like—your slide content always follows along.

Note: Sometimes the body text is a subtitle, other times it's a bullet list or a regular paragraph. The precise function and formatting of the text depends on the master slide you select, but the text neverthe-less makes the transition to the new layout when you change the master slide.

Adding an Image

The image from the new master slide makes things prettier, sure, but that photo of a dawn landscape doesn't exactly relate to the topic at hand. It's not supposed to, though—it's just a *media placeholder* waiting for you to drop in your own picture. You add pictures to Keynote just like you do in Pages and Numbers, via the Media Browser. Click the toolbar's Media button to bring it up, and click the Photos tab to browse your iPhoto library. Choose a picture and drop it on top of the placeholder in your slide, and Keynote replaces the placeholder with the new image, as shown in

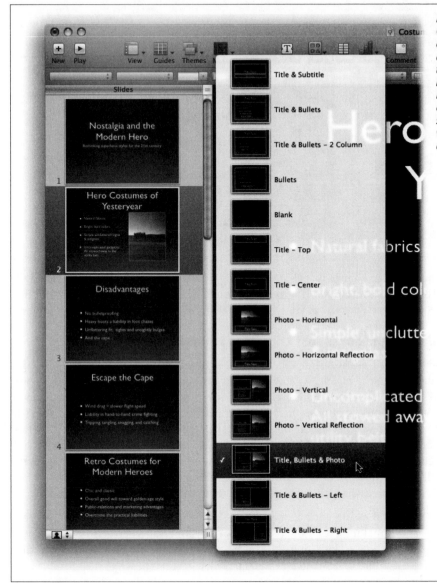

Figure 12-4:
Change the layout of the current slide by choosing a new master slide from the Masters pop-up button in the toolbar. Every theme has its own collection of master slides, giving you a variety of prepared designs to choose from.

Figure 12-5. If you prefer, you can also add pictures by dragging them from a desktop folder or by going to Insert → Choose and browsing to the file to include.

Just like Pages' placeholders, Keynote automatically sizes the picture to fit the placeholder's dimensions, cropping some of the photo if necessary. When you drag a horizontal picture onto a vertical placeholder, for example, Keynote lops off its sides to keep the vertical layout. If that's not quite what you had in mind, you can change the way the image is cropped by editing the picture's image mask. See page 230 for details.

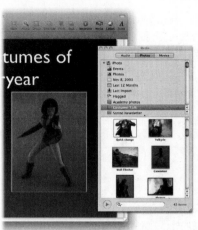

Figure 12-5:
Replace the media placeholder in a master slide by dragging a picture from the Media Browser and dropping it onto the placeholder picture (left). Keynote automatically sizes and crops the picture to fit the placeholder dimensions (right).

In fact, you can change just about anything you want about your picture—and the surrounding text, too. Move it, resize it, rotate it, whatever. You're not locked into any of the prefab layouts of your theme's master slides. That's because…

Slide Design Works Just Like Page Layout

Designing and editing slides in Keynote is nearly identical to creating a page-layout document in Pages. You add and arrange the same set of *objects*—text boxes, pictures, shapes, tables, charts, movies and sounds—on the slide canvas, just as you would compose them on a page in Pages. Click an object to select it; drag it to a new location on the slide; resize it by dragging one of the selection handles along its border; and use the Format Bar or Graphic Inspector to add effects, stroke borderlines, picture frames, and color fills. Chapter 13 gives all the details about how to work with objects in Keynote, but if you're a Pages aficionado, you already have the know-how to understand exactly how it works.

For example, dress up your text-only title slide by adding some images. Since your talk is about making use of the retro styles of bygone superhero fashion—a pair of vintage snapshots of kids dressed as classic superheroes might give the title slide just the right dose of nostalgia. Let's do it.

First, choose a new master slide from the Masters pop-up button. "Photo – Horizontal" gives us what we want: a photo and a title. Keynote provides a placeholder image just as before, but whoops—with less space available for the title text, the whole title no longer fits in the text box, as shown in Figure 12-6. Only part of the text is shown, and the *clipping indicator*—a blue + sign—appears at the bottom of the text box to show that it has more text than can be displayed.

Make your text fit with auto-shrink

One option is to resize the text box: Click it once to select it, and then drag one of the eight selection handles to resize the text box, making it large enough to fit the text. Another option is to change the font size: Select the text box, and choose a new font size from the Format Bar's Font Size pop-up menu. But the fastest option is to use *auto-shrink,* a feature that reduces a text box's font size just enough to squeeze in all its text. Double-click the blue clipping indicator at the bottom of the text box, and the full title springs back into view, albeit at a new, smaller size. With auto-shrink in action, you can continue to add or delete text, and the font size changes on the fly so that the text always fits.

Figure 12-6:
When a text box contains more text than can be displayed (top), Keynote lights up its border and adds the clipping indicator (circled) at the bottom of the text box. Double-click the clipping indicator to activate the auto-shrink feature, and Keynote reduces the font size to make the text fit its box (bottom). Turn off the Auto-shrink checkbox in the Format Bar to return the text to its original size. Of course, you can also turn on the checkbox to auto-shrink instead of clicking the clipping indicator.

Add the snapshots

Add a snapshot by dragging it from the Media Browser and dropping it onto the slide's placeholder picture. Tip the photo askew to give it a more casual feel: ⌘-click one of the picture's selection handles and drag to rotate the picture. Then make it look more like a scrapbook photo by adding a picture frame: Click the picture once to select it, and choose a frame from the Format Bar's Stroke pop-up menu, as shown in Figure 12-7.

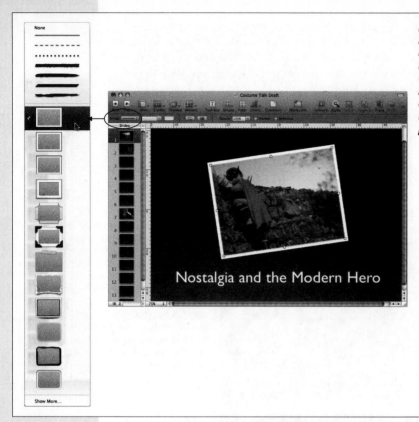

Figure 12-7:
Keynote makes it easy to add a picture frame to a photo, text box, shape, or movie. Click the object once to reveal its selection handles, and choose the frame style from the Format Bar's Stroke pop-up menu.

Add a second snapshot by dragging another picture into the slide from the Media Browser. The first image retains its placeholder powers; if you drop your second picture on top of the first, the second picture will replace it. That's handy when you want to try out different pictures in the same place, but that's not what you want here. Instead, drop the photo onto a blank portion of the slide, and Keynote adds your picture as a new image object on your slide. Drag the picture into position, and resize it by dragging its selection handles. Rotate the image and add a picture frame just like the first picture. Drag the two pictures on the slide to arrange them into just the right composition, and you've got a sweet little vignette of super kids for your title slide, shown in Figure 12-8.

Adding other objects to your slides

You're not limited, of course, to adding only images to slides. You can use iWork's whole range of objects:

- **Sound and video.** Drag media files into your slides from the Media Browser's Movies and Audio tabs (see page 451 for more about movies and page 455 for audio).

Figure 12-8:
Add additional image objects to your slide by dragging new pictures from the Media Browser. Arrange objects on the page by dragging them into position. Because Keynote treats each object in its own layer, the objects appear to stack on top of each other like a scrapbook. For more on organizing object layers, see page 429.

- **Text boxes.** Add more text boxes to your slides by clicking the Text Box button in the toolbar (see page 433).

- **Shapes.** Choose a shape from the toolbar's Shapes button to add shapes to your slides (see page 448).

- **Tables.** Click the toolbar's Tables button to insert a table grid (see page 449).

- **Charts.** Bring numbers to life with a colorful graph (see page 449). Paste one in from Numbers, or build a chart from scratch by choosing a chart type from the toolbar's Charts pop-up button.

Going back to the master slide layout

If your custom slide layout should ever spin out of control—what were you thinking with that fuchsia/chartreuse color scheme?—you can always revert to the original master layout. Click in an empty part of the slide canvas so that no objects are selected, and choose Format → Reapply Master to Slide, and your slide elements snap back to their original positions and formatting. (Any objects you've added that weren't in the original master slide stay put.)

Adding and Inserting Slides

You've already seen how to add slides by clicking the New button at the top left of your screen. You can use the same button to insert slides into the middle of the slideshow, too. In the slide navigator, click the slide that comes immediately before the spot where you want to add a new slide. Click the New button, and Keynote adds an empty slide just after the selected slide.

The new slide uses the same theme and master slide layout as the preceding slide. That is, when you select a slide and click New, Keynote bases your new slide on the master slide for the current slide. If you select a slide with the Gradient theme's Blank master slide and click New, the new slide also has the Blank layout from the Gradient theme.

Note: As you've seen, there's one exception to this rule. When you're on the first slide and it uses the theme's standard title slide, clicking New always gives you the second layout in the theme's master slide list. For subsequent slides, meanwhile, clicking New always creates a slide with the same style as the selected slide.

Keynote also gives you several other ways to add new slides. These methods all do exactly the same thing as clicking the New button in the toolbar:

- Select a slide in the slide navigator and press Return.
- Select a slide and choose Slide → New Slide.
- Select a slide and press ⌘-Shift-N.
- Control-click in the slide navigator and choose New Slide from the shortcut menu.

Creating slides from the Media Browser

You can also create a new slide containing an image, movie, or sound by dragging it into the slide navigator from the Media Browser. The cursor sprouts a green plus sign to show that you're going to add a new slide. When you drop the media object, Keynote gives you a new slide containing only the picture, video, or audio you dropped—as usual, the new slide uses the same theme and master layout as the preceding slide. This works when you drag multiple media objects, too, giving you a quick-and-easy way to build a complete photo slideshow in one fell swoop. For example, select multiple pictures in the Media Browser by ⌘-clicking each picture to use and then drag them into the slide navigator. Just like that Keynote gives you a slew of new slides, one for each picture.

A blank slate

Sometimes you want to start with an empty slide—no text boxes, pictures, nothing—so that you can build your own slide design completely from scratch. For example, maybe you want to build a slide with only a photo, table, or chart and you want a clean canvas to start from. One way to go is to create a new slide and delete all its elements by choosing Edit → Select All (⌘-A) and then pressing Delete. But a less destructive approach is to choose a blank master slide layout for your new slide. All Apple's built-in slides have one—just choose Blank from the Masters pop-up button in the toolbar, and Keynote gives you a master slide devoid of any text or pictures.

Adding Slide Transitions

Most of your Keynote work focuses, of course, on creating a presentation with amazing content. It's all about your slides. But Keynote also makes it easy to think about what happens *between* your slides. Just like you aim for clever transitions between ideas and topics in your talk, Keynote lets you make correspondingly crafty visual transitions. Bold or subtle, ridiculous or sublime, Keynote gives you a range of cinematic effects to shift from one slide to another.

You add transitions in the Slide Inspector. Click the Inspector button in the toolbar and then click the slide icon at the top of the Inspector window to open the Slide Inspector (Figure 12-9). Click the Transitions tab, and choose a transition style from the Effect pop-up menu. This is not the slide's grand entrance, but rather its exit: Keynote applies your selected transition after the currently selected slide—when you play your slideshow, your new special effect moves that slide out of the way and introduces the next one. When you select the effect, the Inspector shows you a preview of how the transition will look when you play the slideshow. Click the preview window to play the transition again.

Note: You'll learn how to play the slideshow in just a couple of pages (and then in lots more detail in Chapter 15). Chomping at the bit to play the slideshow right now? Click the Play button in the toolbar.

Keynote offers lots of different transitions, from old-school movie tricks like wipes, dissolves, and fades, to newer stunts like 3D effects or fancy acrobatics that make objects fly and shimmer across the screen. Browse through the Effects pop-up to find the transition that suits the content and tone of this part of your talk. Find out more about these effects and other animations by making your own transition over to Chapter 14.

Changing the Theme

You chose a theme when you first created your document, but don't sweat the choice too much—Keynote doesn't hold you to your decision. You can select a new theme for any or all slides in your presentation anytime you like. This is handy when you suddenly and unexpectedly discover midway through the project that you completely *despise* your presentation's design—you can switch to a new one with the click of a mouse.

To change the theme for all slides in your presentation, choose Theme Chooser from the toolbar's Themes pop-up menu (or choose File → Choose Theme). Keynote unfurls a slightly modified version of the tried-and-true Theme Chooser that you see when you create a new document, as shown in Figure 12-10. In the "Apply Theme To" pop-up menu, choose All Slides, and choose the new theme and slide size to use. Leave the "Retain changes to theme defaults" option turned on if you've made any formatting changes to any of your slides and you'd like to keep those changes (anything from changing the font to moving the position of a title).

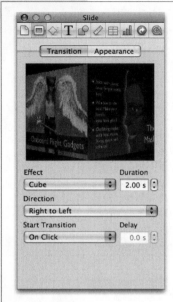

Figure 12-9:
The Slide Inspector's Transition tab lets you add a visual transition from the selected slide to the next one. Choose an effect from the Effect pop-up menu, and Keynote shows a preview (here, the Cube effect creates an illusion that your slides are mounted on a spinning cube). Adjust the length of the transition in the Duration field; change its direction in the Direction pop-up menu; and choose when to trigger the transition in the Start Transition pop-up.

Turn the option off to start from scratch and completely reset the look of your slides to the new theme.

You may occasionally find it useful, too, to change themes for just a selection of slides. Although it's generally a good idea to stick with a consistent style and layout for your slideshow, changing the theme midway through a presentation can help create a strong visual break between topics, marking different acts or chapters of your talk. To give just one slide or a selection of slides a theme makeover, ⌘-click the slides to update in the slide navigator, and follow either of these steps:

- Choose the theme you want from the toolbar's Themes pop-up button. This skips the Theme Chooser window and applies the theme to your selected slides with a single click.

- Choose Theme Chooser from the toolbar's Themes pop-up just as you would if you were replacing the theme for all slides, but choose Selected Slides from the Apply Theme To pop-up menu.

Using the Presenter Notes Pane

As you work through your presentation, you'll almost certainly develop detailed ideas for your talk—ideas that are too detailed to include on the slides themselves, but too important to risk forgetting. For just that reason, Keynote gives you a space for presenter notes, a your-eyes-only cheat sheet to stash notes about each slide.

Choose View → Show Presenter Notes, and Keynote displays the Presenter Notes pane beneath the slide canvas (Figure 12-11). You can use this area to keep anything from a detailed speaking script to brief reminders of what to say

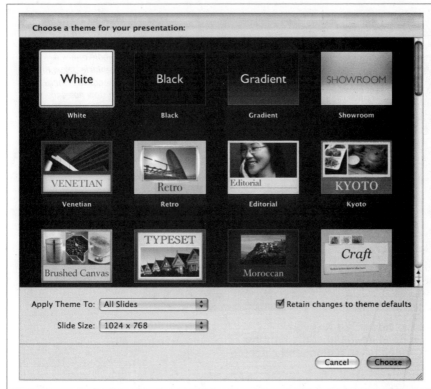

Figure 12-10:
*The Theme Chooser
makes a repeat
performance when you
choose Theme Chooser
from the toolbar's
Themes pop-up button.
When you choose a new
theme and choose All
Slides in the "Apply
Theme To" pop-up menu,
all slides in your
slideshow get the new
look. Change the setting
to Selected Slides to
change the theme only
for the slides highlighted
in the slide navigator.*

during the slide. When you show the slideshow, Keynote's presenter display can feed your notes to you on your own screen—while the audience meanwhile sees only the slides on the room's main screen. See page 498 for more about using the presenter display.

Use the Format Bar to adjust the size, font, alignment, bullet points, and other text formatting for your notes. You can make the notes field larger or smaller by dragging the resize handle in the field's top right corner.

Along with comments (page 461), presenter notes are also a good place to stow "notes to self" about the slides you're creating. Use it as a temporary notepad for chunks of text that may or may not make it into a slide, or as a memo pad where you can keep track of work to do on a slide: facts to check, pictures to update, unhinged allegations to run past the legal department, and so on.

Every slide has its own Presenter Notes field, and you can type or paste as much text as you want into it—a scroll bar appears when your text is bigger than the window. Use the Format Bar, Fonts window, or Text Inspector to format the note text as you would any other text in your slides. If you're using the field for reminders while speaking, for example, you might find it helpful to use a large bold font that you can easily read at a glance.

Figure 12-11:
Choose View → Show Presenter Notes, and Keynote opens a receptacle below the slide canvas where you can stow notes to yourself about the slide. This is an ideal place to keep reminders about what to say during each part of your talk—much, much better than keeping your speaking notes on the slide itself and reading them aloud.

Tip: If you print out your slideshow, you can print the Presenter Notes field, too, although you see only as much of the note as can fit on the page beneath the image of the slide—longer notes get clipped. Choose File → Print, and turn on the Slides With Notes checkbox in the Keynote settings and then click Print. For more about printing your slideshows, see page 515.

Playing the Slideshow

When you've got a draft of your slideshow ready, give yourself a preview screening. In the slide navigator, select the slide where you want to start viewing (the first slide, if you're starting at the beginning) and then click the toolbar's Play button. Keynote takes over your computer's screen, displaying the first slide on a field of black. Advance through the slides by clicking the mouse button or by pressing the space bar, Return, or the right or down arrow key. Back up to the previous slide by pressing the left or up arrow key.

When you advance past the final slide, Keynote exits the full-screen presentation mode, bringing you back to your desktop and the Keynote editing window. If you get impatient to return to the editing window before you reach the end of the slideshow, press the Escape (Esc) key.

There's lots more that you can do while playing a slideshow during a presentation—and Keynote even gives you a special view for rehearsing. For all the details, see page 498.

see page 498.

PRESENTATION STATION

Fade to Black

If you've ever given slideshow presentations with a slide projector, you've probably used a solid cardboard "black slide" as the final slide in your tray. This opaque slide prevents a white screen appearing when you advance to the final slide—and prevents your audience from screaming in surprised agony from this nuclear flash. In Keynote the view of your desktop doesn't sear any retinas, but its appearance is at best unprofessional and at worst embarrassing. (Ahem, shouldn't you have tucked away that *Geeks Gone Wild* folder before the presentation?)

Create a black slide at the end of your Keynote presentation by adding a slide and choosing the Blank master slide. Open the Slide Inspector, click the Appearance tab, change the Background pop-up menu to Color Fill, click the Background color well, and choose pure black from the Color Picker. Now choose ⌘-D to create a second black slide.

Now, when you reach the end of your presentation, the screen goes black—and stays black even if a nervous presenter gives the mouse an extra click.

Browsing and Organizing Your Slides

Now that you've played your rough-draft slideshow in all its full-screen glory, you've no doubt discovered that you have some work to do to reveal the stunning presentation hidden within. Keynote offers several display modes to help you get a big-picture view of your slideshow—or more accurately, lots of little-picture views: slide thumbnails that you can select, shuffle, copy, and delete to whip your presentation into shape.

The Slide Navigator

You've already met the slide navigator, which draws a visual map of your slideshow at the left of Keynote's standard document window. This is where Keynote shows you miniature previews of your slides, and you can work directly with these thumbnails to tweak individual screens or make wholesale changes to the entire show. The slide navigator's appearance varies according to the *view* you select from the View menu:

- **Navigator.** In this view, the slide navigator displays a vertical strip of thumbnails, miniaturized but otherwise identical replicas of your slides. This is Keynote's standard view.

- **Outline.** The slide navigator changes to a text-only view with the titles and text of all your slides. You can edit the text directly in the slide navigator, a fast way to belt out the initial outline of your text. See page 414 for the rest of the story on outline view.

- **Slide Only.** Bye-bye, slide navigator. This view excuses the navigator from the table to make more room for the slide canvas.

- **Light Table.** The slide navigator takes over your entire screen, showing your slides in one big grid for an all-at-once view of your presentation.

In the navigator and outline views, you can adjust the width of the navigator sidebar by dragging the handle marked with two vertical lines at the bottom of the window—drag it to the left to reduce it to its minimum width. As soon as you touch this button with your arrow pointer, the cursor becomes a vertical bar flanked by outward-pointing arrows to indicate that it's ready to move the divider (Figure 12-12). Hide the organizer completely by choosing View → Slide Only. Restore the slide organizer view by using the View menu and selecting one of the other views: Navigator, Outline, or Light Table.

Navigator View

The slide navigator's standard view appears when you open a new Keynote document. This view displays thumbnail versions of each slide, the slide number, and whether slides have been grouped (page 412). When your slides differ visually, Navigator view makes it easy to find your way around your presentation, since it displays a thumbnail image of each slide.

Here you can reorder, delete, or duplicate your virtual slides; as well as lump them into groups to make a long slideshow more manageable, or designate slides for Keynote to skip during the presentation. Click a thumbnail to select it, and Keynote loads it into the slide canvas so that you can see it up close and make changes.

Duplicating slides

You can duplicate a slide—including its contents—so that you can use it in another part of the presentation, or modify it to create a new version of the slide. Press Option while dragging a slide in the navigator; a green ball bearing a + sign appears next to your arrow cursor, telling you that Keynote's about to duplicate the slide. Drag it up or down the column of thumbnails; a blue line and a blue triangle appear as you drag, showing the position the new slide's going to drop into when you release the mouse button.

You can also duplicate a slide by selecting it in the navigator and choosing Edit → Duplicate (⌘-D). Keynote creates a duplicate immediately below your selected slide.

Tip: You can access most of the navigator's commands through Keynote's shortcut menus. Control-click (or right-click) within the slide navigator pane to summon this mini-menu containing commands for New Slide, Cut, Copy, Paste, Duplicate, and so on.

Finally, you can use the Copy and Paste commands to duplicate slides. Select a slide and choose Edit → Copy (or press ⌘-C). Then select the slide just above the spot for your duplicate slide and choose Edit → Paste (or press ⌘-V).

Figure 12-12:
Navigator view displays thumbnail images of your slides in the slide navigator. Here, the thumbnails are shown at their largest size, but you can also select a small or medium view in the Thumbnail Size pop-up menu (A). Make the slide navigator wider or narrower by dragging its resize handle (B).

You can select two or more slides to duplicate at once. Select multiple slides (selected slides display a yellow border) in one of the following ways:

• Drag up or down through the gray area in the slide navigator—on either side of the row of slides—to select a contiguous group of slides.

• Click one slide in the navigator to select it, hold the Shift key and click another slide to select all the slides between the two.

• Click one slide to select it, and then hold the ⌘ key while you click other slides to select your group.

• Click one slide to select it, and then choose Edit → Select All (⌘-A) to select all the slides in your presentation.

Use any of the slide duplication techniques described above to duplicate all the selected slides at once.

Tip: You can use the keyboard to move around in the navigator or select multiple slides. With a slide selected in the navigator—displaying its yellow border—you can use the up and down arrow keys to select the slide above or below it. Press ⌘-up or down arrow to move to the first or last slide in the presentation. Select multiple slides by holding the Shift key while pressing the up and down arrow keys, highlighting slides above or below the selection.

Organizing and grouping slides

The slide navigator makes it easy to shuffle the deck and reorder your slides: Drag a slide up or down in the navigator and drop it into its new order. Move a bunch of slides at once by selecting the whole crowd of them and then dragging. As you drag, a blue line indicates the new position for the slide (or slides) when you release the mouse button.

Attached to that blue line is a downward-pointing blue triangle. If you drag the slide directly up or down, the blue triangle stays lined up with the slide's left edge. But if you drag the slide to the right, the blue triangle jogs over to the right, indicating that Keynote will indent the slide if you drop it there. By indenting a group of related slides, you create a group to help organize your slide collection. You can choose to hide or show a group of slides (the *children*) by clicking the flippy triangle next to the *parent slide* or double-clicking that parent slide (Figure 12-13). Indenting slides and showing or hiding groups is only for your convenience while editing—this organization has absolutely no effect on the slide presentation.

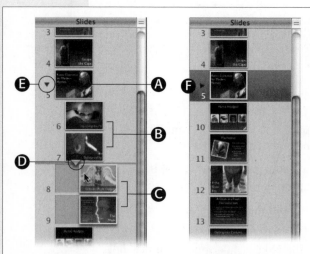

Figure 12-13:
You can divide your presentation into groups of slides to help you organize it—especially useful in longer presentations. When you indent a slide (B) it becomes a child of the parent slide (A). You can add grandchildren (and great-grandchildren, and so on) to this family tree by dragging slides to the right (C). As you drag, the blue triangle (D) indicates the indent position for the slides. If you click a parent slide's flippy triangle (E), Keynote hides all that slide's descendants (F)—here, slides 6–9 are tucked away.

Slide grouping is especially handy when your presentation has a large number of slides. If you create groups of slides for each section of your presentation, you can keep those sections you're not working on hidden—making it much easier to find your place or move from one section of the slideshow to another.

You can make as many indent levels as you need to help organize your slides. Use the following techniques on one slide or a group of selected slides:

- Drag a slide to the right to *indent* it one level, to create a "child" and group it under the slide above.

- Drag a slide to the left to *promote* it, or move it to a higher level, removing it from a group—and making it a "parent" of any slides indented beneath it.

- Press Tab to indent the selected slide to the right; press Shift-Tab to promote a slide to the left.

Note: If you indent a slide that has children, they always move along with that parent slide, retaining their indents beneath it.

Deleting slides

When you're ready to delete a selected slide, or a group of selected slides, from your presentation, press Delete (or choose Edit → Delete).

If you delete a parent slide—a slide above an indented slide or group of slides—Keynote saves the children slides and promotes them to the level of the deleted (or is it deceased?) parent.

You can delete an entire indented group of slides. Click the flippy triangle next to the parent slide to hide the group, and then delete the parent slide. Keynote removes the parent and all its children (and its children's children) from the presentation. If you remove such a family by mistake, press ⌘-Z (or choose Edit → Undo) to restore it to the slideshow.

Skipping slides

Keynote can skip slides you want to remove from the presentation without actually deleting them. You can use this trick to try out two different versions of a particular slide or section you're working on, or to modify a presentation for a certain audience. You can skip a slide or a whole section of the presentation for one audience and then turn it back on for another. For example, your travelogue on Amsterdam could feature the beautiful flower markets and your canal cruise for one audience—and its famous herb-loving coffee shops and red light district for another.

Select a slide or group of slides and choose Slide → Skip Slide. Keynote changes the slide thumbnail into a line in the navigator. You can still select, edit, move, or delete skipped slides—they just don't play in the presentation (Figure 12-14). Bring skipped slides back into the show by selecting them and choosing Slide → Don't Skip Slide. These Skip and Don't Skip commands are also available from the shortcut menu: Select the slide to skip, Control-click anywhere inside the navigator, and choose Skip Slide (or Don't Skip Slide).

Tip: If you have to deliver similar presentations to two or more groups repeatedly, save yourself the trouble of remembering to reconfigure the presentation by just duplicating the entire Keynote file. Then either delete slides or skip slides to tailor the duplicate presentations to the specific audience.

Figure 12-14:
You can skip slides to remove them from the presentation without deleting them, giving you the option to bring them back later. Select the slide to skip, and choose Slide → Skip Slide. Keynote collapses skipped slides to a double line in the slide navigator and removes them from the numbering sequence. Here, two slides have already been skipped.

Outline View

When you get right down to it, a slideshow is really just a fancy outline in disguise, a presentation tool that visually organizes your talk into topics (slides) and subtopics (bullet points). Outline view makes this structure especially clear, making it a good place to marshal your ideas, particularly when you first start organizing your presentation. This lets you shift your attention from the layout of your slides to focus instead on the text and logic of your talk.

Choose View → Outline to display the outline view in the slide navigator. In this view, Keynote displays each slide's number next to a tiny slide icon and the slide's text, if any (Figure 12-15). The outline view displays two kinds of text: the slide title and bullet points. Some slide designs have a subtitle instead of bullet points—but from the outline view's perspective, a subtitle is just a single bullet point. Some master slides display only the title, some only bullet points, some both, and some neither. The outline contains any text you've entered; the master slide you pick determines whether that text makes it to the screen.

In outline view, you can type directly into the slide navigator to add or edit text in your slides. You can add text formatting, too—changing font, size, color, and so on—and the changes appear immediately in the slide canvas. Those formatting changes don't show up, however, in the slide navigator itself, which always uses the same display font no matter what crazy formatting you might apply. Outline view is all about content, in other words, not design.

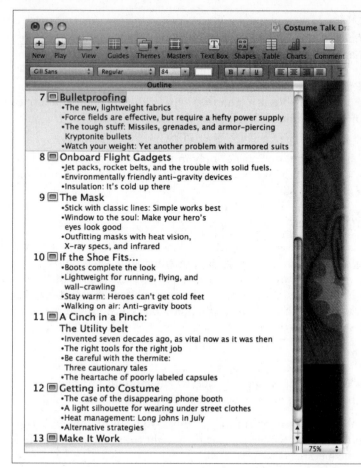

Figure 12-15:
Outline view lets you edit and organize the text of your slideshow directly from the slide navigator. Every slide has a title and one or more bullet points; and the bullet points can have their own indented bullet points, too, letting you nest topics as deeply as you like. You can drag slides or bullet points to reorder them, or drag bullet points from one slide to another.

Tip: You can change the display font and size that Keynote uses for its outline. Choose Keynote → Preferences and click the General button. Use the Outline View Font pop-up menus to make your font and size selections.

Outline view lets you add, delete, move, and duplicate slides, just as you can in Navigator view. Grab a slide by its slide icon and drag it to move it to a new location, for example. This type of slide organization isn't outline view's strong point, though; it's most useful when you add, organize, or delete text; or move text between slides.

Tip: If your lines of text are more than a few words long, widen the slide navigator by dragging the divider handle at the bottom of the window to give your outline some breathing room.

Entering outline text

When you add a new slide in Outline view, whatever you type becomes the slide's title. Press Return and a second slide appears in the outline below the first. If you want a bullet point under your first slide title instead of this new slide, press Tab—the second slide disappears and a bullet point appears in its place. Type your text for the first bullet point, press Return, and then type in the next bullet point. To indent a bullet point an additional level, place the insertion point in that bullet point and press Tab. Bump it back out a level by pressing Shift-Tab.

As you type, your bullet points appear not only in the slide navigator, but in the main slide canvas, too; as you make changes to your outline, Keynote automatically updates the text on your slides.

Moving outline text and bullets

If you drag a slide's icon to the right (or select it and press Tab), it ceases to be a slide and becomes a bullet point beneath the preceding slide—the blue-triangle indent indicator pops up to show just how deeply you're indenting. If the freshly indented slide has bullet points of its own, they come along for the ride, becoming bullet points indented below the slide-turned-bullet. You've just moved the entire slide content, title and all, into the body text of the previous slide. See Figure 12-16 for an illustration.

Going back the other way, when you drag a bullet point all the way to the left (or select it and press Shift-Tab) it becomes a slide; its bullet point text becomes the slide title, and any bullet points below it become bullet points on the new slide.

If your slide has more than one level of bullet points, you can drag them left (or select and press Shift-Tab) to *promote,* or drag them right (or select and press Tab) to *demote* them in the hierarchy.

Move bullet points to a new location in your slideshow by treating their bullets like handles: Select the text of one or more bullet points, grab a bullet (the bullet dot, not its text), and drag it to another position in the presentation—even to an entirely different slide. As you drag, the blue line and arrow guidelines appear and helpfully show you where your bullet points will land when you drop them. (If you Option-drag a bullet point, you copy it to its location, leaving the original bullet in place.)

Selecting multiple bullet points

You can select multiple bullet points, multiple slides, or a combination of both, by dragging your arrow pointer up or down to the left of those items and the outline. As you drag, Keynote highlights the selected items. You can select multiple bullet points that aren't all in a row by selecting one, holding ⌘, and then clicking additional bullet points or slides. Once selected, you can move the group left or right or drag them to a new location in the slideshow.

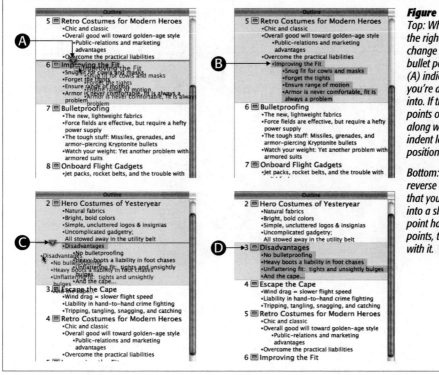

Figure 12-16:
Top: When you drag a slide to the right in the outline, you change it from a slide into a bullet point. The blue triangle (A) indicates the indent level you're about to drop the slide into. If that slide has any bullet points of its own, they move along with it, retaining their indent level in the new position (B).

Bottom: The same process in reverse changes a bullet point that you drag to the left (C) into a slide (D). If that bullet point has subordinate bullet points, they move along with it.

Printing the outline

If having a hard copy of the outline would help organize your slides more easily, Keynote lets you print your outline exactly as it appears in the slide navigator's Outline view. The outline doesn't have to be showing onscreen when you choose File → Print (or press ⌘-P). In the print dialog box, click the Outline button under "Print:" in the Keynote settings and then click the Print button or press Return. For more info about printing Keynote slideshows, see page 515.

Light Table View

Back in the day, slideshow producers had to don white gloves to sort actual 35mm slides by hand and load them into projector trays. This process was impossible without a light table to lay the slides on, shuffle them around into a different order, and decide which ones to cut from the show or send to the lab for duplication. Keynote gives you light table view (Figure 12-17) to do that same organization with your onscreen slides—white gloves required only if you want to make a fashion statement.

In light table view, the slide canvas disappears to make way for the slide navigator, which now takes up the full document window with a grid display of your slides. Pack 'em in by choosing Small in the Thumbnail Size pop-up menu at the bottom right corner of the window—or choose Medium or Large to see more detail in your thumbnails.

Figure 12-17:
Light table view organizes all your slides onto a virtual light box, letting you work with lots of slides at once and giving you a high-level visual feel for your entire presentation. You can change the size of the thumbnails to small, medium, or large in the Thumbnail Size pop-up menu (circled) at the bottom left of the document window.

Apart from the expansive real estate enjoyed by the slide navigator, light table view is otherwise similar to navigator view. You can move, duplicate, or delete slides in this jumbo-sized slide navigator just as you would in navigator view's skinny version. To return to the slide canvas and the view you were using previously (navigator, outline, or slide only), double-click a slide.

Saving Your Slideshow

Hopefully you've been saving your slideshow right from the moment you first created it, tapping ⌘-S obsessively to save your presentation every few minutes…just in case. If not, take care of that crucial bit of business right now. Choose File → Save or press ⌘-S to save your file. The first time you save a Keynote document, the Save dialog box drops into view, letting you choose a name and location to use when saving your new slideshow. If you're not familiar with the Mac's standard Save window, refer to page 22 for a primer.

Automatic Backups

The iWork programs don't have an auto-save feature, which means that Keynote saves your slideshow only when you specifically tell it to do so. Get in the habit of hitting ⌘-S early and often to avoid unpleasant surprises.

One thing you can do, though, for a bit of added protection is to set Keynote to automatically save two versions of your document. Every time you save, this feature saves a copy of the previously saved version of your file so that you always have two copies of your slideshow. To set up this extra safety net, go to Keynote → Preferences, click the General button, and turn on the "Back up previous version option." See page 59 for more about how this feature works.

Opening an Existing Slideshow

Go ahead, take a break, you deserve a little reward after creating your first Keynote slideshow. No really, go have a cupcake and treat yourself to a trashy sitcom. When you come back, though, you'll need to know how to get back to your slideshow masterpiece.

Keynote makes it easy to fetch an existing slideshow right from the Theme Chooser. To get back to a document you were just working on, click the Open Recent pop-up button (Figure 12-18), and choose from your latest projects. You can also get the same set of options by choosing File → Open Recent.

To open a slideshow not included in the Open Recent list, click the Theme Chooser's "Open an Existing File" button, or choose File → Open. The Theme Chooser flips over to reveal the standard Mac OS X file browser to let you choose a file. If you're not familiar with how to use this dialog box to browse for your file, head over to page 35 for a brief tour. You can also double-click the slideshow from your desktop to launch Keynote and open the slideshow.

Figure 12-18:
Click the Theme Chooser's Open Recent pop-up button to reveal the list of your latest projects, and select the one you want to open. Click the "Open an Existing File" button to browse your computer for another slideshow. If you just want to create a new document, double-click a theme to use, and Keynote gives you a new untitled slideshow.

Importing Files from Another Program

Keynote can open slideshows created in Microsoft PowerPoint or the dearly departed AppleWorks 6. When you import these files, Keynote creates a brand new Keynote slideshow based on the original file. That means that any changes you make apply to this new copy; you're not changing the original PowerPoint or AppleWorks document.

Note: Keynote lets you *save* files as PowerPoint documents and a host of other formats, too. See page 517 for the details.

Keynote does its best to maintain the look of the original slideshow, along with all its text, colors, layout, and so on—but you may notice some occasional differences. As you might expect, the more advanced features and formatting included in the original slideshow, the more likely it is that Keynote may have trouble duplicating the slides exactly.

Note: If Keynote runs into trouble during an import, it speaks up, letting you know there was a problem and offering to show you a rundown of the details. If you choose not to review them right away, you can always go back and inspect them later: Choose View → Show Document Warnings to see the list of issues.

Now that you're fortified with that cupcake and you've got your Keynote slideshow open again, you're ready to tackle the nuts-and-bolts details of the program's presentation magic. Enough with the introductions; the next chapter takes you through all of Keynote's nooks and crannies to give you detailed control over every slide's layout.

Laying Out Your Slides

The toughest part of preparing a presentation is really just figuring out what you're going to say. Once you've got that behind you and poured a rough text outline into Keynote, everything that follows is the fun part, the visual candy. This is the design phase, where you craft eye-catching slides to illuminate your presentation's key points. You'll compose your slideshow masterpiece with iWork's colorful palette of layout objects: pictures, shapes, text boxes, tables, charts, and movies—all the same elements that you use in Pages for page layout and in Numbers for designing multimedia reports.

In fact, designing slides in Keynote is practically identical to designing documents in the other iWork programs. You use the very same tools, techniques, toolbar icons, and inspector windows to create and manipulate your design elements. This tight integration of tools is good news, since it means that you don't really have to learn three different programs: Once you've mastered layout in one iWork application, you've mastered it in all of them. There are minor changes from program to program, but the fundamentals remain the same.

This chapter spares your patience (and quite a few trees) by not rehashing every last detail already explained in Chapter 7's exploration of the layout tools in Pages. You'll still learn how to fill your Keynote slides with text boxes, pictures, tables, charts, and the rest, but in cases of overlap, the chapter frequently points you back to the details provided earlier in the book.

Before getting into all that good stuff, though, take a quick diversion into the details of a good hygiene regimen when creating a new slideshow.

Setting Up the Keynote Document

Before you can start creating slides, you first have to create a Keynote document: the container that becomes your virtual slide tray for the presentation. To do so, launch Keynote (or, if it's already running, choose File → New) to open the Theme Chooser. Select a theme and a slide size, and then click Choose (see page 392).

From there, it's a good idea to do some initial housekeeping to establish exactly how you'd like Keynote to present your slideshow, setting the ground rules for how you and your audience will interact with it. The Document Inspector is the place where you take care of these preliminaries. Click the Inspector button in the toolbar to call forth the Inspector window, and click the Document button, the first icon in the Inspector toolbar, as shown in Figure 13-1.

Choosing a Presentation Style

Before you start plugging in your content, you need to think about how you're going to deliver this presentation. Will you be in control of the presentation, advancing the slides manually? Will it play automatically, all by itself? Will the viewer control the show, by clicking buttons onscreen? Keynote can create four varieties of slideshows to satisfy each of these scenarios. Choose one of these presentation styles from the Presentation pop-up menu in the Document Inspector's Document tab (Figure 13-1):

- **Normal.** This choice is the one for a presentation you control yourself, by clicking the mouse, using the keyboard, or using a remote control. Keynote creates this type of show unless you choose otherwise.

- **Hyperlinks only.** Create this kind of Keynote presentation if you want viewers to interact with your show by doing things like navigating from slide to slide, choosing to view different parts of the slideshow, visiting a web page, or creating an email message. Also known as an interactive slideshow, the Hyperlinks only style of Keynote presentation is ideal for self-paced trainings or lessons. See page 514 for more information about using hyperlinks to create this kind of show.

- **Recorded.** The next best thing to being there. In this type of presentation, your slideshow plays like a movie, with a prerecorded narration soundtrack. You prepare the show by recording yourself as you go through each slide; Keynote saves the audio along with your timing for advancing through each slide. When you play the slideshow, Keynote plays back your voiceover narration and moves through the presentation just as you recorded it. This option is available only after you've made a recording in the Document Inspector's Audio tab. See page 512 for the lowdown on recording your slideshow.

- **Self-playing.** Like the Recorded style, this option is also for a presentation that will play all by itself, without human intervention. Instead of saving a recorded presentation, however, slides change automatically after a fixed length of time. You can set the slide interval for the whole show or on a slide-by-slide basis. See page 511 for details on setting up self-playing shows.

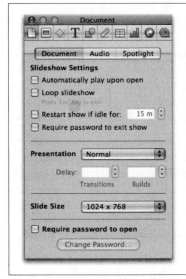
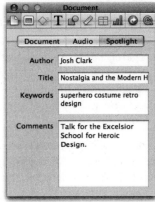

Figure 13-1:
Left: Use the Document Inspector's Document tab to control how Keynote plays your slideshow and to require a password to open it. Choose the presentation style—Normal, Hyperlinks only, Recorded, or Self-playing—from the Presentation pop-up menu.

Right: Click the Document Inspector's Spotlight tab to enter a variety of optional document information. You can assign keywords for searching and comments to remind you, for example, about the document's edit history. The contents of any of these fields show up in a Spotlight search.

Password-Protecting Your Slideshow

God forbid that anyone would see the marketing presentation for Up & Away's new cape-pressing service before it's officially announced. When you're feeling secretive, you can require a password to open your Keynote document. To do this, turn on the "Require password to open" checkbox at the bottom of the Document Inspector → Document pane, and Keynote asks you to provide and verify the password. You can also provide an optional password hint, which Keynote displays after you try to open a document three times with the wrong password.

Keynote also helpfully offers advice for creating a sturdy password. Click the key button next to the Password field, and Keynote opens the Password Assistant window. See page 138 for details about using this feature to choose a secure password.

Note: If you plan to share your document with others, don't forget to send along the password, too, or the recipients won't be able to open it.

A wholly different way to password-protect your slideshow is to require a password to stop it when it's already playing. This is particularly useful for slideshows intended to be used by the general public in a kiosk setting, for example. That way, your kiosk visitors can't turn off presentations using the Hyperlinks Only, Recorded, or Self-Playing presentation modes. This keeps your computer locked and safe in public settings.

To do this, just turn on the "Require password to exit show" setting. Contrary to what you might expect, this slideshow padlock doesn't respond to the same password as the "Require password to open" feature. Instead, when you try to stop a presentation, Keynote requires the name and password of your computer's administrator account in order to complete the action. If you move the slideshow to another computer, the name and password switch to *that* computer's administrator account.

Working with Objects

As described earlier, Keynote, Pages, and Numbers share much more than the box they ship in and the iWork installation disc. They share a common collection of *objects*—the pictures, charts, tables, shapes, text boxes, movies, and sounds that combine to create a designed document. Designing a Keynote slideshow is very much like designing a page-layout document in Pages. Both programs give you a canvas on which you organize and layer individual design elements—the objects— to create the finished composition.

A fundamental difference in Keynote, however, is that there's no such thing as an inline object (as there is in Pages). All objects in Keynote are effectively *floating objects* whose locations are independent of every other object on the slide. You can't nest a shape inside a text box, for example, or a picture inside a shape, like you might do in Pages. Every element of your slide floats free of the rest. (If you're curious, see page 209 for a review of how inline and floating objects work in Pages.)

Apart from that, objects in Keynote follow essentially the same laws of document physics as Pages objects. The rest of this chapter reviews how to work with those objects. Before getting into the specifics of each object type, though, here's a quick review of what they all have in common—how to select, move, and manipulate objects on a Keynote slide.

Selecting Objects

Every object on the page is contained in its own invisible box, and you have to grab this box anytime you want to do something with the object. To select an object and its containing box, click it just once so that its eight selection handles appear around its border, as shown in Figure 13-2. The selection handles indicate that you've selected the object at the *object level*. Now you can move the object, rotate it, and apply other effects.

Note: Free text boxes (see page 433) do not display eight selection handles, just one on the left and right side of the box. All other object types display handles on all four sides and the four corners, too.

By contrast, clicking objects additional times selects the content *inside* the object— the text of a text box or shape, a cell inside a table, the bars of a bar chart, and so on. At that point, you're no longer working with the object as a whole but just certain stuff inside; that means you can no longer move the object or change most of its object properties. To do those things, you have to go back to selecting it at the object level (again, so that you can see its selection handles). If you're working with content inside an object and you want to pull back to working with the object as a whole, press ⌘-Return—just like clicking drills into an object, ⌘-Return pulls you back out. You can also click outside the object to deselect it and then click it just once to select it at the object level.

To select multiple objects at once, Shift-click each object. Or drag across the objects with the mouse to select them: Click in an empty area of the canvas, and drag the mouse to draw a selection box; Keynote selects all objects inside or touching the selection box.

Tip: To select all objects in a slide, click the canvas so that no object is selected and then choose Edit → Select All or press ⌘-A.

Figure 13-2:
Left: Click an object just once to select it at the object level, and Keynote shows its selection handles along the object border. Now you can move, rotate, or add effects to the overall object.

Right: Clicking an object more than once typically selects content inside the object. Here, the text inside the text box is selected, and the selection handles are no longer visible. Now you can edit the text, but you can't move the text box or make changes to the overall object. Press ⌘-Return to pull back and select the text box at the object level.

Moving and Copying Objects

When you boil it down to the basics, designing a Keynote slide is simply about arranging objects on a slide canvas. Move an object to its proper place by selecting it at the object level and then dragging it into position.

Tip: As you drag, the pointer unfurls a banner that shows the X (horizontal) and Y (vertical) position of the object's top left corner relative to the ruler; choose View → Show Rulers (⌘-R) to show the ruler. You can turn this informational feature on or off by choosing Keynote → Preferences and then selecting the "Show size and position when moving objects" in the General pane.

To limit an object's movement to horizontal, vertical, or 45-degree angles, start dragging while holding down the Shift key. For pixel-perfect control, use the arrow keys to move the object a point at a time, or hold down the Shift key while you press an arrow key to bump it over ten points.

To duplicate an object, press Option while you drag. A clone of the object springs out of the original. You can also select an object and choose Edit → Duplicate (⌘-D), and Keynote likewise gives you a copy of the object. This is a nifty trick for adding a duplicate to the same slide, but when you want to put a copy on a different slide, it's Copy and Paste to the rescue: Select the object at the object level, and choose Edit → Copy. Then go to the other slide and choose Edit → Paste, and Keynote deposits your freshly minted copy onto the second slide.

Resizing, Rotating, and Flipping Objects

The selection handles do more than simply advertise that you've selected an object; they also let you change an object's dimensions or rotate it on the page.

To resize an object, drag one of its selection handles. Hold down the Shift key as you drag to maintain an object's proportions. Hold down the Option key to resize an object from its center—the object stays centered on the same point in the slide as you grow or shrink it. You can also specify the exact size of an object using the Metrics Inspector (Figure 13-3): Select the object, and use the Inspector's Width and Height fields.

Tip: If you're using a recent laptop with a multitouch trackpad, you can also resize an object by "pinching" it. Select the object so that its selection handles are visible, and pinch your thumb and forefinger together on the trackpad to shrink the object; open them to make the object larger.

Pictures normally always keep their original proportions when you resize them—no need to hold down the Shift key as described above. If you want to squish and stretch an image into new proportions, however, you can do so by selecting it and turning off the "Constrain proportions" checkbox in the Metrics Inspector.

Give an object a jaunty tilt by rotating it: Hold down the Command (⌘) key while you drag a selection handle. Hold down Shift-Command while you drag to limit the rotation to 45-degree increments, or hold down Option-Command to rotate the selection around the handle opposite the one you're dragging (instead of rotating it around the center).

Tip: If you use a laptop with a multitouch trackpad, you can also rotate the object by putting your thumb and forefinger on the trackpad and twisting them like you're turning a knob. Hold down the Shift key while you do this to restrict the rotation to 45-degree increments.

You can also use the Metrics Inspector: Select the object and spin the Rotate dial, or type a number into the Angle field. The Metrics Inspector also offers the Flip control to turn an object on its head or convert it into a mirror image. Click one of the buttons to do this little somersault.

Figure 13-3:
The Metrics Inspector lets you specify the exact size, position, and rotation angle of the selected object. Click one of the Flip buttons to turn the object on its ear.

Tip: When you flip or rotate a shape that contains text, the text goes along with it; when you're suddenly unable to read your mirror-image text, you can put it back to its original left-to-right position by choosing Format → Shape → "Reset Text and Object Handles".

Connecting Objects

Keynote can yoke two objects to each other with a *connection line,* a special variation on the program's line shape which makes it easy to manage flow charts or organization diagrams. Like a regular line, you can style a connection line's color, style, thickness, and endpoints (adding arrows to one or both ends, for example). The difference is that the ends of the line are always anchored to the two objects. No matter how you might move the object on your slide, the line bends, stretches, and shrinks to maintain the visual link.

To add a connection line between two objects, select the two objects and choose Insert → Connection Line. Style the line using the Format Bar or Graphic Inspector, just like you would with a regular object. For more about connection lines, see page 257.

Styling Objects

Keynote gives you a variety of effects, or *object styles,* to give your objects a graphic makeover: shadows, reflections, borders, background colors, transparency, and more. The Format Bar and the Graphic Inspector give you complete controls over these options. See "Modifying Object Styles" starting on page 264 for the complete story.

Copying and Reusing Object Styles

Behind every great design is a focus on consistency and visual rhythm; having too many variations of fonts, colors, text sizes, and effects quickly contributes to a distracting, crazy-quilt slideshow design. But here's the hitch: Restyling every object just the way you want it can be a time-consuming hassle. Happily, Keynote gives you a few techniques to let you sidestep the manual formatting of each and every object, keeping your design clean and consistent along the way.

Copy Style and Paste Style

After you've styled a shape, picture, movie, or other object exactly the way you want it, you can use it as a model, applying its formatting to another object in your slideshow—even an object of another type, in many cases. Select the object (or table cell or chart data series) whose style you want to use and choose Format → Copy Style, or press Option-⌘-C. Select another object, choose Format → Paste Style (Option-⌘-V), and presto! Keynote transforms the selected object, replacing all its styles and formatting with the style of the original object.

Applying an object style with master slides

Paste Style is handy for updating an individual slide, but it still means a lot of work if you try to use it to update every text box in your 50-slide presentation. When you want to make changes to many objects at once, update the master slide instead, and your changes will be applied to all slides based on that master. Select the object to use as the model, and choose Format → Advanced → "Define Object for Current Master" (the name of this command changes based on the type of object you've selected). This sets the object's properties to be the standard set of properties for your slides. Choose Format → Advanced → "Define Object for All Masters" to make sure the change sticks for *every* slide in your slideshow. For more about editing master slides and creating your own themes, see Chapter 16.

Reapply Master

Instead of updating the master slide with the selected object, you can also do the reverse. Select an object, choose Format → "Reapply Master to Selection", and Keynote strips it of all its unique style changes so that it uses the theme's standard look for the current master slide. To do this for all objects on a slide, click the slide canvas so that no objects are selected and choose Format → "Reapply Master to Slide". If you've moved the title, body text, or any other standard elements from the original slide, this command also restores the original layout.

Paste and Match Style

When you paste an object or text into your slideshow, Keynote normally does its best to match the formatting of the original copy. So, when you paste a table from Numbers, for example, or a text box from Pages, it gets the same styling as it had in the original document. Keynote is just trying to be helpful, but when the result doesn't match the style of your slideshow, or when you inadvertently paste tiny text into your Big Headline, that means more work for you, reformatting the material to match its new context.

Save yourself the trouble by choosing Edit → "Paste and Match Style". When you paste an object, this command automatically applies the master slide's default colors and styles to the pasted object. When you paste text, it uses the same text formatting as the surrounding text.

Layering Objects

When objects overlap, one necessarily covers the other. You can control where objects sit in this stack of layers from the Arrange menu. Select an object and choose the Bring Forward or Send Backward commands to nudge the object higher or lower in the stack, or choose "Bring to Front" or "Send to Back" to move it to the very top or bottom. (The Front and Back buttons on the toolbar do the same thing as the "Bring to Front" and "Send to Back" commands.) For details about working with object layers, see page 260.

Aligning Objects

It sounds mundane, but a big part of elegant design is simply keeping things lined up so that objects adhere to an overall pattern—centered on the page, for example, or aligned in an orderly grid. Like Pages and Numbers, Keynote offers *alignment guides* to help you keep things straight. But it also has a few tricks of its very own to help you size and space objects precisely.

Automatic alignment guides

As you drag an object across the slide, Keynote keeps an eye on its position relative to all the other objects on the slide. When the object you're dragging is close to lining up with another object, an alignment guide materializes, drawing a line between the two objects and "snapping" the object into position to line it up precisely, as shown in Figure 13-4. The alignment guide vanishes when you move past or drop the object.

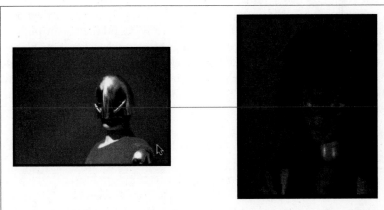

Figure 13-4:
When you're moving an object that is lined up (or nearly lined up) with another object, Keynote snaps it into line and draws an alignment guide through both objects to show you what it's up to. As shown here, Keynote's standard settings line up objects through their center. You can also choose to line them up along their edges by changing preferences in the toolbar's Guides pop-up button, or in the Ruler pane of Keynote's preferences.

These guidelines vary the way they work their magnetic magic depending on your preference settings. In Keynote's standard settings, objects trigger alignment guides when they line up with the *center* of another object (or with the slide itself). If you prefer, you can set it up so that objects snap to the *edges* of other objects instead. This is helpful, for example, if you want to line up objects according to a grid so that their left or right edges are perfectly aligned. Keynote offers two preference settings to change the way that objects snap to alignment guides. You'll find these settings in the toolbar's Guides pop-up button, or in the Ruler pane of Keynote → Preferences (Figure 13-6): "Show guides at object center" and "Show guides at object edges". You can select either, both, or neither. If you turn off both options, Keynote won't display alignment guides at all.

Tip: You can temporarily disable alignment guides by pressing Command (⌘) while you drag an object.

Using relative sizing and spacing guides

A pair of Keynote-only features help you space and size objects equally, too. *Relative spacing guides* pop up and snap an object into place when you're moving it through a location that's spaced evenly with two or more other objects. *Relative sizing guides* appear when you're resizing an object and the object approaches the same height or width as another object, snapping the object to the same size. The whole drama unfolds in Figure 13-5.

To switch the relative guides off, use the Guides pop-up button in the toolbar, or the Ruler pane of Keynote → Preferences; in either place, turn off the "Show relative spacing" and "Show relative sizes" settings. As with the alignment guides, you can temporarily disable the relative guides by pressing the Command (⌘) key while you move or resize an object.

Drawing your own alignment guides

Keynote's automatic alignment guides remain invisible most of the time, showing up only temporarily while you're moving objects. However, you can draw your own alignment guides that stick around and remain visible as long as you like. To add an alignment guide to a slide, chose View → Show Rulers to reveal Keynote's measuring sticks. Click inside a ruler, drag into the canvas, and the cursor pulls an alignment guide in tow behind it. Drop the alignment guide when you have it where you want it. Objects snap to these custom alignment guides just like they do for the automatic guides: They center on the guides when you have the "Show guides at object center" preference turned on, and line up their edges with "Show guides at object edges".

Note: These guides are for your eyes only. They don't show up when you play the slideshow or when you print the slides—only when you're editing your slides.

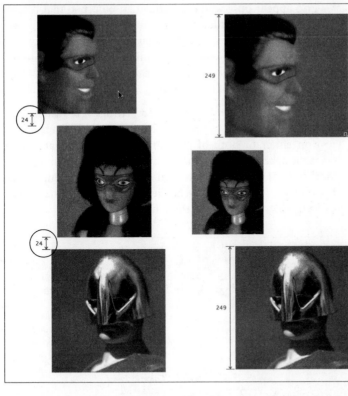

Figure 13-5:
Left: When you move an object through a location where it's evenly spaced with two or more objects, Keynote's relative spacing guides light up and snap the object into position to let you know. Here, the guides (circled) flash on to show that the top picture has moved to be 24 pixels from the middle picture, the same distance separating the middle and bottom pictures.

Right: When you resize an object, the relative sizing guides spring into action when the object approaches the same height or width as another object on the slide, snapping the object to the matching size. Here, the guides alert that the top picture has the same height as the bottom picture.

You create vertical alignment guides from the vertical ruler and horizontal alignment guides from the horizontal ruler. You can move an alignment guide anytime you like by dragging it to its new location; drag it back to the ruler to send it up in a puff of smoke. To hide these guides temporarily, choose View → Hide Guides; get them back by choosing View → Show Guides or dragging a new alignment guide into the slide.

Tip: You can't pull alignment guides from the ruler while you're editing text. Click outside the text box before plucking a fresh guide from the ruler.

The technique described above adds guides only to the currently selected slide and doesn't affect other slides. To add alignment guides to many slides at once, add the guides to the master slide instead; the guides become instantly available to any slide that's based on the edited master slide. For details on editing master slides, check out page 538.

Switching on the master grid

If you're looking for a bit more order and precision for keeping your objects on the straight and narrow, flip on Keynote's *master grid*. Like a sheet of graph paper, this grid scores your slide with regularly spaced lines—except that this grid is invisible.

The lines of the master grid appear only when you move an object so that it lines up with one of the gridlines. As you shuttle the object across the slide, the object snaps to the grid when it gets close to one of the gridlines. Here again, exactly how objects align to the grid depends on the Alignment Guides preferences—choose "Show guides at object center" to center objects on the gridlines, while "Show guides at object edges" lines up the sides of the objects.

The master grid is turned off under Keynote's standard settings. To switch it on and set the grid spacing, choose Keynote → Preferences, and click the Rulers button (Figure 13-6). Turn on either or both of the horizontal and vertical Master Gridlines checkboxes. Set the spacing of these guides by entering a percentage into the horizontal or vertical control. Keynote's standard setting is 10 percent, which adds 10 evenly spaced gridlines across the slide—change it to 5 percent, for example, to make the grid denser with 20 gridlines across the slide.

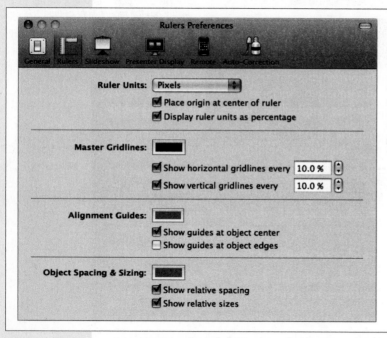

Figure 13-6:
Keynote's Ruler preferences let you control not only the units and display of the rulers, but also Keynote's master gridlines, alignment guides, and relative spacing/sizing guides. To change the color of any of these guides, click its respective color well and pluck a new color from the Color Picker.

Changing the grid and guide colors

Keynote's standard settings go with yellow for its alignment guides and its relative spacing/sizing guides. The master gridlines, meanwhile, are blue—a useful distinction to help you quickly differentiate what's aligning with what. You can change the color of any of these lines in Keynote's Ruler preferences. Choose Keynote → Preferences and click the Ruler button. Click the color well in the Master Gridlines, Alignment Guides, or Object Spacing & Sizing sections to call up the Color Picker and change the color.

One-click object alignment

When you're in a hurry and don't want to fuss with grids and guides, hand the whole thing over to Keynote and let the program align and space a set of objects for you automatically. You do this with the Arrange → Align Objects and Arrange → Distribute Objects menus. See page 258 for the skinny.

Grouping and Locking Objects

Once you have objects placed, sized, and lined up exactly where you want them, you can *group* or *lock* them to make sure that they stay in the same position relative to each other (grouped) or on the slide (locked).

When you group a set of objects, they always travel as a pack. You can move, rotate, and resize them all at once, or add an object build to the entire group so that they appear or disappear from the slide all at once (see page 474 for more about builds). Select the objects to include in a group by Shift-clicking each one, and click the toolbar's Group button or choose Arrange → Group. To disband a group, select it and click the toolbar's Ungroup button or choose Arrange → Group. See page 263 for more info about grouping.

In Pages and Numbers, grouped objects can't be edited individually, but Keynote doesn't have this restriction and lets you get at any member of a group with an extra click. Click the object you want to edit once to select the whole group and then click again to select the individual object. You can now make changes to that object's size, format, rotation, or anything you like without affecting the rest of the group.

Warning: If you apply a build effect (page 474) to a group and then later ungroup the objects, Keynote tosses out the build effect. If you just want to make a quick change to the formatting of one or more of the objects but want to keep the group's build, don't ungroup the objects. Instead, use the technique described above to edit an individual object in the group.

When you lock an object, Keynote glues it down on the slide so that you can no longer move it (or make any other changes to it for that matter). Select the object and choose Arrange → Lock. See page 263 for the details.

Adding and Formatting Text Boxes

Any text in a slide must live within a text box or a shape. Keynote provides three kinds of *text boxes*: title text boxes, body text boxes, and free text boxes. (You'll also learn about *shapes* on page 448.)

- **Title text boxes.** Most Keynote themes contain a number of slide masters (page 398) featuring a title text box. There can be only one title text box per slide. Text you enter in one of these text boxes appears as the slide's title in outline view (page 414). Although they're usually designed to hold a relatively short title, you can actually add as much text as you care to squeeze in.

Note: Title text boxes can use all available text formatting options (described below), except for a quirk with bullets and numbering: The title can't have more than one bullet point.

- **Body text boxes.** You often see body text boxes featured in Keynote slide masters under their alternative moniker, bullet text boxes. Like title text boxes, Keynote permits only one body text box per slide. Text you enter in this kind of text box shows up in Outline view as bullet points, with a bullet for each paragraph. In the slide itself, you can change the bullet style or remove bullets from the slide completely by using the Text Inspector's Bullets & Numbering tab's pop-up menu (see page 439).

- **Free text boxes.** These text boxes take their name from their freedom from the outline (text in a free text box doesn't appear in Outline view) and their freedom from Keynote's slide masters—you typically use free text boxes on an individual slide to supplement a slide master's basic design. Use text boxes to add image captions, callouts, or any text that you want to treat apart from a slide's title or body text.

- **Shapes.** These are the free text box's shapely cousins. You can use any shape (except for the lines) as a text container. Insert a shape by clicking the Shapes button in the toolbar and picking a shape from its pop-up menu, or by choosing Insert and selecting one of the shapes by name. Double-click inside a shape to begin entering text. Like free text boxes, Keynote doesn't display text within shapes in the outline.

Inserting Title and Body Text Boxes

Many slide masters contain a title text box, a body text box—or both. If the slide you're working on doesn't have one of these text boxes, and you want to add one, open the Slide Inspector, click the Appearance tab, and turn on the checkbox for Title or Body. (You can likewise remove one of these text boxes from a slide by turning off its checkbox in the Slide Inspector—although you can remove it more directly by selecting the text box on the slide and then pressing Delete.)

When you remove a slide's title or body text box, you don't really delete it. A slide's title and body text have special standing in Keynote, which considers these fields to be the slide's essential content. Even if you choose to remove the title or body text in the displayed slide, Keynote still includes that info in outline view, for example, stashing it away for safe keeping. If you later decide to restore the title or body text back into your slide—switching to a new slide master, for example, that has those fields—Keynote plugs in the original content for you. This also means that you can change master slides as many times as you like, and the title and body text make the jump right along with you, automatically finding their new position in the layout.

Note: You can't rotate title or body text boxes—these solid content containers refuse to tilt askew. That's not the case with free text boxes and shapes, however; they turn on a dime.

Inserting Free Text Boxes

Unlike every other object in iWork, Keynote's free text boxes have only two selection handles, one on each side. That means you can adjust their width but not their height—at least not with selection handles. Keynote manages the height of free text boxes automatically: As you enter text, these text boxes grow vertically to accommodate all your typing. Likewise, when you delete text, the text box shrinks back down to size.

You have two options for inserting a free text box in your slide. Click the Text Box button in the toolbar or choose Insert → Text Box, and Keynote adds a small text box to the middle of the slide with the word "Text" inside. Now you can reposition the box, adjust its width, and add your own text.

The other way to insert a free text box is to draw it on your slide right where you want it. Press the Option key while you click the Text Box button in the toolbar, or while you choose Insert → Text Box. Release the Option key and position your cursor—which now has the I-beam shape—where you want one corner of your text box, and drag across to the opposite corner. As you drag, Keynote displays a rectangle indicating the new text box's size. Although you can vary the height as well as the width of this rectangle as you draw, just pay attention to its width—since free text boxes adjust their height automatically. When you release the mouse button, the text box outline remains at your desired width, one line high, and with the insertion point blinking—ready for you to enter your text.

Note: If you add a free text box to a master slide, it normally becomes part of the slide background. You've chained it to a spot on the master slide; it displays on every slide created from that master as uneditable text. This type of unchangeable text is useful to display, for example, a company name, copyright information, or a teaching module series title. To make a master slide's free text boxes editable, you can instead designate it as a text placeholder. For more about all of this, see Chapter 16 for details about editing themes and master slides.

Editing Text in Keynote

Tap out your text in Keynote by double-clicking the text to edit (clicking a text box just once selects the text box at the object level; clicking it again lets you edit the text). From there, the basics of text editing are the same in Keynote as it is in the other iWork programs—in other Mac programs, too, for that matter. For a review, head back to "Basic Text Editing in iWork" starting on page 52.

Working with lists and bullets

For better or worse, bullet points are a fact of life for many slideshow presentations, and that means that much of your job editing text in Keynote is really about editing *lists*. Bullet points, nested outlines, and numbered lists—they might take different forms, but they're all lists, and Keynote gives you a few special shortcuts to make quick work of organizing or rearranging them.

You can nest bullet points below other bullet points as outline subtopics. Indent a bullet point to the right by placing the insertion point anywhere in its text and pressing Tab. "Outdent" the bullet point by pressing Shift-Tab.

Select an entire list item by clicking its bullet dot (or number, letter, or other label). Select multiple list items by clicking one item's bullet and then Shift-click another; Keynote selects both list items, plus all of them in between. From there, you can drag the list item(s) by the bullet to a new location:

- Drag up or down to move to a new location in the same list.

- Drag left or right to indent or outdent in the list.

- Drag to another text box to move to another list.

- In Outline view, drag to the slide navigator to move to a different slide.

- Drag to an empty location on the slide canvas to create a new free text box.

Tip: Free text boxes always start out as regular text, with no bullets or numbering. Convert a text box from regular text to a bullet list (or vice versa) by using the Text Inspector → Bullets pane. There you can also change the appearance, spacing, and labeling of your bullet points. For more, skip ahead to page 439.

Clipped text and auto-shrink

Keynote manages overstuffed text boxes differently than Pages, which clips text that won't fit but allows you to flow it into other text boxes (see page 218). In fact, Keynote's free text boxes don't even know the meaning of too much text; the text box keeps growing and growing as you add more content, expanding right off the slide if you keep pouring prose into it. The only way to manage runaway text in free text boxes is to delete some of it, or reduce the font size to make it fit.

Title text boxes, body text boxes, and shapes meanwhile behave somewhat more like Pages, adding a (+) clipping indicator to the bottom selection handle to show that some text is hidden when the box isn't big enough (Figure 13-7). Keynote hides these clipping indicators during the slideshow—their purpose is only to give you feedback while editing.

If Keynote clips your text, you can resize the text box to make it big enough, or you can downsize its font to squeeze more text into the same size. The second option is where Keynote's *auto-shrink* feature looms large, as you saw in Chapter 12. Double-click the clipping indicator, and Keynote instantly adjusts the font size to the largest size that allows the text to fit. Going forward, as you add or remove text from the text box, Keynote stays on the job, constantly calibrating the font size to make sure the text fits. You can tell Keynote to keep its mitts off the size lever and return the text box to its original font size: Select the text box, and turn off the Auto-shrink checkbox in the Format Bar.

Note: The auto-shrink option is available only for title text boxes and body text boxes—not for shapes or free text boxes.

Figure 13-7:
When a text box is too small to accommodate its text, Keynote highlights its border and adds a clipping indicator (circled-bottom) to the bottom of the text box. Double-click the clipping indicator to make Keynote auto-shrink the text to fit inside the box. You can also turn this feature on or off by selecting the text box and clicking the Auto-shrink checkbox in the Format Bar (circled-top).

- Boots complete the look
- Lightweight for running, flying, and wall-crawling
- Stay warm: Heroes can't get cold feet
- Walking on air: Anti-gravity boots

Check your spelling

Keynote normally has its automatic spell checking turned on, flagging misspelled words—or words not in its dictionary—with a red underline. Choose Edit → Spelling → "Check Spelling as You Type" to turn this feature on or off.

Choose Edit → Spelling → Spelling to display the Spelling window for manual spell checking. Keynote shares many elements, including its spell checker, with Pages. See page 113 for the rest of the story on spell checking.

Smart quotes and auto-correction

Keynote can monitor what you type, automatically correcting errors or inserting *smart quotes,* or curly quotes, which curve into a different shape for opening quotes or closing quotes. You can also use Keynote's auto-correction tools to give you quick shortcuts for commonly typed words and phrases. Turn these features on or off in Keynote's Auto-Correction preferences: Choose Keynote → Preferences and click the Auto-Correction button. See page 126 for all the details.

Formatting Text

Once you've got your text into Keynote, you can dress it up by formatting it however you like. Choose a new font, splash your text with some color, make it larger or smaller—whatever you want to do, Keynote provides plenty of formatting tools to give you control over the look of your words. When you select a text box, the Format Bar gives you fast access to the most common text formatting options, shown in Figure 13-8. Keynote applies any text formatting changes you make to the selected text or paragraph, or to what you type next after you make your formatting changes.

Figure 13-8:
You can format text directly from the Format Bar when you select a text box. Its menus and buttons include: font family (A); typeface (B); font size (C); font color (D); bold, italic, and underline (E); align left, center, right, or justified (F); line spacing (G); number of columns (H); and auto-shrink text to fit (I).

- Snug fit for cowls and masks
- Forget the tights
- Ensure range of motion
- Armor is never comfortable, fit is always a problem

When you need more detailed control than the Format Bar provides, turn to the Text Inspector, Fonts window, Format menu, and the ruler. With only a few exceptions, formatting your text with these tools is identical to formatting text in Pages. You'll find those details described in the Pages chapters (especially Chapter 2), but here's an overview of text formatting in Keynote.

The Fonts window

Click the Fonts button in the toolbar or choose Format → Font → Show Fonts to open the Fonts window (Figure 13-9). Find out the full story about the Fonts window on page 62.

Use the controls within this window to do the following:

- Choose a font and see font samples.
- Set the font size.
- Set the font color.
- Set the document color, which is actually the paragraph background color—not to be confused with the text box fill color set in the Graphic Inspector. The document color overrides the text box fill color and is also constrained by the Text Inspector's inset margin setting. In other words, you see the text box fill color in the text box's margin, and the document color behind the block of text.

Figure 13-9:
Click the Fonts button in the toolbar to call up Mac OS X's font-formatting headquarters. If the Preview pane isn't showing, drag the little dot beneath the word Fonts downward to reveal it. Select some text—or an entire text box—to modify it with any of the controls shown here (and described in detail on page 62).

- Choose the text underlining or strikethrough style and color.

- Add a text shadow and adjust its characteristics.

The Text Inspector

Click the Inspector button in the toolbar or choose View → Show Inspector to display the Inspector window. Then click the Text button (the "T" button, fourth from the left) to show the Text Inspector (Figure 13-10). The Text Inspector is divided into three tabs: Text, Columns, and Bullets.

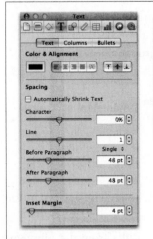

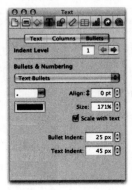

Figure 13-10:
Left: Select some text—or a text box—and use the Text Inspector's Text tab to set the text color, alignment, and spacing of your text.

Middle: The Columns tab gives you control over the number and width of the text box's columns.

Right: The Bullets pane lets you set the bullet style, size, and alignment for your lists. Choose None in the Bullets & Numbering pop-up to convert a bullet point into a regular paragraph, or do the reverse by choosing a bullet style.

The Text Inspector → Text pane offers these controls:

- Set the font color.

- Set the paragraph alignment—left, centered, right, or justified (page 68).

- Turn the text box's auto-shrink feature on or off with the "Automatically shrink text" control (page 436).

- Set the vertical text alignment—top, center, or bottom. (This option has no effect on free text boxes, which automatically adjust their vertical size to fit the text.)

- Set character spacing—the amount of space between each character in the line, also known as tracking.

- Adjust line spacing—the space between each line of the paragraph (page 70).

- Adjust paragraph spacing—the space before or after each paragraph (page 71).

- Adjust the inset margin—the margin around the text inside a free text box or shape.

The Text Inspector → Columns pane lets you change the number of columns of text to display in the text box, including the width of the columns and gutters, the gaps between columns. Working with columns in Keynote works just like it does in Pages; see page 153 for more info.

The Text Inspector's Bullets tab is where you control the look of paragraph bullets or numbers, and it's identical to the Lists tab in Pages' Text Inspector. Here you can swap out your traditional bullet dots for numbers, letters, or spiffy images. See page 87 for details on using this inspector pane and its many bullet styles.

The Format menu

Choose Format → Font in order to do any of the following:

- Show or hide the Fonts window.

- Change the font style (bold, italic, underline, strikethrough, or outline).

- Increase or decrease the font size.

- Adjust tracking, the space between two characters (see page 65).

- Turn ligatures on or off (see page 67).

- Adjust the font's baseline (see page 66).

- Adjust the text capitalization.

Choose Format → Text and select one of the paragraph alignment settings in the submenu: Align Left, Center, Align Right, or Justify.

Choose Format → Text and choose Copy Ruler or Paste Ruler from the submenu in order to copy text box margins, tabs, bullet indents, and paragraph background color (which is labeled Document Color in the Fonts window) from one text box to another. The next section describes how to use the ruler.

Setting margins, indents, and tabs with the ruler

Choose View → Show Rulers to reveal Keynote's vertical and horizontal scales on the top and left sides of the slide canvas. The top ruler displays the bullet alignment, margin settings, and tabs for the selected paragraph. You can use rulers to adjust the text margins and the first-line indent, and set tabs for each paragraph in a text box. So far this system is exactly the same as ruler usage in Pages (see Setting Tabs and Indenting Text, starting on page 72). Keynote adds a new wrinkle—and a new icon—to its rulers: the bullet alignment mark (Figure 13-11).

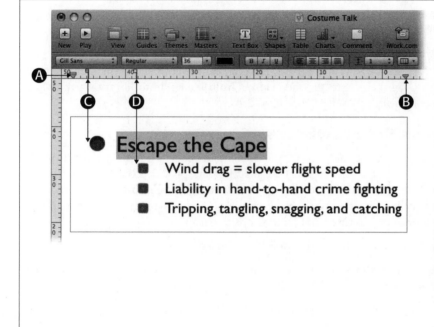

Figure 13-11:
Choose View → Rulers in order to make margin and bullet spacing adjustments with the ruler. Select some text or just place your insertion point within a paragraph, and Keynote displays that paragraph's margins and indents in the ruler. Here, the ruler shows the setting for the "Escape the Cape" bullet point.

The left margin indicator (A) shows the left edge of the text area, where non-bullet text would line up. The right margin indicator (B) shows the right edge. The blue, flag-shaped bullet marker (C) indicates where the left edge of the bullet lines up for the selected text. For reference when you make adjustments, Keynote also displays bullet markers for other paragraphs in the text box (D).

To make any ruler adjustments, place your insertion point within the paragraph you want to adjust, or select text that spans two or more paragraphs. Since text boxes can have more than one paragraph, each text box could have more than one ruler format. Drag the bullet, margin, or tab indicators and watch the effect on the selected text. If you've set an inset margin in the Text Inspector, the inset margin controls the outer limits for the margin settings.

Tabs work in Keynote essentially as they do in Pages, and you can find more details on page 72. Unlike Pages, however, Keynote's Text Inspector doesn't have a special pane for editing tab stops; all tab editing must be done here in the ruler.

Create new tab stops by clicking once on the ruler and dragging the tab into position. Control-click a tab marker and choose one of the four tab styles from the pop-up menu: Left Tab, Center Tab, Right Tab, or Decimal Tab. Or you can just double-click the tab marker repeatedly to cycle through the various tab styles.

There's a hitch to using tabs in text boxes: Keynote reserves Tab and Shift-Tab to indent and outdent bullet points. Ironically enough, that means the Tab key is useless for tabs, but Keynote sidesteps the problem with Option-Tab, which works the way you would normally expect the Tab key to behave, advancing the text to the next tab stop.

Inserting Photos and Other Graphics

You can add just about any kind of graphic file into a Keynote slide. JPEG, PDF, GIF, PNG, PSD, PICT, and TIF are just a few of the graphics formats that Keynote accepts. Drag them onto the slide canvas from your iPhoto library via the Media Browser or from a folder on your hard drive.

Replacing Media Placeholders

Many Keynote slide masters contain *media placeholders* where you can drop pictures, movies, or audio clips. These placeholders provide consistent picture size and placement from slide to slide, and also do some behind-the-scenes magic to automatically size and crop—or *mask*—your pictures to fit. You already got a quick taste of this in Chapter 12, but here's the drill:

1. **Click the New button in the toolbar to add a new slide.**

2. **Choose a master slide with a picture. Keynote updates your slide's layout to reflect your choice.**

3. **Click the toolbar's Media button to reveal the Media Browser.**

4. **Drag a picture from the Media Browser and drop it onto the media placeholder (Figure 13-12), or drag an image file from a folder on your hard drive.**

    Keynote replaces the placeholder picture with your selection, keeping the same size, effects, and dimensions as the original placeholder. Want to try a different picture instead? You can repeat this step as many times as you like, dropping new pictures onto the placeholder until you find the look you want.

Note: When Keynote scales images larger or smaller to fit the placeholder, the result typically looks sharp and tidy. The exception is when you drag a very small low-resolution picture into a placeholder; if Keynote has to blow up the picture to fit, the enlarged image will be fuzzy or pixelated. (Whenever possible, try to work with original images that are at least as large as the slide's display size; this gives you the flexibility to blow up the picture to fill the whole slide if you later decide to do so.)

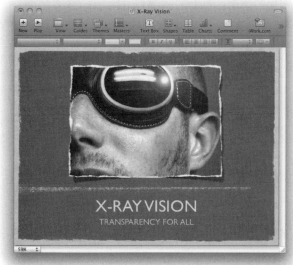

Figure 13-12:

Top: Replace a media placeholder with your own picture by dragging the replacement image from the Media Browser (or a folder from the Finder) and then dropping it onto the placeholder image.

Bottom: When Keynote replaces the placeholder, it keeps the same size, dimensions, and effects as the original placeholder. Here, the vertical image is cropped so that its top and bottom are lopped off to fit the placeholder's horizontal layout, and it gets treated to the same rough-hewn picture frame as the placeholder.

If you're not thrilled by the way that Keynote shrinks and crops your image to fit into the placeholder, you're not stuck with it. You can move, resize, rotate, or style your image however you like, just like any other object. You can also change the way the image is cropped by editing its image mask, which you'll learn about in a just a second.

If you switch to a new master slide after adding a picture to a media placeholder, Keynote keeps your picture and plugs it into the new slide layout, just like it does with the slide's title and body text—but only if the new master slide also has a media placeholder. If you switch to a new master slide without a picture, Keynote tosses your picture out of the slideshow (as always, though, you can get it back with Edit → Undo). Keynote never throws out "regular" pictures, however.

Any pictures that you add to your slides outside of the master's placeholders always stick around in exactly the same location when you switch from master slide to master slide. (The same goes for any object that you add to a slide outside of its title, body text, or placeholders.)

Note: More specifically, Keynote remembers placeholder pictures only when you switch to a master slide with a placeholder that has the same name, or *tag,* as the placeholder on the first master slide. Placeholder tags are set in the Slide Inspector when editing master slides. See page 546 for more details.

POWER USERS' CLINIC

Object vs. Media Placeholders

Although it's distinctly unpopular with Apple's theme designers, who correctly prefer to use media placeholders for pictures, you can also add a picture to an *object placeholder* in a slide. Object placeholders are really a leftover from previous generations of Keynote and, in general, don't have lots of practical application. If you stumble into one or feel the urge to experiment, however, here's the scoop.

As you'll learn on page 449, object placeholders are really intended to be used for tables and charts, but they can also hold media objects like pictures and movies, albeit with somewhat lame results. To add an object placeholder, open the Slide Inspector, click the Appearance tab, and turn on the checkbox for Object Placeholder.

The difference between the two is that media placeholders crop and resize the picture to fill every pixel of the placeholder. By contrast, when you drag a picture to an object placeholder, Keynote resizes the picture but never crops it—the whole picture, in its original dimensions, shows within the object placeholder without any cropping, often leaving empty space inside the placeholder box.

Also, once you drag a picture or movie to an object placeholder, it loses its placeholder powers—unlike media placeholders, you can't continue to add new images until you find the one you want. After you use an object placeholder for an image or movie, it turns into a regular object. The lesson here: Just because you *can* use object placeholders for pictures, it doesn't mean you should. Media placeholders work much better. For more on creating both types of placeholders in themes and master slides of your own, check out Chapter 16.

Adding and Editing Pictures

Don't feel limited to the paint-by-numbers layouts of Keynote's master slides. You can add "regular" pictures to any slide—not just slides based on masters with placeholders—and you can add as many as you like. As you saw in Chapter 12, adding an image to a slide works just like replacing a placeholder, except that you drop the image into an empty part of the slide canvas instead of a media placeholder. You can also select Insert → Choose and then browse to the image file to add to your slideshow. Drag one of the picture's selection handles to resize it, and drag the picture itself to reposition it.

In addition to the usual assortment of formatting, shadows, reflections, and picture frames that you can add to any object via the Graphic Inspector (see page 264), Keynote also gives you some simple editing tools to transform your image:

- **Masks.** Add a mask to an image to crop it, specifying exactly what portion you want to show in your slide. Page 230 reveals the details behind the mask.

- **Instant alpha.** Remove background colors with iWork's instant alpha feature, which turns portions of your picture transparent, handy for creating cutout effects, as shown in Figure 13-13. Page 234 makes it all clear.

- **The Adjust Image window.** Fine-tune your picture's color, contrast, and levels with the Adjust Image window, which gives you sliders to calibrate every aspect of your picture. Turn to page 235 for the color commentary.

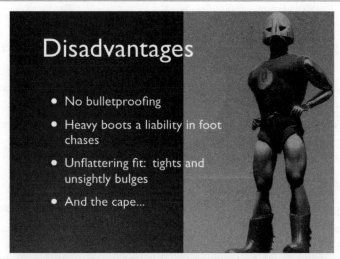

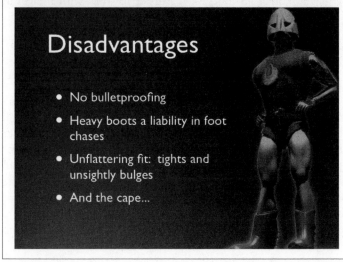

Figure 13-13:
Use Keynote's instant alpha tool to make background colors see-through for a cutout effect. Here, instant alpha removed the solid background color in the photo (top) to let our hero stand on his own (bottom). A white-colored shadow was also added in the Graphic Inspector to give the figure a soft glow.

To use instant alpha, select the picture and click the toolbar's Alpha button. The pointer turns into a crosshair cursor—click and hold the color you want to remove and then drag to expand the selection to include neighboring colors. See page 234 for more information.

Creating new slides from pictures

When you want to fill one or more slides with a picture, drag the picture or group of pictures directly to the slide navigator. Keynote gives each picture a slide of its own using the master directly above your insertion point. If you're building a photo slideshow, for example, start with a blank slide master and drag your pictures into position beneath it in the slide navigator. If you're using pictures that are at least the resolution of your slides (usually 800×600 or 1024×768 pixels), Keynote inserts them full-frame—no resizing needed.

Tip: Keynote places pictures added in this manner on the top layer, so use the Arrange menu to send it to the back if the picture gets in the way of your text boxes.

Managing File Sizes for Image-Heavy Slideshows

Go ahead and fill your slideshows with lush visuals—your slides illustrate your talk, and rich imagery provides your audience with memory cues for recalling your points later. The one downside to packing your slideshow with pictures, however, is that it can pack your hard drive, too. Pictures can be big, which in turn makes for big files. When size matters—if you're emailing your slideshow to someone, for example—Keynote offers some ways to keep a lid on your image-heavy documents.

Up with downsampling: Shrinking big images

Under the standard settings, when you insert an image, Keynote first shrinks very large pictures so that their width fits into the slide (for vertically oriented images, this means that the top and bottom may still spill outside the slide). This process, called *downsampling,* has a pair of advantages: It's easier to work with images at this scale, and they take up less space in your document file.

Note: This process doesn't affect the original image file from your iPhoto collection or hard drive; it just applies to the image imported into your slideshow.

Keynote ships with downsampling turned on, but every once in a while, this normally helpful feature might get in your way. Downsampling reduces the overall size of the image which means removing pixels and, with them, some of the finer details of your picture. If you want to use a tiny detail of a large picture, for example, your downsampled image may not look so good when you mask it and then try to blow up the detail. In this case, even clicking the Original Size button in the Metrics Inspector won't help; Keynote considers the downsampled version that it imported to be your original image.

If you prefer to maintain a picture's original size when you add an image, no matter how large the image might be, choose Keynote → Preferences and, in the General pane, turn off the "Reduce placed images to fit on slides" option. Going forward, Keynote inserts image at their full size.

Reducing file size

Are you actually using every pixel of those images you added? If you've shrunk or masked images in your slideshow (almost certainly the case if you've added any pictures by way of a media placeholder), you can tell Keynote to toss those unused pixels over the side. Keynote will save only the smaller version of the picture, shrinking your file size along the way.

You can aim your shrink ray at either individual images or all images in the file. To reduce the file size of a single picture, select the image and choose Format → Image → Reduce File (or Control-click the image and choose Reduce Image File Size from its shortcut menu). To reduce the file size for *all* images (along with shortened videos or audio clips), choose File → Reduce File Size. In either case, Keynote asks if you really want to do it and provides a file-size savings estimate (Figure 13-14). If the file size of the image(s) can't be further reduced, Keynote lets you know that all images are already at their optimal size.

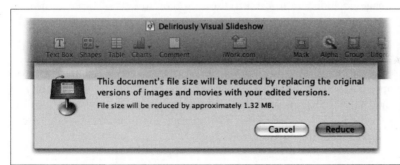

Figure 13-14:
Tell Keynote to reduce file sizes for an individual image (Format → Image → Reduce File) or for all images (File → Reduce File Size). Keynote asks you to confirm the action and lets you know how much space you'll save. Click Reduce to continue.

The one snag after doing this is that you no longer have the rest of the image to work with; as far as Keynote is concerned, the way the picture looks in your slideshow is now the original image. Any bits that you cropped out are no longer available, and enlarging the picture will look clunky at best. That means that it's a good idea to save these steps until you've completed your slideshow and you're fairly sure that you're done working with its images. The *real* original image, however, remains untouched on your hard drive or iPhoto library; if you need to go back to the original, you can simply add the picture to the document again.

Note: Some images will refuse to shrink. Images used in image fills (page 269) or with action builds (page 489) are impervious to these weight-loss techniques. The same goes for certain types of image files. Choose View → Show Document Warnings for details about any images that could not be compressed.

Including or excluding theme images

To save room, Keynote normally doesn't package a theme's pictures inside the document file. That's typically the right call: Even if you send a Keynote slideshow to another computer, for example, that computer has to have Keynote installed to run it, which means that it automatically has all of Keynote's built-in themes. The other computer knows where to find its own versions of those images, and the pictures display just fine even though they aren't technically part of the slideshow file itself.

But what if you're using a non-Apple theme? If you created your own theme or found a third-party theme online, those theme images won't be available on other computers—unless you've installed those same themes on those computers as well. In that case, you can tell Keynote to copy the theme images into the document. You can do this only when you first save a slideshow (or when you choose File → Save As to save it under a new name): At the bottom of the Save dialog box, click the Advanced Options flippy triangle, and turn on the "Copy theme images into document" option.

If you *always* want Keynote to copy theme images, choose Keynote → Preferences, click the General button and turn on the "Copy theme images into document" option on the preference panel. When this option is turned on, the option in the Save dialog box is always checked and grayed out—Keynote will always save new files with theme images included until you turn the option off in Keynote's preferences.

Making Shapes

You can create simple geometric shapes, lines, and arrows in Keynote when you click the Shapes button in the toolbar and choose one from the pop-up menu. You can also insert shapes by choosing Insert and selecting a shape by name from the menu, or by Control-clicking (or right-clicking) the slide canvas, choosing Insert, and picking a shape from the pop-up menu.

Tip: You can draw a shape directly in your document by holding down the Option key when you pick a shape from the Shapes pop-up menu. Let go of the Option key, and your cursor changes to a crosshair shape. Click in the slide canvas where you want one corner of the shape to appear and drag to the opposite corner. Pages draws the shape and displays the shape's width and height measurements as you drag.

You can adjust these shapes' borders and fills, giving them colored, gradient, or image fills. And like all other objects, you can adjust their size, opacity, rotation, and so on. Shapes can also hold text—so that they serve as creatively shaped text boxes. Double-click inside a shape and the blinking insertion point appears, ready for you to type or paste in text. Head back to page 435 for a review of text-editing in Keynote.

For the full story on working with shapes, see page 241.

Building Tables and Charts

When you need to present complex information or large amounts of data clearly, tables and charts can help you organize and present that information in an attractive and understandable way. Get started by clicking the toolbar's Table button or choosing a chart from the Chart pop-up button to add the object to your slide and then stroll back to Chapter 8 for a review. Creating tables and charts in Keynote works exactly the same as it does in Pages, although there are a few Keynote-specific niggles worth pointing out.

When you add a table or chart, Keynote normally tumbles it out into the center of the slide—unless the slide has an object placeholder on it. Object placeholders are like media placeholders, except that they're tuned to catch tables and charts when you add them to the page. Add a table or chart to a slide with an object placeholder, and the new object automatically appears in the placeholder at the specified position and size. Object placeholders are normally part of a master slide, but you can add or remove them from individual slides by turning on the Object Placeholder checkbox in the Slide Inspector → Appearance pane. For details on creating master slides and including object placeholders, see page 546.

When designing tables and charts for Keynote, be careful to keep them relatively simple and uncluttered so that they come through clearly on the screen. If you have a detailed table or chart where it's important that you get across every morsel of deliciously dense data, consider sharing it in a separate handout instead; paper does a much better job than a projected screen at presenting high-resolution information.

When you have more than a handful of data points or want to highlight anything more than big-picture trends, it's best to do your crunching in Numbers, and then print it out. In fact, because Numbers is specifically tuned to deal with data, it's almost always a good idea to run your numbers in iWork's spreadsheet and then paste them into Keynote, rather than working with them directly in your slideshow. That's particularly true when it comes to charts, as you'll learn in a moment. The bottom line: If you're just working with a handful of rows and columns, it's fine to do it in Keynote; when you're charting more complicated data or using tables with complex formulas, do your data work in Numbers.

Whatever method you use to get your tables or charts into Keynote, the program's display does have a tasty benefit not available in Pages or Numbers: You can build them gradually on the screen, disclosing a little bit of information at a time until you've revealed the entire table or chart. For example, a table could appear on the screen row-by-row, column-by-column or even cell-by-cell. Likewise, chart data can appear one data series at a time, one data set at a time, or by individual data points. See page 478 for details on creating builds for tables and charts.

Using Numbers Charts in Your Slideshow

The Chart Data Editor for Pages and Keynote (page 314) is simple but clunky, and it doesn't let you add formulas for automatic calculations like you can in Numbers

Smuggling Chart Textures to Other iWork Programs

Keynote has always enjoyed a few more colors and textures than its iWork siblings, and iWork '09 adds a few more to the list. That means that Keynote's Chart Colors window offers several more 3D textures and 2D image fills than in the other iWork programs. If you find yourself admiring the brushstrokes of Keynote's Artistic texture or perhaps marveling at the sturdy roughness of Concrete, you can use them in your Pages and Numbers charts, too, but it takes a few extra steps.

One option is to paste those charts into Keynote and work on them there before pasting them back into the original documents. You can also use the Copy Style and Paste Style commands described on page 428 to copy the background fill of a Keynote object to an object in Pages or Numbers. Finally, yet another option is to drag the textures directly from Keynote's Chart Colors window:

1. In Pages or Numbers, open the document with the chart that you'd like to update with a Keynote texture or image fill.

2. In Keynote, create a chart, select it, and open the Chart Inspector. Click the Chart Colors button to open Keynote's Chart Colors window.

3. Select the fill type and set you want to use in the Pages or Numbers chart.

4. Drag one of the color blocks from Keynotes Chart Colors window and drop it onto one of the data series in the chart in the Pages or Numbers window.

All of the data points for the selected data series fill with the new texture. Repeat this step for other data series in the chart.

charts. This is fine for simple data sets, but it's not ideal for larger collections of numbers. In those cases, save yourself time and frustration by creating your charts in Numbers and then pasting them into Keynote. This is where iWork steps in with a nifty trick, linking up the pasted chart with your original Numbers document so that you can update your Keynote chart automatically. After you revise and save your new data in Numbers, refresh the chart in Keynote, as shown in Figure 13-15, and you're up-to-date.

To use your Numbers chart in Keynote:

1. **Create a chart in Numbers (Chapter 22), and save the Numbers spreadsheet.**

   Keynote can't link to an untitled Numbers document. Be sure that you save the spreadsheet before copying the chart.

2. **Select the chart in Numbers and choose Edit → Copy.**

3. **In Keynote select the slide where you want to insert the chart, and choose Edit → "Paste and Match Style", and Keynote adds the chart to your slide.**

   Use the "Paste and Match Style" command instead of plain old Paste to insert the chart with your slideshow theme's standard colors and styles. This makes your chart blend in with your presentation's overall design. If you prefer to keep the chart style exactly as it is in the original Numbers spreadsheet, however, choose Edit → Paste.

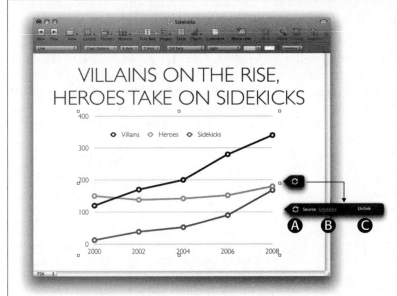

Figure 13-15:
When you select a chart pasted from Numbers, Keynote displays a pointer arrow with a Refresh button (A). Click the button to reload the latest data from the original Numbers spreadsheet.

Click or drag the dot at the end of the arrow to expand it, revealing a link to the original Numbers file (B) and the Unlink button (C). When you click the link, the spreadsheet file opens in Numbers, where you can make changes to the original data. When you click Unlink, Keynote cuts the tie with Numbers, and the chart is no longer linked.

After you paste a Numbers chart into Keynote, you can update its data as usual from the Chart Data Editor, but you can also go back to the source, refreshing the chart's data directly from the original Numbers spreadsheet. When you select the chart, Keynote indicates that it's linked to a Numbers spreadsheet by showing an arrow pointer immediately to the right of the chart. Click the Refresh button to reload the data from the Numbers document, replacing all the data in Keynote's Chart Data Editor for the chart. Be careful here: If you've made any changes to the chart in Keynote, those changes are wiped out when you reload the data from Numbers.

Should you decide that you no longer want to link back to the original Numbers document, click the Unlink button in the expanded link arrow, and Keynote severs the tie. Going forward, you'll edit the chart's data only in the Chart Data Editor.

Note: Sorry, there's no similar feature to link up tables between Numbers and Keynote—only charts.

Adding Movies

Add a little motion to your picture show by screening a movie. Keynote lets you add video to your presentation—if you're feeling avant garde, you can even add several movies per slide (though the performance you get with multiple movies depends on your computer's processing power).

To add a touch of the silver screen to your computer screen, click the toolbar's Media button to open the Media Browser, and click the Movies tab. Choose a movie, and drag it onto the slide canvas. The Media Browser shows only movies you've stored in iPhoto, iMovie, and your Movies folder. Add other movies by dragging their icons from a folder on your hard drive onto the slide canvas, or select Insert → Choose to browse to a file on your computer.

Keynote's media placeholders (page 442) welcome movies as well as pictures. When you drop a movie onto a placeholder, Keynote sizes and positions the movie to fit into the placeholder's border as closely as possible, adding picture frames, shadows, reflections, and any other effects the placeholder might carry with it. However, Keynote doesn't crop and squeeze movies to make them fill the entire dimensions of the placeholder as it does with pictures; the movie always keeps its same relative proportions.

Wherever you drop the movie on the slide, it becomes a regular object—just like a picture or shape—and you can resize, rotate, add a shadow, or change its opacity just like any other object. Resize the movie by dragging one of its selection handles, and reposition it by dragging the movie itself.

Note: Many movies start with a black screen and fade-in. In this case, the movie shows up on your slide as a black rectangle unless the movie is set to display a different *poster frame* in the QuickTime Inspector. Think of the poster frame as the movie poster that advertises your movie; it's the frame of video that Keynote displays before you tell it to start playing the video. Keynote's standard settings, however, start playing the movie as soon as the slide appears; if you stick with those settings, it's best to set the poster frame to the first frame in the movie. Otherwise, when the slide appears, the poster frame appears briefly on screen before the movie begins playing—making a jumpy beginning to your smooth fade-in.

Playing Movies

The QuickTime Inspector (Figure 13-16) is your virtual editing studio for preparing your movie screening. Here you control the length, volume, and playback preferences for the selected video:

- **Start & Stop.** Drag the left handle of this slider to the frame where you want your video clip to start. The right handle marks the end.

- **Poster Frame.** Drag the slider to the frame of the video you want to show before the movie starts playing.

- **Start movie on click.** Under Keynote's standard settings, the movie starts playing as soon as you get to its slide in the presentation. Turn the "Start movie on click" option to make Keynote wait until you click before it starts playing.

- **Repeat.** When you set this option to None, the movie plays through to the end and stops. Set to Loop, the movie plays to the end and immediately starts again at the beginning—over and over. If you choose Loop Back and Forth, the movie plays to the end, switches into reverse, plays backwards to the beginning, and then plays forward again—over and over. You might find this setting useful for a time-lapse movie of a rosebud opening or the clip of your son in the high-diving competition.

- **Volume.** Use this slider to hush the movie from its full recorded volume; pushing it all the way to the left mutes the sound.

Figure 13-16:
The QuickTime Inspector is your master projectionist, controlling all the technical details of your video's playback—from where it starts and stops to whether it loops. You can use the controls at the bottom of the QuickTime Inspector to play, rewind or fast forward through the movie while you're editing.

Use the controls at the bottom of the QuickTime Inspector to preview the movie while editing. You can use these controls to play, pause, rewind, or fast-forward; or move to the first or last frame of the movie. You can also just double-click the movie on the slide canvas to play—single-click to pause it.

The QuickTime Inspector, of course, doesn't do you much good while you're actually presenting. Instead, Keynote gives you a set of video controls that appear when you point to the movie on the slide during your presentation (Figure 13-17). Under Keynote's standard settings, these controls are always available, but you can turn them on or off in the Slideshow preferences pane: Choose Keynote → Preferences and click the Slideshow button. Turn the checkbox on or off for "Show playback controls when pointer is over a movie".

If you prefer not to sully your pristine slideshow with mouse pointers and video controls, you can instead use the keyboard to drive your movie during the presentation. Press or hold the keys listed in Table 13-1 to shuttle through the video—the selections may seem random when you read them on the page, but they make more sense when you rest your fingers on the J, K, and L keys. (No need to press Command or any other key while using these keys, just press 'em solo to control your video.)

Table 13-1. *Keyboard Controls for Movie Playback*

Key	Action
J	Hold down to rewind
K	Press to pause; press again to continue playing
L	Hold down for fast-forward
I	Press to jump to the start of the movie
O	Press to jump to the end

Figure 13-17:
When you play your slideshow, Keynote always lets you use your mouse on slides with movies; point to the movie to reveal video controls, which you can use to pause, play, rewind, or fast-forward your video. Drag the ball in the scrubber bar left or right to move quickly to a certain portion of the video.

Keynote gives you a varying set of controls depending on how much space you give it. If you size the movie very small, only the pause button and scrubber bar will be shown, for example. The controls dissolve away when you move the mouse off of the movie.

Managing Multimedia Files

Under the standard settings, Keynote always copies any audio or movie files you include in your presentation into the Keynote document. This is exactly what you want if there's any chance that you might show your presentation on another computer (a possibility you should always plan for, in case your laptop gives up the ghost just as you step to the podium).

The downside, though, is that these audio and movie files can turn your Keynote slideshow into an enormously large file. If you prefer to save disk space and don't want Keynote to import these media files into your document file every time, you can tell it not to: Choose Keynote → Preferences, click the General button, and turn off the "Copy audio and movies into document" option. That lets you choose what you'd like to do on a file-by-file basis, but you have to do this when you first save the file. At the bottom of the Save dialog box, click the Advanced Options flippy arrow, and turn the checkbox on or off for the "Copy audio and movies into document" option. (This option is checked and grayed out if the general preferences are already set to always copy audio and movie files into the document.)

Tip: If you didn't set this option the way that you want it when you first saved the file, you can choose a new setting by saving the file again. Choose File → Save As, give the file a new name, and choose your preference under Advanced Options before clicking Save. Doing this duplicates your Keynote file—but the new version now contains any movie or sound files.

Assuming that you do keep the audio and video files in your document, though, you can still take some steps to reduce the file size. When you shorten the length of a video clip by changing its start and stop end points, you can tell Keynote to leave the unused portion on the cutting room floor, discarding the unused portions from your file. To do this for an individual movie, select the movie and choose Format → Image → Reduce Movie File Size. To do this for all movies in the slide-show in one fell swoop, choose File → Reduce File Size; this also trims audio clips and images, too (see page 447 for what this means for your slideshow's pictures).

Making Noise: Sounds and Soundtracks

You can add sound—music, narration, or sound effects—to a Keynote presentation in three different ways: as a soundtrack for the entire show, as a song or sound effect for a single slide, or as voiceover narration for an auto-playing slideshow. This section focuses on the first two types: adding soundtrack and audio files to your slideshow. For details about recording narration for *recorded slideshows,* see page 512.

The sound files you add to your slides can be single iTunes or GarageBand songs (which don't have to be actual songs—they can be just sounds), a whole playlist, or one or more audio files you have in a folder on your hard drive. Keynote under-stands a wide range of sound files, including MP3, AIFF, AAC, and others.

Adding a Soundtrack

A Keynote *soundtrack* starts playing right from the first slide, and plays through all the slides for as long as the song or playlist lasts. Since a soundtrack affects the whole Keynote document, it doesn't matter which slide you choose when you set it up.

Start by preparing the soundtrack. If you're using more than one song or sound file, assemble them in an iTunes playlist. If your soundtrack consists of a single song or sound file, it doesn't have to be in iTunes—but having it there does make it easier to insert. Then:

1. **Open the Document Inspector and click its Audio tab.**

   If your soundtrack is in iTunes or GarageBand, open the Media Browser and choose the Audio tab—or, in the Document Inspector, just click the iTunes Library button.

2. **Drag a song or a playlist from the Media Browser into the Document Inspector's Audio well (Figure 13-18).**

   If your song or sound file isn't available in the Media Browser, drag the sound file from a folder on your desktop instead.

   You can select and drag multiple songs or playlists into the Audio well at once. But if you're concerned about the order in which Keynote plays your songs, you should really go back into iTunes and create a new playlist with all the music or sounds you need, in the proper order, or you might not get the results you expected.

Tip: GarageBand loops often make for convenient soundtracks because they're specifically designed to sound seamless when they loop end to end. For details on working with GarageBand and loops, open GarageBand and choose Help → GarageBand Help.

3. **Select whether or not you want the song to repeat.**

   Choose Play Once in the Document Inspector's Audio pop-up menu if you want your selected soundtrack to play through once; choose Loop if you want it to play over and over again. The third choice, Off, disables the soundtrack without removing it from the slideshow. You might find this choice useful when you want to play a silent version of your slideshow, or to turn off the music while you're editing.

4. **Use the Document Inspector's Volume slider to reduce your soundtrack's volume. Click the Play button to preview your audio and set the volume level.**

   You should reduce the volume of your overall soundtrack, for example, when you want to add voice-over narration or sound effects for individual slides—which just happens to be the next topic.

Figure 13-18:
When you drag a sound from the Media Browser, drag it to the left or right before dragging upward. If you drag vertically, you select multiple songs. As you drag, Keynote shows a thumbnail of the song's album art if available. Drop the song in the Document Inspector's Audio well to create a soundtrack for the entire slideshow. Then use the Audio pop-up menu to choose whether the soundtrack loops or plays repeatedly, or to turn the soundtrack off.

Adding Sound to a Single Slide

Sound that you add to an individual slide plays only while that slide is onscreen. You can add more than one sound to a slide to layer sounds. For example, you might want to add sound effects or narration over a background music track. Keynote normally plays sounds you add to a slide as soon as the slide appears, and keeps playing it until the sound ends or you advance the slide. However, you can adjust this behavior in the QuickTime Inspector or by using slide builds to play the sound after a preset time interval or to stop the sound early as described on page 481.

Tip: It's not possible in Keynote to play audio for just a selected set of slides. You can either use a soundtrack to play audio through all slides, or you can play audio on a single slide, but you can't create audio for a limited selection. If that's something you really want to do, the only workaround is to add audio to a single slide and then use builds to change your content on that single slide, faking the look of multiple slides. For more on builds, see page 474.

To add a sound to a slide, drag a song or playlist anywhere into the slide canvas, including into a media placeholder, from any of these sources:

• The Media Browser's Audio tab

• The iTunes window

• A folder on your desktop

You can also select Insert → Choose, select a sound file on your hard drive from the Open dialog box, and then click Insert.

To signal that your slide has audio, Keynote represents the sound file with a loud-speaker icon on the slide canvas. You can move the sound icon anywhere on the slide—it's visible only when you're editing; Keynote doesn't show it when you play the slideshow. Double-click the icon when you're editing the slide to play the sound, and single-click it to pause.

Control your playback of single-slide audio clips with the same QuickTime Inspector knobs and sliders that you use for movies (page 452). Although the inspector's Poster Frame slider is inactive for sound files, the rest of the controls work just the same way:

• **Start & Stop slider.** Drag the left handle to the point where you want to start playing the clip; drag the right handle where you want Keynote to cut out.

• **Repeat pop-up menu.** None plays the sound through once without repeating. Loop plays the sound over and over until you advance the slide. Loop Back and Forth plays the sound through forward and then plays it backwards—over and over until you advance the slide. You'd want to choose this last setting for your presentation investigating satanic messages hidden in rock 'n' roll songs.

• **Start movie on click.** Turn on this option to make Keynote wait until you click to start playing the sound; otherwise, it starts playing as soon as the slide appears.

• **Volume slider.** Reduce the playback volume for this sound. You can't make a sound any louder than it originally was, only quieter.

The playback controls at the bottom of the QuickTime Inspector let you preview the sound while you set the volume. (Keynote can't add playback controls to the slide itself; the only start/stop controls are the ones you choose in the inspector window and when you add builds.)

Working with Hyperlinks

Keynote can turn almost any object on a slide—text boxes, images, shapes, table cells, or movies—into a *hyperlink*. Taking a cue from familiar web links, you can also turn individual words into hyperlinks. Clicking a hyperlink beams you away to a new onscreen location, a teleporter built right into your slideshow. Tell Keynote to take you to any of these places when you click a hyperlinked object:

• A specific slide in the presentation

• A different Keynote document

• A web page in your web browser

• A new, preaddressed email message in your email program

• The end of the slideshow, returning you to Keynote's edit mode

Among other things, hyperlinks provide the navigation when you're building a kiosk presentation or any slideshow where your viewers click buttons to steer through the slides on their own (a self-paced lesson, a product catalog). If you're creating a hyperlinks-only presentation (see page 514), you have to create hyperlinks to move from one slide to the next—clicking the mouse button or using the space bar doesn't work. You can create a menu or table of contents, for example, so the viewer can navigate to different parts of the slideshow and add "forward" and "back" buttons to each slide.

To create a hyperlink, select some text or an entire text box, image, shape, table cell, or movie; open the Hyperlink Inspector, turn on the "Enable as a hyperlink" checkbox, and then select the type of hyperlink from the Link To pop-up menu (Figure 13-19). Keynote displays a hyperlink icon—a blue ball, bearing a white arrow—on any object you've turned into a hyperlink. This icon shows only while you're editing the slideshow, not during the presentation.

The Hyperlink Inspector's settings change depending on the type of hyperlink you select. When you choose Exit Slideshow, Keynote shows you no additional options; clicking the hyperlink simply ends the slideshow, depositing you back in edit mode. The other options, however, require more info as described below.

Linking to Slides

Use hyperlinks to create doors between individual slides in your presentation, letting you skip from slide to slide by clicking the links you create. Choose Slide in the Link To menu. From there, you can choose Next slide, Previous slide, First slide, Last slide, Last slide viewed, or Slide [slide number].

The "Last slide viewed" selection can be useful for a button on a menu slide, for example, to return the viewer to the slide they were viewing before they came back to the menu—like the beloved Back button in your web browser.

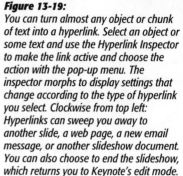

Figure 13-19:
You can turn almost any object or chunk of text into a hyperlink. Select an object or some text and use the Hyperlink Inspector to make the link active and choose the action with the pop-up menu. The inspector morphs to display settings that change according to the type of hyperlink you select. Clockwise from top left: Hyperlinks can sweep you away to another slide, a web page, a new email message, or another slideshow document. You can also choose to end the slideshow, which returns you to Keynote's edit mode.

The "Slide [slide number]" choice can jump to any slide in the slideshow. Type the slide number in the box, or use its pop-up menu to pick the slide number. If you later change the order of the slides, Keynote keeps up with you by changing the hyperlink's slide number so that it continues to point to the same slide. For example, if you choose slide 15, but you later shuffle your slides so that it's now slide 12, the hyperlink updates to point to slide 12.

Surfing the Web

Let your slideshow travel the Web with this most familiar brand of hyperlink, a web link. Choose Webpage in the Link To pop-up menu, then enter the URL—the web address—in the URL field. When you enter this address, feel free to skip the http:// part—just start with www and Keynote fills in the rest.

If you've selected a word or phrase for your hyperlink, that text shows up in the Display field. Changing this text updates the text in your slide, and vice versa. Likewise, if you're in text-entry mode in an empty text box, shape, or table cell—with the insertion point blinking—then anything you type into the Display field appears at the insertion point. Keynote underlines any text you've made a hyperlink, both on the slide canvas while you edit, and in the slideshow. If you've selected an entire object for your web link, the Display menu is grayed out and empty.

When you click a web link during your presentation, you step out of Keynote. Your web browser fires up and takes you to the selected web address. This means that your desktop is visible, but Keynote itself hides so that your presentation isn't visible during your surfing session. After your jaunt around the Web, click the Keynote icon in the Dock to resume your presentation where you left off.

Automatic hyperlinks

Under its standard settings, Keynote automatically detects email and web addresses, and turns them into hyperlinks. So, whenever you type an email or web address, Keynote underlines it and turns it into a hyperlink. If you want to stop this process, you can turn off this feature. To do so, choose Keynote → Preferences and then click the Auto-Correction button. Two checkboxes control Keynote's hyperlink behavior:

- **"Automatically detect email and web addresses"**. Turn this option on to make Keynote hyperlink any email or web page address that begins with "www," "ftp," or "http" without a visit to the Hyperlink Inspector.

- **"Underline text hyperlinks on creation"**. Turn on this option to make Keynote underline all email or web address hyperlinks—whether they were automatically detected, or you created them in the Hyperlink Inspector.

Linking to Other Slideshows

Jump right into another slideshow by adding a hyperlink to another Keynote document. Clicking one of these links during a presentation takes you to the first slide of the target slideshow.

Choose Keynote Slideshow from the Link To pop-up menu, and click the Choose button. Locate the file on your hard drive in the Open dialog box, and click Open. Keynote adds the file's path to the Name field—though you probably see only a small part of the path in the small window. To read the entire path, hold your arrow cursor over the Name field to reveal it in a pop-up tool tip.

The Display field works the same way as it does for a web page link (described above).

Sending Email

Choose Email Message from the Link To pop-up menu to create a link that opens a new message in your email program—preaddressed, with the subject line filled in, ready to begin writing a message. This can be a handy way to get instant feedback from viewers of a self-paced lesson, or to collect contact information from potential customers at a trade show. Enter the email address for the message in the To field, and enter a subject line for the message in the Subject field.

MEMORY LANE

Web View in the Rearview

Previous versions of Keynote offered a feature called *web view,* which let you embed a screenshot of a web page in your slideshow; Keynote could reach out to the Web to update this snapshot on demand. Alas, this feature was removed in iWork '09.

This change means that when you want to include screenshots of web pages, you have to take them yourself. Fortunately, Mac OS X gives you a program called Grab to make it easy to take *screen grabs,* a picture of your entire screen, a single window, or a specific portion of your screen:

1. In your web browser, open the page you want to include in your slideshow.

2. Launch Grab from your Mac's Applications → Utilities folder.

3. In Grab, choose Capture → Window.

   Like any good photographer, Grab gives you a moment to pose before clicking the shutter. Take a moment to get your browser window sized and prepped just the way you want it.

4. Click Grab's Choose Window button, then click the browser window.

Grab snaps its picture, opening the resulting image in a new window.

5. Choose File → Save As to select a location to save your image.

   Grab saves your image as a TIFF format image file.

6. In Keynote, select Insert → Choose, browse to the picture you just saved, and click Insert.

You can also use a keyboard shortcut to copy a screenshot to your clipboard without ever using Grab: Press ⌘-Shift-Control-4, and your cursor turns into a crosshair. Drag across the portion of the screen to copy, and release the mouse. Go to your Keynote slide, and choose Edit → Paste to add the screenshot to the slide. (Want to grab the whole window? Instead of dragging when you see the crosshair, press the Space Bar, and the cursor turns into a camera. Click the window to grab, and your Mac copies its picture to the clipboard.)

To make your screenshot clickable so that it also takes you to the actual web page, select the image in Keynote, and add a web link in the Hyperlink Inspector.

The Display field works the same way as it does for a web page link (described above).

Note to Self: Add a Comment

Keynote doesn't offer the same kind of detailed change-tracking that you'll find in Pages, but it does let you add sticky-note comments to your slides—a quick way to leave yourself reminders or let colleagues suggest changes for your presentation. One useful way to use comments, for example, is to slap them on your slides after doing a first-pass run-through of your presentation (see page 378)—quick, casual notes to capture your first impressions of where changes need to be made: "Needs better transition," "Got lost here," "Where are the stats?" and so on.

To add a comment to a slide, click the toolbar's Comment button or choose Insert → Comment. Keynote adds a yellow sticky note on top of your slide (Figure 13-20). Type your suggestion, reminder, or hare-brained idea, and Keynote scrawls it onto the comment in the Mac's handwritten-ish Marker Felt font.

Tip: Not a fan of yellow sticky notes? Change a comment's color by clicking the comment and choosing a new fill color from the Format Bar or Graphic Inspector.

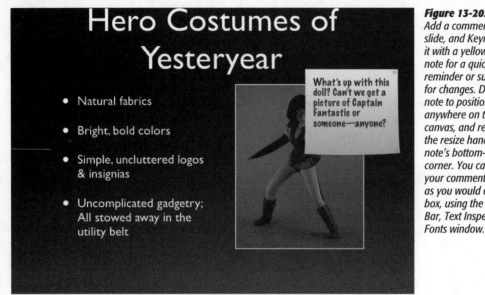

Figure 13-20:
Add a comment to a slide, and Keynote slaps it with a yellow sticky-note for a quick visual reminder or suggestion for changes. Drag the note to position it anywhere on the slide canvas, and resize it with the resize handle in the note's bottom-right corner. You can format your comment text just as you would edit a text box, using the Format Bar, Text Inspector, and Fonts window.

Like objects, comments are added on top of the slide canvas, so your new comment may obscure parts of your slide, but you can use the commands in the Arrange menu to move the up or down in the layer stack. Drag the comment where it's most useful on the slide, and resize it by dragging the resize handle in its bottom right. Delete the comment by clicking the X close icon in the top right of the note. Hide comments without deleting them by choosing View → Hide Comments; bring them back with View → Show Comments.

Comments never appear in the slideshow you show to your audience, but if you have a presenter display set up while making a presentation, you can make the comments appear there. Be careful, though; you can't move the comments during the presentation, so they may hide parts of your slide that you'd like to be able to see during your talk. In general, you're better off using presenter notes for comments and reminders you want to keep handy during your talk. While comments sit in the frame of your slides, presenter notes keep to themselves in a separate pane. For the details, head back to page 406.

Tip: To print slides with your comments visible, make sure the comments are showing on the slide canvas before you print. Choose View → Show Comments.

Changing Slide Backgrounds

Every master slide has a background that matches the other slides in its theme. It's usually a good idea to stick with these matching slide backgrounds for the sake of maintaining a consistent appearance throughout your slideshow. However, you may want to set off different segments of a presentation with different themes, or sometimes create a slide that diverges completely from the status quo.

To change the slide background, open the Slide Inspector and click the Appearance tab. The bottom section of the Inspector controls the slide background. Most slides that are part of a theme use an image fill background. Click the upper pop-up menu in the Background section and choose one of the following background fill types:

- **None.** As you might expect, this choice removes the background entirely, rendering the background white. This is as close as you can get to the retina-burning white screen of a jammed slide projector. Unless you're going to be filling this white space with a lot of text or objects, it's probably not a very good choice. Unlike the printed page, in the projection business white space is not your friend.

Tip: The None option is more useful when you want to export the slideshow in QuickTime format (see page 519) for use in another video project. In that case, the background is actually transparent, so your slides and animations appear on whatever background you use in your video.

- **Color Fill.** If you choose this, a color well appears in the inspector. Click the color well to summon the Color Picker, where you can choose a solid color for the background.

- **Gradient Fill.** Choose this style to create a gradient—a gradual blending from one color into another. Keynote displays two color wells in the Inspector in order to choose those two colors. In addition, you can control the angle of the shifting colors with the Angle knob, the direction arrows, or by typing an angle directly into the angle measurement box. See page 267 for details.

- **Image Fill.** Choose this option if you want a photograph or other image for a slide background. Image Fill is probably selected if you're working on a slide that's part of a theme—the theme background is an image. Keynote displays an image well at the bottom of the Inspector. To use your own image for a background, drag an image file from your hard drive or from the Media Browser into the image well, or click Choose and select an image file from the Open dialog box that appears.

The lower pop-up menu in the Background section of the Slide Inspector determines how Keynote displays your chosen image in the background. The various scaling options let you choose to display the picture at its original size, scaled to just fit the background, scaled and cropped to fill the background, stretched to fill the background, or—if it's a very small original—tiled over the background. See page 269 for more details on how image fills work.

• **Tinted Image Fill.** This final choice in the background fill menu is a variation on Image Fill in which you can blend a color with the image in order to, for example, make a rosy sunrise picture even rosier. This is also the trick for dimming a background image by tinting it black or white. You'll find details on page 271.

Adding Slide Numbers

You can add the Keynote equivalent of a page number—a slide number—to any slide. Open the Slide Inspector's Appearance tab and turn on the checkbox for Slide Number. Keynote inserts the slide number, centered, at the bottom of the slide as a free text box. You can reformat the number or reposition this text box just like any other free text box. But unlike other text boxes, you can't add text or replace the number—since Keynote updates the number if you move the slide to a different position in the show. If you want your slide number to read, "Slide number 5," for example, you have to add another free text box to hold the words "Slide number."

If you want to use slide numbers throughout your presentation, you probably want to add the slide number to your slide masters, as described on page 541.

And speaking of slide masters, dear reader, that's exactly what you are now—a master of Keynote slide design. How'd you like that transition? And hey, *speaking of transitions*... That's one of the primary subjects of the next chapter, which introduces motion, animation, and yes, slide-to-slide transitions. You'll take your new black-belt knowledge of creating lovely but static slides and mix in some motion. Turn the page to learn how to make your slides dance, shimmy, and shake across the screen.

Animating Your Slides

Over the course of the last few chapters, you've written, organized, and designed your slides into the perfect presentation. Congratulations—you've no doubt got an elegant and insightful slideshow on your hands. But even after all your care and attention, your presentation still isn't all that different from an old-fashioned slide-show—a collection of static slides that march past your audience one after the other. It's time to make some waves in your slides' still waters by adding motion to your presentation, animating your slides with *transitions* and *builds*.

Transitions work their magic *between* slides, moving you from one slide to the next with effects that range from subtle dissolves to bombastic explosions that send objects flying on and off the screen. Builds, on the other hand, happen *within* individual slides, letting you pull the strings of objects and bullet points to make them appear, disappear, move, grow, shrink—and generally dance on your slide.

Besides adding some visual excitement to your slideshow, transitions and builds can help you present your information more clearly, add drama, signal changes in topic, and—if you use them wisely—give your slideshow a professional polish. This chapter takes you through Keynote's special-effects laboratory to show you how to add slide transitions and program your objects for builds.

Adding Transitions

Until you add a transition between slides, Keynote switches instantly from one slide to another—a quick change known as a *hard cut* to film editors. Transitions soften the hard cut, easing from one slide to another with a visual effect. Keynote offers 27 transition styles to choose from, and you owe it to yourself to try 'em all just so you know what's available. Be adventurous in your experimentation but judicious in what you actually choose for your final presentation. Go easy on the flash and sparkle—you're building a presentation, after all, not a pinball machine. You don't want your audience to walk away impressed by your fancy transitions—but unable to remember your message.

Transitions serve two very different purposes in a slideshow: They can create smooth and subtle segues from one slide to another, or they can provide dramatic punctuations that highlight the break between slides. When you choose transitions, think about whether your goal is to move smoothly to the next slide, provide a noticeable break between topics, or startle the audience with your visual derring-do.

Consider your message and your audience as you choose transitions. If your presentation is a morale booster for the cheerleading team, you can probably get away with anything. But if you own a funeral home and your presentation to the bereaved describes the various services you offer, you might want to drop the rah-rah sizzle in favor of a more reserved set of transitions. If you have any doubt about which transition to use, err on the side of simplicity.

To insert a transition between two slides, you add it to the *first* slide in the pair. It can help to think of transitions as graceful exits—you apply a transition to a slide to determine exactly how it passes the torch to the next slide. In the slide navigator, Keynote indicates transitions by adding a small blue triangle to the bottom-right corner of thumbnails (Figure 14-1).

Tip: Because transitions control the flow to the next slide only, you can't create a transition into the *first* slide of the presentation. If you want to start with a transition, you need to create a blank slide for the beginning of the show and transition from that to your "real" first slide.

To add a transition, select the slide(s) to work on, and then go to the Slide Inspector → Transition pane (Figure 14-2). (When you add a transition to several slides at once, it becomes the exit transition for each of the selected slides.) Choose your transition style from the Effect pop-up menu, which divides the available styles into several categories. At the very top of the menu, choose None to strip the slide of any transition, reverting to Keynote's standard hard cut. Below that, the Effect pop-up menu offers a list of Recent Effects, showing the last few transitions you used in your slideshow. Consider this a subtle encouragement to reuse the same transitions rather than cramming as many variations as possible into your slideshow. Transitions are like fonts: You usually need only one or two styles in a single presentation.

After those options, the Effect pop-up finally lists the full menu of transitions, starting with Keynote's fanciest effects (Magic Move, text effects, and object effects) down to more traditional 3D and 2D effects. Start by exploring the relatively commonplace 2D effects and then gradually climb up the Effects menu to more complex transitions.

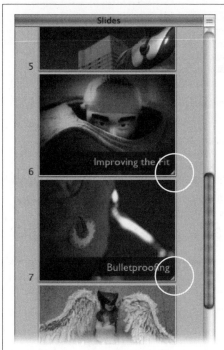

Figure 14-1:
Keynote reminds you that you've added a transition to a slide by adding a tiny blue triangle to its thumbnail in the slide navigator (circled). When you play the slideshow, the transition appears between the indicated slide and the slide that follows.

Note: Depending on your computer and its video card, you may see another section at the bottom of the menu titled "Effects that can't play on this computer". Since Keynote's fancier transitions require a lot of video horsepower, older Macs with underpowered video hardware can't always handle them all. But just because they won't play on your computer doesn't mean you can't use these transitions in your slideshow. If you transfer the slideshow to a computer that does have the necessary hardware, the transitions play just fine; on other computers, they appear as simple dissolves.

If you find that you nearly always use the same transition between slides, save yourself some time by adding that transition to your master slides. This makes your selected transition the standard offering for all slides based on the masters you select. For more on editing master slides, see page 538.

Switching Slides with 2D and 3D Effects

Unlike the other transition categories, which add effects to individual objects on your slides, 2D and 3D transitions apply a single effect to the entire slide, treating each slide as a single card rather than a collection of elements: The whole screen sweeps away at once to make room for the next. These effects are also the most traditionally cinematic, featuring many styles that have been (or once were) reliable standbys in Hollywood editing rooms.

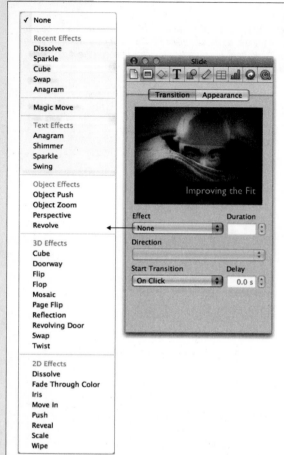

Figure 14-2:
You control and preview slide transitions from the Slide Inspector's Transition tab. Choose a transition from the Effect pop-up menu, and Keynote plays it for you in the Preview window. Click the Preview window to play the transition again.

Change how long the transition lasts using the Duration field. You can set transition durations anywhere from a fraction of a second up to 60 seconds—but most of them look best in the 1- to 2-second range. Many transition effects move from one side of the screen to the other, move in or out, and so on. Use the Direction pop-up menu to choose which way the effects move.

The Start Transition pop-up menu controls whether Keynote switches to the next slide only when you click the mouse or press the space bar (choose "On click") or automatically after a specified amount of time (choose "Automatically").

The 2D effects in particular offer a range of effects inspired by the early years of the silver screen (see Figure 14-3):

- **Dissolve.** The first slide fades out as the next fades in, so that one slide appears to melt into the next.

- **Fade through color.** The first slide fades to a solid-colored screen (black, for example) and then the next slide fades in. Choose the color to use with this effect carefully. With a very short Duration setting and a non-black color, this effect seems to "flash" the next slide into existence. Use a longer duration, fading through black, to create a languorous transition familiar to old Hollywood.

- **Iris.** A growing or shrinking circle reveals the next slide. When you choose Out from the Direction pop-up, the next slide sprouts from the center of the first. When you choose In, the first slide disappears in a shrinking spotlight to reveal the next.

- **Move In.** The next slide flies in from the side or corner, gliding over the first slide, which stays in a fixed position in the background.

- **Push.** The next slide pushes the first out of the way. Keynote slides the two screens up or down, left or right, as if they were on a single, continuous strip.

- **Reveal.** The first screen slides away to reveal the next. This transition is like the Move In effect, except that the *first* slide moves while the second remains fixed in the background.

- **Scale.** This effect combines a dissolve with an effect that causes one of the two slides to grow or shrink, depending on the direction you choose:

  — **Up** makes the next slide spring from the center of the screen.

  — **Down** makes the first slide shrink into the center.

  — **In** makes the next slide fall into the frame from extreme close-up to full screen.

  — **Out** makes the first slide zoom toward the viewer and fade out.

- **Wipe.** The first slide disappears as if you were wiping it away with a giant squeegee, revealing the second slide behind it. You can wipe from any side or corner.

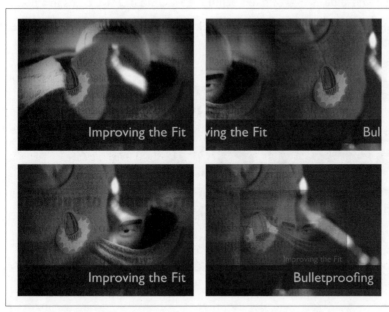

Figure 14-3:
Keynote's 2D transitions recall old-school movie techniques. Clockwise from top left: Iris uses a growing or shrinking circle to reveal the next slide (here, the second slide appears in a spotlight growing from the center of the slide); Push nudges the first screen to the side to make room for the next; Scale dissolves the two slides while shrinking or enlarging one of them (here, the first slide shrinks away to the center of the screen); and Wipe clears away the first slide to reveal the second one beneath it.

Keynote's 3D effects create the illusion of depth (see Figure 14-4), giving the sense that your slides are moving through space rather than on a flat plane:

- **Cube.** The screen appears to turn as if it were a block with the two slides pasted onto neighboring sides.

- **Doorway.** The first slide splits open at the middle like a pair of doors and the next slide zooms forward across a slick reflective "floor".

- **Flip.** The slide flips like a postcard, revealing the second slide on the reverse. You can flip it from side to side, top to bottom, or bottom to top.

- **Flop.** The first slide folds at the middle as if it were the two-page spread of a calendar (when you choose "Top to Bottom") or a book (when you choose either "Left to Right" or "Right to Left"). The effect reveals the second slide as if it were the next two-page spread in the book.

- **Mosaic.** The first slide fractures into 35 tiles, and they turn in a wave to reveal the second slide displayed on the flip side of the tiles.

- **Page Flip.** The first slide peels away from one corner, as if you're turning a page to reveal the second slide behind it.

- **Reflection.** This is like the Cube effect viewed from *inside* the cube. The two slides look like they're joined at a corner; they zoom out and rotate across a reflective surface to bring the second slide into view.

- **Revolving Door.** The first slide spins out of view to reveal the second—as if the two slides were mounted on revolving doors spinning in front of you.

- **Swap.** The first slide swings out and behind the second like two cards in a deck.

- **Twist.** Keynote wrings the slide like a towel, twisting it to reveal the next screen on the other side.

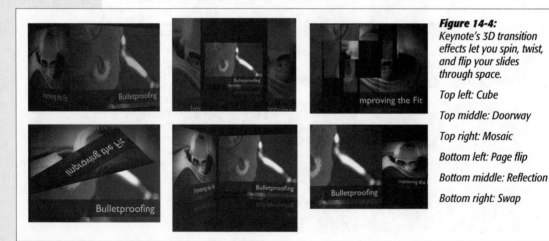

Figure 14-4:
Keynote's 3D transition effects let you spin, twist, and flip your slides through space.

Top left: Cube

Top middle: Doorway

Top right: Mosaic

Bottom left: Page flip

Bottom middle: Reflection

Bottom right: Swap

Adding Object Effects

While the 2D and 3D transition effects move slides as single cards on the screen, *object effects* move every object on your slide individually. Every screen element—even individual bullet points, in some cases—moves independently as you switch to a new slide. Object effects are at their most dramatic for transitions between slides with several images or other objects on each screen and when both slides have the same background.

Object effects are often best used when you're continuing on the same or similar topic as the previous slide. That's because they make it look as if you remain on a single slide while words and pictures move on and off. Individual objects swap out for other objects, creating the illusion that you're not changing slides so much as changing specific elements—introducing new points rather than an entirely new topic.

Object effects include:

- **Object Push.** Like the 2D Push effect, the first screen slides out of the way to make room for the second. Here, however, the objects on the slide move in a staggered sequence, so that every bullet point, image, chart, and table moves on and off the screen at its own pace.

- **Object Zoom.** Every object from the first slide zooms out (in turn) at the viewer and gets replaced by the objects from the second slide, which zip into place from the far distance.

- **Perspective.** This one scatters your slide elements to the wind as the next slide's objects fly in from all slides. The first slide tilts into the distance and its graphics fly in all four directions while the second slide's elements scramble to assemble (Figure 14-5).

- **Revolve.** Every object on the first slide flips like a sheet of paper to disappear, while the individual elements of the second slide flip to reveal themselves.

Figure 14-5:
The Perspective object effect dispatches every graphic and bullet point on the first slide (left) in all directions as the elements of the new slide fly in (middle) to assemble into the complete second slide (right).

Wordplay with Text Effects

Like object effects, *text effects* create slide transitions by transforming individual objects—this time, though, the effect focuses only on the slides' text, right down to animating individual letters. Other graphic elements dissolve in and out to complete the transition.

The result is a clever replacement of one word or phrase with another. This is perfect for slides with large, prominent text, like two title-only slides where you want to show movement from one concept to another: "Consumption" transforms to "Conservation"; "Bruce Wayne" changes to "Batman"; and so on. For best results, make sure that the text on both slides is in the same font and font size; with the exception of the Anagram effect, it's a good idea to make sure the text is in the same spot on the slide, too. The text-effect transitions include:

- **Anagram.** Use this one when the text on the two slides contains several of the same letters; Keynote shuffles the letters from the first slide into place for the second slide. (If the two slides don't share any letters, you might be disappointed, since you're not giving this effect any material to work with.) The Direction pop-up menu lets you choose between Straight Across, which slides the letters left and right, or Arcing, which makes the letters hop into place.

- **Shimmer.** This effect lights up the words on the first slide in magic pixie dust, making them transform dazzlingly into the words on the second slide.

- **Sparkle.** This transition lights a fuse under your slideshow, sending a field of sparks running across the text on the first slide, changing it to the text on the next slide as it goes.

- **Swing.** Text boxes on the first slide swing as if hanging from their top edges, spinning up and around and transforming into the words on the second slide, which swing for a moment before coming to a halt.

Magic Move Transitions

Keynote's object and text effects make for useful transitions when you're replacing the objects on one slide with completely new ones. But what about when you have the same object on both slides? That's where *Magic Move* comes in, gracefully animating a graphic from slide to slide. While an object effect would sling all of one slide's objects offscreen to make room for the next slide, the Magic Move transition is more discriminating. The "magic" kicks in when Keynote identifies images, shapes, or text boxes that appear on both slides and glides them—voilà!—to their new locations on the second slide. Meanwhile, other objects from the old slide dissolve away as new ones fade in.

Say that your title slide features the enormous and impressive logo of SuperMega-Corp, and the second slide repeats the logo, this time tucked away in the bottom-right corner. With the Magic Move transition (Figure 14-6), the logo coasts smoothly down into the corner, shrinking as it goes, as the rest of the slide's new content fades in. Did you catch the sleight of hand that Keynote sneaked into that last sentence? It not only *moved* the logo, it shrank it, too. Magic Move lets you move, resize, rotate, and fade objects from slide to slide. Flip them, add shadows, change color fill, add reflections—Magic Move "tweens" all these changes, morphing the object into its new look.

The secret behind Keynote's magic trick is that the transition works only when you start with the *same* image, shape, or text box on both slides. Keynote is pretty clever about figuring out which objects are the "same," but for the most foolproof

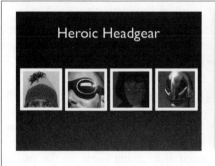

Figure 14-6:
The Magic Move transition finds objects that appear on both slides and moves them smoothly to their new spots on the second slide. This is a good way to draw attention to one graphic among many. Here, the helmet image on the right side of the first slide moves, grows, rotates, and sprouts a reflection in the Magic Move transition to the second slide. The other images dissolve away as the text of the new slide fades in.

results, it's a good idea to copy the object from one slide to the next. You can do this by pasting an object from the first slide to the second slide, or by duplicating the *entire* first slide and then modifying its contents to make the second. As far as Keynote is concerned, the clones on the two slides are now linked. No matter how you might bump them around and change their object properties on either slide, the Magic Move transition keeps up, gliding the object from one slide to the next.

Note: Magic Move doesn't work with tables, charts, movies, or grouped objects. Also, it doesn't work on shapes or text boxes if you change the text they contain.

For best results with Magic Move, follow these steps:

1. **Create your first slide with all the elements that you want to use.**

2. **Select the slide in the slide navigator and duplicate it by choosing Edit → Duplicate.**

3. **In the duplicate slide, change one (or more) of the objects on the page by repositioning, resizing, rotating, or changing its opacity, color, reflection, or shadow.**

   You can change the object's *properties*, but not its *content*. Magic Move works only on objects that have the exact same text (for text boxes or shapes) or picture on both slides. Other objects simply dissolve in and out during the transition.

4. **Add any other objects you want on your new slide, and delete any objects you don't.**

5. **Select the first slide and choose Magic Move from the Slide Inspector's Effect pop-up menu.**

   When you play the slideshow, the shared objects morph to their new locations and sizes on the second slide.

Old-School Transitions

Want even more transitions? Keynote keeps a few older effects tucked away in the basement. These transitions, considered "obsolete" in Apple's words, are vestiges of previous versions of Keynote. With the factory settings, these animations are hidden so you only get to choose from the most modern, fancy-pants effects. But all the oldies are there if you want 'em: Go to Keynote → Preferences and, in the General pane, turn on the "Include obsolete animations in choices" option. Keynote adds such classic transitions as Confetti, Burn, and Falling Tiles, among many others. Despite the "obsolete" label, these effects work just fine—Apple simply thinks you're better off (and decidedly more stylish) using some of the fresher effects. Turning on this option also adds additional effects for object builds, the subject of the next section.

Adding Object Builds

While slide transitions create animations between slides, *object builds* add animations *within* a slide. Builds got their name because they originally did just one thing: gradually added elements to a slide, *building* it up block by block until the whole slide was in place. Although builds' features have expanded with each generation of presentation software, this building function is still very much at the center of what builds do. This lets you do things like make bullet points appear one by one; bring pictures, shapes, or other objects onto the slide individually or in groups; or gradually display a pie chart slice by slice as you talk through each of its elements.

These industrious construction workers are called *build ins* because they add new objects to your slide. Their counterparts—the demolition workers—are called *build outs* and, as you might guess, their role is to remove objects from a slide. Both types of builds can be strictly practical, simply popping the object on or off the screen. But Keynote provides lots of eye candy you can use to introduce objects into slides, with an impressive selection of animation styles that make your graphics plunge, blaze, pop, and sparkle as they materialize onscreen. (As with transitions, discretion is advised when creating object builds. It's nice to have all these options available, but not every slide needs its text to appear as if it's been shot from a machine gun or whirled in a Cuisinart.)

Builds aren't only about grand entrances and exits, however. *Action builds* let you move objects from place to place on a slide—and shrink, grow, or rotate them while you're at it. A particularly clever type of build, the *smart build*, focuses on images, letting you create a photo slideshow *inside* your slide. But let's not get ahead of ourselves. Every builder needs a good foundation, and for Keynote builds, it all begins with build ins and build outs.

Creating Build Ins and Build Outs

The basic process for creating object builds on a slide is to select an object—a text box, picture, or shape, for example—and use the Build Inspector to control how and when each object appears and disappears from the slide. The build in (when objects appear on the slide) and the build out (when objects disappear from the slide) are completely separate operations. You can have either one without the other, or you can have both (or none at all).

The basics of setting up a build are a lot like adding a transition, except that you apply the effect to an individual object:

1. **Select an object on the slide that you want to build.**

    The object you pick can be any kind of text box, a single bulleted item, a picture, chart, table, movie, or sound file.

2. **Open the Build Inspector (Figure 14-7). Click the Build In tab to determine how this object appears on the slide, or the Build Out tab to determine how it disappears from the slide.**

3. **Click the Effect pop-up menu to choose an animation style for your build.**

    The Appear and Disappear effects give you a plain-vanilla entrance and exit, respectively; the rest of the selections offer a dizzying array of equally dizzying effects that make the object fly, materialize, spin, and twirl in and out of view. As you browse these effects, Keynote displays each effect in the Preview window. To see an effect again, click the Preview window.

4. **Choose a direction for your effect in the Direction pop-up menu, if applicable.**

    Like transitions, many build effects let you choose whether an object makes its entrance from the left or right, by plunging down from above, and so on. Use the Direction pop-up menu to give your object its stage directions.

5. **Tell Keynote how much time you want it to spend performing the effect.**

    Enter a number of seconds in the Duration field, or use its up and down arrow button.

That's it—you've just added a basic build to your slide! Enjoy its full onscreen effect by playing the slideshow. If you created a build *in*, the slide first appears without the object when you play the slideshow. Trigger the build by clicking your mouse or pressing the space bar; instead of advancing to the next slide as Keynote normally would, your object materializes onscreen. Likewise, when a slide contains a build *out*, the object is initially included on the screen and clicking the mouse or pressing the space bar sends the object on its way.

When you add several builds to the same slide, Keynote normally marches through them one at a time; each time you click during your presentation, Keynote triggers the next build. After all the builds are complete, clicking advances to the following slide.

You can control the order that builds take place on a slide using the Build Inspector's Order pop-up menu—or drag builds up or down in the inspector's Build Order Drawer, which you open by clicking the More Options button. You can also make builds happen simultaneously or trigger them automatically after a specific amount of time. For the full story on controlling build order, see page 484.

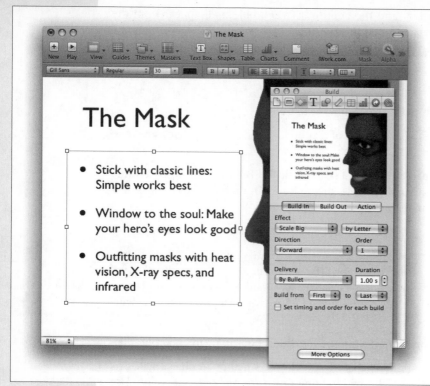

Figure 14-7:
When you add a build to a text box, you can choose to make Keynote show or hide its bullet points one at a time. Choose an option from the Delivery pop-up menu to give each bullet point its own moment to shine.

Tip: You can also add a build to a set of grouped objects (see page 433 for details on Keynote's Group command). When you do this, the entire group builds in or out as if it were a single object. Be careful, though: If you ungroup the objects, then Keynote tosses out the build; even if you regroup the objects later, you have to add the effect all over again. One workaround for this is to copy the group's build settings before you ungroup the objects: Select the group, choose Format → Copy Animation. Then, after you regroup the objects, choose Format → Paste Animation to restore the group's build settings. See page 494 for more about copying builds.

When you first create your build, the animation applies to the entire object (or group). The whole text box, for example, materializes or vanishes at once when you play the slideshow. With the exception of pictures, however, all objects contain additional content elements—bullet points, graph bars, table rows, and so on—and you can make Keynote reveal these elements individually instead of all at once. The specific options vary according to the type of object you're working with, as explained in the following sections.

Building text boxes and shapes

Body text boxes, free text boxes, and shapes offer options that let you build the text bullet by bullet or paragraph by paragraph. When you're giving your presentation, that means you can reveal each bullet point as you discuss it (so your audience doesn't read ahead), or get rid of each bullet when you're done talking about it.

The result is that each bullet point gets its very own build—clicking the mouse or pressing the space bar steps through the build for each bullet in the text box.

You can control how Keynote reveals the text of the selected text box by choosing an option from the Build Inspector's Delivery pop-up menu (see Figure 14-7). "All at Once" is the standard setting and applies the build to the entire text box at once, with no individual treatment of the content inside. From there, body text boxes get special treatment with three additional bullet options:

- **By Bullet.** Choose this option to build one bullet at a time.

- **By Bullet Group.** For nested bulleted lists, this option steps through each top-level bullet at a time, simultaneously building any bullets indented below it.

- **By Highlighted Bullet.** This method steps through the bullets one at a time like the By Bullet option, but dims preceding bullets so that only the current bullet is highlighted, as shown in Figure 14-8.

Shapes and free text boxes don't enjoy these various bullet options; they get only the By Paragraph option, which applies a separate build to each paragraph, like the By Bullet feature above. Title text boxes can contain only a single paragraph, so they don't get the extra build options enjoyed by other text boxes.

Tip: *Some text effects let you further choose how to apply the effect—making it happen letter by letter, word by word, or all at once. Dissolve, Flip, Move Out, Pop, and Scale Big all let you make the choice; just select from the pop-up menu to the right of the Build Inspector's Effect pop-up menu.*

Figure 14-8:
As you build a text box with the Highlighted Bullet Delivery option selected, Keynote fades previous bullet points and highlights the most recent one.

When you choose one of these bullet or paragraph Delivery options, the Build Inspector reveals the "Build from" pop-up menus. The standard setting is "First to Last", so that Keynote builds every item in the text box. If you want to apply the effect to only *some* of the items in the text box, choose the bullet numbers to start and end in the two pop-up menus.

Keynote normally treats all the builds for a text block as a single group, building the items one after the other as you click through them in your presentation. However, you may want to blend in other builds as you step through your list. Say you want to reveal a new picture every time you go to a new item in a product list. To do that, click "Set timing and order for each build" in the Build Inspector and Keynote shows every bullet point as its own item in the Build Order Drawer so you can reorder each one individually. For details on ordering builds, see page 484.

Note: While you can change the order of builds for individual bullets to interweave them with other object builds, text builds can only happen from the top down. You can't make the last bullet build before the first, for example.

Building tables

Tables are chock full of content bits and pieces—rows, columns, cells, and the text inside them. Keynote gives you a variety of ways to gradually show or hide these elements, letting your content take its place at the table little by little. With the following techniques, you can build dramatic tension as you reveal your table data and build up to the final column, for example, to show this year's sales figures for—*wait for it!*—utility belts, capes, and X-ray vision goggles.

To begin, select a table, use the Build Inspector to choose whether to build in or build out, and then select a build effect, direction, and duration as described above. Then choose one of the following table build options from the Delivery pop-up menu:

- **All at Once.** This is the standard delivery option. Keynote treats the whole table as a single object.

- **By Row.** Choose this option to build in the table one row at a time, starting at the top; or build out the table one row at a time, starting at the bottom. (To go the other direction, choose Bottom Up—explained later in this list—instead.)

- **By Column.** This option builds in the table one column at a time, starting at the left; or builds out the table one column at a time, starting at the right.

- **By Cell.** Select this option to build in the table one cell at a time, left to right and top to bottom. When building out, this option removes cells one at a time beginning at the bottom right.

- **By Row Content.** This option first builds in the entire table, but with all of its cells empty, then fills in the cells' contents row by row. When building out, Keynote reverses the process, removing the contents of each row from the bottom up and finally removing the entire, now-empty table.

- **By Column Content.** Like By Row Content, this option first builds in the empty table and then fills in each column's content. When building out, Keynote removes the contents of each column before deleting the table's framework.

- **By Cell Content.** Choose this option to build in the table's structure followed by the cells' contents, one cell at a time starting at the top left. When building out, Keynote removes the contents of each cell starting at the lower right before finally removing the table's framework.

- **Bottom Up.** This option is the same as By Row but in reverse order. Build ins add the table one row at a time starting from the bottom. Build outs remove the rows from the top (which is a little confusing given the name of this option).

- **Bottom Up – Content.** This option has the same effect as By Row Content but in reverse—it builds in from the bottom up, and builds out from the top down.

No matter which delivery options you choose, all the table's elements share the same build effect. Building in and building out, however, are separate actions, so you can make a table leave the slide in a different way than it arrived. You could, for example, build in the table by row content with the Move In effect, and then build out by column with the Dissolve effect.

To coordinate or interweave the builds for your table with those of other objects, turn on the Build Inspector's "Set timing and order for each build" checkbox. As with bullets in text builds, this option lets you change the build order of each table element or specify its own build timing. For details on controlling build order, see page 484.

Building charts

Like tables, you can build a chart into or out of a slide all at once—like any other object—or gradually, to dramatically assemble or disassemble the chart from its various elements. Throw a pie across your slideshow by sending the wedges of a pie chart flying, or make the columns of your bar chart stand up one at a time. The order is determined by the order your data appears in the Chart Data Editor (see page 314).

To begin building a chart, select the chart and use the Build Inspector to choose either build in or build out, a build effect, direction, and duration. Then choose one of the following chart build options from the Delivery pop-up menu. For 2D charts, your options are:

- **All at Once.** This is the standard delivery option; Keynote treats the chart as a single object.

- **Background First.** Choose this option and Keynote builds in the chart in two steps: first the background, axes, and gridlines; then the chart's data.

- **By Series.** Select this option and Keynote first adds the chart's background and then adds its data, one data series at a time.

- **By Set.** When you choose this option, Keynote first adds the chart's background and then adds its data, one data set at a time.

Tip: Need to brush up on the difference between data series and data sets? See page 313.

- **By Element in Series.** With this option, Keynote first adds the chart's background and then adds each data point, one data series at a time.

- **By Element in Set.** You guessed it—Keynote first adds the chart's background and then adds each individual data point, one data set at a time.

- **By Wedge.** This option is available only for pie charts. Choose it, and Keynote adds the pie chart to the slide one slice at a time.

Note: Keynote gives you only three options for area charts: All At Once, Background First, and By Series. When you build a pie chart, you get only two choices: "All at Once" and By Wedge.

3D charts offer the same set of delivery options listed above—for Keynote's 2D build effects, at least. Keynote also adds several remarkable 3D effects that provide a dramatic drumroll for your three-dimensional data, letting viewers seemingly swoop and swirl around the chart as it comes into view. These effects are listed under a separate 3D category in the Effect pop-up (Figure 14-9):

- **Crane.** Swoops into the chart as it spins and grows, like a Hollywood crane shot. Build outs do the same thing but pull *back*.

- **Grow.** The bars, lines, or wedges of your chart sprout into view for build ins, and shrink away for build outs.

- **Radial.** For pie charts only: The wedges fly into the center for build ins, and explode out for build outs.

- **Rotate.** The chart spins horizontally into place.

- **Rotate & Grow.** Two great tastes that grow great together: This one combines the Grow and Rotate effects into a single simultaneous effect.

- **Z Axis.** The chart pushes into the slide as if nudged in from the audience's side of the screen. For build outs, the chart zooms toward the viewers and out of the screen.

With 3D effects, Keynote giveth, and Keynote taketh away; except for the Grow effect, these 3D builds have fewer delivery options than their 2D cousins. Most of the 3D effects have just two: "All at Once" and Cascade, which gradually reveals all the data points in a wave.

No matter what build effect you choose when you build a chart, the chart's background and data elements all use that same effect. But you can choose different build effects for building in and building out.

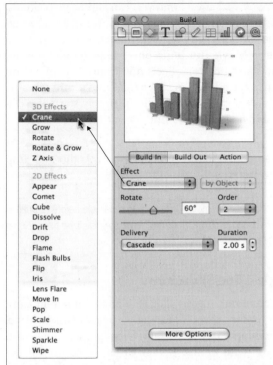

Figure 14-9:
3D charts get special treatment in the Build Inspector, with a special category of 3D effects for build ins and build outs.

If you include the chart's legend on your slide, it's treated separately from the chart itself and gets its own build. You can group the legend and chart together by Shift-clicking both to select them and then choosing Arrange → Group; this lets you combine them into the same build, but then you're limited to the "All at Once" delivery option. You're better off creating separate builds—one for the legend and one for the chart—and then using the Start Build pop-up menu (see page 486) to choose whether the legend appears before, after, or at the same time as the chart. You'll learn more about coordinating builds later in this chapter.

When you add builds for charts, as with tables and text, you can reorder and set timings for individual chart elements' builds. Just turn on the Build Inspector's "Set timing and order for each build" checkbox.

Controlling Movies and Sounds with Builds

When you add a sound or movie to a slide, it normally starts playing automatically as soon as the slide appears and plays until the clip is finished or you move on to another slide. Using builds, you can take control of exactly when audio or video starts playing on your slide. When you add a build in to a movie or sound, the clip starts playing only when the build occurs. Likewise, a build out makes the clip stop playing.

Movies have the usual assortment of visual effects that you can add to their builds, so you can add the Dissolve effect, for example, to make a movie materialize on screen as it starts to play. Movies also have a pair of effects that are unique to them: Start Movie (for build ins) and Stop Movie (for build outs). Unlike build ins and build outs for other objects, these start-and-stop effects don't move the movie on or off screen. Choosing Start Movie for a build in means the movie still takes its place on the slide as soon as the slide appears—the build in simply starts the clip playing. Similarly, choosing Stop Movie for a build out doesn't remove the movie from the slide; it just stops the action.

Meanwhile, the *only* effects available for sound objects are Start Audio and Stop Audio, since sounds don't appear onscreen.

Note: When you add a build to a movie, the onscreen movie controls aren't available before its build in or after its build out. The builds effectively activate and deactivate the movie so it can't be played, even when you click it. See page 453 for info about playing movies during your presentation.

Using Smart Builds for Single-Slide Slideshows

As you've seen, building objects in and out of your slide isn't all that different from creating transitions between slides. In fact, if you're feeling particularly masochistic, you could even put your entire presentation into a single slide, piling it high with objects and fading them in and out with builds. It's far easier, of course, to use Keynote as it was intended, putting each screen on its own slide. But there's one special exception where it's sometimes desirable to pack a mini slideshow into a single screen: pictures.

Keynote gives you an easy method, called *smart builds*, to cycle through a set of photos on a single slide, without having to individually set and sequence all their builds. This is especially convenient when you want to show your audience a set of images related to a single theme. If you're doing a marketing pitch for Up & Away, the superhero outfitter, you might use a smart build to show a single-slide tour of your latest secret-fortress listing; or fly through a set of pictures showing the new JetGirl 2600 anti-gravity boots in action. You can set up your smart build to cycle through the pictures automatically while you do your patter for this slide (see page 486), or trigger each picture manually with a click, just like a normal build.

Creating a smart build

To add a smart build to a slide, go to Insert → Smart Build and select the effect you'd like to use for your pictures. Keynote displays the Smart Build editor and puts a smart build "drop zone" on your slide—a blue square with a dashed outline inside (the drop zone is visible only when editing; it disappears when you play the slideshow). Drag pictures from the Media Browser or image files from the Finder and drop them into either the drop zone or the Smart Build window, just like you would add pictures to a media placeholder.

As you add pictures to the smart build, their thumbnails gather in the Smart Build editor, as shown in Figure 14-10. Simply drag and drop these thumbnails into the order that you want them to appear. To remove an image from the smart build, select its thumbnail and then press Delete.

When you play your slideshow, the smart build works just like any other series of builds. Click to advance to the next picture. You can even add a build in or build out to your smart build to make it appear or disappear from your slide with the usual choice of effects.

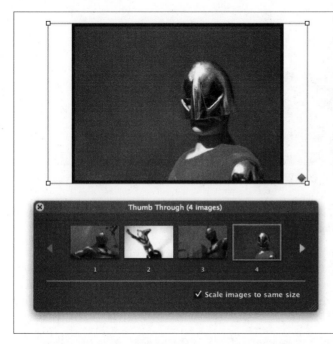

Figure 14-10:
A smart build appears on the page with a blue border and a purple diamond in its lower-right corner. (That's for your eyes only; the border and diamond disappear when you play the final presentation.) When you select a smart build, the Smart Build editor window appears and shows the included pictures as thumbnails. The editor window's title lists the transition effect Keynote will use between pictures, along with the total number of pictures in the smart build.

You can add new pictures by dragging them into either the smart build drop zone or the editor window, and rearrange your mini-slideshow by dragging the thumbnails into place.

Unlike regular image objects, you can't mask or otherwise change the images in a smart build, and you have only very limited control over their size. When the Smart Build editor's "Scale images to same size" checkbox is turned on—the standard state of affairs—Keynote makes all images as large as they can be while still fitting inside the smart build's boundaries. If you turn this checkbox off, the pictures still stay within the smart build, but are sized relative to their original image size, a somewhat peculiar and not particularly useful option. It's best to keep this checkbox turned on and control the image size by dragging the selection handles (the little white squares) along the smart build's blue border.

The Grid and Turntable transition effects add an additional slider to the Smart Build editor window. This slider lets you adjust the relative size of the active and inactive images for these effects, as shown in Figure 14-11.

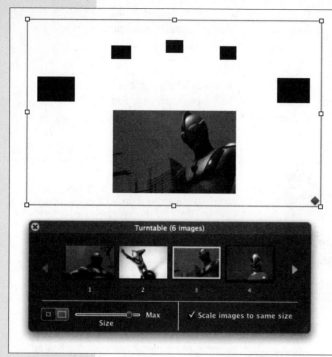

Figure 14-11:
The Turntable smart-build effect rotates pictures so that there's an active image in front, and darkened, inactive images in back. The slider in the Smart Build editor window lets you adjust the size of these two types of images. The button to the left of the slider controls whether the slider adjusts the size of inactive images (click the smaller icon) or the active image (click the larger icon, as shown here).

Editing smart-build settings

You control smart-build transitions from the Action tab of the Build Inspector. Here you can change the effect used to switch pictures, edit the duration of each animation, and fine-tune effect-specific settings. Different build effects have different options, so the settings available here morph into new options when you switch to a new effect.

When you play your slideshow, smart builds normally take you through all the images you've added, but you can choose just a subset of them by selecting their corresponding numbers in the "Build from" and "to" pop-up menus. To customize the build timing for individual images or coordinate their builds with other object builds, turn on the "Set timing and order for each build" checkbox. You'll learn more about automating and coordinating individual builds, including image-by-image transitions in smart builds, in just a moment.

To dismantle your smart build, choose None in the Build Inspector → Action tab's Effect pop-up. Keynote removes the smart build from your slide and deposits all of its pictures onto the slide canvas as regular image objects.

Ordering and Automating Builds

As you gradually turn a once-quiet slide into a symphony of elaborate builds, you'll need to play conductor to keep your animations in organized harmony. The Build Order Drawer is where you compose instructions, coordinating the order and timing of the current slide's builds with precision. Here you can tell Keynote to play certain builds automatically, wait for your click, or launch several builds at the same time.

Open the Build Order Drawer by clicking the More Options button in any pane of the Build Inspector. Keynote slides out a complete list of every build on the current slide (see Figure 14-12). Every time you add a new build to any object on the slide, Keynote adds it to this master list, which acts as the playlist for your slide's performance; when you play the slideshow, Keynote steps through the builds in the order shown here. New builds get automatically added to the end of the list. To change a build's order in this playlist, drag the build to a new location in the Build Order Drawer, or change the number of the build in the Build Inspector's Order pop-up menu.

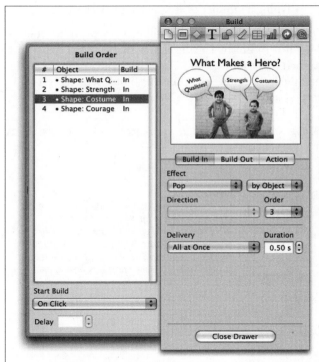

Figure 14-12:
The Build Order Drawer lists all of a slide's builds in the order that Keynote will play them during your presentation. This list shows the order, the object name, and the type of build: build in, build out, the smart build effect, or actions like move, rotate, opacity, and scale (see page 489 for more about action builds). The drawer isn't always wide enough to fit all this info; hover your pointer over an item to show the full entry.

Drag and drop builds to move them to new slots in the list and change their build order. When you click a build, Keynote plays a preview of it in the Build Inspector, and you can use the Start Build pop-up menu at the bottom of the drawer to tell Keynote how you want to trigger the build.

Click an item in the Build Order list to preview its build in the Build Inspector; you can step through the list to watch how the slide will behave during your presentation. Select a build to edit its settings. For example, selecting a build out opens the Build Inspector → Build Out tab so you can change the effects for that build. To delete a build, select it and then press Delete.

Playing Builds Automatically or Simultaneously

The standard behavior for a build is to play only after you click the mouse or press the space bar during your presentation. In other words, Keynote normally waits for your signal before continuing to the next build on the list. However, you can give Keynote the go-ahead to play builds on its own, or to trigger multiple builds at the same time, by using the Start Build pop-up menu at the bottom of the Build Order Drawer. To do this, select the build you want to edit, and then choose one of these options from the Start Build menu:

- **On Click** starts the build when you click the mouse or press the space bar—Keynote's standard behavior.

- **"Automatically after"** starts the build as soon as the previous build finishes (or for the first build, immediately after the slide appears). You can add a pause between the two builds by typing a number of seconds in the Delay box.

- **"Automatically with"** starts the build at the same time as the previous build in the list, without waiting for it to finish. To trigger two builds at the same time, they have to be next to each other in the Build Order list; when you choose this option, Keynote indents the build under the previous build (see Figure 14-13). You can stagger the start by setting a time in the Delay field.

Tip: You can also make several objects build as one object by grouping them: Select all of the objects, choose Arrange → Group, and then create a build for the entire group.

Figure 14-13:
When you choose "Automatically with build #" in the Start Build pop-up, Keynote indents this simultaneous build under the triggering build. Here, three builds are set to run simultaneously with the second build; as the object in build #2 is removed from the slide, three new ones appear.

Mingling Builds of Text, Tables, Charts, and Images

As you've seen, many objects give you the option to build their content gradually, revealing each bullet of a text box with its own build, for example. Similarly, you can create separate build ins and build outs for individual table elements, chart parts, and smart-build images. You trigger this feature by selecting the object and then choosing any option other than "All at once" from the Build Inspector's Delivery pop-up menu in the Build In or Build Out tabs (except for smart builds, that is; for those, every image is always treated with a separate build).

When you choose one of these gradual delivery methods, Keynote's standard behavior is to group all of these "mini-builds" together. In the Build Order Drawer, these builds appear as just two entries—one for the object's first element and another for the other elements, as shown in Figure 14-14. When you play the slideshow, you march straight through all of these mini-builds before moving along to any other builds. For example, if you've chosen the By Bullet delivery method for a text box's build in, you click the mouse to reveal each bullet one at a time during your presentation; only after all of the bullets are revealed can you continue to another build.

Figure 14-14:
When you select By Bullet as the delivery method for a text box's build-in, as shown here, Keynote reveals each bullet one by one. If you leave the "Set timing and order for each build" checkbox (A) turned off, Keynote treats these individual bullet builds as a single block. You have to reveal all the bullets before you can progress to any other builds.

In that case, the build in appears as two items in the Build Order list. The first one (B) controls the appearance of the first bullet. The second one (C) represents the individual builds for the remaining bullets in the text box. Here, the Build Order list shows similar treatment for a table, chart, and smart build.

Treating all of an object's gradual builds as a single, unbreakable block isn't always convenient. You might want to interweave a text box's build in with a pie chart's build in, for example, so you can show a new wedge of the chart as you reveal a corresponding bullet point. Keynote lets you do this with the "Set timing and order for each build" checkbox in the Build Inspector; when you set up the build, turn on this option in the inspector's Build In or Build Out tab. You can also go back and set this option later by selecting the build in the Build Order Drawer.

When you flip the "Set timing and order for each build" switch, Keynote reveals each and every item in the Build Order Drawer so you can reorder and adjust the Start Build settings on these content builds. This lets you sprinkle other builds in between, like mingling the text-box and pie-chart builds in the earlier example (Figure 14-15).

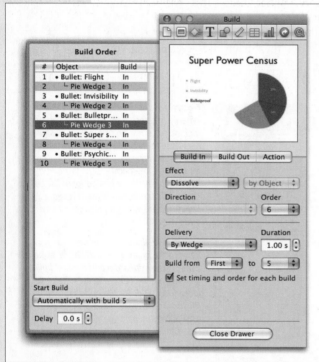

Figure 14-15:
Turn on the Build Inspector's "Set timing and order for each build" checkbox to reorder the individual content builds for an object. Here, a pie chart's wedges are set to display simultaneously with each bullet of a text box.

These freshly liberated builds don't *quite* have their full independence, however. First, they all have to use the same effect settings: Changing the build effect for one bullet, for example, changes it for all the bullets in the text box. Also, while Keynote lets you reorder these builds to mix them with other objects' builds, the content always has to build in the same order within the object itself:

- Text boxes always build top to bottom; you can't move the second bullet's build above the first.

- Charts always build in the order they were entered in the Chart Data Editor.

- Tables always build in the order determined by the Build Inspector's Delivery pop-up menu; you can't scramble the order in which rows, columns, or cells appear.

- Smart builds always build images in the order you set in the Smart Build editor.

Adding Animations with Action Builds

So far, the builds you've seen have been one-way trips on or off the slide, but Key-note also lets you create your own custom builds called *action builds* to move, rotate, fade, and resize pictures without making them wander on or off the slide. With a click of the mouse, Keynote turns you into a skilled animator, making your objects skitter and whirl to any spot on the slide. You can program an object to perform multiple actions simultaneously or one at a time to create elaborate effects and trajectories. Make an object move to the corner of your slide, for example, as it also spins and grows. Or make the object travel to one side of the slide, pause, and then move along to its next station when you're ready.

Tip: Action builds are a lot like the Magic Move transition (page 472). If you find yourself confusing the two, remember: action builds are for moving an object within the *same* slide, whereas Magic Move is for transitioning to a *new* slide. (Action builds also let you create more elaborate animations, as you'll see.)

To add an action build, select the object you want to animate and then go to the Build Inspector's Action tab and pick an action from the Effect pop-up menu: Move, Opacity, Rotate, or Scale. Keynote adds a second, transparent version of the object to your slide. This see-through clone is the Ghost of Object Future, showing you a preview of how and where the object will wind up when the action is over. The Build Inspector also sprouts a few controls based on the action you selected. You can use those controls if you like, but it's actually much easier just to work with the ghost object directly.

If you want to move the object to a new location, for example, just drag the ghost where you want it to go. Rotate it by ⌘-clicking one of the ghost's selection handles and drag. Resize by dragging a selection handle, and change its opacity by adjust-ing the opacity in the Format Bar. You get the idea: Work on the ghost object until you've arranged it on the slide the way you want the object to look when it finishes its action animation. After each change you make, the Build Inspector's Preview window shows you how the build will look.

See what happened? Even though you may have chosen Move as the action, you can still pile all the other effect types onto the same animation so they all happen simultaneously. Behind the scenes, Keynote actually adds a separate build action for each effect, but it's clever enough to schedule them to happen at the very same time. Look in the inspector's Build Order Drawer and you'll see that it lists separate builds for the move, rotate, scale and opacity builds, all set to happen simulta-neously (see Figure 14-16). You'll learn more about setting up multiple action builds in a moment.

Note: If you're working with a picture object, you'll see several more effects listed in the Effects pop-up menu in addition to those mentioned above. These are all smart build effects, and choosing one of them converts the picture into a smart build—just as if you'd chosen an effect from Insert → Smart Build and dropped the picture inside. These smart build effects no longer appear after you add an action to the picture.

Figure 14-16:
When you add an action build to an object, Keynote shows you a ghost version of the object to indicate its future position. Here, the picture is set to move, rotate, and shrink (or scale) when Keynote plays this build. A red line shows you the path the object will follow to its new location. In the Build Order Drawer, Keynote indicates that the rotate and scale actions will happen at the same time as the move action.

As with any other type of build, you can remove an action build by selecting it in the Build Order Drawer and pressing Delete. If you decide, for example, that you don't want to rotate the object while you're moving and scaling it, click the Rotate item in the Build Order Drawer and press Delete. The Preview window plays your action again, and you'll see that the object no longer rotates during its animation. You can also select the ghost in the slide canvas and press Delete; Keynote removes the build action and any other builds set to appear simultaneously with it.

After you're done constructing your build and you deselect the object, it looks like any other object; Keynote doesn't show its ghost version, only its initial position on the slide. The only indication that the object is special is a red diamond with a black dot in the object's lower-right corner. Click the red diamond and Keynote once again reveals the object's ghost image (or several of them, if the object has more than one build action). Click the ghost object again to work on it, or press Tab to toggle between the ghost image and the original object—handy when the ghost object and original overlap.

Tip: To keep the object's motion path and ghost images visible even when it's not selected, Option-click the red diamond. The ghosts no longer get spooked when you deselect the object—they stick around until you click the red diamond again.

Moving Objects Along a Path

Keynote plays a game of connect the dots when you use a Move action to nudge an object across the slide. When you first add the action, you're just working with two dots—the start position and the destination. Keynote draws a red line between the two points to show you the *path* it will follow, a straight line from start to finish. If you prefer to take the scenic route, however, you're not locked into the straight and narrow. You can make an object zig-zag or follow a curved path, too.

To make the object zig-zag, you add additional *nodes* to the path—the "dots" that Keynote connects as it moves the object. Add a node by holding down the Option key while you click the path; the pointer turns into a pen tip, and Keynote adds the new point to the line. Drag the node to a new spot on the slide canvas, and Keynote updates the red trail to show you the object's new course. While you're working with a straight line, this new point on the itinerary adds a hard corner to the path, but you can throw a curve into the mix by clicking the curved Path button in the Build Inspector (circled in Figure 14-17). Keynote updates all the nodes in your path to make the object meander gently through every point.

When you click a curved node, it sprouts two handles, which let you control the shape of the curve. Drag the handles to bend your curve just so (to change the length of both handles at once, hold down the Option key while dragging one of them). You can change an individual node from straight to curved, and vice versa, by double-clicking it. That goes for the two endpoints, too; when you turn an end-point into a curved node, however, it has only one handle to control the shape.

Tip: You can move the entire motion path, along with its start and destination points, by dragging the path itself.

If editing a motion path sounds suspiciously like editing the points of a shape (page 245), that's because motion paths and shapes are close cousins. In fact, you can even use a shape to define your path instead of drawing it by hand—a huge timesaver when you want an object to trace out a circle or ellipse. To do that, insert the shape that you want your object to follow, Shift-click the shape and the object to select them both, and then choose Format → Shape → "Make Motion Path from Shape". Keynote removes the shape from the slide and turns it into the motion path for the object's new action build. From here, you can edit the points of the path just as you'd edit a path you drew yourself. Figure 14-18 tells the whole story.

Tip: If you want a shape to move along the path sketched out by another shape, you can use the same technique. The shape in front is the moving object, and the shape in back defines the path; choose the shape you want to use for the path and click the toolbar's Back button (or choose Arrange → "Send to Back"). Then select both shapes and choose Format → Shape → "Make Motion Path from Shape".

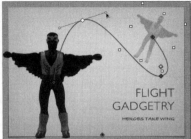

Figure 14-17:
Change the shape of the path for an object move by Option-clicking the path. Keynote adds a new point, or node, to the path, which you can drag to any part of the slide canvas to change the object's course. In both of the slides shown here, two nodes have been added to the path, but the nodes on the right are curved.

Double-click a node to switch it from a straight point to a curved point, or vice versa. You can also make a path curved or straight with the Build Inspector's Path button (circled). Change the shape of a curved line by clicking a node and dragging its handles (right).

If you want the object to pause its motion at some point in its journey, you can add additional move actions, each one a separate action build. In your presentation, for example, you would click the mouse once to move the object to its first location, then click again to move it to the next. Doing this means that you string multiple action builds together. As it happens, that's the very next topic.

Multiple Action Builds

Keynote lets you add as many actions to an object as you can muster. You've already seen that you can apply multiple effects to an object at once, making it move, resize, rotate, and fade all at the same time, for example. You can also create actions that happen as separate events, stringing them together back-to-back, or weaving them with other objects' builds. During your presentation, for example, you could move an object to one place on the slide, and then click the mouse to trigger other builds, click the mouse again to move the object to a second location, and so on.

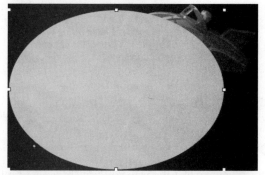

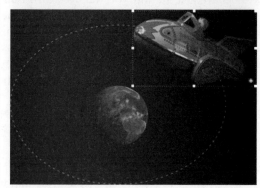

Figure 14-18:
*Use a shape to set an object's course in an action build. Here,
an impressively futuristic rocket orbits the earth.*

*Top: The slide starts with two image objects: the rocket and
the earth.*

*Middle: Add an ellipse shape to the slide. Shift-click the ellipse
and the rocket to select both, and then choose Format →
Shape → "Make Motion Path from Shape".*

*Bottom: Keynote adds a move action build to the rocket
object, tracing the outline of the original ellipse, which is no
longer an object on the slide.*

To add an additional action build to an object, click the Add Action button in the
Build Inspector → Action tab or click the red-diamond + button in the lower-right
corner of the ghost image. Keynote adds another ghost to the slide to show that
you're working with a new action. Make your changes to the ghost image to set
how the object should wind up at the end of its new action. Figure 14-19 shows
you an object with several move actions.

Your new actions show up in the Build Order Drawer with the rest of the slide's
builds, and they work the same way, too. Drag and drop them in the list to change
their order, and use the Start Build pop-up menu to choose how Keynote should
trigger each stage of the object's actions.

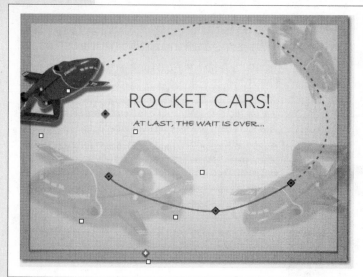

Figure 14-19:
When you add multiple action builds to an object, Keynote represents each one with its own ghost image. Here, a picture of a rocket car moves three separate times from its original location in the top-left corner. When you play the presentation, the rocket pauses at each spot until you trigger the next move.

When you're editing the slide, select a ghost image to edit its path; Keynote shows you the selected path segment as a solid red line, and the others as dashed lines. To add still more actions, click the red-diamond + sign in the last ghost image (bottom left).

Copying Builds to Other Objects

Once you've got an object trained to behave just the way you want it with a build in, build out, or series of action builds, you can copy all those builds to another object in your slideshow, making it behave exactly the same way as the original object. Simply select the object that you set up with your builds and then choose Format → Copy Animation; then select the other object and choose Format → Paste Animation. And with that, your objects' mind-meld is complete: The second object takes on all of the build know-how of the original, absorbing even lengthy strings of action builds. (Note that this method replaces any builds that the target object might have had before.) Use the Build Inspector's Build Order Drawer to fine-tune when and how those copied builds should take place.

Now hold onto that spirit of sharing and move generously along to the next chapter, where you'll learn about the different ways you can share your presentation with others. From playing the slideshow in front of an audience to distributing it on paper or over the Internet, the next chapter is all about getting the word out.

Sharing Your Slideshows

By now, you've discovered the dirty secret of Keynote presenters everywhere: Building a Keynote slideshow turns out to be more fun than work. Tinkering with Keynote's visual effects as you combine your own content with Apple's elegant themes—it's so addictively creative that it sometimes seems as if simply *making* a slideshow is reason enough to use Keynote. Chances are, though, you're not building a slideshow just for kicks. The whole goal of a Keynote slideshow is to *share it* with others, screening it on a computer monitor or projection screen—for an audience of one or a teeming multitude. It's presentation time, and this chapter plumbs every detail of running your slideshow for a live audience, as well as setting it up to play on its own in full, automated glory.

Keynote provides several other ways of getting the word out, too, including printing and exporting your presentation in various file formats that can be opened by other programs or posted on the Web. Fire up the projector, warm up that printer, and ready your Internet connection—this chapter gives you the lowdown on sharing your gorgeous slides onscreen, on paper, and on the Web.

Setting Up the Presentation

First things first, you have to get both Keynote and your computer ready for the big show. The specific backstage preparations depend on exactly how and where you'll display the slideshow. For most presentations, you're the one in the spotlight, driving the slideshow as you speak in person to your audience—a class, a board of directors, or a room of fez-topped conventioneers, for example. Preparing and playing a live slideshow is where this chapter begins, but starting on page 510, you'll also learn how to set up your slideshow to play on autopilot or let your viewers navigate it themselves by clicking onscreen buttons. No matter which of these methods you use, however, your first stop should be Keynote's display settings to choose your slideshow preferences and set up the presenter display.

Note: See page 422 for details on configuring your slideshow to play in normal, self-playing, recorded, or hyperlinks-only mode.

Setting Slideshow Preferences

Some of Keynote's preferences apply only when you play the slideshow, so be sure to review them before show time. Choose Keynote → Preferences, and click the Slideshow button (Figure 15-1). Keynote presents you with a hodgepodge menu consisting of options affecting a range of presentation aspects, from how and where your slides should be projected to when your pointer should be allowed onscreen. Figure 15-1 shows a reliable, standard selection for live presentations, and the following list runs down your options.

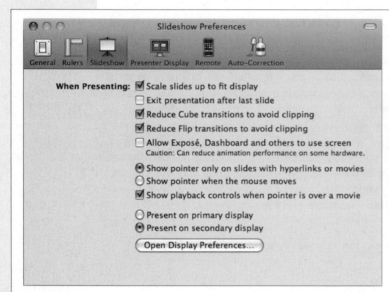

Figure 15-1:
The settings for the Slideshow Preferences shown here are a good configuration for live presentations. The "Scale slides up to fit display" option makes your slides show full-screen, without a black border around the edges. Turning off the "Exit presentation after last slide" option keeps the last slide in your presentation onscreen even if you accidentally click the mouse or press the space bar after you're done. The two checkboxes to reduce Cube and Flip transitions keep these animations from careening off the screen. Give Keynote sole control of your video screen by turning off the "Allow Exposé, Dashboard and others to use screen" setting.

• **Scale slides up to fit display.** Turn on this checkbox in order to make your slide image as large as possible, filling the available height without leaving any black border. You usually want this checkbox turned on, although it means that your slides may lose some of their image quality. An even better option is to make sure that your display's resolution matches the size of your slideshow. See page 396 for details about setting and choosing a slide size.

- **Exit presentation after last slide.** When you turn on this checkbox, Keynote returns to its editing mode when you advance past the last slide in your slide-show. For a live presentation, it's a good idea to turn this checkbox off, to keep the last slide in your presentation onscreen even if you accidentally click the mouse or press the space bar. This is like putting a visual padlock on your slide-show so that you don't accidentally slip out to your desktop. This prevents the dramatic finale of your presentation from being ruined by a view of the Key-note editing window, your cluttered icons, or the desktop picture of your wife at the Halloween party (really, you're the only one who ever finds it funny). When you're ready to exit the slideshow, just press the Escape (Esc) key.

- **Reduce Cube transitions to avoid clipping; Reduce Flip transitions to avoid clipping.** Turn on these two checkboxes in order to slightly reduce the size of Key-note's animations during the Cube and Flip transitions. These preferences only matter, of course, if you actually use the Cube and Flip transitions in your slide-show—and even then, the effect is extremely subtle. These animations actually extend beyond the normal slide boundaries, using some of the slide border to dis-play the transition. If you turn on the first checkbox to scale your slides up to fit the display, then you should turn on both of these checkboxes as well.

- **Allow Exposé, Dashboard and others to use the screen.** This option lets you use Mac OS X's Exposé and Dashboard features during your slideshow, but at the expense of some video performance. Unless you specifically plan to use these features during your presentation, it's a good idea to leave this option off.

- **Show pointer only on slides with hyperlinks or movies.** Choose this standard setting to keep the pointer hidden from view except when you actually need it—to click a hyperlink or control a movie's display.

- **Show pointer when the mouse moves.** If you choose this option instead, you can make the arrow cursor visible any time you move the mouse. This option is useful if you want to point things out on your slides during the show. But since the merest touch of the mouse makes the pointer appear, this also means that clicking your mouse to advance slides will often make the pointer appear; if you turn this option on, use the space bar, the right arrow key, or a remote control to advance slides instead of clicking the mouse.

Tip: When playing your slideshow, you can also show or hide the cursor by pressing the C key.

- **Show playback controls when pointer is over a movie.** Turn this option on to get complete access to a movie's playback controls. See page 453 for more info about playing movies during your presentation.

- **Present on primary display.** The last two radio buttons determine which screen displays your slideshow if you have a second display connected to your com-puter (for example, a video projector connected to a laptop) *and* you've set your computer up for *dual display*. Dual display means that the two screens display different action—usually the slideshow on the audience screen and a special presenter view on a screen that only you can see. You'll learn more about these technical display details on page 501; for now, choose this option only if you really want to view your presentation on the Mac's primary display (the secondary display is usually the best choice).

- **Present on secondary display.** This is the typical choice when you're presenting your slideshow on a second display or projector.

- **Open Display Preferences.** Click this button to open your Mac's System Preferences Display pane in order to set your display resolutions, color depth, and—if you're using two displays—the screen arrangement (see page 502).

Setting Up the Presenter Display

When you really want your presentation to look effortless—when you want to be sure you hit every point and anticipate every transition—Keynote has a solution: Cheat. Your favorite presentation software gives you a crib sheet called the *presenter display,* where you can sneak a look at your notes, monitor how much time you have left, and preview upcoming slides. In order to use this for-your-eyes-only control panel during your presentation, you display your presentation on two screens—a big screen for your audience and another screen (often your laptop) for your cheat-sheet presenter display. But even when you don't have a second screen for the presentation itself, the presenter display can be useful *before* you give your talk, while you rehearse.

Choose Play → Rehearse Slideshow, and Keynote reveals the presenter display, shown in Figure 15-2. When you are in fact rehearsing, you can use this screen to practice and time your presentation and make sure that your presenter notes (page 406) have all the info you'll need.

Playing a slideshow from the presenter display

From the presenter view, you can play and control the slideshow just as you would when you view the normal slideshow. You'll learn all the down-and-dirty details about playing slideshows on page 504, but here's the gist to get you started:

- Advance to the next slide by clicking the mouse or by pressing any of these keys: the space bar, Return, right arrow, or down arrow.

- Go back to the previous slide by pressing the left arrow or up arrow.

- Exit the slideshow and return to edit mode by pressing Escape (Esc).

- Press R to reset the timer.

To jump to a different part of your slideshow, use the presenter display's *slide switcher.* Open the switcher by moving the mouse to the top of the presenter display, and a menu slides down. Click the Slides icon, and Keynote reveals a strip of slide thumbnails across the top of the screen. Use the scroll bar to browse the slides, and double-click a thumbnail to make it the current slide.

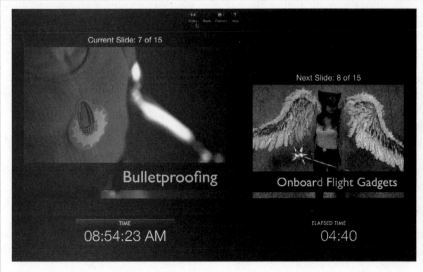

Figure 15-2:
Keynote's standard settings for the presenter display shows you the current slide as well as the next slide, smaller and to the right. A clock shows you the current time, while another shows you the time elapsed since you moved off your title slide.

Advance the slideshow as you normally would, by clicking the mouse or pressing the space bar, but the presenter view also gives you more onscreen controls to jump to a specific slide or pause the show and fade the audience screen to black. Access these additional options by pushing the pointer up to the top of the screen; a toolbar slides down, as shown here.

Tip: For the fastest trip to and through the slide switcher, use the keyboard. Press the equal sign (=), the plus sign (+), or hyphen (–) to bring up the slide switcher. Use the right- or left-arrow key to move forward or back through the thumbnails, or press the up- or down-arrow key to move to the first or last slide. When the slide you want to go to is highlighted, press Return to make it the current slide.

Customizing the presenter display

Figure 15-2 shows Keynote's standard view of the presenter display, featuring the current slide, the next slide, the current time, and the elapsed time since you moved off the title slide. You can resize and reposition every item on the screen, and add additional info, too. To customize the presenter display, point the cursor at the top of the screen and a four-icon menu drops down from the edge. Click the Options button, and choose Customize Presenter Display. Keynote lays down a yellow-striped construction strip across the top of the screen and opens the Customize Presenter Display window, a palette of options for showing or hiding the various cockpit controls in the presenter display (Figure 15-3).

Tip: You can also get to this view directly from edit mode by choosing Play → Customize Presenter Display, or by clicking the Customize Presenter Display button in the Presenter Display panel of Keynote → Preferences.

Drag any of the display elements to a new spot on the page, and resize them by drag-ging the resize handle in their lower-right corners. You can even overlap these win-dows if you have a small screen; click an overlapped window to bring it to the front.

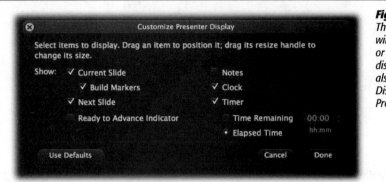

Figure 15-3:
The Customize Presenter Display window gives you controls to reveal or hide elements of the presenter display (these checkbox options are also available from the Presenter Display panel of Keynote → Preferences).

Add or remove information to your presenter display by turning options on or off in the Customize Presenter Display window:

- **Current Slide** shows the slide that your audience sees, including the current state of the slide's builds if it has them.

- **Build Markers.** When the current slide has builds, this option shows you bul-lets below the slide to indicate how many builds remain on the slide. As you advance through each build, Keynote dims the corresponding bullet to show you it's been played, leaving the bullets for remaining bullets aglow.

- **Next Slide** shows a preview of the next slide.

- **Ready to Advance Indicator.** When your slide has builds, Keynote doesn't show their complete animations on the presenter display. Instead, it takes you directly to the end state of the build's animation. To you, it looks like the animation has already completed as soon as you click ahead, even when your audience is still watching the build. For long-lasting builds, this can be inconvenient, because you can't see when the animation is done. The "ready to advance" indicator takes care of this by showing a red bar across the top of the presenter display while Keynote is still building; it turns to green when Keynote is waiting for your signal to move along to the next build.

- **Notes.** Shows the presenter notes for each slide. To scroll through these notes, press the U (up) or D (down) key, or use the scroll bar on the right side of the presenter notes pane.

Tip: Whatever you choose for the Notes option, your sticky-note comments are always visible on the slide previews in the presenter display, if they were visible before you started the slideshow (View → Show Comments). In no case, though, are your comments visible in the audience view. For more on comments, see page 461.

- **Clock** shows the current time.

- **Timer** shows either the time remaining or the elapsed time. The timer starts ticking as soon as you move off the first slide. For the time-remaining option, set the time from which to count down in the Time Remaining field.

If you want to go back to Keynote's stock arrangement after you've made changes, click Use Defaults. When you're happy with your presenter display arrangement, click Done in the Customize Presenter Display window.

Using the presenter display during the presentation

Now that you've got your presenter display just so, all that remains is to tell Keynote that you actually want to use it during your presentation. You'll need a second display, of course, and you'll also have to set up your Mac for dual display, which you'll learn to do in the next section. From there, go to Keynote → Preferences, and click the Presenter Display button. Turn on the "Use alternate display to view presenter information" checkbox. This tells Keynote to show the presenter display on your second screen—or, more specifically, the screen that you *didn't* pick in Slideshow Preferences back on pages 497–498. If you chose to display the slideshow on the secondary display, in other words, turning on this option will show the presenter view on the primary screen (your laptop, for example).

Using the edit view during the presentation

If you're giving a presentation in which you plan to jump around from slide to slide in different parts of the slideshow, consider using a different kind of presenter display: the Keynote editing window. In the Presenter Display Preferences, turn off the checkbox marked "Use alternate display to view presenter information". Choose View → Light Box to cram as many thumbnails as possible into the slide navigator. If you use the Notes field (View → Show Presenter Notes), enlarge it so you can see as much of the notes as you need to during the talk. With this view on your presenter screen, you can jump to any slide during the presentation by clicking its thumbnail in the navigator.

Connecting a Second Display

The easiest way to present a Keynote slideshow is right on your computer's screen—something you've probably been doing all along as you create a slideshow—by clicking the Play button in the toolbar to view your work in progress. If your audience is very small—two or three people—this method can work well. If you have your presentation on a laptop, you can take it to your audience and be ready to present at a moment's notice—perfect for the road-warrior salesman or college recruiter. When your audience is larger, though, it's time to connect your computer to a large monitor or video projector.

Your first decision is about what you'd like to show on the two screens. You've got two options here:

- **Mirror** your computer's screen to the second screen so that you and your audience see exactly the same thing.

- Set up a **dual display** so that you can show your audience the slideshow on the big screen while you use the presenter display on your computer. This is how the pros roll. (Apple also calls this "extended desktop.")

> **Note:** Not all Macs have the video horsepower to manage a dual display. MacBook, MacBook Pro, and MacBook Air laptops can all do it and so can their ancestor, the G4 PowerBook. However, some older Macs, like the iBook and iMacs before the Intel models, can only mirror your computer's screen.

Once you know how you'd like to set up your display, you're ready to hook it up:

1. **Attach the second display or projector to your computer, using the cable adapter—nicknamed a dongle (page 384)—if you need it.**

2. **Choose Keynote → Preferences, click the Slideshow button, and then click Open Display Preferences (or choose → System Preferences, and then click Displays).**

3. **Click the Arrangement tab in the Preferences window.**

   If you don't see an Arrangement tab, that means that your Mac can't detect the external monitor. Make sure that the monitor is turned on and plugged into your Mac, and then click the Detect Displays button in the Displays tab.

4. **If you're setting up your slideshow for mirroring, turn on the Mirror Displays option (your Mac typically switches to this mode automatically when you plug in an external display), and skip ahead to step 6.**

5. **If you're setting up your slideshow for dual display, position the screen images to control how your computer's desktop spans the two displays.**

   Setting the arrangement of the two displays isn't too important for Keynote presentations. Its purpose is mainly for people who are lucky enough to have two monitors that they can use to create a larger desktop—or virtual monitor—on which to work. When you're setting up the typical Keynote dual display arrangement, it's most important to set the *primary display* (the one with the menu bar that you see) and the *secondary display* (the one your audience views). Drag the menu bar from one screen image to the other to make either display primary—usually, you'll want to make your computer screen the primary screen.

6. **Click the Display tab.**

   Two Display windows appear, one for each of your displays. Select a display resolution from the Resolutions list, and a color depth from the Colors pop-up menu for each display.

If you're using mirroring—either because your computer doesn't support dual display mode, or because you prefer to see exactly the same thing your audience sees—use the same resolution and color depth for each display. For best results when you use screen spanning, your Keynote slide size should be the same as the screen resolution for the display you'll be using for the slideshow presentation.

Most video projectors use either 800×600 or 1024×768 pixels resolution— which match the standard sizes for most Keynote themes. Set your display resolution to match your projector's resolution. If you created your Keynote slideshow at a lower or higher resolution, Keynote can scale the slideshow up or down to fill the screen. Keynote scales down automatically if the slides are larger than the screen. Use Keynote's Slideshow Preferences (see page 496) to scale up to fill the screen if the slides are smaller than the screen.

Note: If you don't get an image on your second display when you plug it in–or if the display doesn't sync with your computer, resulting in a squashed, stretched, or unstable image–first try restarting the display. If that doesn't work, leave the display connected and restart the computer to bring it into synchronization.

When you're set up for dual display, Keynote gives you a quick way to swap displays when you're playing your slideshow: Press the letter X on your keyboard, and the two displays switch roles—the one showing your slides now gets the presenter display and vice versa. You can also make this switch from the presenter display's toolbar by clicking the Options button and choosing Swap Displays. For more on the presenter display, see page 498.

Connecting Your Audio Output

If your slideshow contains sound and you're presenting to a group of people instead of just a single viewer, you need some kind of sound amplification. Many video projectors have a built-in amplifier and speaker that can work in a pinch for a small group. In most cases, however, you need something with a little more oomph and a lot more fidelity. Depending on the size of your presentation space, your amplification system could be a set of tiny external computer speakers, a public address system capable of filling Yankee Stadium, or anything in between.

Connect your computer's audio output jack to the amplifier's input. The type of cable you need to link the two depends on the input connections on the speakers, amplifier, or PA system. The computer's end of the cable requires a 1/8 inch stereo miniplug (the kind on your iPod headphones, for example). The amplifier end probably requires the same miniplug or a pair of RCA plugs (those are the red and white plugs you often find plugged into the back of stereos). It's good to have one of each of these cables in your bag.

Choose → System Preferences, click Sound, and then click the Output tab. Adjust the Output volume slider to about 80 percent and play part of your slideshow that contains audio. Use the volume control on the amplifier or PA system to adjust the sound to a comfortable level.

If you're lucky enough to have sound professionals in charge of your audio setup, they'll take care of the connections and be able to adjust the volume during the presentation. If you're on your own, then either you or a helper should be able to adjust the volume during the show, in case people in the back can't hear, or you notice those in the front stuffing Kleenex in their ears.

Set Up the Remote Control

If you plan to use Keynote Remote to drive your slideshow with your iPhone or iPod Touch, you first need to link your iPhone to the computer running Keynote. Take a minute to do that in advance of your talk, and make sure it actually works—before your audience begins to arrive. Likewise, make sure you have the iPhone display set the way you want it—if you plan to refer to presenter notes during your talk, set it to portrait display mode; otherwise, use landscape. Finally, be sure that your iPhone is charged so that it doesn't wink out in the middle of your presentation. See page 507 for complete details about setting up and using Keynote Remote.

If you're using a different remote control, the same idea holds: Make sure the thing works. Turn it on, and click through a few slides just to be sure.

Playing Keynote Slideshows

Dim the house lights, raise the curtains, and cue the applause sign, it's show time at last. With the spotlight on you and your pitch, the last thing you need is a complicated set of controls for moving through your slides. Happily, Keynote makes it dead-easy to advance through your slides using the keyboard or a remote control.

To get started, open the Keynote document, and select the first slide in the show using the slide navigator or by choosing Slide → Go to → First Slide. (You can also select a different slide if you'd like to start somewhere in the middle of your presentation.) Now start the show: Click the toolbar's Play button, choose Play → Play Slideshow, or press ⌘-Option-P. Your first slide flickers onto the screen, and you're on.

Tip: You can set up your slideshow to begin playing automatically as soon as you open the document, not a bad idea for slideshows you've finished editing. Open the Document Inspector, and turn on the "Automatically play upon open" option. That way, Keynote opens directly to the first slide and launches into your slideshow, completely bypassing the editing screen–the "man behind the curtain" whom it's best to keep tucked away from your audience. To stop the show and bring up the editing view, press the Escape key, Q (for quit), or period [.].

Controlling the Presentation

The basics are easy, and the controls work exactly the same whether you're using the presenter display or normal slideshow mode. Keynote gives you lots of different ways to handle the most common actions—moving forward and backward—so that you don't have to hunt around the keyboard guessing. It doesn't matter which method you use for this basic navigation, just go with whatever feels comfortable. Here's the scoop on these essential needs:

- **Advance** through your slideshow by clicking the mouse, clicking your remote control, or by pressing the space bar, Return, the right-arrow key, the down-arrow key, or N (for next).

- **Go back** by pressing the left-arrow key, the up-arrow key, Delete, or P (for previous).

- **Exit** the slideshow by pressing the Escape key, Q (for quit), or period [.] (as in: the end, period).

Tip: If you're using a keyboard with an extended keyboard, pressing Home always takes you back to the very first slide, and pressing End zips you over to the last.

Navigating through builds

When you've set up slides with builds that are set to build "on click," then advancing as described above first steps through each of these builds before moving on to the next slide. If you're trying to move quickly though a bunch of slides with builds, this can feel like wading through mud. To skip the builds and just move to the next slide, press] (right bracket).

It's a similar story for going back through slides with builds, except that the "go back" commands listed above jump you back to the beginning of all builds on the current slide. To step back one by one through the current slides' builds, press [(left bracket).

Hopping around the slideshow with the slide switcher

While you were building your slideshow, you no doubt grew fond of your good friend, the slide navigator, for helping you quickly move around your slideshow. When you're making your way through your full-screen slideshow, you might miss the navigator when you need to leap to a new spot during your slideshow presentation. That's where the *slide switcher* comes in—the slide navigator's onstage cousin. Use the slide switcher to jump to another slide anywhere in the presentation; it slips down from the top of the screen when you call it, letting you browse thumbnails of all of your slides (Figure 15-4).

Press the + sign or equal sign (=) to display the slide switcher; it already has the next slide selected (press the − sign or hyphen to display the slide switcher with the previous slide selected). Or type a slide number to open the slide switcher with that slide selected.

When the slide switcher appears, use left or right arrow keys, or the + or − sign keys, to move forward or backward through the slides in the switcher. Alternatively, use the slide switcher's scroll bar or type a slide number to jump to that slide.

As you move through the thumbnails in the slide switcher, Keynote highlights each one with a yellow outline, but keeps the main slide unchanged. When you've found and highlighted the slide you need, press Return or double-click it to go to that slide. Keynote closes the slide switcher and changes the main view to the new slide.

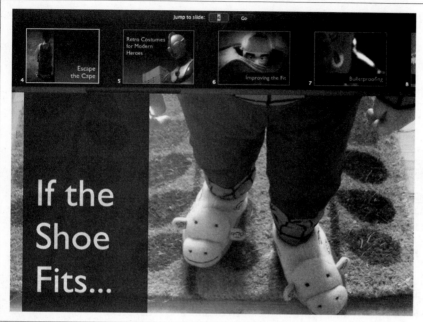

Figure 15-4:
Press the equal [=], plus [+], or minus [–] keys to open Keynote's slide switcher. Then use the + or – keys, or click the slide switcher's arrows, to move in either direction through the slideshow. You can also type a slide number to move directly to that slide. When the slide you're after is highlighted, press Return to close the switcher and move to that slide. If you decide you don't want to switch to another slide after all, click outside the switcher or press the Esc key to close the switcher.

Playing movies

Double-click a movie to start and stop playing it. If you've enabled movie playback controls in Slideshow Preferences (page 497), hover the mouse over the movie and use the controls that appear at the bottom of the movie. See page 453 for more details about playing movies during your presentation.

Opening links and other programs

Use the mouse to click hyperlinks, just like you would on a web page. If the hyperlink opens an email message or a web page, Keynote pauses, hides the slideshow, and switches to your email program or Web browser. When it's time to switch back to the slideshow, press ⌘-Tab or click the Keynote Dock icon (which now displays a green Play button).

You can likewise break out of your slideshow to use another program by pressing H (for hide), which hides the slideshow and takes you back to the last program you were using. From there, you can use your computer normally to open files or run other programs, without ever revealing your Keynote editing screen. Head back to the slideshow, which is waiting for you where you stopped it, by pressing ⌘-Tab or clicking the Keynote icon in the Dock.

Pausing the show

You can freeze a slideshow—even midway through a build—by pressing F. To do the same thing but also dim the screen to black, press B. (In the presenter display, you can also do this by pushing the pointer to the top of the screen to reveal the option menu, and then click the Black icon.) To make the screen white instead, press W.

Thaw out your frozen show and resume playing by pressing any key.

Calling up the keyboard cheat sheet

If all of these keyboard options are making your head hurt, you don't necessarily have to memorize them. Just be sure you know the basics: how to go forward, backward, and exit your slideshow. From there, if you get stuck during your presentation, call up the keyboard commands by pressing the question-mark [?] or slash [/] key. Keynote reveals a window listing all the keyboard commands available while you're playing a slideshow. (It's not exactly the classiest thing to do during a talk, but hey, if you're stuck, you're stuck.) In presenter mode, you can also call up this cheat sheet by moving the pointer to the top of the screen to reveal the option menu, and then click the Help button.

This detailed window lists all of the keyboard commands reviewed here, plus a few extras for power presenters. Often, though, the true power presenters aren't anywhere near their keyboard—they're roaming the stage to engage more directly with their audience, flipping through their slides with the help of a remote control. If you happen to have an iPhone or iPod Touch, then you've got the best of both worlds—a remote, with a miniature presenter display built in.

Keynote Remote with iPhone or iPod Touch

On the very same day that Apple released iWork '09, the company also made Keynote Remote available on its iTunes App Store. It's a program for iPhone and iPod Touch, specifically designed to control Keynote '09 presentations. It's a handy addition to your presenter toolkit and, for just 99 cents, the price is certainly right. Just like Keynote's presenter display, Keynote Remote shows you the current slide and, depending on your settings, either the next slide or the presenter notes for your current slide (Figure 15-6). Move forward and backward by swiping the screen, swiping your slides back and forth. Easy.

Before you get started setting it up, there are a few minor caveats to get out of the way. First, just because you're using your iPhone as a remote control doesn't mean that it stops being a phone. If someone calls in the middle of your talk, even if you have your ringer off, you still have to accept or decline before you can continue driving your slideshow. It's a good idea to forward your calls to another number before you start presenting, but at the very least, set the phone to vibrate.

Also, Keynote Remote works by connecting to your computer over a WiFi network. If either your iPhone or computer has a spotty connection to the network, you may get stranded mid-stage without a working remote. This can be remedied, though, with a bit of advance planning; see the box "Wimpy WiFi?" on page 508 for the details.

Finally, as svelte as these handheld devices might be, the iPhone and iPod Touch are still fairly hefty relative to the standard presentation remote. You may even find that you need two hands to make it work, particularly when you use Keynote Remote in landscape mode. If you like to travel light when you're onstage, you might prefer to use a standard remote control instead of the iPhone (see page 387 for a rundown of remote-control options). That said, if you'd like to have your presentation notes with you without being chained to your computer, the iPhone and iPod Touch are pretty much as small as they could be for that use, and you'll probably find it worth toting around. Assuming that's the case, you're ready to get started.

POWER USERS' CLINIC

Wimpy WiFi?

Keynote Remote whispers its instructions to your computer over a WiFi wireless network—in order to work, your phone has to be connected to the same WiFi network as your computer. But what happens when you don't have WiFi access, or there's only a weak signal, or enthusiastic conference-goers are soaking up all the bandwidth? If the network's not sturdy, all you've got in your hand is a good-looking phone; your iPhone as a remote is kaput.

Don't despair. When you don't have a reliable WiFi network to count on, you can make your own using your Mac's built-in *computer-to-computer network* feature:

1. Click the AirPort network icon in the menu bar, and choose Create Network.

   If you don't have an AirPort icon in the menu bar, choose → System Preferences, and then click Network. Click AirPort, and turn on the "Show Air-Port status in menu bar" option.

2. Give your new network a name—"Remote Possibility", perhaps—and pick a channel from the pop-up menu.

3. Turn on the Require Password checkbox, and type a password for your network. Click OK.

   For a short presentation like this one, it's okay to use the weaker encryption, "40-bit WEP (more compatible)", which also allows you to enter a short five-character password, easy to type on your iPhone.

4. Your Mac is now producing its own private WiFi network; now you just need to connect your iPhone or iPod Touch.

Tap the Settings icon on your iPhone, and choose Wi-Fi. Select your new network, type the password, and you're done. You've now got a private, reliable wireless connection direct to your computer.

Linking your iPhone to your computer

Keynote won't let just any old iPhone start pushing its buttons. It insists on a formal introduction first, a process called *linking*:

1. **Make sure that Keynote is accepting Keynote Remote connections.**

   Go to Keynote → Preferences, and click the Remote button. Turn on the "Enable iPhone and iPod Touch remotes" option.

2. **Make sure that your iPhone or iPod Touch is connected to the same WiFi network as your computer.**

   Tap the Settings icon and then choose Wi-Fi to select the network.

3. **Tap the Keynote Remote icon on your iPhone to launch the program, and tap the Link to Keynote button to display a four-digit pass code (Figure 15-5).**

4. **Return to Keynote's Remote Preferences window on your computer, where you'll see your iPhone listed. Click Link.**

   Enter the four-digit code from your iPhone into the window to complete the authentication and grant permission for that iPhone to control your slideshow.

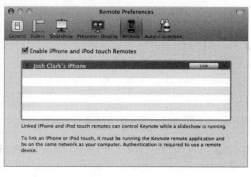

Figure 15-5:
Left: When you tap Keynote Remote's "Link to Keynote" button, your iPhone displays a four-digit pass code.

Right: Give that pass code to your computer in Keynote's Remote Preferences window; click the Link button next to your iPhone and type in the number to complete the link. You can unlink the device anytime by clicking Unlink next to the iPhone name.

Playing the slideshow with Keynote Remote

After you link your iPhone, Keynote Remote shows that it's connected to your computer. Tap the Play Slideshow button, and your computer starts playing the open Keynote document; if you've got more than one slideshow open, the one in the top window starts playing. On the computer's screen and to your audience, the slideshow looks just as it would if you'd started playing it from the keyboard.

On the iPhone, you'll see one of two views, depending on your settings (Figure 15-6). In portrait mode, you see the current slide, with your presenter notes displayed below; drag or flick through a slide's presenter notes to scroll through them. In landscape mode, you see the current slide and next slide (or build)—no presenter notes. Swipe the screen to flick the slides forward and back.

Click the Options button at the top left, and Keynote shows you three buttons: First Slide, End Show, and Settings. Click Settings to change the computer that you're controlling, the orientation (portrait vs. landscape), and whether to include the presenter notes in the portrait display.

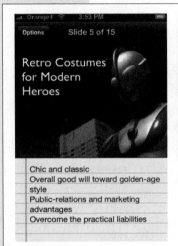

Figure 15-6:
When you control a slideshow with your iPhone and Keynote Remote, you can choose between a portrait display (left) and a landscape display (right). Both views show the current slide (or build), and the portrait display can optionally include presenter notes, while landscape shows the next slide or build. In either view, swiping the screen moves you forward or back through the slideshow.

Creating Self-Playing Slideshows

If letting your iPhone run your slideshow isn't enough and you want still *more* automation, Keynote is ready for you. Self-playing or kiosk slideshows put your Keynote presentation on autopilot. They play completely automatically, advancing each slide and build according to the timings you set. Kiosk presentations are usually set to loop, playing over and over again to display your latest product, explain a museum exhibit, or embarrass attendees at your 20th high school reunion.

Tip: Even though these kinds of slideshows are completely automatic, Keynote still responds to certain keyboard commands during the presentation. You can keep viewers from stopping the presentation by requiring a password (see page 423), but they'll still be able to pause it using the F, B, or W keyboard shortcuts. The only foolproof way to prevent viewers from meddling with the slideshow is to remove the keyboard—or in the case of a laptop, cover it.

Keynote has two flavors of self-playing slideshow:

- **Timed slideshows** advance automatically based on timings that you provide for individual slides or a standard slideshow-wide setting.

- **Recorded slideshows** let you make a voice-over narration while you advance through your slideshow; Keynote saves your entire performance and plays back your slides and your silver-voiced narration exactly as you recorded them.

You select one of these slideshow modes by picking a presentation style in the Document Inspector, as you learned way back on page 422. Even though both of these types of slideshows play all by themselves, Keynote reserves the term *self-playing* for the timed slideshow in the Document Inspector's Presentation pop-up menu; select Self-playing to create a timed slideshow or Recorded to create a recorded slideshow. (The Recorded option is grayed out until you record your voice-over narration, which you'll learn about in a moment.)

Timed Slideshows

When you turn your presentation into a timed slideshow by choosing Self-playing in the Document Inspector's Presentation pop-up (Figure 15-7), Keynote will play all transitions and builds automatically according to the timetable you set. In the Document Inspector's Transitions field, set the number of seconds Keynote should wait before starting a transition to the next slide (for slides with builds, this countdown starts after the last build is complete). In the Builds field, set how long to wait before starting each build on the slide.

Figure 15-7:
In the Document Inspector → Document tab, pick "Self-playing" in the Presentation pop-up to turn your presentation into a timed slideshow. Set the presentation's standard settings in the two Delay fields for transitions and builds; you can override these settings for individual slides in the Slide Inspector and Build Inspector.

These document-wide settings apply to transitions and builds set to begin "on click." If you've already customized transitions and builds for individual slides to happen automatically, Keynote will respect those custom settings and play them just as it would for a normal slideshow. That means that you can use the Document Inspector settings to set standard timings but create special timings for individual slides:

- **Transitions.** Open the Slide Inspector to the Transition tab, set the Start Transition pop-up menu to Automatically, and enter the number of seconds you want to display the slide in the Delay box. Keynote allows a maximum delay of 600 seconds.

- **Builds.** Open the Build Inspector's Build Order drawer, set the Start Build pop-up menu to "Automatically after", and enter the time delay in the Delay box—up to 60 seconds.

Recorded Slideshows

Recorded slideshows capture your voice and presentation for posterity, playing it back exactly as you saved it. Before you can turn a normal presentation into a recorded slideshow, you first have to make the voice-over narration, where you do your patter as you advance through the slideshow. Keynote records both the audio and your slideshow timing, tying the two together to play them back like a movie. This is a good way to distribute a polished view-only presentation, or to capture a live presentation to share later on YouTube, for example. (See page 531 for more about exporting slideshows to YouTube.)

Tip: When you're making a recorded slideshow, it's best to wait to record until the very end of the editing process, when you're sure that the design is complete and the slides are in their final order. If you make changes after recording your voice-over, it can put the slideshow out of sync, requiring you to rerecord it.

To record a voice-over narration:

1. Select the slide where you want the recording to start. (After you complete your recording, when you play the slideshow, it will always start at this slide.)

2. Open the Document Inspector → Audio tab, and click Record (Figure 15-8); or choose File → Record Slideshow.

   Keynote starts up your slideshow, and a red light in the top-left corner of the screen tells you that recording is in progress, with a meter showing your input volume.

3. Start giving your presentation, speaking clearly to record your narration, and advancing through each slide as you normally would.

4. Continue to the end of the slideshow (or at least until the last slide you want to include in the self-playing show). Press the Escape key to stop the slideshow and save your voice-over recording.

5. **Switch to the Document Inspector → Inspector tab, and choose Recorded from the Presentation pop-up.** This option becomes available only after you record narration.

Figure 15-8:
After you create the narration for a recorded slideshow, the Document Inspector → Audio tab shows that there's a saved recording. Listen to your voice-over by pressing the Play button, remove it by pressing Clear, or rerecord by selecting the slide where you want to start, and then press Record. You can also adjust the playback volume here.

After recording the narration and setting the presentation type to Recorded, you can review your handiwork by clicking the toolbar's Play button. No matter what slide is selected when you click Play, a recorded slideshow always starts at the first slide where you started your narration. Likewise, it always ends on the slide where you stopped the recording.

Tip: If you click Play in the toolbar and you don't hear your narration, you probably haven't chosen Recorded as the presentation type. Review step 5 above.

If you don't like part of your recorded slideshow, you can rerecord the whole thing, or pick a slide in the middle where you want to start rerecording. Select the slide where you want to start recording your next pass, and click Record in the Document Inspector → Audio tab.

If you already made a voice-over for the selected slide, Keynote gives you two options:

• **Record from Beginning.** This means you're starting from scratch, throwing out the original recording and starting over from the selected slide.

• **Record & Replace.** This option lets you replace the end of your original recording, starting with the selected slide. Keynote keeps all the narration for the slides that came before the selected slide and then tacks your new narration onto the audio afterward. This is the way to go when you want to pick up your narration in the middle of the slideshow.

If you're starting your rerecording on a slide that wasn't included in your original narration, Keynote offers the same "Record from Beginning" option to start from scratch. Instead of "Record & Replace", however, Keynote now offers "Record & *Append*", which lets you add the slide and your new narration to the end of your previous recording.

Tap, Tap. Is This Thing On?

To get your voice into the Macintosh, you need a microphone. Most Macs have built-in microphones—but don't be tempted to use them to record narration. The quality's poor and they pick up a lot of noise from the computer. Instead, consider using an external microphone to give your slideshow the audio it deserves; consumer-level microphones are inexpensive ($100 or less) and deliver much better results. If your Mac has an analog audio input jack and you've already got a microphone, you can plug it right into your computer (although you might need an adapter cable to plug into the Mac's 1/8-inch stereo mini plug).

If your Mac doesn't have an audio input jack, you'll need a USB microphone like the G-Track from Samson (*www. samsontech.com*), the Snowball from Blue (*www.bluemic. com*), or the MXL.006 from Marshall Electronics (*www.mxl*

usb.com). You can also use a telephone operator-style headset that plugs into your Mac's USB port, like the headset made by Plantronics (*www.plantronics.com*). Bonus: You can also use a headset for online game-playing or making calls over the Internet with programs like Skype or Apple's iChat.

Once you've plugged in your microphone, you can set your input levels in your Mac's System Preferences. Choose → System Preferences, and click the Sound button in the Hardware pane. In the Sound Preferences window, click the Input tab and select your microphone. Adjust the input volume, and when you're happy with the silky sounds of your own voice, close the window.

Setting Up Hyperlinks-Only Slideshows

Instead of feeding your presentation to your viewers with an automated slideshow, you can make the whole thing self-serve. In a hyperlinks-only slideshow, people help themselves to your presentation's buffet, navigating through the slideshow at their own pace by clicking onscreen buttons to move from slide to slide.

You can't simply turn a normal presentation into a hyperlinks-only presentation the way you can with a self-playing presentation. You have to plan ahead for this kind of slideshow when you design and create your slides, because hyperlinks-only presentations require you to provide one or more hyperlinks on every slide (see page 458).

Once you've created a slideshow containing hyperlinks on every slide, you can turn it into a hyperlinks-only presentation. Open the Document Inspector, click the Document tab, and choose "Hyperlinks only" from the Presentation pop-up menu.

Tip: If you're creating a slideshow with "forward" and "back" buttons on every slide, give yourself a shortcut by adding those buttons to your master slides (you'll learn about editing master slides on page 538). Use arrow shapes as your buttons, for example, and add hyperlinks to each: In the Hyperlink Inspector, choose Slide from the "Link To" menu, and then pick "Next slide" or "Previous slide."

In this kind of presentation, Keynote expects viewers to navigate with hyperlinks—the normal slide-advancing techniques and keyboard shortcuts don't work. The only keys the program responds to are the Escape key and the period (.), which stop the slideshow; and the question mark (?) and the help key, which summon the now-useless Presenter Keyboard Shortcuts window, listing all the commands you can't use in a hyperlinks-only presentation.

Printing Slides and Handouts

Printing isn't the first thing that pops into your mind when you think of presentation software, but printing your slideshow is extremely helpful—or even essential—in certain circumstances. You'll find printing useful in order to do any of the following:

- Provide a printed handout of some or all of the slides so your audience members can make notes during the presentation, but not be distracted by mindlessly copying information from the screen.

- Print your slideshow-in-progress, along with your draft presenter notes, for review by your team members, or for your own use so you can study it on the subway or before the big event.

- Print your slideshow outline so you can run your text by the legal department.

Choose File → Print, and Keynote unfurls the Print dialog box. If it's just a tiny window with two pop-up menus, click the blue arrow next to the Printer menu to reveal Keynote's print options in their full glory (Figure 15-9). Choose your printer in the Printer pop-up menu. If you want to print more than one copy, enter the number of copies in the Copies box. If you want to print less than the whole slideshow, enter a slide range, like 3 to 12, in the From and To boxes (or select the "Print selected slides only" option described in the option list below). To print just one slide, enter its number in both boxes.

Choose Keynote in the menu displayed under the page range fields to reveal all of Keynote's options for printing your slideshow. The left column lets you choose the big-picture layout for your printout:

- **Individual Slides.** Choose this style to print one slide on each page at maximum size.

- **Slides With Notes.** Use this style to print one slide on the upper half of each page with the slide's presenter notes on the lower half.

- **Outline.** Select this style to print out only the outline, just as it appears in the outline pane (sorry, free text boxes don't make the cut).

- **Handout.** Choose this style to print between two to six slides on a page, using the pop-up menu to determine the number. Keynote arranges the slides from top to bottom on the left side of the page, in a layout that's intended for taking notes next to each slide. Turn on the checkbox marked "Add divider lines" to include a

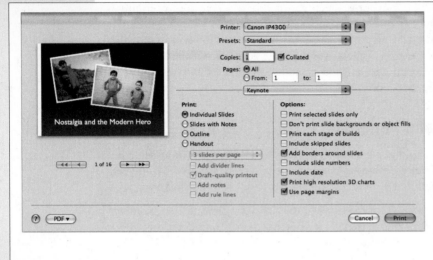

Figure 15-9:
The Mac's print dialog box looks different depending on which version of Mac OS X you're running. Here, Mac OS X Leopard shows a preview of your printed document at left; click the arrow keys to flip through all the pages that will be printed. At the right, Keynote-specific printing options are shown. To switch to other printer options, make another selection from the pop-up menu labeled Keynote.

separator line between slides. Turn on the checkbox marked "Draft-quality print-out" to speed up printing. For most handouts, it's a good idea to turn on both of these checkboxes. The "Add notes" option plugs your presenter notes into the space at the right, and "Add rule lines" inserts lines into the note area—for those of us who otherwise can't figure out how to write straight.

Tip: The Handout layout option is the only one of Keynote's options that offer multiple slides per page. If you're after more of a grid layout, however, you can get that by choosing the Individual Slides option and then picking Layout from the pop-up menu under the page range fields. There you'll find options for squeezing multiple pages onto a single sheet of paper, perfect for printing a light-table-style grid of slides. Unfortunately, the Print dialog box's preview doesn't show you this alternate layout after you've chosen it. You have to actually print or choose "Open PDF in Preview" from the PDF pop-up button to see the final layout.

Use the checkboxes under Options to determine how Keynote prints the slides. These options are available for all of the printing styles except Outline, which doesn't print slide images.

- **Print selected slides only.** This option prints only the slides you selected in the slide navigator when you chose File → Print. To select multiple slides in the slide navigator, ⌘-click or Shift-click the slide thumbnails to print.

- **Don't print slide backgrounds or object fills.** This option saves ink and makes your slides more legible at smaller print sizes. If you use light text on a dark background, never fear; Keynote switches the text color to black so that you can still read it. Turn this checkbox on unless you absolutely need to see backgrounds and fills in your printout.

- **Print each stage of builds.** When you turn on this checkbox, Keynote prints each slide build as a separate slide. You can leave this option turned off if you use builds only to gradually add bullet points to a slide. However, you might turn on this option when you build slide elements in and out repeatedly, which would leave you—if you turn this checkbox off—with a printout showing a confused pile of elements in the slide.

- **Include skipped slides.** If you've removed any of your slides from the presentation by skipping them (Slide → Skip Slide), turn on this checkbox and Keynote includes them in the printout.

- **Add borders around slides.** Turn on this option to print a hairline border around each slide to show the slide's outline—useful if it has a white background or if you've turned on the "Don't print slide backgrounds or object fills" option.

- **Include slide numbers.** This option is another one you probably want to turn on to print the slide number next to each slide image.

- **Include date.**

- **Print high resolution 3D charts.** This option enhances the print quality of 3D charts.

- **Use page margins.** This option makes sure the slide borders stay within the printer's print area.

Note: Keynote doesn't have the usual File → Page Setup option to select your paper size and orientation. Instead, these options are tucked away in the Print dialog box. To change these settings, choose Page Attributes from the pop-up menu that says Keynote when the Print dialog box first appears. Keynote's standard page orientation is landscape (horizontal). This orientation is the way to go if you're printing full slides, but for notes, handouts, and outlines, vertical orientation's probably a better choice.

Got it? Click Print, and you're done.

Exporting to Other Formats

Keynote allows you to export your slideshow to a variety of file formats, making your presentation accessible on computers that don't have Keynote installed—or to heathens who don't own Macs. You can save your presentation for editing and viewing in PowerPoint or Keynote '08, or you can export it for browsing as a PDF, a collection of HTML files, a QuickTime movie, or as a thicket of JPEG, PNG, or TIFF image files.

Note: Previous versions of Keynote could save slideshows as Flash, too. This feature was removed in Keynote '09.

Saving as PowerPoint

The 800-pound gorilla of presentation software is, of course, Microsoft Power-Point. Keynote can save slideshows in PowerPoint format which people can view and edit on any computer—Mac or Windows—that has PowerPoint. Although PowerPoint uses the same file format on Mac and Windows, these two operating systems handle fonts and graphics in completely different ways, which you'll surely notice when you view your presentation on a Windows computer.

Equally frustrating are the inconsistencies when you export from Keynote to Power-Point on the Mac. Many of Keynote's transitions and builds don't display properly—or at all—because PowerPoint doesn't know the corresponding effect. Keynote does the best with what's available, mapping effects to similar effects when it can; otherwise, transitions are replaced with a standard dissolve. Some bulleted text may disappear, the appearance of fonts and graphics can change, and movies and sounds may not display as you intended. In other words, nearly all of Keynote's panache is vulnerable to this translation because PowerPoint doesn't know all of Keynote's tricks. If you need to play your presentation on a computer that doesn't have Keynote installed and you want to preserve Keynote's visual splendor, export it as a Quick-Time movie; you can play and control it just like the original Keynote slideshow.

Still, there are times you want to—or have to—save your slideshow in PowerPoint format. Unlike a QuickTime export, you can edit a Keynote slideshow you've exported to PowerPoint like any other PowerPoint presentation. Just limit yourself to simple transitions and build effects—in other words, avoid all the cool stuff that Keynote does so well. That way, your slideshow can make the transition from Keynote to PowerPoint with little change.

Keynote gives you two ways to save a PowerPoint presentation:

- Choose File → Save As and, in the Save dialog box, check the Save Copy As checkbox and choose PowerPoint Presentation. (If you don't see this option, click the blue downward-facing arrow at the top of the dialog box to get the expanded view.)

- Choose Share → Export, and click the PPT button, and then click Next. Keynote rolls out the Save dialog box (Figure 15-10).

Tip: You can leave the name of the document the same as the Keynote file's name. Keynote appends the .ppt extension to the name so that you—and your Mac—can tell the different versions apart.

Saving as Keynote '08

If your friends are doing a poor job keeping up with the Joneses—that would be you—when it comes to upgrading to the latest version of iWork, you can save your slideshow as a Keynote '08-friendly file. Choose File → Save As, turn on the Save Copy As checkbox, and choose iWork '08. New features included in iWork '09, such as new transitions or build effects, will not of course make the leap to this older format, so your slideshow may lose a bit of visual flair when you do this.

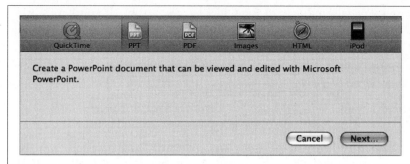

Figure 15-10:
*When you choose Share →
Export, Keynote presents its
various export options. Pick
one of the formats, and then
click Next to either select more
options or open the Save
dialog box.*

Sorry, your pals are out of luck if they're using an even older version; your best option is to export as PowerPoint and then let the laggards import that into their version of Keynote.

Creating a QuickTime Movie

When you export a Keynote slideshow as a QuickTime movie, you can preserve all your transitions and builds, since QuickTime actually creates a movie, frame by frame, while Keynote plays your slideshow. Unlike a traditional movie, though, this is a movie that you can control like your original slideshow. A QuickTime movie gives you the same presentation options as you have for your regular Keynote slideshow—you can click to advance slide by slide and build by build, or save it as a self-playing, recorded, or hyperlinks-only slideshow. (Choose View → Enter Full Screen in QuickTime Player to show your slideshow at full strength.)

Better yet, when you save a presentation as a QuickTime movie, you can play it on any computer that has QuickTime Player installed. QuickTime is Apple's media authoring and viewing software, so the player software comes on all Macs—and also on any Windows PC with iTunes installed. You can also download it free and install it on Windows machines: Download the latest version for Mac or Windows at *www.quicktime.com.*

QuickTime lets you save your presentation in various sizes and qualities, ranging from large files with full-quality video down to small files more suitable for a web page.

Tip: Keynote also creates QuickTime movies for two of its other export options, too. Choose iPod in the Share → Export dialog box to make a movie optimized for your iPod or iPhone (page 527), or choose Share → Send To → iWeb and choose Video Podcast to send a QuickTime movie to your iWeb site (page 532).

To get started choose Share → Export, and click the QuickTime button to reveal the export options for this format (Figure 15-11). Begin by picking a presentation style from the Playback Uses pop-up menu. These options perfectly mirror the presentation styles available in the Document Inspector for Keynote slideshows (page 422):

• **Manual Advance.** Similar to Keynote's normal presentation style, you advance through the slides and builds by pressing the space bar or arrow keys, clicking the mouse, or clicking Play in the QuickTime controls. (If you have a white Apple Remote for your Mac, you can also use it to advance a QuickTime movie, pressing Play to move to the next slide.)

- **Hyperlinks Only.** Advance through the slideshow by clicking hyperlinks that you create when you design the slideshow (page 458).

- **Recorded Timing.** This is the same as Keynote's recorded presentation style; to use this option, you first have to record voice-over narration (page 512).

- **Fixed Timing.** When you view this kind of QuickTime slideshow, you have absolutely no manual control—every slide and build advances automatically. This kind of movie is like Keynote's timed self-playing presentation (page 511), except the build duration and slide durations are the same for the entire slideshow—you can't vary the timing on individual slides.

  When you choose this option, Keynote gives you more fields to control the display. In the Slide Duration field, enter the number of seconds each slide should remain on the screen after all its builds are complete; in Build Duration, enter the number of seconds that should separate each build on the slide. In the Repeat pop-up menu, choose: None to make the slideshow play just once; Loop to make it play continuously; or Back and Forth to play backward when it reaches the end, then forward when it hits the beginning, and so on.

Whatever playback style you choose, check the "Enter full screen mode when opened" option to make the slideshow take up the whole screen instead of letting QuickTime open it in a window. You might not want to do this if you choose a small, low-quality file size in the settings below, because the movie won't look very good at full screen. But if you save the movie as a full-quality file, this option will look great—the next best thing to presenting the slideshow in Keynote itself.

Select a size and quality for the movie from the Formats pop-up menu. Keynote displays the details for the current setting beneath the two checkboxes.

- **Full Quality, Large.** When you choose this setting, QuickTime creates the best quality movie, at 24 frames per second (fps), with the same pixel dimensions as your slides. As always, high quality means large file size—and this setting creates the largest files.

- **CD-ROM Movie, Medium.** Choose this option to create a movie with a smaller file size—suitable for including on a CD-ROM, for example. These movies have half as many frames—12 fps—which makes your transitions and movies appear jerkier than the silky smooth flow of the full-quality option. This setting produces movies that are one quarter the size of the full quality movies, creating a 400×300 pixel movie from your 800×600 pixel slides.

- **Web Movie, Small.** Opt for this setting to sacrifice presentation size and quality in order to make a movie small enough to include on a web page or send via email. To achieve this small file size, QuickTime quarters the movie size once again, resulting in a 12 fps, 200×150 pixel movie from your 800×600 pixel slides.

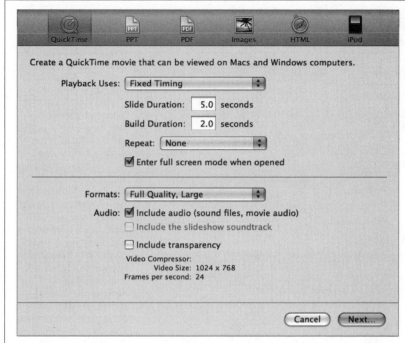

Figure 15-11:
Select options from the QuickTime export pane to determine the movie's type and quality. When QuickTime creates a Fixed Timing movie, you can set the slide and build duration, and whether or not the movie loops. These settings override any you may have set in Keynote's various inspectors.

- **Custom.** Choose this setting if you prefer to "roll your own" QuickTime settings in order to produce some other blend of size and frame rate, use a different video compressor, or alter the movie's audio quality, as explained in Figure 15-12.

Tip: If the slideshow includes an audio soundtrack, the QuickTime movie will keep on playing until the audio finishes. If your slideshow is a lot shorter than the audio, consider using a shorter audio file for your soundtrack.

If your slideshow includes any sound, turn on the checkbox marked "Include audio" to include it in the QuickTime movie. If your slides' background is set to None (see page 463), turn on the "Include transparency" option to export the movie with a transparent background. This is handy if you want to include your QuickTime movie inside another video project—or even another Keynote slideshow—to composite your slides seamlessly onto another background. (Some transitions won't display properly with this option on—so if you turn it on, review the transitions in your QuickTime movie after the export.)

When you've set all the QuickTime options, click Next to open the Save dialog box. Then name the movie, select a destination folder, and click Export.

The Export to QuickTime window appears, displaying each slide as QuickTime churns through every slide to convert your slideshow into a movie. If you're exporting at full quality, you have the pleasure of watching QuickTime process

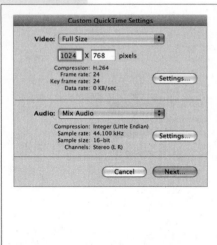

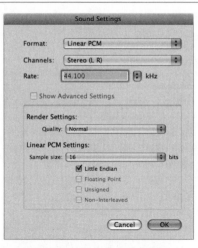

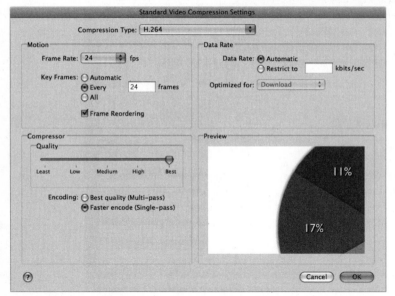

Figure 15-12:
If Keynote's three off-the-rack QuickTime formats don't provide the fit you desire, choose Custom to create the ultimate bespoke export. The Custom QuickTime Settings dialog box (top left) lets you set a custom movie size, and its two Settings buttons lead to the Video Compression Settings (bottom) and Sound Settings (top right) dialog boxes, with which you can tweak QuickTime's video and audio behavior. You can choose from a bewildering array of quality settings and audio and video compression schemes, or codecs—compression/ decompression algorithms. QuickTime could use a Missing Manual of its own to help sort out all these settings—but until then, you can learn about them from Apple's collection of QuickTime resources at www.apple.com/ quicktime/resources/.

each frame as it turns your slide transitions and builds into 24 fps motion pictures. This might be a good time to go out for some fresh air, mow the lawn, or see what's on TiVo.

When Keynote finishes exporting, double-click the new QuickTime file to open it in QuickTime Player. If you've saved your slideshow as a fixed-timing or recorded-timing movie, it starts playing immediately. If you saved it as a manual-advance or hyperlinks-only slideshow, the first slide appears and awaits your command.

Saving as PDF

If you want to share your slideshow with people who don't have Keynote, and you'd like to use a format that's more universal than PowerPoint or QuickTime, Keynote lets you export your slides as a PDF document, which pretty much any computer can open. Every Mac can read PDF files with OS X's Preview program, and Adobe makes free versions of its Adobe Reader program for virtually any computer operating system—making PDF the best bet for a universally readable file. Along with exporting your slideshow as a HTML web page, PDF is a good option when you need to distribute your slideshow to the masses, no matter what software they might (or might not) have installed.

Alas, all of your soaring transitions and builds are brought to a standstill in a PDF file, which reduces your slideshow to a collection of static images. That means, of course, that your viewers don't see any transitions, builds, or movies; or hear any sounds. But they can see all your text and images, making PDFs a useful way to solicit comments from your coworkers before the presentation, or distribute the slides to your workshop attendees afterwards. Exporting to a PDF also preserves any hyperlinks in your slideshow, so you can still navigate a PDF for hyperlinks-only slideshows, for example.

To create a PDF document from your slideshow with the Export command, choose Share → Export, select PDF, and Keynote rolls out the PDF export options (Figure 15-13). Select your settings, and click Next. Give your file a name, pick a destination folder in the Save dialog box, and then click Export.

Exporting Slides as Image Files

Keynote can turn your slideshow into a collection of individual image files—one for each slide or build. You'll find this ability handy when someone asks you to email a copy of just one or two of your slides, or if you want to include a few of your slides in a Pages document as part of a handout, or on your website. Keynote can create image files in three different formats:

- **JPEG** is the most popular compressed image format. JPEG compression can yield files that are a small fraction of the original file size, although at some sacrifice of image quality. Keynote lets you adjust the quality (and file size) of JPEG images—the higher the quality, the larger the image file.

- **PNG**, pronounced "ping," is designed for use on web pages. Like JPEG, PNG also compresses the image file, but produces a higher-quality image.

- **TIFF** image files aren't compressed—and therefore have the highest possible image quality, but also the largest file size.

Tip: Keynote can also export your slide images directly to iPhoto as a new photo album. For details, see page 534.

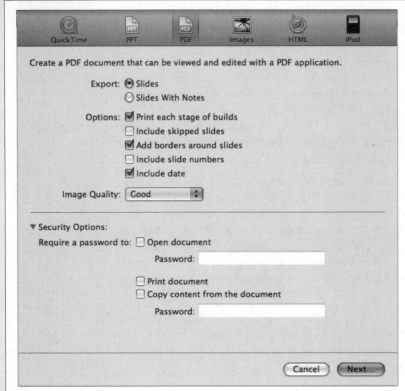

Figure 15-13:
The PDF export settings provide many of the same options as Keynote's Print window (page 515). In addition, you can choose the image quality; select a lower quality to reduce the file size— the lowest option, Good, is fine for viewing onscreen, Better works well for basic printing, and Best is ideal for final-draft high-quality printing. The security settings let you require a password for certain activities.

To export images, choose Share → Export, and click the Images button. The Image Export dialog box appears (Figure 15-14). To create an image from each slide in the slideshow, click All. If you want to create images from just some of the slides, click the From button and enter a range of slide numbers in the two boxes. To create an image of just one slide, enter that slide number in both boxes.

Turn on the "Create an image for each stage of builds" checkbox if you need individual image files for each of your slide builds. Use the Format pop-up menu to select the type of image file: JPEG, PNG, or TIFF, and then click Next to bring up Keynote's Save dialog box.

Enter a name for your images in the Save As box. As Keynote saves each of your slide images, it appends a number to the name you enter here—resulting in, for example: rocket-boots001, rocket-boots002, and so on.

Select a destination folder. If you want to keep your slideshow images together in their own folder, click New Folder, give the new folder a name, and then click Create. Finally, click Export, and a progress bar appears to give you an indication that Keynote's toiling away, converting your images.

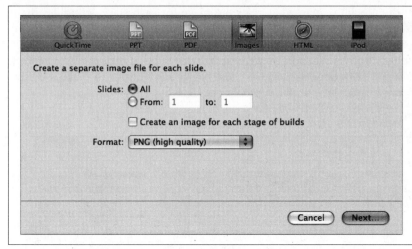

Figure 15-14:
Set the slide range and format for an image export, and choose whether to make individual images from each build. It's often a good idea to make a sample export of one slide in each format and compare their quality, so you can judge the three qualities.

Exporting a Slideshow as a Web Page

Everybody's got a Web browser, which means that everyone can view your slideshow when you export it as a web page. Right up there with saving your presentation as a PDF file, HTML is an ideal format for distributing your slideshow far and wide without running into software compatibility trouble. You can view the slideshow right in your browser, clicking the mouse to advance or using the optional navigation buttons to move back and forth.

Like exporting a PDF file, though, the resulting web page is stripped of your slideshow's transitions, build effects, movies, and music. In this format, your slideshow becomes a collection of still pictures—the same pictures, in fact, that you would get from exporting the slides as images, only presented together on a web page. Also, and this might seem strange for a web page, any hyperlinks in your slideshow don't make it through the export; clicking your slides advances to the next slide or build, period.

Tip: Saving a slideshow as a web page isn't the only way to share it on the Web. You can display an exported QuickTime movie on a web page, for example, and Keynote also offers several easy options tailored for sharing the presentation online at sites like iWork.com, YouTube, or via your own iWeb site. See page 515 for details.

The size of the resulting web page matches the slide size in the Document Inspector (page 528). To make sure that the slideshow can fit into the browser window, you'll get the best results by setting that size to 800×600 before doing the export. With that done, you're ready to go: Choose Share → Export, and click the HTML button.

The HTML Export dialog box appears (Figure 15-15). To make your web page include every slide in the slideshow, click All. If you want to create images from just some of the slides, click the From button and enter a range of slide numbers in the two boxes. To create an image of just one slide, enter that slide number in both boxes.

Turn on the checkbox marked "Create an image for each stage of builds" if you need individual slides for each of your builds. Turn on "Include navigation controls" to add forward/back buttons to the web page, as well as a "home" button to take you back to the first slide—otherwise, the only option is to click the slides to move forward. It's a good idea to use these navigation buttons to make it crystal-clear to your viewers how to move around the slideshow.

Use the Format pop-up menu to select JPEG or PNG as the picture format for your slides, and then click Next to bring up Keynote's Save dialog box.

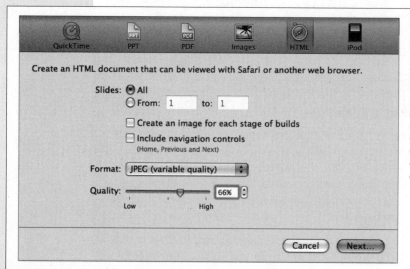

Figure 15-15:
Choose your display settings for exporting your slideshow as an HTML web page. When you select JPEG as the image format, the Quality slider lets you find the right balance between file size and image quality. Try exporting just one or two slides at different quality levels to experiment and find the lowest acceptable setting.

Enter a name for your web page in the Save As box, select a destination folder, and then click Export.

Sharing your exported web page

Keynote saves your web page as a HTML file, but also saves a folder of files alongside it, using the same name you provide in the Save dialog box. This folder contains the pictures of each of your slides and needs to travel along with the HTML file in order for browsers to show the complete page. If you're sharing your new web page on a website, be sure that you upload both the file and the folder to your web server.

Actually, a website isn't a requirement for sharing your web page. You can also email it to others or distribute it on a CD, and your viewers can open the page in their browser from there. The one catch is that you always have to include both the HTML file and its accompanying folder. For email, that means that you have to compress these files into a single file, a zip file; on the other end, your recipients will unzip the file to get at your web page. To zip it, go to the Finder and locate the HTML file and the folder. Select both of them by ⌘-clicking each one, and then choose File → Compress 2 Items; your Mac creates a file named Archive.zip. You can send that zip file via email.

Exporting to iPod or iPhone via iTunes

Keynote's final export option is labeled iPod in the Export dialog box (Figure 15-16), and it's really a stripped-down version of the QuickTime option that just happens to add the movie to your iTunes library. From there, you can sync the movie to your video iPod or iPhone.

Movies on the iPod can play only straight through—you don't have the same options to control them manually or by hyperlinks that you have for a regular QuickTime movie. Keynote offers you either fixed-timing or recorded playback options in its Playback Uses pop-up menu. (For details on these, see page 519 in the Creating a QuickTime Movie section.) Choose whether you'd like to include audio in the movie, and then click Next.

Figure 15-16:
Exporting an iPod movie creates a small QuickTime movie optimized to play on your video iPod or iPhone. The settings are an abridged version of the QuickTime options; Keynote handles all the size and compression settings to make it the right format to fit in your pocket.

Keynote's Save dialog box appears. Enter a name for the movie in the Save As box, pick a folder for the file, and click Export. The Export to QuickTime window appears and shows you Keynote's progress through your slideshow. When its work is complete, Keynote launches iTunes and imports the movie into your library.

Emailing Slideshows

Sending your Keynote documents via email is probably the most common way that you share your slideshows—possibly even more than presenting them to crowds of adoring fans. Keynote makes emailing an easy process, letting you export the file and open an email message with the file already attached, with just one click.

Choose a file format—Keynote, PowerPoint, or PDF—from the Share → Send via Mail submenu, and Keynote opens Mail, your Mac's email program. A new message window appears with your file already attached, ready to be addressed and mailed.

Note: This command is tuned to use Mail. If you use another email program, you'll have to go the long way 'round: Export the file (to send in a non-Keynote format), create a new mail message in your favorite email program, and attach the file manually.

The caveats mentioned earlier about exporting your slideshow as PowerPoint or PDF apply here, too: The result may not exactly match your original Keynote slideshow. Also, emailing a PDF with this method doesn't give you all of the options that you have when you create a PDF from the Share → Export dialog box. Instead, Keynote makes its formatting decisions for you in order to create the smallest file size—the same results you'd get by exporting the file with build stages excluded and the image-quality option set to "Good." For finer control over the export process, use Share → Export instead, and then create your email message manually.

Note: If you added a password to your Keynote file, this password isn't added to emailed PDF and PowerPoint files, only to the Keynote version. If security is important for your document and you don't want to send the Keynote format, the only password-protected option is to first export the file as PDF and then email the file manually. Choose Share → Export and pick PDF to start the export. Flip the triangle next to Security Options and select your password preferences.

Sharing Your Slides Online

From collaborating with team members before your presentation to sharing your brilliance with the world after the fact, posting your slideshow online makes it easy for others to find your work. Keynote offers built-in tools to fast-track your presentation to the Web: Share and collect feedback at iWork.com; post a movie version of your slideshow on YouTube; or add the slideshow to your own iWeb site or blog.

Using iWork.com with Keynote

Whether you want to share a slideshow with coworkers, distribute lecture notes to your class, or run a presentation by your team, iWork.com is a nifty way to do it. The Web-based service is specifically designed to help you share a document with a small group of viewers to collect their feedback. Many of us typically do that by circulating a document in email, but feedback can be difficult to track that way. And with Keynote's media-heavy files, you're often working with files big enough to make email servers choke. Loading your slideshow to a site like iWork.com solves both problems, providing easy file-viewing and a single location for gathering comments.

For detailed info about using iWork.com, head back to page 332 for the full review. Meanwhile, here's the quick lowdown, with a few notes specific to using iWork.com with Keynote slideshows. To send a slideshow to iWork.com:

1. **Open the slideshow in Keynote, and choose Share → Share via iWork.com.**

   If Keynote prompts you to sign in, enter your Apple ID and password. See page 333 for details on these gatekeeping items.

2. **In the iWork.com invitation window (Figure 15-17), type the names or email addresses of the people you'd like to view the slideshow, and enter the subject and message text for the invitation email.**

3. **If you choose to allow downloads from iWork.com, click Show Advanced to choose the file formats to offer.**

   The standard offerings are iWork '09, PowerPoint, and PDF, but you can choose any combination that you like and also add iWork '08 to the mix.

4. **Click Share, and Keynote cranks away at the upload, showing its progress and the estimated time remaining.**

   For big files—especially files with audio and video—this can take quite a while. Go read a Dostoevsky novel, and come back when you're done.

5. **Keynote lets you know when it's done sending the file to iWork.com and offers to take you there. Click the View Document Now button to go.**

   You can go to the page later from the Shared Documents screen: Choose Share → Show Shared Documents. You'll also receive an email with a link to the document page at iWork.com.

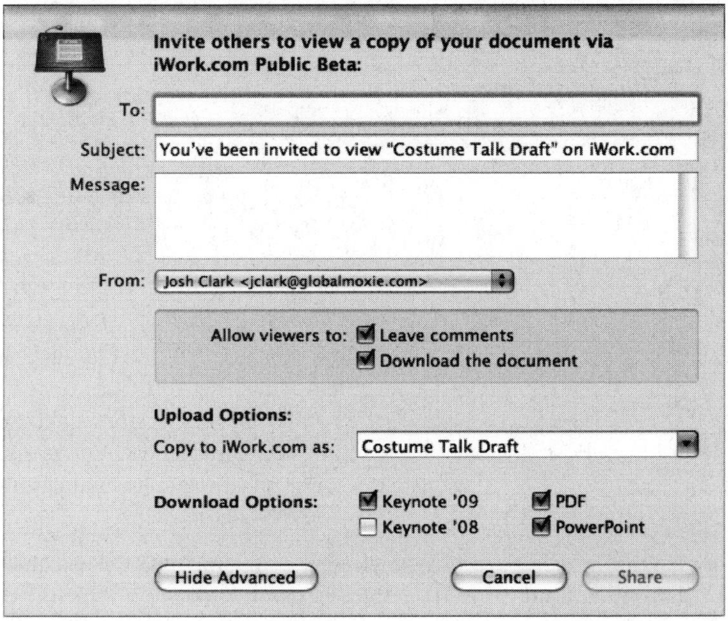

Figure 15-17:
To invite people to view your Keynote slideshow at iWork.com, choose Share → Share via iWork.com, and Keynote displays the iWork.com invitation window. Type your guests' names or email addresses in the To field, and type the subject and message text for your invitation. Choose whether to allow visitors to leave comments or download the slideshow; click Show Advanced to reveal the file name and download options shown here.

Keynote slideshows in iWork.com don't dance and wiggle they way that they do when you watch them in Keynote with all of your builds and transitions. Instead, viewing your slideshow at the iWork.com website is very much like looking at a PDF version of the slideshow (in fact, under the hood, that's exactly what it is).

Still images replace movies; there's no audio; and slides have no builds or transitions. Apart from that, this static version of your slideshow (Figure 15-18) looks exactly the same on the Web as when you designed it—with all the pictures, fonts, and charts just as you placed them.

Tip: Even though you can't see the full-motion effects in your browser, you *can* see them when you download a Keynote or PowerPoint copy of the slideshow from iWork.com and play them on your computer.

Figure 15-18:
The iWork.com view of your Keynote slideshow offers the same layout as it does for Pages and Numbers documents: an optional slide navigator at left (click Show Navigator if you don't see it), the current slide in the middle, and information about the slideshow and its viewers at right. Jump from slide to slide by clicking a thumbnail or using the navigation arrow buttons.

Comments are slightly different in Keynote than in Pages; instead of anchoring to specific text, comments float free on the slide.

To add a comment to a slide, there's no need to select a specific part of the slide to comment on as you do in Pages. In Keynote, comments float free on the slide, not anchored to any particular text. To add a comment, click the Add Comment button at the top of the screen, and a yellow sticky note appears on the slide: Type your comment and click Post. To add a reply to another comment, click the Reply button in the comment box. As in Pages, iWork.com puts a comment indicator on thumbnails in the Navigator to show that those slides have comments.

When you download the slideshow in the Keynote '09 format, the document includes all of the comments added in iWork.com. (Comments are not included in PowerPoint, PDF, or Keynote '08 documents; they're also not included in the Keynote '09 file if you set the original file to require a password before sending it to iWork.com.)

YouTube

If iWork.com documents are aimed at small groups of friends and coworkers, YouTube movies are just the opposite—videos aimed at getting the attention of the whole world. You can add your Keynote slideshows to YouTube's boisterous collection of online movies—an easy way to share your slideshow and allow others to embed it in their own blog or website, too.

Note: Before you can add your own motion-picture masterpiece to YouTube, you have to create a YouTube account. If you don't have one yet, visit *www.youtube.com* for more information.

Choose Share → Send To → YouTube, and Keynote shows you a form to provide your YouTube account information and details about the movie (Figure 15-19). Click Next, and Keynote asks you a few questions about how you would like to format your slideshow movie.

Note: Choose carefully from the "Size to Publish" pop-up menu. The Mobile size can be viewed on the iPhone and iPod Touch, but Medium can't.

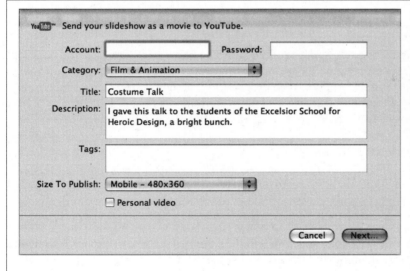

Figure 15-19:
Choose Share → Send To → YouTube to share your slideshow as a movie on the super-popular video-sharing website. To get started, enter your account details, and type the title, category, and description of your slideshow. In the Tags field, type keywords that describe your slideshow's topics; these will help people find it when they search on the YouTube website.

Choose a movie size from the "Size to Publish" pop-up menu. Keynote offers two choices—Mobile (480×360) and Medium (640×480). If you don't want your movie to be seen by anyone but you or by viewers you've designated, turn on "Personal video".

Just like exporting a movie for iPod, your YouTube movie can be one of two presentation styles: Fixed Timing or Recorded. (Recorded is grayed out until you make a voice-over narration for the slideshow; see page 512.) For Fixed Timing movies, choose timings for these two settings:

- **Slide Duration.** The number of seconds you want the movie to pause before advancing to the next slide (this countdown starts after the last build on the slide, if any).

- **Build Duration.** The number of seconds you want the movie to pause between builds.

If your slideshow has an audio soundtrack, include it in the movie by turning on "Include the slideshow soundtrack"; ditto for "Include the slideshow recording" to include your recorded voice-over narration, if any.

Click Next, and Keynote treats you to a screenful of legalese from YouTube. Click Publish to agree to the website's legal terms and conditions, and Keynote churns out the movie and uploads it to YouTube. When it's done, Keynote lets you know that it has left your movie in YouTube's capable hands—and that it might be a few minutes before the site can process it and make it ready to play. Click the View button to go to the YouTube web page listing your uploaded videos, where you can wait for your movie to be ready… just like lining up outside for the big summer blockbuster on opening day.

iWeb

Don't let all this talk about sending your slideshow to iWork.com and YouTube distract you from proudly posting your Keynote creation on your very own site. If you happen to use Apple's iWeb program to maintain your website, blog, or podcast, Keynote can send it right over as a Keynote document, PDF, or QuickTime movie, even creating a video podcast of your slideshow in full swing.

Note: This feature requires iWeb '08 or later.

Choose Share → Send To → iWeb, and Keynote asks how you'd like to pack up your slideshow for the Web. Choose an option from the File Type pop-up menu:

- **PDF.** When it's important to make sure that anyone and everyone is able to open and view your slideshow, PDF is the best option to choose, although it removes all animations, audio, and video from your slideshow. Keynote offers you the same formatting options you get when you choose PDF from the Share → Export window (see page 523).

- **Keynote Document.** This shares a copy of your original document, but of course it can be viewed only if your website visitor uses Keynote.

- **Video Podcast.** This is a QuickTime movie's fancy-pants alter ego, a movie that appears not only on your website but also in your site's *podcast feed*. When visitors subscribe to your podcast, their podcast program—iTunes, for example— automatically loads your videos (and now your slideshows!) as soon as you add them to your site, allowing them to watch your movies the moment they're available. When you choose the Video Podcast option, Keynote offers you the same formatting options you get when you choose iPod from the Share → Export window (see page 527).

Whatever format you choose, Keynote saves a separate copy of the file for iWeb; any subsequent changes that you make won't appear on the iWeb site unless you resend the slideshow later. When you've made your choice, click Send, and Keynote beams your document over to iWeb. If you haven't yet set up a site in iWeb, it asks you to select a template to use and creates a site. If you've already got multiple sites, iWeb asks you which site you want to edit. A brand new page opens with a thumbnail image of your document.

Tip: For more details about using iWeb to build web pages, launch iWeb and choose Help → iWeb Help.

Shipping Your Slides to Other iApps

You've already seen how you can send your slideshow to iTunes (page 527) and iWeb; Keynote plays matchmaker with several other "iApp" programs, too, letting you use your slideshow in iChat, iDVD, iPhoto, and GarageBand.

Sharing Slides in iChat Theater

When you combine Keynote and iChat, you don't have to be in a darkened room to share your slideshow—you don't even have to be in the *same* room. Instead, a feature called *iChat Theater* lets you transmit your presentation across the Internet in a video chat. Pitch your marketing presentation while you sit at home in your pajamas; you control the slideshow from your desktop, and your audience watches it on theirs, listening to your voice as you take them through your spiel. You can give the presentation to anyone with whom you could normally have a video chat.

Note: You need Mac OS X 10.5 or later to use iChat Theater. For help with using iChat, launch the iChat program and go to Help → iChat Help.

If you already have a video chat underway, you can fire up your slideshow in iChat Theater by dragging the Keynote file's icon from your desktop and into the video chat window. Otherwise, follow these steps to start your slideshow:

1. **In iChat, choose File → Share a File with iChat Theater.**

   iChat opens the "Share with iChat Theater" window. Browse your hard drive to find your Keynote document, and click Share.

2. **A window appears in iChat asking you to start a video chat. Pick a buddy from your buddy list, and then click Buddies → Invite to Video Chat.**

Keynote opens and loads your slideshow, and the first slide of your slideshow is displayed in the iChat video window. Now you can use the usual set of Keynote controls to advance through your slides, just as if you were giving your presentation in front of a live audience. On the other end of the iChat, your slideshow fills your buddy's video screen. When your slideshow is finished, close the Keynote control window, and you return to a regular video chat.

iDVD

Burn, baby, burn your slideshow onto a DVD. Keynote can save your slideshow as a movie that you can use to create a new movie project in iDVD, or add to an existing project. The result is a big-screen version of the QuickTime export option, with all the fancy wrapping that you can add to videos in iDVD.

Choose Share → Send To → iDVD. Keynote slides out a window where you can set your video options:

- **Video Size.** Select Standard or Widescreen to determine the shape of your slideshow.

- **Playback Uses.** Choose Manual Advance, Recorded Timing, or Fixed Timing—all of the options that you normally have with a QuickTime export (page 519), except for hyperlinks-only.

- **Audio.** Turn on this checkbox to include sound with your slideshow. (This option is grayed out when you've chosen Manual Advance.)

Click Send, enter a file name for your movie, and click Export. Keynote cranks through your slideshow, converting it to a QuickTime movie, and then opens the file in iDVD, where you can create your dynamite DVD.

iPhoto

If you like the idea of exporting your slides as images (page 523), but think it's just too messy to scatter them into a folder on your desktop, you can keep things neat and tidy by adding them to a new iPhoto album instead:

1. **Choose Share → Send To → iPhoto.**

   Keynote offers you the same formatting options that it offers in the Images pane of the Share → Export window.

2. **Choose your image settings, and click Next.**

3. **Keynote asks for a name for your new iPhoto album. Enter a name, and click Send.**

   iPhoto launches and imports your slide images into the new album. (Nifty side benefit: This means your slides are also now available in the Media Browser, available to any of your iWork apps on demand.)

GarageBand

Apple's music-making software, GarageBand, isn't just for making tunes. You can also use it to add audio to a timed or recorded version of a slideshow movie. GarageBand is your Mac's sound studio, and you can use it to mix your own narration, music soundtrack, zany morning-zoo sound effects, whatever. Technically, you can do this for any QuickTime movie—there's nothing special here about Keynote slideshow movies—but Keynote makes it easy to export your slideshow movie to GarageBand in a format particularly suited for video podcasts or playing on your iPod. If you're meticulous about the audio of your podcasts, make GarageBand a way station on the way to your website:

1. **Choose Share → Send To → GarageBand.**

   Keynote offers you the same formatting options that it offers in the iPod pane of the Share → Export window (page 527).

2. **Choose your presentation timing (slide and build durations) and click Send.**

3. **Give your video a name and choose a destination folder to save it. Click Export.**

   GarageBand opens and creates a new document with your slideshow as a movie track. You're ready to lay in your soundtrack—John Williams, eat your heart out.

With all this attention on sharing your slideshow with audiences, websites, and even other software programs, there's one important person who's been left out: You. Never fear, you can use Keynote to share with yourself, too, by making it easy to reuse the elegant slide designs you've created. Just like Apple's theme designers have shared their skills with you, you can do the same by creating your own Keynote themes that you can use again and again or—why be greedy?—share with others, too. Turn the page to learn how.

Customizing Keynote Themes

Don't be fooled by the good looks of Keynote's theme library—it's a lot more than a pretty face. Sure, Apple's elegant themes look great (and they make you look great, too), but deep down, they're all about productivity and efficiency. Using one of these themes lets you skip the big-picture design phase and get right to work on your material. And when you use a theme, each of your slides is based on a master slide, which means you can instantly apply changes to a whole batch of slides by updating that master layout—or by changing the standard look of the theme's text, charts, and other objects. Customizing themes, in other words, lets you work smarter and faster, sidestepping the need to make changes to individual slides, object by object, over and over again.

When you customize a theme—or build one from scratch—you only have to do it once. You can save your creation as its own theme to use it again for other documents, and Keynote adds it to the Theme Chooser, giving you yet another starting point for building your slideshows: a standard theme for your company's marketing presentations, your school's slideshows, or just a blank slideshow with the standard settings configured the way you like. Share your theme with others or, if you suffer from a debilitating fear of document design, install a theme created by someone else. You can find lots of additional themes online, for free and for sale (see page 548).

This chapter tours Keynote's theme machinery, showing you how to create and modify themes and install new ones.

Keynote Theme Basics

Whether your design is baroque or basic, every slideshow is based on a theme, which boils down to a collection of prefab slide designs called *master slides,* each with its own layout and standard settings (slide background, fonts, object fills, and so on). Master slides lay the foundation for the overall layout and look of each slide in your presentation; you can change the layout of an individual slide by choosing a different master slide from the toolbar's Masters pop-up button. If you later edit a master slide's layout or settings, the changes automatically appear on all the slides based on that master.

When you edit a theme, you're really just editing its master slides—updating the layout or background, adding a logo or copyright notice, switching the standard colors of its charts, and so on. You can also build a theme from the ground up, creating new master slides from scratch.

To work with a theme's master slides, you first have to open the master slide navigator. In the toolbar, click the View button to Show Master Slides, or, in the slide navigator, drag the Slides pane separator, as shown in Figure 16-1. The navigator shows thumbnails of all of the master slides for the slideshow's theme—the same thumbnails that show up in the toolbar's Masters menu.

Master slides have a few special features, but for the most part, they look and work just like regular slides when you edit them. Select a master slide in the navigator, and Keynote displays it on the slide canvas, ready to edit like a normal slide.

Modifying a Theme

Keynote comes with 44 themes, and for any given project, chances are that at least one or two of these themes will come mighty close to the design you'd like to use. When a theme is "close but not quite," you can change it by editing its collection of master slides.

Note: When you edit these master slides in your slideshow, you're not making changes to the original theme, only to the way it looks in this slideshow. Other slides using the theme continue to use the theme's original set of master slides. You can, however, save your changes as a separate custom theme; see page 547.

Importing Master Slides

You can modify or add your own master slides to a theme, as you'll soon see, but don't overlook the lazy route: swiping the work of others (or at least of other slideshows). Keynote makes it easy to borrow master slides from other Keynote themes and documents. In fact, Keynote does this every time you apply a new theme to one or more slides in a slideshow: When you change a slide's theme by choosing from the toolbar's Themes pop-up button, Keynote pours all the master slides from the second theme into the master slide navigator. Keep adding new themes, and you keep adding new master slides, too.

Figure 16-1:
Left: Drag the pane separator (circled) down to reveal the master slide navigator.

Right: Click one of the master slides to modify it, duplicate it (press Return or choose Edit → Duplicate), or delete it (press Delete).

This can get a bit cumbersome, though. Sometimes you want only one or two of these master slides, not the theme's whole collection. To import just a single master slide to your slideshow, do one of the following:

- In another Keynote document, find a slide that's based on the master slide you wish to import, and drag it from *that* slideshow's slide navigator into the current slideshow's slide navigator, along with all of your regular slides. Keynote adds that slide to the slideshow and adds its master to the bottom of the master slide navigator.

- In another Keynote document, find a master slide you want to import and drag it from that slideshow's master slide navigator into the current slideshow's master slide navigator.

After you've imported the master slide into Keynote, it's yours to use, reuse, or modify, as if it had been part of your slideshow's original theme all along.

Modifying Master Slides

When you make a change to a master slide, the change cascades through every slide that uses the master slide. This makes it easy not only to change the layout and styles of these slides, but to add new standard content, too. For example, when you add a free text box or picture to a master slide, Keynote automatically adds it to the slides that use that master, making it a one-step process to add a slide number, logo, or footer text to lots of slides at once.

Note: If you want to create a new master slide without modifying the layout of any existing slides already in your slideshow, see "Adding New Master Slides" (page 542).

Each master slide holds some combination of the following layout elements and standard settings:

- Position of title and body text

- Background text and graphics

- Placeholders for pictures, movies, text, charts, and tables

- Standard text settings (fonts, bullet styles, and so on)

- Standard object settings (line styles, color fills, and the like)

- Slide transition styles

- Object builds

- Alignment guide positions

Note: Unlike regular slides (where you can select several in the slide navigator to apply changes to a bunch of slides at once), you can select only one master slide at a time. If you want to change the background of all your slides, for example, you need to do that one at a time, stepping your way through the whole collection. Take a deep breath, and prepare to apply the same background again and again. And again.

Changing any of those attributes on a master slide instantly affects the appearance of the slides generated from it. Move the title text box to a new location and change its color, and the titles of all of the slides based on that master switch to the new position and color, too. The exception is when you've already applied custom formatting to an individual, non-master slide. In this example, if you've already moved one slide's title to a new location, that slide won't get updated automatically when you move the master slide's title. Local changes on individual slides, in other words, override changes made at the master-slide level, while objects still in the master's original location get updated to reflect the change.

Tip: To make a slide come back in line with its master, choose Format → "Reapply Master to Slide".

In addition to simply changing what's already on the master slide, you can add new objects, too. Add an image object for your logo, a free text box for your copyright footer, or a shape as a decorative container around the whole slide. Think of your new objects like wallpaper; these elements appear on your slides as uneditable background objects—you can change their content only from the master slide, not from the regular slide.

The exceptions are the small handful of special objects controlled by the Slide Inspector: the title text box, the body text box, and media, text, or object place-holders. These portions of the slide are, of course, designed to be edited, so they don't simply sink into the background like other objects you add to a master slide. You turn them on and off from the Slide Inspector, which gets a new name and a slightly different look when you're editing master slides, which brings us to…

The Master Slide Inspector

When you select a master slide in the master slide navigator, the Slide Inspector bows out and gets replaced by the Master Slide Inspector (Figure 16-2). As in the Slide Inspector, the Appearance tab determines whether the slide displays the title and body text box, as well as an object placeholder (see page 546) and slide number. Turn the checkboxes on or off to toggle the display of these elements.

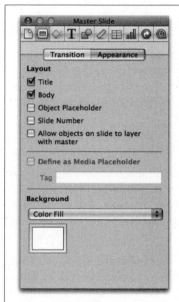

Figure 16-2:
The Master Slide Inspector replaces the Slide Inspector when you're editing a master slide, giving you new options in the Appearance tab, shown here. Include the various content objects on the master by turning on the associated checkboxes in the Layout section. Use the Background pop-up menu to choose whether to include a background fill, and if so, what kind.

If you want to add a transition—so that every slide you create from this master slide has a built-in transition—click the Transition tab and set it up just as you would for a single slide. (This sets a standard transition for slides based on this master, but you can change it or eliminate it on individual slides.)

The Master Slide Inspector also teaches the normal Slide Inspector two new tricks:

- **Allow objects on slide to layer with master.** This option lets you interact with a master slide's charts, images, shapes, and other objects when you edit your regular slides. Normally, when you add an object to a master slide, it becomes part of the background of your slides—you can't edit them, and they always float below any new content you add to your slides. This is normally quite convenient and makes it easy to add background images, like a company logo or "DRAFT COPY" watermark. However, when you want to interleaf regular slides' objects with the master slide's objects, turning on this checkbox lets you do just that.

• **Define as Media/Text Placeholder.** This lets you turn a picture or movie object into a media placeholder, or a text box or shape into a text placeholder. Select the object and then turn on this checkbox. For more details, see page 545.

Adding New Master Slides

The easiest way to create your own master slide is to find one that's similar to what you'd like to create and use it as a starting point. If you prefer to start from an empty slide, choose a blank master slide as your model.

In the master slide navigator, select the master slide you want to use as the basis for your new slide, and duplicate it using any of these methods:

• Click the toolbar's New button.

• Choose Edit → Duplicate.

• Press Return.

• Choose Slide → New Master Slide.

No matter which way you duplicate the original master slide, Keynote makes a carbon copy of it and displays its thumbnail in the master slide navigator. Double-click the new master slide's name—it's something like "Master #12" or "Blank copy"—and give it a more descriptive name. Then make changes to your new master slide as described in the previous section.

Changing Standard Object Styles

Every master slide has its own settings that determine the standard attributes of free text boxes, shapes, images, tables, and charts. So every time you add a new shape to a slide based on the same master slide, for example, it uses the same graphic styles—the fill color, line stroke, shadow, and so on. The same goes for all other objects, too.

You can change any of these styles by choosing an object with the exact formatting you want and then telling Keynote to start using that as a model instead. You can make this change for individual master slides or for the entire theme. From then on, anytime you insert a new object into your slideshow, it appears exactly the way you want it to—with the font, background color, outline, and so on, that you've defined. Say you don't like your theme's color scheme for shapes; here's how to change your slideshow's standard settings for new shapes:

1. **Insert an object into your slide.**

   It doesn't matter whether you insert this shape into a master slide or a regular slide. If you add it to a master slide, however, be sure to remove it when you're done so it doesn't appear on every slide based on that master—unless that's what you want.

2. **Format the shape with all the styles you want new shapes to have.**

   Choose a fill color, stroke style, shadow, font style, and so on.

3. **Choose Format → Advanced → "Define Shape for All Masters".**

   You've just defined the standard style for new shapes you add to your slide-show. To limit this change to objects added only to slides based on the current master, choose Format → Advanced → "Define Shape for Current Master".

You can similarly change the standard settings for every other type of Keynote object—insert the object, adjust it to your liking, and then define it as the default style in the Format → Advanced menu. Going forward, new objects you add to your document will mimic the formatting of that object.

Note: When you define the standard settings for an object type, all the other objects in the slideshow update to reflect the change. When you change the color of your default shape, for example, all other shapes change color, too, except for any that were explicitly set to use a different color. In other words, all shapes still using the original standard settings change to the *new* standard color.

Defining standard chart styles

Charts offer some complexities—and therefore some extra settings—you don't find in other objects. You can set the chart's size and the relative placement of its legend, and you can (sort of) independently choose the styles used by Keynote's various types of charts.

Start by adding a chart to the slide and setting the attributes you want it to use (Chapter 22 has complete details about formatting and styling charts). Resize the chart and position the legend so they're both sized and positioned the way you'd like new charts to appear in this theme. With the chart still selected, choose Format → Advanced → "Set Chart and Legend Geometry for All Masters".

Keynote gives you 19 varieties of charts to choose from, and you're supposed to be able to define a standard style for each chart type. At least that's the plan—it's a bit buggy in practice. You're supposed to create a chart in each of the 19 styles, format it the way you want it, and then choose Format → Advanced → "Define [chart type] for Current Master" (or "for All Masters").

However, when you define any one of the chart styles, it overrides settings you've defined in the other chart styles. Specifically, colors that you define for column, bar, and area charts also apply to their stacked counterparts, so default colors are always the same for both "regular" and stacked charts of each type. With that one exception, all of the remaining default settings apply to all chart types. So if you set up a chart with a certain number of gridlines for one chart type, the remaining chart types also get those same gridlines as their standard setting, no matter what settings you've given them previously.

In practice, this means that you should use the "Define [chart type] for Current/All Masters" command to set most default settings for all charts at once, and then set the chart's primary colors one at a time for each chart type.

Reverting to the Original Theme

Whoa, who'd have thought that mustard yellow, hot fuchsia, and mud brown would make such an ugly combination? If your attempts to embroider your theme with a few elegant touches have instead butchered it beyond recognition, Keynote lets you head back to square one and restore the original theme settings:

1. **To restore defaults to only certain slides, select them in the slide navigator** (Command-click to select multiple slides).

2. **Head to File → Choose Theme.**

    In the Theme Chooser, select the original theme and presentation size.

3. **Turn off the "Retain changes to theme defaults" option.**

4. **Choose All Slides or Selected Slides from the Apply Theme To pop-up menu.** Then click Choose, and Keynote restores the master slide defaults for the selected slides.

Building Themes from Scratch

Creating a brand new theme is really the same as modifying an existing theme, but with a bit of initial pruning and planning. Start out with just a single blank master slide: Create a new Keynote document from any theme—it doesn't matter which—and then choose View → Show Master Slides to open the master slide navigator. Delete all of the master slides except for one blank slide (you have to delete them individually, since Keynote doesn't let you select more than one master slide at a time). Now you have a clear space to build your theme's foundation.

Create a "Master" Master Slide

To make sure that you keep your background and text styles consistent from slide to slide, it's a good idea to create a *master* master slide—a model that you'll use as the basis for each of the master slides you create. That way you can duplicate this master slide to make new masters, and those slides will automatically inherit this slide's text and background settings. Get these settings right on this first master slide and you won't have to change them for subsequent slides.

To get started, select the master slide in the slide navigator. Then, in the Master Slide Inspector:

1. **Click the Appearance tab and use the Background pop-up menu to select a color, gradient, or image fill for your slide backgrounds.**

2. **Turn on the title, body text, and slide number checkboxes to add those text boxes to the master slide.**

3. **Click the Transition tab and choose a standard transition style, if any, from the Effect pop-up menu.**

With the title, body text, and slide number options turned on, you now have those three main text boxes on your slide. Set the size and position of these text boxes and—more importantly—format the font, text, and bullet styles for each text box the way you want them to appear throughout your theme. If you're feeling thorough, format each of the body text box's five indent levels differently so you can highlight their different levels of importance. If you always add builds to your body text boxes—making the body text appear bullet by bullet, for example—you can add those builds to the master slide to make that standard behavior (see page 474).

Tip: When setting a master slide's text formatting, it's particularly useful to have some sample text to work with. Create a regular slide in the slideshow, apply your master-in-progress to this sample slide, and add text and images to it. Then, as you make changes to the master, periodically switch to your sample slide to see the results.

Even if you don't plan to have all of these text boxes on every master slide you build (and you almost certainly won't), place these boxes in spots where you think most slides will use them. This is particularly important for the title text box; you don't want the title hopping around when you switch master layouts in your slideshow.

Finally, add any other background elements that you want to appear on every slide. Add these as regular image objects, text boxes, or shapes—for example, your company logo, a photograph, copyright text, or company tagline. Turn down the opacity of these objects to fade them if you plan to put text and other content on top of them in your slides. When you have your background objects in place, *lock* them so you don't accidentally select or move them: Select the objects and then choose Arrange → Lock.

With your "master of masters" complete, you're ready to start building your various master slides. Simply duplicate this original master slide for each new master you want to create, modifying each one to give it a unique layout.

Adding Text and Media Placeholders

When you first add objects to a master slide, Keynote adds them as background objects: Images, free text boxes, and other objects show up as fixed and uneditable on your regular slides. That's great for logos, watermarks, and other permanent fixtures, but not so wonderful if you're looking for variety. That's where *placeholders* come in. As their name suggests, these stand-ins simply show where text, images, audio, and movies should go—you replace them with your real content when you edit the slide.

Text boxes and shapes set to be *text placeholders* show up on your slides as regular objects, ready for you to edit their text. *Media placeholders,* on the other hand, have the extra smarts to know how to squeeze and stretch pictures and movies: When you drop a picture or movie onto a media placeholder, Keynote automatically replaces the placeholder with your selection, sized and positioned to fit the placeholder's dimensions.

You can add as many placeholders as you like to a master slide. To create one, add an object to the master slide and then select the object. In the Master Slide Inspector → Appearance tab, turn on the "Define as Media Placeholder" checkbox for a picture or movie, or the "Define Text Placeholder" checkbox for a shape or text box.

Naming placeholders with tags

The Tag field immediately below the "Define as Media/Text Placeholder" checkbox is optional, but it plays an important role. A *tag* gives your placeholder a name that tells Keynote how to translate placeholder content across different master slides. When placeholder objects have the same name, this tells Keynote that these placeholders should share content when you switch master-slide layouts.

For example, when you edit your slideshow and switch a slide's layout by choosing a new master slide, Keynote automatically transfers your title and body text to the new layout. But it transfers placeholder content only if both master slides contain text or media placeholders with the same tag. If each master slide has a media placeholder tagged "Illustration," then a picture in the placeholder will make the transition when you switch a slide's master. If the two master slides have different tags for their placeholders (or if the new master slide doesn't have a placeholder at all), then Keynote tosses out the picture and it doesn't show up in the new layout.

Because of this, it's a good strategy to be consistent and descriptive in the way you tag your placeholders. When master slides share placeholder names, it gives you more flexibility to change master slides without losing content in the switch.

Note: Because tags identify placeholders between master slides, you can't repeat tags on the same master slide. Every placeholder on a slide has to have its own unique tag.

Adding masks to media placeholders

Keynote's standard behavior when you drop an image into a media placeholder is to resize the image so it fits inside the placeholder without getting cropped. You'll always see the full original image, in other words, but it may not fill the whole placeholder; for example, dragging a horizontal picture into a vertically oriented placeholder leaves empty space above and below the picture.

To have Keynote automatically crop and resize pictures to fill the placeholder's exact dimensions—like Pages' placeholders do—add a mask to the placeholder image in the master slide. When you drop an image on a masked placeholder, Keynote fills the *entire* mask window with your picture. See page 230 for details about working with image masks.

Adding Object Placeholders

Object placeholders work like text and media placeholders, but they're designed to hold tables and charts. When you add one of these objects to a slide based on a master with an object placeholder, the table or chart drops automatically into the placeholder at the specified position and size. (You can drop images, movies, and audio into object placeholders, too, but after you do that, they'll no longer "catch" tables and charts.)

To add an object placeholder to a master slide, select the slide in the navigator and turn on the Object Placeholder option in the Master Slide Inspector → Appearance tab; Keynote adds the placeholder to the slide. Then simply position the placeholder where you want it and adjust its size.

Note: If you share your themes (page 548), it may not be immediately obvious to other Keynote users how to take advantage of your object placeholders, because they don't actually do much placeholding. Unlike text and media placeholders—which display sample text and pictures as visual cues to show you how to use them—object placeholders are empty, showing up only as gray-outlined boxes until you add charts or tables to the actual slide. This might be why Apple's own themes never use them.

Defining Your Theme's Object Styles

After you have a few master slides under your belt, you're ready to set the standard object styles for your objects, as described earlier on page 542. In the slide navigator, create a new slide from the master slide you're working on. Then insert and modify each type of object to create its standard appearance:

- **Free text box.** Enter some text in the box and then select and format that text. Set the background fill, the outline stroke, shadow, and opacity for the text box.

- **Shape.** Insert a shape, enter some text in it, and then select and format the text. Then set the background fill, the outline stroke, shadow, and opacity for the shape.

- **Image.** Insert an image and adjust its stroke, shadow, opacity, and reflection.

- **Table.** Insert a table and adjust its size, rows, columns, borders, headers, footers, and so on.

- **Chart.** Go through each of the chart types, styling each the way you want it to appear. See page 543 for some caveats about defining standard chart styles.

Choose Format → Advanced → "Define [Object] for Current Master" to save these standard properties only for slides based on the current master slide. Or choose Format → Advanced → "Define [Object] for All Masters" to save these standard properties for the whole theme. After you define an object's styles, you can delete it from the slide before inserting the next type of object you want to define.

Saving Custom Themes

After you've gone to all the trouble of modifying or creating your own master slides, they still exist only within that one Keynote document. But if you save them as a theme, they're available whenever you want them, right in the Theme Chooser.

Before you save your theme, though, take a few minutes to put together some sample slides in the document. These slides show up in the Theme Chooser when you skim your theme's thumbnails for a preview. As you build up your theme collection, these preview slides become invaluable reminders of just what the theme looks like. For example, previews for the Apple-designed themes all include a slide with a sample table and another with a chart to show the theme's default style for each.

When you're ready to go, choose File → Save Theme and give your new theme a name. If your theme's master slides contain sounds or movies, turn on the "Copy audio and movies into theme" checkbox at the bottom of the Save dialog box. Turning on this checkbox can make your theme's file size much larger, but it ensures that if you move your theme to a different computer or plan to share it with others, the audio and video files tag along for the ride.

Keynote's standard spot for saving themes is in a folder named Themes buried deep in your hard drive. Themes saved there automatically show up at the bottom of the Theme Chooser. You don't *have* to save your themes in Keynote's Themes folder, though. From the Save dialog box, select any destination folder you like, and then click Save. Even though the theme won't show up in the Theme Chooser, you can still open it from the Finder to create a new slideshow in Keynote.

Note: Keynote saves its theme files with the .kth file extension.

Sharing and Buying Themes

Now that you've created your own eye-popping Keynote theme, it's time to share it with your friends and coworkers. Send along your template as an email attachment, on a CD, or put it online to share with the world. First, though, you have to dredge up the theme file, buried deep in Keynote's theme basement. If you saved your theme in Keynote's standard location, you can get to it by navigating to this folder: *[your Home directory]→Library→Application Support→iWork→Keynote→Themes*. When someone sends you a new Keynote theme, you install it by dropping it into that same folder.

Whether or not *you* decide to share your creations, lots of other people are doing it. Apple's built-in Keynote themes includes a wide variety of designs, but there are hundreds, maybe thousands of other professionally designed templates for you to discover. Type *Keynote themes* into Google to find an ever-growing collection of theme developers. You'll find some of the best from the following companies:

- **Jumsoft.** *www.jumsoft.com*

- **Keynote Theme Park.** *www.keynotethemepark.com*

- **Keynote Pro.** *www.keynotepro.com*

- **One Eyed Goldfish.** *http://www.oneeyedgoldfish.com*

Part Three:
Numbers '09

3

Creating a Numbers Spreadsheet

Don't be fooled by its name: Numbers has a mind for math, sure, but the iWork spreadsheet program does much more than just crunch digits. If you've always thought of spreadsheets as the exclusive and arcane domain of the Accounting Department down the hall, think again. Numbers can juggle figures for the most demanding spreadsheet jockeys, but you can also use it to store and organize just about any kind of information.

A spreadsheet is a list machine: Use it for to-do lists, contact lists, event planning, team rosters, product inventories, invoices—anything you might put into a list or table, you can put in a spreadsheet. And then Numbers can make your list dance. Once you've plugged your data into Numbers, you can sort it, filter it, categorize it, or combine it with data from other lists. Numbers isn't just a fancy calculator, in other words; you can use it as your own private *database*—a place where you store, manipulate, and view data from all kinds of different angles.

And of course Numbers can do math, too. When your data happens to take the form of digits—class grades, your check register, a valuation of assets minus depreciation—Numbers churns through your calculations, updating your totals as you add and edit data. The program knows more than 250 *functions,* feats of mathematical gymnastics that range from simple addition to complex accounting algorithms.

But all that is standard stuff, describing the basic work of spreadsheet programs for the last three decades. What's novel about Numbers is its attention to visual design; your spreadsheets have never had such great-looking figures. Just like the other iWork programs, Apple gave considerable care to making it easy—even fun—to design stunning spreadsheet documents. Mix your data tables with color-ful charts, photos, and graphics, and they're suddenly multimedia presentations (Figure 17-1). You even know how to do it already: Laying out a Numbers document is just like creating a page-layout document in Pages, or a slideshow presentation in Keynote. Drop design elements onto the spreadsheet canvas as *objects,* nudge them into place, and style them with colors, picture frames, reflections, shadows—you name it.

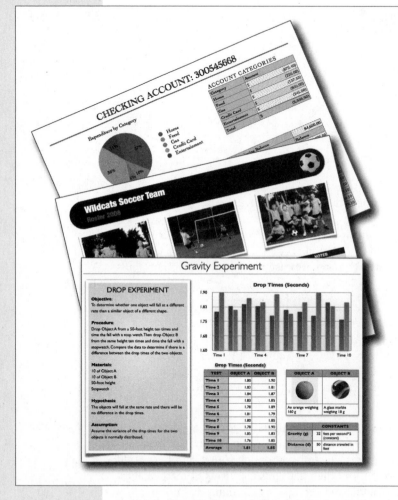

Figure 17-1:
In Numbers spreadsheets, you're not limited to gray columns of figures. You can add photos, charts, and text to create slick multimedia presentations. Apple's built-in templates offer stylish examples: Here, the Checking Register, Team Organization, and Gravity Lab templates show off some of the possibilities.

In this ballet of objects, *tables* are always the star in a Numbers spreadsheet. You already met these data grids in Pages (Chapter 8) and Keynote (Chapter 13), where they played only supporting roles. In Numbers, tables take the spotlight as the organizing elements for your data. The program's interface is designed for work-ing efficiently with table cells, adding a few tricks that you won't find in Numbers' iWork cousins.

This chapter gets you started with a high-level introduction to Numbers' features, showing you how to create, save, and print a basic spreadsheet, followed by a tour of a more complex and graphical report.

Picking a Numbers Template

As with the other iWork programs, your Numbers journey starts at the Template Chooser. When you launch Numbers or choose File → New to create a new document, the Template Chooser appears and tempts you with a selection of 30 spreadsheet templates (Figure 17-2).

Tip: If you find yourself turning to the same template again and again, you can cut out the Template Chooser by picking a standard template to use every time you open a new document. Go to Numbers → Preferences, click the General button, and then turn on the "Use template" option in the For New Documents section. Click Choose and select your standard template from the Template Chooser. After you do this, you can call up the Template Chooser any time by going to File → "New from Template Chooser".

Numbers templates play a different role than templates in the other iWork programs. In Pages and Keynote, templates define only the *look* of your document. While some Pages templates are designed for newsletters or reports, for example, you can fill them with any type of text or images. Numbers templates provide a similarly colorful and elegant selection of templates, but nearly all of them are intended for very specific purposes.

If you want to build an invoice, a workout tracker, a family budget, or a check register, Numbers has you covered with a template for each. Those templates are preloaded not only with a layout of page elements, like all iWork templates, but also with calculations designed to achieve the specified task. Their utility, in other words, comes from the particular jobs they've been programmed to do. As you'd expect, the Workout Tracker template can tally the number of days you've exercised, chart your running pace, and track your weight-lifting repetitions, but it can't help much with collecting your accounts receivable—that's an entirely different kind of legwork.

Unless a template specifically targets the same goal as your current project, it doesn't have much immediate use to you, at least not in the same sense as the fill-in-the-blank templates in Pages and Keynote. But even in such cases, Numbers templates are ideal demonstration documents, and they include sticky-note comments that give you hints about how they work. As you make your way through the next few chapters, be sure to browse the Template Chooser's offerings to explore how Apple pieced together the formulas and functions that make these templates tick. (You'll learn all about formulas and functions in Chapter 20 and Chapter 21.)

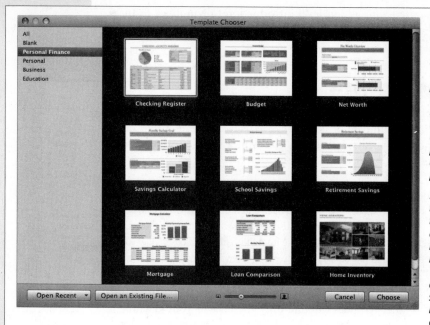

Figure 17-2:
When you launch Numbers or create a new spreadsheet, the Template Chooser prompts you to select a template for the new file. Pick the Blank template to get a basic grid, or choose one of Apple's prefab designs to accomplish one of their preprogrammed tasks.

Skim your cursor over a template's preview image to get a look inside, and double-click to open a new, untitled document based on that template. To open a file you've already created, make a selection from the Open Recent pop-up menu, or click "Open an Existing File" to pick a file on your hard drive.

When you select a category in the Template Chooser's left pane, Numbers shows you a preview of related templates in the main window. Run your pointer across the face of a template thumbnail to flip through its contents and get a preview of its chart and table colors. Double-click a template (or click it once and then click Choose) and a fresh, untitled document zooms out, based on the template you chose.

Tip: Even if you don't plan to use a template for its advertised purpose, you still might choose it for its styles—its color scheme and standard formatting. You can always wipe out a template's contents to start from scratch but still get the benefit of its good taste.

Your First Basic Spreadsheet

Up & Away, Megaville's leading superhero outfitter, has decided to invest in the next generation of heroes by launching a sidekick academy to train aspiring teen do-gooders. Enrollments have already surged beyond expectations, and the academy's new staff is struggling to keep up. The future of Megaville depends on these youngsters' talents, but the future of the sidekick academy depends on staying organized during this crucial startup phase. The first task is to create a contact list of all of these eager enrollees. Specifically, what's needed is a single place to track the sidekicks' "mask names" as well as their real names, ages, email addresses, phone numbers, and street addresses. It's Numbers to the rescue!

Gimme a Grid

To get started with your new spreadsheet, double-click the Blank template in the Template Chooser. Numbers opens a wide window containing a single *table*—an empty grid constructed from rows and columns that chop the table up into blocks called *cells* (Figure 17-3). Numbers labels its columns with letters (A, B, C...) and rows with numbers (1, 2, 3...). Columns and rows intersect in cells, giving each cell an address. Combine the column letter and row number to make a cell coordinate: For example, D4 is the cell in column D, row 4.

This table is where you'll enter the sidekicks' information. Each row will hold the info for one sidekick, with the cells of each column holding a single piece of contact info: first name, last name, age, and so on. You'll set up these rows and columns in just a moment, but first take a moment to get acquainted with your Numbers workspace.

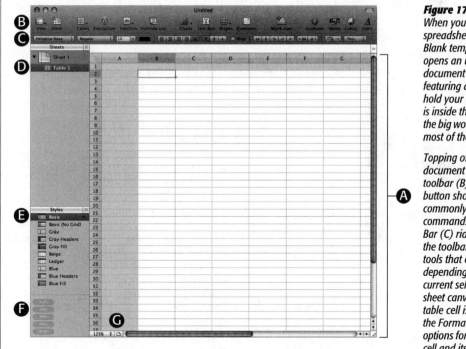

Figure 17-3:
When you create a new spreadsheet from the Blank template, Numbers opens an untitled document window featuring a large table to hold your data. The table is inside the sheet canvas, the big workspace that fills most of the window (A).

Topping off your document window is the toolbar (B), featuring button shortcuts to commonly used commands. The Format Bar (C) rides along below the toolbar with a set of tools that changes depending on your current selection in the sheet canvas. Here, a table cell is selected, so the Format Bar shows options for formatting that cell and its table.

At the left of the window, the Sheets pane (Figure 17-3, label "D") lists each sheet of your spreadsheet, along with the tables and charts on each one (see page 568). Below that, the Styles pane (Figure 17-3, label "E") lists a set of predesigned table styles that let you change the look of a table with the click of a button (see page 565). At the bottom, the Instant Calculation panel (Figure 17-3, label "F") shows the results of several calculations when you select more than one table cell (see page 565).

If you want to take a really close look at your data, you can zoom in. Choose a magnification level from the pop-up menu at the bottom left of the sheet canvas (Figure 17-3, label "G") to make your view larger or smaller, or choose Zoom In (⌘->)or Zoom Out (⌘-<) from the View → Zoom submenu.

The Toolbar and Inspectors

If you've already explored Pages and Keynote, then Numbers puts you in familiar surroundings. The layout, icons, and controls of the spreadsheet document window share lots of features with your word-processing and slideshow documents— starting with the toolbar, Format Bar, and inspectors.

The toolbar

At the top of the window, the Numbers toolbar offers quick access to 15 commonly used commands. You'll learn more about each of these buttons in the coming chapters, but Table 17-1 gives a quick tour. You can hide and reveal the toolbar by clicking the Tic Tac button at the top right of the window.

Like the other iWork programs, Numbers lets you customize the toolbar by adding, deleting, and reorganizing its buttons. To set it up just the way you want, Control-click the toolbar and choose Customize Toolbar to see your options. Page 40 has more details about this important bit of interior decorating.

Table 17-1. Numbers' Standard Toolbar Buttons

View · Sheet	*View* offers options for changing the document window display, and the *Sheet* button adds a new sheet to your spreadsheet (and to the Sheets pane). See page 568 for an intro to working with sheets.
Tables · Reorganize · Function · Formula List	Choose a table template from the *Tables* pop-up button, and Numbers adds a new table to the current sheet (see page 582), The *Reorganize* button sorts and filters table data (see page 642); the *Function* pop-up button adds a calculation to the selected cell (see page 564); and the *Formula List* button toggles the display of all of the formulas in your spreadsheet on and off (see page 697).
Charts · Text Box · Shapes · Comment	These object buttons insert a new chart (Chapter 22), text box (page 806), shape (page 806), or comment (page 600), respectively.
iWork.com	The *iWork.com* button lets you share your spreadsheets online.
Inspector · Media · Colors · Fonts	The *Inspector, Media, Colors,* and *Fonts* buttons summon the Inspector, Media Browser, Color Picker, and Fonts window, respectively.

The Format Bar

The Format Bar tags along below the toolbar, displaying an ever-changing choice of tools depending on your current selection in the sheet canvas. In Numbers, you spend most of your time working in tables and table cells, and so the Format Bar typically displays options for styling the text, data, colors, and borders of table data. But when you select another object type—a chart, text box, shape, or picture—the Format Bar updates its buttons and menus to show options that are specific to that object. If you prefer to give up this convenient strip of tools to save a little room, you can send it on its way by choosing View → Hide Format Bar. To bring it back, choose View → Show Format Bar.

The inspectors

As in all the iWork programs, Numbers relies on its 10 inspectors to direct every aspect of your document. Click the toolbar's Inspector button to open the Inspector window, and switch between inspectors by clicking the toolbar buttons lining the top of the Inspector window. (If you're not sure what a button is for, hover your pointer over the button to see its name.) This floating control panel gives you quick access to controls otherwise tucked away in the menus—along with a few that are unique to the inspector. You'll learn all about the inspectors and their many options in the coming pages and chapters.

Tip: To open a second (or third or fourth) Inspector window, choose File → New Inspector or Option-click one of the inspector buttons at the top of the Inspector window.

Working with Table Rows, Columns, and Cells

When you add data to your spreadsheet, you stow every piece of data in a table cell. *Cells* are formed by the intersections of *rows* and *columns,* which are the main organizing elements of your tables. Cell data can be just about anything: words, numbers, dates, time durations—whatever. In your sidekick spreadsheet, you'll stash a single snippet of info about each sidekick into each cell.

Tip: Before you even get started, it's a good idea to save your file right away. Choose File → Save and choose a name and location for your file. After that, make it a habit to tap ⌘-S to save the file every few minutes…just in case. For more info on saving your spreadsheets, see page 570.

Labeling your data in header rows and columns

The first thing you need to do is to figure out what data will go where. Start by naming your table's columns and rows. When you create a new spreadsheet using the Blank template, Numbers gives you a table with a *header row* and *header column,* which you use to label your table. The program shades each of these to set them apart from the rest of your table where you'll store the actual info (the *body rows and columns).* You'll learn all about the special role of header rows and columns on page 634. For now, just think of them as the places where you label your data.

Don't confuse the header row and header column with the table's *reference tabs*, the lettered and numbered labels at the top and left sides of the table (Figure 17-4). As you'll learn, those tabs let you select and edit an entire row or column at a time, and each one also acts as a handle that you can grab to move its corresponding row or column. You'll get a glimpse of reference tabs in action in a few pages, and you'll learn much more about them in the coming chapters.

In your contact list, every sidekick's personal info will be listed in a single row, with the data divided into columns. Start by labeling those columns: Click the table's top-left cell—the first cell of its header row, called cell A1 (column A, row 1)—and type *Mask Name*, the label for the first column. Hop to the next column to the right by pressing Tab or the right-arrow key, and then type the label for the next column. Repeat the steps until you've labeled all the columns you plan to use, as shown in Figure 17-4.

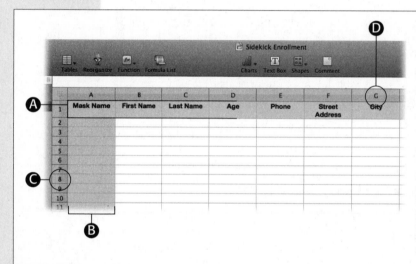

Figure 17-4:
Use the header row (A) and header column (B) to label your table's rows and columns. Here, the header row's cells label the columns with all the pieces of contact info for the new sidekick recruits.

Don't confuse header cells with the table's reference tabs, which likewise label the rows and columns with numbers for row tabs (C) and letters for column tabs (D). As you'll see, reference tabs help you to work with whole rows and columns at once.

See how the contact info is chopped up into elements? First name and last name are split apart, as are the street address, city, state, and zip. Although you could combine all of this info into a single cell, you're giving yourself more options by splitting them up. Separating the last name from first name lets you sort sidekicks by last name, for example, and isolating the city lets you look up sidekicks in a specific town. You could always add more columns to split this info later, but doing it up front saves you time and headaches. In other words, labeling your table is more than just being fastidious: You're really planning how you'll organize and access your spreadsheet's data.

Note: You don't *have* to set up your table data in tidy rows and columns. If you're feeling ornery, you can take a scattershot approach and add info to cells willy-nilly. But creating an orderly, tabular structure as shown in Figure 17-4 makes your data organized and, as you'll see in the following chapters, infinitely malleable. Oddly enough, creating a rigid structure actually makes the info more flexible.

Selecting and editing cells

The next chapter goes into all the down-and-dirty details of navigating and editing tables in Numbers, but the basics are straightforward: When you're working in a table, skip ahead to the next cell by pressing Tab or the right-arrow key. Press Shift-Tab or the left-arrow key to throw the machinery in reverse and jump one cell *back* (to the left). Use the up- or down-arrow keys to move—you guessed it— up or down. You can also click a cell to select it. (See page 582 for a roundup of other ways of selecting and moving around in tables.)

Tip: In many cases, you can use Return to move down to the cell below the selected cell and Shift-Return to move to the cell above. There are a few special considerations for the Return key, though; page 589 has the details.

Once you've selected a cell, just start typing to replace its contents. That's fine when you're filling in a cell for the first time as you just did with the header row. But when a cell already contains data, you wipe it out as soon as you start typing, replacing it with your new info. To edit a cell's contents instead of replacing it out-right, double-click the cell or press Option-Return.

That's all you need to know to start entering data; now you're ready to add your first enrolled sidekick, Wonder Lad. His info goes in the first row below the header row; type his contact info into each column in row 2. Uh oh, Wonder Lad has already run into his first crisis: Some of the cells are too small, causing some cells to run into each other and the street address to be clipped. Never fear, no cell can hold Wonder Lad; even though there may not be enough room to *display* the complete info in all the cells, it's still in there. In this case, you just need to make the column wider; Figure 17-5 shows you how. (See page 592 for more on handling content that's too large to display.)

If you find yourself squinting to see the text in your spreadsheet's tiny boxes, you can adjust the magnification level in the pop-up menu at the bottom-left corner of the sheet canvas. You can also do your typing in the *Formula Bar,* the text field just above the sheet canvas (Figure 17-6). The Formula Bar displays the contents of the selected cell in a large font size and gives you ample room to work, which is handy when you have a particularly long piece of info—or a lengthy formula, as you'll learn in Chapter 20. When you're done, press Return or Tab to store your changes in the table cell (don't just click another cell to leave the Formula Bar or you'll accidentally add a *cell reference,* another topic you'll learn about in Chapter 20).

Congratulations, you've got a bona fide spreadsheet on your hands. It's not much of an academy with just one sidekick on the books, though. Go ahead and add the rest: Jump down to the next row and add the info for the next sidekick, and then continue along through your list until all your sidekicks are on board.

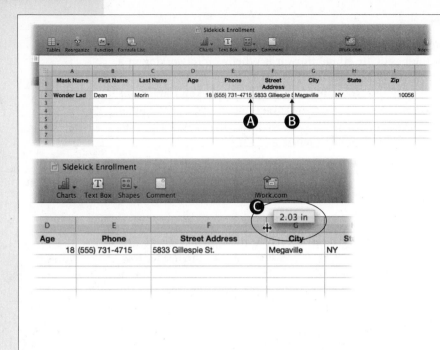

Figure 17-5:
Top: The cells in Numbers' standard table are often too small to display much text. Here, the phone number runs right up against the next cell (A), and the street address (B) is lopped off.

Bottom: To make a column wider or narrower, point to the right border of its reference tab until the cursor turns into a bar with two arrows (C). Drag the border to the right to make the column wider, or to the left to make it narrower—or double-click the border to make it expand so the cell is just wide enough to fit its contents. As the column expands, Numbers reveals the clipped info.

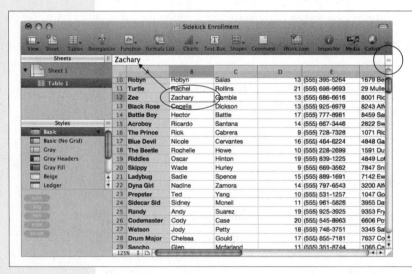

Figure 17-6:
When you crave a little elbow room, do your editing in the Formula Bar instead of directly in the cell. The Formula Bar always shows the contents of the selected cell; just place your insertion point and type away. You can resize the Formula Bar by dragging the handle on the right (circled) to make it larger or smaller.

Working with Address Book

If you've already got the sidekicks' contact info in your Mac's Address Book program, Numbers makes it easy to pull it into your table. Just drag an address card from Address Book, drop it into your table, and Numbers adds the info in a fresh row, using your column headings as hints for what info goes where (see Figure 17-7). In this example, Numbers recognizes First Name, Last Name, Phone, Street Address, City, State, and Zip. Fill in the remaining fields and you're done. See page 625 for the full story on using Address Book info in Numbers.

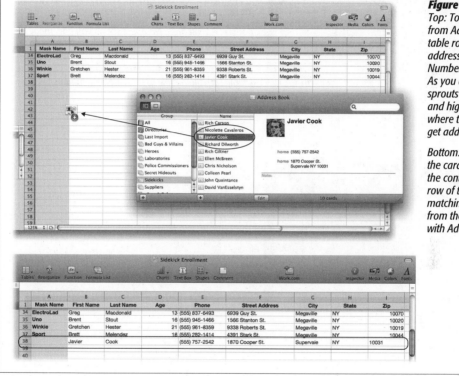

Figure 17-7:
Top: To add a contact from Address Book to a table row, drag the address card into the Numbers sheet canvas. As you drag, the cursor sprouts a green + sign and highlights the table where the contact will get added.

Bottom: When you drop the card, Numbers adds the contact in the last row of the table, matching column names from the header row with Address Book fields.

Adding and removing columns and rows

When you first opened your Numbers document, you got a table with 13 columns (A–M) and 45 rows. You're not using the last four columns (J–M), though; if you find all those empty boxes distracting, you can close them up by dragging the handle at the top-right corner of the table, just to the right of the last column reference tab, circled in Figure 17-8. Drag it left to resize the table and remove the empty columns, or drag it right to expand the table and add new columns.

Adding or removing empty rows from the bottom of the table works the same way, but this time you drag the handle at the *bottom* of the row reference tabs, at the bottom left of the table. Drag the handle up to remove empty rows or down to add new ones.

To add or remove both rows and columns at the same time, drag the handle at the bottom-right corner of the table instead.

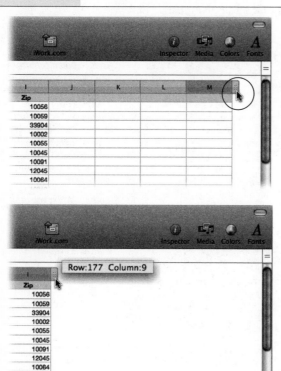

Figure 17-8:
Top: To close up unused columns, grab the handle at the far right of the column reference tabs and drag it to the left.

Bottom: As you drag, Numbers shows you how many columns and rows are in your table. Release the mouse button when the table is the size you want. You can also add new columns by dragging the handle to the right, or simply click the handle to add one new column.

You can't use this trick to delete rows or columns whose cells already contain data, however; Numbers stops resizing the table as soon as it runs into a filled row or column. That's a safety mechanism that prevents you from accidentally deleting data. You can override the safety by holding down the Option key while you drag, and Numbers removes rows or columns, empty or not. You can also select a cell in the row or column you want to delete and then choose Table → Delete Row or Table → Delete Column, but a faster route is to use the pop-up menu tucked away in every reference tab (see Figure 17-9).

You can likewise use a reference tab's pop-up menu to *add* a neighboring row or column. Add a new row by choosing Add Row Above or Add Row Below, add a new column by choosing Add Column Before or Add Column After. But because you'll use these commands often, do yourself a favor and learn the keyboard short-cuts (these work only when you've selected a cell, not when you're actually editing its text):

- Press **Option-right-arrow** from any cell to add a new column to the right.

- **Option-left-arrow** adds a new column to the left.

- **Option-up-arrow** adds a new row above.

- **Option-down-arrow** adds a new row below.

There's plenty more to learn about adding, deleting, rearranging, and resizing rows and columns—you'll find complete info starting on page 631.

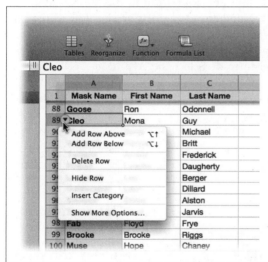

Figure 17-9:
Point to the reference tab for a row or column and an arrow appears, signaling the presence of the tab's shortcut menu. You don't have to Control-click here: Just click the arrow and a pop-up menu appears with several options for working with the row. Choose Delete Row to remove it, or choose Add Row Above or Add Row Below to insert a new row. You get similar options when you reveal a column tab's pop-up menu.

Sorting your spreadsheet

Now that you've packed your spreadsheet full of eager young heroes, it's a snap to get them in order. In fact, it's never been so easy to manage such a big group of adolescents. To make your sidekicks line up by last name, choose Sort Ascending from the reference-tab menu for the Last Name column. Numbers instantly shuffles your sidekicks into alphabetical order by last name. To sort by Mask Name instead, choose Sort Ascending from the pop-up menu for the Mask Name column.

Note: Numbers doesn't include the header row when it reorders your table, only the rows below. The header row always stays fixed at the top of your table.

You can also create more detailed sorting rules, even telling Numbers to filter out some rows as it goes—to show only sidekicks older than 16, for example. Numbers calls this process *reorganizing*, and you'll learn all about it on page 642.

Fast Math: Quick Formulas and Instant Calculations

You may have heard this news already: Spreadsheets are good at math. Numbers can manage incredibly complex *formulas* to display calculated values in any cell of your spreadsheet. You'll see a whiz-bang example of formulas in action later in this chapter, and you'll get the full story in Chapter 20 and Chapter 21. But before you go all Einstein on your spreadsheet, the simple truth is that most spreadsheet formulas aren't exactly rocket science. Most folks put spreadsheets to work by adding columns of figures or doing other basic math. Numbers makes it especially easy to do these common calculations with its *quick formulas,* six predefined operations that you can apply to a row, column, or group of selected cells.

To display the average age of enrolled sidekicks, for example, select the header cell for the Age column, click the Function pop-up button in the toolbar, and then choose Average (see Figure 17-10). Numbers adds a new shaded row to the bottom of your table—a *footer row*—and displays the average age in the Age column of the new row. (It turns out that 15.204545455 is a fine age to be a sidekick.) Want to display the youngest age instead? Select the Age header cell and then choose Minimum from the Function pop-up button; Numbers updates the column's footer cell to let you know that 9-year-olds are your youngest students.

Tip: Here again, don't confuse the header cell with the reference tab. The shortcut trick described above involves selecting the header cell (here, the cell labeled Age). If you click the reference tab instead (the tab labeled D in Figure 17-10), you select the whole column, and the quick formulas in the Function menu are grayed out.

Figure 17-10:
Apply a quick formula to an entire row or column by clicking its header cell and selecting a formula from the toolbar's Function pop-up button. When you add the Average function to the Age column, as shown here, Numbers adds a footer row to the table and displays the average in the Age column (shown in bold text at the bottom).

After you add a quick formula to your table, Numbers doesn't just forget about it. A formula is a smart placeholder that updates whenever relevant cells change (in this example, values in the Age column). If you add a new row or change any of the age values, the formula updates the cell to reflect the change. Using quick formulas on header cells as shown here is an easy way to tally whole rows or columns, but you can also use them to tally *any* selection of cells. To learn more about putting quick formulas to use, see page 674.

What's that? *Quick* isn't fast enough for you? When that's the case, Numbers rolls out *instant calculations,* a constantly updating dashboard of tallies based on your current selection of cells. The Instant Calculations pane is located at the bottom left of the document window. The pane's display is grayed out when you have fewer than two cells selected, but it lights up when you highlight numbers in more than one cell, showing you the sum, average, minimum, maximum, and count (the number of numbers) for your selection. Figure 17-11 shows an example, and page 672 lets you in on some nifty tricks you can do with instant calculations.

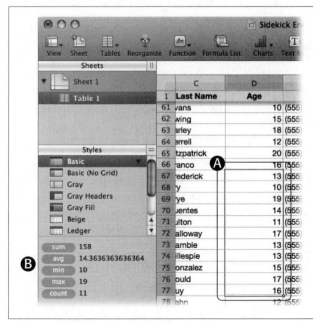

Figure 17-11:
When you select more than one cell (A), the Instant Calculation pane (B) shows stats for that group. From top to bottom, the pane lists the sum, average, minimum value, maximum value, and the count of selected cells. (These tallies don't include empty cells or cells with non-numeric values.) These instant calculations are a great way to glance at common stats about a select group of numbers—without having to add formulas to the spreadsheet.

Changing the Table Style

When you create a spreadsheet using the Blank template, Numbers starts you off with a simple grid, its header row and column displayed in gray. As you'll learn in Chapter 19, there are lots of ways you can dress up your table—styling its text, colors, and borders, and even adding shadows or pictures. Numbers tries to anticipate your style needs, however, so that you don't have to trouble yourself with the window dressing.

Every template, including the Blank template, comes loaded with several prefab *table styles*. To change the table style, click anywhere in the table and then choose an option from the Styles pane at the left of the document window. Presto! Your table now has alternating row colors, or blue headers, or no grid, or shaded cells. Anything on this menu of style options is yours to command. You can also create your own table style to add to this set of options; see page 663 for details about working with table styles.

Fancy Formulas and Glitzy Graphics

Even if Numbers stopped at the features you've already seen, you'd get a ton of good value there. You can squeeze lots of utility out of a homely grid like your sidekick contact list and other grids like invoices, expense reports, and accounting ledgers. But Numbers lets you create more than just simple grids: When you tune-up your spreadsheet with more sophisticated formulas and mix in some high-octane graphics, your workhorse columns of numbers turn into a multimedia report or an interactive cockpit that lets you monitor your stats.

You'll learn about these advanced techniques later in the book—formulas in Chapter 20, charts in Chapter 22, and other multimedia layout fun in Chapter 23. But just to see what's possible, take a quick spin through Apple's Grade Book template (which might come in handy for your sidekick academy). Choose File → "New from Template Chooser", click the Education category, and then double-click the Grade Book template. Numbers creates a new, untitled document based on the template (Figure 17-12).

The top of the spreadsheet looks familiar enough: a simple-looking grid. It's a table of grades with one student's grades on each row, lined up in a column of assignments. The header row shows the "weight" of each assignment (how much the assignment's score counts toward the final grade). The Total column uses those weights to calculate the final score, and the Final Grade column shows the corresponding letter grade.

Things get more interesting when you look at the bottom of the sheet, which features two more tables and a chart. See what's happening here? The sheet canvas holds more than one table, effectively letting you put lots of mini-spreadsheets onto a single sheet. The sheet works just like a page-layout document or a Keynote slide: You can drop pictures, charts, shapes, text boxes, and of course tables onto the sheet—as many as you like wherever you want.

Tip: To add an additional table to your sheet, click the toolbar's Tables pop-up button and choose a table template; Numbers drops a new table at the bottom of the sheet. For more about adding tables, see page 582.

When you add multiple tables to a sheet, the tables can stand alone, showing their own info independent of the rest, or they can talk to each other and swap data.

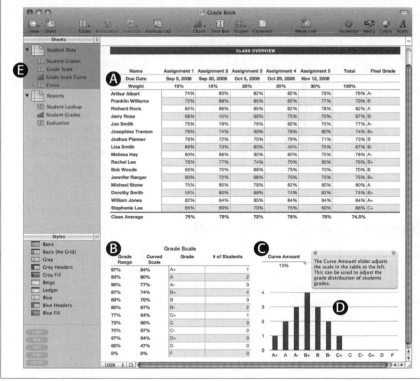

Figure 17-12:
The Grade Book template features three tables and a chart on its first sheet. Through the magic of formulas, the tables all share information. The top table (A) displays the students' grades, using the grade range scale in the Grade Scale table (B), which also counts the number of A's, B's, C's and so on from the top table (A). The Grade Scale table (B) adjusts the grade levels based on the amount in the tiny Curve Amount table (C). The chart (D), meanwhile, displays the grade curve, a visual graphic of the counts shown in the Grade Scale chart (B). All of these page elements are listed in the Sheets pane under the icon for this sheet (E).

Here, for example, the top table includes formulas that pluck information from the Grade Scale table to determine each student's letter grade in the last column. The Grade Scale table gets something in return, fetching info from the top table to count the number of students with each letter grade. The chart in the lower right, meanwhile, displays the same info graphically.

Curve Amount is the last table on the sheet, a little two-cell organism that indicates the amount to adjust the distribution of the grades. Click the Curve Amount percentage to edit it, and a slider materializes (see Figure 17-13). Drag it left or right, and the tables and chart all update on the fly to show the results of your revised grading curve. Changing the curve percentage, in other words, sets off a chain reaction that ricochets through the tables, updating several values at once.

This sounds complicated and looks impressive, but don't be daunted. It's really just a handful of well-placed formulas in table cells that monitor values in other tables and update when information changes. Moving the slider back and forth turns the whole thing into a machine for visualizing classroom grades on a curve. In Chapter 21, you'll explore how to craft formulas like this to make one table process or summarize the data of another. For now, just consider this template a demonstration of what's possible with Numbers—spreadsheets can be *much* more than simple grids.

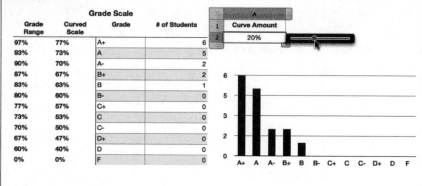

Grade Scale					
Grade Range	Curved Scale	Grade	# of Students		
97%	77%	A+	6		
93%	73%	A	5		
90%	70%	A-	2		
87%	67%	B+	2		
83%	63%	B	1		
80%	60%	B-	0		
77%	57%	C+	0		
73%	53%	C	0		
70%	50%	C-	0		
67%	47%	D+	0		
60%	40%	D	0		
0%	0%	F	0		

Figure 17-13:
Clicking the Curve Amount value in the Grade Book template unfurls a slider that you can use to adjust the curve value. As you move the slider, it changes the grade levels in the Grade Scale table, which in turn updates the chart and (though you can't see them here) the students' grades in the top table.

Organizing Your Data with Sheets

Once you start adding more tables to your spreadsheet, the sheet canvas can get crowded fast. To keep things clear and your message focused, you can organize your tables, charts, and other data into multiple sheets. Like adding a new slide to a Keynote slideshow, a new sheet gives you a fresh slate to display and work with your data. From its name, you might think that a sheet is a single page, but that's not the case; when you print it, a sheet can span several pages. A sheet is more like a chapter than a page, a way to organize your data around distinct themes for your spreadsheet's presentation:

- A company's financial statement might have separate sheets for the balance sheet, income statement, and cash flow.

- A lab report might have a summary sheet graphing the results of an experiment, with subsequent sheets displaying the raw data.

- The organizer for a Little League coach might include the team roster and contact info on the first sheet, the team schedule on the second, a summary of players' hitting stats on the third, and the detailed data for all at-bats on the fourth.

- Your personal spreadsheet for contact info might divide contacts into separate sheets for business, friends, and family.

To add a new sheet, click the Sheet button in the toolbar or choose Insert → Sheet, and Numbers gives you a clean sheet with a single table. The sheets are listed in the Sheets pane along with all their tables and charts, as shown in Figure 17-14. When you add a new sheet, Numbers automatically assigns it a name; if you're happy with such lyrical names as Sheet 1, Sheet 2, and Sheet 3, then you're all set. If you prefer something more descriptive, you can change the name by double-clicking it in the Sheets pane and typing a new name.

Note: You can also enter a new name in the Sheet Inspector's Name field. You'll learn more about the Sheet Inspector on page 574.

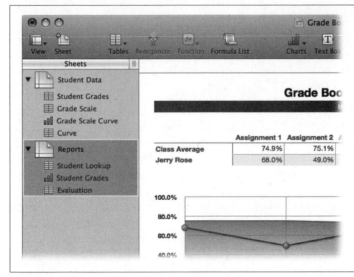

Figure 17-14:
The Sheets pane shows the sheets in your Numbers document, with the tables and charts for each one listed below. The current sheet is highlighted—here, it's the Reports sheet of the Grade Book spreadsheet. To collapse a sheet's list of charts and tables, click the flippy triangle next to its icon.

Shuffling Sheets in the Sheets Pane

Use the Sheets pane to move through your sheets: Click a sheet, and Numbers loads it into the sheet canvas. To shuffle the order of your sheets in the Sheets pane, drag a sheet's icon to a new position, or ⌘-click sheets to select several and then drag to move them as a group. You can also use the Sheets pane to copy a sheet, including all of its data and objects, using any of these methods:

- Option-drag a sheet's icon and Numbers adds a copy of the sheet wherever you drop it in the Sheets pane.

- Select a sheet in the Sheets pane and then choose Edit → Duplicate. Numbers adds the copy immediately *after* the selected sheet.

- Select a sheet in the Sheets pane and choose Edit → Copy or Edit → Cut. Select the sheet immediately *before* the spot where you want to copy the sheet (it can even be in a different Numbers document), and then choose Edit → Paste.

If you have several sheets, each with several tables or charts, the Sheets pane can become a long, rambling list. To squeeze sheets into a more compact view, click the flippy triangle next to each sheet's icon and Numbers hides the sheet's listing of tables and charts. Click the triangle again to display the full listing.

To delete a sheet and its contents, select it in the Sheets pane and press the Delete key. Tread carefully: When you do this, you delete the sheet's tables *and* all of their data.

Note: You can also use the Sheets pane to select, copy, and move tables (page 583) and charts (page 805).

Saving Your Spreadsheet

Choose File → Save or press ⌘-S to save your spreadsheet. The first time you save a Numbers document, the Save dialog box drops into view, letting you choose a name and location for your new file. If you're not familiar with the Mac's standard Save window, flip back to page 22 for a review.

If you want to share your spreadsheet with folks who use Microsoft Excel, Numbers makes it easy to save a copy in Excel format. Just choose File → Save As and, in the Save window, turn on the "Save copy as" option and pick Excel in the neighboring pop-up menu. (If you don't see this option, click the blue arrow at the top of the Save dialog box to reveal the extended view.) Click Save, and Numbers saves a separate version of your spreadsheet as a .xls file. That file's just a *copy*, though; after you save it, you return to your original Numbers document, and any changes you make don't make their way into the Excel version. To freshen the Excel copy, choose File → Save As again and save another copy of your document in Excel format. For more on saving your spreadsheet in other file formats, including possible translation troubles, see page 817.

Automatic Backups

Numbers, along with the other iWork programs, lacks an auto-save feature, which means that keeping your file safely stored on your hard drive is up to you and your ⌘-S reflex. Get in the habit of hitting this crucial keyboard combo every few minutes in case some digital disaster strikes.

You can get a bit of additional protection by telling Numbers to automatically save a *second* version of your document every time you save. This feature saves a copy of the previously saved version of your file so that you always have two copies of your spreadsheet. To set it up, go to Numbers → Preferences, click the General button, and then turn on the "Back up previous version" option. See page 59 for more about how this feature works.

Password-Protecting Your Spreadsheet

One shudders to consider what could happen if the home addresses of Megaville's future generation of heroes fell into evil hands. When your spreadsheet contains sensitive information, Numbers lets you lock it up with a password.

To add a password, open the Document Inspector (shown in Figure 17-16): Click the toolbar's Inspector button to open the Inspector window, and then click the inspector's Document button (the first one on the left). Turn on the "Require password to open" checkbox, and Numbers prompts you to enter and confirm a password, as shown in Figure 17-15. From now on, when anyone opens the spreadsheet, Numbers asks for the password. If you enter the wrong password three times in a row, Numbers displays the password hint you supplied.

To update the password, click the Change Password button at the bottom of the Document Inspector and follow Numbers' instructions by entering the old and

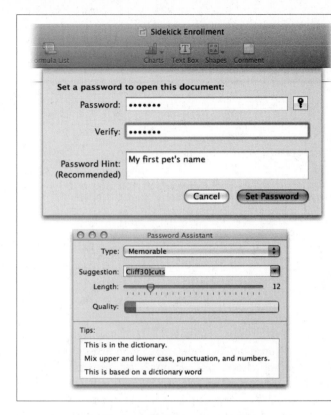

Figure 17-15:
When you turn on the "Require password to open" checkbox in the Document Inspector, Numbers asks you to enter and confirm the password. Add a hint that Numbers can display in case you forget the pass phrase.

Click the key icon next to the Password field and Numbers brings up the Password Assistant, which rates the security of your password as you type, offering suggestions along the way.

new passwords. You can lift the password protection completely by turning off the Document Inspector's "Require password to open" checkbox; then enter your password one last time, and Numbers lowers the gate.

Adding Search Keywords

The Document Inspector (Figure 17-16) also offers four fields you can use to supply background info about your spreadsheet, which is useful for adding internal notes that don't appear in the sheet canvas itself. Perhaps even handier is the fact that your Mac indexes these fields for Spotlight searches, so providing relevant keywords can help you track down your file later. The Document Inspector provides fields for title, author, keywords, and comments. The title field has no effect on the actual filename of your document; the info here is just for internal use.

Opening an Existing Spreadsheet

When you're ready to return to a saved document, choose File → Open to reveal the standard Mac OS X file browser and select a file. If you're not familiar with using the Open dialog box to browse for your file, jump back to page 35 for a quick tour.

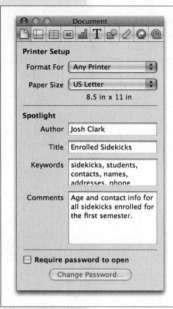

Figure 17-16:
The Document Inspector lets you choose the paper size and preferred printer when you're ready to commit your data to paper (see page 573 for more about preparing to print). You can also enter Spotlight search keywords and password-protect your document.

Numbers also makes it easy to get your mitts on a saved spreadsheet right from the Template Chooser. To fire up a document you were working on just recently, click the Open Recent pop-up button and choose one of your latest projects. (You can also get the same set of options by choosing File → Open Recent.) To open a spreadsheet not included in that list, click the Template Chooser's "Open an Existing File" button and the Chooser flips over to reveal a file browser, the same one you see when you choose File → Open.

You can also double-click the spreadsheet's file icon from your desktop, or drag it onto the Numbers icon in the Dock to launch Numbers and open the file.

Importing Files from Another Program

Most of the world, alas, doesn't use Numbers as their everyday spreadsheet program. Microsoft Excel is far and away the world's most popular spreadsheet program, and sooner or later someone will ask for your spreadsheet as an Excel file. Fortunately, all the iWork programs speak Microsoft, and Numbers can open Excel files and translate them into Numbers spreadsheets. Ditto for these other file formats, too:

- **AppleWorks 6** spreadsheets

- **CSV** (comma-separated values)

- **Tab-delimited text**

- **OFX** (Open Financial Exchange), a file format commonly provided by banks and financial institutions for use with personal finance software like Microsoft Money

Importing one of these files works very much like opening a regular Numbers document: Choose File → Open and select the file. Numbers imports the file and opens it as a new Numbers document. When you save the file, that means you save it as a *Numbers* document unless you specifically save a copy of the file in another format (see page 817).

Numbers does a good job of importing Excel files, especially when the spreadsheets are reasonably straightforward. But if you're importing complex spreadsheets with sophisticated formulas, Numbers may run into trouble. Numbers can't display formula calculations for functions it doesn't know, of course, and although Numbers has been adding functions at an impressive pace, Excel still has far more tricks in its function library than Numbers does. Excel has a few other advanced tricks, too, like pivot tables and macros, that spreadsheet jockeys might depend on. If you use an Excel spreadsheet that relies on those features or certain arcane functions, you may be disappointed when you open it in Numbers.

When Numbers realizes it's struggling to import certain elements of a file, the program lets you know, offering to list any elements that might not have made the trip as expected. If you choose not to review these messages right away, you can check 'em out later by choosing View → Show Document Warnings.

POWER USERS' CLINIC

The Missing Macro

Scripts and *macros* have long been the dark art of the spreadsheet world—homegrown mini-programs that you build into a spreadsheet document to automate complex actions or calculations. For years, applications like Microsoft Excel have allowed spreadsheet wizards to create these custom timesavers. In corporate and scientific settings, scripts often handle processes that require more complex logic than you can pack into a spreadsheet formula. Excel's macros are written in a programming language called *Visual Basic for Applications* (VBA).

Unfortunately, Numbers doesn't speak VBA, which means it can't understand Excel's macros. In fairness, though, neither does Excel. The latest version of Excel for Mac OS X, Excel 2008, dropped support for VBA macros, although Microsoft promises to bring it back in the next version. For

now, though, that means Mac users who want to use Excel macros are out of luck unless they have a copy of Excel 2004 kicking around.

For the ambitious macro-maker, however, Numbers '09 adds new support for AppleScript, the built-in Mac OS X scripting language that lets you program your applications to do various tasks. Numbers' AppleScript powers aren't as expansive as Excel's VBA capabilities, but it's a promising first step for building macros in the iWork spreadsheet program.

Using this scripting support requires AppleScript programming know-how, however—a topic outside of the scope of this book. To learn more about using AppleScript, visit *www.apple.com/applescript* or pick up a copy of *AppleScript: The Missing Manual*.

Previewing Your Spreadsheet in Print View

The way your Numbers spreadsheet looks onscreen doesn't typically reflect how it'll look when you print it. Spreadsheets often have many more rows and columns than can fit on a single sheet of paper. But unlike Pages, which shows you a true-to-life view of every page break for lengthy text documents, Numbers normally keeps its page breaks to itself while you're editing. That's a good thing—when you're updating a data-dense table, the last thing you want to do is dodge page margins and leap across page breaks. Better for your info to be displayed seamlessly, without interruption.

Eventually, though, you'll want to see what your document looks like on paper before you send it to the printer. Numbers gives you a separate view—*Print view*—that lets you organize how your document will look on the printed page (or when you export your spreadsheet to a PDF file, for example). This view shows you where page breaks appear and lets you move and resize objects until you get the layout you want.

Before jumping into Print view, though, make sure you've got your document and sheet layout set up the way you want them.

Page Setup

Unlike most Mac programs, Numbers doesn't offer the tried-and-true Page Setup option in its File menu, the place where you normally set your paper size, preferred printer, and page orientation. Instead, those details are handled in the Document and Sheet Inspectors: Choose the page size and printer in the Document Inspector's Printer Setup area (Figure 17-16).

With the exception of the page size (which applies to your whole document), Numbers handles all your print settings on a sheet-by-sheet basis. You manage these settings from the Sheet Inspector (Figure 17-17): In the Sheets pane, select the sheet you want to edit, and then click the toolbar's Inspector button to open the Inspector window. Click the Sheet button—the second from the left—to reveal the Sheet Inspector.

Because sheets can be both wider and longer than a single page, the final printed result is often a tiled collection of pages. Your sheet might be three pages wide by five pages tall, for example. The Page Layout section of the Sheet Inspector lets you choose how to organize those pages. The left pair of buttons let you switch between portrait (vertical) or landscape (horizontal) page orientation. The right pair lets you choose the order in which Numbers prints the "tiles" of your sheet: The left button prints your pages in columns from top to bottom; the right button prints in rows, left to right down the sheet.

The Sheet Inspector lets you number a sheet's pages independently of the other sheets. To start a sheet at a specific number, choose "Start at" and enter a number in the field. Otherwise, just leave the setting at "Continue from previous sheet" to number your pages straight through.

You set the margins for the sheet here, too. If you want Numbers to print your sheet as close to the page's edge as possible, turn on the Use Printer Margins checkbox. When you do that, Numbers grays out the margin settings to let you know that the sheet effectively has no margins.

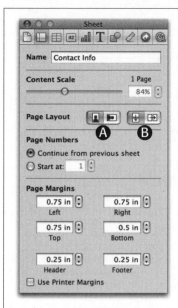

Figure 17-17:
The Sheet Inspector lets you rename the selected sheet and control the sheet's print settings.

The Content Scale slider is available only in Print view and lets you make the sheet's contents larger or smaller to fit the printed page. The number of pages displayed here is also active only when you're in Print view, showing you the number of pages in the current sheet (when you're not in Print view, it always says "1 page"). The Page Layout buttons let you choose portrait or landscape orientation (A) and the order to print pages (B), as explained below.

In the Page Margins section you can adjust individual margins or, if you prefer to print as close to the edge of the page as your printer will allow, turn on the Use Printer Margins checkbox.

The Page Margins settings control the spacing between the edge of the paper and your sheet's content. These settings don't affect the spacing of any *headers* and *footers,* the captions that ride along at the top and bottom of your pages to carry the document title or page number, for example. The header and footer margins are independent of the top and bottom margins you set here; they measure the distance from the edge of the page to the start of the header or footer. For example, if you set the top margin to 1 inch and the header margin to 0.5 inches, the header would start 0.5 inches from the edge of the paper, and the spreadsheet content would start 1 inch from the edge of the paper. If the header runs long and extends beyond that 1 inch margin, it nudges the body text down, so your content always appears below the header. You'll learn more about headers and footers in the next section.

Working in Print View

Print view lets you see the current sheet's page breaks and make adjustments to its layout and scale to make the sheet more printer-friendly. Switch to Print view by clicking the page icon at the bottom of the document window; when you do, Numbers reveals two new controls shown in Figure 17-18. (You can also flip to this print perspective by pressing ⌘-Option-P or choosing View → Show Print View or File → Show Print View.) To exit Print view, repeat the same step again (the commands in the View and File menus now read Hide Print View).

When you switch to Print view, Numbers chops up the sheet into page "tiles," showing you exactly how it will look when you print it or export it to a PDF file (see page 820). If your sheet is *wider* than a single page, it spills into one or more additional columns of pages on the right. If your sheet is *taller* than a single page,

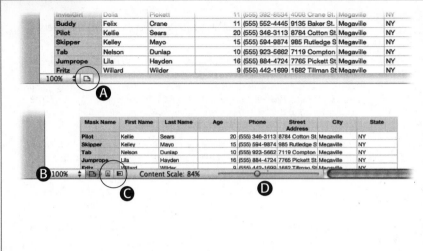

Figure 17-18:

Top: You can switch to Print view by clicking the page icon at the bottom of the document window (A).

Bottom: To signal that you're in Print view, Numbers highlights the page icon in blue and adds two controls next to it, which are also repeated in the Sheet Inspector. The Page Layout buttons (C) let you switch between portrait and landscape orientation for the current sheet. The Content Scale slider (D) shrinks or expands your content to make it fit your pages.

Don't confuse the Content Scale percentage with the View percentage (B), which lets you zoom in and out of your document but only affects your onscreen view, not the way your sheet prints.

it spills into one or more additional rows of pages on the bottom. When a table spans more than one page, Numbers repeats its header rows or columns to help you keep your place. Figure 17-19 shows what all of this looks like.

Tip: If you don't want to repeat the display of header rows or columns when you print the sheet, turn off Table → "Repeat Header Rows on Each Page" or Table → "Repeat Header Columns on Each Page". (These menu commands are checked when they're turned on and unchecked when they're off; they're grayed out when you don't have a table selected.)

You can work in Print view just as you normally would, editing table content or adding new objects like charts, pictures, shapes, and text boxes. It's best, however, to reserve Print view for managing the *layout* of your document rather than editing its data—the visual gaps created by the page breaks can make it frustrating to work with data. Where this perspective really shines is in preparing your document to look its best on the printed page.

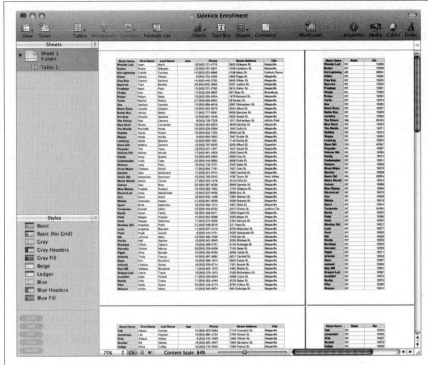

Figure 17-19:
*Print view shows you
how the current sheet will
get printed. Here, Print
view shows that the
sidekick contact list is too
wide to fit a single
portrait page–its last two
columns, State and Zip,
spill over to a second
column of pages on the
right. The header column
is repeated on those
right-hand pages, just as
the header row is
repeated on the pages
below. To squeeze the list
into the width of a single
page, adjust the Content
Scale slider at the bottom
of the document window
or in the Sheet Inspector.*

*You can zoom in or out
of this tiled view using
the View pop-up menu in
the bottom-left corner of
the sheet canvas.*

Scale the print size of your content larger or smaller to make page breaks appear
where you want them (or not at all). You do this by using the Content Scale slider
at the bottom of the document window or in the Sheet Inspector. To resize individual objects, select them and drag their selection handles or change the Size field
values in the Metrics Inspector. You can likewise move an object from page to page
by dragging it—or by cutting and pasting—just as you normally would on the
regular sheet canvas. Chapter 23 gives the lowdown on selecting and moving
objects, and page 584 covers resizing tables.

Note: The Content Scale slider has no effect on what your sheet looks like onscreen when you're not in
Print view. However, when you resize or move individual objects on the canvas in Print view, you *do*
change their size and position in the regular view as well.

Adding headers and footers to a sheet

Print view is also where you add and edit the sheet's page headers and footers, text
that repeats at the top and bottom of every page of the sheet. You can use these
recurring strips to display any text you like, but they're often used to display the
page number, document title, and date. (Sorry, you can't put pictures or other
objects in headers or footers—just text.)

The header and footer areas aren't easy to spot before you add text to them. To make them visible in Print view, choose View → Show Layout and Numbers makes the header and footer outlines visible as gray boxes. (Layout view also adds borders around the page margins and text boxes.) To add your text to a header or footer, place the insertion point in the outlined text field and type away. You can format this text like you format text in any iWork document, using the Format Bar, Text Inspector, and Fonts window. (See Chapter 2 for tips on editing text in iWork.)

Headers and footers are unique to each sheet. While they show up on every *page* of the sheet you're working on, headers and footers don't roll over to the pages of other sheets: Changes that you make in one sheet don't appear in the rest. To repeat a header or footer in *every* sheet of your document, you have to copy and paste its text into each sheet.

Tip: You don't have to turn on Layout view to edit headers and footers, it just makes them easier to spot. Numbers also highlights their border when you hover your pointer over a header or footer; click when the border appears to place the insertion point inside.

You can put your own text in a header or footer, but you'll typically want to use one or more *formatted text fields,* special placeholders that automatically update the text with the current page number, page count, filename, or date and time. (You can add these special text snippets anywhere you like in your spreadsheet, but headers and footers are a popular choice.) Place the insertion point in the header or footer, and then choose any of the following options from the Insert menu:

- **Page Number.** When you choose Insert → Page Number, you add the current page number to the page. When you add this text field to headers and footers, the number changes on every page. The Page Number field stays alert, too, keeping an eye on your changes and updating the number if the field slips to a new page. When you first add a page number, it displays Arabic numerals (1, 2, 3...) but you can change it to alphabetical order or Roman numerals by Control-clicking the page number and choosing an option from the pop-up menu.

Note: Page Number fields follow whatever numbering rule you set in the Sheet Inspector for the current sheet (see page 574).

- **Page Count.** This kind of field lists the total number of pages in your spreadsheet. To add text that looks like "Page 1 of 3," for example, type the word *Page* followed by a space, then insert a Page Number field, then type *of* with spaces on either side, and finally add a Page Count field.

Note: This field gives unreliable results when you use the Start At numbering option in the Sheet Inspector for any of your sheets.

- **Date & Time.** Choose Insert → Date & Time to add the current date in this format: Saturday, December 6, 2009. Double-click the date, and a little window zooms out to let you change the date format, add the time of day, or set a different date. If you want Numbers to set the date to the current time every time you open the spreadsheet, turn on the window's "Automatically update on open" option. When you're done making your changes, click anywhere outside of the edit window to send it packin'.

Tip: The only date-format option that combines both date and time is this long-form option: January 6, 2010 1:17 PM. If you want to display both date and time but use a different format for either one, insert *two* Date & Time fields, formatting one for the date and the other for the time.

- **Filename.** Choose Insert → Filename, and Numbers adds the document's filename. If you later save the document under a new name, the field updates automatically to reflect the change. Under Numbers' standard settings, the filename includes its file extension (*Sidekick Enrollment.numbers*, for example). To change this, double-click the filename and turn off the "Always show filename extension" option in the pop-up window that appears. This window also lets you show the complete location of the file on your computer: Turn on the "Show directory path" option if you're into that sort of thing. When you're done, click anywhere outside the edit window to close it.

Printing Your Spreadsheet

When you've arranged your pages just the way you want them and sprinkled them with headers and footers, choose File → Print and then click the Print button. You'll find more info about printing in Chapter 24 (page 815).

With a clean, sorted, printed spreadsheet on your desk, your mission to get the sidekick academy organized and off the ground is well underway. But new challenges await, dear reader. Make sure you're prepared for them by learning everything there is to know about editing and formatting your tables; it all starts on the next page.

Editing Tables in Numbers

If spreadsheets are all about efficiency, then the tables they contain are the key to number-crunching nirvana. Tables help you plow through calculations in a snap; they organize and reorganize your info quickly; and they squeeze your data into a compact display. For all that Numbers can do for you, though, much of the spreadsheet work boils down to data entry and table formatting, and that part's up to you. It's *your* turn to be efficient: To get the most out of your spreadsheet, you need to be nimble as you edit your data. This chapter shows you how.

The last chapter already gave you a quick intro to typing into tables and working with rows and columns. Now you'll take a deeper look at wrangling table objects, editing table cells, working with Numbers' data formats and exploring a bevy of shortcuts for entering data quick. By the time you're done, you'll be spinning around your table faster than a game of musical chairs. Let's get to it.

Working with Table Objects

In Numbers, tables are *objects,* just as they are in Pages and Keynote. If you've already made your way through the rest of this book, objects are already old friends. They're the building blocks of every iWork document, the design elements that you slide across the page—or in this case, the sheet canvas—to create your layout. In Numbers, tables are the main focus, and you may frequently have spreadsheets where a single table is your one and only object. But no matter how many or few you pile into your document, you have to know how to select and edit these guys in order to work on your spreadsheet.

Note: You'll learn more about working with other types of Numbers objects—pictures, text boxes, shapes, movies, and sounds—in Chapter 23, hot on the heels of a whole chapter on chart objects in Chapter 22.

Selecting a table object tells Numbers that you're ready to edit it, but what part exactly? Tables have many different elements (rows, columns, cells, the data inside, even the borders between cells), and you can select any of them individually. Selecting the table at these different levels lets you edit the table in different ways, but blocks you from editing it in others. Understanding how to select a table and its parts—and move quickly among them—is the first step to becoming a fleet-footed spreadsheet jockey.

Adding a Table

First things first: You need to have a table before you can select it. Whenever you create a new spreadsheet document, Numbers already has a table set for you on the sheet canvas—sometimes several, depending on the template you use (page 553). If you start from the Blank template, for example, Numbers gives you a single table grid, selected and ready to go. When you add a new sheet (page 568), Numbers likewise gives you a fresh table to get you started.

To add a new table to the current sheet, click the toolbar's Tables pop-up button or choose Insert → Table, and Numbers shows you a menu of predefined tables (Figure 18-1). Your choice of tables varies according to the template you used to create your document, but each option comes stocked with its own visual style and structure. Some even contain content to get you started, including header text or formulas. Just like document templates give you a head start with the design of your overall spreadsheet, these predefined table templates do the same with your new table. (You can add your own preformatted tables to this list, too, as you'll learn on page 667.) Choose a table, and Numbers deposits it at either the bottom or right edge of the sheet.

Tip: You can also create a brand-new table based on cells, rows, or columns of another table: Select the elements to use in the original table, and drag them to a blank part of the canvas. You'll learn more about this on page 620 (for copying and moving cells) and page 640 (for rearranging rows and columns).

Selecting Table Elements

You can work with a table at several different *selection levels*, each of which lets you edit or format the table in different ways. At each level, Numbers gives you visual cues to let you know what part of the table you're working with. When you first create a table, open a new document, or click anywhere among a table's cells, Numbers selects the table at the *cell level*. This is where you'll spend most of your time—the level at which you'll skip through your table's data to add new values—but selecting the table at other levels has its uses, too. Here's a quick tour.

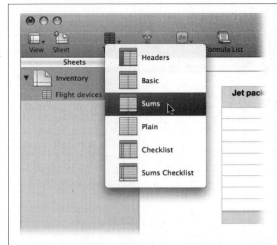

Figure 18-1:
The Tables pop-up button in the toolbar holds a selection of prefab tables, each with its own style and layout. To add a new table to your sheet, choose one of these tables, and Numbers gives you a fresh grid to work with. When you add the Sums table, for example, Numbers gives you an empty table with header and footer rows, with the footer cells prestocked with formulas to add the values of body cells in the column above. When you add data to any non-header cell, the footer cells update automatically, as shown here. For more about formulas, see Chapter 20.

PAIN POINT

Big Tables Bog You Down

Numbers '09 introduces significant speed improvements over its predecessors, but it still gets winded when it comes to very large tables. As you start working with tables containing tens of thousands of rows, Numbers shows the strain. Opening the file requires long waits, scroll bars lag and stutter, and recalculation of formulas can take several seconds.

When you're feeling weighed down by a single big table, try adding a new one. Numbers often speeds up quite a bit when you split large data sets into multiple sheets or tables. By doing that, you give the program less to lift at once—fewer rows to process, less figures to juggle. Not all data can be broken up easily into slices like this, of course, and it's certainly not the most convenient way to manage your info, but managing multiple tables is often less of a headache than wading through a sluggish interface.

Selecting the table object

When you select a table at the table or *object level,* you're working with the entire table as a whole. You can't edit the table's content at this level, but you can move the grid across the canvas, resize it, or apply formatting changes to the whole she-bang—to change the font, for example, or add borders or backgrounds to the entire table. (You'll learn more about all the various options for styling your table on page 656.)

Use any of these methods to select a table at the object level:

- Click its name in the Sheets pane.

- When the table is unselected, hold the cursor *over the edge* of the table. When it turns into an arrow with four compass points (Figure 18-2), you can click to select the table, or drag to move it.

- When one or more table cells are already selected, you can either press ⌘-Return or click the Table handle, the gripped area at the table's top left corner.

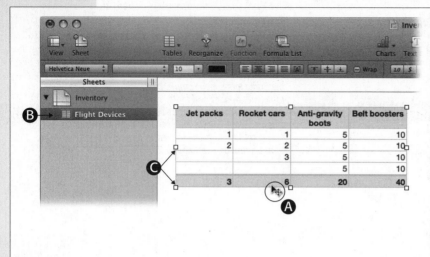

Figure 18-2:
When you hold the cursor over the edge of an unselected table or one that's already selected at the object level, the cursor turns into an arrow with four small compass points (A). Click to select the table at the object level, or drag to move it to a new location. You can also select a table by clicking its name in the Sheets pane (B). However you do it, the presence of the table's eight selection handles (C) signals that it's selected at the object level.

When a table is selected at the object level, it's shorn of its reference tabs (page 558) and its row and column handles. Instead, the eight selection handles sprinkled along the table's border show that you've selected the table—that's the only indication, in fact. If you drag any of these selection handles, you'll resize the table, although probably not in the way you'd like. The most common way to change a table's size is by adding or deleting rows and columns (see page 632). Here, though, resizing the table changes its overall size without changing the number of rows and columns. The height and width of those rows and columns shrink and grow as you change the table's shape and size. You can similarly change the table's size by selecting it and setting its overall height and width in the Metrics Inspector.

To delete a table—*along with all its data*—select it at the object level and press Delete.

Selecting cells

When you move the cursor over a table's cells, the pointer turns into a white cross, signaling that it's ready to select a cell. Click any cell to select it, and Numbers highlights the cell to let you know that it's active. The table also sprouts reference tabs and four *table handles* at its corners (unlike the eight square selection handles that you see when selecting at the table level, table handles really look like handles, complete with grips that practically compel you to grab them). When you select a cell, the cell's reference tabs also light up to help pinpoint the active cell. Figure 18-3 gives you the picture.

Note: Unlike Pages or Keynote, Numbers tables don't have to be selected at the object level before you can select a cell; just click anywhere inside a table to select one of its cells.

	A	B	C	D
1	Jet packs	Rocket cars	Anti-gravity boots	Belt boosters
2	1	1	5	10
3	2	2	5	10
4	✛	3	5	10
5			5	10
6	3	6	20	40

	A	B	C	D
1	Jet packs	Rocket cars	Anti-gravity boots	Belt boosters
2	1	1	5	10
3	2	2	5	10
4		3	✛ 5	10
5			5	10
6	3	6	20	40

Figure 18-3:
*Top: When the cursor floats over a table's cells, it takes on
a cross shape to let you know that it's ready to select a cell.
Numbers adds a blue outline to the current selection and
highlights the reference tabs for the cell's column and row.
Bottom: To select more than one cell at once: Drag across
the cells to select them; shift-click neighboring cells; or
⌘-click non-adjacent cells.*

*The table's lettered and numbered reference tabs appear
only when you're working inside a table, and they bring
with them four gripped handles at each corner. Click the
Table handle in the top left corner to select the table at the
object level, or drag it to move the table to a new location.
Drag the remaining three handles to add or remove
columns and rows.*

From here, any changes you make apply only to the selected cell and the text
within. At the cell level, you can set the background and borders of individual cells,
for example. Be careful here, though: Numbers implicitly selects the full text of the
selected cell—if you start typing as soon as you first select it, you'll replace any data
inside. If that's not your plan, click inside a selected cell (or press Option-Return),
and Numbers places the insertion point inside the cell, letting you add or edit the
existing cell content. Now you're no longer at the cell level but the *text level,* and
you can apply text formatting to individual words or characters within the cell.
You can tell that you've selected a cell at the text level when you see the blinking
insertion point in the cell, or if text is highlighted inside the cell. You'll learn more
about editing and formatting cell data starting on page 590.

Tip: The simple way to think about selecting tables, cells, and content is that clicking drills deeper into a
table, and ⌘-Return pulls back out. Click a cell to select it, and click it again to edit the text inside. Press
⌘-Return to pull out of this editing mode (Numbers selects the whole cell), and press ⌘-Return again to
select the entire table at the object level.

When a cell is selected, use the Tab, Return, and arrow keys to jump to a neighboring cell. (You'll find more details about navigating table cells on page 588.) To
select more than one cell at once, drag across the range of cells you want, and
Numbers outlines the entire block of selected cells. You can also select neighboring cells by shift-clicking them or by pressing Shift-arrow to expand the selection
to the cell next door. To select or deselect non-adjacent cells, ⌘-click the cells. To
select all cells in the table, select one or more cells *at the cell level,* not the text level,
and then choose Edit → Select All, or press ⌘-A. (Selecting all cells in a table isn't
quite the same as selecting the table at the object level; once again, to do that you
press ⌘-Return to pull back from the cell level to select the table at the object level.)

Selecting rows or columns

Select an entire row or column by clicking its reference tab, as shown in Figure 18-4. (If you don't see the reference tabs, select any table cell to make them appear.) When you select a row or column, you can work a range of magic on them—move the selection to a new location in the table, delete the whole row or column, hide it temporarily, apply formatting to all its cells or borders, and more. You'll find all the details about working with rows and columns starting on page 631.

Tip: Shift-click the reference tabs to select multiple neighboring rows or columns; ⌘-click to select non-adjacent rows or columns.

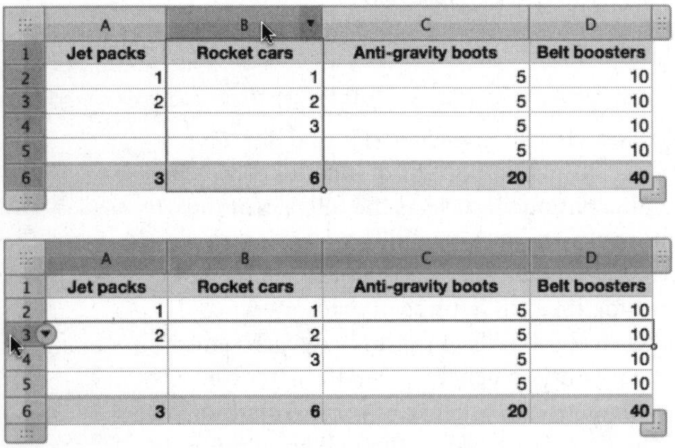

Figure 18-4:
Top: Click the lettered reference tab at the top of a column to select the entire column.

Bottom: Click the numbered reference tab at the left of a row to select the entire row. Avoid clicking the arrow at the right side of the tab when you do this, or you'll only display the tab's pop-up menu.

Moving and Copying Tables

You can drag a table anywhere you like on the sheet canvas, but the method varies depending on how (and whether) you selected the table:

- If the table isn't selected, or if the entire table is selected at the object level, hold the cursor over the edge of the table. The cursor turns into the four-point arrow shown in Figure 18-2 to signal that it's ready for heavy lifting: Grab the table and drag it to its new location.

- If a table cell is selected so that the reference tabs are visible, drag the table using the Table handle in the upper-left corner.

Tip: If nothing happens when you try to drag the Table handle, you're probably not clicking the actual handle but instead clicking a *frozen header row:* a floating set of column labels. Turn to page 637 for more about these cool numbers, and in the meantime try scrolling back up to the top of the table until the grips reappear on the Table handle. Or press ⌘-Return to select the table at the object level and grab the table by its edge, as described in the first point above.

Hold down the Shift key while you drag to limit the move to a straight horizontal, vertical or 45-degree route. Hold down the Option key while you drag to create a new copy of the table; the table clone leaps out of the original table and lands wherever you drop it.

To nudge a table ever so slightly, select it at the object level and use an arrow key (any direction) to move it just one point. Hold down the Shift key while you press the arrow to bump the table ten points per key press.

To move the table to a precise location, use the Metrics Inspector. To do so, select the table, click the toolbar's Inspector button, and click the Metrics icon in the Inspector window. Use the arrow buttons or type new values in inches in the X and Y Position fields to position the table's top left corner horizontally and vertically. (Don't bother trying to rotate or flip the table using those controls in the Metrics Inspector; in Numbers, tables are immune to such antics.)

Tip: Choose View → Show Rulers (⌘-R) to see the rulers. You can change the units used in the rulers and Metrics inspector in the Rulers pane of the Numbers → Preferences window.

To move a table to a different sheet, select its name in the Sheets pane and then drag it (or Option-drag to create a copy) to a new position below another sheet. Numbers installs your table in its new home on the new sheet. Switch to that sheet by clicking it in the Sheets pane, and position the table wherever you want it to go. You can also paste the table to move it to a new location: Select the table and choose Edit → Copy or Edit → Cut, switch to the new sheet, and choose Edit → Paste.

Note: If you move a table to a new sheet and other tables contain formulas that refer to the moved table, those formulas keep up automatically, following the table to its new address. More about formulas in Chapter 20.

Naming Tables

Every Numbers table has a name that's displayed in the Sheets pane and can optionally be displayed above the table. The default table names aren't exactly charged with personality (Table 1, Table 2, and so on), and you can change them to make them more descriptive. Double-click the name in the Sheets pane, and type its new moniker. You can also edit the name of the selected table in the Table Inspector. If you're not sure which table is which, click anywhere in the table whose name you want to change, and Numbers highlights its name in the Sheets pane. The reverse also works: click a table in the Sheets pane and Numbers selects that table in the canvas.

When you have more than one table or chart on a sheet, you can rearrange the order of their names in the Sheets pane by dragging their names into a new position. This has no effect on their layout in the sheet canvas; it's just a way to soothe your own personal organizational eccentricities. (What *does* have an effect, however, is dragging a name to a different sheet; doing that moves the table or chart to the other sheet, as you've already seen.)

Note: On any sheet, no two tables can share the same name. That's because table names aren't just decorative labels, they're unique identifiers that you can use to refer to tables in formulas, as you'll discover in Chapter 20.

Numbers can use the table name to automatically label your table for you. Turn on the Name checkbox in the Format Bar or in the Table Inspector, and the table name appears just above the table. If you don't immediately see the table name, it's probably hidden behind the table's reference tabs; click outside the table to deselect it, or press ⌘-Return, and the reference tabs will go away to reveal the table name.

To change the font and text style of this name label, double-click the name to select it; the text doesn't highlight the way that most text does, but Numbers draws a light gray border around it, and the Format Bar switches to text-only formatting options, as shown in Figure 18-5. Use the Format Bar, Fonts window, and Text Inspector to style the text as you wish.

Tip: To increase the distance between the table name and the table itself, increase the After Paragraph spacing in the Text Inspector.

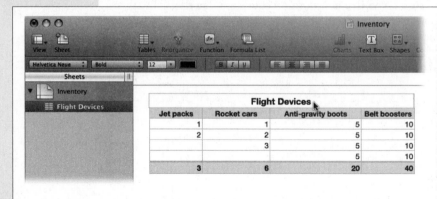

Figure 18-5:
Click the table name to select it for formatting, and Numbers draws a faint gray outline around it to let you know that you've got the name selected. The Format Bar updates to show text-formatting options. From left to right, select the font family, typeface, font size, color, font style, and text alignment for the title.

Navigating Table Cells

Like pretty much everything on your Mac, you can select table cells by pointing and clicking with your mouse. When you start facing down hundreds or thousands of cells in your spreadsheet, however, clicking to edit each one turns into serious exercise. Rather than developing an over-muscled mouse arm, put your energy into committing some crucial keyboard shortcuts to memory. Once you've selected a table cell, you can move all over your table without lifting a finger from your keyboard.

The Tab and arrow keys are your greatest allies, letting you hop to the cell next door. Click Tab to select the cell to the right; select Shift-Tab to move to the left.

When you're working at the cell level, you can similarly use the arrow keys to select the cell in the corresponding direction—up, down, left, or right. (See the box "Where Does the Arrow Point?" to sharpen your arrow skills.)

Where Does the Arrow Point?

The range of your keyboard's arrows changes depending on your current selection level. When you have a cell selected at the cell level, the arrow keys bump you over to select the next cell (left, right, up, or down). When the cell is selected at the text level, however, the arrows instead move you around *inside* the cell.

When you're motoring through your cells for the first time, for example, you can just use the Tab and arrow keys to move to each one, type your data and then tab or arrow to the next cell. Even though you're typing text into the cell, it's still selected at the cell level, not the text level, and your arrows take you to the next cell. That's because text-level editing is triggered only when you click inside a selected cell or press Option-Return to edit the cell's existing text. In that case, your arrows no longer target neighboring cells. Instead, they shuttle you around the text *inside* the cell.

To make your arrows shoot outside the cell again, press ⌘-Return to leave text-level editing behind, selecting the cell at the cell level. Or press Tab or Shift-Tab to move to the next cell to the right or left; Numbers selects the new cell at the cell level, and your arrows get their cell-leaping powers back.

Hopping Rows with the Return Key

Under Numbers' standard settings, you can also use the Return key to move to a new cell. Pressing Shift-Return moves you to the cell above, and pressing Return moves you *somewhere* in the row below. Exactly where Return lands you, however, depends on what you've been up to. Normally, the Return key takes you down to the cell below your current selection. But when you've been using the Tab key to navigate between cells and editing content anywhere along the way, pressing Return selects the cell just below the one where you started tabbing, as shown in Figure 18-6. This is especially useful if you're in a marathon data-entry session, adding many rows of content: When you tab through the columns of cells in each row, *entering data in at least one of the cells,* and then press Return, Numbers jumps you down to the first column of the next row, ready for your next entry. (If you press Return from the last row, Numbers adds a new row for you automatically.)

Note: The Return key's column-tracking behavior works only when you use the Tab key to move between columns. If you use the mouse or arrow keys to move from cell to cell, the Return key simply moves you down to the cell immediately below.

The Return key stops its grid-skipping behavior when you turn off the "Return key moves to next cell" checkbox at the bottom of the Table Inspector (Figure 18-7). In that case, the Return key no longer moves you around the table and instead adds a carriage return inside the text of the selected cell. This is useful when you want to add paragraphs of lengthy notes to a table's cells (see page 594 for more on working with paragraphs, line breaks, and tabs inside cells).

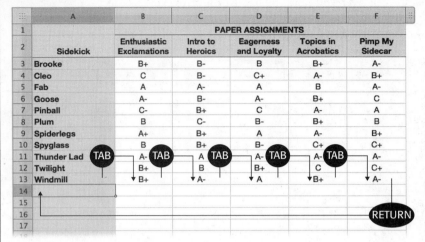

Figure 18-6:
When you tab from cell to cell and then press Return, Numbers moves you down to the next row, selecting the cell in the same column where you started tabbing. That's frequently the first column of the row, as shown here, but it doesn't have to be. If you click a column in the middle of the row and tab through several cells, pressing Return selects the cell in that same middle column, one row below.

Although the label on this option mentions only the Return key, it affects the behavior of the Tab key, too. Specifically, it changes what the Tab key does when you're in the last column of the table. Normally, when you press Tab from a cell in the last column, Numbers adds a new column, so you can just keep rolling along to the right, creating new columns as you go. When you turn off a table's "Return key moves to next cell" checkbox, however, pressing Tab from the last column instead takes you down to the first column of the next row (Numbers adds a new row for you if you're already in the last row). This row-hopping behavior translates to Shift-Tab, too: When the "Return key" option is off and you press Shift-Tab from the table's first cell, you teleport down to the last cell of the table.

Editing Table Cells

Now that you've got the hang of moving around your table cells, it's time to fill them up with data. As you learned in the last few pages, typing into a cell works slightly differently when you have the cell selected at the cell level versus the text level. When you select the cell at the cell level (by clicking it once or moving to it with the Tab or arrow keys), your typing replaces any data already in the cell. If you instead want to edit that data, you should make your changes in the Formula Bar, or select the cell at the text level—click inside the selected cell or press Option-Return—before you start typing.

When you make changes in the Formula Bar, Numbers keeps the cell selected at the cell level. Your changes appear in the cell itself only after you finish editing in the Formula Bar; press Return or click the Formula Bar's Accept button to store your changes.

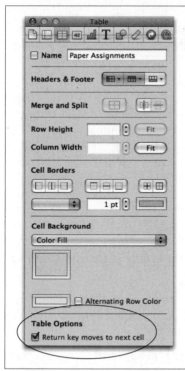

Figure 18-7:
The Table Inspector is home to the "Return key moves to next cell" checkbox (circled), which controls whether you can use the Return key to skip from row to row. Turning this option on or off affects the behavior of the Tab key in subtle ways, too, changing what Numbers does when you press Tab from the table's last column.

By contrast, when you select the cell at the text level, Numbers places the insertion point inside the cell itself and lets you edit the text. Editing data inside a cell works just like text editing everywhere in iWork—and in most Mac programs, for that matter. For pointers, head back to page 52 for a review of basic text editing. When you're done typing the cell data, press ⌘-Return to pull back to the cell level, or press Tab to continue on to the next cell.

To delete a cell's contents, select it at the cell level and press Delete. This clears the value in the cell, but leaves its formatting behind—any borders or fill color sticks around. To strip out all the formatting, too, choose Edit → Clear All, or cut the cell to the clipboard by choosing Edit → Cut. (See page 656 for details about adding borders and backgrounds to cells.)

Undoing Your Typing

As usual, you can use the Edit → Undo (⌘-Z) command to take back any changes that you might make (see page 58 for a review of the Undo and Redo commands). However, after you've typed into a cell selected at the cell level, Undo behaves differently than you might expect. In that case, Numbers treats your typing as *two* steps: 1) deleting any data inside the cell, and 2) adding the new typing. This means that when you press ⌘-Z, Numbers undoes your typing, but not the deletion: *The cell is left empty.* You have to press ⌘-Z a second time to get your original value back.

If you're still editing the cell when you change your mind, you can dodge this two-step undo by using the Escape (Esc) key instead. Pressing Escape always cancels any changes that you're making to the current cell, reverting it to its original value.

Handling Data That Doesn't Fit

Table cells can be a tight squeeze (realtors call it "cozy"), and your data won't always fit into its small quarters. In that case, Numbers clips the data to show only a portion of it. The original data is still stored safely away; Numbers simply compacts its *display* to fit the available space in your table. The way that Numbers works this sleight of hand depends on the type of data inside the cell, as shown in Figure 18-8. Specifically:

- If the value is a date or time, a + clipping indicator appears.

- If the value is a decimal number, Numbers rounds its display to a number that fits. For example, 3.88888888888 might display as 3.88889 to squeeze into a narrow cell (the number of decimal places in the display depends on the width of the cell).

- If the value is a whole number, it's displayed using *scientific notation,* which shows the number multiplied by ten to the power of a displayed exponent, where the exponent is displayed following an "E" in the number.

  Huh? In case your high school algebra textbook disappeared long ago, here's another way to put it: Scientific notation tells you how many spaces the decimal point should be moved to the right or left to get a "traditional" decimal display. For example, 888,888,888 might become 8.89E+08, which your algebra teacher would have written as 8.89×10^8 (that "E" stands for "exponent"). In plain language, that means that the leading eight should be followed by eight decimal places. A negative exponent moves the decimal to the left.

- If a decimal or whole number still doesn't fit after getting squeezed as described above, a + clipping indicator appears.

- For text values, no clipping indicator appears, and you can see only content that fits inside the cell's boundaries.

Letting text content spill into neighboring cells

When a cell has the Wrap checkbox turned off in the Format Bar or in the Cells Inspector, Numbers allows *text* to spill over into cells next door (numbers, dates, and times never spill). This happens only when the neighboring cell is empty. If the neighbor contains data, however, Numbers lops off the display at the cell boundary. Figure 18-8 shows all this in action.

When you turn on the Wrap checkbox, text never spills out of the cell. Instead, text wraps to a new line when it hits the cell boundary. Numbers also flexibly expands the height of the table row as you add additional lines of text to the cell—unless the row has been set to a fixed height, in which case the text gets clipped at that height.

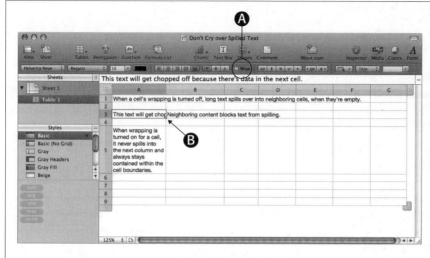

Figure 18-8:
Turn off a cell's Wrap checkbox (A) to allow its text to spill out into neighboring cells when those cells are empty, as shown here in the top line. When the cell next door contains data, however, text doesn't spill and instead gets clipped to remain inside its cell boundaries (B).

Behind the scenes, the data remains intact. When you select a clipped cell at the cell level, as shown here, the Formula Bar shows the full content. (For very long content, adjust the height of the Formula Bar by dragging the handle at its right side.) The cell itself doesn't reveal the clipped content until you select it at the text level by double-clicking or pressing Option-Return.

Sizing rows and columns to fit your values

If cell values aren't visible because columns or rows are too narrow, use the Fit buttons in the Table Inspector to adjust their size automatically to fit the content. Click the Fit button next to the Column Width field to adjust the width of the current column to fit all fields. You can also choose Table → "Resize Columns to Fit Content", or use this super-handy shortcut: Double-click the border to the right of the column's reference tab, and the column adjusts its width to fit.

Doing the same for a row similarly adjusts its height to fit the height of the content within; it also makes the row flexible so that it grows and shrinks as you add and remove content. In fact, this is Numbers' standard behavior unless you specifically resize a row to make it a fixed height. If you do that, you can return the row height to its normally limber flexibility by clicking the Row Height's Fit button in the Table Inspector, or choose Table → "Resize Rows to Fit Content". Just like columns, rows also give you a shortcut for this: Double-click the bottom border of the columns' reference tab to make the row resize to fit. For more on resizing rows and columns, see page 638.

Merging table cells

When content spills out of its cell as shown in the top line of Figure 18-8, it might look like you can edit it by selecting any of the cells it crosses, but that's not the case. No matter how Numbers might display a cell's data, it still "lives" only in the original cell, and that's the cell you must select to edit it. Even though the A1 cell extends all the way over to the F column, you can click only cell A1 to edit it; clicking cell B1, C1, or any of the others in that row will add content to that other cell, not the long text spilling out of A1.

That's not always convenient. When you know that the cell's content will always span a specific range of cells, you can *merge* those cells into one big strapping mega cell. Numbers knocks down the walls between the merged cells, and now you can click anywhere inside the newly expanded cell to edit it. This is useful for titling multiple columns, for example. To add a single title above three columns, you'd merge the cells of those three columns in the top row so that the merged cell spans the three columns below.

To merge cells, select two or more neighboring cells, and choose Table → Merge Cells, or click the Merge button in the Table inspector, shown in Figure 18-9. Numbers merges the content of the cells, too, replacing the old column divisions with tabs and row divisions with carriage returns.

You can merge both rows and columns at once—to make a 2×2 block, for example—but the cell selection must always form a rectangle. The cells also have to be the same type; they must all be body cells, or all header cells (page 634), or all footer cells (page 637).

Tip: You can also merge cells by selecting the border between two cells and pressing the Delete key. For more about selecting table borders, see page 657.

Paragraphs, Line Breaks, and Tabs

Because the Return and Tab keys have special roles to help navigate your table cells, you can't use them as is to add a new line or tab stop to a table cell. In most cases, you'll just include brief snippets of data in your cells—numbers, short text labels, names—but occasionally you may want to include longer text, for a column of notes about students at the sidekick academy, for example.

To add a new line to a cell, press Option-Return. (If the cell is selected at the cell level, pressing Option-Return selects it at the text level; pressing it while editing text inserts a paragraph break.) To add a tab stop to a cell, press Option-Tab.

Tip: If you're after a line break instead of a paragraph break, press Option-Shift-Return. Page 71 explains the difference between the two. (Alas, unlike Pages, Numbers doesn't have a Show Invisibles command to show you when you've used a line break or a paragraph break.)

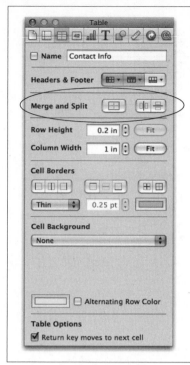

Figure 18-9:
Merge selected cells into a single-cell organism by clicking the Merge button, the left button in the Table Inspector's Merge and Split section. Click the button again to "unmerge" the merged cell, or deselect the Table → Merge Cells command.

Next door on the right, the Split button takes the opposite action, dividing each selected cell into two equal halves. Click the left side of the button to split cells vertically into columns; click the right side to split horizontally into rows. Any text in the original cell goes to the topmost or leftmost cell in the new pair.

When you can't spare the brain cells to remember the Option key modifier, you can also edit your text in the Formula Bar, which not only provides a roomier environment for editing cell data, but also gives you line break and tab buttons, too. Clicking them inserts a line break and tab respectively. Figure 18-10 shows you the lay of the land.

To make the Return key perform its regular duty—inserting paragraph returns—turn off the "Return key moves to next cell" option in the Table Inspector. When you do that, as you learned a few pages ago, pressing the Return key now starts a new paragraph in the table cell and no longer jumps you to the next table row. Likewise, Shift-Return adds a line break instead of moving you up a row.

For lengthy notes, you'll almost certainly want to turn on the cell's Wrap option to allow text to wrap at the column boundary instead of continuing on a single line. Turn on the Format Bar's Wrap check box or the Cells Inspector's "Wrap text in cell" option.

Formatting Text

You can format the text of table cells with all the familiar font styles you've already seen in Pages and Keynote. Choose a new font, shade it in a new color, make it larger or smaller, add extra line spacing, change its alignment—Numbers provides plenty of formatting tools to shape the look of your cell data. No matter whether you've got a cell selected at the object, cell, or text level, the Format Bar gives you fast access to the most common text formatting options, shown in Figure 18-11.

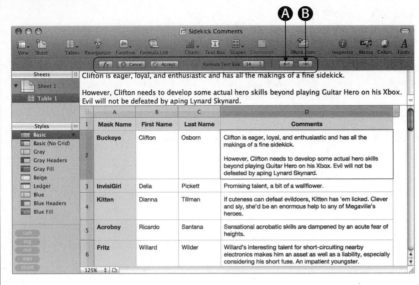

Figure 18-10:
When you're working inside the Formula Bar, the Format Bar displays six buttons. At the far right are the Line Break (A) and Tab (B) buttons. Click those buttons to insert a line break or tab into the cell's text.

Choose a new text size from the Formula Text Size button to make the Formula Bar show its text larger or smaller. This doesn't affect the size of the text in the cell itself, only what you see while editing in the Formula Bar. The Cancel and Accept buttons do as you'd expect, discarding or storing your cell edits. (You'll learn about the Function Browser button at the left in Chapter 702.)

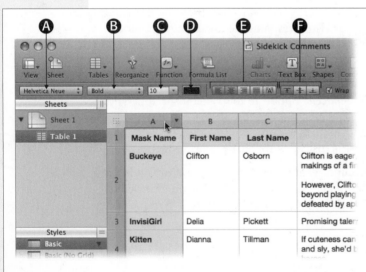

Figure 18-11:
Use the Format Bar to style the text of selected cells. Here, the first column is selected so that any changes apply to all text in every cell of the column. The Format Bar's menus and buttons include: font family (A); typeface (B); font size (C); font color (D); align left, center, right, justified, or automatic (E); align top, middle, or bottom (F).

Choosing automatic alignment positions content according to its data type (right for numbers and dates, left for text, centered for Boolean values). Here, the left and center alignment buttons are both highlighted to show that the selected cells are formatted with a mix of alignments (the header row is centered, while the rest of the cells are left-aligned).

Numbers applies your formatting changes to all the cells included in the selection: When you have the table selected at the object level, all text in *all* cells updates to reflect your changes. Select a row or column, and your changes hit the text in all its cells. When you select just a portion of a single cell's text, you focus the change only on that selected text—to give a single word a **bold** or *italic* text style, for example, or to increase the line spacing of the current paragraph.

When you need more detailed control than the Format Bar provides, turn to the Text Inspector, Fonts window, Format menu, and the ruler. With only a few exceptions, formatting your text with these tools is identical to formatting text in Pages. You'll find those details described in the Pages chapters (especially Chapter 2). Here's an abbreviated tour of text formatting in Numbers.

The Fonts window

Click the Fonts button in the toolbar or choose Format → Font → Show Fonts to open the Fonts window (Figure 18-12). Find out the full story about the Fonts window on page 62.

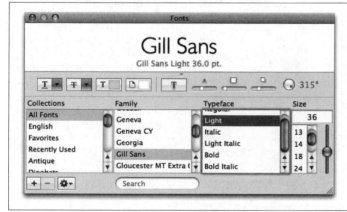

Figure 18-12:
Click the Fonts button in the toolbar to call up Mac OS X's font-formatting headquarters. If the Preview pane isn't showing, drag the little dot at the top of the window, below the title bar, to reveal it. Select some text–or an entire cell or table–to modify it with any of the controls shown here (and described in detail on page 62).

Use the controls within this window to do the following:

- Choose a font and see font samples.

- Set the font size.

- Set the font color.

- Set the paragraph background color—this is not the same as the cell's fill color (see page 659), although the two settings have nearly identical effects.

- Choose the text underlining or strikethrough style and color.

- Add a text shadow and adjust its characteristics.

The Text Inspector

Click the Inspector button in the toolbar or choose View → Show Inspector to display the Inspector window. Then click the Text button in its toolbar to show the Text Inspector. The Text Inspector is divided into three tabs—Text, Columns, and Bullets—but most of the options you're likely to use in a table are offered up in the Text tab, shown in Figure 18-13.

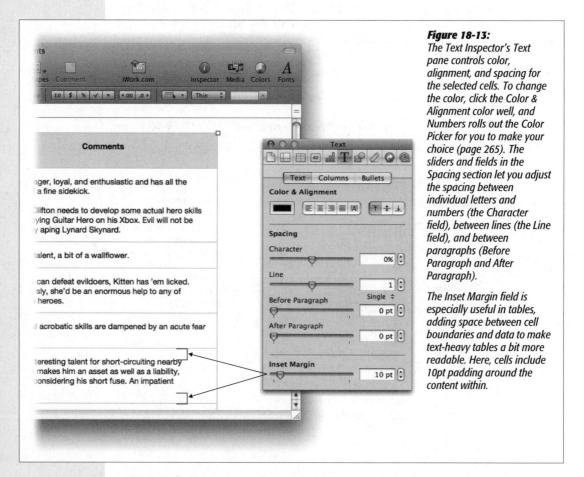

Figure 18-13:
The Text Inspector's Text pane controls color, alignment, and spacing for the selected cells. To change the color, click the Color & Alignment color well, and Numbers rolls out the Color Picker for you to make your choice (page 265). The sliders and fields in the Spacing section let you adjust the spacing between individual letters and numbers (the Character field), between lines (the Line field), and between paragraphs (Before Paragraph and After Paragraph).

The Inset Margin field is especially useful in tables, adding space between cell boundaries and data to make text-heavy tables a bit more readable. Here, cells include 10pt padding around the content within.

The Text Inspector → Columns pane lets you change the number of columns of text to display in the text box, including the width of the columns and gutters, the gaps between columns. It's unlikely that you'll need to have more than one column in a table cell, but, hey, it's your spreadsheet. (You're more likely to do this in text boxes; see page 806.) Working with columns in Numbers works just like it does in Pages; see page 153 for more info.

The Text Inspector's Bullets tab is where you control the look of paragraph bullets or numbers, and it's identical to the Lists tab in Pages' Text Inspector. Here you can swap out your traditional bullet dots for numbers, letters, or spiffy images. See page 87 for details on using this inspector pane and its many bullet styles.

The Format menu

Choose Format → Font in order to do any of the following:

- Show or hide the Fonts window.
- Change the font style (bold, italic, underline, or outline).
- Increase or decrease the font size.
- Adjust tracking, the space between two characters (see page 65).
- Turn ligatures on or off (see page 67).
- Adjust the font's baseline (see page 66).
- Adjust the text capitalization.

Choose Format → Text and select one of the paragraph alignment settings in the submenu: Align Left, Center, Align Right, Justify, or Auto Align Table Cell. This last option aligns text based on its data type. Text aligns left, numbers and dates align right, and Boolean values align center.

Setting margins, indents, and tabs with the ruler

You can set margins, tabs, and indents for individual paragraphs of a table cell using the ruler. To do this, select the cell at the text level by double-clicking the cell or by selecting it and pressing Option-Return. Choose View → Show Rulers to reveal Numbers' vertical and horizontal measuring sticks on the top and left side of the sheet canvas, as shown in Figure 18-14. The top ruler displays the margin settings, indent, and tab for the selected paragraph. Use the ruler to adjust the text margins and the first-line indent, and set tabs for each paragraph in a text box, exactly as you would in Pages (see Setting Tabs and Indenting Text, starting on page 72).

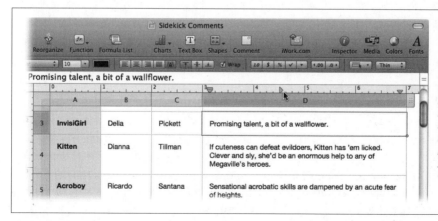

Figure 18-14:
Choose View → Rulers in order to make margin and tab adjustments with the ruler. Select a cell at the text level, and Numbers displays the margins and indents for the selected paragraph in the ruler. Add a tab stop by clicking in the ruler, as shown here.

Unlike Pages, however, Numbers' Text Inspector doesn't have a special pane for editing tabs; all tab editing must be done here in the ruler. Create new tabs by clicking once on the ruler and dragging the tab into position. Control-click a tab marker and choose one of the four tab styles from the pop-up menu: Left Tab, Center Tab, Right Tab, or Decimal Tab. Or you can just double-click the tab marker repeatedly to cycle through the various tab styles.

Adding Comments

Flag a table cell with a comment to leave yourself a reminder, give someone else feedback, or offer others instructions on how to use the spreadsheet. To add a comment to a cell, select the cell at either the cell or text level, and click the Comment button in the toolbar or choose Insert → Comment. A yellow *comment balloon* materializes, floating above the table but anchored to the cell by a yellow line. The line points to the cell's new *comment indicator*, a yellow triangle in the cell's top right corner, as shown in Figure 18-15.

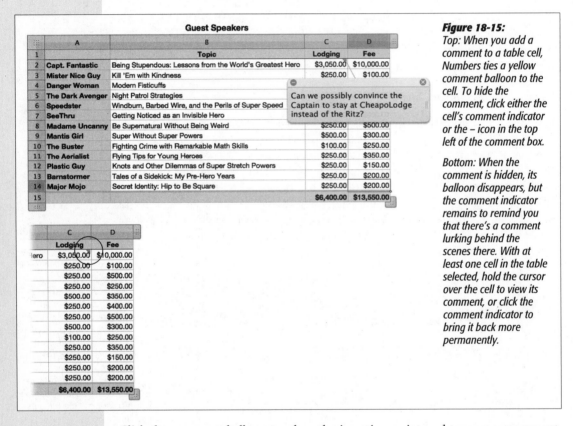

Figure 18-15:
Top: When you add a comment to a table cell, Numbers ties a yellow comment balloon to the cell. To hide the comment, click either the cell's comment indicator or the – icon in the top left of the comment box.

Bottom: When the comment is hidden, its balloon disappears, but the comment indicator remains to remind you that there's a comment lurking behind the scenes there. With at least one cell in the table selected, hold the cursor over the cell to view its comment, or click the comment indicator to bring it back more permanently.

Click the comment balloon to place the insertion point and type your comment, using the usual collection of text-formatting tools to style your text however you like. Drag the balloon by its top edge to move the comment to a new location on the sheet. Wherever you might drag it, the comment's elastic line remains firmly tethered to the table cell, always pointing to the relevant content.

To hide an individual comment, click the – button in the comment balloon or click the cell's comment indicator, as shown in Figure 18-15. To hide all comments, choose View → Hide Comments; bring them back by choosing View → Show Comments. To remove the comment permanently, click the X Delete icon in the comment balloon's top right corner.

Adding sticky notes outside of tables

You can also add one or more general comments to the current sheet, rather than to a specific table cell. To do so, deselect all tables by clicking a blank part of the sheet canvas, and click the Comment button in the toolbar or choose Insert → Comment. Numbers adds a big yellow sticky note on top of your sheet, as shown in Figure 18-16. Drag the comment to position it wherever you'd like, or delete it by clicking its X Delete icon.

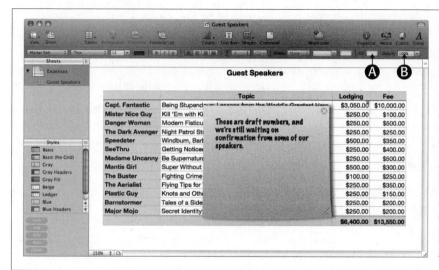

Figure 18-16:
When you add a comment with no table cell selected, Numbers adds a big sticky note to your sheet canvas. As usual, you can use the Format Bar and other text-formatting tools to style the comment's content. Unlike the cell-specific comment bubbles, however, you can also change the color of the sticky note by changing its fill color (A) or make it transparent by changing its opacity setting (B).

Printing comments

You can include comments when you print the spreadsheet just by leaving the comments visible (View → Show Comments) when you choose the File → Print command. When you hide comments (View → Hide Comments), Numbers prints neither your comments nor the yellow comment indicators in table cells. For more on printing your document, see page 815.

Check Your Spelling

Numbers normally has its automatic spell checking turned on, flagging misspelled words—or words not in its dictionary—with a red underline. Choose Edit → Spelling → "Check Spelling as You Type" to turn this feature on or off.

Choose Edit → Spelling → Spelling to display the Spelling window for manual spell checking. Numbers shares many elements, including its spell checker, with Pages and Keynote. See page 113 for all the details about how to run a spell check on your spreadsheet.

Using Different Types of Data

Numbers has a discriminating nose for data. It can sniff out the difference, for example, between numbers and names in your grade book, or between dates and checkboxes in your to-do list. For Numbers, this data detection isn't just a fussy party trick, it's a job requirement. When you start sorting your data down the road and, especially, when you start building formulas and charts based on your data, Number has to know when you're giving it numbers to crunch, text to sort, or dates to schedule. Numbers sees the world in five shades of data:

- **Ordinary text.** This data type includes headings, notes, descriptions, or any text that Numbers can't place as one of the other data types.

- **Numbers.** This data type is the main ingredient of most spreadsheets and includes prices, integers, fractions, percentages, and any other type of numeric data. Numbers offers lots of different display options for numbers.

- **Dates and times.** This data type includes calendar dates (like December 6, 2009), time of day (like 12:26 p.m.), and the combination of both (December 6, 2009, 12:26 p.m.). You can enter and display this info in a variety of formats.

- **Time duration.** A length of time, like weeks, hours, or even milliseconds.

- **True or false values.** This on-or-off data type is also known in nerd circles by its chirpier name, *Boolean* values. Behind the scenes, these values are either TRUE or FALSE (in all caps), but you'll typically see them in Numbers spreadsheets as a simple checkbox (see page 621). You might use these values in to-do lists to mark items complete, in grade books to mark pass/fail, or in complex formulas that evaluate conditions (see Chapter 21).

Most of the time, you don't have to give these data types a second thought, since Numbers is clever at automatically figuring out the *data type* of each cell, just by looking at its information and formatting. As it does this, it displays your data in subtly different ways. You can get a hint of how Numbers interprets your data by looking at its cell alignment, for example, as shown in Figure 18-17.

As you can see in Figure 18-17, numbers and dates can display in several different forms. Numbers for example can include a comma (or not) to mark off thousands, a percentage sign, a currency symbol, or even hour, minute, and second units. Dates are equally flexible, showing the same moment in time in a variety of different formats.

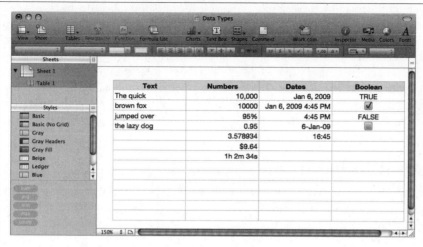

Figure 18-17:
*Numbers changes the
text alignment (left, right,
or center) of your entry
based on the type of
data that you add to a
cell. Text aligns to the
left, numbers and dates
to the right, and Boolean
values stay centered.
That's just the standard
treatment, however, and
you can change this
formatting however you
like (see page 604).
Here, for example, the
header cells are centered
even though they contain
ordinary text.*

You can explicitly control the display of this info by setting cells' data format, as you'll learn on page 604. Until you do that, though, Numbers makes its own call on how to format the data. With number data, the info is generally displayed as you enter it, but sometimes with minor differences. If you enter an amount with a dollar sign, for example, the figure is always displayed with two decimal places, even when you add more decimal places, as shown in Figure 18-18. Dates are especially obstinate in this regard. No matter how you might enter a date—1-6-09, 1/6/09, or 6-Jan-09—Numbers converts it to the standard date format—Jan 6, 2009, for example—until you explicitly tell it to format the cell's date a different way.

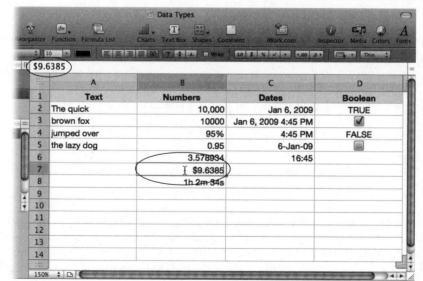

Figure 18-18:
*In Figure 18-17, the
circled cell displayed as
$9.64, even though the
original entry was
$9.6385. Selecting the
cell displays its true
value in the Formula
Bar; double-clicking the
cell to select it at the
text level displays the
actual value in the cell
itself, as shown here.
When you go back to
selecting the value at
the cell level (or no
longer have the cell
selected at all), the
value reverts to the
$9.64 display.*

Don't get flustered by these display changes. It's only for show. Behind the scenes, Numbers keeps your original data just as you entered it, for numbers at least; you can see that's the case by double-clicking a cell to select it at the text level, and Numbers shows your original entry. In other words, the way Numbers *displays* your data isn't necessarily the same as the way it *stores* it. No matter how it displays your data, the important thing to know is that Numbers treats all numbers, dates, and times the same when it comes to calculations. When you enter a currency as $9.6385, it may show up in the table as $9.64, but it will still count as $9.6385 when Numbers does its math.

Choosing Cell Formats

The way your cell displays its data is called the *cell format*. Most cells start life using Numbers' *automatic* cell format, which detects the data format to display as described above, but you can tell Numbers to use a specific data format for any or all of your cells.

To change the data format, select the cells to update—if you select one or more rows, columns, or tables, you can choose the data format for all their contained cells in one swoop. Choose the data format with any of these methods, all shown in Figure 18-19.

- Click the Number, Currency, Percentage, or Checkbox button in the Format Bar.

- Choose an option from the Cell Format pop-up button in the Format Bar.

- Choose an option from the Cell Format pop-up menu in the Cells Inspector.

Note: The Format Bar's Checkbox button adds a special checkbox control to the selected cell. The Slider, Stepper, and Pop-Up Menu options in the Format Bar's Cell Format menu likewise add their own special controls. You'll learn more about this on page 621.

It's OK if you add data to a cell that doesn't match your selected cell format. Nothing breaks or explodes—Numbers just treats the data like ordinary text. So, if you have a column set to display with the currency cell format, and you enter a date into the cell, Numbers can tell it's not currency, and won't treat it like a price. But it won't treat it like a date either, just text displayed exactly as you entered it, so it won't do the magic formatting tricks that it would normally do when you enter a date into a cell with the automatic or date-and-time format.

Tip: You can also explicitly tell Numbers to treat a cell value as ordinary text—and to display it exactly as you type it—by setting it to use the text cell format. You'll learn more about that on page 611.

For most cell formats, the Cells Inspector offers a handful of additional display options related to that specific format. When you decide to wing it with the automatic cell format, these Cells Inspector options likewise change depending on the detected data type. When Numbers thinks you're dealing with a date, for example,

Figure 18-19:
Set the format of selected cells by clicking the Number, Currency, Percentage, Checkbox, or Cell Format buttons in the Format Bar (A). The Cell Format pop-up button reveals the remaining cell formats; here, a date format is chosen for the selected column. You can also set the format by selecting from the Cells Inspector's Cell Format pop-up menu (B).

it offers the date-formatting options in the Cells Inspector. What follows is a tour of Numbers' many cell-format options.

The number cell format

When you use the number format, you can specify the number of decimal places to display, as well as whether and how to format the thousands separator and negative values.

The Format Bar's Number button is the cell-format button labeled 1.0, and it gives you a shortcut to a common set of display settings for numbers. Clicking that button formats selected cells to display two decimal places, a thousands separator, and the – minus symbol for negative numbers. Use the Decrease Decimal Places and Increase Decimal Places buttons to the right of the cell-format buttons to adjust the number of decimal places displayed. Figure 18-20 shows the whole story.

Note: Don't be thrown by the fact that this is the only cell format labeled "number." Most of the other cell formats are meant to be used with numbers, too. The currency, percentage, fraction, numeral system, and scientific formats all work with the number data type (and only that type).

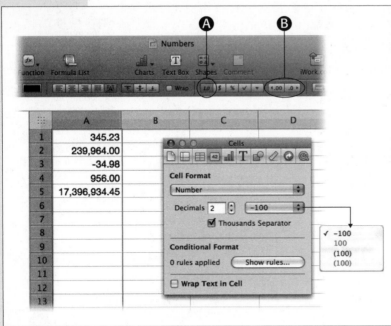

Figure 18-20:
The Format Bar's Number button (A) might be better labeled 1.00 instead of 1.0, since clicking it sets selected cells to display two decimal places—as well as the thousands separator and the – minus sign for negative numbers. Make Numbers display more or fewer decimal places by clicking the Format Bar's decimal-place buttons (B); the left one adds more decimal places and the right takes 'em away. If a data value has more decimal places than you set here, Numbers rounds the value for you.

The Cells Inspector also lets you fine-tune these settings, providing a choice of formats to use for negative numbers and the option to turn the thousands separator on or off.

The currency cell format

When you've got your mind on your money and your money on your mind, the currency format is the one for you. It works just like the number format but adds a currency symbol ($, €, £, ¥,…). Clicking the Format Bar's Currency button is the fastest route for setting your cells to use dollar values, for example, automatically displaying numeric values with a $ symbol. Like the Number button, the Currency button also sets selected cells to display two decimal places, the thousands separator, and the – minus sign for negative numbers. You can likewise adjust the number of decimal places by using the Format Bar's decimal-places buttons.

Note: Numbers chooses the symbol displayed on the Currency button based on your Mac OS X System Preferences (see the box on page 608). If you live in the U.S., the currency button shows the $ dollar symbol. In Europe, it shows the € Euro symbol. Whatever symbol you see is the symbol that Numbers will use in the selected table cells when you click the Currency button.

If you want to use a different currency than the one offered by the Currency button, you can turn to the Cells Inspector, where all the money in the world is at your command. Under Numbers' standard settings, the Cells Inspector offers you a choice of 25 currencies. If you can't find the one you're looking for, you can request the full listing in the Numbers → Preferences window: Click the General button and turn on the "Show complete list of currencies in Cells inspector" checkbox. When you do that, the Cells Inspector offers a loooong listing from the Afghani to the Zloty.

The Cells Inspector additionally lets you change the number of decimal places to display, turn the thousands separator on or off, and choose the format for displaying negative numbers. Turn on the Accounting Style checkbox to display the currency symbol at the left edge of the cell instead of immediately next to the value.

The percentage cell format

Click the % Percentage button in the Format Bar to display numbers followed by the percentage sign. This is more than a simple cosmetic change; formulas treat these figures as percentages—*25%* is counted as *0.25,* for example. Numbers takes this into account, too, when you apply the format to cells that already contain data: A cell with the value of *5* in automatic format becomes *500%* when you switch to the percentage format. The value makes the transition unchanged, however, if you had entered it as *5%* (with the percentage sign) in automatic format. When you add a new value to a cell that already has the percentage format applied, Numbers treats the value as a percentage (entering "5" displays 5% and, behind the scenes, the number is treated as 0.05).

Like the Number and Currency buttons, the Percentage button also formats selected cells to display two decimal places, the thousands separator, and the – minus sign for negative numbers. You can adjust any of these settings in the Cells Inspector, and change the number of decimal places using the decimal-place buttons in the Format Bar.

The date and time format

Set selected cells to display the date and/or time by clicking the Cell Formats pop-up button in the Format Bar and choose an option from the Date & Time submenu as shown back in Figure 18-19. If you don't see the format you'd like to use there, the Cells Inspector offers a wider selection of options.

Tip: Numbers takes its standard date and time formats from Mac OS X's System Preferences (see the box on page 608). You can also create your own custom date format, as described on page 611.

Human beings have lots of different ways to represent dates and times, and Numbers does its best to be flexible about how you type them. You can type the full date (like January 6, 2009), for example, or you can type an abbreviated date using dashes or slashes (01-06-2009 or 1/6/09). Whichever of these ways you do it, Numbers recognizes your entry as a date and displays it according to the date format you select in the Format Bar or Cells Inspector.

If you don't provide a year (Jan 6 or 1/6), Numbers assumes you mean the current year. If you provide a year but only two digits, Numbers assumes you're talking about the new millennium when the year is less than 50 (1/6/09 is 2009), but otherwise you slip back to the last century (1/6/51 is 1951). Entering the year with four digits, of course, clears up any ambiguity.

Note: If you enter a date that doesn't exist (June 31, 2009, for example), Numbers treats it as ordinary text instead of a date.

Times are a bit more straightforward. You simply use numbers separated by a colon. If you enter two numbers in this format (8:45), Numbers treats them as hours and minutes. Add a third number, and Numbers treats them as seconds (8:45:35). This format works as-is for 24-hour times (14:23), but be sure to add pm to the time if you're using a 12-hour clock and working past noon (2:23 pm). Numbers is lenient about how you add am and pm; you can leave out the space (2:23pm) or enter it in capital letters (2:23 PM), or both.

To enter *both* date and time, separate the two with a space, and Numbers swallows both at once, happily digesting this combination, for example: 1/6/09 2:23 pm. In fact, Numbers *always* stores both a date and a time for your entry, even if you enter just one or the other. When you enter only a date, for example, Numbers sets the time to midnight; when you enter only a time, Numbers assumes you mean today.

However you decide to type your dates and times, the Cells Inspector ultimately determines what's shown. If you have the Time Format field set to None, no time will be displayed even when you enter one, and the same goes for the Date Format field. As usual, of course, Numbers doesn't forget the date or time that you enter, even if it doesn't show it. If you later change the format to display the missing info, Numbers still has the complete date and time stowed away and hauls it out to display according to your preferences.

UP TO SPEED

Regional Rules

Your Mac knows where you live and how folks there do things. All the iWork programs, including Numbers, take cues from the Mac OS X System Preferences to manage things like date and time formats, currency, and whether or not you're a fan of the metric system.

When Numbers is working with dates, for example, it knows that Americans think of the third day of May as 5/3, while Brits prefer 3/5, and it interprets your entry accordingly. In the same way, Numbers assumes that you prefer to work with dollars as a standard currency when you're in the US but switches over to the dinar when you happen to be in Tunisia.

The International pane of your Mac's system preferences is the control panel for all these format decisions, not only for iWork but for every other well-behaved program on your computer. The settings that you choose there don't have to correspond to where you actually live—change them to anything that you like.

To make a change, go to ⌘ → System Preferences and click the International button. From there, click the Format tab, and choose any region to switch to its local date, time, number, currency, and measurement conventions. This tab also lets you choose your own custom date and time format, or switch over to the Buddhist, Hebrew, Islamic, or Japanese calendar system.

The duration cell format

Use the duration format to display a period of time in units varying from weeks at the high end to microseconds on the other. The standard setting is hours, minutes, and seconds. For example, you can format the duration field to display three hours, nine minutes, and 15 seconds as 3:09:15, 3h 9m 15s, or 3 hours, 9 minutes, 15 seconds.

Select the cells to format, and choose Duration from the Cell Format pop-up menu in the Format Bar or Cells Inspector. Use the Units slider in the Cells Inspector to select the three time units to display, and use the Format pop-up to tell Numbers how you want to display your selected units (Figure 18-21).

Note: You can, of course, use durations in formulas—to add and subtract amounts of time, for example. Especially handy: When you subtract one date-and-time value from another, you get a duration value. For more on doing math with dates, times, and durations, see page 739.

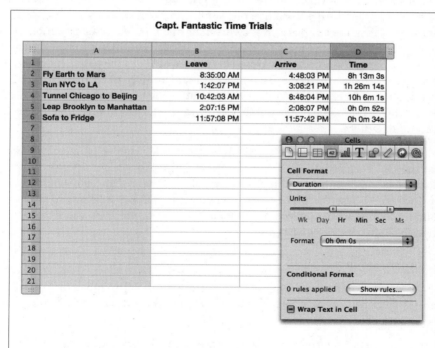

Figure 18-21:
The right column of this table is formatted to display the duration between the departure and arrival times in the previous columns. The width and position of the Units slider sets the units to use. Here, it's set to display hours, minutes, and seconds, the standard setting. Drag the slider all the way to the left to display weeks, days, and hours, or all the way to the right to display minutes, seconds, and milliseconds. You can stretch or squeeze the slider to display more or fewer units: Drag the handle on the left or right end of the slider to resize its width to cover the units you want to include.

The fraction cell format

Use the fraction format to replace the decimal portion of a number with a fraction. For example, 10.5 displays as 10 1/2 when the format is halves, 10 2/4 when the format is fourths, and 10 4/8 when the format is eighths. You can use the denominator of your choice or let Numbers pick the fraction closest to the actual decimal value.

To apply the fraction format to selected cells, choose Fractions from the Cell Formats pop-up menu, and select an accuracy level from the submenu that appears. The same choices are also available in the Cells Inspector. The accuracy level determines how detailed you'd like the fraction to be, from one digit in the denominator (1/8) to two digits (1/24) to three digits (1/553). You can also choose to have the fractions displayed with a fixed denominator (halves, quarters, eights, sixteenths, and so on), and Numbers rounds your number to the nearest value using that denominator. As with rounding in other number formats, fractional rounding is just for display purposes—Numbers always remembers the "real" value for you.

The numeral system cell format

When counting in multiples of ten just seems so *been there,* switch to a whole different number system. The numeral system format displays numbers in binary, hexadecimal, or any other counting system from base 2 to base 36. If you have no idea what binary or hexadecimal numeral systems are, then chances are you'll never need this cell format, but here's the gist. The base of a counting system determines how many digits you use; our familiar decimal system uses base 10, for example, and each digit's "place" represents units of ten raised to the power of 1, 2, 3, and so on—that means units of 10, 100, 1,000, 10,000. Other numeral systems work the same way, but with a different *base* instead of 10. In the base 2 (or binary) system, there are only two digits 0 and 1: The binary number 10 represents 2^1, or 2, 100 is 2^2, or 4; 1000 is 2^3, or 8; and so on. No matter what numeral system you use, however, the actual *value* of the number is the same, it's just *displayed* in a different counting system.

To switch selected cells to a different numeral system, choose Numeral System from the Cell Format pop-up menu in the Format Bar or Cells Inspector. In the Cells Inspector's Base field, choose the base value of the system you want to use, from two to 36. Use the Places field to choose the number of digits to display, including leading zeroes. If you select Base 2, 8, or 16, you can also choose an option for displaying negative values.

The scientific cell format

Use the scientific format to display very large or very small numbers in compact form (as described on page 592, Numbers also uses this format when it needs to squeeze a number's display into a narrow column).

To define a scientific format that displays two decimal places, select one or more cells, click the Cell Formats button in the format bar, and then choose Scientific from the pop-up menu. To change the number of decimal places, use the Decimals field in the Cells Inspector. As usual, Numbers rounds the number to fit the specified number of decimal places, but only for display; the precise actual value remains safely stowed away for use in formulas or if you choose to change the display format later.

The text cell format

The text format tells Numbers to treat a value like ordinary text, making it display your data exactly as you entered it. This is convenient, for example, when your data might contain values that Numbers would otherwise interpret as another data type. If you enter the product number 1883-12-13 into a cell with the automatic cell format, for example, Numbers assumes that you're entering a date: December 13, 1883. (In fact, it even changes the value of the data behind the scenes, converting your entry into 12/13/1883.) Setting the value as ordinary text tells Numbers not to mess with the value and display it as you entered it: 1883-12-13. Setting the cell explicitly as text tells Numbers not to treat it as one of its special data types.

Tip: Even when a cell is set to another format—automatic, number, date and time, whatever—you can still tell Numbers to treat its value as ordinary text. Start the cell's value with an apostrophe (*'1883-12-13*), and Numbers treats the value as text (Numbers doesn't display the apostrophe itself).

Creating a Custom Cell Format

Numbers' built-in cell formats should cover just about every need you'll have for displaying data. But if you're feeling especially exacting about how you want to display a certain bit of info, Numbers lets you build your own *custom format* for displaying numbers, text, or data. This is convenient, for example, if you want to show millions of dollars as $3.5M instead of $3,503,493—or display your own custom units like miles or km. When you create a custom format, Numbers adds it alongside the standard formats—listed in the Cell Formats pop-up menu in the Format Bar and in the Cells Inspector. That means you can continue to use it down the road in cells anywhere in your spreadsheet.

Note: Numbers adds custom formats to the current spreadsheet only; they aren't automatically available in other documents. If you paste a cell with a custom format into another spreadsheet, however, the custom format becomes available there, too. Also, when you save your document as a template, any new spreadsheets that you create from that template also have the custom format available. For more on saving templates, see Chapter 25.

To define your own cell format, select one or more cells (it doesn't matter if they're empty or filled) and then choose Custom from the Cell Formats pop-up menu in either the Format Bar or the Cells Inspector. You can also choose Format → Create Custom Cell Format. Numbers rolls out the Custom Format dialog box. This window has two different views depending on the type of format you want to build. Choose Number & Text from the Format pop-up menu to see the view shown in Figure 18-22; choose Date & Time to get a different set of options, which you'll see in a moment.

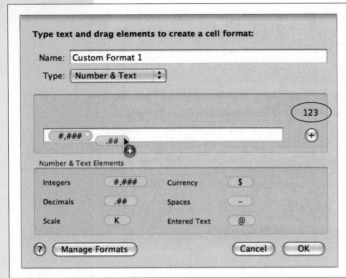

Figure 18-22:
The Number & Text view of the Custom Format dialog box lets you build a format by dragging number and text elements from the bottom pane into the format field. A preview (circled) shows what the format will look like in the table cell. You can also add any text that you like by typing directly into the format field. To remove a number or text element from the format, click it, and press Delete.

Type a name for your format in the Name field, and click OK to apply the format to the selected cell. Numbers adds the new format to the Cell Formats pop-up menus.

Building a custom number format

You construct a custom number format out of *number elements,* which together represent how to display every aspect of the number you enter into a cell. One number element shows a currency symbol, for example, while others show the integer portion of the value, the decimal portion, and so on (you'll find out about all the different types in just a moment). You mix and match these number elements to tell Numbers the order and content to display in the cell as part of your custom format: A dollar sign, followed by the number in millions, followed by two decimal points, for example.

Every number element is represented by a capsule in the bottom pane of the Custom Format dialog box. Add a number element to your custom number format by dragging its capsule from the bottom pane and into the format field just above, then drag and drop your capsules within the format field into the order you want them to appear. After you drag a number element to the format field, its capsule sprouts an arrow inside. Click the arrow to show the element's pop-up menu where you can fine-tune the display of that element (the number of decimal points or the currency symbol to use, for example).

The Custom Format dialog box includes five number elements, plus the Entered Text element (spaces are considered number elements, although you can also use the space bar to add spaces directly into the format field). As you'll see in the next section, the Entered Text element displays the value that you type into the cell exactly as-is, but Numbers doesn't let you combine Entered Text with any of the number elements. A custom number format, in other words, cannot contain the Entered Text field, only some combination of the five number formats and any custom text that you type directly into the format field (you might use custom text to display unit measures, for example, like "tbsp" or "cups" in a recipe spreadsheet, or USD after a dollar amount).

Note: If you drag elements into an order that doesn't make sense (decimals before integers, for example), Numbers warns, "Invalid format," in the preview area. Specifically, Numbers doesn't like it when you put integers and decimals out of order or when you insert scale, currency, or space between integers and decimals.

Number elements include:

- **Integers.** This element controls the display of the numbers to the left of the decimal point. The pop-up menu for this element lets you choose whether to show or hide the thousands separator. To display zeros or spaces in front of the integer when it has fewer than a particular number of digits, choose "Show Zeros for Unused Digits" or "Use Spaces for Unused Digits" from the pop-up menu. Then increase or decrease the number of zeros or hyphens displayed by choosing "Add Digit," "Remove Digit," or "Number of Digits." For example, when the number of digits is set to 5 and the "Show Zeros" option is selected, the Number format displays *00100* when you enter *100*. You can also increase or decrease the number of digits by selecting the number element and pressing the up or down arrow key.

- **Decimals.** This element displays the numbers to the right of the decimal point. You can choose to display these as numbers or fractions by choosing Decimals or Fractions respectively from the element's pop-up menu. After making your choice, choose the pop-up menu again to choose the number of decimal places to display or the fractional unit to use (halves, quarters, eighths, and so on). You can also adjust the number of decimal places by selecting the element and pressing the up or down arrow key. If you never want to display decimals, leave this number element out of the format, and Numbers will always round the display to the nearest integer.

- **Scale.** Use this element to display the units of a number (percentage, hundreds, thousands, millions, billions, trillions, or scientific). Choose the scale to use from the element's pop-up menu. When you apply your format to a cell that already has number data, Numbers updates the display to take the new units into account. For example, if your custom format is set to display numbers in thousands, applying it to a cell with the value 3,000 changes its display to "3" (or "3K" if you choose the K shorthand).

- **Currency.** This element adds a currency symbol to the number format; choose the symbol to use from the element's pop-up menu.

- **Spaces.** Use this element to control the amount of space displayed between elements. Choose a width from the element's pop-up menu: Normal adds a standard space, Wide adds an em space (page 77), and Narrow adds a sixth of an em space. A fourth width, Flexible, left-aligns elements preceding the space and right-aligns elements that follow it. You can add more than one space to the format field with these options, but only one of them can be Flexible.

Numbers lets you turn your custom number format into a shape shifter so that it shows a different format depending on the value of the cell. This is especially handy for defining the format for negative numbers—adding a – negative sign or parentheses around numbers less than zero—but you can add a custom format for a variety of other conditions, too. To do this, click the + button to the right of the format field, and Numbers reveals a new format field and condition pop-up menu, as shown in Figure 18-23.

Figure 18-23:
Click the + button to the right of the format field to add a format condition. Select the condition from the pop-up menu above the new format field, and add the elements you want to use for this format. Here, the custom format adds parentheses around negative numbers. To add more conditions, click a + button again; to remove a condition, click its – button.

Building a custom text format with predefined text

Custom text formats let you display predefined text before or after a cell's value. For example, you could add "Notes:" before each entry in a column of comments. Drag the Entered Text element into the format field as the placeholder for the cell's value, and type your predefined text before or after. You can't combine the Entered Text element with any of the number elements; you can mix it only with text that you type directly into the format field.

When you're done, enter the format's name in the Name field and then click OK. Numbers applies the format to the selected cells and adds it to the Cell Formats pop-up menus.

Building a custom date and time format

To create a custom date or time format, choose Date & Time from the Type pop-up menu in the Custom Format dialog box (Figure 18-24). Drag the elements you want to include into the format field (Figure 18-24). As with numbers, many of the date and time elements have pop-up menus that let you fine-tune their display. For the month, for example, the pop-up menu lets you choose whether Numbers should display its full name, an abbreviation, or a number. For hour, you can choose 12 or 24 hour time and whether numbers less than ten should include a leading zero. Open any element's pop-up menu to reveal its options.

When you're done, enter the name of your new format in the Name field, and click OK. Selected cells get the new format right away, and Numbers adds the format to the Cell Formats pop-up menus.

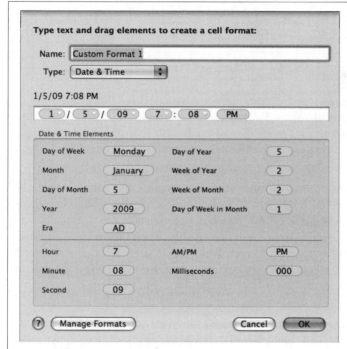

Figure 18-24:
Choose Date & Time from the Type pop-up menu to reveal the options for creating custom date and time formats. It works just like adding number or text formats: Drag each element you want to include into the format field. Add dividers like slashes, dashes, spaces, or commas by typing them directly into the format field. As you make changes, a sample date immediately above the format field previews your custom format.

Managing Custom Cell Formats

When you add new formats to your spreadsheet, Numbers lists their names in the Cell Formats pop-up menus in the order you added them. You can edit their names, rearrange their order, or delete them from the list by clicking the Manage Formats button in the Custom Format dialog box, or by choosing Format → Manage Custom Cell Formats. Numbers reveals a dialog box for managing your collection of cell formats, as shown in Figure 18-25.

Note: When you delete a custom format, Numbers removes the format from the Cell Formats menus, but any cells using the format continue to display it. To switch them to another format, select the cells and make a new choice from the Cell Formats pop-up menu in the Format Bar or Cells Inspector.

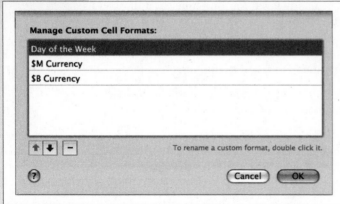

Figure 18-25:
Choose Format → Manage Custom Formats to edit your collection of bespoke data formats. To rename a format, double-click it and type the new name. To move a format to a new location in the list, select it, and use the arrow buttons at the bottom left to move it up or down (dragging them has no effect). To remove a format's listing from the Cell Formats menus, select the format and press the – delete button, or press Delete on your keyboard.

Editing a custom format

To make changes to a custom format after you've saved it, click a cell using that format and then click the Show Format button in the Cells Inspector, or choose Custom from the Format Bar's Cell Format menu. The Custom Format dialog box reappears. Make your changes to the data format by rearranging, adding, or removing its format elements.

To replace the existing format in the Cell Format menus, leave the original name in the Name field and click OK. Numbers asks if you want to replace the existing cell format; yep, click Replace. Numbers updates the selected cell with the new format. Going forward, when you choose this custom format from the Cell Format menu, Numbers applies the revised format. However, any cells that still have the old format keep that format until you specifically update them: Select the cells and choose your custom format from the Cell Format menu in the Format Bar or in the Cells Inspector.

If you're editing a custom format and want to save your changes as a new format, change its name and then click OK. Numbers applies the updated format to the selected cells and adds it to the Cell Format menu, keeping the original custom format, too.

Add It Quick: Data-Entry Shortcuts

Let's face it, typing row upon row of data into a spreadsheet can be dreary work, and time-consuming, too. To ease the pain, Numbers adds several time-savers to help fill your grid quickly, even suggesting entries when the program thinks it knows where you're headed with a cell value. This section surveys those speedy shortcuts.

Auto-Completing Entries

Many spreadsheets repeat information from row to row. In a spreadsheet detailing course enrollment at the sidekick academy, for example, columns for department and class name will inevitably include repeated values in several rows. Typing the name of the required course "Enthusiastic Exclamations" for the 200th time would try even the most battle-hardened typist. Holy déjà vu!

Happily, Numbers takes note of these reruns and, when it looks like you might be typing a text value it's already seen, the program offers to fill it in for you (only for text, though, not for numbers, dates, or times). Numbers does this by watching what you type, comparing it to previous entries in the same column, and when it recognizes the beginning of your entry, offers to *auto-complete* it, as shown in Figure 18-26. The suggested text appears highlighted after your insertion point. In Figure 18-26, for example, the insertion point is located after the "E" and Numbers suggests the remaining text "nthusiastic Exclamations" along with two other alternatives.

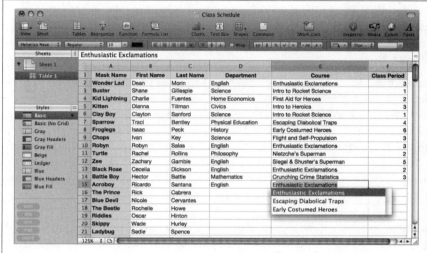

Figure 18-26:
As soon as you start typing text into a cell, Numbers scans the cells directly above in the same column to suggest values that match your entry. Here, typing E brings up all the class names that start with E. When there are multiple entries, as in this case, you can use the up and down arrow keys to select the matching entry from the pop-up menu and then press Tab or Return to accept the selected entry. Or keep typing to winnow the entries. When there's only one match, then Numbers offers no pop-up menu, showing its suggestion inside the cell where you're typing; press Tab or Return to accept the suggestion and move to the next cell.

You can use the text Numbers suggests, or keep typing to override its suggestions. You can also press the Delete key to dismiss the auto-suggested text and type the remainder of your text however you like.

Tip: If you find this feature to be more noisy than helpful, turn off "Show auto-completion list in table columns" in the General pane of the Numbers → Preferences window.

Auto-Correction and Smart Quotes

Numbers can monitor what you type, automatically correcting errors or inserting *smart quotes,* or curly quotes, which curve into a different shape for opening quotes or closing quotes. You can also use Numbers' auto-correction tools to give you quick shortcuts for commonly typed words and phrases. Turn these features on or off in Numbers' Auto-Correction preferences: Choose Numbers → Preferences and click the Auto-Correction button. See page 126 for all the details.

Autofilling Cells

Numbers is clever at spotting patterns, and you can use that talent to fill a run of neighboring cells with sequential numbers, days, or months. *Autofilling* lets you use the content in one or more cells to add values to the cells around it. You can use autofill to simply copy the value and formatting of a single cell, but the feature is especially useful for adding a series of values that increment from cell to cell like a counter.

Whenever you select one or more cells, Numbers gives you a Fill handle—a little circular control at the bottom-right corner of the selection box, as shown in Figure 18-27, top. When you hold the cursor over the Fill handle, it turns into a black cross to signal that it's ready to autofill. Drag the Fill handle over the cells you want to fill, and any data, cell format, formula, or background fill associated with the selected cell is pasted into those cells, replacing any previous values they might have contained. You can autofill up or down along the same column, or left or right along the same row, but you can't drag diagonally to autofill a block of cells.

Note: When you copy a formula into a new cell—whether by moving, pasting, or autofill—Numbers updates the formula's cell references to reflect the new location. You'll learn all about formulas in Chapter 20; for details, see "Copying or Moving Formulas" on page 691.

You can also autofill several cells with the same value by selecting a range of neighboring cells and choosing Insert → Fill → Fill Right, replacing all the cells with the leftmost value in the selection. Similarly, choose Fill Left to fill the selected cells with the rightmost value, Fill Down to use the top value, or Fill Up to use the bottom value.

Note: Comments are unaffected by autofill. Comments in the original cell don't get copied to the others, and comments in the other cells remain behind even as the cells' content is replaced.

Cloning individual cells like this is useful when you're setting up a table and want to copy cell formatting or initial cell values. But autofilling really earns its supper by saving you time building simple lists with regular increments: 1, 2, 3…; 5, 10, 15…; A, B, C…; Jan, Feb, Mar…; you get the idea.

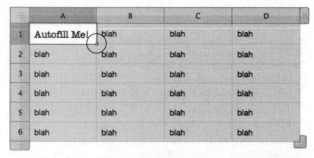

Figure 18-27:
Top: Cell selections always offer the circular Fill handle at the bottom right of the selection box.

Bottom: Dragging the Fill handle along a row or column autofills neighboring cells with the value and cell formatting of the original cell.

To do this, select two cells before dragging. For example, if two selected cells contain 1 and 2, Numbers adds the values 3 and 4 when you drag through the two adjacent cells. And if two selected cells contain 5 and 10, the values 15 and 20 are added when you drag through the adjacent two cells (values are incremented by five). Likewise, if two selected cells contain A and B, Numbers adds the values C, D, E, and so on when you drag the Fill handle into new cells.

This works with days, months, and dates, too: Select just one date cell, and drag the Fill handle into neighboring cells to increment the date day by day. When you select two cells and drag the Fill handle, Numbers increments the value by the interval between the two dates. If seven days separate the dates in the selected range, then Numbers bumps each autofilled value up by a week. Figure 18-28 shows examples of using autofill to create several different types of lists.

Autofilling doesn't set up an ongoing relationship among cells in the group. After autofilling, you can change the cells independently of each other. (If you *do* want to create a relationship among the cells, you'll be better off setting up a formula instead of using autofill to generate your sequential list; see Chapter 20.)

Note: If you choose more than two cells with an irregular interval (or cells with text values), autofilling simply repeats the pattern of the selected cells: If you select cells containing 1, 2, and 5, for example, dragging the Fill handle adds 1, then 2, then 5, then 1, then 2, then 5, and so on to the new cells.

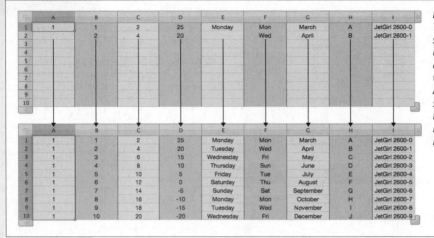

Figure 18-28:
This before-and-after snapshot shows the effects of using autofill on different types of values and patterns. Autofilling with the cells shown in each column in the top table gives the results shown in the bottom.

Copying and Moving Cells

While you can use autofill to copy a single cell's content into adjacent cells, it doesn't help when you want to copy a cell's content farther afield, or work with a whole block of cells. For that, Numbers provides a few different methods for copying and moving cells.

You can move cells within a table, to another table, or to another spot on the canvas to create a whole new table of their own. To start, select the cell(s) to move, and move the cursor near the edge of the selection—it turns into a hand to signal that it's ready to take hold of the selected cells. Drag the selection to its new location in any table; the ghostly image of the original cells follows the cursor as you drag, and Numbers highlights the cells where the selection will land if you release the mouse button. When you've dragged the cells to the desired position, drop them. Numbers replaces any existing content with the original cell content, formatting, comments, everything; meanwhile, Numbers empties out the original cells, stripping them bare not only of their values but also all formatting. If you drag the selection to the canvas instead of inside another table, Numbers adds the cells to the canvas as a brand new table.

If you're moving cells far enough that dragging is a hassle (or if you're moving them to a different sheet), Numbers offers a pair of commands that lets you queue up cells to move and then zap them to their new location in two separate steps. Select the cell(s) to move and choose Edit → Mark for Move (Shift-⌘-X). Numbers highlights the selection in orange to show that it's ready to launch. Then navigate to the destination cell on your spreadsheet, choose Edit → Move (Shift-⌘-V), and Numbers ships the marked cell(s) to the new location.

To copy the cells instead of move them, hold down the Option key while you drag. The cursor sprouts a + sign in a green bubble to let you know that it's duplicating instead of moving the selection. As before, Numbers replaces the values and formatting of the destination cells, but this time the original cells remain intact.

Pasting table cells

You can also copy or move selected cells by going to Edit → Copy or Edit → Cut, selecting the destination cell(s), and then choosing Edit → Paste. If no cells are selected when you paste, Numbers adds the pasted cells as a new table. Otherwise, Numbers pastes the cells into the selected location, replacing the data values, formatting, and comments of any cells that stood there before. Exactly how the cells are pasted, however, depends on how you've selected the cells at the destination. Figure 18-29 tells the story.

As Figure 18-29 shows, no matter what collection of cells you select at the destination, Numbers always fills all of them—even if that collection doesn't fit the dimensions of the cells on the clipboard. This turns out to be a convenient way to fill an entire row or column with a single value, formula, or display format: Copy a single cell to the clipboard with the value and formatting you'd like to apply. Then click the reference tab for the destination row or column to select it, and choose Edit → Paste. Numbers fills in *all* the cells with clones of the original.

Tip: The same trick works if you just want to paste cells' formatting but not replace their content. Instead of using the regular Copy and Paste commands, however, Choose Format → Copy Style and Format → Paste Style. If you want to paste only the cell value without changing the underlying style and format of the destinations cells, choose Edit → Paste Values.

Numbers also lets you paste cells so that they nudge other cells out of the way instead of replacing them. Choose Insert → Copied Rows or Insert → Copied Columns, and Numbers moves existing cells aside before pasting the rows. (This works best when you've copied an entire row or column.)

Adding Special Controls to Cells

One pitfall of working with large amounts of data is the inevitable typo. Numbers gives you a few controls that can help reduce fat-finger keyboard errors, keeping your data tidy and making the process of data entry a bit friendlier in the process. These options add checkboxes, sliders, "steppers," and pop-up menus—familiar visual devices that provide an alternative to typing values manually. To add these controls to selected cells, choose one of them from the Cell Format menu in the Format Bar or Cells Inspector.

Using checkboxes for Boolean values

Everybody knows what a checkbox means: yes or no, complete or incomplete, on or off. Don't look now, but that checkbox is what your neighborhood geek calls a Boolean indicator. Checkboxes are so familiar that it might seem a little overwrought to apply such a fancy term to them, but a Boolean value's simple choice of TRUE or FALSE is really just an on/off switch, like a checkbox. Numbers lets you use checkboxes as a friendly way to flip that Boolean switch. Turn a checkbox on to set the cell's value to TRUE, or turn it off to set it to FALSE.

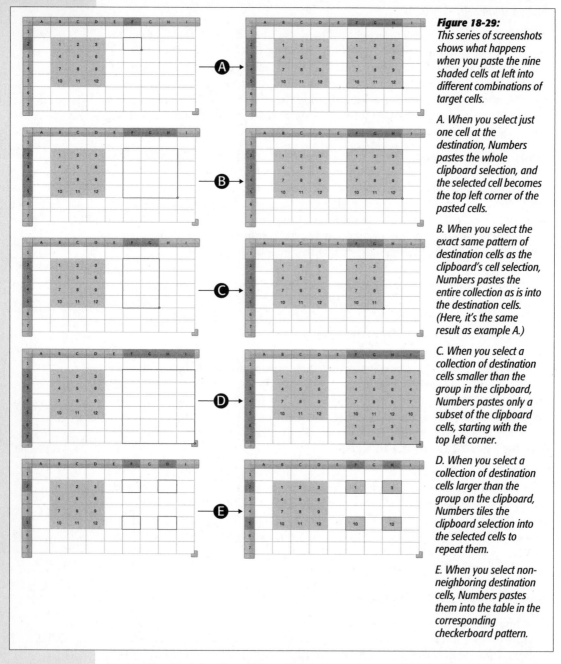

Figure 18-29:
This series of screenshots shows what happens when you paste the nine shaded cells at left into different combinations of target cells.

A. When you select just one cell at the destination, Numbers pastes the whole clipboard selection, and the selected cell becomes the top left corner of the pasted cells.

B. When you select the exact same pattern of destination cells as the clipboard's cell selection, Numbers pastes the entire collection as is into the destination cells. (Here, it's the same result as example A.)

C. When you select a collection of destination cells smaller than the group in the clipboard, Numbers pastes only a subset of the clipboard cells, starting with the top left corner.

D. When you select a collection of destination cells larger than the group on the clipboard, Numbers tiles the clipboard selection into the selected cells to repeat them.

E. When you select non-neighboring destination cells, Numbers pastes them into the table in the corresponding checkerboard pattern.

But really, Boolean shmoolean. Although you can indeed put these TRUE/FALSE values to use in formulas and to filter your content—you'll learn about this in Chapter 21—you'll usually just appreciate the visual utility of having checkboxes in your spreadsheet. Figure 18-30 shows a simple example of checkboxes in a to-do list. Click a checkbox to toggle it on or off.

To add a checkbox to selected cells, click the Checkbox button in the Format Bar, or choose Checkbox in the Cell Format pop-up menu in the Cells Inspector. If any cells already contain a TRUE Boolean value, their checkboxes are turned on. Otherwise, any existing values are replaced with FALSE, and their checkboxes are switched off.

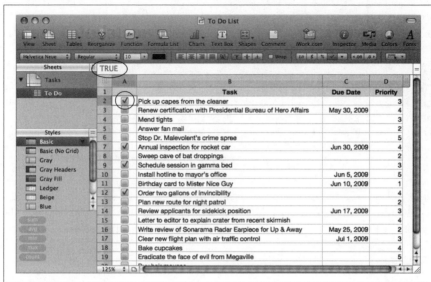

Figure 18-30:
Use checkboxes to indicate complete items in a to-do list, for example. Behind the scenes, turning on a checkbox sets the cell's value to TRUE. Unchecked boxes are set to FALSE.

Using sliders for numbers

Add a slider to a number cell and Numbers lets you change its value quickly with a flip of the wrist. Sliders are particularly valuable when you have a cell hooked up as part of a formula and want to test "what if?" scenarios to see how the rest of your spreadsheet's values change as you gradually change one cell's value. The Grade Book template that you saw on page 567 is a good example of this. Figure 18-31 shows that same slider again, along with the controls in the Cells Inspector that make it tick.

To add a slider to selected cells, choose Slider from the Cell Format pop-up menu in the Format Bar or the Cells Inspector. The Slider works with any type of number format (number, currency, percentage, fraction, scientific, or numeral system), and you can choose which one to use in the Cells Inspector. The inspector also offers several other settings for controlling the display of both the slider and cell value it controls.

Note: The slider is 100 pixels wide, which means that it can contain, at most, 100 "steps" or increments and this limitation overrides whatever value you might put into the Cells Inspector's Increment field. If you set the minimum value to 1, for example, and the maximum to 200, the increment will be 2, even when you set the Increment field to 1, because it's not possible to move the slider less than one pixel at a time.

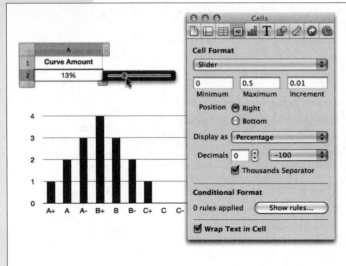

Figure 18-31:
Sliders make their presence known only when you click a cell with the Slider format (they don't show if you select more than one cell). Move the slider's position with the mouse or arrow keys. Here, the Grade Book template slider lets you set the number of points to adjust grade scores.

The Cells Inspector controls the behavior and appearance of the cell, including the minimum and maximum values of the slider's range. The Increment field sets the amount the cell value increases or decreases as you nudge the slider right or left. Set the Position field to display the slider below the cell or to the right. The Display As field determines the type of number format to show in the cell, and Decimals sets how many decimal places to display.

You're not obliged to use the slider. You can edit the cell value just as you normally would, by typing directly into the cell, although you can't go outside the range set by the minimum and maximum values in the Cells Inspector.

Using steppers

A stepper control adds up and down arrows next to a cell when you select it. Like a slider, a stepper lets you set a range and a fixed increment for number values. While a slider is useful for moving quickly through a range of values, a stepper is better for carefully nudging values by specific increments. Figure 18-32 shows what the Grade Book template looks like with its slider replaced by a stepper.

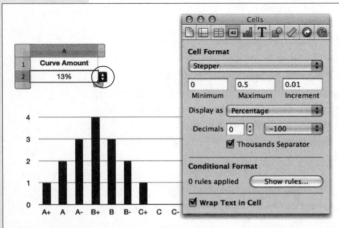

Figure 18-32:
A stepper control adds up and down arrows to the right of the selected cell. Click the arrows or use your keyboard's arrow keys to bump the value according to the increment set in the Cells Inspector. You can also type values directly into stepper cells, but Numbers automatically corrects any typed values to fit the increment specified in the Cells Inspector. This makes a stepper a good way to force values to fit specific steps or units.

Using pop-up menus for predefined values

Like the many pop-up menus in Numbers itself, pop-up controls let you offer a fixed selection of values for a cell. When you select a cell formatted with a pop-up menu, like the one shown in Figure 18-33, a disclosure triangle appears to the right; click the triangle to reveal the available options. To trigger the pop-up menu from the keyboard, select the cell and press the space bar, use the up or down arrow keys to move through the options, and press Return or Space to make your selection.

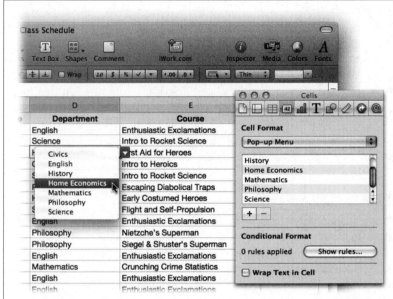

Figure 18-33:
Cells with pop-up menus sprout a translucent handle with a downward arrow when you select them. Click the arrow to reveal the pop-up menu with the allowed values for the field. Add or remove menu items from the pop-up menu by clicking the + or – button in the Cells Inspector listing. Double-click a value to give it a new name. The Cells Inspector doesn't provide an option to reorder values; to juggle the display order, you have to add, delete, and rename the menu items.

Whenever possible, you should format cells for pop-up menus *before* entering their data. When you add a pop-up menu to a cell that already has a value, that original value is wiped out, and replaced by the number 1, the first in a standard set of placeholder menu options (1, 2, and 3). You can likewise run into trouble changing the menu options for pop-up menus for cells that already contain values. Pop-up cells *must* contain values in the option list; if you rename or delete the option for a cell's current value, Numbers changes the cell's value to the first value in the list. Be careful.

Using Address Book Info

Numbers is on close terms with Address Book, your Mac's contact compendium, a relationship that can save you heaps of time when you're building a contact list in your spreadsheet. Drag an Address Book card or group into your spreadsheet, and Numbers slurps up the info automatically. Numbers also speaks fluent vCard, a common format for saving an individual's contact info to include in email messages, for example.

Creating a new table of contacts

Drag one or more address cards—or even better, a group card—into a blank area of the sheet canvas, and Numbers adds the info as a brand new table with contacts listed in rows and address info in columns. The table doesn't look like much at first, showing only four columns of data: Last Name, First Name, Phone, and Email. Moreover, those initial Phone and Email fields are ambiguous; they can be from the entry for work, home, or other. (Numbers takes the "first available" info for those fields, but which field that might be depends on how you entered the data.)

Under the surface, though, the new table contains the complete contact info for all your contacts—Numbers is simply holding them back as *hidden columns*. To view the hidden columns, select the table, and choose Table → Unhide All Columns. Numbers reveals all 65 address columns listed in Table 18-1, including specific email and phone columns for home, work, and other. Alas, now you've probably got more info than you wanted: Go ahead and delete any columns you don't need (page 633).

Tip: When you drag an address card or group card from Address Book, be sure you drag it *sideways* out of the Address Book window. Dragging up or down instead selects additional cards.

Adding contacts to an existing table

When you drag an address card or group card into a table with a header row containing one or more names matching Address Book field names, Numbers adds the contacts as a new row in the table. (See page 634 for complete details about header rows.) It doesn't matter where you drag the card into the table; Numbers always adds each contact as a new row at the bottom of the table.

Note: You can't add contacts to a table that has no columns with Address Book field names. If you drop a card into such a table, Numbers ignores it and instead adds a new table as if you had dropped the card directly onto the sheet canvas.

In these new contact rows, Numbers fills in the cells only for columns named for Address Book fields; the rest are left blank. Table 18-1 lists the column names that Numbers looks for. In many cases, Numbers accepts an alternate name (Surname instead of Last Name, for example), and those substitutes are listed in Table 18-1, too.

Tip: For addresses, Numbers offers an option that combines and formats all the address info (street, city, state, and zip) into a single cell. Use Address, Home Address, Work Address, or Other Address as column names to display this consolidated contact info. The plain Address name, like the generic Email and Phone fields mentioned earlier, uses the "first available" address and could be the address for home, work, or other.

Table 18-1. *Address Book Column Names*

Address Book Field Name	Numbers Also Recognizes...
Prefix	Name title, Name prefix
Last name	Last, Surname
First name	First, Given name, Forename
Suffix	Name suffix, Professional suffix, Academic suffix
Nickname	
Maiden name	
Job title	
Department	Job department
Company	
Phone (first available number)	
Main phone	
Work phone	
Home phone	
Mobile	Mobile phone, Mobile telephone, Cell phone, Cell telephone, Cellular, Cellular telephone, Cellular phone
Home fax	
Work fax	
Pager	Beeper
Other phone	
Email (first available address)	Email address
Work email	
Home email	
Other email	
URL (first available URL)	
Work URL	
Home URL	
Other URL	
Birthday	
AIM (first available address)	IM, IM handle, IM name, IM address, Chat, Chat handle, Chat name, Chat address
Work AIM	Work IM, Work IM handle, Work IM name, Work IM address, Work chat handle, Work chat name, Work chat address
Home AIM	Home IM, Home IM handle, Home IM name, Home IM address, Home chat, Home chat handle, Home chat name, Home chat address
Other AIM	Other IM, Other IM handle, Other IM name, Other IM address, Other chat, Other chat handle, Other chat name, Other chat address

Table 18-1. *Address Book Column Names (continued)*

Address Book Field Name	Numbers Also Recognizes...
Yahoo	
Work Yahoo	
Home Yahoo	
Other Yahoo	
Jabber	
Work Jabber	
Home Jabber	
Other Jabber	
Address (first available address)	
Street address (first available street address)	Street
City (first available city)	Town
State (first available state)	State
Zip	Zip code, Postal code
Country (first available country)	
Work address	
Work street address	Work street
Work city	Work town
Work state	
Work zip	Work zip code, Work postal code
Work country	
Home address	
Home street address	Home street
Home city	Home town
Home state	
Home zip	Home zip code, Home postal code
Home country	
Other address	
Other street address	Other street
Other city	Other town
Other state	
Other zip	Other zip code, Other postal code
Other country	
Note	Notes
Image	

Importing OFX Files for Bank Data

Numbers makes it similarly easy to quickly import personal financial data into your tables. Many bank websites allow you to download account info as a file in the Open Financial Exchange (OFX) format. Depending on the type of account, these files might list financial transactions like withdrawals and deposits, cleared checks, bill payments, investments, and so on.

Tip: OFX is a file format commonly used by Quicken and Microsoft Money, Redmond's personal finance software. If your bank's site doesn't specifically offer a download for OFX, look for a download for Money instead; that's probably an OFX file.

You can add OFX data to a spreadsheet in one of three ways:

- **Create a brand new spreadsheet.** Choose File → Open and select the OFX file. Numbers creates a spreadsheet with two tables—one with your account data and one with your transaction details.

- **Add a new table to a spreadsheet.** Drag the OFX file from your desktop into a blank area of your sheet.

- **Add to an existing table.** Drag the OFX file from your desktop into a table whose header row includes one or more column names matching OFX transaction categories. Numbers adds a new row to your table for each transaction, filling in any columns that match OFX categories. (If you're not sure of these category names, drag the file into a blank part of your sheet to create a new table and borrow the column names from that table.) To maintain a check register, for example, you can use the Checking Register template in the Template Chooser's Personal Finance category; drag an OFX file from your desktop into the check register table, labeled "Checking" in the template.

Organizing Tables in Numbers

Now that you can spin your way across tables faster than a can-can dancer, you've got all the know-how you need to fill up your grids with lots of juicy data. But all that info is only useful if you can pluck it back out again, and that's where a little organization goes a long way. Once you've got your data loaded into a table, it's time to go to work to massage it into shape—structuring it, sorting it, searching it, filtering it. This chapter shows you all the ways that Numbers can help you tidy your tables and find the right info at the right time.

This organizational effort is about more than shuffling data, though: A pristine table also *looks* clean, and this chapter also shows you how to make your data more accessible (and your tables prettier) with the judicious application of borders and background fills. Once you've transformed your gray numbers into shapely figures, Numbers makes it easy to perform the same makeover miracle again and again by storing styles and saving your own predefined tables for later reuse. Before you dig into this interior decoration, though, you'll learn about organizing the structure of your table, starting with rows and columns.

Working with Rows and Columns

Filling table cells quickly is all well and good—after all, that's how you'll spend most of your time as you work with your spreadsheet. But although cells may be where you actually sling your data, it's the rows and columns that hold the whole thing to together and keep your info organized. Good row and column management makes for good table manners. It's also efficient. This section shows you the fastest ways to add, insert, delete, resize, and hide rows or columns, letting you grow or prune your table quickly as the need arises.

Note: As you squeeze and stretch a table's rows and columns, its overall size naturally changes, too. When you have other tables or objects on the sheet, Numbers nudges the positions of those objects relative to your growing or shrinking table. This prevents the table from running over other objects when it gets larger, or from creating too much space between objects when it gets smaller. You can prevent Numbers from doing this in the General pane of the Numbers → Preferences window: Turn off the "Automatically move objects when tables resize" checkbox.

Adding and Deleting Rows or Columns

When you've selected one or more of a table's cells, the table sprouts four gripped handles at its corners; you can use three of them to add or remove cells at the edges of the table by dragging. With the exception of the top-left handle—the Table handle, which moves the table to a new position—the others resize the table as you drag, adding or removing rows or columns as you go. (The Table handle is visible only when the first row and column are onscreen.) Figure 19-1 gives you the lay of the land.

Note: Numbers won't let you add rows when you're filtering table content (see page 644). In that case, the row handle won't drag, and the row and column handle will move only left or right (see Figure 19-1 for pointers to these different handles). To start adding rows again, remove the filtering criteria from the table's Reorganize window to turn off row filtering.

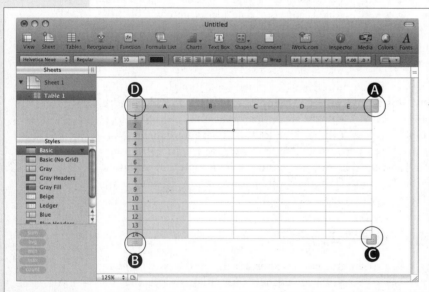

Figure 19-1:
Drag the column handle (A) to the left or right to remove or add columns; if you click without dragging, Numbers adds just one column to the table. Drag the row handle (B) up or down to remove or add rows; click to add one row. The row and column handle (C) does double duty, working changes on both rows and columns as you drag. Drag the Table handle (D) in the top left to move the entire table, without changing the number of rows or columns.

Numbers also adds new rows and columns as you edit your table, giving you new cells as you bump up against the table's boundaries by pressing Tab or Return. See page 589 for the details.

Deleting rows or columns containing data

You can use the table's handles to remove only empty rows or columns. When you try to drag the handle through a row or column that contains data, Numbers throws on the brakes and will go no farther. That's a good policy, since it prevents you from carelessly chucking entire swaths of data with an ill-considered flick of the wrist.

To remove a row or cell that contains data, you have to be more explicit about it. When you hold down the Option key while dragging the handle, that flips off the safety, and Numbers deletes rows or columns whether or not they contain content. You can also delete rows or columns with menu commands. Select a cell (or a series of neighboring cells) in the row(s) or column(s) to delete, and choose Table → Delete Rows or Table → Delete Columns. Numbers throws out the offending rows or columns and cinches up the table around them. (You can also choose these commands when you have entire rows or columns selected, but it's not necessary; selecting a single cell inside a row or column is enough to tell Numbers which one you want to delete.)

The Delete command is also available in the reference tab pop-up menu for the row or column (Figure 19-2). These menus hold a handy collection of tools for working with rows and columns. When a single cell is selected, the menus offer the Delete Column or Delete Row command. When you select more than one cell in neighboring rows or columns, the options change to Delete Selected Columns or Delete Selected Rows.

Note: Pressing the Delete key deletes only the data inside selected cells, not the cell containers themselves.

Inserting rows or columns

The table's handles let you add rows and columns at the end of the table, but that doesn't help you when you want to insert rows or columns in the *middle* of the table. You'll find yourself doing that frequently, especially for rows, so it's a good idea to get familiar with the Option-arrow keys—the keyboard shortcuts for inserting new rows and columns:

- Add a row above the selected cell by pressing **Option-Up Arrow** or by choosing Table → Add Row Above.

- Add a row below the selected cell by pressing **Option-Down Arrow** or by choosing Table → Add Row Below.

- Add a column to the left of the selected cell by pressing **Option-Left Arrow** or by choosing Table → Add Column Before.

- Add a column to the right of the selected cell by pressing **Option-Right Arrow** or by choosing Table → Add Column After.

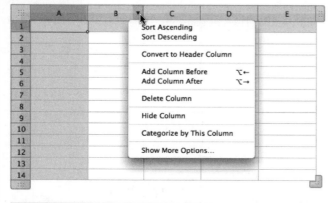

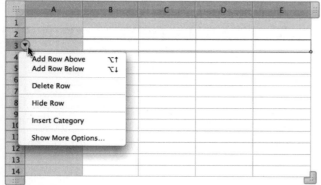

Figure 19-2:
Every column and row has its own pop-up menu tucked away in its reference tab. To trigger one of these pop-up menus, point to the reference tab for the row or column you want to edit, and a menu arrow appears. Click the arrow to pop open the menu for the row or column, and make your selection. (This also happens to be the very same menu that you get when you Control-click a reference tab.)

When you select cells in multiple rows or columns, these commands add the same number of rows or columns as your selection. For example, if you want to add three rows to your table, select cells in three neighboring rows, and press Option-Up Arrow or choose Table → Add Rows Above; Numbers adds three rows above your current selection. The same works for columns: When you press Option-Left Arrow or Option-Right Arrow with cells selected in several columns, Numbers adds the same number of columns before or after the selection.

You can also add a single row or column from the reference tab pop-up menu, which offers the same commands as the Table menu: Add Row Above and Add Row Below for row reference tabs, and Add Column Before and Add Column After for column reference tabs. Unlike the Table commands and Option-arrow keystrokes, however, these reference-tab commands always insert just one column or row, no matter how many rows or cells might be selected.

Working with Header Rows and Columns

For all but the most basic tables, it's just plain polite to label your data and provide a formal introduction between your info and your reader. Header rows and header columns handle this bit of etiquette. Header rows always ride at the top of tables, their cells labeling the columns below. Header columns meanwhile anchor the left side of tables, their cells labeling the rows stretching off to the right, as shown in Figure 19-3. Most tables have either a header row or a header column, often both. You can format these headers with whatever background or border you like (see page 656), but Numbers typically starts you out by shading them to stand out from the other rows and columns, known as the table body.

Note: When a table contains both header rows and header columns, they have some shared real estate where their cells intersect in the top left of the table. In that case, those cells are considered to be part of the header row. Header columns appear below any header rows.

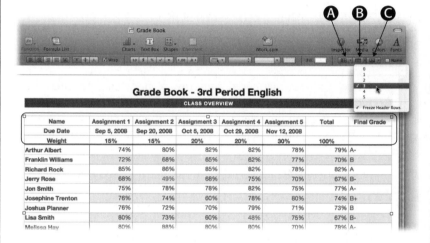

Figure 19-3:
This grade book table has three header rows (circled) and a header column consisting of student names. Choose how many header rows and columns to display (or remove them entirely) by selecting from the Header Column (A) or Header Row (B) pop-up buttons in the Format Bar. You can add up to five header rows or columns. This run of buttons also includes the Footer Row button (C), which you'll learn about in the next section.

Header rows and columns not only help your spreadsheet readers understand your data—they help Numbers figure it out, too. By labeling your data with these header elements, you give Numbers a *name* for your rows and columns, and the program uses these names in a variety of ways. You've already seen how Numbers uses the header row to identify columns when you import contact info (page 625) and financial transactions (via OFX files, page 629). The header row plays a similar role to organize your data when Numbers works with Pages to create mass mailings (page 169).

When you learn about formulas in the next chapter, you'll see that Numbers also uses these row and column names to refer to specific cells when it works its mathematical magic. Header cells also provide shortcuts for applying a quick formula to an entire row or column. More on all this in Chapter 20.

Finally, header rows and columns are also persistent: When a table spans more than one page, Numbers repeats its header rows and columns on each of those pages when you print the sheet. This helps you and your readers keep your bearings as you flip from page to page. You can preview this effect (or turn it off) in Print View (page 573).

Because of the special status of header rows and columns, you add them to a table in a different way than you add normal rows and columns. The Format Bar provides Header Row and Header Column buttons to add and remove a table's header elements, as shown in Figure 19-3. When a table doesn't have a header row or header column, click the corresponding button to add one; click it again to remove it. You can also click the menu arrow next to one of the buttons to choose how many header rows or columns you'd like (choosing *0* removes any header rows or columns). These button menus are also repeated in the Table Inspector, which you can likewise use to add or remove header rows and columns. You can also choose how many header rows or columns display by choosing a number from the Table menu's "Header Rows" or "Header Columns" submenu.

You can also convert a mild-mannered body row or body column into a header, often a good idea after you've imported an Excel or CSV file, for example. To perform this amazing feat, open the reference tab pop-up menu for the topmost body row or the leftmost body column, and choose Convert to Header Row or Convert to Header Column.

Once you have a header element in place, you can use it to add even more header rows or columns. This works just like inserting a regular row or column: Select the header row or column and use an Option-arrow combination to insert a new header row or column; or choose one of these options from a header's reference tab menu: Add Header Row Above; Add Header Row Below; Add Header Column Before; or Add Header Column After.

Tables can have as many as five header rows and five header columns. Stacking header rows or columns in this manner gives you an additional display option, which is nice, but its real utility comes in when you want to build formulas that use some portion of the header cell—units of measure, for example, or the weight of a test score in an overall class grade. In that case, adding another header lets you isolate part of the row or column label to use in a formula. Here again, you'll find out more about formulas in the next chapter. No matter how many header rows or columns your table has, they always have to appear at the very top and left of the table.

While adding a header row or column is a different process than for a regular row or column, you delete them the same way: Choose Delete Row or Delete Column from its reference tab pop-up menu, or select it and choose Table → Delete Row or Table → Column.

Note: Be careful when you delete header rows or columns. Although you can always add header elements back to the table, any content that was in the original header row or column won't come back with it. Removing a header element sends its contents to the data boneyard.

Freezing header rows and columns

As soon as you start working with more than a casual sprinkling of data, it doesn't take long before your tables extend well beyond the height or width of a single screen. As usual, of course, your scroll bars have you covered to help you shuttle around your sheet. But since the header row and header column are tied firmly to the top and left of the table, scrolling away from the first row or column means that your data labels slip out of view, too. And right on cue, you immediately forget what the heck all those columns of numbers stand for.

Happily, Numbers can put that forgetful scenario on ice by *freezing* your header rows or columns. When you enable this cool feature for a table, then scroll its header row or column off the screen, Numbers freezes the header element in its tracks, stopping it at the edge of the visible sheet canvas to float above the rest of the table below. This keeps your data labels in view even when the "real" header is hundreds of rows offscreen. Figure 19-4 shows a frozen header row. To create one for yourself, select the table, and then choose Table → Freeze Header Rows or Table → Freeze Header Columns. These options are also available in the Header Row and Header Column buttons in the Format Bar and Table Inspector.

Note: You can't freeze headers in Print view, only in the standard editing view.

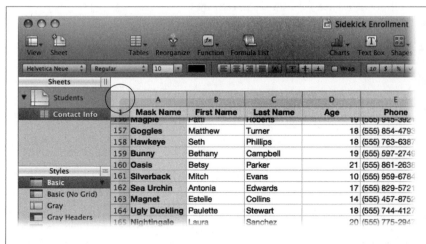

Figure 19-4:
With the Freeze Header Row option turned on, the first row of this table floats above the other rows, keeping the column labels in view. Notice that the region in the top left corner (circled) where you would normally find the Table handle no longer sports a grip. In fact, it's no longer a handle, and you can't use it to move the table to a new position as you normally would. The gripped handle returns when you scroll back to the top of the table and the header row unfreezes.

Adding Footer Rows

As you might guess, the footer row is the header row's opposite number, staking out the bottom row of the table. Although footer rows don't quite have the same heady importance as their column-labeling counterparts, they're often deployed to display column sums or other calculations for the cells above. In fact, as you'll

---

learn in the next chapter, that role is where the footer row's one and only superpower comes in: It can "catch" quick formulas that you add to header cells, automatically calculating the rows above. See page 675 for the details.

Apart from that, adding a footer row to tables is simply a way to draw attention to the bottom row(s) of the table. You can add up to five footer rows to a table, and Numbers typically shades them to set them apart from the body rows. Add one or more footer rows by choosing a number from the Footer Rows pop-up button in the Format Bar (Figure 19-3) or the Table Inspector. You can also choose a number from the Table → Footer Rows submenu.

If you choose zero from any of these menus, you remove all footer rows from the table. You can likewise delete a footer row by choosing Delete Row from its reference tab pop-up, or by selecting the row and choosing Table → Delete Row.

Resizing Rows and Columns

Adjust the size of rows and columns by dragging the boundary between reference tabs. When you point the cursor between two reference tabs, the pointer turns into a thick line with arrows, signaling that it's ready to push the boundary for you. To resize a row, drag the bottom border of its reference tab; to resize a column, drag its tab's right border. As you drag, Numbers displays the new height or width in inches (or whatever unit you've selected in the Ruler pane of the Numbers → Preferences window). Figure 19-5 shows an example.

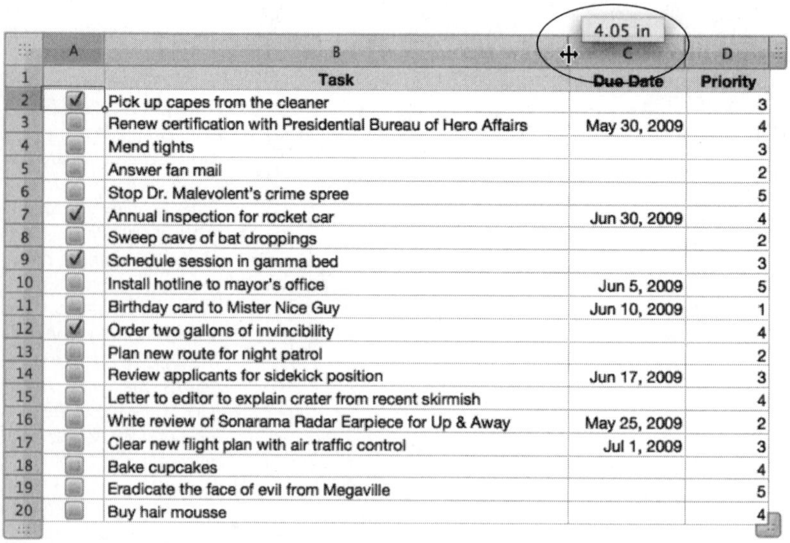

	A	B	C	D
1		Task	Due Date	Priority
2	✓	Pick up capes from the cleaner		3
3		Renew certification with Presidential Bureau of Hero Affairs	May 30, 2009	4
4		Mend tights		3
5		Answer fan mail		2
6		Stop Dr. Malevolent's crime spree		5
7	✓	Annual inspection for rocket car	Jun 30, 2009	4
8		Sweep cave of bat droppings		2
9	✓	Schedule session in gamma bed		3
10		Install hotline to mayor's office	Jun 5, 2009	5
11		Birthday card to Mister Nice Guy	Jun 10, 2009	1
12	✓	Order two gallons of invincibility		4
13		Plan new route for night patrol		2
14		Review applicants for sidekick position	Jun 17, 2009	3
15		Letter to editor to explain crater from recent skirmish		4
16		Write review of Sonarama Radar Earpiece for Up & Away	May 25, 2009	2
17		Clear new flight plan with air traffic control	Jul 1, 2009	3
18		Bake cupcakes		4
19		Eradicate the face of evil from Megaville		5
20		Buy hair mousse		4

Figure 19-5: *Resize the width of a column by dragging the right border of its reference tab left or right. Here, the cursor indicates that Numbers is ready to resize the Task column; dragging left makes it smaller, and dragging right makes it larger. All the while, a yellow tool tip shows the new width of the column.*

Making rows or columns the same size

You can also use the same method to resize several rows or columns at once: Select all the rows or columns you'd like to squeeze or stretch by Shift-clicking or ⌘-clicking their reference tabs. Resize *one* of the selected rows or columns (drag the right border of a column's reference tab, or the bottom border of a row's reference tab). During the drag itself, only the one row or column will change size, but as soon as you release the mouse button, the other selected rows or columns snap to the new size, too.

If you're not a precision mouse jockey but still want to fix the size of rows or columns to a very precise height or width, the Table Inspector lets you specify the exact size. Select the rows or columns to adjust, and use the arrows in the Column Width or Row Height field to adjust the size, or type the values directly.

All the methods mentioned so far change the overall size of the table, too. Making rows and columns larger makes your table swell; making them smaller makes your table shrink. When you want to resize rows or columns without changing the overall size, Numbers offers two commands that spread out row and column sizes evenly. Choose Table → Distribute Rows Evenly or Table → Distribute Columns Evenly, and Numbers makes all selected rows or columns the same size within the available space, without changing the size of the table footprint. Apply these egalitarian commands when you have an entire table selected at the object level, and Numbers makes *all* rows or columns in the table the same size.

Note: The Distribute Evenly commands are grayed out when you have just one cell, row, or column selected.

Tailoring row and column size to your content

When you want to tighten rows or columns as much as possible while still showing all your content, Numbers can resize them automatically to fit the exact size of your content. This is handy for revealing clipped content (page 592) or eliminating unused white space. Double-click the reference tab's right border, or choose Table → "Resize Columns to Fit Content" (or click the Fit button in the Cells Inspector), and Numbers adjusts the width of the selected column to precisely fit its widest content. This is a one-time thing; Numbers won't continue to update the column width to fit your content, at least not until you again choose Table → Resize Columns To Fit Content.

It works differently with rows. Unless you set rows to a specific height, Numbers always adjusts row height to fit your content. Rows grow as you add new lines (when text wrapping is on) or make the font size larger, and they shrink when your content shrinks. They're always a *flexible height,* in other words, until you explicitly drag them to a new size or set their height in the Table Inspector. After you do that, they cease to be flexible and, as a result, their fixed height can clip cell contents or leave unused white space. To make the row height flexible again for selected rows, double-click the reference tab's bottom border, choose Table → "Resize Rows to Fit Content", or click the Fit button in the Table Inspector.

Note: For pointers on handling content that's too big for a cell, head back to page 592 for a review.

Moving Rows and Columns

Move a row or column to a new location by dragging its reference tab. The tricky part is that you have to click the reference tab once before dragging. If you drag an unselected reference tab, you'll only select neighboring rows and columns. Instead, click the reference tab, release the mouse button, and *then* drag. As you drag, Numbers shows a heavy blue guideline to show you where the row or column will land when you drop the mouse. Release the mouse, and Numbers inserts the row or column in its new location, closing up its old position. This trick also works for moving several neighboring rows or columns, as shown in Figure 19-6.

Note: You can't move header rows, header columns, or footer rows. Their special status means that they're always anchored in place. You can, however, move or copy the *cells* inside headers and footers. See page 620 for a roundup of techniques for moving and copying cells.

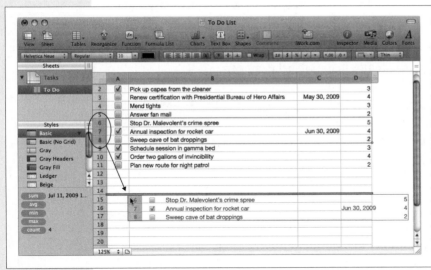

Figure 19-6:
To move one or more rows to a new location, select the row(s) by clicking their reference tabs (circled). Shift-click or Shift-drag the reference tabs to select multiple neighboring rows. Drag the reference tab of a selected row up or down to move it to a new location, as shown here with a selection of three rows. As you drag, a heavy blue guideline shows you where the rows will land when you drop them.

Numbers doesn't limit you to moving rows and column only within the same table. You can drag them by their reference tabs to other tables, too. Or drop them into a blank location on the canvas to create a whole new table.

To *copy* the column or row instead of moving it, hold down the Option key while you drag, or use the clipboard:

1. Select the row or column by clicking its reference tab.

2. Choose Edit → Copy or press ⌘-C.

3. Select the row or column immediately *after* the location where you want to insert the copied row or column.

4. Choose Insert → Copied Rows or Insert → Copied Columns, and Numbers inserts the row or cell into its new location.

In contrast to Edit → Paste, these Insert menu commands wedge a new column or row into the table before the selected cells; Paste replaces the selected cells.

Hiding and Unhiding Rows and Columns

Information can enlighten, for sure, but too much can also overwhelm or make it difficult to focus. When you're working with a sprawling set of data, Numbers lets you temporarily sweep parts of it away so that you can work with just the relevant info for the task at hand. You do this by *hiding* rows or columns. This is invaluable, for example, when you have a very wide table with lots of columns, but you care about only a few of them just now and want them all to fit on your screen without scrolling.

Note: You already saw this effect in action on page 626 in the discussion of Address Book info. When Numbers adds a new table of contacts to your spreadsheet, it hides all but four of its 65 columns to avoid flooding your sheet with obscure contact fields.

To hide a row or column, choose Hide Row or Hide Column from its reference tab pop-up menu. When you have cells selected in multiple rows or columns, the command turns into Hide Selected Rows or Selected Columns, which makes all those rows or columns vanish. This disappearing trick is only an act; the data is all tucked safely away behind a digital curtain. Formulas that use a hidden cell continue to work, and sorting takes hidden fields into account. You can tell that your hidden rows or columns are still lurking behind the scenes because Numbers safely holds their reference tabs in reserve: When you hide columns C and D, for example the displayed reference tabs skip directly from B to E, signaling that the rows in between are hidden.

Note: Numbers won't hide rows or columns that contain merged cells.

Bring your hidden data back into the open by choosing Unhide All Rows from any row's reference tab pop-up menu, or Unhide All Columns from any column's pop-up. These commands are also available in the Table menu. Numbers also offers two ways to unhide only specific rows or columns:

• To show rows or columns hidden in a selected range of rows or columns, select the rows or columns around the hidden data and then choose Unhide Selected Rows from the pop-up menu of any of the selected rows or columns.

- To reveal hidden data that's immediately adjacent to a row or column, go to the reference tab pop-up menu for that row or column, and choose "Unhide Rows [numbers]" or "Unhide Columns [letters]".

- If only one column is hidden, you can unhide it from any column's reference tab pop-up by choosing "Unhide Column [letter]"; ditto for rows.

Note: If you copy a Numbers spreadsheet into Pages or Keynote, any hidden rows or columns don't make the trip. Unhide all data that you want to include before you send the table on its way.

Reorganize: Sort, Filter, Categorize

It doesn't matter how tangled, disordered, or generally cluttered your spreadsheet data might be. Numbers can give you an instant makeover. On your command, Numbers sweeps in to *sort* your table rows into any order you like, *filtering* out irrelevant data along the way, and *categorizing* your data neatly by column values to let you quickly focus on the information that matters most.

This luxury means that you don't have to give any particular thought to the specific order of your data as you enter it. Just get your info into the table willy-nilly and, once it's in there, let Numbers sift and sort it for you. Not only is Numbers an adept organizer, it's also a great *reorganizer.* You're not stuck with any single view of your data; you can sort it this way and then that way, or filter out certain data and then bring it back to focus on a new area.

Numbers lets you sort, filter, and categorize your table rows from a single control panel—named, appropriately enough, the *Reorganize window* (Figure 19-7). To open this titan of tidiness, select the table to edit and click the toolbar's Reorganize button. (Don't be put off if you think this button looks like a boozy martini glass; Numbers is more clear-headed than that. The funnel icon is meant to convey the point that Numbers will filter and focus your data.)

Tip: When you have more than one table in your spreadsheet, you use the same Reorganize window to work with all of them. Select the table to edit, and the title bar at the top of the Reorganize window updates to show you which table it's working on.

Sorting Rows

The top pane of the Reorganize window is devoted to your table's sort order, the sequence in which you want your rows are displayed. This pane lets you pick a column and arrange the table's rows in ascending order (A, B, C…1, 2, 3) or descending order (Z, Y, X…3, 2, 1) according to the values in that column, the *sort column.* Figure 19-7 shows you what it looks like to sort the sidekick contact list alphabetically by Mask Name. In that case, Mask Name is the sort column, and all the rows line up according to their values for that column.

Note: Rows always keep all of their column values when you sort them, so that the entire row of data values shuffles to its new location in the list. Just because you're sorting *by* a column, in other words, doesn't mean that you're sorting *only* that column. The sort column's value determines the order of the rows, and the rows themselves stay whole.

Figure 19-7:
The Reorganize window is split into three panes for sorting (circled), filtering, and categorizing. To reorder the table, choose the column to sort by in the left pop-up menu, and choose "ascending" or "descending" in the right pop-up. Choose "Sort entire table" in the pop-up menu below the sort criteria to sort all rows, or choose "Sort selected rows" to reorder only the rows you specify. When you make a change to any of these menus, Numbers immediately updates the table. If you later make changes to the table, come back to the Reorganize window and click Sort Now to reapply the sort order.

An even faster way to sort your table rows is to use the reference tab pop-up menu for the sort column—the Mask Name column, in this example. Choose Sort Ascending or Sort Descending from the column's pop-up menu, and Numbers updates the rows according to that order. Going this route always reorders all rows of a table; you can't sort only selected rows as you can from the Reorganize window.

What happens when there's a tie? You can give Numbers additional instructions for what to do when two rows have the same value in the sort column. In that case, you can set up a second, "backup" sort order that handles these tied values. Say that you want to sort your sidekicks alphabetically by last name; for youngster heroes who happen to share the same name, you can order those matches alphabetically by first name. Figure 19-8 shows you how.

A few observations about how Numbers sorts its data: When a column contains a mix of text and numbers, numbers always come before letters. When you sort in ascending order, for example, numbers always come before text; the reverse is true when you sort in descending order. When you're sorting dates or times, Numbers

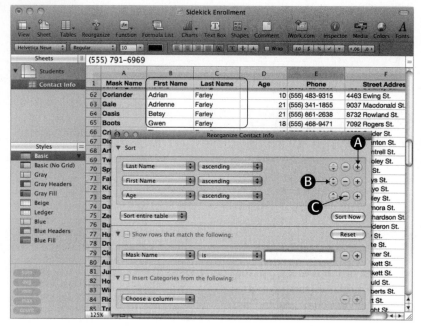

Figure 19-8:
Add additional sort criteria to tell Numbers what to do in case of a tie by clicking the + button (A) to the right of the sort info. Numbers inserts new sort menus; choose the column and order to add. Here, Numbers sorts the table by last name, first name, and then age. The entire table is sorted by last name; first name comes into play only when two sidekicks have the same last name, like the Farleys shown here. Numbers sorts them by first name. If two sidekicks have the exact same name, Numbers would further sort them by age.

To shuffle the order of your search criteria—to sort by first name instead of last name, for example—use the arrow buttons (B) to move a sort up or down in the list. Click the – button (C) to remove the sort criteria.

pays attention only to their chronological order. (Dates don't get sorted alphabetically by month name, for example; January is always before February.) Empty cells always wind up at the bottom of the sort order, no matter whether you're sorting in ascending or descending order.

Note: Numbers doesn't include header and footer rows when it sorts a table. These special rows always stay glued to the top and bottom of the table.

Filtering Rows

You've already seen that you can manually hide a table's rows by making a selection and telling Numbers to tuck them out of view (page 641). The Reorganize window puts a new spin on this by handling it for you automatically, filtering the displayed rows based on the rows' column values. For example, you can use this tool to show only incomplete items on your to-do list, or zoom in on tasks that are due within the next week.

Say that you're planning a field trip for 15-year-old sidekicks to visit the mighty League of Goodness headquarters, and you need to contact their parents for permission to go on the outing. You want to make your contact list show only sidekicks who are 15 years old. The Reorganize window has you covered, as shown in Figure 19-9.

Note: Numbers triggers the filter only after you choose a column and define a rule in the Filter pane. Typing a matching value into the rule field isn't enough; press Return or Tab after you type the value to make Numbers go ahead and update the table.

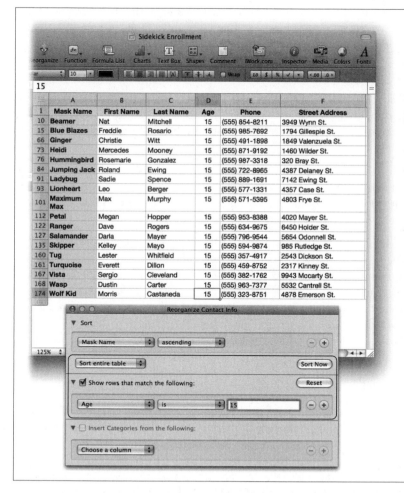

Figure 19-9:
The middle pane of the Reorganize window filters content based on conditions you set for certain column values. Here, the table is set to display rows only if the age value is 15. Numbers keeps the original row numbers in the row tabs, a subtle reminder that there are hidden rows.

You can winnow the list even further by adding additional conditions: Click the + button to add a new rule; or click the – button to remove it. Disable your filter by turning off the "Show rows that match the following" checkbox, and Numbers brings back your missing rows. It still remembers your filter rules, though, and you can go back to them by flipping the checkbox on again. To wipe out all filter rules, click Reset.

Unlike sorting, which only reorders the table when you tell it to, filtering updates the table anytime you make any changes. If you edit a value so that a row no longer matches the filter rules, Numbers whisks the row out of view. Alas, the always-on nature of a table filter means that Numbers doesn't let you add any new rows to the table. To resume adding new table rows, you have to switch the filter off: Turn off the "Show rows that match the following" checkbox in the Reorganize window, or click the Reset button to clear the filter rules completely.

Categorizing Rows

It's often convenient to group rows together when they share the same value in a column. A spreadsheet of Little League players, for example, should be able to list players by team. Similarly, revenue figures for a company's sales reps might be usefully clustered by state, maybe subcategorized by city, too. Filtering can help you zoom in on these groups one at a time—showing all Little League sluggers for just one team, for example—but that's not exactly a home run if you want to flip quickly between teams (you'd have to update the filter each time). Similarly, the sort feature is a swing and a miss. Although a good sort order can at least line up your ball players team by team in a single view, you still have a lot of scrolling to do to jump from team to team when you have lots of players in each team.

In Numbers, *table categories* solve that problem, divvying your table into topic headings that make it easy to browse rows in clusters of logical groups. Numbers can create these categories for you automatically by using the values in one or more columns.

Say that you're organizing the class rosters for the sidekick academy. You've created a table that includes a row for every student for every class period during the day. With five class periods per day, and 200 students, that's 1,000 rows—a bit unmanageable to browse easily. Categories to the rescue!

Click the toolbar's Reorganize button to open the Reorganize window. The bottom pane of the window offers to categorize the table using the values in any column—now known as the *category column*. Choose Department as the category column, for example, and Numbers adds a *category row* for each unique value in the Department column, grouping rows with matching values underneath. Each of these category rows gets a flippy triangle that you can use to toggle the display of its contents. As usual when working with rows or columns, the reference tab pop-up offers a faster way to add table categories. Instead of using the Reorganize window, open the pop-up menu for the category column you'd like to use and choose "Categorize by This Column". Either way you do it, Figure 19-10 shows the result.

You can expand or collapse all categories at once by choosing Expand All or Collapse All from the reference tab pop-up menu of any category row. If any one of the category rows are expanded to show their content, all category rows offer only the Collapse All option; Expand All is offered only when all categories are collapsed. As you'll learn on page 649, you can also create subcategories beneath category rows. If you choose Expand All or Collapse All in a subcategory row's pop-up menu, Numbers expands or collapses only that subcategory level, leaving parent categories unchanged.

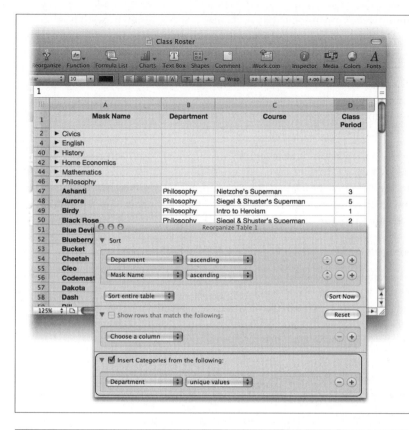

Figure 19-10:
When you choose a category column in the Reorganize window's bottom pane (circled), Numbers adds a category to the table for every value it finds in the chosen column. Here, the table is categorized by department, so Numbers groups rows together when they have the same value in the Department column. Every category is headed by a category row, which has a flippy triangle that lets you hide or reveal its contents. When you first add categories, all flippy triangles are always open to show all rows. Here, all departments have been tucked away except for the Philosophy department, whose flippy triangle is open.

Tip: When you click a category's flippy triangle to hide or show its contents, Numbers has the annoying habit of jumping you to whatever cell is currently selected, even if that cell is far away from the category you're trying to view. To avoid being beamed clear to the other side of your spreadsheet, select a cell in the category row before clicking its flippy triangle.

When you add categories, Numbers doesn't automatically sort these categories into any particular order. It simply adds the categories in the order that it finds each value in the table. If you want to have the categories displayed alphabetically, for example, you should sort the table by the category column—the Department column in our example. You can sort the rows either before or after adding the categories, it doesn't matter which. If you do it after, Numbers will update the category order for you. To sort the rows within each category, add a second sort rule as described back on page 643. In the class roster example shown in Figure 19-10, rows are sorted by Mask Name within each Department.

Moving rows between categories

After you categorize a table, Numbers constantly monitors your changes to keep all rows in their correct category. If you change the value of a row's category column,

---

Numbers bumps the row immediately to its new category. In our example, changing a student's Department cell from History to Mathematics moves her immediately out of the History department and into algebra territory alongside other students in the Mathematics department. You can make the same change by dragging and dropping; when you move a row by dragging its reference tab to a new category, Numbers changes the value of the row's category column to match its new home. So, in this example, dragging our forlorn student from History to Mathematics changes her row's Department column to Mathematics, too.

Numbers does a similar bit of auto-entry for you when you insert a new row (page 633) inside a category. In that case, Numbers fills in its category information for you—here, the value of the Department column. That's not only a timesaver, but it also ensures that the row stays put in the current category, at least until you decide to change the value of the row's category column.

Adding more categories

When you change a row's category cell to a new value that's not shared by any other row, you actually create a new category, or in this example, a new academic department. Remember, Numbers maintains a separate category for each unique value in the category column, so adding a brand new value adds a brand new category. Numbers adds a new category row to the table and moves the edited row in place below it.

You can also add a new category using the reference tab pop-up for any category row. The specific command to choose varies according to the row you've selected:

- **Category row.** When you choose Add Category Above or Add Category Below from the reference tab pop-up of a category row, Numbers inserts a new category immediately above or below the selected row. The new category gets a name like "Item 1" and contains a single row with the value "Item 1" in the category column. Change that value to whatever you'd like to name your new category.

- **Single body row.** Choose Insert Category from a body row's pop-up menu to add a new category row immediately above (the option is grayed out for the first row of an existing category). The new category gets a name like "Item 1", and Numbers accordingly sets the category column value to "Item 1" for all rows below the new category row up until the next category. In other words, choosing Insert Category splits the current category in two: The rows above keep their current category value, and the rows below get a new one, "Item 1". Edit the category name in the new category row to change this value to anything you like.

- **Multiple body rows.** Select more than one row (they don't have to be next to each other, but they do have to be in the same category), and choose "Create Category from Selected Rows" from the pop-up menu of one of the selected rows. Numbers gathers all the selected rows into a new category with a name like "Item 1". The new category finds its home immediately above the category where you selected the rows. Edit the name in the category row to change the category title.

Tip: If you choose the Insert Category or "Create Category from Selected Rows" command before you've selected a category column in the Reorganize window, Numbers adds a new column to the table and sets it as the category column. This is convenient when you haven't yet created a column to hold your category values. After doing this, the table is split into two categories with names like "Item 1" and "Item 2". Edit these names in the category rows.

Adding and managing subcategories

You can further organize your rows by adding subcategories. In the sales rep example mentioned earlier, you might categorize your reps by state and then add city subcategories. In our class roster example, it would be useful to subcategorize the department listings by individual course, so that you can see the specific list of students enrolled in each course. The fastest way to add a new subcategory is to use the reference tab for the subcategory column (the Course column, for example), choosing "Categorize by This Column" from the reference tab's pop-up menu. A more deliberate route uses the Reorganize window; Figure 19-11 shows how it's done.

As with main categories, the table's overall sort order sets the sequence in which subcategories are listed. If you want categories and subcategories to be sorted, you should set the sort columns in the same order that you list the category columns at the bottom of the Reorganize window. In Figure 19-11, for example, columns are sorted by Department and then by Course. Within each course, they're then additionally sorted by Class Period and Mask Name.

Using dates as categories

When your category column holds dates or times, you can opt to group them by date range, clustering rows together when the date or time falls in the same day, week, month, quarter, or year. A table of product orders could group orders placed each week, for example, and a project management spreadsheet might group milestone events by quarter.

Get started by choosing "Categorize by This Column" from the date column's reference tab, or select the date column in the Reorganize window's bottom pane. The Reorganize window is also where you choose how you'd like to group the column's values. Figure 19-12 shows the options, and you can see an example of the results in Figure 19-13.

Editing the category row and adding subtotals

When Numbers first adds categories to your table, the category rows have only a single value—the category name in the row's leftmost cell. If you decide to edit that category name, go carefully: Changing that value changes the value of the category column in every row of the category. In the class roster, for example, changing the name of the Science department category to Pseudo-Science changes the Department column of every row in that category to the new (and not entirely convincing) title.

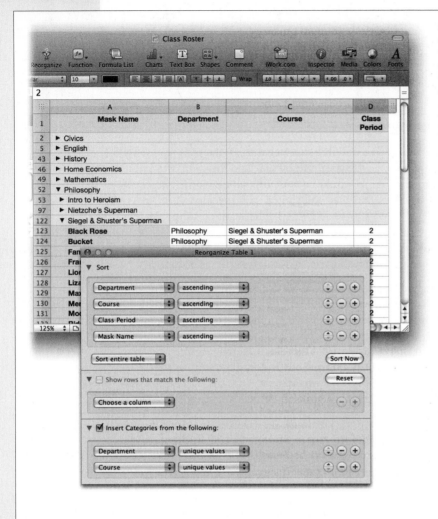

Figure 19-11:
Here, Numbers has added course subcategories to each department category, indenting each course category to show that it belongs to the department above. To add a subcategory, click the + button to the right of a column category in the Reorganize window. The order in which the categories are listed in the Reorganize window determines how they're "nested" in the table. Because the Department column is listed first, it's the main category with the Course column as a subcategory. You can flip this order by clicking one of the arrow buttons next to a column category in the Reorganize window. Clicking the Move Up arrow "promotes" a subcategory higher up the list; in this case, it would make Course the main category and Department the subcategory. Clicking the Move Down arrow does the reverse, "demoting" a category to subcategory status.

The category name is the only cell in the category row that Numbers lets you edit directly, but the program makes up for this restriction by giving the category cells a few other special talents. Select any cell in a category row to reveal a menu arrow at the right side of the cell. Click the arrow to reveal the cell's pop-up menu, which offers several options to display *summaries* of the category's contents, including subtotal values:

- **Category name.** This is the same value that Numbers pours into the row's first cell when it first creates the category. Choose this option to display the category value in another cell, for example. The displayed name is always the same as the value of the category column in all rows for the category.

- **Blank.** Make the cell show nothing at all.

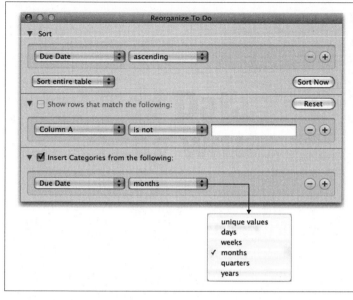

Figure 19-12:
When you categorize rows by date, you can tell Numbers how wide each category's date range should be. Choose "Unique value" to create a category for every individual value in the column—the same effect you've seen with other data types. Choosing one of the other values, however, bundles rows according to the time period of your choice.

- **Subtotal.** The sum of all number values in the selected column for the category.

- **Average.** The average of all number values in the selected column for the category.

- **Minimum.** The lowest numeric value in the selected column for the category.

- **Maximum.** The highest numeric value in the selected column for the category.

- **Count.** The number of values in the selected column for the category.

- **Show function name.** This option is available when you've also selected one of the five computations listed above (subtotal, average, minimum, maximum, or count). When you turn this option on, the cell displays the name of the operation along with its tally ("Count: 5").

Note: The subtotal, average, minimum, and maximum calculations work their magic only on number values, not dates, times, durations, or text. Count tallies any non-empty cells of any data type. When you use the average calculation, you might end up with a value loaded with decimal points; to quiet the decimal noise, adjust the cell format for the body cells in that column (the category row takes its cell format automatically from its member cells, so reducing the number of decimal points in those cells reduces it in the category row, too).

When you choose one of these options for a cell in any category row, Numbers applies the change to all other category rows at that category level as well as any subcategories (parent categories are not affected). This all-for-one approach turns category rows into a repeating summary line that gives you a quick and consistent report on each category. Figure 19-13 shows a simple example.

Product	Department	Date to Order	Gross Price	# to Order	Total Cost
▼ April 2009	Count: 6				$30,908.53
Spraytech Web Pistol	Deterrence	Apr 3, 2009	$279.95	12	$3,359.40
JetGirl 2600 Anti-Grav Boots	Flight	Apr 12, 2009	$899.95	10	$8,999.50
Cosmic Energy Ring	Alien Exotica	Apr 20, 2009	$4,999.95	2	$9,999.90
BlinkAway Invisibility Aerosol	Invisibility	Apr 23, 2009	$129.99	12	$1,559.88
Forcefield Bracelet	Defense	Apr 25, 2009	$385.99	15	$5,789.85
BulletsAway Invincibility Pills	Defense	Apr 30, 2009	$12.00	100	$1,200
▼ May 2009	Count: 4				$8,549
High-Frequency Alert	Communication	May 10, 2009	$89.95	10	$899.50
Sonarama Radar Earpiece	Vision	May 13, 2009	$375.00	10	$3,750
Verticality Wall-Climbing Kit	Surveillance	May 15, 2009	$279.95	5	$1,399.75
FastFlight Rocket Belt	Flight	May 25, 2009	$499.95	5	$2,499.75
▼ June 2009	Count: 2				$551,199.90
Lunar 5000 Moon Station	Alien Exotica	Jun 3, 2009	$275,000.00	2	$550,000
Bat Signal	Communication	Jun 10, 2009	$599.95	2	$1,199.90

Figure 19-13:
This table shows planned orders to restock inventory over three months, with items categorized monthly by order date. The left column of each category row has the category name ("April 2009"). The second column is set to display the count of items in the category, with the "Show function name" option turned on. The last column is set to show a subtotal of the cost of all items in the category.

Numbers gives you only limited options to format column rows. Although you can format their size, text color, and font, you can't edit their borders or change more advanced text options like paragraph spacing or inset margin. A convenient way to set category rows apart is to set a unique fill in the Graphic Inspector (page 659), a change that Numbers does allow for these finicky table elements. As with editing cell values, any formatting changes that you make to one category row applies to all of them in the same category level.

Removing categories

To temporarily hide categories for the selected table, turn off the "Insert Categories from the following" checkbox in the Reorganize window. Numbers returns to its normal, uncategorized view. Bring your categories back by turning the option on again. You can likewise work this category toggle switch by choosing Table → "Disable All Categories or Table" → Enable All Categories.

To remove the categorization more permanently, click the – button next to each category or subcategory in the Reorganize window. Or click this button for just a selection of categories when you want to continue categorizing but using fewer columns (and thus fewer subcategories). You can also stop using a specific column as a category column by choosing Delete Categories from the reference tab pop-up menu for the column.

Note: Don't get scared off by the "Delete" language for removing categories. You won't actually delete any of your data; you're only removing the category rows and the organization they impose.

Find & Replace

Even after you've sorted, filtered, and categorized your spreadsheet into a set of perfectly groomed and organized tables, it's not always easy to put your hands on the exact piece of data you're looking for. As you plump your data into a giant haystack, the individual needles get harder and harder to find. Happily, Numbers' search features make quick work of hunting down wayward data, and its Find & Replace utility lets you change these results to transform found words and phrases into something else. When you need to change the name of the sidekick academy's "Gamma Rays for Health and Fitness" course to "Risks of Reckless Irradiation," Find & Replace updates all references in the class roster faster than you can say, "glowing green sidekicks."

Finding Data from the Search Pane

To launch your search, choose Edit → Find → Show Search, or press ⌘-F. Numbers pops open the Search pane, the starting point for all your spreadsheet's search expeditions, located just below the sheet canvas at the bottom of the document window. When you first open the Search pane, Numbers automatically puts your cursor in the Search field. Type the word or phrase you want to find and, as you type, the Search pane lists your results, as shown in Figure 19-14. To hide the search pane, press ⌘-F again, or choose Edit → Find → Hide Search. You can also slide the pane closed by dragging its resize handle down at the top right corner of the Search pane.

To jump to a specific search result, click its listing in the search pane, as shown in Figure 19-14. You can also step through results one at a time by using the up and down arrow keys, or by choosing Edit → Find Next (⌘-G) or Edit → Find Previous (Shift-⌘-G).

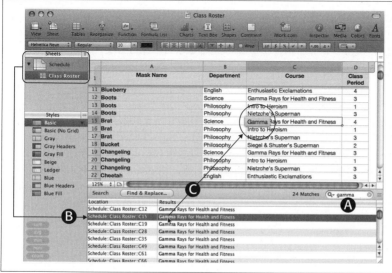

Figure 19-14:
Type the word or phrase you're looking for into the Search field (A), and the Search pane lists all the matches it finds. The Location column (B) shows where each match was found, including the sheet and table, if applicable. Click a result in the Search pane, and Numbers jumps to that location in your spreadsheet, briefly flashing the term to help you find it on the screen (C).

In Numbers' standard settings, the Search pane includes partial matches in its results. For example, when you search for "ray" to find references to the gamma-ray class, Numbers also shows you results for the sidekick name Gray**son** and the course for sewing **ray**on costumes. To find only whole-word matches, click the magnifying glass in the Search field, and choose "Whole word" from the pop-up menu that appears. When you do that, Grayson and rayon disappear from the search results, but so does "rays"; update your search term to "rays" to include matches for the plural form. To be similarly exacting about uppercase and lowercase letters, choose "Match case" from the Search field's pop-up menu. When you do that, Numbers shows search results only when they match the uppercase and lowercase letters of your search terms exactly.

When it hunts for your search results, Numbers checks the values of cells for matches—for cells with formulas, that means it checks against the *calculated* value of the cell, not the text of the formula itself. To search formula text, you can use the Find & Replace window, as you'll learn in a moment—or you can use the search tools in the Formula List (see page 697).

Tip: Searching for dates is a bit tricky, because Numbers sees dates in only one format: 5/30/2009. If you search for "May" or "May 30" or "5/30/09," the search won't turn up any results, even when the cell format is set to display the month name. When you're searching for a date, that means you should always enter it in that MM/DD/YYYY format.

The Find & Replace Window

When you want to replace found text with something new, click the Find & Replace button at the top left of the Search pane, and Numbers reveals the Find & Replace window. Despite its name, you don't *have* to replace text that you find with this window. You can use it simply to *find* text, too, which you may want to do to limit the search to the current sheet or to search formula text—two options not available from the Search pane. Most of the time, though, you'll find yourself using the Find & Replace window to put both parts of its name to use, to morph matching text into a new word or phrase. Figure 19-15 shows you how to fill out the Find & Replace fields.

When you're sure that you definitely want to replace all instances of the Find text with the Replace text, click Replace All, and Numbers rockets through your spreadsheet, making the changes. If you have the "Repeat search (loop)" checkbox turned off, Numbers searches forward from your current location and stops when it reaches the end of the document or current sheet. Turn the checkbox on to make Numbers loop around to the beginning of the document, making its replacements until it reaches the current location again. Normally, when you're replacing all occurrences of your search text, you should have this option turned on.

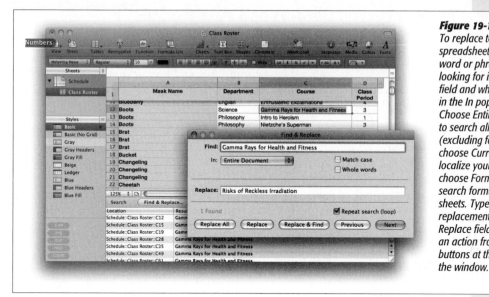

Figure 19-15:
To replace text in your spreadsheet, enter the word or phrase you're looking for in the Find field and where to search in the In pop-up menu. Choose Entire Document to search all sheets (excluding formula text); choose Current Sheet to localize your search; and choose Formulas Only to search formula text in all sheets. Type the replacement text in the Replace field, and select an action from the buttons at the bottom of the window.

If you want to review individual instances of the search text before replacing them, click Next, and Numbers takes you to the first match. (If you can't see the match, it could be hidden behind the Find and Replace window—it's a good idea to move the window out of harm's way when you're running your search.) If you don't want to replace the text, click Next again to hop along to the next match. Otherwise, click Replace or, even better, click Replace & Find to make the replacement and then jump to the next match.

Tip: The Replace and Replace & Find buttons both do exactly what they say they do: They replace the current selection with the text in the Replace box. That's perfect when the text that you want to replace is already selected. But when you're just starting a search, that's probably not the case, and you'll get an unwanted result: Clicking Replace & Find adds the replacement word at your current insertion point before looking for the word you want to find. To avoid surprises, always begin a session by pressing the Next button before pressing either Replace button.

Finding formula elements

Choose the Formulas Only option in the Find & Replace window's In pop-up menu to shine Numbers' searchlight into your spreadsheet's formulas. This is the only way to search formula text from the Find & Replace window—the other search-in options (including Entire Document) search only calculated values, not the actual text of the formula. Using this feature, you can find and/or replace cell references, operators, functions, you name it—any part of the formula that you want to find or change. You'll learn more about formulas in Chapter 20.

Make It Pretty: Borders and Backgrounds

Like any other object in iWork, you can add borders, fills, and other effects to your table to make it colorful or subdued, flashy or conservative. More than just dressing up your table, well-placed background fills and borderlines make your tables more readable, too, guiding your reader's eye through the columns of a row or demarcating header rows and columns.

When you apply color fills or borders to other types of objects, Numbers colors or adds lines around the *entire* object. You can do that with tables, too, but you can also add these styles to individual rows, cells, or columns. In this respect, every cell acts as its own object that you can style however you like. Before you start styling each and every one of your cells individually, though, it's a good idea to start at the object level, applying a uniform background and border format to the entire table. This gives your table a design foundation and establishes consistency. From there, you can make formatting changes to individual rows, columns, or cells as you like. Whatever level of the table you're working with, this section explores how to fine-tune your table's lines and colors.

Tip: Once you have the text, color, and borders of a table or cell formatted just the way you want it, you can use it as a model for others. Select it and choose Format → Copy Style. Select one or more other cells or tables and choose Format → Paste Style, and Numbers applies the formatting. You can also save a table's formatting in the Styles pane; see page 665.

Styling Cell and Table Borders

Tables take their visual form from the griddle lines that crisscross their surface, outlining the rows, columns, and cells inside. Because these rules slice clear through the table from top to bottom, from far left to far right, they each give the impression that they're unbroken divisions. In fact, Numbers sees every gridline as a series of short segments laid end to end, each spanning the height or width of a cell. These are called *border segments,* and you can select any of them individually to change their color, thickness, or style—or hide them completely.

When you combine all neighboring border segments, you've got the boundary of an entire row or column, which Numbers calls a *long border segment.* You can style long border segments all at once, too, to add a borderline below a header row, for example. Or you can style all border segments for the entire table to add uniform gridlines throughout.

With all the many possible segment combinations to choose from, it's important to tell Numbers exactly which ones you mean to format. You do that by selecting one or more border segments, just like you'd select a cell, row, or column before making changes to it.

Selecting table borders

When you select a table at the object level, all its border segments are implicitly selected. When you use the format tools described on page 658 on a table that you've selected in its entirety, the changes update every border segment in the table. Often, however, you'll want to format only some of the border segments—adding a strong border to the outside edges that frame the table, for example, and a light treatment for inner borders.

The Format Bar and Table Inspector both offer tools to select specific table borders, letting you choose gridlines relative to the box that outlines your current selection. Figure 19-16 gives you a tour of these options.

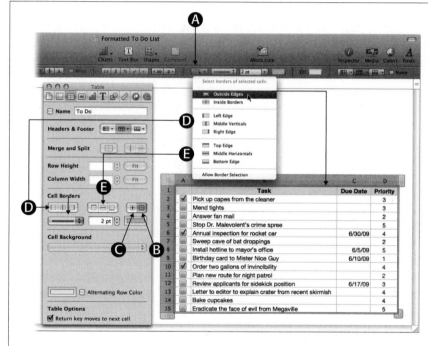

Figure 19-16:
Choose an option from the Borders pop-up menu (A) in the Format Bar, or click a Cell Borders button in the Table Inspector to select one or more borders relative to the current selection. Numbers highlights the selected borders by outlining them in blue. Here, with the entire table selected, the Outside Edges option selects all four borders around the outside of the table. The Outside Edges button (B) in the Table Inspector is correspondingly highlighted.

Choosing Inside Borders from the Format Bar's Borders menu, or clicking the Inside Borders button (C), would choose every border segment except the outside edges. The vertical options (D) let you choose among the far left or far right border of the current selection, or all vertical borders inside the selection. The horizontal options (E) similarly let you choose between the top or bottom border of the selection, or all horizontal borders within.

Figure 19-16 shows the border selection for the outside edges of an entire table. When you select a different table element, the border options choose segments next to (or within) that selection only. When you select an entire column for example, the Outside Edges option affects the four sides of the column. The same goes for selecting a range of adjacent cells, or just a single cell: The box formed by your current selection determines which borders are selected when you choose an option from the Borders pop-up menu or click a Cell Borders button in the Table Inspector.

Tip: When you have at least one border segment selected in a table, choose Edit → Select All (⌘-A) to select all the table's border segments.

When you turn on the Allow Border Selection option in the Table menu or in the Borders pop-up menu in the Format Bar, you can select border segments simply by clicking them. You'll know that the cursor is ready to select a border when it changes from a cross shape to a thick line with two arrows. Click a border once to choose the long border segment for the entire run of the row or column, and click it again to select only the border segment for a single cell. Continue clicking the border segment to switch back and forth between selecting the long and short segment. To add additional border segments Shift-click or ⌘-click the segments to add; deselect border segments by doing the same thing.

Allowing border selection gives you a few extra perks, too: You can now resize rows and columns by dragging their borders directly—you're no longer limited to using the reference tab's border. You can also merge cells by selecting a border segment and pressing Delete; the cells on either side of the border collapse together (see page 594 for more on merging cells).

Tip: Allowing border selection is convenient when you're first setting up a table's border styles, but once you're done, turn this feature off. It's all too easy to select a border when you mean to select a table cell. Turn it off by choosing Disallow Border Selection in the Table menu or in the Borders menu in the Format Bar.

Formatting table borders

With your table cells selected, use the controls in the Format Bar or Table inspector to add borders to your table, as shown in Figure 19-17.

You can also use the Stroke settings in the Graphic Inspector to set the border style, weight, and color. These settings work exactly as they do in the Format Bar and Table Inspector, only in a different inspector and with a different label.

When a table is selected, Numbers always highlights its cell borders to help you make your way through the cells, even if you haven't styled borders to appear. You can see how the table will actually look when it prints by deselecting the table: Click the sheet canvas anywhere outside of the table.

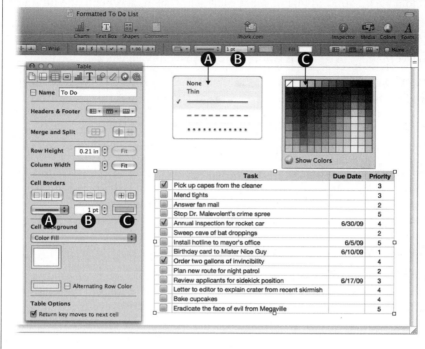

Figure 19-17:
Use the pop-up menus in the Format Bar or Table Inspector to adjust the appearance of the selected border segments: The Stroke pop-up menu (A) offers a selection of stroke styles, or choose None to hide the selected border; the Line pop-up menu (B) controls the thickness of the border; the color well (C) lets you choose a color. The Format Bar offers only a limited selection of swatches in its color well; you can choose one of them, or click Show Colors to open the Color Picker and choose from millions of colors (see page 265). Clicking the color well in the Table Inspector likewise opens the Color Picker.

Background Colors and Images

Add a background fill to the entire table, or only to individual rows, columns, or cells to set them apart from the rest of the table (think header and footer rows) or to create a visual rhythm with alternating rows. Just like any other object in iWork, tables and their elements can accept solid colors, gradients, or images as their backgrounds. You decide which by choosing a background style from the Cell Background pop-up menu in the Table Inspector. You can do the same thing by choosing a fill style from the Graphic Inspector's Fill pop-up menu like you would for a shape or text box. If you're adding a solid background color, you can also use the Fill pop-up menu in the Format Bar to choose the color. For all the filling possibilities, see page 265.

Note: Unlike other objects, tables don't get the advanced-gradient option for fill style.

Before you start styling individual cells, select the table at the object level so that its selection handles appear, and choose a background to apply to the entire table. This is the backdrop color that floats behind all your table cells; any backgrounds that you additionally add to rows, columns, or cells will layer on top of this table background. In other words, when you add a background to the entire table *and* to individual cells, the cell background "wins" and that's the one you see.

To add a background to one or more cells, select them, and apply the fill style to the selected cells. You can also apply background colors to selected cells by drag and drop:

1. **Select the cells to color. (If you're coloring just one cell, you can skip this step.)**

2. **Click the Colors button in the toolbar or choose View → Show Colors to display the Color Picker.**

   See page 265 for a complete tour of the Color Picker.

3. **Select a color, adjust its opacity, and drag from the swatch into the table's selected cells.**

   Pages displays the green + sign ball next to your arrow cursor as you drag, and outlines the table cell beneath it in blue, indicating its readiness to receive the color when you release the mouse button.

Adding images to table cells

The only way Numbers lets you add an image to a table cell is as a background image. You can do this by choosing Image Fill or Tinted Image Fill in either the Graphic Inspector or the Table Inspector. For the latter, make your selection from the Cell Background pop-up button and select an image file to use, as described on page 269.

But there's an easier way to add the background image: If you have the picture in iPhoto or Aperture, use the Media Browser. Click the Media button in the toolbar and then click the Photos tab. Browse through your library to find the image to include, and drag it into the table cell. Numbers automatically sets the fill style to Image Fill with the new image, setting the image size to Scale to Fit. (Numbers also gives an image the same treatment if you paste it into the table cell.) If you prefer a different image size for your picture, change the setting in the Table Inspector or the Graphic Inspector.

Alternating row colors

Adding subtle color variations to odd and even table rows makes it easier for your reader to track across the columns of a row—an especially big help for wide tables with lots of columns. To do this, select the table at any level, turn on the Alternating Row Color checkbox in the Table Inspector, and choose a color by clicking the neighboring color well. Numbers applies the color to every other row of your table (the other rows get whatever background you set at the object level for the table).

More specifically, Numbers applies the color, just *under* your table rows. These colors are always painted on top of the background that you choose at the table's object level, but underneath any background that you add to individual cells. If you don't immediately see your alternate row colors, that probably means that they're covered by backgrounds in individual cells. Setting the fill style for those cells to None will let your alternating colors shine through.

Tip: When you add alternate row colors, you typically no longer need horizontal borderlines between rows. Having both only adds visual noise. Turn off horizontal borders by setting the stroke style to None for the table's middle horizontals. See page 657 for details on selecting those borders.

You can use alternating rows in combination with any kind of cell background, but the alternating rows always use a solid color. For example, if you have the table set to display an Image Fill background and you add an alternating row color, odd rows display the image background, and even rows have the solid color of your choice. You can soften this effect by adjusting the opacity of the alternate row color. The Checking Register template does this to good effect, as shown in Figure 19-18.

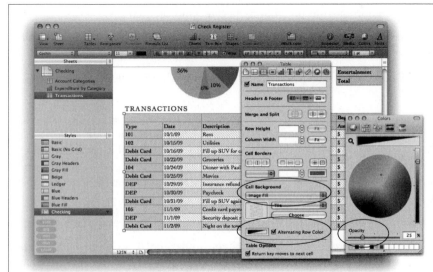

Figure 19-18:
This table in the Checking Register template has a check-patterned background image. It also has alternating row colors, but the opacity of that color is reduced to 25 percent, allowing the pattern to show through, albeit with a faint tint. To change the opacity of the alternating color, click the color well next door to the "Alternating row color" checkbox to reveal the Color Picker. Use the Opacity slider to make the color transparent.

Conditional Formats for "Content Alerts"

Cell formatting isn't only about aesthetics; they can also be part of your own homegrown data surveillance system. Numbers lets you add tripwires to cells to trigger a change in formatting when the cell's value meets a certain set of conditions. You might make the cell with your bank balance turn bright red, for example, when your funds get dangerously low (an event that might meanwhile make *you* turn a sickly green). You can similarly highlight to-do items whose due dates are closing in, or revenue figures for sales reps who've met their monthly quota.

Note: You can't set conditional formatting for summary cells in a category row.

To apply conditional formatting, you select one or more cells and then define rules to trigger new formatting. Each rule specifies its own visual effect to associate with cells when they meet the rule's conditions. You might make your checking account balance turn amber when it dips under $250 and then bright red and bold letters when it goes under $50, for example. When the cell doesn't meet any of the conditions you add, nothing happens, and the cell simply displays as it normally would. Here's how to set it up:

1. **Select one or more cells.**

2. **Choose Format → Show Conditional Format Rules, or click the "Show rules" button under Conditional Format in the Cells Inspector.**

   Numbers opens the Conditional Format window, shown in Figure 19-19.

3. **Choose an option from the "Choose a rule" pop-up menu.**

   The options in the top section of the menu apply tests to numeric values. Options in the middle section are for text values. The "With dates" option is for dates.

4. **Type the value to trigger the new cell formatting in the field next to the pop-up menu.**

   You can also use the value of another table cell as a test value for the rule; Numbers monitors the values of both cells and triggers the conditional formatting when the condition is satisfied. To choose the other table cell, click the blue oval in the value field. The cell reference field appears; click the table cell whose value you'd like to use, or type a cell reference (the cell's coordinates—C3, D5, G9, and so on), and press Return.

5. **Click Edit to choose the formatting to apply when cells meet the rule's criteria.**

   Choose a text color, font style (bold, italic, underline, or strikethrough), and fill color for the cell. As you make your choices, Numbers shows you a preview of how the cell will look. Press Done when you've got it just so.

6. **To add additional rules, click the + button and repeat steps 3 through 5 above.**

When you apply more than one rule to a cell, it's possible that the cell's value could meet more than one of the conditions. In that case, Numbers manages the overlap by applying the formatting of the topmost matching rule. If that rule doesn't have any of the format styles specified (text color, font style, or fill color), then Numbers finds the next matching rule that does have that rule. So, if the first rule has the text color and font style specified, but no fill color, Numbers goes down through the list of matching rules until it finds a fill color to use.

To remove a rule for a selected cell, click the − button next to the rule in the Conditional Format window, or click the Clear All Rules button.

Figure 19-19:
The cells in the In Stock column are set to highlight when stock dips below 10 items as a reminder that it's time to reorder. Below the rule, Numbers shows a preview of how the formatting will look for cells meeting the condition. To add another formatting rule for the selected cells, click the + button to the right of the rule.

Working with Table Styles

As you settle into a groove with your spreadsheets, you'll likely develop a set of consistent visual habits for formatting your tables, using the same color schemes, border styles, and font choices over and over again. That steady consistency is a good thing; it not only reinforces the professional brand or personal style of your documents, but it also gives regular readers of your documents (including you) subtle cues for understanding different parts of your data. It's a good practice, for example, to craft a visual system that distinguishes different kinds of tables. Tables that contain only summary calculations from other tables' data might use a gray background to indicate that they shouldn't be edited. Tables for income might use pale green headers, and tables for expenses pale red. Static reference data might have a pale yellow background. You get the idea.

The last few pages have shown you how to do exactly that type of table formatting, styling the colors, borders, and text of individual tables. But as you add more tables to your spreadsheet and more documents to your collection, you'll find that meticulously reformatting every single table to match your personal preferences quickly becomes a dreary chore.

Numbers anticipates this problem by letting you save and reuse *table styles,* predefined collections of formatting rules that you can apply to any table with the click of a mouse. Add a table, click a style, and presto, you've got the colors, borders, and fonts you like to use. If you later decide that you need to make the headers for that table style a slightly darker shade of cinnamon, you can update the style, and the change cascades through all the other tables in the document that use the style. Table styles, in short, make quick work of formatting (and reformatting) the common visual characteristics of your tables, ensuring along the way that your tables maintain a consistent look.

Applying Predefined Table Styles

Every Numbers template comes with its own collection of table styles, and you can put them to use right away. Just select a table, and click a style in the Styles pane at the left of the window. Figure 19-20 shows an example.

Tip: You can also apply a style by dragging its name from the Styles pane and dropping it on top of any table, selected or not. (Oddly enough, if you have a table selected but drop a style onto a different, unselected table, then *both* tables change their style.) Change the style of *every* table in a sheet in one fell swoop by dropping the style name onto the sheet's icon in the Sheets pane.

Applying a table style changes the font, color, and border formatting without touching the cell content or data formats of the edited table. Specifically, table styles dress up the following table attributes:

- The table's background color or background image
- The background and text formatting for body cells
- The stroke, color, and opacity of the table's inner borders and outside edges
- The background, text formatting, and borders for header rows, header columns, and footer rows

When you apply a style to a table, it takes on all the style's characteristics for the table elements listed above—unless you've specifically styled one of those elements for the table already. If you set a table's header row to be a lovely chartreuse, for example, the header row will doggedly remain chartreuse when you change the table style. Numbers treats as sacred any formatting that you specifically make to a table's elements, and it protects those changes, called *style overrides,* when you change table styles.

Numbers will only discard your overrides when you specifically tell it to do so. In the Styles pane, click the downward arrow to the right of the style that you want to apply, and Numbers reveals the style's pop-up menu (Figure 19-21). Choose "Clear and Apply Style" from the pop-up menu, and Numbers clears out any custom text, color, or border formatting that you've added to the table before applying the new style as a fresh coat of paint.

Tip: If you don't see the downward arrow next to the style in the Styles pane, be sure that you have a table selected, and point to the style name. The arrow fades into view.

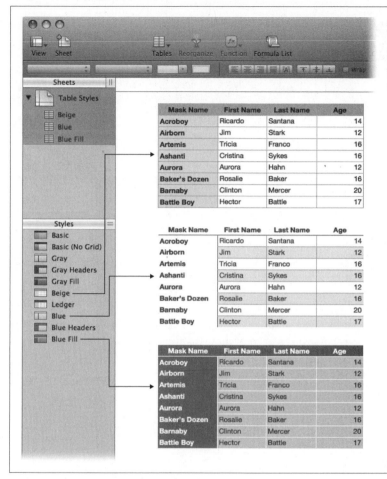

Figure 19-20:
Click a predefined style in the Styles pane to change the look of the selected table. Here, three versions of the same table show off three different table styles.

Creating and Modifying Table Styles

The formatting recipes in a spreadsheet's table styles aren't set in stone; you can alter their ingredients to suit your own taste or cook up an entirely new graphic treat. After you've applied a style, you can continue to make your own custom formatting changes to the table; Numbers adds them to your table as style overrides. You can save these modifications as your own new table style or use them to replace an existing style.

Tip: If you wind up blending a visual disaster, you can revert to the original style by using the "Clear and Apply Style" command described above, or by choosing Format → Reapply Table Style.

When you save a table style, Numbers doesn't save the styles of each and every cell and border segment in your table. If you have several different body cell formats, for example, Numbers saves only one of them for use in the table style. For the

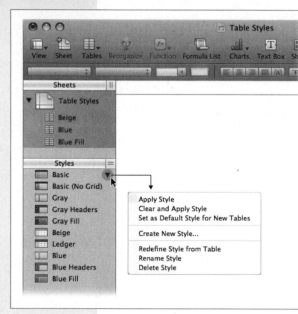

Figure 19-21:
Point to a style name in the Styles pane to reveal its menu arrow. Click the arrow to summon the style's pop-up menu, offering several options to work with the style, which you'll learn about in the next few pages. The Apply Style option sets the style for the selected table, the same as clicking the style name in the Styles pane.

most consistent results, keep it simple and use the same consistent format for all cells and border segments within each of these distinct categories:

- Body cells
- Header rows
- Header columns
- Footer rows
- Category rows
- Inner borders
- Outer edges

After you've fine-tuned the font styles, background, and border colors of your table, you can replace an existing style by choosing "Redefine Style from Table" in the style's pop-up menu in the Styles pane. Every table in your spreadsheet that uses that style updates instantly to reflect your modifications. As usual, however, Numbers treats any style overrides in those tables as sacrosanct. If you want to clear overrides, you have to use the "Clear and Apply Style" command individually on those tables.

To create a new style instead of replacing an old one, choose Create New Style from the pop-up menu of any style in the Styles pane. Numbers prompts you to enter a title for your style. Type a name and press OK, and Numbers adds the new style to your Styles pane.

Whenever you add a new sheet to your document, Numbers automatically gives you a new table using your spreadsheet's default table style. To make Numbers use your brand new style (or any other style) for these tables, choose Set as Default Style for New Tables from the style's pop-up menu.

To rename a style in the Styles pane, choose Rename Style from its pop-up menu and type the new name. To rearrange styles in the Styles pane, drag them to a new location. Delete a style from the list by choosing Delete Style from its pop-up menu; if the style is in use in your spreadsheet, Numbers asks you to choose another style to replace it.

Tip: The table styles that you customize in the Styles pane are available only within the current spreadsheet document. To make a style available in another document, paste a table with that style into the other spreadsheet, and Numbers adds the style to the second document's Styles pane. You can also make all your styles available to new documents by saving your spreadsheet as a template. For details, see Chapter 25.

Capturing Reusable Tables

Table styles are a big timesaver for duplicating the general *look* of a table, and much of their utility is related to the fact that they're completely oblivious to the content of the table. You can apply a new table style to any table, no matter what its size, content, or cell format. Often enough, though, you'll find yourself building multiple tables that share not only the same color or border styles, but the same column organization, formulas, and data structure. In that case, table styles only help so much; they're all style and no substance. What you really need is access to pre-formatted tables that already have the column layout, formulas, and starter content you routinely use.

That's exactly what the toolbar's Tables pop-up button offers you. When you add a new table with that button, Numbers gives you a selection of tables to choose from, some of them already formatted with cell formats for checkboxes or simple formulas to handle sums in the footer row. All of Numbers' built-in templates have a selection of these starter tables, but they're naturally very general. You can add tables of your own to address specific needs and common requirements.

For example, say that you store all your expense reports on separate sheets of a spreadsheet. Every time you file your expenses after a long weekend in Vegas—er, work trip to Omaha—you have to recreate the same expense report table. Having quick access to a blank expense report from the Tables button would be ideal. To do it, start out by creating a blank expense report form. Design a table decked out with all the header cells, borders, formulas, and placeholder content you'd like to have in place whenever you put a fresh expense report table in place. Get it ready to the point where the only thing missing is the unique info you'll enter for each expense report.

When you have your model table in place, choose Format → Advanced → Capture Table. Numbers rolls out the dialog box shown in Figure 19-22. Enter the name you'd like to use for the table in the Tables menu, and click OK. You can now clone your expense report table anytime you like by selecting it from the list of pre-defined tables that appears when you click the Tables button in the toolbar or choose Insert → Table.

Note: Your new addition to the Tables menu is available only from the current spreadsheet. To make your reusable tables available in other spreadsheets, save your document as a template. See Chapter 25 for details.

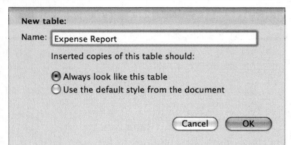

Figure 19-22:
When you capture a table to include in the Tables pop-up button, Numbers asks you how it should style new tables. Choose "Always look like this table" if you want Numbers to be faithful to your rendering. If you want the table to blend in a bit more, choose "Use the default style from the document" to use your spreadsheet's standard table style to apply colors, borders, and font styles to new tables.

To rearrange, rename, or remove tables in this list of prefab tables, choose Format → Advanced → Manage Tables. Double-click a name to change it; select a table in the list and click the up or down arrow button to move it to a new location; or click the – button to remove a table. Click Done when you've got the list just so.

Using Formulas

Just on its own, a grid is good. You've got your data organized and sorted, all in one place. And now that you know how to build and style this baby, you can show it off with panache. But your table doesn't *do* much yet. Isn't a spreadsheet supposed to balance your checkbook, manage your company's budget, make you dinner, and find you true love? Although Numbers might not offer any love potions, it does have all kinds of other *formulas* to set your grid in motion.

In Numbers, formulas are responsible for the fundamental numbers work behind your spreadsheet, mixing and mashing your raw data to surface facts, figures, and bottom-line tallies. Formulas are equations that you add to cells to make them calculate: add up columns, average grades, or figure the net present value of an investment. A formula's calculations can range anywhere from very simple math (1+1) to complex constructions that gather values from other tables or apply sophisticated financial algorithms. This chapter gets you started at the shallow end of that pool, getting you acquainted with Numbers' basic arithmetic before you move onto the gee-whiz formula magic you'll find in the next chapter.

Whether your math is simple or sophisticated, Numbers makes the *process* of adding and editing formulas easy, giving you lots of ways to build and insert these number-crunching gizmos into your table cells. You can compose an elaborate formula by hand, sure, but you can also drag-and-drop common calculations into a table or add up a column with just a click. This chapter tours all of these techniques.

Formula Basics

On the surface, a formula cell looks just like any other. It displays the results of its calculation and looks for all the world like all the other cells whose values you typed directly into the table. Under the hood, though, the actual value of the cell is an equation—the formula—that tells Numbers how to generate that cell's value. To see the formula, select the cell, and Numbers displays its formula in the Formula Bar, as shown in Figure 20-1.

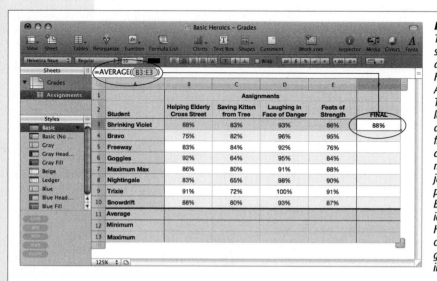

Figure 20-1:
This table shows students' scores for assignments in the Basic Heroics class at the Up & Away sidekick academy. The selected cell in the last column shows the average score for the first student. Although its displayed value looks mild-mannered enough—just a simple percentage—the Formula Bar reveals its secret identity as a formula. Here, the formula calculates the average grade from the four cells in the row.

Don't worry just yet about the structure and vocabulary of the formula in Figure 20-1; you'll learn about the construction and building materials of formulas later in this chapter. For the moment, it's important to understand only a few basics about the way formulas work:

- **A formula lives in a single cell.** Even when a formula uses the values of other cells in its equation—to add up a column of numbers, for example—the formula always sits in the cell where the result is displayed.

- **Formulas always stay up to date.** Numbers constantly monitors your spreadsheet for changes. Whenever you make a change in your table, the program hustles to update the results of any affected formulas. Editing a number in a column of cells, for example, instantly changes the value of the cell showing that column's total.

- **You can use formulas with any data types.** Although you'll typically use formulas for numbers, they aren't strictly limited to math. Formulas can work their magic on dates, text, and time durations, and they can even take direction from the TRUE/FALSE on-off switch of Boolean values.

- **The Formula Bar lets you view and edit a cell's formula.** As you'll soon see, Numbers offers many ways to add a formula to a cell. But once you've placed it, viewing the guts of the formula always works the same way: Select the cell to display the formula in the Formula Bar. You can edit it there, too, or double-click the formula to use the Formula Editor. You'll learn more about editing formulas starting on page 680.

Instant Calculations

Before you add a single formula to your table, Numbers is already spoilin' to do its math, running numbers even when you don't ask for them. The action happens in the Instant Calculation pane at the bottom left of the document window, where Numbers offers constant commentary on your current selection of cells. When you select two or more cells containing numeric values, the Instant Calculation pane lights up to show a set of tallies for the selected cells. Figure 20-2 shows the Instant Calculation pane in action.

Tip: Select multiple cells by ⌘-clicking, Shift-clicking, or Shift-dragging across the cells to include. You can also select an entire row or column by clicking its reference tab. For more on selecting table elements, see page 582.

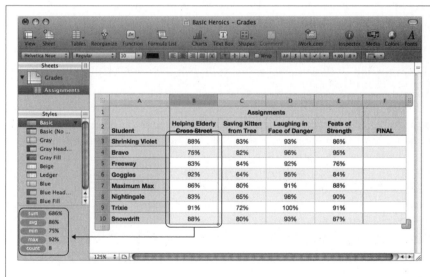

Figure 20-2:
When you select two or more cells containing numeric values, the Instant Calculation pane shows the sum, average, minimum value, maximum value, and overall count (the number of cell values) of those values. Empty cells or cells with non-numeric values are ignored. Although that's what you'd expect for most of these number-focused calculations, it might surprise you for count: When you select a bunch of text cells, count says you have no values selected. It can see only numbers, dates, and times.

You can select any combination of cells to make the Instant Calculation pane do its thing. Choose multiple columns or rows, for example, or select a block of cells several columns wide and several rows deep. The cells don't have to be next to each other, either; select any cells in the table by ⌘-clicking them, and Numbers still pours their values into its instant-calculation mill.

Having an always-on calculator in plain view is handy for doing a quick check on the status of any group of cells you might fancy, but its display is fleeting. As soon as you click away to another cell or otherwise change your selection, the Instant Calculation pane changes its display to capture the tallies for the new group of cells. That's fine when you're after a one-time check, but it's less convenient when you frequently want to see a calculation for a specific set of cells. In that case, it makes sense to give the calculation a permanent home in your table. As it turns out, that's exactly what formulas do.

Creating Formulas from Instant Calculations

The Instant Calculation pane gives you an easy way to turn its snapshot tallies into formulas in your table cells. The little capsules next to each tally in the Instant Calculation pane are more than just labels; they each have a formula hidden inside. Drag one of these *calculation capsules* and drop it into any cell of the table to add that formula to the cell.

For example, say the instructor of the Basic Heroics class is more comfortable leaping into the jaws of doom than working a spreadsheet. (Hey, we've all known that feeling at some point.) He's got the table of grades that you saw in Figure 20-2, but needs help figuring their averages and maybe getting a little more insight into how the class is doing from assignment to assignment. He's asked for your help, and now's your chance to be the hero.

You'll start by displaying the overall average score for a single assignment, along with the lowest and highest scores for that assignment. To hold your formulas, add three footer rows to the bottom of the table, by choosing 3 from the Footer Rows pop-up button in the Format Bar (see page 638). Label these rows "Average", "Lowest", and "Highest", as shown in Figure 20-3. Make the Instant Calculation pane show the tallies for the first assignment by selecting its scores, and then drag the calculation capsule for average, minimum, and maximum into the corresponding cells in the first column's footer rows.

Tip: The cell where you drag the capsule doesn't have to be in the same table as the selected cells; you can add the formula to any table you like.

As you can see at the bottom of Figure 20-3, the cell where you drop the calculation capsule gets more than just a simple numeric value. Numbers doesn't just copy the *result* from the Instant Calculation pane; it adds a corresponding *formula* to the cell so that it always shows an accurate tally of the scores in that column. Change any of the scores above, and the tallies update to reflect the change.

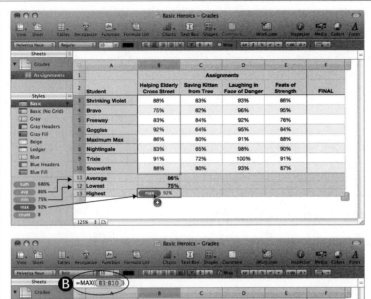

Figure 20-3:
Top: Grab an instant calculation by its capsule, and drag it into a table cell. The cursor balloons into a green + bubble to show that it's about to add the calculation to the cell. Release the mouse button, and Numbers adds a formula to the cell, replacing any previous value it might have contained.

Bottom: After you drop a calculation capsule into a cell, Numbers switches focus and selects the target cell (A) where you dropped the capsule. The Formula Bar shows the formula that's been added to the cell (B), and Numbers lights up the cells included in the formula with a pale glow (C).

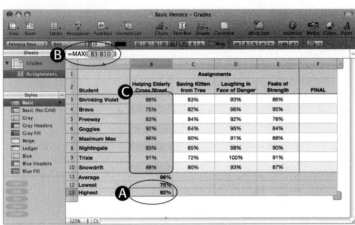

The formula, in other words, plants the instant calculation inside your table, linking it to the specific cells you selected when you dragged the calculation capsule into place. Here again, it's not yet important to understand the jargon or format of the cell's formula; you'll learn all about that later in this chapter. In fact, the whole point of this drag-and-drop maneuver is that you don't *have to* deal with the formula at all; Numbers builds it for you automatically.

Tip: You can delete a formula from a cell in the same way you'd delete any other value: Select the cell and press the Delete button.

Dragging calculation capsules into a table makes quick work of formulas when you want to show a calculated result in just one cell. But when you have lots of cells to fill in, all this drag-and-drop mousework turns into a tedious chore. In the Basic Heroics table, for example, the remaining three assignment columns still have nine empty cells in the footer rows, all waiting for formulas. Instead of dragging a calculation capsule into each and every cell, you can instead copy the formulas from the first column into the neighboring columns.

Sure, you can copy and paste the cells, or Option-drag them, but autofill is the fastest route. You'll find complete details about autofill on page 618, but here's how to use it here: Select the three cells in the first column's footer row, and grab the circular autofill handle in the bottom right corner of the selection box. Drag the autofill handle to the right across the neighboring three columns, and Numbers fills them with formulas. Figure 20-4 shows the result.

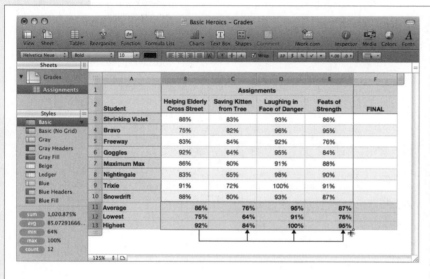

Figure 20-4:
Use autofill to copy formulas from one column to another. As you drag across the columns, Numbers inserts formulas into the cells, but customizes them for each column to work with the scores in the cells directly above. With that done, you have a nice collection of footer columns to show how the class did with each assignment. The averages, for example, tell you that the class overall has trouble saving kittens but excels at laughing in the face of danger.

See what happened there? Numbers was clever enough to guess that you didn't want to repeat the same calculation over and over for the same cells in the first column. Instead, it updated the formulas in each of the columns to run their numbers on the column above. Now you've got a tidy set of calculations at the bottom of each column to summarize what's going on with the scores above. When Numbers copies formulas that work with other cells in the table, it automatically shifts to use cells *relative* to the formula's new position. You'll find out more about copying formulas, as well as this theory of relativity, on page 691.

Adding Quick Formulas

Plunking a formula into a cell and then copying it into neighboring cells works just fine, but because repeating a formula is such a common activity, Numbers provides a shortcut in the form of *quick formulas*. Like instant calculations, quick formulas offer fast access to common actions, but they're specifically tuned for inserting formulas into your table—and best of all, they can add formulas to lots of cells in one swoop. You can use these one-click wonders on any selection of neighboring cells in the same row or column, but they're especially clever when applied to header or footer cells, instantly adding row or column tallies to your table.

You can apply a quick formula by selecting one or more cells and choosing a *function* from the Function pop-up button in the toolbar, or from the Insert → Function submenu. Functions are the predefined calculations that Numbers knows how to do. As you'll learn in the next chapter, Numbers knows over 250 functions, many of them managing complex algorithms appropriate to the financial or engineering worlds. Quick formulas, however, stick to the basics, giving you easy access to six of the simplest and most commonly used functions:

- **Sum** adds up the selected cells.

- **Average** calculates the mean value of the cells.

- **Minimum** displays the lowest value among the cells.

- **Maximum** displays the highest value among the cells.

- **Count** shows the number of numeric or date/time values in the cells (text values aren't included in the tally).

- **Product** multiplies all the cells.

Note: Like instant calculations, quick formulas ignore empty cells and non-numeric values (except in the case of Count, which also tallies date and time values).

Using Quick Formulas with Header and Footer Cells

When you select a cell in a table's header row and choose a calculation from the toolbar's Function button, Numbers runs that calculation against the column's body cells, showing the result in the footer cell of the same column (Figure 20-5). Choose Sum, for example, and the footer cell adds up the column. Pick Average, and the footer shows the column's mean value. In other words, the footer cell always "catches" the result of the calculation that you add to the header cell (while the header cell itself is unaffected). Behind the scenes, of course, Numbers has simply added a formula to the footer cell—a *quick* formula, since it's done with just a single click. Any value or formula already in the footer cell is replaced. If the table doesn't have a footer row, Numbers obligingly adds one for you.

This trick becomes even more useful when you select multiple header cells and then make a selection from the Function button. Numbers inserts a formula into the footer cell of each column, each one applying the calculation only to the values in its own column.

Note: Numbers lets you add multiple quick formulas only when you select *neighboring* cells. If the selected cells aren't immediately adjacent, all options in the Function menu are grayed out.

Adding quick formulas to rows

You can add quick formulas to body rows using the same principle, by selecting cells in the table's header column and then picking a function from the toolbar's Function button. Numbers runs the calculation for each of the selected rows and

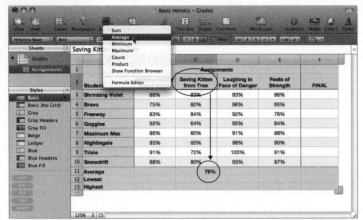

Figure 20-5:
Top: Select a header cell and choose a calculation from the Function pop-up button in the toolbar. Numbers adds a quick formula to the column's footer cell, showing the result of the calculation when applied to all of the body cells in the column. When there are multiple footer rows, as shown here, the function always goes into the top one.

Bottom: If you select and then apply a quick formula to the header cells for all four assignment columns, Numbers inserts a formula into all of their footer cells, each one showing the result for its own column.

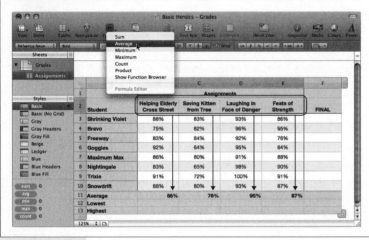

puts the results in the *last* column of the table. That's a subtle but important difference from working with cells in the header row, which always adds the formula in the footer row. There's no such thing as a footer *column,* so Numbers does its best and assumes that you want to treat the last column of the table as the results column. If the last column already contains values for any of the selected cells, Numbers adds *another* column to the table and puts each row's formula there.

These are reasonable assumptions for Numbers to make, but it means that you have to be careful about reapplying quick formulas to the header cells for individual rows. In Figure 20-5, for example, if you select a student name and pick Average from the Function button, Numbers adds the average score into the FINAL column, the last column of the table. Perfect, that's the result you were after. But if you select that same student again and choose Average (or any other function) one more time, you'll probably get something different than you anticipated: Numbers adds a new column, since the FINAL column is already occupied for that row. The formula instead gets inserted in that new column and includes the cell from the FINAL column in its calculation.

Adding quick formulas directly to footer cells

Selecting a footer cell and applying a quick formula generally works as you might expect. Numbers inserts a function into the footer cell to run the selected calculation on all the column's body cells. It's the same result, in other words, as if you had chosen the function with the column's header row selected: Both routes add the same formula to the footer cell.

The one advantage to adding the quick formula directly to footer cells instead of using the header cell is that it's the only way to add calculations to additional footer rows when you have more than one. In the Grades table for the Basic Heroics class, for example, there are three footer rows to display the average, lowest, and highest scores. Applying quick formulas from the header row updates only the top footer row. To add a quick formula to the second or third footer row, you have to do it directly, as shown in Figure 20-6.

Tip: You *can* use the header row to add formulas to multiple footer rows, but you have to plan ahead: Add a quick formula to the header cell when you have just one footer row. Then insert a new footer row above the current footer row, and add another quick formula. Rinse and repeat.

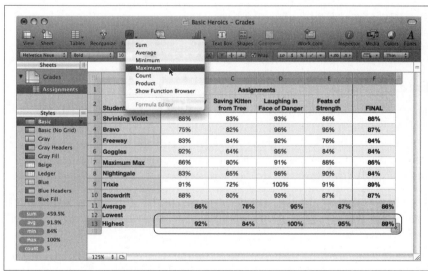

Figure 20-6:
When you select one or more footer cells and pick a function from the Function pop-up, Numbers adds a function to each cell, applying the calculation to the values from each column. When you have multiple footer rows, as shown here, the values in the other footer rows are not included in the calculations—only the body cells are included.

Using Quick Formulas with Body Cells

As you've seen, quick formulas are at their most useful in header and footer cells to quickly tally entire rows and columns. But you can put them to work in body cells, too, to add formulas that run calculations on any range of cells that you choose. As with header and footer cells, you can use quick formulas to get the sum, average, minimum, maximum, count, or product of the selected cells. When you apply a quick formula to body cells, Numbers inserts one or more formulas into your table, but the exact cell (or cells) where the formula lands—and which values are tallied—depends on the cells you've selected when you pick a function.

TROUBLESHOOTING MOMENT

Oh, My Achin' Footer

Adding a quick formula to footer cells always works just as described when the selected footer cells are empty or when you select just a single footer cell. However, under certain other conditions, the resulting quick formula might veer off course—or at least away from what you expect.

For example, when you select multiple footer cells and one or more of the cells contains a non-formula or its formula does not apply to the entire column of body cells above, Numbers doesn't add new formulas to the selected cells. Instead, Numbers inserts a formula in the cell to the *right* of the selected footer cells (adding a new column if necessary). This formula shows the results of the calculation applied to the values of the *footer cells*, not the columns above.

You'll get a different result if you apply a quick formula to a single cell that already has a formula that works with some range of cells other than the column above. (You'll learn about how to do this later in the chapter.) In that case, Numbers updates the cell's formula to use your selected function, but continues to work with the formula's original range of cells. In other words, when you apply a quick formula to a footer cell, it doesn't reset the range of cells to use the column above. (If it's already working with the column above, then there's no problem.)

If these aren't the results you're looking for, you can simply clear the selected footer cells and start from scratch: Select the cells, press Delete, and pick the function you want to apply from the toolbar's Function button.

Note: To apply a quick formula, the selected cells must form a rectangle. You can choose a single cell, a 3×3 block, a column of five cells, and so on, as long as the selection forms a regular shape of neighboring cells.

Adding a quick formula to a single cell body

When you add a quick formula with just a single body cell selected, Numbers inserts your formula into that cell. But the range of cells that go into the formula's calculation depends on what's going on elsewhere in the cell's row and column. Numbers takes a close look at the cell's neighbors to figure out what it should do, running through the following checklist in this order:

- **Are there values above the selected cell?** If yes, the formula's calculation is applied to all body cells above the selected cell. If you choose the Sum function, for example, the selected cell adds up the values of all body cells above.

- **No? Well then, are there values to the left of the selected cell?** If yes, the formula uses all body cells to the left of the cell. If you pick the Product function, for example, the selected cell shows the result of multiplying all body cells to the left.

- **None of the above?** Back to step one: The formula runs its calculation against all body cells above the selected cell, even though they're all currently empty. Of course, there's really no point in applying a formula to empty cells, but when you start filling them up with data, your formula will be there to welcome them.

Note: Unless the cell is a footer cell, you can't replace a manually typed value with a quick formula. If a cell has a non-formula value in it, you have to delete that value before you can add your quick formula.

Adding a quick formula to a range of cells

When you select multiple cells and add a quick formula, Numbers adds a formula into one or more adjacent cells to tally only the cells you've selected. The selected cells themselves remain untouched; they're simply used as the values in your new formula's calculation. This is a convenient way to add calculations for any set of neighboring cells in your table. Here again, though, the exact place that your new formula lands depends on how you've selected the cells.

When you've selected multiple cells all in the same row, Numbers inserts your quick formula into the cell immediately to the right of the selected cells—but only if it's an empty cell. If the cell to the right already has a value, Numbers won't over-write it. Instead, Numbers inserts a new column into your table, immediately to the right of the selected columns, and adds the value in the new column, as shown in Figure 20-7. Similarly, if there is no column to the right (when the selection includes the table's last column), Numbers adds a new column at the edge of the table to hold the new formula.

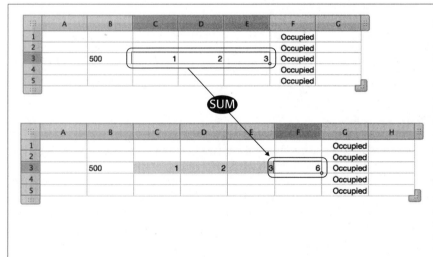

Figure 20-7:
When your selection includes more than one cell, all in the same row, adding a quick formula inserts a formula immediately to the right of the selected cells. The formula runs its calculation–here, a sum–on only the cells in your original selection. When that cell is already occupied, Numbers inserts a new column to hold the formula, nudging the previously neighboring column over to the right.

It works the same way when you add a quick formula with multiple cells selected in the same *column*, too. In that case, Numbers inserts the formula into the cell immediately below the selected cells. If that cell already has a value, Numbers inserts a new row immediately below the selection to hold the new formula value. If the selection includes the last row so that there is no row below, Numbers like-wise adds a new row to the table to hold the formula.

Numbers prefers working with columns. When your selection includes a block of cells spanning *both* columns and rows, Numbers adds a formula to each of the cells in the row immediately below your selection to tally the columns above. Each of these formulas tally only the selected cells in the same column, as shown in Figure 20-8. If any of the cells in the row below have values in the selected columns, Numbers adds a new row and inserts the formulas there. Similarly, if the selection includes cells in the last row so that there is no row below, Numbers adds a new row to the table to hold the formulas.

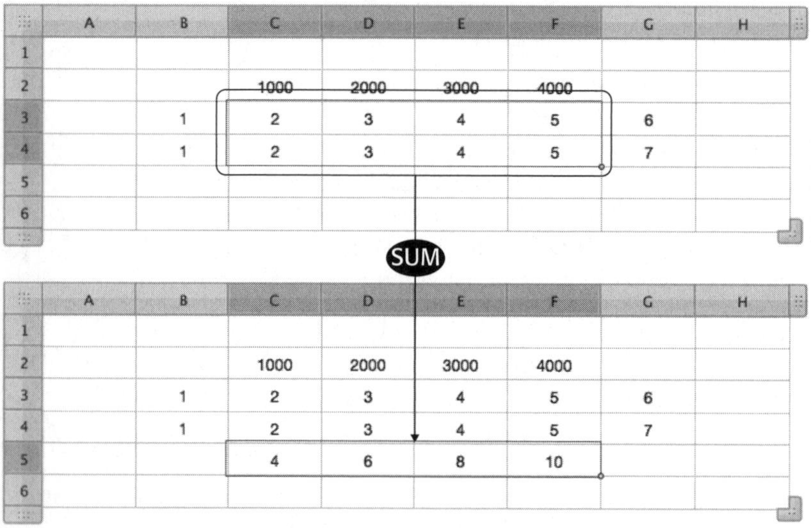

Figure 20-8:
When you choose a quick formula with a selection of cells spanning both columns and cells, Numbers adds formulas to the cells in the row below. Each one of the formulas applies its calculation to the selected cells in the same column.

Editing Formulas

When you're doing very simple math on neighboring cells—adding up a row or column, for example—quick formulas are all you need. However, as helpful as this automatic formula mixology might be, Numbers' quick formulas and instant calculations can handle only very simple equations. When you require something even slightly more sophisticated—another type of calculation or working with nonadjacent cells—it's time to build your own formula. This section introduces you to the basics of editing formulas, along with the tools that Numbers offers for making the job go easier.

Anatomy of a Formula

A formula is an *equation,* a statement that says, "this cell's value is equal to this calculation." To signal its status as an equation, every formula starts with the = sign. Numbers figures out the value of whatever follows that = sign and presents it to you in the cell containing the formula, the *formula cell.* The simplest possible formula is:

    =1

Numbers strains its mighty math muscles to evaluate the right side of the = sign and arrives at the startling conclusion that the value is in fact one. The cell's value is thus treated and displayed as one.

Note: Technically, the cell's "real" value is the formula itself. But for display purposes and when the cell is used in other cell's formulas, Numbers considers its value to be the calculated value.

Setting a cell's value to a specific number by using a formula is not especially exciting or even terribly helpful (it's of course easier to type that value directly into the cell and dispense with the = sign entirely). Things start to get more interesting when you give Numbers some math to work with. Again, let's keep it simple to start:

    =1+1

Once again, Numbers puts its genius for figures to work, this time deciding that the calculated value of the cell is two, as shown in Figure 20-9.

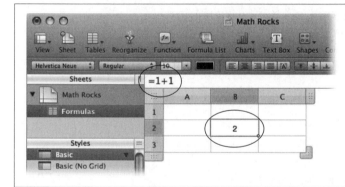

Figure 20-9:
Select a formula cell to reveal its underlying equation in the Formula Bar. Here, a cell with the formula =1+1 shows its calculated value, which is—ah, you already know the answer— two.

You get the idea: Whatever value pops out of the right side of the = sign becomes the displayed value for the cell. It's worth underlining, though, that a formula *must* start with an = sign in order to be treated as a formula. If you enter simply *1+1* into a cell (with no = sign), Numbers treats the entry as text. Instead of calculating its value, the cell simply displays 1+1.

Numbers' arithmetic operators

Way back in grade school, at least one of your beloved math teachers tried to teach you the word *operator,* the technical term for the + sign, − sign, and all the other symbols that tell you to make one number perform some mathematical transformation on another. Just like the equations you recall so fondly from your school days, Numbers relies on operators to understand how you'd like it to do its math. Table 20-1 shows the list of operators that Numbers understands, along with examples of how to use them.

Note: Numbers also has another kind of operator, the *comparison operator,* which lets your formulas make some simple logic decisions. You'll learn more about these tiny morsels of artificial intelligence on page 745.

Table 20-1. *Numbers' Arithmetic Operators*

Operator	Description	Example	Result
+ (plus sign)	Add two values	=2+2	4
– (minus sign)	Subtract one value from another	=4–1	3
* (asterisk)	Multiple two values	=2*3	6
/ (forward slash)	Divide one value by another	=10/2	5
^ (caret)	Raise one value to the power of another value	=10^2	100
% (percent sign)	Divide value by 100	=5%	0.05

Numbers lets you use these arithmetic operators to do only, well, arithmetic. You can't use them with text. Much as we'd all occasionally like to take back our words, for example, this formula only confuses Numbers:

```
="conversation with boss" - "comment about hideous tie"
```

You might wish the result were *huge pay raise* (or maybe, *get job back*), but Numbers returns only an error when you try to do math on text values. You'll learn more about error messages and how to cope with them on page 696.

Understanding the order of operations

When you add more than one operator to a formula, you're actually giving Numbers several calculations to do in a single line. The formula =1+2+5, for example, requires two calculations:

1. **Add one and two to get three.**

2. **Add five to get eight.**

That's a straightforward example and it's easy to understand the result. But when you start adding ever more operators to a formula—subtracting, dividing, multiplying, and exponentiating (*exponentiating!*) all at once—it's important to understand the *order of operations.* That's the set of rules that Numbers follows to figure out the order in which it will tackle the various calculations in your formula. For example, what's the value of this formula?

```
=25 - 5 * 2
```

The answer is 15, although you might have thought the answer was 40 if you didn't follow the tried-and-true order of operations that your algebra teacher taught in high school. In case your memories of algebra class are vanishingly distant, here's a quick review. Numbers attacks every formula in this order:

1. **Calculations inside parentheses**

2. **Percent, from left to right**

3. **Exponents, from left to right**

4. **Division and multiplication, from left to right**

5. **Addition and subtraction, from left to right**

Let's walk through an example to see how this works in practice. Consider this formula:

```
=1 + 16 / 2 ^ 3 * 4 - 2
```

There are no parentheses or percentages here, so Numbers skips to the third item in its list, calculating exponents. Numbers does its magic on 2^3 to get 8:

```
=1 + 16 / 8 * 4 - 2
```

Division and multiplication from left to right are up next. First up it's 16/8 to get 2:

```
=1 + 2 * 4 - 2
```

...followed by 2*4 to get 8:

```
=1 + 8 - 2
```

Finally, Numbers is down to addition and subtraction from left to right: 1 plus 8 is 9. Subtract 2, and Numbers arrives at its final result:

```
=7
```

You can control the order of operations (or simply make it easier for you to read and organize your formula) by adding parentheses, which group calculations together so that Numbers figures the value inside before running through its regular order of operations. Take a look at how broadly a single pair of parentheses can affect the value of the sample equation above:

```
1 + (16 / 2) ^ 3 * 4 - 2 = 2,047
1 + 16 / 2 ^ ( 3 * 4 ) - 2 = -0.996
1 + 16 / 2 ^ 3 * (4 - 2) = 5
```

In formulas, parentheses must always travel in pairs. If you include just one parenthesis without its companion to "open" or "close" the pair, Numbers will complain with an error message.

Meet the Formula Editor

Numbers shows its affection for formulas by wrapping them in their own sleek editing field. Numbers admits you to this luxury suite when you select a cell and type the = sign as the first character, signaling that you've started to type a formula. This triggers the appearance of the almighty Formula Editor (Figure 20-10), a wide text field that hovers above the selected cell, expanding as you enter your (often lengthy) formula text. The Formula Editor also pops up when you select a formula cell at the text level, by double-clicking it or pressing Option-Return.

Tip: Although the Formula Editor always appears immediately on top of the cell you're editing, you can move it anywhere on your screen. When you hover the cursor over the left side of the Formula Editor, it turns into a hand to show that Numbers is ready to give it a push. Drag the Formula Editor wherever you like.

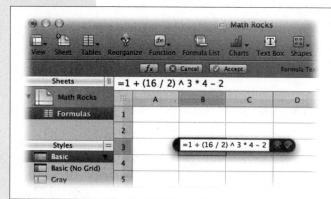

Figure 20-10:
The Formula Bar appears when you start editing a formula inside a table cell, popping up to float above the cell itself. As you type, the cell expands to the right, giving you room for lengthy formulas.

Type your formula into the Formula Editor's text field and, when you're done, press Return, press Enter, or click the Formula Editor's Accept button (the one with the green check icon). You can also press Tab or Shift-Tab to commit your changes and move to the next cell. But what you *shouldn't* do to save your formula is click another cell when you're done editing. Normally, when you're editing a cell, clicking any other cell stores your changes and selects the clicked cell. However, when you're editing a formula in either the Formula Editor or the Formula Bar, clicking another cell *includes* that cell in the formula itself. You'll learn more about cell references in the next section.

Should you change your mind midway through adding or editing a formula, just close the Formula Editor and reset the cell to its original value by pressing Esc or clicking the Formula Editor's Cancel button, the one shaped like a red X.

The Formula Editor is convenient because it gives you a wide view to edit your formula within the cell itself. Although this does give you more elbow room than a regular table cell to compose your formula, the Formula Editor still doesn't provide as much space for editing as the Formula Bar above the sheet canvas. You can use the Formula Bar interchangeably with the Formula Editor—just select a cell, click the Formula Bar to place the insertion point, and type away. Adjust the bar's height by dragging the resize handle at the far right of the Formula Bar up or down—or double-click the handle to make the Formula Bar adjust its size automatically to fit the cell's formula or contents. You can also change the font size of the Formula Bar by picking a size from the Formula Text Size pop-up menu, which appears above the Formula Bar when you've selected it.

Using Cell References

Now that you've got formulas doing a bit of math, you can see that any table cell can operate as a high-falutin' calculator. But even with all the fancy operators you explored a few pages back, if your calculations use only constant numbers (1, 2, 3, …), the results aren't really all that different from the very first =1 formula you saw a few pages ago. Because you're using plain old constant numbers in these math calculations, the "answer" to your equation is always the same, no matter how you might change the spreadsheet around that table cell. It's a calculation, sure, but it doesn't respond to the spreadsheet environment around it.

By contrast, formulas become much more flexible and useful once you start to fold in the data you've entered elsewhere in your spreadsheet. You already saw Numbers doing this with instant calculations and quick formulas earlier in this chapter. Naturally, you can do the same with your own formulas, too. To do that, you use *cell references,* placeholders in your formula that point to values in other cells in your spreadsheet.

Think of cell references as coordinates, identified by combining the name of the cell's column with the name of the cell's row. Remember the game Battleship? In the game, your hidden playing board is a grid where you lay out your ships—just like the data in your table. Players call out coordinates, trying to hit each other's battleship: *A9! C12! F4!* It works the same way with your table: The letter of a column's reference tab combines with the number of a row's reference tab to give you the location of a cell. Plug in the right coordinates, and you hit the bull's eye ("You sank my subtotal!").

When you include a cell reference in a formula, you tell Numbers to fetch that cell's value and use it in the formula's calculation. The simplest example is =A1, which tells Numbers to set the value of the formula cell to the same value found in cell A1. More often, though, you'll use cell references in various math equations, adding them as value placeholders where you would traditionally use constant values. Instead of =2+2, for example, you might have the formula =B2+C5, which tells Numbers to add the values of those two cells. If the values of those cells change, Numbers spots the update automatically and recalculates the formula; your formula cell, therefore, always reflects the latest data in your spreadsheet.

Say you're working on getting a handle on per-student expenses at the new sidekick academy, and you've put together a table to calculate the cost of each student's school uniform. You've started to build a basic grid to figure the cost of each uniform accessory, as shown in Figure 20-11.

Figure 20-11 shows the formulas for the three cells that require calculations—they're really just plain old formulas that happen to use cell references instead of constant values. There's something else interesting going on here, too. Take a close look at the formulas in the Tax and Total columns, and you'll see that they reference cells that in turn have formulas referencing other cells—a chain reaction. If you change the value in the Number column, for example, the Subtotal column updates to reflect the new value; that in turn triggers a change in the Tax column; and the Total column updates to tally the new values in both columns.

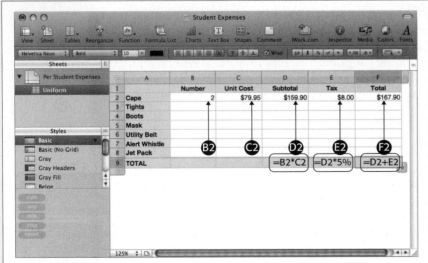

Figure 20-11:
This table lists the cost of each accessory of a sidekick's uniform. The Subtotal column for each item shows the number of items times the unit cost; the Tax column shows the five percent sales tax on the subtotal; and the Total column shows the subtotal plus the tax.

Those three columns all use cell references to figure their values using the formulas shown here.

Adding cell references to formulas

When you're editing your formula, you can add cell references by typing their coordinates, just like the formulas shown in Figure 20-11. But really: A1, B5, G3, R2D2, C3PO? Huh? While coordinates are an efficient way to pinpoint the locations of cells, they're not especially meaningful as *names*. This makes them hard to remember and, as a result, you might be prone to make mistakes when working with them directly. Numbers lets you sidestep these dreary coordinates and identify cells in a few different ways when you edit your formula.

The most direct route is to click the cell you want. When you're working in the Formula Bar or Formula Editor, clicking any cell inserts its cell reference into the formula. (Numbers reminds you that you're in this cell-reference mode by adding a *fx* function symbol to the usual white-cross cursor when you hover over other cells.)

If you're so blazingly efficient that you prefer not to let your fingers leave the keyboard to work the mouse, you can instead use the keyboard to browse to the cell you want to include: While you're editing a formula, hold down the Option key and use the arrow keys to navigate the table. As you pass through cells, their cell references appear in the formula at the insertion point. When you land on the cell you want, release the Option key, and Numbers adds the cell reference to your formula.

You can also add a cell reference by typing the cell's plain-language name, constructed from your own header labels. When your table has a header row and/or header column, you can combine those header-cell values to build coordinates instead of using the reference-tab letters and numbers. The result is a friendlier version of the cell's letter-number coordinates. In the table of uniform expenses, for example, the "full name" of cell B2 is "Number Cape", cell D5 answers to "Subtotal Mask", and so on.

The Plus Side of References

You can use cell references however you like in any formula or function—they're interchangeable with the constant values you used to plug into equations in your high-school math class. But Numbers makes it especially easy to use cell references to *add* cell values. In fact, unless you give the program a hint that you're not doing addition, it assumes that's exactly what you're up to.

To create a formula that adds any group of cells in your table, just select the formula cell, type the = sign, and start clicking table cells. As you go, Numbers inserts the cell references into your formula, automatically wedging the + sign between them, giving you an instant sum.

If the values to add are all neatly tucked together in neighboring cells, it's even easier: Select the formula cell, type the = sign, and drag from one end or corner of the cells to the opposite end or corner. Numbers adds up the values in the dragged selection, but this time it dispenses with the + sign in your formula and instead uses the SUM function with a *range reference* to describe your cell selection. You'll learn more about functions in Chapter 21 and range references on page 21, but for now all you need to know is that the formula adds up all of your selected cells.

In fact, these are the names that Numbers prefers to work with, too—a helpful convention since these long-form names tend to be more meaningfully descriptive of the cell's *content* than just its *location*. Even if you enter a cell reference into a formula using its letter-number coordinate, Numbers displays its full name when you go back and select the cell, as shown in Figure 20-12.

Tip: Prefer short nicknames to long formal ones? Babs over Barbara? B2 instead of "Q1 2009 Revenue"? Tell Numbers to keep it short and use the letter-number coordinates for names instead of header cells: Go to Numbers → Preferences, click the General button, and turn off the "Use header cell names as references" option.

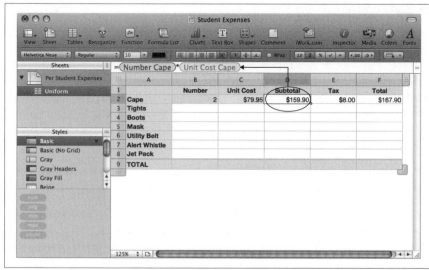

Figure 20-12:
In its standard settings, Numbers always displays cell references using header cell values where available. Here, the Cape row's Subtotal cell refers to the cells formerly known as B2 and C2 by their long names: "Number Cape" and "Unit Cost Cape".

These header names aren't just for display; you can use them when you're typing your formula, too. Because these names can run long, Numbers gives you some editing help by offering to auto-complete cell and row names as you type. After you type three characters, a pop-up list of suggestions appears if those first three letters match a header name (or the name of a table or sheet, as you'll learn shortly). Figure 20-13 shows this feature in action.

Note: Numbers doesn't offer its auto-completion suggestions when you turn off the "Use header cell names as references" checkbox in Numbers → Preferences.

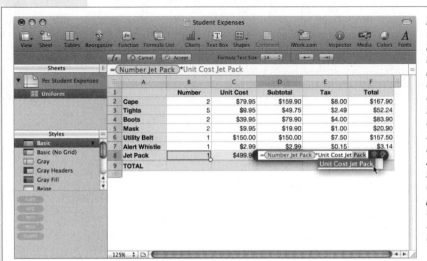

Figure 20-13:
When you're typing a cell reference and the first three or more characters match a header or column name, Numbers offers to auto-complete it for you. Here, Numbers offers to complete Jet Pack to polish off the cell reference for "Unit Cost Jet Pack." To accept the suggestion, press Tab or click the suggestion in the pop-up menu. To ignore the suggestion, press Delete or just keep typing.

Viewing and editing cell references

However you wind up adding a cell reference to your formula, it shows up in the Formula Bar and Formula Editor as a colored *reference capsule* with the cell's name or reference-tab coordinates inside. Each reference capsule gets its own color, and when the formula cell is selected, Numbers color-coordinates them with the corresponding cells in the table, highlighting those cells in matching colors. This color-by-numbers trick makes it instantly clear which cells you're using in the formula. To make sure a formula is operating on the cells you expect, just click the formula cell, and the included cells light up.

The highlighted cells are more than just a visual reference, though. You can also drag them to change the cell reference in your formula. When you're working in the Formula Bar or Formula Editor, Numbers dresses each referenced cell with a selection box, complete with a circular handle in the lower-right corner (Figure 20-14). When you hover the pointer near the selection-box border of one of these cells, it turns into a hand; drag the selection box to a new cell, and Numbers updates the cell reference in your formula to point to the new location.

This hand-grabbing drag-and-drop is the very same technique that you'd normally use to move a cell's contents to a new spot. But when you're editing a formula, the cell's contents stay put, and the only thing that moves is the cell-reference selection box. Similarly, dragging the circular handle on a cell-reference selection box doesn't replace the contents of the cell's neighbors as it would when you use the autofill handle in normal editing mode. Instead, the handle expands the cell-reference selection to the cell's neighbors, highlighting multiple cells. This creates a *range reference*, which you'll learn about on page 717.

Tip: Selection boxes appear around a formula's referenced cells only when you're *editing* the formula; simply selecting the formula cell isn't enough. To trigger this feature, place the insertion point in the Formula Bar, or open the Formula Editor by double-clicking the formula cell or pressing Option-Return.

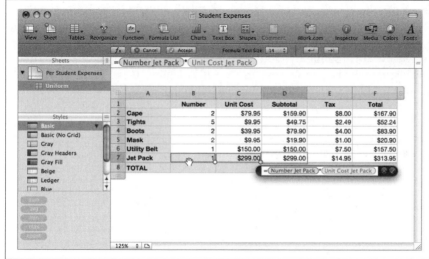

Figure 20-14:
When you're working in the Formula Editor or Formula Bar, selection boxes appear around referenced cells. To change a cell reference to point to a different cell, hover the cursor over the border of the cell you want to change. When it turns into a hand, drag the selection box to a new cell, and Numbers updates the formula with the revised cell reference.

Of course, you can also change a cell reference directly from the Formula Bar or Formula Editor. Click a reference capsule to select it, and Numbers highlights the selection box around the corresponding table cell. Double-click a capsule to edit its cell-reference address, or hold down the Option key and use the arrow keys to move the reference's selection box to a new cell in the table. To remove a cell reference from your formula, select its capsule and press Delete. You can also drag a selected capsule to a new location in the edit field to move it to a different position in the formula.

When you hover the pointer over the cell-reference capsule, a menu arrow appears on its right side, giving you access to a pop-up menu where you can switch among *relative* and *absolute* versions of the cell reference. You'll learn more about these alternate formats on page 693 in the discussion of copying formulas.

Note: You won't get much mileage from these reference capsules if you take them outside of their formula. When you drag a reference capsule outside of the Formula Bar or Formula Editor, it loses its magical abilities and turns into plain text. Dragging a reference capsule into a table cell, for example, replaces that cell's value with the capsule's cell-reference name. Dragging it into a blank part of the sheet canvas instead creates a text box, likewise containing the cell-reference name. In both cases, the cell reference remains intact in the formula.

Referencing cells in other tables or sheets

Numbers doesn't limit your formulas to using cells from the same table, or even from the same sheet. You can mix and match data from any table in your document, which is especially handy for displaying summaries of data calculated elsewhere in the spreadsheet.

For example, you've made good progress in detailing the per-student expenses at the sidekick academy, breaking out expenses into separate tables for housing, field trips, special projects, and the like. Now you'd like to show all of those table tallies in a single executive summary. You've created a table at the top of the sheet to list each expense category and its cost, as shown in Figure 20-15. To fill in the Cost column, you add cell references to the cells showing the final tally from each table. For the Uniform table, for example, the cell showing the final total is F8, or "Total TOTAL". To indicate that the cell is from another table, the cell reference starts with the table's name ("Uniform"), followed by two colons and the cell coordinates. Either of these cell reference styles does the trick:

```
= Uniform :: F8
= Uniform :: Total TOTAL
```

Tip: The table name is optional if there's only one cell in the spreadsheet with that name. For example, if the Uniform table is the only one with a cell named Total TOTAL, you can drop the table name from the cell reference, and Numbers will still find it.

You can type these foreign-table cell references manually into your formula, but those foreign names can be a mouthful. Numbers eases the effort by offering the same kind of auto-completion suggestions that it offers for header cells; after you type the first three letters of a table name, Numbers pops up its suggestions to complete the entry for you.

As usual, though, the most direct way to add a cell reference is simply to click the cell. When you're working in the Formula Bar or Formula Editor, clicking a cell *anywhere* in the spreadsheet adds that cell reference to your formula. If you need to scroll to get to the reference cell, the Formula Editor stays put, floating above as you scroll the sheet below. This lets you continue editing the formula even if the formula cell itself is no longer in view. After you press Return or click the Accept button to store the formula, Numbers springs you back to the formula cell's location in the spreadsheet.

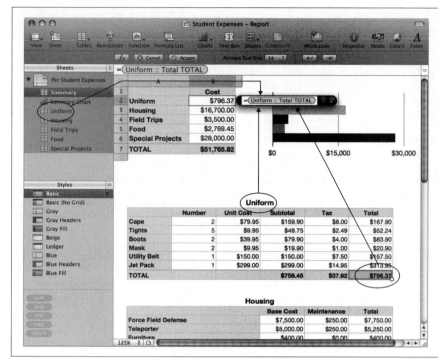

Figure 20-15:
Adding a table name to a cell reference lets you point to a cell in a separate table. Here, the summary table at the top of the sheet displays the value of the total-cost cell in the Uniform table. The table name is the same name that appears in the Sheets pane and, optionally, above the table.

This applies to adding cell references for tables that live on an entirely different sheet of your spreadsheet, too. After you've started editing a formula in either the Formula Bar or Formula Editor, click another sheet's icon in the Sheets pane, select the cell to reference, and Numbers inserts the cell reference into your formula. As you switch sheets, the Formula Editor remains onscreen, floating above the action. When you press Return or click the Accept button to store the formula, Numbers returns you to the formula cell on the original sheet.

References to other sheets often—but not always—add the sheet name to the beginning of the cell reference:

```
Sheet Name :: Table Name :: C5
```

Tip: If you're typing out a cell reference to a cell on another sheet, Numbers offers auto-complete suggestions for sheet names, just as it does for tables and header cells. You have to specify the sheet name only when there's more than one table in the document with the same name. When that's not the case, you can drop the sheet name and just use the table name. (When Numbers inserts cell references for other sheets, it uses this abbreviated form when it can.)

Copying and Moving Formulas

When you're working with straight-up text or numbers, copying and moving data around your table doesn't require much planning, and the results are rarely surprising. Whether you drag a cell, copy it, paste it, or autofill its value, the data

Dancing Sheet to Sheet

Fans of keyboard shortcuts have yet another alternative for selecting cells in other tables and sheets:

1. With the insertion point in the Formula Bar or Formula Editor, hold down the Option and Command (⌘) keys and tap Page Down (or Page Up) to flip through the tables in your spreadsheet, including those on other sheets. (On laptops without Page Down or Page Up keys, press ⌘-Fn-Option-down-arrow or ⌘-Fn-Option-up-arrow, respectively.)

2. When you land on the table you want, release the ⌘ key, but hang onto the Option key.

3. While holding Option, use the arrows to select the cell to reference.

4. Release the Option key, and Numbers inserts the cell reference into your formula.

If you find it hard to remember all the steps to this dance, you can also start by typing the name of the table, letting Numbers auto-complete it for you to speed things along. Once the table name is in place, Option-arrow to the cell, following steps 3 and 4 above.

---

lands in its new location looking just as it did in its original spot—Numbers' copy machine always makes a perfect duplicate. With formulas, however, it's not always clear what "perfect duplicate" means, especially when cell references are involved. When you plunk a formula into a new location, Numbers sometimes makes changes to those cell references in an effort to anticipate your needs. As you shuffle formulas around your spreadsheet, it's important to understand how and when Numbers modifies your formula to blend in with its new surroundings—and how you can control those changes.

The important distinction is moving vs. copying. When you *move* the original formula cell to a new location, Numbers leaves its cell references untouched; the formula continues to point to the exact same cells that it did in its new location. You move a cell when you drag it to a new location with the hand cursor or when you use the Edit → Mark for Move and Edit → Move commands (see page 620).

However, when you *copy* a cell by pasting, autofilling, or Option-dragging, Numbers updates the formula's cell references so that they point to different cells relative to the formula's new location. Say that you have a formula in cell A1 that contains a reference to the cell next door at B1. When you copy the formula down to the next row (cell A2), Numbers updates the formula's cell reference to point to cell B2. Numbers assumes that the *relative position* of the referenced cell is more important than the actual original address. Even though the copied cell is in a new spot, it still points to the cell next door.

This turns out to be a huge timesaver when you want to repeat a formula in many cells—to tally all the cells in each row or column, for example. The Basic Heroics grade sheet from earlier in the chapter offers an example, as shown in Figure 20-16. Instead of updating each of the formula cells for every row, you can copy them quickly using autofill (page 618), and Numbers handles the cell reference updates for you.

Note: You might think that cutting and pasting moves a cell, but Numbers considers all pasted cells to be *copies* of the original. That means the cut-and-paste combo gets the copy treatment, not the move treatment, and Numbers updates cell references accordingly. The exception is when you cut or copy the *text* of a formula from the Formula Editor or Formula Bar. When you paste the text of that formula into a new cell, all of the cell references remain exactly as they were in the original.

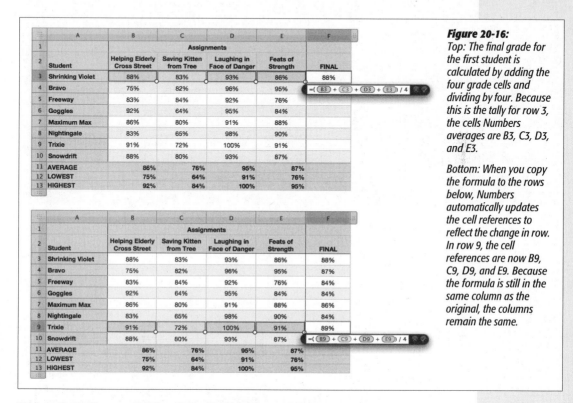

Figure 20-16:
Top: The final grade for the first student is calculated by adding the four grade cells and dividing by four. Because this is the tally for row 3, the cells Numbers averages are B3, C3, D3, and E3.

Bottom: When you copy the formula to the rows below, Numbers automatically updates the cell references to reflect the change in row. In row 9, the cell references are now B9, C9, D9, and E9. Because the formula is still in the same column as the original, the columns remain the same.

Using Relative and Absolute Cell References

Numbers manages this graceful maneuver by treating your cell addresses as *relative cell references*. Even though you provide specific cell coordinates in your formulas, Numbers reads them as flexible directions based on the location of the formula cell. In the grade sheet example, as far as Numbers is concerned the formula really says, "Add *the four cells to the left,* and divide by four." When you copy the cell to a new location, the references update to match.

This relative treatment of cell references is great—except when it's not. Sometimes you do actually mean what you say, and you might want to refer to the same, specific cell even when the formula is copied to a new location. For example, say that you're arranging for three foreign exchange students to attend the sidekick academy. Everyone's very excited to welcome sidekicks Big Ben, Sacre Bleu, and Mr. Roboto, but you have to figure out the cost of school uniforms in pounds, euros,

---

FREQUENTLY ASKED QUESTION

Tracking a Moving Target

What happens if I use a cell reference in a formula, but I later move that cell to a new location?

When a cell moves to new digs, Numbers knows its forwarding address and quietly updates cell references in all formulas to point to the new location. For example, say that you have this very simple formula:

    =C3

If you move the C3 cell to C4, the formula updates accordingly to refer to cell C4. The same applies even when you move a cell only indirectly, by adding or deleting rows or columns elsewhere in the table so that the cell gets nudged to a new position.

Numbers *won't* track a cell, however, if you cut and paste its value to a new location. When you're moving a cell and need formulas to follow along, you have to move it without using the Clipboard. A good substitute for cut and paste is to select the cell and choose Edit → Mark for Move. Then select the new location and choose Edit → Move. It works just like cut and paste, but lets formulas follow the cell to its new home. (You can also get the same effect by dragging the cell to the new position.)

You can also throw Numbers off course by deleting a row or column that contains a referenced cell. When that happens, Numbers complains that the formula contains an "invalid reference," signaling that the original data behind the cell reference has gone missing.

and yen. So you plug a currency conversion into your table and—whoops!—your table cells light up with error messages, as shown in Figure 20-17. (For help dealing with error messages, see page 696.)

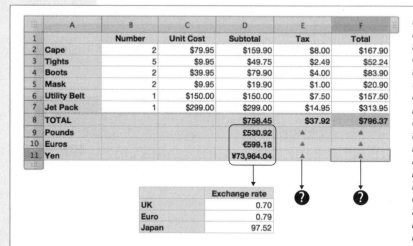

Figure 20-17:
In the Subtotal column, the three bottom footer rows contain formulas that multiple the value in the TOTAL row (the top footer row) by an exchange rate from the table below. This works great in this column, but when you copy the formulas to the neighboring columns, Numbers updates the columns in the cell references, too. Because those columns don't exist in the exchange-rate table, Numbers throws up its hands and tosses error messages into those cells.

In this example, you want it both ways: You want the cell reference for the dollar value (the value in the TOTAL row) to update so that you're always working with the value in the current column. But you *don't* want the cell references to update for the exchange rates; those should always take their value from the same column in the exchange-rate table.

When you don't want Numbers to use relative cell references, you use an *absolute cell reference* instead. This nails down the cell reference to a fixed spot in your sheet, making Numbers use the same cell no matter how you might place or copy the formula cell. You mark a cell as absolute by putting a $ sign before its cell coordinates. In Figure 20-17, for example, the exchange rate for UK pounds sterling is in cell B2 (or "Exchange Rate UK", using its header-cell name). That means the absolute cell reference for this cell is B2 (or "$Exchange Rate $UK"). You can type these $ signs directly into the cell reference in the Formula Bar or Formula Editor, but you can also change the reference style with a jiggle of the reference capsule: Every reference capsule has a pop-up menu that lets you select the reference style to use. Figure 20-18 shows this menu in action.

Tip: You can also click the reference capsule once to select it (or place the insertion point either immediately before or after the reference) and then press ⌘-K to cycle through the reference options—relative, absolute, absolute row, or absolute column. (More on those last two options in a moment.)

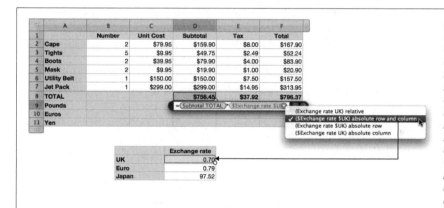

Figure 20-18:
When you move the cursor over a reference capsule in the Formula Editor or Formula Bar, a menu arrow appears; click it to reveal the pop-up menu to select the reference style to use. Here, the formula to calculate the subtotal value in pounds sterling is set to use an absolute cell reference for the UK exchange rate.

Go ahead and update the Subtotal column's formulas for the Pounds, Euros, and Yen rows to use absolute references for the exchange-rate cell. Now you can copy those three cells into the neighboring columns to get the correct, error-free results.

Working with mixed cell references

Easy as that approach is, it still takes a few more steps than necessary, requiring three different formulas in each row before you can copy them into the neighboring two columns. With a small tweak, you can create just one formula and then copy it into all nine cells, saving you some legwork.

The trick is to mix relative and absolute addresses within a single cell reference—fixing the row but not the column, or vice versa. Eagle-eyed reader that you are, you no doubt noticed that the pop-up menu in Figure 20-18 has four options for reference styles: Relative, absolute row and column, absolute row, and absolute column. The last two options let you glue down just the row or column respectively, while allowing the other "half" of the cell reference to remain relative.

Instead of adding a $ dollar sign in front of *both* column and row coordinates, these *mixed cell references* display it in front of only the fixed half of the address.

In your exchange-rate table, for example, all the formulas use the same row (the TOTAL row) for the base dollar values, although the column changes with each column. This means that if you craft a cell reference to use an *absolute row* (the TOTAL row) and a *relative column,* you could copy that reference to all nine currency-conversion cells, and they would point to the correct location. The exchange-rate cell reference is the reverse: The column must be fixed to use the "Exchange rate" column every time, but because the currencies appear in the same order in both tables, the row can remain relative. In the Pounds cell of the Subtotal column, this formula winds up looking like this:

```
=Subtotal $TOTAL * $Exchange rate UK
```

The $ sign in front of "$TOTAL" and "$Exchange rate" show that those row and column references are fixed; they'll remain unchanged when you copy the formula from cell to cell. When you copy the formula cell one row down to the Euros column, for example, Numbers updates the relative row in the "$Exchange rate UK" cell reference to use the Euro row below. The cell reference for "Subtotal $TOTAL", however, is fixed to use the TOTAL row, so it remains unchanged:

```
=Subtotal $TOTAL * $Exchange rate Euro
```

What about when you copy the original formula cell to the right, into the Tax column? Numbers updates the relative column of the "Subtotal $TOTAL" cell reference to use the Tax column. But because the "$Exchange rate" column is fixed in "$Exchange rate UK", it remains the same. So the copied formula in the Tax Pounds cell looks like this:

```
=Tax $TOTAL * $Exchange rate UK
```

Finally, copying the formula to a new row *and* column combines both changes. The copied formula looks like this in the Tax Euro cell, as shown in Figure 20-19:

```
=Tax $TOTAL * $Exchange rate Euro
```

Copying the Value, Not the Formula

If you just want to copy the computed *result* of a cell's formula instead of the formula itself, you can sidestep all this fuss about cell references. Select the cell, choose Edit → Copy, and choose Edit → Paste Values. The displayed result of the original cell shows up in the new cell without its formula—a mild-mannered value without the formula cell's special abilities.

Coping with Formula Errors

As clever as Numbers can be, it's not hard to confuse it when you don't follow its rules or speak its language correctly. The program expects your formulas to be formatted correctly, to use cell references for cells that actually exist, and to provide

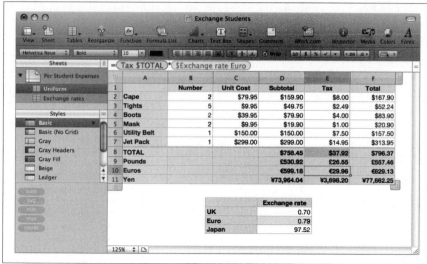

Figure 20-19:
By carefully mixing absolute and relative cell references in the formula of the Subtotal Pounds (D9) cell, that formula could be copied to the other eight currency conversions in the bottom right of the table so that their cell references point to the right place. Here, the formula in the Tax Euros (E10) cell points to the correct dollar and exchange-rate cells.

values that let it complete the actions you request. When that's not the case or when Numbers otherwise can't make sense of your formula, it complains by putting a red triangle—the error icon—in the middle of the cell.

Click the icon to see the error message, which provides brief details about what got Numbers mixed up (see Figure 20-17, for example). Often the message gives you enough information to go on, and you can quickly find and fix the error. When you get the vaguely worded message, "The formula contains a syntax error", that usually means that you've got something out of order in your formula. Check to make sure that all of your parentheses match up, that you've got arithmetic operators where they should be, and that all of your function arguments are properly separated with commas (page 712).

Some problems aren't so nasty that they merit the error icon. In that case, Numbers flags the cell with a warning indicator, a blue triangle in the cell's top left corner. For example, you can tell Numbers to show warnings if a formula references an empty cell—useful when you want to be sure that all data values have been provided. To do this, choose Numbers → Preferences, click the General button, and turn on the "Show warnings when formulas reference empty cells" option. Like the error icon, the warning indicator displays details about the warning when clicked.

Browsing and Searching Formulas

As you start adding more and more formulas to your spreadsheet, it can sometimes be difficult to recall what comes from where. In fact it's not always immediately obvious even *which* cells contain formulas; formula cells, after all, look just like their neighbors and so keep a low profile. When you need to get a handle on your growing collection of formulas, click the Formula List button in the toolbar or choose View → Show Formula List, and the formula list materializes in a new pane at the bottom of the document window.

The formula list is a modified version of the Search pane (page 653) but focuses solely on formula cells, organizing them by sheet and table and showing their location, computed results, and formula text, as shown in Figure 20-20.

Tip: Numbers offers an option to print the formula list when you print the rest of your spreadsheet. See page 816 for details.

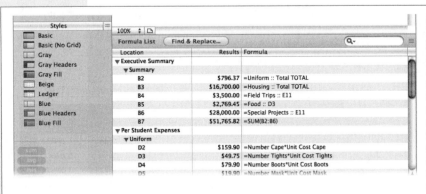

Figure 20-20:
The formula list lets your browse all of your spreadsheet's formulas. To hide the results for any sheet, click the flippy triangle next to the sheet name; ditto for table names. To jump directly to any listed cell, click once on its entry in the list. To open the Formula Editor for a formula, double-click its entry.

To search inside your spreadsheet's formulas, type your search term into the search field at the top right of the formula list, and then press Return. Numbers displays the results in the pane below. To restore the list to its full glory, clear the contents of the search field by deleting the text or pressing the X icon in the right side of the search bar.

To make sweeping substitutions across multiple formulas, you can summon the Find & Replace window, described on page 654, by clicking the Find & Replace button at the top of the pane. When you open the window from the formula list, the "Formulas Only" option is selected, ensuring that your changes will be limited only to formula text, not to other data.

Note: To use the Find & Replace window on formulas, you must have its Formulas Only option selected. Choosing either of the other two options—Entire Document or Current Sheet Only—makes Numbers do its search-and-swap on regular data values only.

Advanced Data Crunching with Functions

You can get lots done in your spreadsheet simply by mixing formulas with the ingredients you've seen so far: cell references, operators, and constant values. You could put down this book right now and be wildly productive with Numbers—the whole world of basic algebra is your oyster. But the great thing is that you don't *have* to do the algebra (or eat the oyster, for that matter). Numbers gives you more than 250 predefined calculations called *functions* that juggle figures for you so you don't have to construct the equations yourself. They can even do a few tasks for you that are flat out impossible to do with straight-up arithmetic.

Functions can handle a range of jobs including simple two-plus-two addition, converting teaspoons to tablespoons, and figuring out an asset's depreciation. They're not limited to working with numbers, either. Functions can transform text, traverse the calendar, construct sentences, make logical decisions, and sift through tables to find certain values. This chapter shows you how to put this remarkable collection of timesavers to use in your formulas. You'll start with the most common tasks and move on to sophisticated strategies for wrangling data across multiple tables in your spreadsheet.

How Functions Work

Think of Numbers' function library as an army of math-minded elves waiting to do your bidding. Each elf has a specific job it knows how to do; you give it the raw materials it needs to do that job—a set of numbers to average, for example—and it comes back with the answer. You don't have to understand *how* it gets the answer or what equations and incantations it performs behind the scenes; just give it your figures, and it hands you the result. Every one of your little minions has a name and even brings along its own basket to hold the raw materials you provide.

The busiest and most popular of all spreadsheet functions is without a doubt SUM. You've already seen this little guy in action several times in the previous chapter. SUM's job is simple: It adds the numbers you put in its metaphorical basket, a pair of parentheses that you add immediately after the function name. For example, this formula adds the numbers inside the parentheses and returns the value 10:

```
=SUM(4, 2, 3, 1)
```

Every function has to be followed by a pair of parentheses in order for you to give it your data. Inside the parentheses is the place where you ask the question you want answered. The raw materials you pour into a function's parentheses are known as its *arguments*. They get along better than their confrontational name suggests, even lining up in a specific order to feed the function the info it needs. Some functions, for example, require a specific set of arguments in a defined order; you have to ask your question in precise terms. The CONVERT function, for example, takes a number in one unit and converts it to another. To make a cell display the number of miles in five kilometers, for example, you put the question to CONVERT with a specific series of three arguments, like so:

```
=CONVERT(5, "km", "mi")
```

In this example, the arguments are the number that you want to convert (5), the current units of that number (km), and the units in which you would like the answer (mi). CONVERT obligingly lets you know that the answer is 3.107 (and many decimal places more, too). You can type arguments directly into the formula or, more commonly, represent some or all arguments with cell references. Figure 21-1, for example, shows a table that lets you perform any unit conversion you'd like by editing the values of the table cells.

Note: Don't worry, you don't have to memorize all of the function names and the arguments they require. Numbers makes it easy to put your hands on that info when you need it, as you'll learn when you meet the Function Browser on page 702.

Whether you type your arguments directly or use cell references, there are a few rules to keep in mind as you build your argument list:

- **Arguments go inside parentheses.** Every function name has to be followed by parentheses containing the function's arguments. As usual in a formula, these need to be a pair of matching open and closed parentheses.

- **Arguments are separated by commas.** It's just like your English teacher taught you: separate items in a list with commas. (As you'll learn on page 706, however, a special kind of cell reference called a *range reference* can represent several cell references at once, sidestepping the need for a long list of comma-separated values.)

Note: If your Mac is set to use a comma instead of a period as the decimal separator (in the International pane of your Mac's System Preferences), use a semicolon instead of a comma to separate arguments.

	A	B	C	D
1	Number	Old Unit	New Unit	Conversion
2	5	km	mi	3.10685596118667
3	12	cup	gal	0.75
4	77	F	C	25
5	76	in	cm	193.04
6	2	tbs	tsp	6
7	2	day	mn	2880

=CONVERT(A2,B2,C2)

Figure 21-1: *The CONVERT functions in the last column of this table pluck their arguments from the first three columns using cell references. Changing a value in any of those columns changes the result in the last column. Instead of converting from tablespoons to teaspoons in row six, for example, you could change the units in columns B and C to pints and quarts (pt and qt). Numbers updates the conversion's result accordingly.*

- **Text arguments go inside quotes.** Like the CONVERT example above, any text value has to go inside quotation marks. Cell references aren't considered text, even though their values might contain text. (Don't put cell references inside quotation marks or they'll stop working as references.)
- **White space is your friend.** Functions can get complex, but you can at least make them easier to read and edit by giving them a little space to breathe. Feel free to sprinkle spaces, tabs, and line breaks into your formulas to create visual breaks between arguments, operators, and functions. Numbers ignores extra spacing except inside quotation marks or cell references, so the only effect your spaces have is to make your life easier.

Arguments can even include other functions or calculations. The formula to display the mile equivalent of five kilometers could also be written like any of the following alternatives, where the first argument always calculates to 5:

```
=CONVERT( SUM(2, 3), "km", "mi" )
=CONVERT( SUM(C2, C3), "km", "mi" )
=CONVERT( (10 / 2), "km", "mi" )
=CONVERT( AVERAGE(4, 6), "km", "mi" )
```

Remember the order of operations from the last chapter (page 682)? Numbers always does calculations inside parentheses first, and that includes the parentheses that hold function arguments. In the examples above, this means that Numbers figures the value of the first argument (5) before it sends the function on its way to fetch the final value. This lets you use functions, or any calculation, interchangeably with constant values in your argument list.

In fact, that's true anywhere in your formula, which means you can combine functions with arithmetic operators just as you would with constant values or cell references. For example, these formulas all return the same result:

```
=5
=10 / 2
=SUM(4, 6) / 2
=SUM(4, 6) / AVERAGE(1, 3)
```

To add a function to your formula, you can simply type the function name and arguments directly into the Formula Bar or Formula Editor, just like the examples you've seen so far. It doesn't matter whether you type the function name in lowercase letters, all caps, or a mix of the two—Numbers recognizes them in any of these formats. As soon as you type the function name and the opening parenthesis, however, Numbers immediately sets the function name in capital letters; so when you type *sum(*, it instantly snaps to attention and becomes SUM(. This all-caps display is the accepted convention for spreadsheet function names, but more important, it helps set function names apart from the rest of your function, making the whole thing easier to read.

Adding Functions with the Function Browser

Typing functions into the Formula Editor by hand works well enough for common, easy-to-remember functions like SUM. But when you cobble together more complex functions—or when you're not sure of the function name or even if such a function exists—a little help is in order. The *Function Browser* lets you thumb through Numbers' entire library of functions, where each one is listed with a complete description of its arguments and what the function does, as well as examples. When you find the function you want, Numbers inserts it into your formula, including labeled placeholders for the function's arguments.

You can open the Function Browser by doing any of the following:

• When you're working in the Formula Bar or Formula Editor, click the Function Browser button (labeled *fx*) above the Formula Bar.

• With any cell selected, click the toolbar's Function button and choose Show Function Browser from its pop-up menu.

• With any cell selected, choose Insert → Function → Show Function Browser.

• Choose View → Show Function Browser.

The Function Browser, shown in Figure 21-2, consists of three panes that organize your view of the function library. The top left pane groups functions into categories, including the All category, for when you want to drink from the fire hose, and Recent, which helps you focus on your commonly used collection of functions (or at least the last ten of them). When you choose a category, the top right pane lists the functions alphabetically by name. Click a function, and the bottom pane offers a detailed description of it, including tips and examples.

Figure 21-2:
When you're working in the Formula Bar or Formula Editor, click the Function Browser button (circled) to open the Function Browser window. Browse the functions using the two top panes, and read the description of a function at the bottom by clicking its name in the top-right pane. To insert a function into your formula, double-click its name or select it and then click Insert Function.

Browsing function categories is a good way to get acquainted with the many possibilities that functions offer, but don't take the category names too literally. The Engineering category, for example, might seem daunting to literature majors, but that category happens to include the CONVERT function—as useful to home cooks counting the number of tablespoons in a quarter cup as it is to physicists converting joules to ergs. Similarly, the serious-sounding Statistics category includes the commonly used AVERAGE and COUNT functions.

Because these category names are a bit loose, the Function Browser's search bar is often the most efficient way to find the function you're looking for. This miniature search engine scours functions' description text, so even if you don't know a function's name, searching for a word related to what you want it to *do* typically helps you find what you need. Type your search term into the field at the top right of the window, press Return, and the Function Browser switches to a two-pane display, with matching functions listed at the top and the description pane at the bottom. To return to the regular category display, clear the search field.

Tip: Limiting your search term to just one word often gives you the best results. That's because the Function Browser's search bar treats all searches as *phrases,* which means you'll see results only when a function's description includes the exact text you type. When you type *convert minutes,* for example, Numbers won't find a function whose description includes "convert a value to minutes," even though it contains the words *convert* and *minutes.* Better to search simply for *minutes.*

When you find your function, double-click it to add it to the formula for the selected cell, or click Insert Function. (Nothing at all happens, however, if you have *more* than one cell selected; to add a function from the Function Browser, you can have only one cell selected.) The Function Browser inserts more than just the function name into your formula; it also gives you *argument placeholders* to remind you what info the function needs and, where applicable, in what order. These placeholders show up as gray capsules; pointing to one of them displays a brief description of its purpose, as shown in Figure 21-3. Numbers displays placeholders for optional arguments more faintly, letting you know that you can safely ignore them if you like.

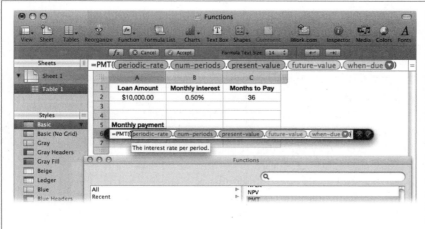

Figure 21-3:
When you insert a function into a formula from the Function Browser, Numbers gives you argument placeholders to fill in. Each one has a terse label, but you can get a more helpful description by hovering your cursor over the placeholder (or by reading the even more helpful description in the Function Browser). Numbers displays required arguments in dark gray, and optional arguments in a lighter color. Here, the PMT function will calculate the monthly payment for a loan when you provide the periodic interest rate, the number of periods to pay, and the present value of the loan (the amount you owe).

To fill in an argument placeholder, click to select it and then type a value. You can also use a cell reference: Click a capsule to select it and then click the cell you want to use for the argument value, or hold down Option and use the arrow keys to navigate to the cell you want to use. In the PMT function in Figure 21-3, for example, you would use cell B2 for the periodic rate, cell C2 for the number of periods, and cell A2 for the present value of the loan. The resulting formula will tell you what your monthly payment would be to pay off your $10,000 loan in three years. (For another example of the PMT function at work, check out Numbers' built-in Mortgage template, which shows you monthly payments under a variety of interest rates and payment schedules.)

Note: Because capsule shapes often signal that you can drag an element, you might be tempted to drag an argument placeholder into a cell to try to use that cell as the value. Resist that urge; you'll only replace the cell's value with the name of the placeholder. Instead, click the placeholder capsule and then click the cell whose value you want to use.

Some argument placeholders (like the *when-due* placeholder in Figure 21-3) contain pop-up menus that list all the argument's allowed values; click the capsule's menu arrow to see your choices. Hovering the cursor over any of the choices displays a brief description of what the value stands for, just like with the argument placeholders themselves.

Pasting Examples from the Function Browser

Many of the detailed function descriptions in the Function Browser (and in Numbers' Help window) include one or more ultra-useful examples of table cells actually using the function (see Figure 21-4). This is generally the case for functions like the PMT example above, which requires specific arguments in a fixed order. When you see these examples, you can copy and paste those table cells (including their headers) directly into your spreadsheet to give you a head start in building the function and the cells that feed it.

Pasting these examples works like pasting any other group of table cells in Numbers. When no cell is selected, Numbers creates a new table to hold the pasted cells. Otherwise, Numbers pours the cells into the selected table, replacing the selected cells with the pasted example. (For more on copying and moving table cells, see page 620.)

Tip: Use Edit → "Paste and Match Style" instead of the straight-up Edit → Paste command when pasting these cells. This ensures that the font and text styles of the pasted cells match those of your spreadsheet, instead of the Function Browser's text styles.

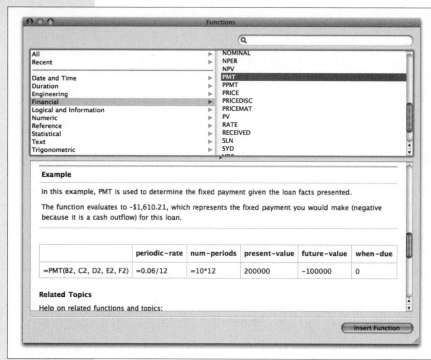

Figure 21-4:
*The detailed descriptions
in the Function Browser
often include working
examples that you can
paste directly into your
document. Here, a two-
row table illustrates the
PMT function at work. To
add the example to your
spreadsheet, highlight
the table and then
choose Edit → Copy.
Next, select the spot
where you want to paste
the cells in your
document, and then
choose Edit → "Paste
and Match Style".*

Using Cell Ranges in Functions

All of the function examples you've seen so far have used cell references with the
same comma-separated format as any other argument. That works fine when you
have just a small handful of arguments—to add the values of four cells, for example:

```
=SUM(B1, B2, B3, B4)
```

But that's actually longer than just doing it directly with the plus sign:

```
=B1 + B2 + B3 + B4
```

And either method becomes hideously long when you decide to add a column of
10,000 values. In the time it would take to type or click all the cells, you may as well
just add up the values yourself. Happily, Numbers provides a shorthand called a
range reference that lets you point to any collection of neighboring cells—a *range*.
Many functions accept range references as arguments, including SUM, which adds
up all the cells described by the range. To provide a range reference, you give
Numbers the cell reference for the top-left and bottom-right cells in the range, separated by a colon. (If it's a single-column range, then your job is to name the top
and bottom cells.) B1:B4, for example, describes adjacent cells in a column—a
reference to cells B1 and B4 *and* the cells in between (B2 and B3). These two
formulas return the same result:

```
=SUM(B1:B4)
=SUM(B1, B2, B3, B4)
```

Even though a range reference is just a single argument, in other words, it actually "unpacks" into several values. You can even string multiple ranges together by separating them with commas just as you would with any other argument. For example, these two formulas give you the same result:

```
=SUM(B1:B3, C10:C12)
=SUM(B1, B2, B3, C10, C11, C12)
```

A reference to adjacent cells in a row works the same way. B2:E2 refers to cells B2, C2, D2, and E2. Cell references can similarly describe a block of cells: D6:E10 gives you rows six through 10 in columns D and E, ten cells in all. Figure 21-5 gives you the full picture.

Tip: Be careful that you don't accidentally include the formula cell in one of its range references, or Numbers will choke up an error. You're not allowed to refer to the formula cell in its own formula. (You also can't refer to another cell that depends on that formula cell for its value.)

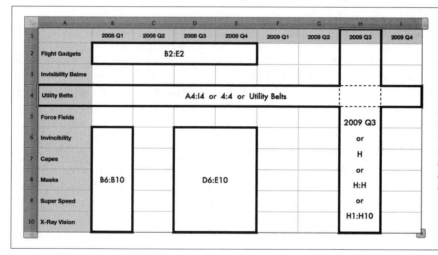

Figure 21-5:
Use cell ranges to describe blocks of adjacent cells, including cells in a row (B2:E2), in a column (B6:B10), or in a block (D6:E10). You have a few more options for referring to all cells in a row or column, where you can instead use the reference-tab label or header cell value to describe the range.

Unlike working with individual cells, Numbers doesn't give you the option of using header names when you refer to cells in reference ranges. You have to use the letter-number coordinate format for cells. Numbers lifts that restriction, however, when you want to create a reference to *every* cell in a row or column. In that case, you can just refer to the row or column by its header name alone to create a *row reference* or *column reference*. If column H of your table is labeled "2009 Q3," for example, either of these formulas adds up every cell in that column:

```
=SUM(H)
=SUM(2009 Q3)
```

When you leave off the row coordinate of a cell reference, in other words, it turns into a range reference for the entire column. You can do the same thing to add up

---

rows, too. If the second row of your table is labeled "Flight Gadgets," you can add up all its values like so:

```
=SUM(Flight Gadgets)
```

It doesn't work quite the same way as columns, however, when you want to refer to rows by their reference-tab numbers instead of their header names. That's because Numbers reads =SUM(2) as the *number* 2 instead of the sum of all cells in *row* 2. To clear up the confusion, you use a *row range,* which indicates all cells in the specified range of rows; since you just want one row, the start and end row is the same. Here's how you tell Numbers to add all the cells in row 2:

```
=SUM(2:2)
```

If you want to add all the cells in *multiple* rows or columns, you simply indicate the first and last to include, using the reference-tab letters and numbers for your row and column references:

```
=SUM(B:D)
=SUM(2:4)
```

Note: When you select entire rows or columns of cells using row and column references, the range typically includes the header and footer cells, too. This is no problem for the SUM function, which simply ignores text values, but it could cause confusion (or at least an error or warning message) for functions that expect only numbers. When you want to exclude header and footer cells, use a specific cell range instead of a row or column reference.

Adding Cell Ranges to Formulas

You can type range references directly into your formula, just as you can with cell references. As usual, the most direct (if not necessarily the fastest) way to indicate a range of cells is to point them out with your mouse. With the insertion point inside the Formula Bar or Formula Editor, drag your cursor across a range of cells from one end to the other, and Numbers inserts the appropriate range reference into your formula.

Note: Range references don't mean anything to Numbers if they're outside a function's parentheses. It's a common mistake, for example, to try to add a group of cells by including only a cell range in a formula (like =B2 + C2:F2), but that won't work. Always be sure to include your range references as a function argument: =B2 + SUM(C2:F2)

You can also trace out a cell range without lifting your hands from the keyboard. Press and hold Option, and then use the arrow keys to move to one end of the range. Then, while still holding down the Option key, press and hold Shift while you use the arrow keys to expand the selection. When you've selected the range you want, release the Shift and Option keys, and Numbers adds the range reference to your formula. Or release only the Shift key and, while still holding the Option key, use the arrows to reposition the entire cell range on the table.

When you're working in the Formula Bar or Formula Editor, Numbers highlights the referenced cell ranges in the table, using the same color as their reference capsules in the formula—just as it does for single-cell references. These cell ranges are bordered by a selection box that you can drag to a new spot in the table. (Dragging a range's box updates only the range reference's address in the formula; it doesn't affect the data in the cell range.) To shrink or expand the area of the range reference, drag the circular handle at the bottom right of the selection box, circled in Figure 21-6.

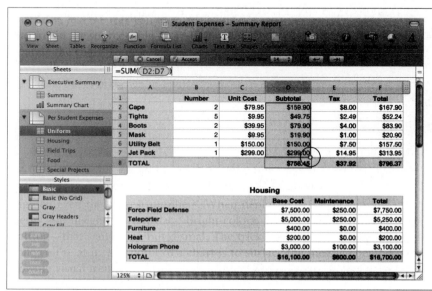

Figure 21-6:
When you place the insertion point in the Formula Bar or Formula Editor, you can adjust the location and size of the formula's cell ranges by dragging their borders (to move them) or the circular handles (to resize them) at the range's bottom right.

Common Math Functions

Numbers offers a wide range of functions for managing your adventures in arithmetic, including lots of advanced functions tailored for accountants, statisticians, and rocket scientists. Although these brainy beauties are often crucial to folks working in a specific field, these functions are too esoteric for the general public, often requiring specialized knowledge even to understand *why* you might use them. Some of these topics would require a whole other book (and possibly a graduate degree) to explain. If you wouldn't know a multinomial coefficient from a multinational coffeehouse, then chances are you'll never use anything close to all the functions iWork offers. As a result, this book doesn't delve into these deep, dark nooks and crannies.

Instead, this section provides a review of commonly used math functions. Although this treatment only scratches the surface of the function library's numerical know-how, you can, as always find a complete list of all iWork formula functions in the Function Browser.

Tip: The Numbers Help menu also includes a handy overview of functions, including introductory material for working with financial and accounting functions. To check it out, choose Help → "iWork Formulas and Functions Help".

The Quick-Formula Functions and Basic Math

In the last chapter's review of instant calculations and quick formulas, you met the most popular functions in Spreadsheet Land. SUM, COUNT, MAX, MIN, AVERAGE, and PRODUCT are the most commonly used math functions, which explains their privileged status in the toolbar and (except for PRODUCT) in the Instant Calculations pane. In addition to using these functions in quick formulas, you can also include them in your own custom formulas, and many of them have other closely related functions that you might consider as alternatives (MEDIAN instead of AVERAGE, for example). This section provides a quick tour of these basic functions.

SUM: Adding Numbers

The SUM function will almost certainly be in the heaviest rotation in your function playlist. This function's one and only job is to add up what you hand to it. As discussed earlier in the chapter, its arguments are simply the set of values to add, which you can enter directly or represent with functions, cell references, or cell ranges. Here are some examples:

```
=SUM(A1, D4)
=SUM(A1:D4)
=SUM(A1, B1:D4, 200, 15.1, 35%)
```

Tip: Because Numbers uses commas to separate arguments, don't use commas in your numbers when writing functions. If you do, Numbers reads a number like 1,200 as two separate arguments. For example, SUM(1,200, 3) gives you 204, not 1,203. In other words, what you need to write is SUM(1200, 3).

SUM ignores text values and empty cells, but it *can* work with dates and durations. You can even use SUM to add durations to a date to get a whole new date. With this and one or two other date-specific exceptions, however, you can't mix and match data types. You should work with either numbers or durations, but not both at once. To find out more about doing math with dates and times, see page 726.

Note: SUM also has a discerning cousin, SUMIF, which adds values in cell ranges only when they meet certain conditions. You'll learn more about conditional functions starting on page 731.

COUNT, COUNTA, and COUNTBLANK: How many?

The COUNT function, of course, counts the number of values you give to it, but only if those values are numbers or dates. You can give it other data types, but COUNT quietly ignores them, passing them over to tally only the numbers, dates, and durations in its inbox. For example, the following formula returns 3 because it contains only three numbers; the text and Boolean values get ignored:

```
=COUNT(1, 2, 3, "text", TRUE)
```

When you include one or more range references as arguments for COUNT, the function counts all of the cell values inside. Assuming that all six cells in the range A1:B3 contain numeric values, this formula returns 6:

```
=COUNT(A1:B3)
```

If you want to count cells that contain *any* type of value, including text and Boolean values, then use COUNTA instead ("A" stands for "all"). This function works the same way as COUNT but includes every value and non-empty cell that you give it.

When you find yourself in the throes of nihilism, COUNTBLANK lets you focus instead on the emptiness, returning the number of *empty* cells in a range. Unlike the other counting functions, COUNTBLANK accepts just one argument, a range reference:

```
=COUNTBLANK(A1:B3)
=COUNTBLANK(C)
=COUNTBLANK(4:4)
```

Note: Like SUM, COUNT also has a COUNTIF counterpart that lets you add conditions about which values it should count.

MAX and MIN: Finding the biggest and smallest

The MAX and MIN functions bust out the record books to award the honor for biggest or smallest value in a collection. Like COUNT, these functions accept a list of values, cell references, and cell ranges and then go to work—but only on numbers, dates, and durations (they ignore text and Boolean values). MAX returns the largest number or latest date in the collection, and MIN returns the smallest number or earliest date. For example, this formula examines six cells and hands back the largest value:

```
=MAX(B2:D3, E4, F5)
```

Note: MAX and MIN don't let you mix data types in a single operation. You can compare numbers, dates, or durations, but don't combine them into one calculation.

If you want to include text and Boolean values in the mix, use MAXA or MINA. (Like COUNTA, the "A" is for "all"). However, MAXA and MINA still dispense only numeric values, so don't think that you can use them to find the lowest and highest text values, alphabetically speaking. Instead, text values are assigned the value 0, which may be useful if you want to treat the word "None" as 0 instead of ignoring it, for example. In MAXA and MINA calculations, the Boolean value TRUE counts as 1 and FALSE counts as 0. Empty cells, however, get ignored.

LARGE, SMALL, and RANK: Ranking values

If you think LARGE, SMALL, and RANK is the name of the new Jack Black movie, think again. These three functions let you work with cell values based on their rank in a collection of values. While MAX and MIN let you find only the bookend values for a range of cells, LARGE and SMALL let you find the value that's a specified number of steps from the largest and smallest.

LARGE and SMALL both require two arguments: the range of cells to work with and the ranking of the value to fetch. In the LARGE function, the ranking refers to the number's position when the collection is ordered from large to small. For SMALL, it's the reverse. This formula, for example, finds the second-largest value in a range of cells:

```
=LARGE(B2:B15, 2)
```

LARGE and SMALL can look up the rankings for numbers, dates, and durations, but you can't mix those data types. All cells in the range must have the same data type, or Numbers complains with an error.

While those two functions look up a value based on its rank, RANK does the opposite: It looks up the rank of a value in a range of cells. This formula finds the rank of cell B3 (from highest to lowest) in the range B2:B15:

```
=RANK(B3, B2:B15)
```

Tip: You can also rank values in reverse order, so that rank 1 has the lowest value in the list—when you're ranking golf scores, for example. To do this, add a third argument to the RANK function, setting it to FALSE or 0.

Figure 21-7 shows both the RANK and LARGE functions at work. Say you're pulling together some data about the villains of Megaville and want to show the ranking of each villain by their despicable amount of property damage. In row 2 of the property table, Bruiser's property damage value is shown in cell D2, so you can discover that he's ranked eighth in mayhem using this formula:

```
=RANK(D2, Property Damage)
```

Copy that formula down the Damage Rank column to fill in the rest of the rankings. To call out the top three offenders a bit more, you decide to show the top three damage amounts in a separate table. Those values use the LARGE value to display the first, second, and third highest amounts—for the highest amount, the result is the same as using the MAX function:

```
=LARGE(Property Damage, 1)
=LARGE(Property Damage, 2)
=LARGE(Property Damage, 3)
```

Tip: It would be more enlightening to have Numbers fetch the names of the villains responsible for those damage rankings, too, showing that the evil Dr. VanEsselstyn is the scourge of Megaville. You can do that by using lookups, a topic you'll discover on page 744.

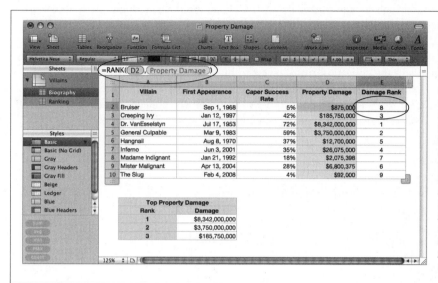

Figure 21-7:
The Damage Rank column in the top table uses the RANK function to find the position of the cell next door in the values of the overall Property Damage column. Although this is information that you could find by sorting the table by its Property Damage column, showing the rank is useful when you want to sort your table some other way. Here, for example, the table is sorted alphabetically by villains' names.

AVERAGE and MEDIAN: Finding the middle value

The average value of a set of numbers is, of course, the sum of the values divided by their count (how many there are). This is something you could easily do with SUM( )/COUNT( ), but Numbers is all about saving you time, so it provides the AVERAGE function to return the mean value (another name for "average") of a collection. AVERAGE accepts a bunch of arguments for processing, and these values may be constants, cell references, range references, or other functions. For example:

```
=AVERAGE(A1, B2:B9, 39.4)
=AVERAGE( C3, SUM(A2:A6) )
```

AVERAGE ignores text and Boolean values, working only with numbers, durations, and dates. In fact, one area where AVERAGE outdoes what you might do with SUM( )/COUNT( ) is when you want to average dates and times. Throw a bunch of dates at AVERAGE, and it finds the "average date" for the group. This has relatively dubious value for more than two dates or times, but it's handy to find the middle point between a pair. Just don't mix numbers, durations, and dates—you have to use the same data type throughout.

Note: The AVERAGEIF function lets you choose to include or exclude values from the average based on a condition of your choice. You'll learn more about this gatekeeper on page 737.

If you want to include text and Boolean values in the calculation, the AVERAGEA function does just that. Just like MAXA and MINA, AVERAGEA treats text and Boolean FALSE as 0, and Boolean TRUE as 1.

A common companion of the average value is the *median*. When you have a few unusually high or low numbers in the collection, which might skew the average value, the median can often give a better picture of where most of the group is actually centered. Instead of boiling the numbers down to a common value as AVERAGE does, MEDIAN finds the middle number in the group. If you ordered the numbers in the collection from lowest to highest, the median would be the number in the center, so that half the numbers in the group are less than the median and half are greater. If there's an even number of values in the collection, MEDIAN averages the two middle numbers to get the median. Here are some examples:

The median of 1, 2, 3, 4, and 5 is 3:

```
=MEDIAN(1, 2, 3, 4, 5)
```

The median of 1, 2, 3, 4, 5, and 6 is 3.5:

```
=MEDIAN(1, 2, 3, 4, 5, 6)
```

The median of 7, 7, 7, 7, and 999 is 7:

```
=MEDIAN(7, 7, 7, 7, 999)
```

Like AVERAGE, the MEDIAN function can work with dates and time durations, too, but ignores text and Boolean values (and there's no MEDIANA alternative).

Multiplying with PRODUCT

The PRODUCT function is a simple replacement for the * multiplication operator (page 682) in the same way that SUM replaces the + operator. Give PRODUCT a collection of values, and it multiplies them together—as long as they're numbers. PRODUCT ignores *all* non-numeric values. This formula multiplies 3, 5, and 10 and hands back the value 150:

```
=PRODUCT(3, 5, 10)
```

Just like the other functions reviewed in this section, PRODUCT can also accept cell references and range references, which let you multiply lots of values in a hurry:

```
=PRODUCT(B1:B15)
```

QUOTIENT and MOD: Divide and conquer

While PRODUCT is more or less a shorthand for the * operator, QUOTIENT does something more than simply act as a substitute for the / division operator. In fact, it often returns an entirely different result than the division operator would. QUOTIENT does *integer division,* which means it lops off the result's decimal value and returns only whole numbers. While 13/5 gets you 2.6, QUOTIENTs' answer is 2:

```
=QUOTIENT(13, 5)
```

This is the kind of division that you learned in grade school where your answer to 13 divided by 5 would be "two with a remainder of three." If you also want to get at that remainder number, you'll have to remember that the high-falutin' name for the remainder is the *modulus*. That's where the MOD function gets its name, and it works just like the QUOTIENT operator except that it returns the remainder. This formula confirms that the remainder of 13/5 is in fact three:

```
=MOD(13, 5)
```

Rounding Numbers

Many numbers, even when very small, are nevertheless unmanageably long thanks to the digits that stretch off to the right of the decimal point. When it comes to *displaying* this fractional portion of a number, Numbers bends to the space available, rounding numbers to fit the enclosing cell (page 592) or letting you set a cell's data format (page 604) to give you control over where to plant a number's decimal point. If you adjust a cell's data format to display its value with three decimal places, for example, then it rounds 3.14159 to 3.142. When you futz with this display format, however, the rounding is only for show; under the hood, the original value is retained, and you can use the cell's value in calculations without losing any precision.

In most cases, that's what you want. But sometimes you need to change the underlying value, too, so that the rounded value gets used in calculations, not just for display. Likewise, if you're doing a calculation inside a formula and need to use a rounded result for another calculation in the same formula, Numbers' display settings won't help you.

Finally, Numbers' standard rounding method rounds numbers up if the next digit is 5 or greater, but what if you want to use a different method? Rounding to the nearest multiple of five, for example? Or always rounding down instead of up? It turns out that there are *lots* of ways to round numbers, and your trusty spreadsheet program gives you no less than 10 functions to bump numbers up or down to the value or decimal accuracy you want. This section takes you through the options.

Simple rounding with ROUND, ROUNDDOWN, and ROUNDUP

The ROUND function is the most commonly used rounding function, because it applies the traditional rounding method, just like your grade-school math teacher taught you. ROUND bumps numbers up when the next digit is five or greater and down when the next digit is less than five. For example, it rounds the number 1.5 up to 2, and the number 1.4 down to 1. ROUND accepts two arguments, the number to round and the number of decimal digits to keep:

```
ROUND(number-to-round, number-of-digits)
```

For example, this formula returns the number 8.46:

```
=ROUND(8.4579341, 2)
```

If you set the number of decimal digits to a *negative* number, the function rounds numbers to the left of the decimal point—rounding to the nearest 10, 100, 1,000, and so on. Another way to think of it is that a negative number in this argument determines how many zeroes appear at the end of the rounded whole number. For example, setting the number of digits to –2 rounds to the nearest hundred; the result has two zeroes to the left of the decimal point. This formula returns 2500:

```
=ROUND(2463.3, -2)
```

As their names suggest, the ROUNDDOWN and ROUNDUP functions always round numbers up or down (respectively), no matter what the next digit is. These alternatives take the same arguments as ROUND, letting you choose how many decimal digits to keep. For example, ROUNDDOWN(1.99, 0) returns 1, and ROUNDUP(1.01, 0) returns 2.

As far as these three ROUND functions are concerned, rounding up really means moving the number away from zero, and rounding down means moving it closer to zero. Because of that, when you work with negative numbers, rounding up actually makes the number *smaller:* –1.5 rounds to –2.

Note: A quirky pair of functions named EVEN and ODD offer a variation on ROUNDUP, rounding a number up to the nearest even or odd number, respectively. For example, EVEN(2.1) gives you 4, and ODD(2.1) gives you 3.

Lopping off decimal digits with INT and TRUNC

The INT (integer) and TRUNC (truncate) functions don't bother with rounding at all. They simply snip off a number's digits at a specified point, ignoring the pruned portion completely.

INT is really a specialized version of TRUNC. Its job is to take a single value and lop off all numbers to the right of the decimal point: 5.954 becomes 5. TRUNC, on the other hand, lets you specify the number of decimal places to keep when you bring out the carving knife. That means these two formulas deliver the same result—5:

```
=INT(5.954)
=TRUNC(5.954, 0)
```

If you instead wanted to shorten the number to one decimal point, this formula would give you 5.9:

```
=TRUNC(5.954, 1)
```

These functions are useful when you're dealing with units that always travel in whole numbers. For example, if your calculations tell you that the average classroom at the sidekick academy can accommodate 20.5 students, INT turns that into 20 so your space planning doesn't include splitting hapless sidekicks down the middle.

Note: At first glance, these functions look like they do the same thing as ROUNDDOWN, and that's true for positive numbers. When you work with negative numbers, though, the behavior is different. While ROUNDDOWN turns −1.5 into −2, INT simply ignores the decimal place and returns −1.

MROUND, CEILING, and FLOOR

The ROUND family of functions is handy for rounding numbers to the nearest decimal or whole number, but what if you want to round a number to some other unit? When you want to round values to the nearest multiple of five or prices to 50-cent increments, MROUND does the trick. MROUND takes two arguments: the number you want to round and the increment (or *factor)* you want to use.

```
MROUND(number-to-round, factor)
```

When you're rounding 128 to the nearest multiple of five, for example, this formula tells you the value is 130:

```
=MROUND(128, 5)
```

The CEILING and FLOOR functions play the ROUNDUP and ROUNDDOWN roles for MROUND, always rounding either up or down to the increment you specify. Using FLOOR for the previous example rounds 128 *down* to 125:

```
=FLOOR(128, 5)
```

One place where these three functions are useful is for calculating prices at round-ish numbers like increments of 25 cents. This formula, for example, rounds the price in cell B2 to the nearest 25-cent value:

```
=MROUND(B2, 0.25)
```

Transforming Text in Formulas

Numbers has a mind for math, sure, but it's also got a talent for juggling words and rearranging letters. The program's many text functions let you work with your cells' text entries to clean up your data, combine prose into new constructions, or pluck a snippet of text from the middle of a longer passage.

The way you'll most commonly work with your text values is to combine them into entirely new values. In the same way that you add numbers with the + operator, you combine text with the *&* operator, which glues two bits of text together. In Numbers, text snippets are called *strings* and combining them is called something only a geek could love: *concatenation.* It works just like addition, only with strings instead of numbers. This formula, for example, concatenates a first name and last name into a full name, putting a space in between for good measure:

```
="Walter" & " " & "Kovacs"
```

FREQUENTLY ASKED QUESTION

Totally Random

How do I generate random numbers?

When you need a quick collection of random numbers for your spreadsheet, turn to the RAND and RANDBETWEEN functions, which pluck numbers from thin air. You might put the resulting numbers to use to build a pop quiz for your math students, or to sort a table in random order, for example.

RAND takes *no* arguments and gives you a random number between 0 and 1 (but never equal to either). For example, this formula returns results like 0.3682823833:

```
=RAND( )
```

More often, though, you'll want a number within some range other than 0 and 1. You can get that by multiplying times the range of numbers you want. To get a random number between 0 and 25, for example, use:

```
=RAND( ) * 25
```

When you want integers between and *including* 1 and 25, you need to do an additional sleight of hand, using INT to chop off the decimals and then add 1:

```
=INT( RAND( ) * 25 ) + 1
```

Because that starts to get messy, Numbers gives you the RANDBETWEEN function, which returns a random number between (and including) its two arguments. This lets you reduce that last noisy example to:

```
=RANDBETWEEN(1, 25)
```

Whichever method you use, you'll soon see that Numbers has a thing for generating random numbers. Every time you add or change *any* formula in your document, Numbers recalculates each and every random number in your spreadsheet, plugging in a new value. The randomness just keeps on coming. To avoid this, you can copy and paste the random numbers back into your document as regular values so that they stop recalculating. To do that, select the cells, choose Edit → Copy and then, with the cells still selected, choose Edit → Paste Values.

Did that earlier mention of shuffling a table's entries in random order pique your interest? To do that, fill a column with random numbers and then sort the table using that column (see page 642 for details about sorting).

That's a bit odd on its own; normally, you'd just type *Walter Kovacs* directly into the cell. But this method becomes much more useful when those first and last name values are replaced with cell references.

```
=B2 & " " & C2
```

Figure 21-8 shows how you can use that recipe to create a new column of full-name values when your table contains columns for first and last names.

As these examples show, you can mix and match both cell values and "literal" text strings in your formulas. The important thing to remember when you type strings directly into the formula is that they need to be contained in quotation marks.

When you combine cell values into a text string, they can contain any type of data—numbers, dates, durations, whatever. When you do that, Numbers converts the value to text, using the same display format as the original cell, even when that's not necessarily that cell's complete underlying value. For example, say the value of cell B2 is 35.4325, but it displays $35.43 because it's set to the currency format. In that case, the following formula returns "Price: $35.43":

```
="Price: " & B2
```

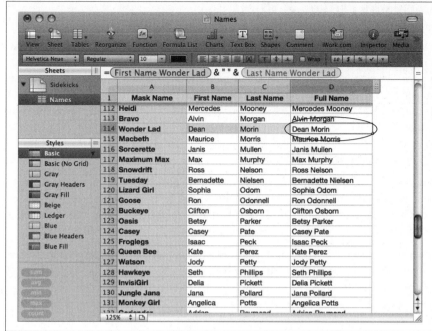

Figure 21-8:
You can use a formula to combine the text values of cells into a single value, like the full names of all the sidekicks at the academy. The formula for Wonder Lad uses the & operator to combine his first and last names with a space in between.

Tip: If you want to use a different format than the one imposed by the cell's data format, then you can use the FIXED or DOLLAR formats to do exactly that. See page 725.

Whatever data types you pour into a concatenation, they always come out as text on the other side. To Numbers, the *numeric* value of "Price: $35.43," for instance, is zero.

When you're feeling especially wordy, you can use the CONCATENATE function, which does the same thing as the & operator, combining the arguments into a single string in the order listed:

```
=CONCATENATE(B2, " ", C2)
```

Note: Sorry, no range references allowed in the CONCATENATE function, only single-cell references.

You can use these methods to glue together as many text strings as you like. Other times, though, you want to rearrange, extract, or substitute text inside a single string. The following pages describe the most commonly used functions for transforming and manipulating text strings. In addition, you can find several others, along with their descriptions, in the Function Browser's Text category.

Working with Portions of Strings

While concatenation lets you stitch strings together, a host of other functions let you slice and dice your text to find and use just a section of a string in your formula. Just as you can combine first and last names into a single full name, you can also go in reverse, splitting a single full name into first and last names. You can even perform a text transplant, surgically removing a portion of the text and replacing it with something else—a miniature Find & Replace right there in your formula cell.

LEFT, MID, and RIGHT: Extracting text

The LEFT, MID, and RIGHT functions let you pluck a portion of text from a string. You choose the number of characters to use from the beginning, middle, or end of the string, and the function returns that slice of text. (These functions leave the original string or cell value untouched and intact.)

When you give LEFT a string and a number of characters, for example, it returns that number of characters from the very beginning (or "left") of the string, leaving aside any text that follows:

    LEFT(string, string-length)

One use of this is to display a brief excerpt from a lengthy text value. If cell B2 contains the entire text of the Gettysburg address, for example, the following formula makes it display only the first 30 characters (including spaces)—"Four score and seven years ago":

    =LEFT(B2, 30)

RIGHT works exactly the same way but returns the text from the end of the original string. When used on the Gettysburg Address cell, this formula returns "shall not perish from the earth.":

    =RIGHT(B2, 32)

Note: If the string length that you give LEFT or RIGHT is the same or longer than the length of the original string, the functions return the entire original string.

Unlike the other two functions, MID isn't tethered to either end of the string. The MID function fetches a run of text from anywhere within the original text. To do this, though, you have to tell MID where you want to start your new string and where you want to end it. You do that by supplying three arguments:

    MID(string, start-position, string-length)

The start-position argument is the number of characters (including spaces, line breaks, tabs, and so on) from the start of the original text. Numbers counts the first character of the string as 1 and moves along from there. The string-length is the number of characters to extract. This formula returns *b*, for example:

    =MID("abc", 2, 1)

LEN, FIND, and SEARCH: Counting characters

The only hitch with the LEFT, RIGHT, and MID characters is that you need to know the precise location and length of the text that you want to grab. Splitting a column of full names into first and last names, for example, is tricky because all the names start and stop at different places in each string. Happily, Numbers gives you three functions that can help you do your letter-counting research to pass the appropriate numbers along to your text-extracting function.

The LEN function (short for LENgth) tells you how many characters are in a string. This formula, for example, returns 3:

    =LEN("abc")

Say you want to trim very long cell entries using the LEFT function and add an "…" (ellipsis) afterward to show that the entry has been clipped. But you don't want to add an ellipsis if the original string is so short that it doesn't *need* to be reduced. The solution is to check the string's length before you clip it, using LEN in combination with the IF function to make the call. You'll learn all about IF starting on page 732, but for now here's a quick example:

    =IF(LEN(B2)>30, LEFT(B2,30) & "...", B2)

This tells Numbers to check to see if the text in cell B2 is longer than 30 characters and, if so, display the first 30 characters followed by an ellipsis. If the text is shorter than 30 characters, Numbers displays the original value of cell B2.

Where LEN is a one-trick pony, always counting to the end of the string, FIND and SEARCH are more flexible. Their job is to find a snippet of text within a string and tell you its position. These functions accept three arguments:

    SEARCH(search-for, source-string, start-position)

The first argument is the text you want to find in the original string: the source string that you provide in the second argument. The third argument—the position where you want to start your search—is optional; if you leave this argument out, Numbers uses the value 1 to start at the beginning of the string. This formula helps you discover that the word "shall" starts at character 16 of the string:

    =SEARCH("shall", "Search and you shall find")

Note: If there's more than one instance of the search text in the original string, SEARCH and FIND both return the position of the first match, counting from the left.

SEARCH and FIND work exactly the same way, except that FIND is more of a stickler. FIND requires *exact*, case-sensitive matches and doesn't allow wildcards (see "Something Wild for Searching Text" on page 741). SEARCH, on the other hand, ignores the difference between upper- and lowercase letters and lets you include wildcards for more flexible searching. Unless it's important to match the case of the text you're hunting for, SEARCH provides the most hassle-free experience.

The project of splitting full names into first and last names gives you a chance to see several of these functions working together. Figure 21-9 shows the final result, using the values in the Full Name column to create separate values for first and last names.

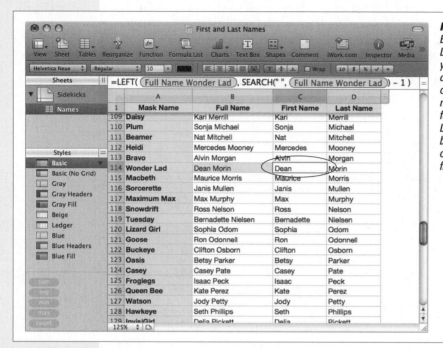

Figure 21-9:
By combining SEARCH, LEFT, RIGHT, and LEN, you can pluck the first and last names from a cell containing only full names. Here, the LEFT function extracts Wonder Lad's first name, Dean, by taking all the characters before the first space in the name.

There are a few steps involved to arrive at the formulas that extract these names. The names split on spaces, of course, so to find the end of the first name, you start by finding the position of the first space in the string. For Wonder Lad, that search looks like this:

```
SEARCH(" ", Full Name Wonder Lad)
```

This formula returns 5, the position of the space immediately after the first name. If you subtract one from that value, you have the length of the first name, enough information to use LEFT to grab it. This formula returns Wonder Lad's first name, Dean:

```
=LEFT( Full Name Wonder Lad, SEARCH(" ", Full Name Wonder Lad) - 1 )
```

The last name starts one character after the space you found in the first step, so you know its position from the start of the string. To use RIGHT to retrieve that last name, however, you need to know its position relative to the *end* of the string. To find the number of spaces to count back from the end of the string to the beginning of the first name, you subtract the space's position from the length of the string:

```
LEN(Full Name Wonder Lad) - SEARCH(" ", Full Name Wonder Lad)
```

That's the length of the last name. Giving that length to RIGHT extracts the name:

```
=RIGHT( Full Name Wonder Lad, LEN(Full Name Wonder Lad) - SEARCH(" ", Full
Name Wonder Lad) )
```

After you've plugged those formulas into Wonder Lad's new columns for first and last name, you can copy them into all of the other students' rows, too, for a tidy collection of split names.

Note: This is a fairly simple example that works best when all names contain only one space. For names with more than one word, these formulas put the first word in the First Name column and all the rest in Last Name.

SUBSTITUTE: Replacing text

The SUBSTITUTE function finds and replaces text in a string, returning the new-and-improved value. The function takes three arguments and an optional fourth:

```
SUBSTITUTE(source-string, find-string, replace-string, occurrence)
```

The first argument is the original string, the second is the string you want to find, and the third is the replacement text to add to the string. The fourth *occurrence* argument is optional and tells Numbers to replace only a specific instance of the text when there are multiple matches. For example, if there are three occurrences of the *find-string* text in the original string, setting the occurrence argument to 2 tells Numbers only to replace the second one. If you leave out the occurrence argument, Numbers replaces all instances of the text.

This formula, for example, displays "Larry, Moe, and Shemp":

```
=SUBSTITUTE("Larry, Moe, and Curly", "Curly", "Shemp")
```

The search is case-sensitive, so the *find-string* text has to match the uppercase and lowercase letters of the original text in order to trigger the substitution. If the find-string text isn't anywhere to be found, the function returns the original string untouched.

Note: The replacement text in a substitution doesn't have to be the same length as the text it replaces: All strings can be whatever size you like.

Cleaning Up Text

Data entry is, alas, a human endeavor, and so it's prone to lots of odd little mistakes—extra spaces, mistyped characters, inconsistent capitalization. Numbers' functions can help you tidy up these typos or otherwise help transform the format of text to meet your specific needs.

UPPER, LOWER, and PROPER: Changing capitalization

Numbers give you three functions to nudge the case of your characters up, down, or a combination of the two. (You can also tell Numbers to adjust the *displayed* capitalization for one or more cells by using the commands in the Format → Font → Capitalization menu, but that doesn't change the text in the actual data as the functions in this section do.)

All three functions take a single argument—the value of the original string—and return the text with its new capitalization:

```
=UPPER(B2)
```

Here are your three capitalization options:

- **UPPER** returns an all-caps version of the original string.

- **LOWER** returns a lowercase version of the original string.

- **PROPER** returns a string with the first letter of every word capitalized and the rest lowercase.

TRIM: Snipping extra white space

Just a single extra space in your data can gum up formatting, choke data lookups (page 744), and foil text substitutions. The TRIM function cleans your data up around the ears, getting rid of extra spaces. Specifically, it removes all spaces before the first character, all spaces after the last, and any double-spaces anywhere in the middle. The result is a spic-n-span text string where every word is separated by only a single space.

TRIM accepts a single argument—the text you want it to tidy up—and returns the trimmed string. This formula returns "Space: the final frontier":

```
=TRIM( "   Space:   the final frontier   ")
```

Formatting Numbers in Text

When you treat a number as text, Numbers has to decide how to format it in your string. As you've seen, the way a number is displayed in a cell is often different than the actual number that's stored away. The real number is always a plain, unadorned figure with no formatting. Even when a currency cell displays $1,250.05, the number's actual value may be something like 1250.04934—no $ dollar sign, no thousand separator, and lots more decimal digits. Right there, Numbers already has two choices about how it should include the number in a string when you call on it: Does it use the formatted currency value or the actual value?

Numbers always guesses that you want the formatted value. If the currency amount mentioned above is in cell B2, then this concatenation results in "Only $1,250.05":

```
="Only " & B2
```

That's a pretty good guess, but it's not always what you'll want. Maybe you'd like to round the number to the nearest dollar, leave off the thousands separator, or eliminate the currency symbol. Numbers gives you two functions—FIXED and DOLLAR—that set the formatting of your number when you use it in a text string.

Note: Even though text and numbers are different data types behind the scenes, Numbers is clever about switching a value's type when it sees that's what you want to do. As described above, when you use the & operator on two numbers to combine them as text, Numbers knows that they should be treated as text strings, and does just that. Likewise, you can add two text strings when they look like numbers. When you have a string like "42" or "$9.99," Numbers is smart enough to know that it should treat it as a number if you try to use it in math. In other words, the program figures out that "42" + "$9.99" = 51.99. You never have to explicitly change a number into text or vice versa unless you want to format a number a certain way (the topic of this section).

FIXED and DOLLAR: Data formats inside formulas

The FIXED function takes a number and turns it into a string based on the specific formatting rules you supply. The function lets you specify the number of decimal places to include and whether or not to include the comma thousands separator in the string. FIXED takes three arguments:

```
FIXED(number, decimal-places, no-commas)
```

The first argument is the number you want to format; the second is the number of decimal places you want it to round the number to (this works just like ROUND on page 715); and the third option excludes a comma thousands separator when you set it to TRUE or 1. (The comma is included if you set the third argument to FALSE or 0.)

Both of the last two arguments are optional. If you leave out the decimal-places value, Numbers rounds to two decimal places. If you leave out the no-commas argument, the comma thousands separator is included in the string.

To return to the previous example, where a currency-formatted cell contains the value 1250.04934, using FIXED on the cell ignores the cell's currency formatting and instead uses the formatting you choose. The following use of FIXED returns a string with the full number value and no comma separator so that the final formula is "Only 1250.04934":

```
="Only " & FIXED(B2, 5, TRUE)
```

This version rounds to the nearest whole number and adds the comma separator to get "Only 1,250":

```
="Only " & FIXED(B2, 0)
```

The DOLLAR function works the same way but adds the $ sign to the value and offers no third argument to include or exclude the thousands separator:

```
DOLLAR(number, decimal-places)
```

Using DOLLAR on the B2 cell containing 1250.04934 gets the string $1,250.05 in this formula:

```
=DOLLAR(B2)
```

Working with Dates and Times

We all understand our calendars and datebooks as grids of days, blocks of time that you can add and subtract. You probably do this math all the time: three days from now; a week from tomorrow; a year ago Tuesday; fifteen shopping days until Christmas. This kind of "date math" is crucial to planning projects and coordinating with others. Turns out that Numbers is great at date math, making it easy to, for example, fetch a date that's a certain number of days (even specifically *business days)* from another date.

Numbers is particularly good at this because it understands calendars differently than us humans. While we think of a date as a day and a time as a specific moment on the clock, Numbers doesn't distinguish between the two. A date is a time is a date. When you enter a date into Numbers, you're entering a time, too; you might not do it explicitly—the time may not even be visible in your spreadsheet—but it's there. If you don't enter a time yourself, then Numbers assumes you mean 12:00 a.m. (midnight) on the date you entered. Likewise, when you enter a time, there's a date attached to it. If you don't specify the date, then Numbers assumes you mean today. In other words, every date in Numbers is actually a very precise moment in time, right down to the millisecond.

For Numbers, the calendar is just one big rolling conveyor belt, measured in milliseconds. This makes it easy for Numbers to move back and forth in time—whether you want to leap ahead a few years or jump back a few seconds, Numbers just rolls the conveyor belt back or forth and spits out the new time in any format you want, as a date, a time, both, the day of the week—whatever.

This section introduces you to doing math with dates, times, and durations, and explains functions you can use to get information about any moment in time that you care to zoom in on. Fire up the time machine—it's time to explore Numbers' date functions.

Note: This section covers most of Numbers' date and time functions, and certainly the most common ones. To check out the stragglers not included here, check out the "Date and Time" category in the Function Browser.

Doing Math with Dates and Times

Numbers provides several functions for working with dates and times, and you'll learn all about them in the next few pages. First, though, there's a lot you can do with the arithmetic operators and math functions you've already seen. This section explores how you can add, subtract, average, and order dates, times, and durations.

Frequently, this section uses the term *date value*, but that's simply shorthand for "date-and-time value." Any math that you can do with a calendar date, you can also do with a time of day. As explained earlier, Numbers doesn't see the difference.

Tip: Don't forget that when your formula returns a date, time, or duration value, you can adjust that value's formatting by editing the cell format in the Cells Inspector.

Adding or subtracting durations from a date value

When a formula adds a duration value to a date value, Numbers returns a brand new date value equal to the original date moved into the future by the amount of time in the duration. Add a day to January 8 and Numbers returns January 9. Add an hour to 3:00 p.m. and Numbers returns 4:00 p.m.

This is a convenient way to set the due date on an invoice, for example. When you put today's date in row B3, this formula returns the date 30 days in the future:

```
=B3 + "30 days"
```

As the example above shows, you can just type a duration and its units directly into the formula, but *you have to put it in quotes.* You can type the duration's units in any of the formats shown in Table 21-1—they're the same units you can use to type a value into a cell using the duration cell format (page 609).

Tip: Numbers lets you use a shorthand for working with durations in days. When you add a regular number to a date, Numbers interprets the number as days: "1/8/2010" + 2 gives you the date January 10, 2010.

Table 21-1. *Duration Units*

Duration	Accepted units
Week	week, weeks, wk, wks, w
Day	day, days, d
Hour	hour, hours, hr, hrs, h
Minute	minute, minutes, min, mins, m
Second	second, seconds, sec, secs, s
Milliseconds	millisecond, milliseconds, ms

You can mix and match the durations that you add, either in the same text string or in several. If you want to find a time a certain number of days, hours, minutes, and seconds later than the time shown in cell B4, for example, any of these formulas will do it:

```
=B4 + "1d 1h 2m 30s"
=B4 + "1 day" + "1:02:30"
=B4 + "1 day" + "1 hour" + "2 minutes" + "30 seconds"
```

Of course, you can also use a duration value from a cell reference, too:

```
=B4 + B5
```

Subtraction works the same way to move back in time from a fixed date:

```
=B4 - "3 days"
```

Note: Numbers doesn't let you add two dates (although you *can* subtract one date from another, as you'll see shortly). This means that you can't include more than one date when adding durations.

The ability to add durations to a date to get a new date makes it convenient to rough out a timeline for project planning, as Figure 21-10 demonstrates.

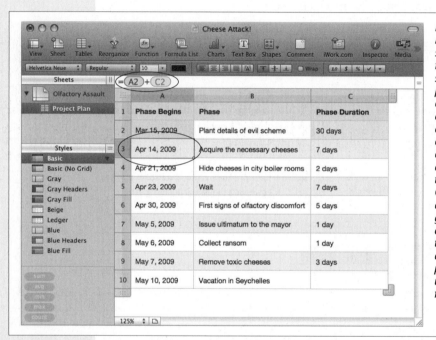

Figure 21-10:
Mister Malevolent is sketching out a timeline for his most insidious scheme yet. To start, he puts a date in the left column of the first row and an estimated duration in the right column. In the next column, he adds the date and the duration from the previous row. Copying the formula down the date column gives the estimated start dates of each phase of the plot. Adjusting the duration of any of the phases automatically updates every date that follows in a ripple effect.

WORKDAY: Leave your weekends out of it

For project plans like Mister Malevolent's dairy-based scheme, it's often more accurate to count only *business* days so the project plan doesn't include weekends. (Even super villains enjoy a day off—what's the point of all that evil if you can't kick back?) That's where the WORKDAY function comes in, ready to monitor your office hours and protect your weekends.

The WORKDAY function accepts three arguments: the date you're counting from, the number of workdays you want to add or subtract, and an optional argument of excluded dates:

```
WORKDAY(date, work-days, exclude-dates)
```

The second argument of the WORKDAY function can be either a regular number (the number of days) or a duration value. A number of days is straightforward and easy to understand: 2 means two workdays, period. When you use a duration value, however, it gets trickier. No matter what time unit the duration value is displayed in—days, weeks, or milliseconds—Numbers first translates the value into days and then plugs that value in as the number of workdays. If your duration is displayed in hours, for example, you might be tempted to think those are work hours—making 24 hours the same as three business days, for example. But that's *not* how it works. In that case, Numbers translates 24 hours into 1 day, which tells WORKDAY to count one workday from the start date.

In Mister Malevolent's project plan, you can replace the formula that adds the date and duration from the row above with the WORKDAY function. Here, the duration field is set to display the number of days, so the confusion described above isn't an issue. For example, the formula for row 3, where Mister Malevolent acquires the necessary cheeses, would be:

```
=WORKDAY(A2, C2)
```

The WORKDAY function's optional *exclude-dates* argument is useful to add holidays or other days when working is so out of the question that Mr. Malevolent would get positively medieval on you if you asked him to work then. This argument can be a cell or range reference to one or more date values, or you can type it as an *array* of dates, like so:

```
=WORKDAY( A2, C2, {"4/12/2009", "5/1/2009"} )
```

Tip: To find the number of workdays between two dates, use the NETWORKDAYS function: NETWORK-DAYS(*start-date, end-date*). Not to be confused with a yet-to-be invented function that performs some kind of social hobnobbing; this puppy returns the net number of days between start and end date.

Subtracting one date value from another

When you subtract one date or time value from another, the result is a duration value, a useful way to quickly see the elapsed time between two dates or times—the time it takes Wonder Lad to run the 40-yard dash, the billable hours you worked for a client before lunchtime, the number of days until you go on vacation.

Using math functions with date values

As mentioned earlier in this chapter, the SUM, MAX, MIN, and AVERAGE functions all work with dates and durations, too. You can use MAX or MIN to find the latest or earliest date or time in a series, or use AVERAGE to find the midpoint between two dates. The SUM function adds dates, durations, and numbers, with the same result you've just seen for using the + operator with those values. Whether you use SUM or + with dates and durations, a few caveats apply:

• You *can't* sum date values with other date values.

- You *can* sum a date value with durations, as long as only one date value is involved.

- You *can* sum a date value with regular numbers as long as only one date value is involved (numbers get treated like durations in days).

- You *can't* sum regular numbers with durations unless one of the values is also a date. (In that case, the numbers are treated like days.)

Building Dates and Times in Formulas

You can use cell references in formulas to refer to date values, as you've seen, but you can also add them directly to your formulas. The most direct way to do this is to add a date or time (or both) as a text string. You can type this string in any of the formats that you'd type a date or time into a table cell (see page 607). For example, any of these formulas return the date value for January 9, 2010:

```
="1/8/2010" + 1
="January 8, 2010" + 1
="01-08-2010" + 1
="1-8-10" + 1
```

Numbers also provides four functions to insert a date value into a formula. TODAY and NOW both insert the current date. TODAY sets the time to 12:00 a.m., and NOW sets the time to, you guessed it, the current time. The values inserted into these functions update each time you open the spreadsheet or add or update a new function. Neither of these functions requires any arguments, but you still have to include their parentheses. For example, this formula shows you the amount of time that's elapsed since the day began at midnight:

```
=NOW( ) - TODAY( )
```

You could insert these functions into a formula cell to display today's date on an invoice or other correspondence, or use a Date & Time formatted text field to do the same job (see page 579).

Building a date using the string formats shown above is almost always the easiest way to go, but Numbers also gives you the DATE and TIME functions that you can use to construct date values:

```
DATE(year, month, day)
TIME(hour, minute, second)
```

For the DATE function, the year value has to be the *full* year. If you enter *10* thinking you're going to get 2010, you'll be 2000 years off—Numbers sets your date to the year 10; enter *2010* instead.

Extracting Date and Time Info

Numbers provides a slew of functions to give you lots of details about any individual date or time value:

- **YEAR(date).** The four-digit year.

- **MONTH(date).** The number of the month. MONTH("April 15, 2010") returns 4.

- **MONTHNAME(date).** The name of the month.

- **WEEKNUM(date).** The number of the week within the date's year.

- **DAY(date).** The numeric day of the month.

- **DAYNAME(date).** The weekday name. You can also use a number from 1 to 7 as the argument: DAYNAME(1) is Sunday, for example, and DAYNAME(7) is Saturday.

- **WEEKDAY(date).** Returns a number from 1 to 7 corresponding to the day of the week for that date. The standard setting sets Sunday to 1, but you can use an optional second argument to set Monday to 1 and Sunday to 7—WEEKDAY (date, 2)—or set Monday to 0 and Sunday to 6—WEEKDAY(date, 3).

- **HOUR(date).** Returns the hour as a number from 0 to 23.

- **MINUTE(date).** Returns the minute.

- **SECOND(date).** Returns the second.

- **DUR2DAYS(duration).** Converts a duration value to the number of days.

- **DUR2WEEKS(duration).** Converts a duration value to the number of weeks.

- **DUR2HOURS(duration).** Converts a duration value to the number of hours.

- **DUR2MINUTES(duration).** Converts a duration value to the number of minutes.

- **DUR2SECONDS(duration).** Converts a duration value to the number of seconds.

- **DUR2MILLISECONDS(duration).** Converts a duration value to the number of milliseconds.

What IF: Adding Logic to Formulas

All the functions you've seen so far have performed straight-up calculations. They've taken a set of values, worked a predefined transformation on them, and returned the value, no questions asked. For the functions in the Function Browser's "Logical and Information" category, however, asking questions is the whole point. These discriminating functions sit your data down for an interview, ask probing questions, and then decide what to do based on what they discover:

- *"Is your grade higher than 93 percent? Yes? Congratulations, you get an A."*

- *"Have you paid your January bill? No? The amount goes into accounts receivable."*

- *"Has this check cleared? Yes? Add it to the reconciled balance in the check register."*

This category of functions imposes true-or-false conditions on your data: If yes, do this; if no, do that. It's like the game Twenty Questions: The "questions" these functions ask can be complex, but the answers are always simple: yes or no. It sounds basic, but the result can be quite powerful, even letting you sift through mountains of data to pluck out summaries of what's found within. Before tackling the mountains, though, you'll start with a molehill, learning how to set a single cell's value based on one or more conditions.

Setting Conditions with the IF Function

The IF function is Numbers' general-purpose decision-maker. It checks to see if some *condition* is true and, based on the outcome, it does either one thing or the other. You make this kind of decision every morning: If it's raining, you take an umbrella on the way out the door; otherwise, you leave it at home. The IF function makes the decision look like this:

```
=IF(Is it raining?, Take umbrella, Leave umbrella at home)
```

The IF function takes three arguments: the condition to be examined, the "yes" value, and the "no" value. If the condition is true, the function hands back the "yes" value; otherwise, the "no" value. The decision path is simple—just two options; the trick is knowing how to set the right condition.

Using comparison operators

A condition is a statement that is either true or false. Two is less than one: FALSE. Two plus two is four: TRUE. These are examples of Boolean values: TRUE.

Remember Boolean values? You learned about the data type with the funny name way back in Chapter 18 when you read about cell formats. As you discovered then, you can use a checkbox to set a Boolean TRUE/FALSE value in a spreadsheet cell. The other way to create a Boolean value is to build a condition using Numbers' *comparison operators*. Table 21-2 lists all these operators, which you can use to build conditions for your IF functions (and a few others, too).

Table 21-2. Numbers' Comparison Operators

Operator	When you're asking if...	Example	Result
=	Two values are equal	1=2	FALSE
<>	Two values are not equal	1<>2	TRUE
>	The first value is greater than the second	1>2	FALSE
<	The first value is less than the second	1<2	TRUE
>=	The first value is greater than or equal to the second	1>=2	FALSE
<=	The first value is less than or equal to the second	1<=2	TRUE

The Example column in Table 21-2 shows a range of simple conditions using numbers, but conditions can use a wide range of values on either side of the operator: cell references, functions, text strings, dates, functions, a calculation—anything that returns a value that can be compared. A condition that asks if A2 is equal to B2, for example, looks like this:

```
A2 = B2
```

To ask if A2 is more than double the sum of column B, you'd do this:

```
A2 > SUM(B) * 2
```

Tip: You might recognize these comparison operators as symbols from math class, but Numbers puts them to work with text, dates, and times, too. The greater-than and less-than operators compare text alphabetically (a is less than b), and dates and times chronologically (yesterday is less than tomorrow).

You can put these conditions into the IF function's argument list just as you see them here. For example, this formula tells you whether A2 and B2 contain the same value, and displays the word Equal in a cell if so and Unequal if not:

```
=IF(A2=B2, "Equal", "Unequal")
```

The condition in the function's first argument can be anything you like as long as it results in a TRUE or FALSE Boolean value. Since checkboxes set Boolean values, for example, that means you can use a cell reference as your condition argument when the cell contains a checkbox. Figure 21-11 shows a very simple example of this.

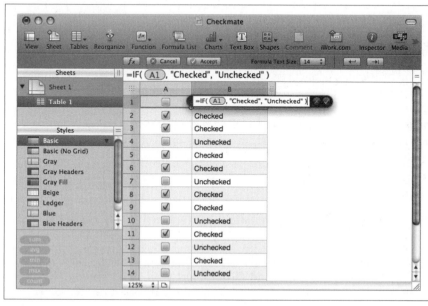

Figure 21-11:
Any Boolean value can be used as a condition in the IF function, including the values of checkbox cells. The second column of this table displays its value depending on whether the checkbox next door is turned on or off.

The example in Figure 21-11 isn't exactly the most practical use for deploying a checkbox to control calculations. A check register offers a slightly more sophisticated example. Say that you're keeping all your checking-account transactions in a table. As usual, when it's time to balance your checkbook by comparing your Numbers check register with your bank statement, your outstanding checks prevent your balance from matching up. Adding a column to store the running balance of cleared transactions will help make sure that you're in sync with the bank. You can use a checkbox and an IF function to automatically update that balance, as shown in Figure 21-12.

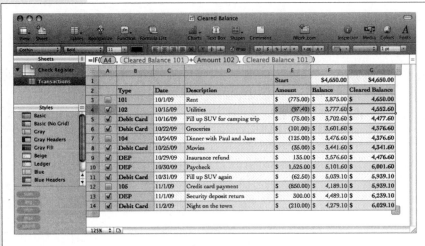

Figure 21-12:
Click the checkbox in the left column to indicate that a transaction has cleared the bank. The formula in the Cleared Balance column adds the transaction value to the column's running balance only if the checkbox is turned on; otherwise, it keeps the previous row's balance. Since the column tallies only cleared transactions, the balance at the bottom of that column should be the same as the balance at the bank.

Testing multiple conditions with AND and OR

A handful of Numbers' functions are specifically designed to be used as conditions in IF functions, and always return Boolean values. You can use these functions to build more complex conditions than what you might do with a single comparison operator. The AND and OR functions are particularly helpful here, letting you combine several comparisons at once to see if any or all of them are true:

- **AND** accepts two or more conditions as its arguments and returns TRUE if *all* of the conditions are true. If even one of the conditions is false, the function returns FALSE.

- **OR** also accepts two or more conditions but returns TRUE if *any* of the conditions are true. A single yes vote carries the day.

Say you've loaded a table with info about all the promising singles who've responded to your latest personal ad. If this effort is all about finding your sugar daddy or mama, you could set up a "Make a date" rule based on the contents of the Income (B) and Occupation (C) columns. When you're seeking a successful rock guitarist, the condition one of your suitors has to meet might look like this:

```
AND(B2>100000, C2="Rock Guitarist")
```

Tip: Don't include commas in your argument numbers. If you type *100,000* in the function above, Numbers sees the comma as an argument separator, and suddenly you're looking for someone who makes anything more than $100/year. And baby, you're too good for that riff-raff.

If an astronaut would also suit your profile, you could change the second argument to an OR function:

```
AND( B2>100000, OR(C2="Rock Guitarist", C2="Astronaut") )
```

As you see here, you can combine AND and OR functions to build fairly complex conditions. In this example, the function returns TRUE only for an income of more than $100,000 *and* an occupation of either guitarist *or* astronaut (no wonder you're still single). Because the whole shebang returns a TRUE or FALSE value (the result of the AND function), it qualifies as a condition that you can include in your IF function.

```
=IF(
    AND(
        B2>100000,
        OR(C2="Rock Guitarist", C2="Astronaut")
    ),
    "Make a date!",
    "Keep looking"
)
```

Tip: As you start building even mildly complex IF functions, they quickly devolve into lengthy tangles of parentheses, commas and operators. To keep yourself sane and have a chance at making sense of your own formulas, it's a good idea to apply some extra formatting as shown in the example above.

Numbers ignores any white space that you add between the elements of your functions—including spaces, returns, line breaks, and tabs. The Formula Bar even anticipates this need by giving you buttons to press to insert line breaks and tab stops. Put those buttons to good use with some wisely placed indents to break out your conditions and arguments. You can also press Option-Return or Option-Tab to insert line breaks and tab stops from either the Formula Bar or Formula Editor.

Other condition functions

In addition to AND and OR, Numbers provides a handful of other TRUE/FALSE functions that you can use as conditions in your IF functions:

- **ISBLANK** returns TRUE if the cell-reference argument is empty, otherwise FALSE. For example, ISBLANK(A1).

- **ISERROR** returns TRUE if the argument results in an error, otherwise FALSE. To see if you're going to hit a "division by zero" error, for example: ISERROR(A1/B1).

- **ISEVEN** returns TRUE if the argument is an even number.

- **ISODD** returns—you guessed it—TRUE if the argument is an odd number (as in "not even" rather than "peculiar").

- **NOT** flips the value of a Boolean value. NOT(TRUE) returns FALSE, and NOT(FALSE) returns TRUE.

The IFERROR function is typically handier than ISERROR because it handles the case where you'd normally use ISERROR, only in less space. IFERROR takes two arguments, testing the first to see if it returns an error. If you're error-free, the function returns the value of that first argument; otherwise, it returns the value of the second argument. For example, say you want to dodge the dreaded "division by zero" error that so often finds its way into table cells. Here are two examples of how you'd use the two functions to dodge the error by inserting 0 into the cell when division isn't possible:

```
=IFERROR(A1/B1, 0)
=IF( ISERROR(A1/B1), 0, A1/B1 )
```

Nesting IF functions to give multiple instructions

So far you've seen how an IF function can choose between two options. That might be useful in a grade-book scenario if you want to show whether a student has passed or failed Basic Heroics. But it would be even better if you could figure out the actual letter grade based on his final percentage grade. You can do just that by *nesting* IF functions, fitting one into another like a series of Russian dolls. For example, you already know how to find out whether a grade is an A:

```
=IF( F3 >= 90%, "A", "Not an A" )
```

When you replace the no value "Not an A" with another IF function, you can give Numbers additional conditions to try:

```
=IF( F3 >= 90%, "A", IF(F3 >= 80%, "B", "Lower than B") )
```

Numbers tries that second IF function only when the first condition is false: It's not an A, is it a B? As soon as it hits a true condition, the function returns the true-value argument for the corresponding IF function. If none of the conditions are true, the false-value argument of the final IF function is returned ("Lower than B" in the example above). You can keep on nesting values to get all your grades. With a little extra formatting, that looks like so:

```
=IF(     F3 >= 90%, "A",
     IF( F3 >= 80%, "B",
     IF( F3 >= 70%, "C",
     IF( F3 >= 60%, "D",
     "F" ) ) )
   )
```

As you start stacking up parentheses with formulas like this one, it's important to make sure that every opening parenthesis is matched by a closing parenthesis and vice versa. Numbers helps you track your parenthetical progress by highlighting the matching open parenthesis every time you type a closing one in the Formula Bar or Formula Editor.

Tip: As you might guess, this can get pretty hairy when you add more than just a few nested IF functions. When you have *lots* of conditions you want to test, it's probably better to create a separate table that maps one value to another (the minimum grades for each grade level, in this example) and then do *lookups* against that table. That's the approach the Numbers' Grade Book template uses; you'll learn more about lookups starting on page 744.

COUNTIF, SUMIF, and AVERAGEIF for Smart Summaries

For such a simple concept, the IF function is extraordinarily flexible, but it still has its drawbacks. Most notably, it's lousy at trying to process lots of values inside a *range* of cells. If you want to do something simple like show a count of how many A's were handed out in the Basic Heroics class, IF can't manage the job. It doesn't know how to sift through the grade column to test each individual cell value and then add up the matching values. For that type of job, you need to turn to IF's bean-counting cousins COUNTIF, SUMIF, and AVERAGEIF.

These functions do the same basic job as COUNTA, SUM, and AVERAGEA, except that those sans-if counterparts blithely include each and every value in the specified range. By contrast, the COUNTIF, SUMIF, and AVERAGEIF functions let you set a condition that each value has to satisfy in order to be included in the calculation. When you're counting the grade column, for example, COUNTIF lets you limit the count to values that match the letter A.

All of these functions require two arguments: the range of cells to calculate and a condition to use to test each of those cells. This formula counts all "A" values in the range F3:F28:

    =COUNTIF(F3:F28, "=A")

The condition in the second argument looks different than the ones you've seen so far—not only is it quoted, but it's missing the left side of the = comparison operator. That's because Numbers treats each value in the first argument's range as the left side of that condition. It steps through each value individually and plugs it into the comparison. If the value is A, it's counted; otherwise, Numbers moves on to the next value.

If you don't include a comparison operator in the second argument, then Numbers treats the whole argument as a value to match, the same as if you had included the = comparison operator. That means that you could write your A-counting formula like this, dropping the = sign:

    =COUNTIF(F3:F28, "A")

Now that you're just dealing with plain values in that second operator, you can put anything you like in there—a cell reference, a function, a number, text. When that comparison value matches a value in the specified range, Numbers adds it to the tally. To count all cells in the range that match the value of one specific cell, for example, you do this:

```
=COUNTIF(F3:F28, C2)
```

You can also construct a condition by building a text string that looks like a condition. If you decide you want to count values that are greater than the C2 cell value, for example, you can't just use ">C2" as the condition, because Numbers thinks you're talking about the *text* C2, not the cell. Instead, you can build the condition text by combining ">" with the value of the C2 cell like so:

```
=COUNTIF( F3:F28, ">" & C2 )
```

Adding and averaging a row or column based on values of another

You can use SUMIF and AVERAGEIF to do the same kind of thing as the COUNTIF examples shown above, tallying the values of a range when those values meet a certain condition. For example, you might use AVERAGEIF to do the average of only passing scores in a Grades column:

```
=AVERAGEIF(Grades, ">60%")
```

Often, though, it's more useful to add or average a row or column when *another* column meets a condition. Say you have a table containing a list of customers' unpaid invoices. With hundreds of outstanding bills, it would be handy to have an easy way to look up the total owed by an individual customer. Using categories (page 646), you could group and subtotal invoices by customer name, but you want a system where you can just type in a customer name and see the total amount they owe.

To allow exactly this kind of calculation, SUMIF and AVERAGEIF take a third optional argument. When you provide it, you tell Numbers that you want to set your "if" condition on a different range of cells (the *test values*) than the ones you're actually adding up (the *add values*). When you use this format, the cell range in the first argument is the collection of test values that determine whether to add individual cells in the third argument, which is also a cell range:

```
=SUMIF(test-values, condition, add-values)
```

This might sound complicated, but it's easy to understand when you see it in action. In the invoice example, you want to add Amount Due values only when the Customer Name column in the same row matches a specific customer. So the formula would look like this to add up the amount owed by Acme Anvils:

```
=SUMIF(Customer, "Acme Anvils", Amount Due)
```

But why edit the formula every time you want to see the amount for a different customer? Better to let yourself simply type any customer name into a cell and make the formula look up their balance. To do that, swap out "Acme Anvils" with a cell reference, with the result shown in Figure 21-13:

```
=SUMIF(Customer, A2, Amount Due)
```

Note: The two cell ranges have to be the same height and width. In the formula above, the ranges are both full columns, so they're the same size. When you're working with a more specific range of cells, however, be sure that they're the same dimensions. For example, using A1:A8 and B2:B9 works just fine (both are a column of eight cells), but combining A1:A3 and B1:B2 results in an error because they're different heights.

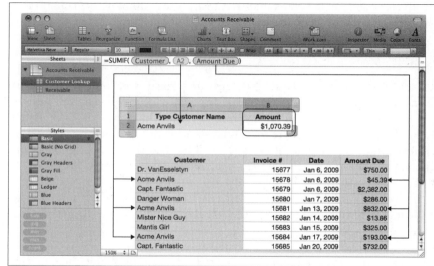

Figure 21-13:
When you type a customer name into the top table (cell A2), the formula in the Amount cell (circled) fetches the customer's invoice amounts from the bottom table and adds them up for a tidy summary of the amount due.

An especially common use of SUMIF works in combination with checkboxes—adding a column of numbers, for example, when their values are either checked or unchecked. This lets you add a running tally to checklists, or work through "what if?" scenarios: What's the outstanding balance of your unpaid expenses this month? How much will it cost to do your selected home improvements this year? What are the expenses for the wedding guests who have RSVP'd? This is a common enough scenario that the Blank template even gives you a predefined table dedicated to checklist addition. Choose Sums Checklist from the Tables pop-up button in the toolbar, and Numbers gives you a table that adds up the last column of figures for checked rows only. Behind the scenes, it's the SUMIF function that makes that table tick.

Adding more conditions: COUNTIFS, SUMIFS, and AVERAGEIFS

COUNTIF, SUMIF, and AVERAGEIF are great at zeroing in on a slice of your data, but they're limited by their ability to apply only one "filter." In the invoice example you just saw, SUMIF can winnow the invoices based on one condition, the customer name. But what if you also want to limit the results to invoices more than 30 days old, to show the total past due? In that case, you need to add a second condition, which you can do by adding an "S" to your trusty COUNTIF, SUMIF, and AVERAGEIF functions.

In SUMIFS and AVERAGEIFS, the first argument is the range of cells to tally, followed by two or more arguments that describe the test values and conditions:

```
=SUMIFS(add-values, test-values1, condition1, test-values2, condition2, ...)
```

In the invoice example, the add-values argument is the Amount Due column and you want to set conditions on the Customer and Date columns. A first pass at this looks something like this:

```
=SUMIFS(Amount Due, Customer, A2, Date, "<1/6/10")
```

That does the job, adding up amounts only for invoices with the matching customer name and dates from before January 6, 2010. But that means you have to edit the formula every time you want to refresh the past-due amount. Yuck. Better instead to have the formula figure the 30-day date for you. You can build the condition text within the function itself, but you'll need to rely on a little bit of the date math you learned back on page 727, subtracting 30 days from NOW( ):

```
"<" & ( NOW( ) - "30d" )
```

Plugging that condition into the function, you get:

```
=SUMIFS( Amount Due, Customer, A2, Date, "<" & ( NOW( ) - "30d" ) )
```

You could keep on adding additional pairs of test values and conditions, too, to winnow down the conditions even further. But you could also have fewer—all of these IFS functions work just fine with only one condition. When you do that, the result is the same as doing a SUMIF with its single condition, although the order of the arguments is different. This formula, for example, does the same thing as the SUMIF formula that you saw in the last section to tally one customer's amount due:

```
=SUMIFS(Amount Due, Customer, A2)
```

It's worth noting, too, that the test-value ranges don't have to be different than the range of cells you want to add up. This is useful, for example, if you want to do your math on values in a specific range. To add up the amount due on invoices billing between $50 and $100, for example, you could do this:

```
=SUMIFS(Amount Due, Amount Due, ">50", Amount Due, "<100")
```

This tells Numbers to do both its addition and tests on the same column, adding only values that are more than $50 but also less than $100.

The AVERAGEIFS function works the same way, averaging the values in the first argument based on the test values and conditions that follow. The COUNTIFS function, however, follows a different pattern, completely tossing out the first argument you use in SUMIFS and AVERAGEIFS, so that the arguments contain only test values and conditions:

```
=COUNTIFS(test-values1, condition1, test-values2, condition2, ...)
```

With its marching orders in hand, COUNTIFS steps through the test-value cell ranges and increments its counter every time all the conditions are true. This is especially useful for setting conditions in columns; COUNTIFS delivers the count for all rows where the value is true. To show the count of Captain Fantastic's past-due invoices (older than 30 days), this formula does the trick:

```
=COUNTIFS( Customer, "Capt. Fantastic", Date, "<" & (NOW( )-"30d") )
```

GEM IN THE ROUGH

Something Wild for Searching Text

The COUNTIF, SUMIF, and AVERAGEIF functions (as well as their "IFS" siblings) know a special trick for matching text values: They let you use *wildcards* to find loose matches. Just like wildcards in a card game can represent any card you want, these little jokers are stand-ins for any text character. Numbers has two wildcards:

- The **?** (question mark) matches any single character. "?uper" refers to any value that begins with a single character followed by "uper." *Super* and *duper* match, but *pauper* doesn't because it starts with *two* characters before "uper" (you'd need "??uper" or "p?uper" to match pauper).

- The ***** (asterisk) matches any number of characters, or none at all. "astro*" refers to any value that begins with "astro," including astro itself. *Astronomy, astroturf,* and *astronaut* all match, but *gastronomy* doesn't. To match all these options, including *gastronomy*, "*astro*" does the trick, matching any value that contains "astro" anywhere in the word.

To generate a count of Megaville heroes whose names start with "Super" for example, you'd use COUNTIF on a column of names. If the column was named Hero, the formula would look like this:

```
=COUNTIF(Hero, "Super*")
```

(In Numbers, wildcard text matches aren't case-sensitive. "Super" matches "super" and "SUPER".)

This turns into a bit of a headache when you actually want to search for text that includes a question mark or asterisk—Numbers treats your ? and * as wildcards. To signal that you want to treat these characters as actual text, add a ~ tilde in front of them:

```
=COUNTIF(A2:A9, "Question~?")
```

Pulling it all together: Using IF math to summarize data

Say that baseball season is in full swing at the sidekick academy (sorry, no superpowers allowed on the field). The coach of the Sidekick Academy Sidecars has asked you to help track a few of the team's basic batting statistics. He has diligently recorded each and every batting appearance of every Sidecar player into a simple table with hundreds of entries (see Figure 21-14), but he needs help plucking out the stats for individual players. Coach has called you in to pinch-hit as team statistician.

Figure 21-14:
Coach's simple table shows every batting appearance for the season. If a player gets a hit, the base number is entered in the Base column (4 is a home run). Walks and strikeouts are indicated with checkboxes, and if a hit drives any runners home, the number is noted in the RBI (runs batted in) column.

	A	B	C	D	E
1	Player	Base	Walk	Strikeout	RBI
2	Wonder Lad	1	☐	☐	
3	Battle Boy	2	☐	☐	
4	Drum Major		☐	☑	
5	Buckeye		☑	☐	
6	Skippy	1	☐	☐	2
7	Spyglass		☐	☐	
8	Spiderlegs		☐	☑	
9	Fast Track	1	☐	☐	
10	Hocus Pocus		☐	☐	
11	Wonder Lad	2	☐	☐	
12	Battle Boy	2	☐	☐	1
13	Drum Major		☐	☑	
14	Buckeye		☐	☐	
15	Skippy	1	☐	☐	
16	Spyglass		☐	☐	
17	Spiderlegs		☐	☑	
18	Fast Track	1	☐	☐	
19	Hocus Pocus		☐	☐	
20	Wonder Lad		☑	☐	

Create a separate table to hold your summary stats. The table will show at bats, numbers of hits, batting averages, and tallies for singles, doubles, triples, home runs, walks, strikeouts, and RBIs, as shown in Figure 21-15. When you're done, the table will consist almost entirely of COUNTIF, SUMIF, and COUNTIFS functions to gather the statistics for each individual player.

Note: It's typically a good strategy to put this table on a separate sheet for your polished report, letting you tuck all the raw data out of sight in the back. For this example, though, both tables stay within easy view on the same sheet.

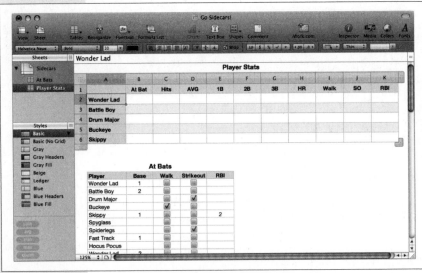

Figure 21-15:
The Player Stats table at the top of the sheet will hold the individual stats culled from the At Bats table below. In each row, formulas will use the player's name in the left column to boil down the individual stats with the help of the COUNTIF, SUMIF, and COUNTIFS functions.

Start by building the statistics for a single player, the amazing Wonder Lad. Add his name to the left column, and you'll use that cell to gather and tally his info from Coach's data table. Since you'll be using this same player condition in nearly all of the functions in this row's cells, it's a good idea to use absolute references (page 693) for the referenced columns. That way, you can reuse the condition text in all your columns. Your condition will look for rows in the At Bats table that contain the player's name (Wonder Lad in cell $A2) in the Player column (At Bats :: $Player).

The number of at bats is a simple count of all of Wonder Lad's batting appearances. Since Coach has listed every appearance in its own row, you can get that stat by using all the times Wonder Lad's name appears in the table. COUNTIF is the tool for the job:

```
=COUNTIF(At Bats :: $Player, $A2)
```

Note: Baseball statistics sticklers will no doubt be pained by the inclusion of walks in the at-bats tally, but we're keeping things simple here.

Hits are a count of all Base column values higher than zero. That means you're counting rows that match two conditions (in the Player column and the Base column). Time to call COUNTIFS from the bullpen:

```
=COUNTIFS(At Bats :: $Player, $A2, At Bats :: $Base, ">0")
```

The 1B (single), 2B (double), 3B (triple), and Home Run columns are also counts of the Base column, but require matches for specific values—the number of bases in the hit. Here are the formulas for the four columns:

```
=COUNTIFS(At Bats :: $Player, $A2, At Bats :: $Base, 1)
=COUNTIFS(At Bats :: $Player, $A2, At Bats :: $Base, 2)
=COUNTIFS(At Bats :: $Player, $A2, At Bats :: $Base, 3)
=COUNTIFS(At Bats :: $Player, $A2, At Bats :: $Base, 4)
```

AVG is the batting average—nothing fancy here, just the Hits cell divided by the At Bats cell (C2/B2). But it's a good idea to make sure you avoid a division by zero error, which would happen for players who haven't yet stepped up to the plate:

```
=IFERROR(C2/B2, 0)
```

The Walks and SO (strikeouts) columns are counts of checked (TRUE) values in the corresponding columns of the At Bats table:

```
=COUNTIFS(At Bats :: $Player, $A2, At Bats :: Walk, TRUE)
=COUNTIFS(At Bats :: $Player, $A2, At Bats :: Strikeout, TRUE)
```

The RBI value is the sum of the player's runs batted in from the At Bats table:

```
=SUMIF(At Bats :: $Player, $A2, At Bats :: RBI)
```

You've now got an entire row of Wonder Boy's personal batting stats. To get the rest of the team, fill in the left column with player names, and then copy the cells from the Wonder Boy row. Select the row's body cells, and drag the Fill handle down to the bottom of the table, as shown in Figure 21-16 for five players.

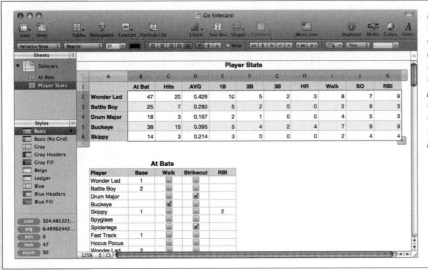

Figure 21-16:
When you copy the body cells from Wonder Lad's row, Numbers brings the formulas along with them, calculating each player's individual stats. Each row uses the player name in the left column to look up all the player's numbers.

From a giant mess of unordered data, you've plucked out every player's batting stats in a matter of minutes. Now that you've got it all in a tidy summary table, you can further sort and filter the table to see which players have the most home runs, top batting average, and so on. Even better, the stats stay up to date: As Coach continues to add batting appearances to his At Bats table, the summary table reflects every hit and homer. Count that a home run for IF functions.

Looking Up and Fetching Cell Data

The data-matching functions you saw in the last section—COUNTIF, SUMIF, AVERAGEIF, and their variations—are terrific at working with data in groups and tallying up matches in the aggregate. But because their job is to find a match, work it into a calculation, then zip along to the next match, they're all about the bottom line. They can't share the content or location of individual cell values. That's perfect for summarizing many matching items, but when you want to fetch information related to a single unique table entry (a product, a student, an interest rate, a secret fortress listing), you have to look elsewhere. Specifically, you have to look up.

Lookup functions find data from a specific cell in your spreadsheet based on its content. From there, you can branch out to pluck content from nearby cells. This means you can, on the fly:

- Look up a product by its part number and let Numbers plug its product name and price into a packing list for you automatically.

- Fetch the letter grade that corresponds to a student's percentage score and add it to your grade book.

- Type a company name into your invoice to have Numbers retrieve its address from a table of contact info, plugging it into the invoice for you.

The common feature among these examples is that all involve a prestocked table of reference data (a product catalog, the grade scale, company contact info) where every item, grade level, or company is listed just once. You can then use that storehouse as a kind of card catalog, letting Numbers' lookup functions retrieve info on your behalf about any item inside. The Function Browser groups the lookup functions under the Reference category, and that's the right way to think of them—a collection of fleet-footed reference librarians ready to look up any cataloged snippet of information.

Although you can use lookups on any table cell, retrieving organized reference data is certainly their most common and powerful use. By letting Numbers find and fill in reference data on your behalf, you save yourself the time and potential errors of entering the data manually. Your spreadsheet might even have several of these reference tables; if so, lookup functions can mix and match their data in various and useful ways across your document's sheets. This section shows you how to use these lookup functions and work around some of their foibles.

Using VLOOKUP and HLOOKUP

The two most commonly used lookup functions are VLOOKUP and HLOOKUP which, despite a few quirks, offer the best balance between ease of use and flexibility for this category of functions. These two guys work the same way but see the world from different directions: VLOOKUP and HLOOKUP respectively perform vertical and horizontal lookups. VLOOKUP lets you find a specific *row* in a large table of data, and HLOOKUP seeks out a specific *column*. Once these functions find the row or column you're looking for, you tell them to hand you the value of any specific cell inside.

Because most tables organize individual entries by row, you'll likely use VLOOKUP far more frequently than its column counterpart, and that's where this section will focus. Both, however, work with a similar set of arguments, three of them required and the last one optional:

```
VLOOKUP(search-for, columns-range, return-column, close-match)
HLOOKUP(search-for, rows-range, return-row, close-match)
```

Let's tackle the initial two arguments first, because there's something a little tricky going on here. The *search-for* argument is the value you're trying to find; when you're looking up a product by its part number, for example, this argument is the part number you're trying to find. The second argument is the overall range of cells you're interested in working with. This range has to embrace not only the cells you're searching (the Part Number column, for example) but also the cells whose values you ultimately want to retrieve (the Price column perhaps). This range, then, is always a block of cells—it has to be at least two columns wide for VLOOKUP, or two rows high for HLOOKUP.

An example helps. Say you're putting together a packing list to ship Captain Fantastic his latest order from Up & Away, Megaville's premier superhero outfitter. You have a list of product IDs, and you're using VLOOKUP to find the corresponding prices in your product table, shown in Figure 21-17. The columns-range argument for this lookup should stretch from the ID column to the Price column. The range *could* extend all the way over to the Manufacturer column, but it doesn't have to; it only has to be large enough to include the *search column* (ID) and the *result column* (Price). If you wanted to retrieve the product name instead of the price, then the range could include just the ID and Product Name columns.

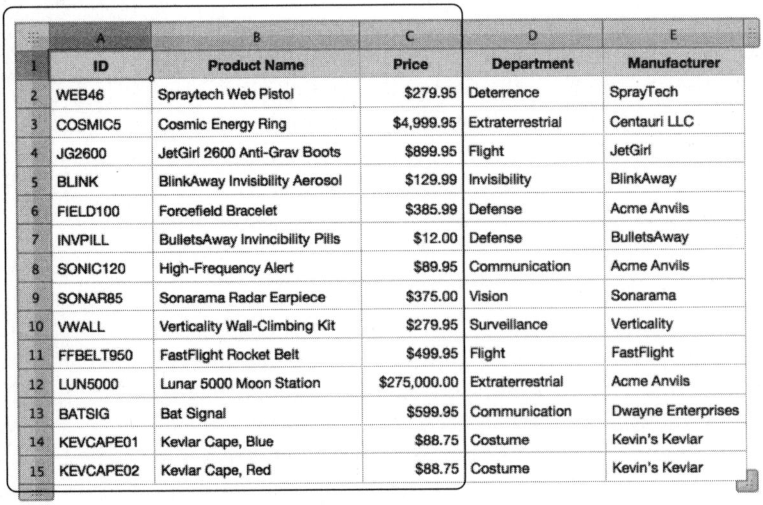

	A	B	C	D	E
1	ID	Product Name	Price	Department	Manufacturer
2	WEB46	Spraytech Web Pistol	$279.95	Deterrence	SprayTech
3	COSMIC5	Cosmic Energy Ring	$4,999.95	Extraterrestrial	Centauri LLC
4	JG2600	JetGirl 2600 Anti-Grav Boots	$899.95	Flight	JetGirl
5	BLINK	BlinkAway Invisibility Aerosol	$129.99	Invisibility	BlinkAway
6	FIELD100	Forcefield Bracelet	$385.99	Defense	Acme Anvils
7	INVPILL	BulletsAway Invincibility Pills	$12.00	Defense	BulletsAway
8	SONIC120	High-Frequency Alert	$89.95	Communication	Acme Anvils
9	SONAR85	Sonarama Radar Earpiece	$375.00	Vision	Sonarama
10	VWALL	Verticality Wall-Climbing Kit	$279.95	Surveillance	Verticality
11	FFBELT950	FastFlight Rocket Belt	$499.95	Flight	FastFlight
12	LUN5000	Lunar 5000 Moon Station	$275,000.00	Extraterrestrial	Acme Anvils
13	BATSIG	Bat Signal	$599.95	Communication	Dwayne Enterprises
14	KEVCAPE01	Kevlar Cape, Blue	$88.75	Costume	Kevin's Kevlar
15	KEVCAPE02	Kevlar Cape, Red	$88.75	Costume	Kevin's Kevlar

Figure 21-17:
The range for a VLOOKUP has to start with the column you're searching (the ID column, in this example) and include the column whose value you want to retrieve (here, that's Price). This means the VLOOKUP range must always be at least two columns wide. The rows described by the range also define the portion of the table that VLOOKUP will search.

You can express this using a column range (ID:Price, in this example) or a specific block of cells (A2:C15). Whichever format you choose, understand that this also describes the rows that VLOOKUP will search inside. You could limit the search to only a specific portion of the table by targeting a specific set of rows. This range, in other words, describes the canvas your lookup works on, including the search column, the results column, and the rows to search.

One other wrinkle: For VLOOKUP, the *left* column in the range *has to* be the column you want it to search. (For HLOOKUP, the *top* row of the range has to be the row to search). In this example, the search column is the ID column, and the range ID:Price tells VLOOKUP that's the case. If you instead wanted to look up a price using the product name, then the Product Name field would have to be the leftmost column in the range: Product Name:Price. This has an important consequence: Because the range has to include both the search and result columns, and because the search column is always the leftmost column of the range, the result column can't be located to the left of the search column. VLOOKUP can fetch the value of cells *only* when they're to the right of the column you're searching. Likewise, HLOOKUP can retrieve cell values only when they're below the search row; no upward lookups. That's not always convenient, and in a few pages you'll learn some alternative strategies for finding values outside the lookup range.

That shortcoming doesn't affect the product ID lookup example, however. You've got the ID column pegged for the left column of the range, and you're ready to search for your first product ID, "BLINK." That means that you've got the first two arguments of your VLOOKUP function defined, just two to go—the *return-column* and *close-match* arguments:

```
VLOOKUP("BLINK", ID:Price, return-column, close-match)
```

The return-column determines which cell value you get back after VLOOKUP finds the row you're looking for; in other words, the thing you're really and truly in search of. This value is also called an *offset,* a numeric value that instructs Numbers how many columns to move over to find the data you're looking for. This number is relative to your selected range: The leftmost column in the range is column 1, the next is column 2, and so on. In our example, the Price column is the third column in the range:

```
VLOOKUP("BLINK", ID:Price, 3, close-match)
```

So far, these VLOOKUP instructions tell Numbers to find the row where the ID column matches the text "BLINK" and then return the value of the Price column. The only thing that remains is to choose *how* Numbers should match "BLINK" when searching through the rows. The final optional argument, close-match, is an on-off switch that determines whether VLOOKUP has to find an exact match or if you'll settle for something that's close:

- **Close Match.** This is the standard setting; if you leave out the close-match argument, this is what you'll get. You can also specify a close match by setting this argument to either TRUE or 1.

  When you go with a close match, you tell Numbers to give you the row most closely matching your search value when no exact match is available. This means that the matching row is the closest value in the search column that is also *less than* the value you're searching for. Think of this as the *Price Is Right* rule: The winner is the bidder with the closest value without going over. (For text, this less-than comparison works alphabetically; for dates and types, chronologically.) This is particularly useful when you're searching a reference table that's organized by ranges of values, as you'll see in the grade-book example on page 751.

- **Exact Match.** Choose this option by setting the close-match argument to FALSE or 0. This option returns a value only when there's an exact match for your search value; otherwise, the function returns an error. (Text matches aren't case-sensitive, however, so you don't have to type the right mix of uppercase and lowercase letters to get a match.)

This is typically the option to use when you're looking for specific items, like the product ID example or to fetch a customer address. In those cases, the closest match usually doesn't help you and can even introduce embarrassing errors. (Whoops! You mistyped the product ID and Numbers inserted the data for the closest match—instead of a cosmic energy ring, a frilly pink tutu is now winging its way to Captain Fantastic.)

To look up the product ID, an exact match is called for, which means that you finally have all the ingredients for your recipe to search for the price of the product with the ID "BLINK." The final formula looks like this:

```
=VLOOKUP("BLINK", ID:Price, 3, FALSE)
```

As usual, things get much more interesting when you replace the "BLINK" search value with a cell reference, letting you look up values based on what you type into your spreadsheet. For example, this whole discussion started with a promise that it would help you fill out Captain Fantastic's packing list. You can do this by putting a packing-list form on one sheet of your document and stashing your product table on another. By adding lookup formulas to this form, you can enter just the product ID, and Numbers will fetch the product name and unit price from the product table, entering those for you automatically. With those values in place, you can use them and refer to them like any other value. In the packing list, for example, enter the number of items for each product, and the Total column figures the final value (C2 * D2). Figure 21-18 shows the result.

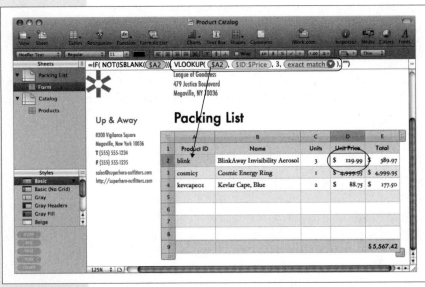

Figure 21-18:
You can add lookups to a form on one sheet to fetch data from a reference table on another. This packing-list form looks up product names and prices when you enter a product ID in the left column. Numbers retrieves the data from the Products table on the next sheet (see Figure 21-17). Here, typing "blink" into cell A2 fetches the name and price for the BLINK product listed in the Products table.

In Figure 21-18, the VLOOKUP that performs this data-collecting errand has been wrapped in an IF function so that it looks up data only when a product ID has been supplied. If you don't do this, VLOOKUP tries to find a match using an empty value, returning either an irrelevant row or an error. In row 2, shown in the figure, the condition for this check is:

```
NOT( ISBLANK($A2) )
```

This literally says, "Is cell A2 not blank?" but when translated to something a bit more graceful, asks, "Is there a value in cell A2?" If yes, do the lookup. If not, insert an empty value. The final IF function looks like this:

```
=IF( NOT( ISBLANK($A2) ), VLOOKUP( $A2, $ID:$Price, 2, FALSE ), "")
```

Matching text with VLOOKUP and HLOOKUP

When you're doing a lookup for an exact text match—like finding the name of a product, company, or client—both VLOOKUP and HLOOKUP let you use wildcards in the search-for value (see "Something Wild for Searching Text" on page 741). This can save time by letting you find a match without having to type each and every character of your search value, which gets tiresome when you're trying to look up the address, for example, of "Abracadabra Excalibur Superhero Rocket Car Company, Inc."

In that case, setting your search term to "abra*" does the trick. Similarly, in the packing-list example you just saw, you could type "bl*" into the Product ID column, and the lookup would still fetch the "BLINK" product information. You can also build the asterisk directly into the VLOOKUP request by adding it to the cell value. For example:

```
=VLOOKUP( $A2 & "*", $ID:$Price, 3, FALSE )
```

Note: Numbers allows wildcards only in exact-match lookups; you can't use them in close-match searches.

Doing this makes it more likely that you'll create a search value with more than one match, though that can certainly happen even with any search value, with or without a wildcard, text or otherwise. No matter what, though, the lookup functions always return just one result. If there are multiple matches, Numbers picks one of them and hands it back to you. When you absolutely *must* look up multiple rows that match a search value, filters (page 644) or categories (646) are your best option.

Managing "left lookups"

As described earlier, VLOOKUP can return cell values only to the right of the search column. In the Products table back in Figure 21-18, this restriction means that you can't look up a product name to get the product ID. The only values available to you when searching in the Product Name column are the cells in the Price, Department, and Manufacturer columns.

When you need to look up a value to the left of the search column—a *left lookup*—you have a few options. First, of course, you can simply move the result column to the right of the search column (see page 620 for info about moving rows and columns). If that's not an option, you can instead use the LOOKUP function, or combine the MATCH and INDEX functions—topics that you'll learn about in the next few pages. Finally, you can also fall back to an ugly but effective kludge: Create a copy of the values you want to find in a brand-new column to the right of the search column.

For example, to look up a product ID by searching for a product name, you'd add a new column to the product table, using a cell reference in each cell to grab its value from the Product ID column, as shown in Figure 21-19, which adds an ID Copy column.

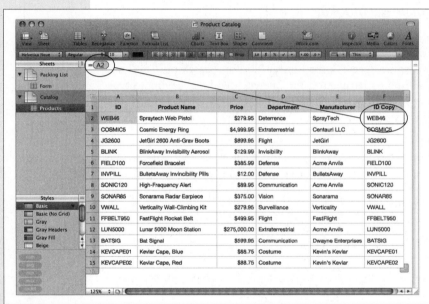

Figure 21-19:
To create a clone of the Product ID column, add a new column to the right edge of the table. In all the now column's body cells, add a simple formula that sets the cell's value to the Product ID cell in the same row.

Now VLOOKUP has a column it can work with when you search the Product Name column. To fetch the ID for the forcefield bracelet, this formula does the trick:

```
=VLOOKUP("Forcefield Bracelet", Product Name:ID Copy, 5, FALSE)
```

Now, though, you have two matching columns—a potentially confusing situation and certainly one that wastes valuable pixel space in your sheet. Sweep the new column under the rug by choosing Hide Column from the reference tab pop-up menu for the ID Copy column. Even though the new column is hidden, the lookup continues to work on its values. (For more on hiding rows and columns, see page 641.)

Using LOOKUP for Easier but Inexact Matches

The LOOKUP function is an alternative to VLOOKUP and HLOOKUP, offering advantages (and one significant disadvantage) over the two standard lookup functions. LOOKUP lets you choose *any* result column or result row from which to fetch a value, no matter what range you choose for your search column or search row. This sidesteps VLOOKUP's left-lookup problem and also dispenses with figuring out the column or row offset for the result cell, giving you a simpler overall syntax. You give LOOKUP three arguments:

```
LOOKUP(search-for, search-where, result-values)
```

The first argument, *search-for,* is the search value you want to match, and the second argument, *search-where,* is the cell range (usually a column) in which to find that search value. When LOOKUP finds a match, it returns the value in the corresponding position in the cell range (usually another column) of the third argument, *result-values.*

This straight-to-the-point format is a big improvement on the relatively indirect arguments of the VLOOKUP and HLOOKUP functions. To find the product ID of the Forcefield Bracelet in Figure 21-17, for example, simply enter this:

```
=LOOKUP("Forcefield bracelet", Product Name, ID)
```

There's a catch, though, and it unfortunately disqualifies LOOKUP from many uses: LOOKUP doesn't know how to do an exact match. It always uses the close-match method, which also means you can't use wildcards with LOOKUP. For the most common lookups like the product catalog example or finding contact info or order history for a specific company, exact match is almost always what you want. That said, the close-match method is useful in some circumstances, and it's worth exploring how you can put it to use.

Doing close-match lookups

These close-but-not-quite matches are especially useful when you have a set of graduated-value categories that contain a range of values—tax brackets, grade scales, and date ranges, for example. When you want to find out which category a value falls into, a close-match lookup can tell you.

That's because close matches always choose the value that's closest to the search value *without going over.* That effectively means that the matched value is the "bottom" of any category range. Figure 21-20 shows examples of close-match search results.

As shown in Figure 21-20, one of the uses for a close-match lookup is to find the corresponding letter grade for a percent score. Head back to the Basic Heroics classroom, where you can help the instructor instantly assign letter grades based on students' final scores. To do that, add a table to hold the grade scale and then add lookups to the GRADE column, as shown in Figure 21-21.

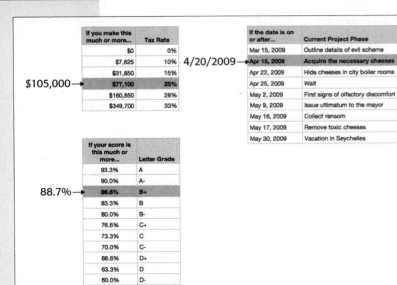

Figure 21-20:
You can use a close match to find where a value belongs in a graduated set of categories. Because a close match finds the closest value equal to or less than the search term, this lets you look up categories based on the bottom value, or "start," of each category: The start of a new tax bracket, the start of a new project phase, the start of a new grade level.

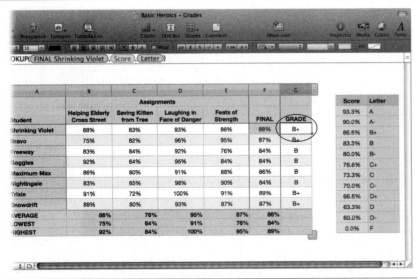

Figure 21-21:
When you add a grade-scale table to the grade book, a simple LOOKUP function lets you find the letter grade associated with each score. Here, Shrinking Violet's grade is found by using her final score for a close-match lookup. The closest match for the 88% grade is 86.6%, a B+.

Figure 21-21 uses the LOOKUP function to find the letter grades in the column. To find Shrinking Violet's grade, the formula is:

```
=LOOKUP(FINAL Shrinking Violet, Score, Letter)
```

Since there's no left-lookup issue involved here, you could also use VLOOKUP with the close-match argument set to TRUE for exactly the same result:

```
=VLOOKUP(FINAL Shrinking Violet, Score:Letter, 2, TRUE)
```

Using MATCH and INDEX to Fetch Any Cell

When you have to do a left lookup *and* you need to do an exact match, then all three of the LOOKUP, VLOOKUP, and HLOOKUP functions let you down. The solution is to turn to the MATCH and INDEX functions, which can fetch any cell in your spreadsheet without the restrictions of the other lookups. However, this combination is a bit more complicated to construct, which typically makes using the other lookup functions more appealing when they'll do the trick.

Combining MATCH and INDEX turns your lookup into a two-man job, where each function handles a separate task. MATCH finds the location of the search cell in your table, and then INDEX uses that info to retrieve the value you're after. In this section, you'll see how to use these functions to do a left lookup to look up a product ID by matching its associated product name, using the product-list example you saw earlier.

The first step is to find the matching row in the table's Product Name column. That's a job for MATCH, which specializes in finding a specific value in a row or column. MATCH accepts three arguments:

```
MATCH(search-for, search-where, matching-method)
```

The first argument, *search-for,* is the value you want it to find, and the second argument, *search-where,* is the range of cells where you want it to look. MATCH can only look in one direction, along a row or along a column, which means that the range for the second argument must be a straight line of cells within a single row or column. You can use a column reference, for example, or specify a range of cells.

The final argument, *matching-method,* tells Numbers how to match the search value and takes one of three values: 0, 1, or –1.

- **Exact match: 0.** Set this argument to 0 to use this method. Just like the exact-match option in the other lookup functions, this finds a value only when it matches exactly. Text values aren't case-sensitive, and you can use wildcards for text searches.

- **Close match: 1.** This less-than-or-equal-to search is the method MATCH uses if you omit this argument, but you can also select it by setting the argument value to 1. As described previously, this match finds the value that's closest to the search value without going over.

- **Modified close match: –1.** This is very similar to close match but flips the condition on its head, finding the value closest to the search value without going *under* the search value. In other words, this flavor of close match finds matching values that are higher than the search value, rather than lower.

Note: If MATCH doesn't find a match, it returns an error message.

To find the location of the row in the Products table that has an exact match for the "Bat Signal" product name, for example, the following MATCH function does the trick, adding the name of the Products table to the cell reference to be clear which cells you're talking about:

```
MATCH( "Bat Signal", Products :: B2:B15, 0 )
```

As Figure 21-22 shows, however, the match doesn't yet tell you much, resulting only in the inscrutable number 12. (The example in the figure replaces the "Bat Signal" string with a cell reference.)

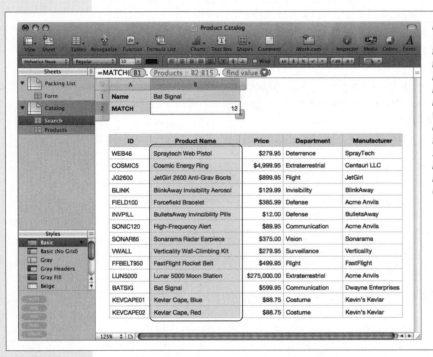

Figure 21-22:
The MATCH function in the B2 cell of the top table searches cells B2: B15 (circled) in the Products table, finding a match for the "Find" value in the B1 cell above. Here, the result for searching for Bat Signal is 12, which indicates that there's a match in the twelfth cell of the range.

The 12 result offered up by MATCH refers to the matching cell's location in the range, counting from the top (or from the left when you're working with a row). That means the cell you're after is in the twelfth row of the range B2:B15. That's mildly interesting, but it doesn't do much for you on its own, since the value you're actually after is the product ID for the Bat Signal. That's where INDEX comes in. The INDEX function returns the value of any cell you want when you supply its row/column coordinates within a range. Since MATCH told you the row of the cell in the B2:B15 range, that gives you enough info to tell INDEX the coordinates of the cell next door, which holds the product ID you're after.

The INDEX function accepts three arguments. (Well, OK, it accepts a fourth optional argument, too—an *area range index*, a topic not covered in this book. For most common uses, only the following three are important.)

```
INDEX(range, row-index, column-index)
```

Note: That third *column-index* argument is optional, and if you leave it out, Numbers assumes you want to work with the first column of your selection. When your range is a column—the most common case—that means that you can always leave off that third argument.

For example, this combination of arguments gets you the cell you're after:

```
INDEX( Products :: A2:A15, 12 )
```

This tells INDEX to take the cell in the twelfth row of the A2:A15 range of the Products table. Since MATCH already told you that the product name is in the twelfth row of the B2:B15 range, you know that the product ID is in the twelfth row of the A2:A15 range. Now the trick is to put it all into a single formula. You can get that by replacing the 12 in the INDEX function shown above with the original MATCH function.

Stepping back a bit, all of this means that the big-picture recipe for using INDEX and MATCH to do an exact-match lookup on any search and result column looks like this:

```
=INDEX( result-values, MATCH( search-for, search-where, 0) )
```

For the specific example you're working with in the product-catalog example, that translates to this formula, as shown in Figure 21-23:

```
=INDEX( Products :: A2:A15, MATCH( B1, Products :: B2:B15, 0 ))
```

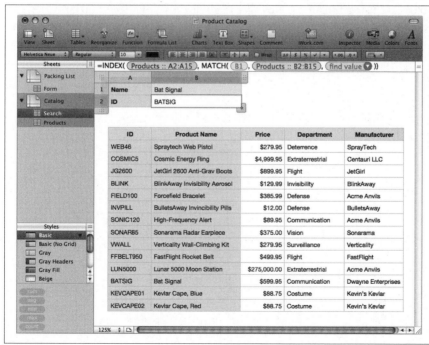

Figure 21-23:
Typing Bat Signal into the Find cell now turns up the product ID "BATSIG" in the cell below. Thanks to the combination of INDEX and MATCH, you can do an exact-match lookup on any cells you want, including a left lookup.

Other Lookup Functions

The five lookup functions mentioned here are the heavy hitters of spreadsheet lookups, but you can find several others in the Reference category of the Function Browser. Table 21-3 summarizes a few of the most useful, and you can find complete details on these and others in the Function Browser's description pane.

Table 21-3. More Lookup Functions

Function	Syntax	Description
OFFSET	OFFSET(*cell, row-offset, column-offset*)	Returns the value of the cell (or range of cells) that's a certain number of rows and columns away from another specified cell.
COLUMN	COLUMN(*cell*)	Returns the column number for a specified cell (or the formula cell, if no cell is specified). COLUMN(C2) returns the number 3, since C is the third column of the table.
ROW	ROW(*cell*)	Returns the row number for a specified cell (or the formula cell, if no cell is specified). COLUMN(B4) returns the number 4.
COLUMNS	COLUMNS(*range*)	Counts the number of columns in the range reference.
ROWS	ROWS(*range*)	Counts the number of rows in the range reference.

In this chapter, you've seen how Numbers can work all kinds of transformations on your data using functions. Now get ready for a whole new kind of metamorphosis: Seeing your matter-of-fact data bloom into gorgeous graphs and charming charts. Turn the page to learn how to put a visual spin on your spreadsheets.

Charts: Giving Shape to Numbers

They call economics "the dismal science," but iWork's stunning chart features can brighten even the grayest numbers. When deployed correctly, graphic charts add energy and insight to your data. Bright colors, 3D charts, and effortless chart formatting—that's anything but dismal. The trick is how to hang onto the "science" while you're at it. The point of a chart is to surface the message behind your data, showing visual trends and relationships that may not be immediately evident from staring at the numbers themselves. It takes care to create a graphic that does this well. Great charts tell a complicated story at a glance, but poorly designed charts can confuse and mislead. (Perhaps you want to intentionally mislead—that takes a carefully designed chart, too!)

This is where iWork's remarkable chart features are both a blessing and a curse. Numbers is chock full of options for decorating, labeling, coloring, shading, and even twirling your chart into just about any form you'd like. It's an impressive toolkit, and the results always look polished; you can create a chart in seconds that looks like a whole art department labored over it for hours. The problem is that it's easy to get carried away with the look of the chart and lose track of its message, to sacrifice the substance to the flash. Your charts should be more than a pretty graphic or a splash of color in the annual report. They should enhance the understanding of your data.

The good news is that you can have it both ways, creating gorgeous graphs that also enlighten. This chapter shows you not only how to use these tools, but also why and when. You'll learn about the 19 styles of charts that Numbers offers, how to integrate them with your tables, and how to format them with elegance. The chapter finishes with a review of where to pull back, showing you how a bit of careful design restraint can lend greater sophistication and a sharper point to your charts. But first, the basics.

Adding a Chart to Your Spreadsheet

In Numbers, charts help visualize data from one or more of your tables, showing all of a table's data or just a portion. Because table data feeds your charts, every chart is associated with a table, a link that you create when you first add the chart to your spreadsheet.

To add a chart, first select the table that you want to graph—the *source table*. The way you select the table matters: When you select all of a table's cells, or when you select the table at the object level so that its eight selection handles are visible, Numbers adds a chart that includes all of the table's data. If you create a chart with only a portion of cells selected—even only one cell—then the chart shows the data for that selection of cells. As you'll learn on page 772, you can change the selection of charted cells anytime, so you're not locked into your original choice, but you can save yourself time by making the right selection from the get-go. Figure 22-1 shows the striking difference between creating a chart based on all of a table's cells versus just a single cell.

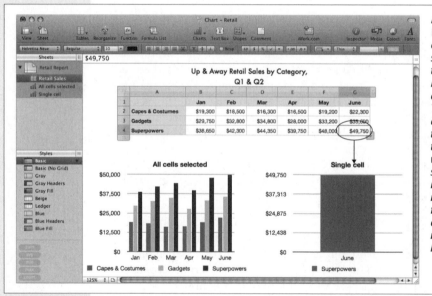

Figure 22-1:
When you add a new chart, it always starts off showing the data for the table's selected cells. Here, two charts show data for the same table. The chart on the left was added with all of the table's cells selected, and the chart on the right was created with only a single cell selected. As a result, the chart on the right shows only the data for that one cell, almost certainly not the insightful graphic you're looking for.

If the table or selected cells are empty, the chart is blank until you add values. If no table is selected when you add a chart, Numbers adds a chart *and* a table to your spreadsheet—a *placeholder chart* that gets you started with some simple example data. You can replace that placeholder data at your leisure to enter your chart data from scratch.

With your table-selection strategy settled, click the Charts pop-up button in the toolbar, and choose the type of chart you'd like to use (Figure 22-2). When you click a chart type, Numbers adds your new chart to the sheet, along with the chart's legend as a separate object (you'll learn more about the legend on page 762).

Drag the chart wherever you'd like it to appear (you can even paste it to a whole different sheet), and resize it using its selection handles. Or you can skip that move-and-resize two-step by *drawing* the chart onto the sheet:

1. **Hold down the Option key, and make your selection from the Charts pop-up button.**

2. **Release the Option key and move the cursor down onto the sheet canvas. It turns into a crosshair shape.**

3. **Drag the crosshair across the canvas to create a chart in the location and size you want.**

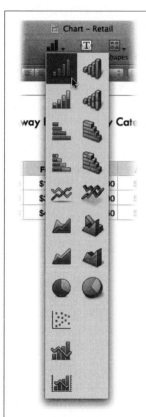

Figure 22-2:
Click the Charts pop-up button in the toolbar to choose from Numbers' 19 styles of charts. (These options are also available from the Insert → Chart menu.) The top eight charts appear in two columns, indicating that they're available in both 2D (on the left) and 3D charts. The 3D versions can add "pop" to your chart, but use them carefully—they can distort your data to produce misleading results (see page 797).

To remove a chart, select it and press Delete. Because a chart is dependent on its source table, you can also remove a chart by deleting its table. When you do this, Numbers will warn you that you're about to nuke the chart, too, and lists the chart(s) connected to the table. Click Delete to continue or Cancel to bail out.

Chart Parts

You'll learn about all the different chart types on page 763, but you first need to get acquainted with some of the anatomical terms for charts. When you add a chart to your spreadsheet with no tables selected, Numbers adds a placeholder chart to your spreadsheet, prestocked with sample data, as shown in Figure 22-3. Think of this starter chart as a floor model to help you get acquainted with how charts work in Numbers. It's a good place to start a tour of the basic features that all charts share for displaying your data. Here's a quick orientation.

The X-axis and Y-axis

The *X-axis* and the *Y-axis* are your chart's horizontal and vertical measuring sticks. All chart types except pie charts have X- and Y-axes, and they serve to give your chart scale and context. One axis corresponds to either your spreadsheet's row or column headings, the *categories* of data you're charting—in Figure 22-3, the column headings for years are charted along the X-axis. The other axis measures the *values* of your data—the number of costumed heroes in two regions of Megaville County, for example.

Tip: Numbers lets you choose the scale of the value axis (the Y-axis in Figure 22-3) as either linear or logarithmic. For mere mortals, linear is what you're looking for, and that's the standard setting. If you like yours logarithmic, select the table and choose Log Scale from the Format Bar's Y-Axis menu, or go to the Chart Inspector → Axis pane and pick Log Scale from the Value Axis pop-up menu.

Data series and data sets

Charts construct a visual story from your data. Like every story, there's a certain series of events that combine to give the whole picture and produce the narrative. In charts, these narrative events are the individual data values plucked from your table, *the data points*. As you saw back in Figure 22-1, a single data point doesn't make for much of a story. Instead, you have to display several data points about your subject in order to draw conclusions about it. Because you show a series of data about your subject, this subject is called the *data series*—the main character of your story.

In Figure 22-4, for example, the chart tells the story of Region 1 and its changing number of heroes over four years. Region 1 is the data series because the data points (the number of heroes) are represented by a *series* of columns, one for each year. The simplest charts, like this one, have only a single data series. Figure 22-3, however, shows a chart with *two* data series, comparing the series of data points for Region 1 to the series for Region 2.

Tip: When you include header cells in your source table, your chart becomes much easier to work with. In a standard chart, its text labels borrow the values of the header cells, making it instinctively clear how the chart is displaying your data.

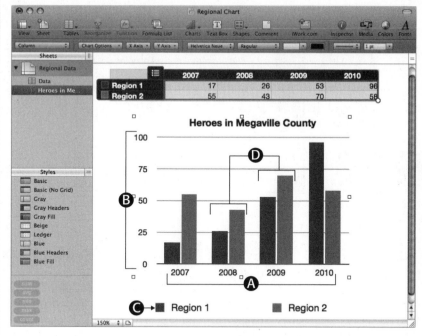

Figure 22-3:
Numbers' placeholder column chart plots two data series, Region 1 vs. Region 2, over four years along the X-axis (A) with values represented along the Y-axis (B).

The numbers behind the chart live in the chart's source table, where each row represents one of the chart's regional data series. The row header cells correspond to the labels in the chart's legend (C), which displays color keys to identify which column represents which data series. When you select the chart, these color keys also appear in the table's header cells.

Each number in the table is a data point, represented by a column in the chart. The numbers from both data series for each year are a data set (D), represented by the paired columns in the chart.

In both charts, the data points for the regions are organized by year. In chartspeak, the years are the *categories,* or *data sets,* of the chart. A data set is a collection of data points for all of the chart's data series. In the charts in Figure 22-3 and Figure 22-4, 2007 is a data set, 2008 is a data set, and so on.

All charts in iWork display one or more data series, but they differ in the way they display their data points. The figures here are column charts, which show data points as, you guessed it, columns. Other chart types, which you'll explore in just a few pages, draw these data points in different ways—as bars, pie slices, coordinates, points on a line, and so on. No matter how they render the data points, however, the bottom line is that they all illustrate the same things: one or more data series, organized into categories of one or more data sets.

Note: Scatter charts are the exception; although they have data series, scatter charts don't organize the data into data-set categories. For more on working with scatter charts, see page 777.

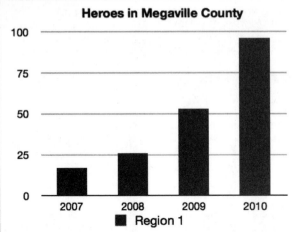

Heroes in Megaville County

Figure 22-4:
*This simple chart has a single data series, Region 1,
showing a series of data points for the region across
four years. The years are the data sets, the categories
that organize the display of the data points.*

In the chart's source table, these data series and data sets are represented by rows
and columns. In Figure 22-3, the rows (Region 1 and Region 2) are the data series,
and the columns (2007, 2008, 2009, and 2010) are the data sets. But Numbers lets
you flip this arrangement on its head, changing chart orientation so that the years
are the data series, and the regions are the data sets. You do this by clicking the
source table's *Data Series button,* which becomes visible only when you select the
associated chart. Click the chart, and a dark frame materializes around the related
rows and columns in the source table. In the top left of this frame, the Data Series
button lets you flip the roles of rows and columns.

Figure 22-5 shows what happens when you do this in the regional heroes chart.
Now the years are the data series: Each year's data is shown in a series, grouped by
regional data-set categories. Numbers notes the new state of affairs by moving the
color keys next to the column headings instead of the row headings. The icon on
the Data Series button also flips to a vertical layout to show that the chart is organized by columns instead of rows. (When the reverse is true, the button has a
horizontal layout.)

The legend

Just like the legend on a map, a chart's *legend* shows what the lines, bars, and symbols
on your chart represent. The legend displays the headings of the rows or columns
containing the data series and can also display the color or symbol used for the
data points on the chart. The legend is a separate object on your page—you can
reposition or remove it without affecting the chart itself. When you move the
chart, however, the legend moves along with it; the only way to position them
independently of each other is to move the legend.

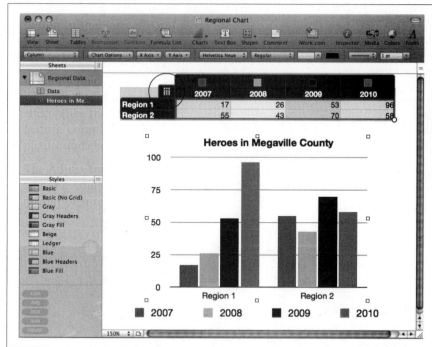

Figure 22-5:
When you select a chart, its source table sprouts a dark outline around the chart's related rows and tables. Click the Data Series button (circled) in the top left corner of this frame to flip the data orientation of the chart. Here, the year columns are the data series, and the region rows are the data sets. Numbers shows that's the case by placing the legend symbols next to the column headers and changing the Data Series button icon to a vertical layout.

To remove the legend (you're actually only hiding it), click to select it, and press Delete, or turn off the Legend option in the Chart Inspector or in the Format Bar's Chart Options pop-up menu. To bring it back, turn the Legend option on in either the Format Bar or Chart Inspector. You'll find out more about editing the legend text on page 780.

Choosing a Chart Type

The first key to creating great charts is picking the right kind of chart for the type of information you're presenting. Now that you've got the hang of how Numbers organizes its charts, you've got the info you need to choose what kind of chart to build. Numbers offers 11 types of charts—throw in the 3D chart styles and you've got a total of 19 styles in all. That's a lot of options, and it's important to understand the strengths of each so you can make the right choice for your data. Here's a quick tour.

Note: For many of these chart types, the Chart Inspector offers a custom set of options for formatting the chart's display. You'll find more details about formatting charts starting on page 784.

Column

Column charts are a good choice for showing simple results clearly. One data series produces one column, while two or more series allow you to compare those series back-to-back. In this example, you can compare sales of three different retail categories over four years.

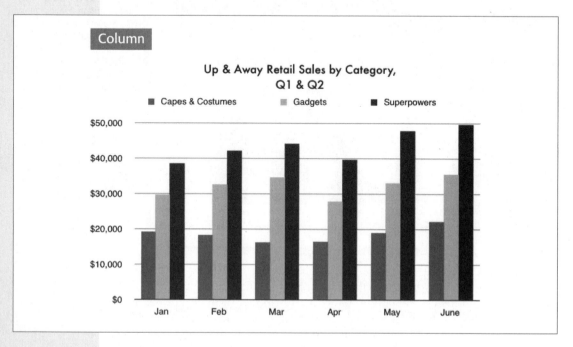

Stacked column

Stacked column charts let you display the cumulative result of multiple data series, one on top of the other. Here, this chart shows the same data as the column chart. Unlike regular column charts, stacked column charts do a poor job of comparing the values of each data series within individual columns, or even to estimate what those individual values might be. Because the emphasis is on the *combined* value of the data sets, use stacked column charts only when the individual values of the data series are less important than the overall combined value.

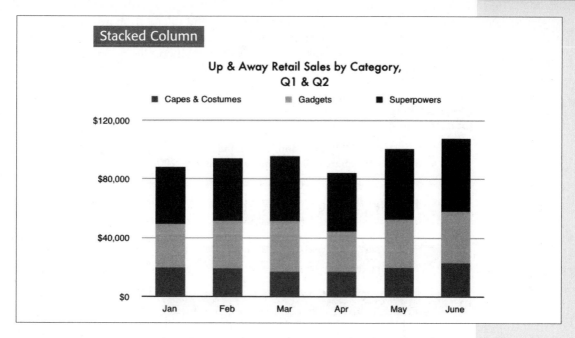

Bar

Bar charts are just like column charts turned sideways. Like column charts, they're also good for comparing simple data. They're particularly effective when you remove the X-axis labels and instead display the values at the end of each bar. This example compares the speed of Captain Fantastic and Wonder Lad in four different time trials.

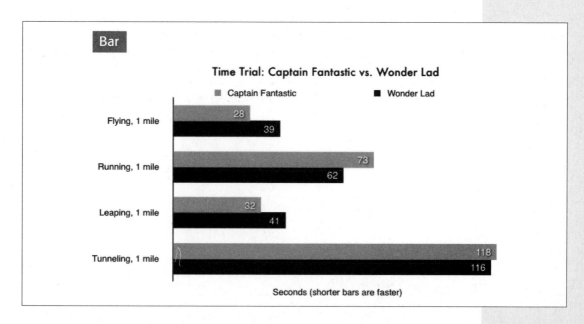

Stacked bar charts line up multiple data series end to end to show their total values, and they have the same pitfalls as stacked column charts. This example shows the quarterly number of awards bestowed by the city on heroes in the League of Goodness.

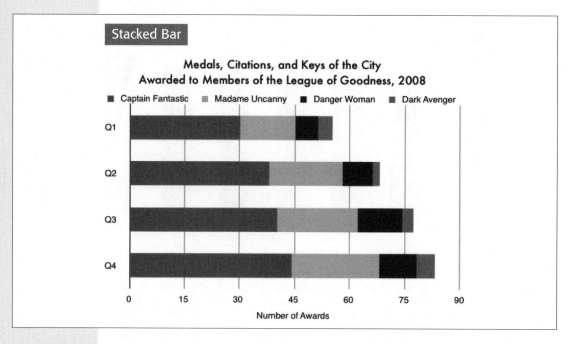

Line

Line charts are typically the best choice for viewing trends over time by plotting continuous data as points and joining them with a line. They're very good for comparing or demonstrating relationships between multiple data sets (although they become confusing if you have more than four or five lines). Line charts can present more data in a compact space than many of the other types of charts and are a good choice when you have a large number of data points to plot.

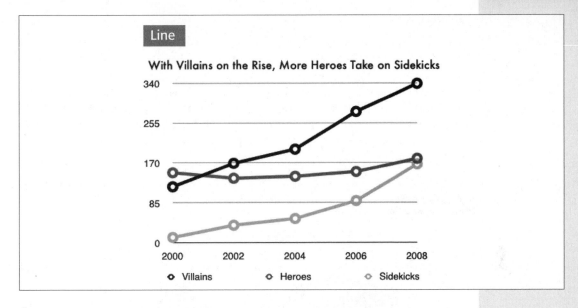

Line

With Villains on the Rise, More Heroes Take on Sidekicks

Area

Area charts are similar to line charts but fill in the space below the charted line with a background fill for each data series. Like line charts, area charts are good at tracking the change in data series value over time. However, be aware that when data series cross, one of the series can disappear behind the other, making its data invisible.

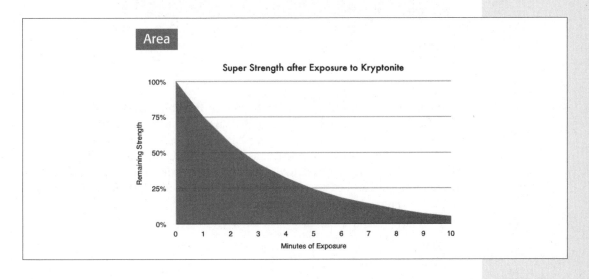

Area

Super Strength after Exposure to Kryptonite

Stacked area

Stacked area charts illustrate the combined values of multiple data series for each data set. Like stacked column and bar charts, these charts emphasize total cumulative value and, as a result, are not great for showing specific values for the individual data series. Because of the continuous flow of the chart data, however, they're better than stacked bar and column graphs at illustrating the changing importance of each data series from data set to data set. Here, for example, you can see the relative increase in huge spiders in Megaville as alien robots and atomic ants declined from peaks in the 1950s and 1960s.

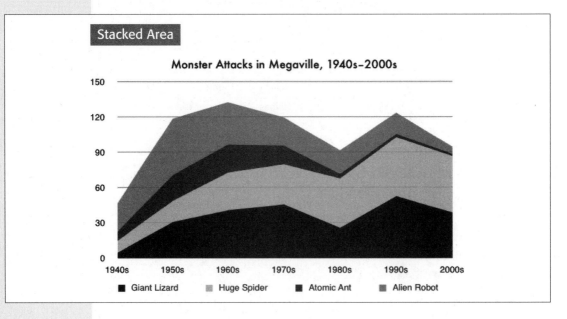

Pie

Pie charts display percentages of a whole—the distribution of super abilities in Megaville's hero community, for example. Pies work best when there aren't too many items to illustrate and your emphasis is showing proportions, rather than specific data values. The downside is that it can be difficult to discern the exact size of each pie slice, making it hard to differentiate slices with similar values. Pie charts use only a single data set: the first data point from each series listed in the Chart Data Editor. Here, one section of the pie is "exploded" to call attention to it.

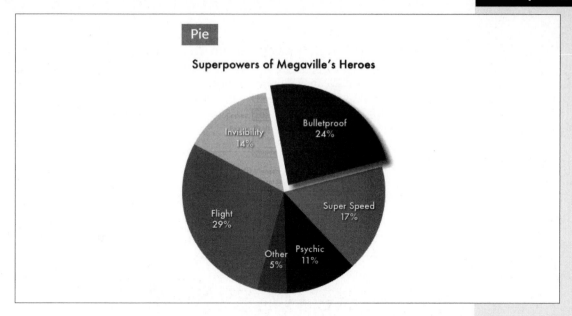

Scatter

Scatter charts plot individual data points and are useful for spotting trends in the cloud of a large data set—as well as surfacing outliers (data points that don't fit the overall trend). A favorite in scientific circles, scatter charts let you plot every data point to its own X and Y coordinates, unlike other chart types where every data series has a value for specific data set categories.

This chart plots the number of monthly skirmishes of Megaville's supertypes by age, showing that heroes are more active than villains but also tend to peak younger.

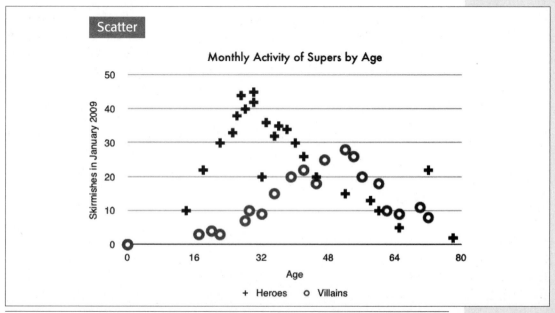

Mixed

Mixed charts display multiple data series in two or more chart styles, as column, line, or area charts. Each series in the chart can have its own style. Here, the data series for the national average of annual monster attacks is shown as an area chart, while Megaville's numbers are shown as a line chart.

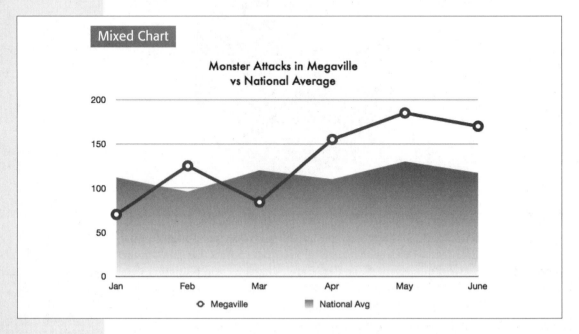

Two axis

Two-axis charts are mixed charts with a twist: One of the data series uses a different Y-axis, allowing you to display data that works in two different units or scales. These two scales are represented by two Y-axes on either side of the chart. In Numbers' standard settings, the first data series in the chart uses the one on the left and the other series uses the right. Meanwhile, each of the data series can have its own chart style—column, line, or area.

This chart uses one axis to plot the number of new supervillains in Megaville with a column chart (with a Y-axis from 0 to 70) and compares it to the unemployment rate, depicted in an area chart (with a Y-axis from 0% to 8%).

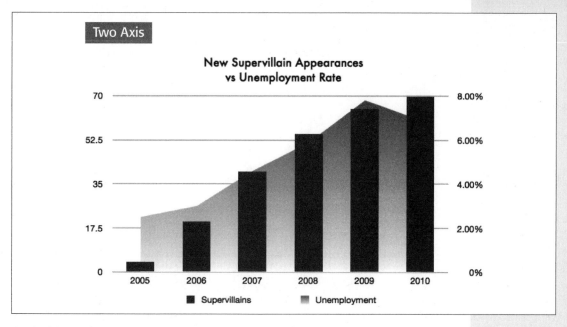

Switching Chart Types

Your very first decision when you add a chart to your spreadsheet is what kind of chart to add—in fact, making that choice is *how* you add the chart. Don't fret too much about making the wrong pick, though; if you later decide that your chart is more of a line chart than a column chart, Numbers makes it easy to switch. The Chart Inspector (Figure 22-6) lets you of the hook.

To open the Chart Inspector, click the Inspector button in the toolbar to reveal the Inspector window, and click the Chart icon in the Inspector. To change the chart type, select the chart and then choose its new look from the Chart Type pop-up button, available from any tab of the Chart Inspector. You can also choose a chart type from any of these other locations:

- The Format Bar's Chart Type pop-up menu

- The Format → Chart → Chart Type submenu

- The Chart Type submenu of the chart's shortcut menu (Control-click the chart to see this menu)

Numbers handles the switch between most chart types gracefully, but you might stumble into unexpected results when you flip in or out of pie charts and scatter charts. That's because these two types use the source table's data differently than the other chart types, which always plot every cell value as its own data point.

Pie charts illustrate only a single data set, and so they show wedges for only the first row or column of the table. The first data point in each series is shown in the chart, but only that first data point. The rest of the table is ignored.

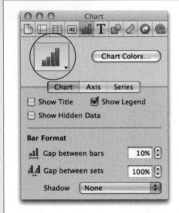

Figure 22-6:
The Chart tab of the Chart Inspector lets you change the type of the selected chart.
Click the Chart Type pop-up button (circled) and choose the new chart style.

Scatter charts meanwhile use every cell's data, but treats *pairs of cells* as individual data points, with adjacent cells combining to provide the chart coordinates for each data point. The first cell is the X-axis value, and the second is the Y-axis value, giving the chart the coordinates to plot. Scatter charts, in other words, require an entirely different data organization in your source table than the other charts, and you shouldn't expect to switch easily with other chart types—at least, not if you expect the results to make sense. For more on working with scatter charts, see page 777.

Working with a Chart's Table Data

A chart's source table provides the raw material for the key points shown in a chart. When you change the data in the table, Numbers immediately updates the chart to reflect the change. Add a new row or column to a table, and the chart grows a new data series or data set. Delete a cell's data, and the chart's data point vanishes, too. Remove the entire table, and the chart goes bye-bye along with it.

But changing the source table's data isn't the only way to change what's shown in the chart. Numbers lets you limit the chart's display to a specific selection of cells from the source table. You can also modify the order of data series in the chart and even incorporate new series from other tables. This section explores the different techniques for managing how your table data makes its way into charts. If you're already happy with the collection of data shown in your spiffy new graph, feel free to skip ahead to page 779 to start working with the chart's labels and formatting.

Tip: When you hide data in the source table (page 641), Numbers typically hides it in the chart, too. But you can choose to chart hidden rows or columns in the Chart Inspector's Chart pane: Turn on the Show Hidden Data checkbox.

Choosing the Charted Cell Range

As you saw on page 758, you can choose the charted cells when you first create a table, but you can also change this selection at any time. Whittling down the selection of charted cells is especially useful when you want to chart only the calculated totals of a table, for example, or to zoom in on just two or three data series to do a focused comparison.

Say that the instructor of the sidekick academy's course in Basic Heroics has asked for your help with charting his students' scores. He has a table of grades that include all of the class assignments for the semester, but he's interested in charting only the grades in his table's Final column. That means the chart should have a single data series (the final score) with its data points (the grades) arrayed into data sets (the students). To do that, you need to tell Numbers to chart only the Final grade column and use that column as the data series. It turns out to be a simple process.

When you select a chart, Numbers highlights the charted cells in the source table, outlining them in blue. This outline has a circular handle at the bottom right corner that lets you grow or shrink the collection of selected cells; you drag the handle to change the selection's size. As you drag, the chart updates to add or remove values from the chart—whatever cells you include in the selection box are the values included in the chart. Figure 22-7 shows how the selection box should look to chart the final grades for the Basic Heroics class.

The only wrinkle is that the circular handle can drag only the bottom right corner of the selection box. That means that you can expand the selection down and to the right, but not up or to the left; the top left corner of the selection remains fixed. To do that, you first have to move the selection and *then* resize:

1. Hover your cursor over the selected cells, and it turns into an arrow with four compass points. (The cursor appears only when there's room to move the selected cells; if all cells in the table are already selected, for example, there's no wiggle room to shift the selection, so no cursor appears.)

2. Drag the selection box so that its top left corner sits in the top left cell you'd like to include in the chart.

3. Drag the circular handle so that the bottom right corner sits in the bottom right cell to include.

Removing Data Series from a Chart

Moving and dragging the selection box to choose a cell range works well when all of your cells are in a tidy block. But what if you want to chart only selected data series, and they don't live next door to each other? Numbers lets you surgically remove data series from your chart without affecting the original data in the source table.

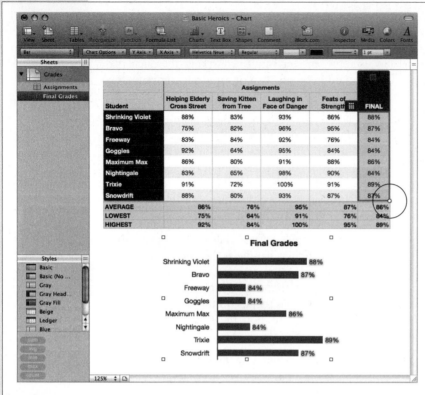

Figure 22-7:
The chart at the bottom of the sheet shows the data from the body cells of the grade table's Final column. The source table indicates this by highlighting those cells when you select the chart. The circular handle at the bottom right of the selection box (circled) lets you resize the box by dragging the right corner.

Here, the selection box has been sized and maneuvered to outline only the students' final grades. The Data Series button at the top of the Final column shows that the chart uses columns as its data series—the Final column's values are the data series, and the students are the data sets.

Say that you're charting six months of retail sales for the departments at Up & Away, the superhero outfitter. You've got five departments charted, but want to do a head-to-head comparison of just two of them. Each of these departments are data series, as shown in Figure 22-8. To remove one of the departments from the chart, select the chart so that the dark border appears around the department names—the data series labels—in the source table. Click the label of the department to remove and press Delete. Numbers removes the data series from the chart (in this case, all of the data points for the selected row). The data remains untouched in the source table but is simply no longer linked to the chart. Repeat that process for every data series you want to remove.

Tip: If you later decide to add the data series back to the chart, you can do so by dragging the cells from the table and into the chart, just as you would if you were adding the data from another table—the topic of the next section.

Adding Data Series from Other Tables

Numbers lets you combine data series from more than one table, allowing you to do a visual summary of information from several tables in your spreadsheet. A simple example: You've been hard at work analyzing the trends of monster attacks

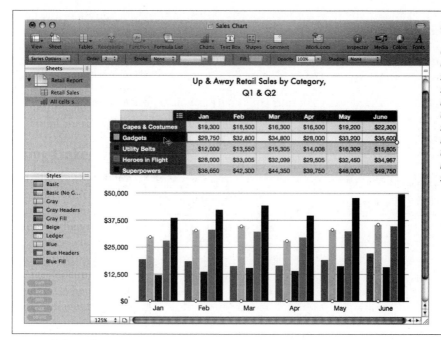

Figure 22-8:
When you select a chart and click the heading of a data series in the source table, Numbers shades the heading and highlights the row's cells to indicate that it has selected the series data. Press Delete to remove that data from the chart but leave it intact in the source table.

in Megaville over the past few decades, and you've got the results stored in two separate tables—one has the figures for giant lizards and huge spiders, the other for atomic ants and alien robots. You'd like to combine the stats from both into a single chart. Here's how to do it:

1. **Create a chart from one of the tables. In this example, doing so gives you half the data you want to chart: the data series for lizards and spiders.**

2. **In the second table, select the cells whose data you want to add to the chart. (Select multiple cells by Shift-clicking or Shift-dragging.)**

3. **Drag the selected cells into the chart, as shown in Figure 22-9, top.**

   When you move the cursor over the border of the selection box for the selected data cells, the cursor turns into a hand, signaling that it's ready to move the cells. Drag the cells to the chart.

When you drop the cells from the second table into the chart, Numbers adds the data to the chart as one or more new data series, and the ants and robots invade the chart to join the lizards and spiders in spreadsheet domination. When you select the chart, Numbers highlights the included cells in both tables.

Dragging and dropping table data into charts can get a little hairy. You have to be careful that all tables treat their data the same way in order for the chart to display the data series consistently. The Data Series button in the table originally used to create the chart—the lizards and spiders chart, in this example—determines whether rows or columns are used as data series. This setting applies to the data contributed by other tables, too. To get the results you want when you drag data from another table, both tables should organize their data the same way. In Figure 22-9, for example, both charts organize their data series (the monsters) in columns and the data sets (the years) in rows.

If your table data doesn't fall into your chart as you expect, you may have to fall back to editing the chart's cell references manually to get the data series organized again. See the box on page 777 for more details.

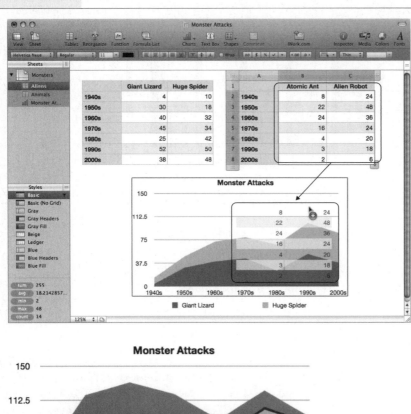

Figure 22-9:
When you drag table cells into a chart, the cursor balloons into a green plus sign to let you know that you're about to add new data to the chart. When you release the mouse button, Numbers adds the new data to the chart as one or more brand new data series. In this case, the two dragged columns turn into data series for ant and robot attacks in Megaville. The resulting chart is shown at bottom.

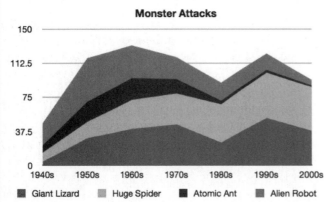

Working with a Chart's Cell References

This section describes lots of marvelous mousework that you can do to collect and shape the data for your chart—drawing boxes around the data cells to include, dragging from other tables, slicing out specific data series. Behind the scenes of all this cell-selecting machinery, Numbers is really just keeping a list of cell references to include in your chart. Every time you add or remove cells to be charted, Numbers updates its internal list of cell references, organizing them by data series.

The Chart Inspector lets you open the hood to climb in and monkey around with these cell references, letting you change the cells used for any data series. This means that you can replace all or part of a data series with a different row or column of data. This is useful, for example, when you have fresh info for a single data series, perhaps from a different table, and want to swap it into the chart without editing the original source table. This is also the only way to update cell references when the source table is located on a different sheet—if you created a chart on one sheet, for example, and then moved it to another, leaving the source table behind.

To do this, select the individual data series to edit by double-clicking one of its data points in the chart (a column, bar, area, or line for the series). Numbers adds circular handles to all of the chart's data points for the series to indicate that it's selected. In the Chart Inspector → Series pane (Figure 22-11 on page 781), go to the Data field, and click the reference capsule representing the range that you want to replace. Drag across the new range of cells that you want to include, or double-click the reference capsule to type the cell reference manually (necessary if you're editing cell references to a table on another sheet). These cells can be from any table in your spreadsheet, and you can also use a comma-separated series of cell or range references. When you make the change, Numbers updates the chart, using the new data for the series.

The Chart Inspector → Series tab also lets you make a similar change to the data series label, choosing a name or cell reference to display the name of the series in the chart. Page 783 covers this in more detail.

Changing the Order of Data Series

Unless you tell it otherwise, Numbers displays your chart's data series in the order they appear in the source table. That means you can change the lineup by shuffling the rows or columns in the source table (see page 640 for details about moving rows and columns). But Numbers also lets you choose a specific order without editing the source table. To change the position of a data series in the chart: Select the series that you want to move by double-clicking one of its data points (a bar, column, line, or area), and pick a number from the Format Bar's Order pop-up menu to set the new position for the series. Choose 1 to make it first in the list, 2 to make it second, and so on. (This menu is also available in the Chart Inspector → Series pane.)

Working with Scatter Charts

Scatter charts interpret and display the source table's data differently than other charts. Every other chart type clusters data points together into data sets, displaying all of your sales results for 2007, for example, then 2008, then 2009, and so on. Every data series has a value for each of these data sets, so the result is very structured, a one-to-one comparison of each data series.

Scatter charts, however, are just that—scattered. They dispense with the orderly presentation of bar, line, and area charts and instead sprinkle data points willy-nilly across the chart canvas. Every data point is actually made up of two values: the X-axis value and the Y-axis value. The chart puts these two values together to plot one data point anywhere on the chart, independent of the rest. This type of chart is particularly good for plotting large data sets and seeking out correlations and patterns from a big cloud of data.

To make this work, scatter charts treat two cells as one data point, requiring two rows or columns for a single data series—one X value and one Y value. To show multiple data series, you add additional two-column or two-row pairs of cells. Figure 22-10 shows an example of a scatter plot with two data series.

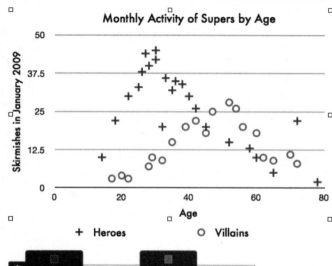

Figure 22-10:
This scatter chart (top) has two data series—Heroes and Villains—represented in the source table (bottom) in two sets of columns. Each cell pair provides the X and Y coordinate of a single data point to plot. When you select the chart, Numbers adds X and Y labels to the columns to help you make sense of the data. The label for each data series is taken from the header cell of the first value in the pair, which Numbers highlights with a dark tab in the source table when the chart is selected.

Here, the X value represents the age of a hero or villain, and the Y value is the number of skirmishes for this particular super. Plotting the two together helps to find a correlation between age and number of monthly skirmishes.

Heroes	Skirmishes	Villains	Skirmishes
14	10	17	3
18	22	20	4
22	30	22	3
25	33	28	7
26	38	29	10
28	40	32	9
27	44	35	15
30	42	39	20
30	45	42	22
32	20	45	18
33	36	47	25
35	32	52	28
36	35	54	26
38	34	56	20
40	30	60	18
42	26	62	10
45	20	65	9
52	15	70	11
58	13	72	8
60	10		
65	5		
72	22		
78	2		

When you create a scatter chart or select the cells that it should use, be sure that you always have an even number of columns or rows—every X value needs a corresponding Y value—or some data series won't display at all. In fact, it's a good idea to enter and organize your X and Y values into a table before creating the chart. The X value is always on the left of the pair when you're organizing data series in columns; it's on the top when you're organizing by rows. (The chart in Figure 22-10, for example, uses columns as data series.) You can switch between using rows or columns as data series by clicking the source table's Data Series button, which appears as a gear icon for scatter charts.

Sharing an X value

The Data Series button also offers an alternative way to organize your data when all of your data points share the same X values on the chart. For example, say that you're doing a study of the woeful effects on sidekicks' chipper enthusiasm from drinking vast quantities of store-brand colas. You take measurements at regular intervals for your entire sample of 100 impossibly wired sidekicks. Because the X value—the time when the measurement was taken—is the same for all entries, you can choose to share this value among all measurements.

To use this feature, select the chart, click the Data Series button in the source table, and choose Share X Values from the pop-up menu. When you do this, the scatter chart no longer sees the table in value pairs. Instead, the first column or row holds X values and the rest hold the Y values for the data series. If the chart is set to use columns as data series, for example, then the first column holds the X values for the entries, and every remaining column holds the Y values for each data series.

When you use this option, in other words, you're back to using a single row or column for each data series—with one additional row or column to hold the X value for all of the series. In the great sidekick cola experiment, each sidekick would be a data series, each with a single row or column showing the measurement taken at each interval.

This approach makes for easier data entry in your source table—you're not repeating the same info over and over again—and also makes the table data easier to read, letting you scan across a single line of data to see the results for each sample period.

Editing Chart Text and Labels

After laboring to collect your data and spin it into a beautiful chart chock-full of insight, don't forget to tell your reader what it means. The text on your chart—the title, the legend, the data labels—is very nearly as important as the data itself, since it's the text that says what those bars, lines, and scatterplot dots represent. When your chart goes to 11, your text should concisely answer the question, "Eleven what?"

This imperative has to be balanced with clear communication—too many text labels can choke a chart with needless clutter. Add just enough text to explain your data and stop there. The Chart Inspector lets you add a variety of text elements, including chart title, chart legend, axis titles, and axis data labels.

The Chart Title

Like tables, every chart has a name that appears in the Sheets pane. When you first add a chart to your spreadsheet, this name appears above the chart. To edit this title, double-click it, or double-click the name in the Sheets pane, and type the new name. If you prefer not to display the title above the chart, turn off the Show Title checkbox in the Chart Inspector → Chart tab or in the Format Bar's Chart Options pop-up menu.

The Chart Legend

The chart's legend is a separate object that you can manipulate independently of the chart. The legend is like a cousin of the text box: You can adjust its fill, stroke, or opacity with the Graphic Inspector, or rotate it with the Metrics Inspector.

The legend displays the labels for the data series. When you first create a chart, Numbers uses the source table's header cells to figure out the names for each data series. If the rows or columns of the data series have no header cells, Numbers throws up its hands and goes with the inspiring names "Untitled 1", "Untitled 2", and so on. Either way, you can change these data series labels by double-clicking the name in the legend and typing the new label. This has no effect on the source table's header cells.

You can also change the label for a data series by selecting the data series in the chart and then typing a name into the Label field of the Chart Inspector's Series tab (Figure 22-11). You select a data series by double-clicking one of its data points (column, bar, scatter plot, line, or area). This selects all data points in the series, and circular handles appear at each data point to signal the selection. With the series selected, type a new name into the Chart Inspector's Label field, and Numbers replaces its label in the legend. Instead of typing a name directly, you can also add a cell reference to the Label field, telling Numbers to use whatever value appears in that cell as the legend label. To do this, place the insertion point in the edit field and click the cell to use.

To dismiss the legend, click to select it and press Delete (or turn off the Show Legend checkbox in the Chart Inspector). If you change your mind later, open the Chart Inspector and turn on the checkbox for Show Legend, or choose Show Legend from the Format Bar's Chart Options pop-up menu.

Axis Titles and Labels

The Chart Inspector's Axis pane lets you add titles and labels to the X-axis and Y-axis to help the viewer understand exactly what data these items represent. You turn these labels on and off in the Value Axis and Category Axis pop-up menus,

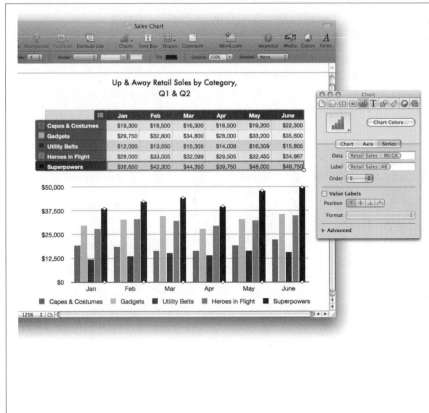

Figure 22-11:
When you double-click the data point of a series, Numbers selects the entire data series, adding circular handles to all of its data points. In this column chart, the Superpowers data series is selected, and every column of the series has the circular handles to indicate the selection. The Superpowers row is also highlighted in the source table.

With the data series selected, you can edit its label in the Chart Inspector's Label field. Here, a cell reference shows that the series uses the Superpowers header cell for its label. You can change it by typing your own text into the field or by placing the insertion point in the field and clicking a different cell to use its value instead.

as shown in Figure 22-12. (These options are also available from the X-Axis and Y-Axis pop-up menus in the Format Bar.)

The *value axis* is the Y-axis in column charts, line charts, and area charts, and the *category axis* is the X-axis because it displays the data-set categories. For bar charts, the situation is reversed. In scatter charts, which have no data set categories, both the X-axis and Y-axis display values. (Pie charts don't have chart axes, so the Axis pane doesn't even exist for that chart type.)

Add a title to a chart's X- or Y-axis to identify the type of values being charted if it's not already obvious from the chart title or data labels. To do so, select the chart and choose Show Title from the Value Axis or Category Axis pop-up. Numbers adds the title to the chart with some placeholder text—replace it with your own text by double-clicking it and typing the new name. To remove the title, deselect Show Title in the relevant axis pop-up menu.

To hide or display labels along the value axis, choose Show Value Labels from the Value Axis pop-up menu. You can choose the maximum and minimum values displayed on the axis by setting values in the Chart Inspector's Max and Min fields;

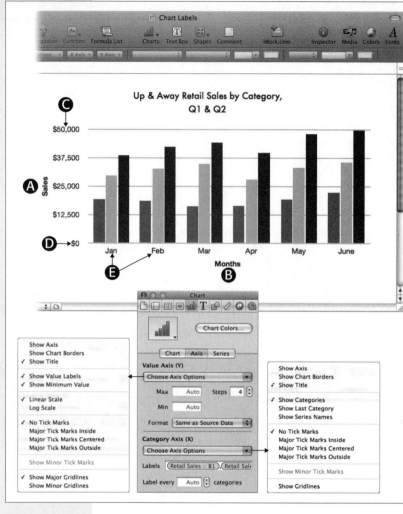

Figure 22-12:
The Value Axis and Category Axis pop-up menus offer options to show labels, tick marks, and gridlines on your charts. The value title (A) and category title (B) are overall labels for the X- and Y-axis. Value labels (C) add measurements to the Y-axis; the Value Axis pop-up offers the option to hide or display the minimum value (D). Category labels (E) show the names of the chart's data sets. Although series names aren't shown here, you can also add a series label (typically the header cell values for your data series) to every data point.

if you leave these fields set to Auto, Numbers automatically adjusts the scale to fit the data values displayed, but always sets the minimum value to zero—unless any of your data points is less than zero, in which case, Numbers sets the minimum to a negative value. You might want to customize these settings in order to, for example, begin the chart at a higher value when all your data points are much higher than zero, or to display a much higher range than your largest data point—to perhaps show how much fund-raising is yet to be done to reach your goal. If you don't want to display the minimum value at all, turn off the Show Minimum Value option in the Value Axis pop-up menu. Choose the data format of these value labels from the Format pop-up menu.

Tip: For a cleaner-looking chart, it's a good idea not to show the minimum value when it's zero. If the minimum value isn't zero, however, you owe it to your readers to include this value label so they can discern the chart's baseline value.

The Steps field sets the number of values shown on the axis. Numbers spaces these steps evenly from the minimum to the maximum value; set the value to 1 if you want to display only the maximum and minimum values. Make sure the maximum value is evenly divisible by the number of steps or you'll end up with a display of inappropriate precision with labels reading, for example, 33.333 and 66.667. (Another option is to change the data format for these labels by selecting them and using the number-formatting controls in the Format Bar to reduce the number of decimal points, for example.)

The Category Axis pop-up menu lets you label your chart's data sets with their category names. Numbers typically has this option turned on for new charts, but you can turn it on or off by choosing Show Categories from the Category Axis pop-up. Choose Show Series Names to add the data series labels to every data point (these are the same labels that appear in the chart legend).

The Labels field immediately below the Category Axis pop-up lets you edit the dataset category names, but you can also do this directly in the chart itself: Double-click a category label in the chart, and type the new name. The Labels field, meanwhile, holds all of the data set labels, separated by commas. Type the names into the field or, even better, select a cell to use instead: Place the insertion point in the field and click a cell to add its cell reference. In Figure 22-11, the Labels field shows that Numbers is plucking the category names from cells in the Retail Sales chart.

When space is short or it's simply not necessary to label every data set, you can adjust the number of category labels by changing the "Label every *n* categories" field to space out the labels along the axis. When you do this, you can make sure that the last category name always displays by picking Show Last Category from the Category Axis pop-up menu.

Turning on more than a few of these labels can make for a mighty crowded axis; you can ease the congestion by displaying a set of labels at a different angle. For example, when you choose the Show Series option with a column chart selected, Numbers adds the series name for each and every column—but there's almost never enough room to squeeze all of those names horizontally along the X-axis. The result is that those labels crowd together in an unreadable and overlapping jumble. The fix is to display the series names vertically or diagonally: Select all of the series labels by double-clicking any one of them, and then choose an angle from the Format Bar's Angle pop-up menu or type an angle number directly into the field. Choose 90°, for example, to display X-axis labels vertically instead of horizontally. You can do this for any series of chart labels.

Data-Point Labels

All charts except scatter plots can slap a label on every data point to show its value, as you can see in Figure 22-13. Select the chart, and click the Series tab to reveal the settings for the specific chart type. Turn on the Value Labels checkbox, and Numbers adds the labels to your chart. If you later decide to get rid of them, flip the switch off on the same checkbox. With the checkbox turned on, you can set the position of the labels relative to the individual data points (bars in column and bar charts, points in line charts and area charts, and slices in pie charts). Choose a data format for your data-point labels from the Format menu.

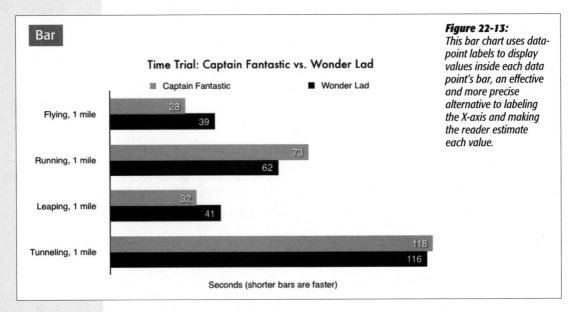

Figure 22-13:
This bar chart uses data-point labels to display values inside each data point's bar, an effective and more precise alternative to labeling the X-axis and making the reader estimate each value.

Changing Text Styles

Change the fonts for the entire chart at once by selecting the chart and choosing a new font from the Format Bar or Fonts window. Change the fonts separately for axis titles, labels, or data-point labels by clicking one of those items to select it. A selection square and two round selection indicators highlight the entire group of labels. Use the Fonts window, Format Bar, or Format Menu to make your adjustments. You can change each set of axis labels only as a group; likewise, you can change data point labels only as a group for each data series. Press ⌘ as you click to select multiple groups of labels.

Formatting Charts

With your chart data organized and labeled, you're finally ready to apply the wow factor to your chart. The graph that you get when Numbers first adds a chart to your spreadsheet is just a starting point—you can alter the appearance of just about every chart element. Like any other object in a Numbers document, you can resize, reposition, or rotate charts, adjust their opacity, and so on. But charts also get privileged treatment in Numbers, with formatting options that other objects don't have: Spin your data in space with 3D effects, add colors and effects to individual chart elements, make pie slices explode from the center, and fine-tune the position of bars and columns. This section tells you how.

Tip: The Chart Inspector and the Graphic Inspector have most of the controls for formatting a chart's appearance, and you may find it handy to have both open at once: Open one Inspector, and then Option-click one of the Inspector buttons at the top of its window to display another. Or choose View → New Inspector when you already have at least one Inspector window open.

Adding 3D Effects

Numbers lets you display your chart as a 3D diorama for your data, offering a slick presentation with a variety of textures that make the chart look like a physical object, with weight and presence. Eight of Numbers' chart types are available in 3D versions. (Sorry, scatter charts, mixed charts, and two-axis charts do not offer 3D versions.)

When you select a 3D chart, the Chart Inspector's Chart pane sprouts new settings, labeled 3D Scene, as shown in Figure 22-14. These settings let you change the viewing angle of the chart to turn it three dimensionally in space, as well as add lighting effects and depth. A second 3D scene controller also materializes next to the chart in the canvas; you can use either controller to tilt and swivel the chart—they work the same.

Tip: To adjust the shadow cast by your 3D chart elements, use the Graphic Inspector's Shadow settings. You can't rotate a 3D chart object the way that you can rotate other objects—you're limited to changing the viewing angle by working the arrows in the 3D Scene control.

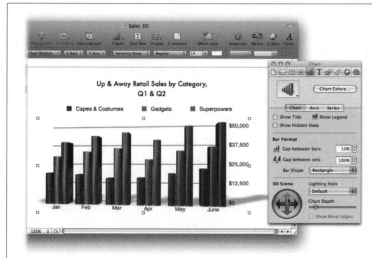

Figure 22-14:
The Chart Inspector's 3D Scene settings let you spin your chart in space: Click the vertical arrow and drag up or down to rotate the chart vertically; use the horizontal arrow to turn it left or right. To turn the chart freestyle, click the center of the arrows and drag.

The Lighting Style pop-up menu lets you change the lighting effects on your chart, and the Chart Depth slider sends the chart back and forth in space, making it deeper or more svelte as you change the setting.

For pie charts, the Show Bevel Edges option rounds the edges of each pie slice to create a subtle boundary between wedges. (Column and bar charts get their own special settings, letting you choose rectangles or cylinders for your bar shapes.)

Enjoy these 3D special effects, but go carefully. Although the result often looks remarkable, it doesn't always do your data any favors. By its very nature, the 3D effect skews the perspective of the chart, changing proportions to make some parts of the graph look larger than they are. If your goal is to offer an accurate view of your data, then 3D charts are *not* the way to go. But here's the thing: It's really *fun* to play with the 3D tool, and it's oddly satisfying to see Numbers spin and tilt your data with its sophisticated 3D modeling effects. And now here's some book saying that you shouldn't frolic with your charts in three dimensions. What gives?

The essential problem is that Numbers' chart data is only two dimensional; adding an artificial third dimension doesn't enhance your readers' understanding of the information. In fact, the skew and shadow of a 3D chart can actually obscure your chart's data by distorting its elements, making it difficult to accurately gauge data values. The bottom line is that these effects are window dressing—albeit incredibly impressive window dressing—that don't add substance to the chart. For all these reasons, 3D effects unfortunately fall into the category of "chartjunk" (see page 796). But if you absolutely cannot resist adding these effects to your chart, at least try to use 'em with restraint and keep the skewed perspective to a minimum: Limit the chart depth and keep the angle relatively flat in the 3D Scene control.

Adjusting Color, Shadow, and Opacity

The right combination of colors and opacity can add visual spark to your charts without distracting from its data. Every chart is made up of groups of objects that you can select and format in different ways. You can change the stroke, fill, and font color, choose an overall background color of the chart, or add elegantly subtle gradients to the bars of your data series.

When you select a chart at the object level so that its eight selection handles are visible, you can change the background color of the overall chart—the area that appears behind the data points. Choose a color from the Fill color well in the Format Bar, or use the Graphic Inspector's Fill section to add a color, gradient, or image fill to the chart background. (This option is available only for 2D charts; Numbers doesn't let you set the background for 3D charts.)

For the chart's data series elements—columns, bars, areas, pie wedges, and lines—Numbers provides a set of preselected palettes that you can use to quickly change the mood of the chart while making sure that the colors come from the same family. Click the Chart Colors button in the Chart Inspector or Format Bar, and Numbers displays the Chart Colors window (Figure 22-15). Choose a fill type from the top pop-up menu:

- **2D Color Fills** provide a selection of palettes with solid colors.

- **2D Image Fills** give you a selection of colored textures.

- **3D Texture Fills** give you a selection of textures intended for use with 3D charts (although you can use them with 2D charts, too).

After selecting your fill type, choose a specific set of colors from the second pop-up menu, and the Chart Colors window displays a preview of the six-color palette. When you find the color set you want to use, click the Apply All button, and Numbers updates your chart with the new colors. You can also apply a color to just one of the data series: Drag the color from the Chart Colors window and drop it on top of a data series element, and Numbers applies the color or texture to all of its data points.

Tip: If you like one of the built-in image fills or texture fills, but want to tweak it to display in a different color, you can add your own tint. Start by adding the built-in fill to a data series, and then select the series and use the Graphic Inspector to switch from image fill to a tinted image fill. Pick a color from the color well, and you've added a custom tint to the Apple-designed texture.

Figure 22-15:
The Chart Colors window lets you browse and select color palettes for your charts. To give a chart a color makeover, select the chart, and click the Chart Colors button in the Chart Inspector. Select the fill type from the top pop-up menu, then the specific color set from the bottom pop-up menu. When you've found a palette you like, click the Apply All button.

If you prefer to craft your own color collection, you can use the trusty Color Picker to shade individual chart elements. Quickly change the fill color of a column, bar, area, or pie wedge by dragging a color from the Color Picker's swatch or palette and dropping it onto the element to change—Numbers updates the data points and legend with the new color. Or, with a chart selected, click once on a column, bar, area, or pie segment to select that element, and Numbers selects all the other bars or columns of that data series, too. Use the Format Bar or Graphic Inspector to change the fill, or add a stroke (in 2D charts only) to outline the column, wedge, or line-chart segment; the stroke also appears in the legend's color square for the data series.

Tip: A great way to add some design nuance to a 2D chart without distracting from the data is to use a gentle gradient to fill your chart's bars, columns, or areas. Choose Gradient Fill from the Fill pop-up menu in the Graphic Inspector.

When you select a chart at the object level, the Graphic Inspector's Opacity slider and Shadow settings affect the chart's columns, bars, areas, or pie segments, but they have no effect on labels or the chart's background fill or gridlines. To change the opacity or shadow for labels, select the labels separately and then use the Opacity slider and shadow controls. To change the opacity of the chart's background, double-click the background to select it (circular handles appear at its corners), and then use the Opacity slider.

Note: Adjusting the opacity of columns, bars, areas, lines, and pie segments is an all-or-nothing affair. Even when you select a single data series, for example, changing the opacity affects the elements for *all* data series.

For bar and column charts, the Chart Inspector → Chart pane lets you choose whether the chart's bars cast shadows as a group, or if each bar has its own individual shadow. Pie charts offer a similar setting for controlling wedge shadows in the Chart Inspector.

Formatting the X- and Y-Axis

Numbers lets you show or hide each of the chart axis lines, as well as add and format their labels, tick marks, and gridlines. Figure 22-16 gives you a tour of these elements.

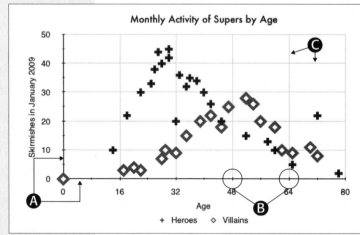

Figure 22-16:
Charts can include several different lines and borders to help your reader make sense of your data. Axis lines (A) are borders that run along the X- and Y-axis, separating the chart canvas from its text. Tick marks (B) notch the axis lines to give a sense of scale. Gridlines (C) score the chart canvas to help your reader eyeball data values.

The Chart Inspector's Axis tab is headquarters for these adjustments, letting you choose settings in the Value Axis and Category Axis pop-up menus to add or remove your chart's various marks and measures. (The options for these menus are also repeated in the Format Bar's X-axis and Y-axis pop-up menus.)

- **Axes.** Choose Show Axis from either axis menu to show or hide the Y-axis or X-axis, the lines that respectively run along the left and bottom of the chart.

You can also choose Show Chart Borders from either menu to display both axes and continue the borderline all the way around all four sides of the chart. (Adding or removing an axis or border is a purely aesthetic choice—the axes on which the chart is built are there whether you show their lines or not.)

- **Tick marks.** Both axis pop-up menus contain several choices for *tick marks,* the scale markings placed along the axis lines. Major tick marks appear at each gridline or label location along the Y-axis, and between each data set along the X-axis. Minor tick marks appear halfway between the major ones.

  Choose No Major Tick Marks to remove all tick marks—major and minor. Choose one of the three Major Tick Marks menu items to display the marks inside the axis line, centered on the line, or outside the axis line. No matter how you display your major tick marks, the minor tick marks follow suit if you turn them on using the Show Minor Tick Marks menu item. Numbers doesn't let you display minor tick marks without their major counterparts.

- **Gridlines.** Gridlines jump out from their associated axis at a 90-degree angle, with the goal to make it easier to gauge the value of data points (for the value axis), or to help separate the data sets (for the series axis). The category axis has a single set of gridlines that line up with its major tick marks; to turn it on, choose Show Gridlines from the Category Axis pop-up. The value axis has both major and minor gridlines: Turn them on by choosing Show Major Gridlines or Show Minor Gridlines from the Value Axis menu. (Minor gridlines are available only when major gridlines are turned on.)

Formatting the value axes for two-axis charts

Their name doesn't exactly shout it out, but two-axis charts actually have three axes for you to work with, the X-axis and two Y-axes. When you select a two-axis chart, the Chart Inspector accordingly gives you a separate group of value-axis settings to control the format of the second Y-axis, as shown in Figure 22-17. The Y1 pop-up menu controls settings for the left axis, and Y2 controls the right. Both axes share the same gridlines (controlled by the Value Axis (Y1) pop-up menu), but the two have their own settings for titles, tick marks, and value labels—including the number of value labels to display.

When you first add a two-axis chart, Numbers starts off by charting the first data series on the left Y-axis and the remaining data series on the right. You can customize this by choosing which axis you want each data series to use. To do this, select a data series by double-clicking one of its data points, and then choose either "Plot on Y1" or "Plot on Y2" in the Format Bar's Series Options pop-up menu. (You can also choose an axis by selecting a data series and picking an option from the Plot On pop-up menu in the Chart Inspector → Series tab.)

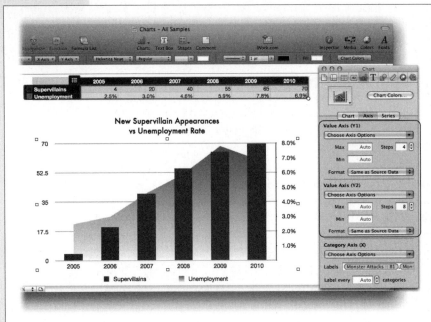

Figure 22-17:
When you work with a two-axis chart, Numbers gives you an additional set of controls in the Chart Inspector → Axis tab to let you format each Y axis separately. The Value Axis (Y1) options pull the strings on the left axis, while the Value Axis (Y2) settings control the right axis. Two-axis charts always start off showing the values of the chart's first data series on the left (Y1) axis and the rest of the data series on the right (Y2). Here, the two axes have a different number of value labels, and the right axis sports a set of tick marks.

Working with Pie Charts

Pie charts slice up your data differently than other chart types. These tasty charts show each piece of source data as a proportion of a whole, representing each data point as a wedge of the pie. That means that pie charts have no X and Y axes, and they can display only one data set—the first data set in the charted cells of your source table.

Practically speaking, that means the pie chart shows data only from the first row or column of the table's selected cells. If the data series are in rows in your source table, Numbers turns the first column into the pie chart, displaying the color keys next to your table's row labels. If the data series are in columns, Numbers turns the first row into the pie chart, showing the color keys next to the column labels. Each slice of the pie represents one of the data points in that set, as a percentage of the total of that data set. Figure 22-18 shows how it works.

Double-click to select a pie wedge, and then drag the wedge to *explode* it, moving it away from the chart's center as if the slice has been carved out. People often use this technique to emphasize a certain segment (or group of segments) of a pie chart to show, for example, what percentage of Megaville's heroes are bulletproof, as shown in Figure 22-18. To group two or more neighboring wedges together in a single exploded slice, select one of the wedges, then ⌘-click the others. Now Shift-drag the wedges away from the center, and they explode together as a single unit. You can also explode wedges using the Explode slider, described shortly.

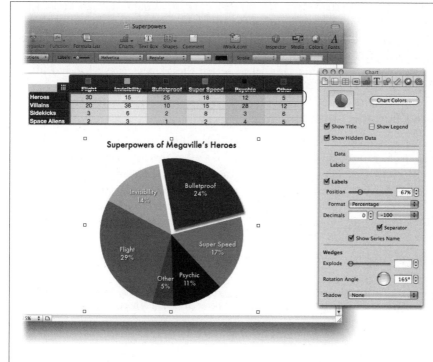

Figure 22-18:
Pie charts can display only one data set. No matter how many data sets you might choose in the source table, only the first one contributes to a pie chart—the others aren't included at all.

Here, the first row's values (circled) are charted; to choose a different data set, change the selection of charted rows (page 773) so that the data set you want falls into the first row. Or click the source tables' Data Series button to switch the data sets from rows to columns—in order to chart the proportions of heroes, villains, sidekicks, and space aliens among Megaville's flying population.

In addition to exploding chart parts, the pie chart also gets its own custom version of the Chart Inspector, shown in Figure 22-18. Unlike the other chart types, the pie's inspector has no tabs; all of its settings are shown in a single view where you can refine the visual flavor of your pie. Most of these settings apply to data series, the individual wedges of the pie chart. To apply your settings to all slices at once, select the chart at the object level; to make a change to just one wedge, double-click to select it. Here's the rundown of the custom settings for pie charts:

- **Labels.** Turn on this checkbox to display the data-point values for each wedge. In Numbers' standard settings, this value is a percentage of the whole, instead of the actual numeric value of the data point, as shown in Figure 22-18. If you want to show the original value, choose a new data format from the Format pop-up menu. Control the position of the labels by nudging the Position slider right or left; increasing the Position value shoots the labels outside the pie, reducing it brings them back in. Finally, choose Show Series Name to show or hide the data series names for the entire chart or for an individual slice.

- **Explode.** Use the Explode slider to move the selected wedge(s) away from the pie, or use the field's up and down arrow buttons, or type the number in the field and press Return. Press ⌘ while you click to select two or more segments in order to explode them at the same time. When the chart is selected at the object level, the slider explodes all wedges at once.

- **Rotate.** Spin a pie chart using the Chart Inspector's Rotation Angle knob. Click and drag the knob to rotate it, use the up and down arrow buttons, or enter a rotation angle in the box and press Return. As you rotate the chart, Numbers keeps the labels right side up as it spins the wedges around the wheel. If you'd rather rotate the chart *and* the labels, open the Metrics Inspector and use its Rotate knob.

Spacing Bar and Column Charts

The Chart Inspector → Chart tab (Figure 22-19) offers custom settings to manage the bar spacing for column and bar charts, as well as their stacked siblings. Adjusting this spacing also adjusts the width of the bars themselves, as Numbers narrows them to make room for the extra space or widens them to fill in narrow gaps. In other words, Numbers does what it can to work within the available space. If you find the bars getting too narrow, give Numbers more elbow room: Resize the chart by dragging its selection handles.

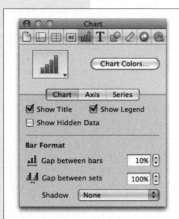

Figure 22-19:
When you're working with a bar or column chart, the Chart Inspector's Chart tab offers settings for adjusting the width between individual bars and between data sets.

The "Gap between bars" setting in the Chart Inspector determines the spacing—if any—between the bars within each data set. Zero percent means no gap, and 100 percent results in a gap equal in width to the bars. The "Gap between sets" box controls the size of the gap between data sets, and here again a setting of 100 percent creates a gap as wide as one of the bars. It usually makes most sense to have little or no gap between bars, and a larger gap between sets. To change the settings, use the up and down arrow buttons next to each box, or type in a number and press Return.

Tip: You can also adjust bar width and spacing by dragging the border of a bar. Drag a bar boundary that borders another bar in the same data set to adjust the "Gap between bars" setting. Or drag the outside border of one of the outer bars in a data set to adjust the "Gap between sets" setting.

Formatting Data-Point Symbols

When you work with line, area, or scatter charts, the Chart Inspector → Series pane lets you choose the symbol you want to use for each data series' data points. Double-click any data point to select its series, and then choose a symbol from the Data Point pop-up menu: circles, triangles, diamonds, squares, and so on. (Choose None to keep a low profile and leave the data points unmarked.) The field next to the pop-up menu controls the size of the symbol; leave the field blank to let Numbers adjust the size automatically, or choose your own point setting to make the symbols larger or smaller. Using the Format Bar or Graphic Inspector, you can also choose the stroke and, for hollow shapes, fill for the symbols.

For line and scatter charts, the Chart Inspector → Series pane also offers options to connect the data points with straight or curved lines.

Choosing Chart Types for Mixed and Two-Axis Charts

Mixed charts and two-axis charts are the multitaskers in the Numbers chart family. Both chart types can display each data series in a different chart style: column, line, or area. In a mixed chart or two-axis chart, select a data series and then choose the chart type from the Format Bar's Series Options pop-up menu. You can also make this selection from the Series Type pop-up menu in the Chart Inspector → Series pane.

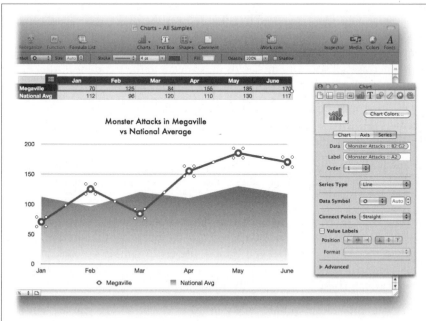

Figure 22-20:
This mixed chart uses a line chart for the Megaville statistics and an area chart for the national average. Here, the Megaville data series is selected, and the Chart Inspector's Series Type pop-up menu shows that it's a line chart. To change it to a different type, choose Column or Area from the menu.

Adding Trendlines

When you have lots of data points, it can be difficult to spot the overall trend at first glance. *Trendlines* help to call out the direction of your data by applying a mathematical model that "fits" your data points, boiling them down to a single line. The resulting trendline is a path drawn across your chart as a kind of visual summary of one or your data series. In Numbers, you can add trendlines for any or all of your data series. There are many mathematical approaches to doing this, and Numbers gives you a choice of which model to use for each trendline.

Note: Trendlines aren't available for stacked charts or pie charts.

To add a trendline to your chart, select the data series you'd like to fit by double-clicking one of its chart elements; or to add trendlines to *all* of your data series, select the chart at the object level. In the Chart Inspector → Series pane, open the Advanced flippy triangle, and click the Trendline tab. Select the type of equation you'd like to use to apply the trendline—the proper choice depends on the overall shape of your data values:

- **Linear.** Gives you a best-fit straight line, appropriate when your data follows a simple linear path.

- **Logarithmic.** Produces a best-fit curved line, appropriate when values increase or decrease quickly, then level out.

- **Polynomial.** Gives you a curved line that follows the peaks and valleys of your data, appropriate when you have rising and falling data, as shown in Figure 22-21. Choose the order of polynomial you want to use in the Order field—increasing the polynomial adds more detail to the trendline. Order 4, for example, produces up to three peaks or valleys in the line.

- **Power.** Produces a curved line appropriate to data that tends to increase at a specific rate. This option can be used only for positive values—data with negative or zero values are a no-go.

- **Exponential.** Gives you a curved line appropriate for data that increases or decreases at increasingly faster rates. Like the power option, exponential can't be used with negative or zero values.

- **Moving Average.** This one acts like a line chart, but draws its line through average data-point values. When you choose this option, enter the number of data points in the Period field that you want Numbers to sample for each trendline point. Numbers uses that number to cluster data points together in groups, and uses the average value as the trendline points.

Numbers lets you add trendline labels to your chart, letting you include the trendline in the chart's legend, show the equation that describes the trendline, or display the R-squared value for a trendline. (The R-squared value is a statistical

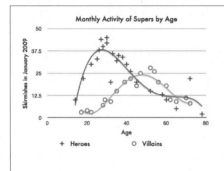

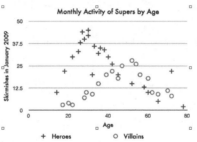

Figure 22-21:
Adding a trendline to the scatter chart on the left calls out the overall pattern suggested by the data, as shown on the right. Here, a polynomial trendline shows a curved line to fit the changing data for the two data series. These lines suggest that heroes are more active than villains but peak earlier in age.

measure of how well the trendline approximates the real data points; its fancy-pants name is the *coefficient of determination*. The value usually ranges from 0 to 1—the higher the value, the better the fit.) To add these labels, click a trendline to select it, and turn on the Label, Show Equation, or R^2 Value checkboxes in the Trendline tab of the Chart Inspector → Chart window. The Label checkbox adds the trendline to the chart legend; type the label's text into the neighboring field.

Note: When you display a trendline's equation or R-squared value, Numbers adds it as a free-floating label inside the chart. Drag it wherever you want it to appear within the chart's boundaries.

Adding Error Bars

When you're charting measurements that may not be precise, you can indicate that by adding *error bars* to your chart. These are little visual caveats that ride along with each data point to show the margin of error, warning the reader that the actual value could lie anywhere within the error bar's boundaries. You can add error bars to any or all of a chart's data series. To add them, double-click a data point to select its data series, or select all data series by selecting the chart at the object level. In the Chart Inspector → Series tab, click the Advanced flippy triangle, and click the Error Bars tab.

Note: Error bars are available for all chart types except pie charts.

The Error Bar settings offer two pop-up menus that determine where and how the error bars are displayed. (For scatter charts, these pop-up menus are repeated twice, allowing you to set up separate error bars for both the X- and Y-axes.) From the first pop-up menu, choose the way you want the error bars to be displayed:

- **Positive and Negative.** Displays full error bars, both above and below each data point.

- **Positive Only.** Displays only the part of each error bar that falls above its data point.

- **Negative Only.** Displays only the part of each error bar that falls below its data point.

From the second pop-up menu, choose the kind of error bar you want to display:

- **Fixed Value.** Displays error bars with the exact same margin of error for every data point; choose that value in the field next door.

- **Percentage.** Displays error bars based on a fixed percentage of each data point's value; choose the percentage in the neighboring field.

- **Standard Deviation.** Displays error bars based on the standard deviation of your data set; choose the number of standard deviations in the adjacent field. *Standard deviation* is a statistical measure of the how close or spread out your data values are. A low standard deviation indicates that the data points tend to be very close to the same average value, while high standard deviation indicates that the data vary wildly across a range of values.

- **Standard Error.** The *standard error of the mean* is similar to standard deviation but instead aims to show how accurately your data reflects the average value of "real world" data—useful when polling a small sample of the actual population, for example. The standard error takes into account both the value of the standard deviation and the sample size: the standard deviation divided by the square root of the number of data points. This always displays a smaller error margin than you'd see with standard deviation, and in general, the larger the sample, the smaller the standard error will be. (Of course, choosing this option over standard deviation doesn't instantly make your data more accurate, even though it shows smaller margins of error; it's simply a different way to measure it.)

- **Custom.** Lets you set error bars based on your own criteria. In the Positive field, specify how far above the data points you want the error bars to extend; in the Negative field, specify how far below the data points you want the error bars to extend. You can also add a cell reference to these fields, handy if you've calculated the margin of error in a table cell; while you're editing the field, click a table cell to add its reference.

Once you've got your error bars in place, Numbers gives you lots of options for formatting their display: Adjust their stroke and endpoints, color, or apply a shadow. Select the endpoints for a data series by double-clicking one of them, and the Format Bar shows the available options. You can also use the Graphic Inspector to apply these styles.

Beware of Chartjunk

With all the tools, labels, decorations, and effects that you can add to iWork charts, it's easy to get carried away. Marbled textures! Shadows! Gridlines! Tick marks! *Three-dimensional exploding pie graphs!* Whoa there, eager chart-maker, you're burying your information under a pile of distracting effects.

Statisticians call this stuff *chartjunk,* unnecessary visual elements that make your graph tough to read or, worse, distort its shapes or perspective in ways that make your audience misinterpret the info. Chartjunk is usually added with the best intentions—to make the chart pretty, to make it appear more "scientific," or just because the graphic tools are so much fun to play with. But don't lose sight of the reason you're making the chart in the first place: to convey complex information efficiently and in a way that draws underlying trends to the surface. If a chart element doesn't contribute directly to that goal, if it's merely ornamental, it's chartjunk. Let it go. Show off the data, not the chart.

Here are some common examples of chartjunk:

- **Shadows and 3D effects.** However you might draw your graphs, the *data* behind iWork charts is two dimensional, drawn from a table of values. Faking a third dimension by adding shadows or perspective only distorts your graph's shapes without contributing meaning, as shown in Figure 22-22.

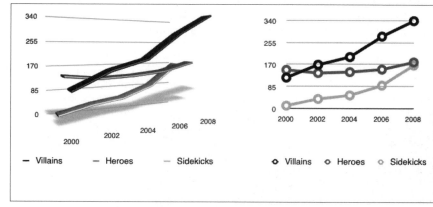

Figure 22-22:
Adding 3D perspective to charts adds no value to the data and instead skews proportions to make it difficult to properly estimate the values shown. Here, a two-dimensional line graph shows much more clarity than its 3D counterpart, whose values jut out of the field, exaggerating their value.

- **Ornamental shading.** Avoid complex patterns when coloring chart elements. Use the Chart Colors window with restraint and avoid its noisier textures (looking at you, wood and marble texture fill).

- **Unnecessary text.** Titles, captions, and labels are important to describe what your chart is about, but pare them down to the bare minimum, giving your readers what they need to understand the data, but no more.

- **Dense, dark, or heavy gridlines.** Gridlines, if used at all, should be a background element. When you have too many gridlines, or when they're too bold, they compete with the data points and make the chart difficult to read—the opposite of their intention. Consider whether gridlines are necessary at all, and if they are, make them skinny, give them a light color, or reduce their opacity.

- **Fancy fonts.** Your chart's labels aren't the main event here—keep their fonts subdued and appropriately small.

Confession time: Even though these elements and features are plainly distracting, something about them is irresistible. On the surface, they seem to lend a quality of slick professionalism. They just seem so…*fancy*. And seriously, it's addictively fun to tinker with the look and design of these charts. Keep in mind, though, that piling your charts with decoration doesn't give them extra authority or value—only the underlying information can do that. In the tough love department, if your information is so dull that it requires vertigo-inspiring 3D effects to give it interest, then perhaps you're not sharing the right information—or maybe you're not presenting it the best way.

The Right Chart (or Table) for Your Data

Every set of data tells a different story, and picking the right type of chart for that story is critical to communicating it effectively. Think twice before using a pie chart, for example. Although the goal of a pie chart is to illustrate proportions of values, it turns out that it's hard to distinguish the relative size of pie slices, particularly when they're close in value. This is especially true for 3D pie charts, which skew proportions. Column or bar charts do a better job of showing relative values, and with a more compact presentation, too, as shown in Figure 22-23.

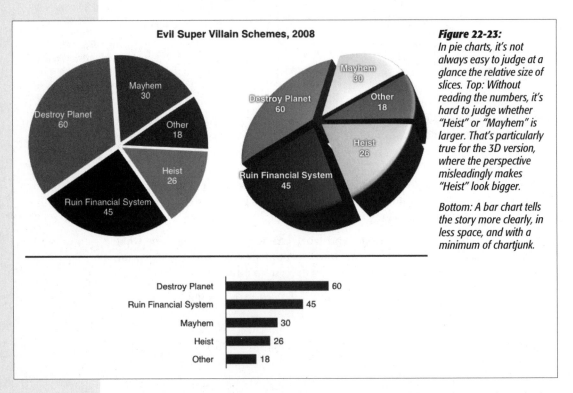

Figure 22-23:
In pie charts, it's not always easy to judge at a glance the relative size of slices. Top: Without reading the numbers, it's hard to judge whether "Heist" or "Mayhem" is larger. That's particularly true for the 3D version, where the perspective misleadingly makes "Heist" look bigger.

Bottom: A bar chart tells the story more clearly, in less space, and with a minimum of chartjunk.

It's even tougher to discern the difference between pie slices when you're asked to compare values in two separate pies. Here again, a column or bar chart makes the comparison clear, as shown in Figure 22-24.

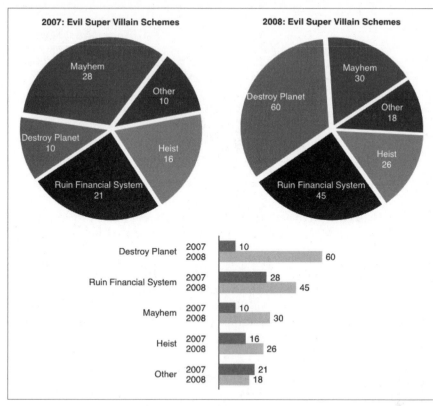

Figure 22-24:
When comparing two data series, don't use two pie charts; it's difficult to quickly scan for value differences, and the relative proportions can be misleading. After a glance at these bar charts, you might think there was much more mayhem in 2007 than 2008, when in fact there was actually less overall (28 vs. 30). Bar or column charts make it easy to see the differences quickly.

Stacked charts present similar problems of estimation. Although they're useful in showing cumulative values for groups of data, it's difficult to visually gauge the values of groups within each stack. This is particularly true as you add more and more values to each stack—only the bottom element in the pile is easy to measure against the Y-axis. When it's important to easily understand the relative values of each element at a glance, an unstacked chart is the way to go.

The exception is area charts, where stacked charts are typically superior to their unstacked counterparts. An unstacked area chart is just a line chart with extra ink; in most cases, that means chartjunk. If the chart tracks more than one data series and their data lines cross, one of the areas will obscure the other so that you can no longer see its data points (adjusting the chart's opacity can help with this, though). A line chart can do the job better than an unstacked area chart, as shown in Figure 22-25.

Tip: Unstacked area charts can still be useful for drawing a contrast with other data as part of a mixed chart, as in Figure 22-20.

Finally, some data may simply be too thin to bother charting at all. Sometimes the best way to convey a set of numbers is just to show it in its raw form, in a table.

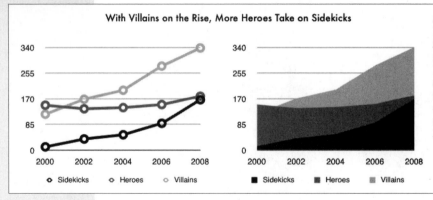

Figure 22-25:
These charts show the same data in a line chart (left) and an area chart. The area chart uses more unnecessary ink to show the same information, and the villain count is obscured for the year 2000.

Just because charts are prettier than tables, after all, doesn't mean they're always more effective. Carefully consider your goal, the nature of your information, and the best way to get your point across.

In general, tables are better than graphs for detailing structured numeric information, while graphs are better for indicating trends, making broad comparisons, or showing relationships. The data in Figure 22-23, for example, is really just a simple list of numbers, and turning it into a chart isn't especially enlightening. A table could do the job just as effectively (Figure 22-26).

Evil Super Villain Schemes, 2008

Destroy the planet	60	33.5%
Ruin the global financial system	45	25.1%
Cause mayhem and inspire chaos	30	16.8%
Simple heists	26	14.5%
Other schemes	18	10.1%
TOTAL	**179**	**100%**

Figure 22-26:
A table often allows more descriptive captions for your data than a chart. When you're working with a small set of simple numeric information, a table can often convey a message with more clarity than a graphic.

None of this is to say that charts aren't useful, or even essential. On the contrary, a terrific graphic can be eye-opening and cut instantly through a vague cloud of data. Numbers gives you the tools to create charts and graphs with exactly that kind of visual insight. But the same tools can also confuse and confound when used carelessly (the same, of course, can be said of pen and paper). Like all great design, the process of creating a clear and simple chart is usually neither clear nor simple. Make sure you give the job the care and thought it deserves and, when in doubt, hold back on the eye-popping effects.

Designing Your Spreadsheet Report

From their very first appearance on personal computers in the late 1970s, spreadsheet programs have always treated serious numbers so... *seriously.* VisiCalc, Lotus 1-2-3, Microsoft Excel—these programs have all presented spreadsheets exclusively as relentless grids of rows and columns, rows and columns, rows and columns. This blandly straightforward approach has the undeniable benefit of putting an unwavering focus on the data. You've got *grids* of numbers, and you've got *charts* of numbers—and that's it. It's all about the data.

When Numbers came along, it introduced something completely new, almost unthinkable, to the spreadsheet world: Design. Numbers blows up the idea of the grid as the single defining design element of a spreadsheet document. While every other major spreadsheet program presents just one grid per worksheet, Numbers lets you have as many tables as you like, arranging them on the canvas wherever they suit you. Instead of treating graphics as an afterthought like other spreadsheet programs do, Numbers gives you the same effortless access to media and design elements that you find in Keynote or Pages.

As the previous chapters have demonstrated, Numbers' tables can work a grid with the best of them, giving single-minded attention to your data and calculations when that's what you're up to. But Numbers can also see beyond the data to the overall design of the *document,* too, making it easy to create eye-catching presentations. Apple's message: The fact that your data is serious doesn't mean you can't have fun with its design.

With Numbers, you can blend your carefully created tables and charts with a variety of multimedia elements to create rousing reports like the template examples shown in Figure 23-1. Using text captions, pictures, and even movies and audio, Numbers lets you illustrate your data with elegance. This chapter shows you how.

Figure 23-1:
Numbers can create all the grids you want, but it can also create graphical reports with pictures, text, charts, shapes—even movies and sound. The Template Chooser (page 553) is a good place to browse for examples and inspiration. Here, the Comparison, Baby Record, and Science Lab templates offer three lively examples.

Working with Objects

Good news! If you've made your way through the Pages or Keynote section of this book, you already know how to design your spreadsheet. Working with the sheet canvas in Numbers is nearly identical to designing a Keynote slide or building a page layout in Pages. Like both of those programs, Numbers clears a workspace for you and lets you arrange *objects* in that space to build a designed document. You even work with the exact same set of tools and building materials, since all iWork programs share a common arsenal of objects: pictures, text boxes, shapes, tables, charts, movies, and sounds.

By now, you probably know the drill: Click an object to select it; drag it to a new location on the page; resize it by dragging one of the selection handles along its border; and use the Format Bar or Graphic Inspector to add effects, stroke border-lines, picture frames, and color fills.

Like Keynote, there's no such thing as inline objects in Numbers, as there is in Pages. Instead all Numbers objects are *floating objects,* which you place on the sheet canvas independently of the rest. That means that you can't add an image or shape inside a text box, for example, as you might in Pages. (You can, however, add images as backgrounds to table cells and other objects, as you'll learn on page 811.)

Because the details of adding and editing all of these objects has been covered else-where in the book, this chapter covers the mechanics of each feature only briefly, pointing you to spots where you can find more substantive discussion. Instead, the main goal here is to spotlight the *possibilities* that these tools offer, offering a hint of inspiration about just how different a spreadsheet can look.

First, though, let's be sure you know the fundamentals of working with objects. For a review of iWork's basic laws of object physics—how to select, move, and manip-ulate objects—head back to Keynote's description of working with objects on page 424. To learn how to style and format objects with the Graphic Inspector, flip back to page 264 to check out modifying object styles in the Pages section.

Got it? Here's your assignment. The science faculty at the sidekick academy for aspiring heroes have decided to lobby for three new departments and a fancy new training facility. They've worked up budgets, projected student enrollment, researched potential funding, and collected a variety of facts and figures to bolster their case. The teachers have collected the info in a big jumble of Numbers tables (Figure 23-2), and they think some thoughtful design may help them make their case better. In awe of your superhuman iWork abilities, the faculty have come to you for help with the layout of the summary page and the detail pages within. Time to spring into action.

Identifying "Back Page" Data

Great reports, like sausages, are at their most delicious when you don't know every last thing that goes into them. Both go down easier if you're spared the gory details. In fact, the essential goal of most final reports is to synthesize and summa-rize data rather than catalog every last detail. The first job of any document design is to figure out the parts of your data you want to emphasize and which can be tucked away.

Chances are, most of your spreadsheets involve totaling and subtotaling numbers to show bottom-line results. Particularly for a report's summary page—and often for inside pages, too—those final tallies are the numbers that matter. Depending on the type of document you're building, you may not even need to share the orig-inal raw data at all; at the very least, you can relegate it to one or more back sheets

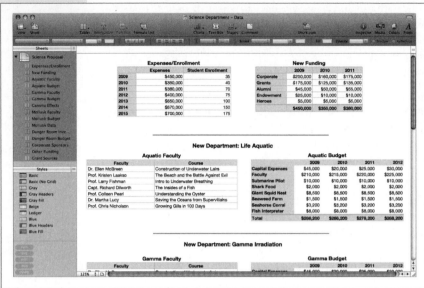

Figure 23-2:
The faculty's spreadsheet contains the raw data for their presentation. It's got some summary data (projected expenses, enrollment, and funding), followed by faculty and budget information for the new departments. There are also some statistics supporting the need for each department and a few tables of details about funding sources. As the designer, your job is to organize this data so that it's easy to understand, helping to forcefully make the faculty's point.

of your document. You can choose whether or not to print those sheets when you're ready to publish. If you're doing a scientific report on an experiment with thousands of measurements, for example, the data for those individual measurements should go on a back sheet while you put the summaries of your findings in sheets up front. Let Numbers sweat over your calculations in a back workshop while you parade the polished results around the showroom.

Your faculty colleagues from the sidekick academy have, alas, passed you a mountain of raw stats: many tables stacked into a single sheet. As you create their presentation report, you'll select the summary statistics to show on the front page, add increasing levels of detail on following pages, and create one or more sheets of "hidden" data that won't be published as part of the final result.

The decisions of what goes where typically evolve over the course of the design rather than all at once, but a few elements are usually immediately obvious. For example, the first thing Capt. Fantastic and the other sidekick-academy trustees will ask is how much this hootenanny is going to cost. The front page should show a chart of the forecasted expenses. As it turns out, this front-page decision also decides one of the tables that will go to the *back* page. Read on.

Hiding Charts' Source Tables

Good candidates for the hidden back page include tables that you plan to chart. As you learned in the last chapter, charts are always paired with a table. But including both the chart and its data is redundant and (often) unnecessary. You need the table *somewhere* in your document to keep the chart alive, but it doesn't have to be on the same sheet. Like the raw data described above, you can tuck charts' source tables on a back sheet and later decide whether to print it as part of your final report.

Here's the catch: You can't cut and paste the table to move it to a different sheet. If you do that, you temporarily remove the table from the chart and, when that happens, Numbers deletes the chart with it. Instead, you should move the table to the other sheet by *dragging* it in the Sheets pane. You can likewise do the same thing to move a chart to a new sheet.

For example, say that you've created a new Summary sheet for the science faculty presentation, and you've created a two-axis chart to show forecast expenses and student enrollments at once. Now you want to move the source table to a back sheet so that it doesn't clutter up the summary page. First, be sure that you've got your chart just the way you want it, paying special attention to the range of cells it's charting in the source table—it's difficult to change the charted cell range after you separate the chart from its source table (see page 777). When you're ready, create a sheet called Chart Data, for example, and drag the source table to the new sheet in the Sheets pane, as shown in Figure 23-3.

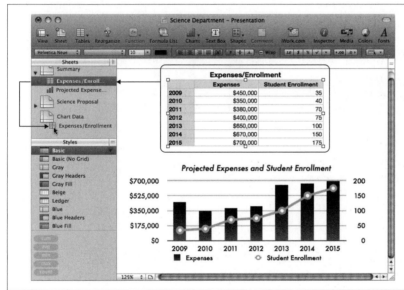

Figure 23-3:
To safely move a chart's source table to a new sheet, select the table in the Sheets panel and drag it below the target sheet's icon. Here, the Expenses/ Enrollment table is moved to the Chart Data sheet.

You're off and running with one organizational decision behind you. You've got a standalone chart on the summary page, and you've knocked off one of the tables that the faculty gave you. Now to tackle the rest. The process for deciding what goes where always varies according to individual and project, but a good approach when you're getting started is often to dash off some brief text that defines what you're trying to do—a summary of findings or statement of purpose. Even if this text doesn't wind up in your report, words often bring focus and help surface the key data to highlight. For the summary page of the faculty's presentation, you'll start with a title and some brief proposal text. Click back to the Summary sheet and get ready to do some typing.

Adding Text Callouts

To add a *text box* to your spreadsheet, click the toolbar's Text Box button or choose Insert → Text Box, and Numbers drops the object into the middle of the canvas, with the placeholder word, "Text". Go ahead and type something a bit more expressive, as shown in Figure 23-4.

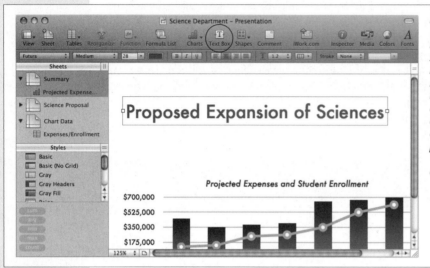

Figure 23-4:
This text box displays the title of the Summary sheet. Add a new text box by clicking the Text Box button in the toolbar, and Numbers deposits a two-handled object into the sheet canvas with the inspiring placeholder prose, "Text". Double-click to edit the text.

Numbers text boxes work just like free text boxes in Keynote (page 435). Unlike every other object in Numbers, these objects have just two selection handles, one on each side. That means you can adjust their width but not their height—at least not with selection handles. Numbers manages the height of text boxes automatically: As you enter text, these text boxes grow vertically to accommodate all of your typing. Likewise, when you delete text, the text box shrinks back down to size.

Tip: You can also add a text box by *drawing* it directly onto the canvas. Option-click the Text Box button in the toolbar and release the Option key. Position your cursor—which now has the I-beam shape—where you want one corner of your text box, and drag across to the opposite corner. Numbers draws a rectangle indicating the size of the text box, but only the width "sticks," since Numbers always sizes the height of text boxes to fit the text inside. When you release the mouse button, the text box outline remains at your desired width, one line high, and with the insertion point blinking—ready for you to enter your text.

Use the Format Bar, Fonts window, or Text Inspector to format and style your text. For more details about formatting text in Numbers, see page 595.

Drawing Shapes

Text boxes work well for all kinds of text—titles, labels, captions, lengthy descriptions—but when you want text to have a bolder presence on the page, *shapes* make for great alternatives. In fact, shapes are really just text boxes with a couple of special privileges: You can size shapes to any height you wish, and of course you can assign them any shape, giving you more flexible display options than a text box.

The ability to size a shape to any height adds an interesting advantage over text boxes because it lets you use the shape as a container for more than just the text inside. Figure 23-5 shows an example: The rectangle shape holds the proposal's intro text but also stretches to extend its border around a table of expected funding sources.

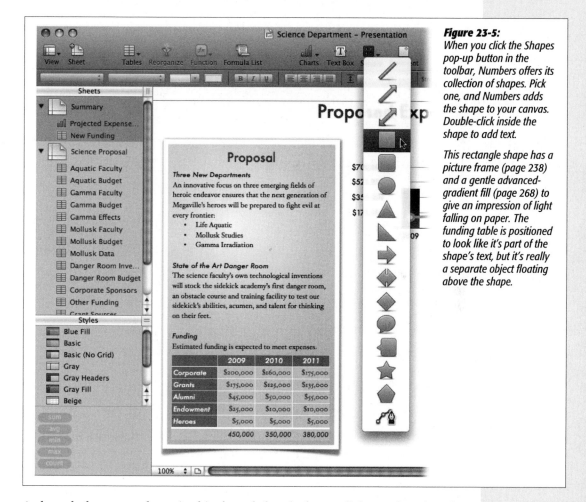

Figure 23-5:
When you click the Shapes pop-up button in the toolbar, Numbers offers its collection of shapes. Pick one, and Numbers adds the shape to your canvas. Double-click inside the shape to add text.

This rectangle shape has a picture frame (page 238) and a gentle advanced-gradient fill (page 268) to give an impression of light falling on paper. The funding table is positioned to look like it's part of the shape's text, but it's really a separate object floating above the shape.

As hoped, the proposal text in this shape helps shed some light on the other elements that should appear on the summary sheet. The text emphasizes the three new departments, suggesting that this cover page should include some content—perhaps some images or stats—to feature the new Life Aquatic, Mollusk Studies, and Gamma Irradiation departments. Adding three columns to fill out the bottom right corner of the page should work nicely, and here again shapes can help.

Shapes can play lots of useful roles beyond glorified text boxes. They're especially versatile as background elements to provide a color, texture, or gradient behind one or more design elements. Figure 23-6 shows how shapes create three shaded column backgrounds for the department content.

Tip: Like text boxes, you can add a shape to your spreadsheet by drawing its exact location and dimensions onto the sheet canvas. Hold down the Option key and select a shape from the Shapes pop-up button or the Insert → Shape submenu. Release the Option key and move the cursor into the canvas; it's now shaped like a crosshair. Drag the crosshair from one corner of your shape's position to the opposite corner, and Numbers adds the shape for you.

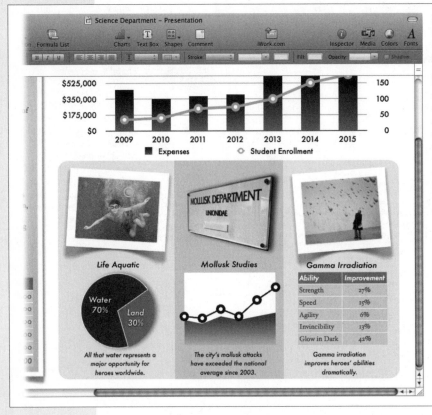

Figure 23-6:
Put shapes to work as visual "containers" for design elements. When you position a shape behind other objects, it adds a background or border for those objects. Here, a wide rounded rectangle surrounds all three department columns, with a single darker rectangle striping the middle to create three column backgrounds.

Shapes are, of course, also useful simply as shapes. Add arrows or stars to call attention to elements of the design, or create your own custom shapes and squiggles to draw any form you want. From there, you can adjust the shape's border and fill, giving it a colored, gradient, or image fill. For all the details about working with shapes, see page 241.

And hey, what do you know, adding that department content rounds out the cover sheet for your report, shown in its full glory below. The ever-attentive reader will also notice that these departments also managed to sneak in a new type of design element: Photos and other graphics are the next topic in this chapter.

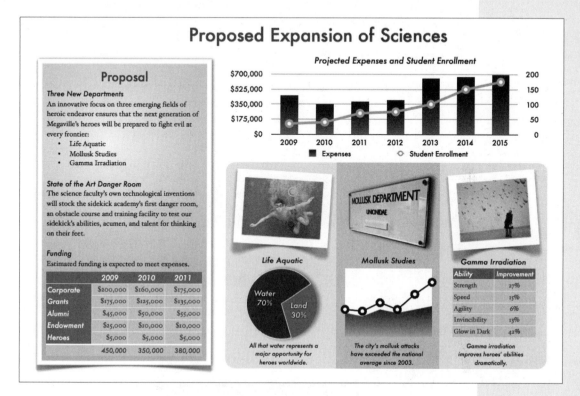

The final design of the proposal's cover page mixes a brief prose intro, a smattering of important big-picture stats, and teasers for the benefits of the proposed departments. The whole thing works as a kind of magazine-cover intro for the detailed data that will be presented within.

Along the way, the Life Aquatic and Mollusk Studies department columns added two new charts whose source tables were also tucked away on the back sheet, just like the table for the chart at the top of the layout.

Inserting Pictures

As you start designing the inside pages of spreadsheet reports, the content inevitably becomes denser, giving way to more traditional columns and rows of grid data. That makes the judicious use of design elements even more important, not only to set the personality and tone of your report but also to add visual breaks for the reader, making it easier to digest the page as a whole. Pictures are especially helpful here, and Numbers, like all the iWork programs, gives you fast access to your iPhoto image library (and Aperture, too, if you have that software installed).

To add a picture from iPhoto, Aperture, or Photo Booth, click the Media button in the toolbar to summon the Media Browser (Figure 23-7). Click the Photos tab, browse to the picture to use, and drag it to a blank spot on the sheet canvas. The cursor grows a green + sign to let you know that you're about to add the picture to the canvas. Drop it where you want it to appear. If the picture you want to use isn't in iPhoto or Aperture, you can insert a picture from anywhere on your hard drive by selecting Insert → Choose and browsing to the file to include, or by dragging the file's icon into your spreadsheet from the Finder.

Note: Be careful about where you drop your photo when dragging from the Media Browser. If you drop it onto a shape, Numbers turns that shape into an *image mask* for your picture, cropping the picture into the selected shape and removing the shape from your layout. More on image masks in just a moment.

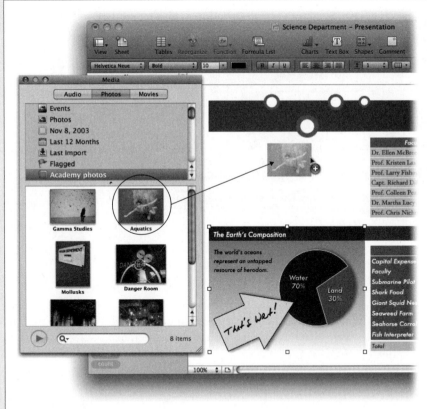

Figure 23-7:
The Media Browser offers you a convenient tunnel into your iPhoto library. Click the Photos tab to browse your library, including all of your albums. When you find the picture to use, drag its thumbnail into the Numbers document window and drop it where you want the picture to go.

After you place your photo, move or resize the picture as you like. In addition to the usual assortment of styles, shadows, reflections, and picture frames that you can add to any object via the Graphic Inspector, Numbers also gives you some picture-specific editing tools to transform your image:

- **Masks.** Add a mask to an image to crop it, specifying exactly what portion you want to show in your spreadsheet. Page 230 reveals the details behind the mask, or you can cut to the chase by selecting the picture and clicking the Mask button in the Format Bar, or choosing Format → Mask. You can also choose Format → Mask with Shape to crop your picture along the contours of the selected shape. Figure 23-8 shows the result of masking with a rounded rectangle.

- **Instant alpha.** Remove background colors with iWork's instant alpha feature, which makes portions of your picture see-through, handy for creating cutout effects (like the Mollusk Department sign in Figure 23-7). Page 234 makes the feature completely transparent, or give it a try right away by selecting the picture and choosing Format → Instant Alpha.

- **The Adjust Image window.** Fine-tune your picture's color, contrast, and levels with the Adjust Image window, which gives you sliders to calibrate every aspect of your picture. Turn to page 235 for the scoop.

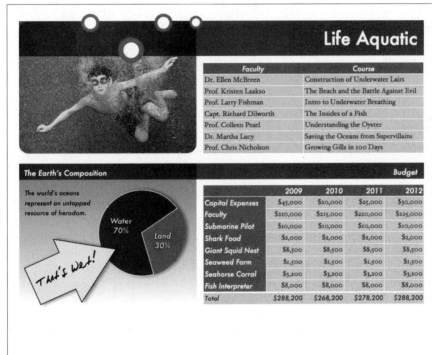

Figure 23-8:
The photo at top left has been cropped with the Format → "Mask with Shape" command, using a rounded rectangle to take the edge off its corners. A few other fun things are happening here, too: The bar across the top of the page has reduced opacity, giving it a translucent effect on top of the photo. Shapes are used to good effect here, with circles as playful bubbles at the top, an arrow callout at the bottom, and a rectangle giving form to the left column with a subtle gradient background fill. The entire left column acts as illustration while the right column gets down to business.

Adding Pictures to Table Cells

When you want to create a grid of pictures or otherwise add illustrations to your table, you can add images to table cells, too—kind of. When you drag a picture from the Media Browser into a table cell or paste a picture into a cell, Numbers adds it to the table as a *background image,* adding the picture as the fill image for the cell. Any content in that cell displays on top of the picture, and the picture itself replaces any previous fill color or fill image the cell might have had before.

You can't resize, mask, or otherwise work iWork's normal picture magic on fill images, but you can adjust its display somewhat in the Graphic Inspector. When you select the cell and visit the Graphic Inspector, you'll find the Fill pop-up menu set to Image Fill, with the image set to the cell's picture. Pick a scaling method from the pop-up menu to change how Numbers sizes the picture in the cell. The standard setting is Scale to Fit, which squeezes the entire image into the cell. For details about the other options and more about image fill, see page 269.

Working with Placeholder Images

If you're building your document on top of a template from the Template Chooser and the template includes pictures, Numbers makes it easy to quickly replace those photos with your own without throwing the layout out of whack. Those pictures are almost always *media placeholders,* temporary stand-ins filling out the design until you make a better offer. You can tell for sure by hovering your cursor over the picture; a tooltip materializes to tell you to replace the picture with your own image. To do just that, drag a picture from the Media Browser or the Finder to replace it. Numbers automatically sizes, positions, and styles your picture to match the placeholder's layout. (This often means that the photo is masked, too; see page 230 for details about how to edit the image mask if you'd like to make a change to how the picture is cropped.)

Reducing File Size

As the number of pictures in your spreadsheet starts to rival the number of table cells, you'll likely notice your document's file size expand at the waist. Images can be big; when you add lots of them, they can weigh down the spreadsheet and make it difficult to send via email. When things get heavy, Numbers has a way to help trim down your document size.

First, though, save your document; this technique won't work otherwise. After that, choose File → Reduce File Size to make Numbers cut any unused pixels from your spreadsheet. Here's what that means: Normally, Numbers keeps a copy of the full original image inside the document. This lets you shrink, enlarge, and mask the picture—and then later choose to undo it all to return to the original image in its full glory any time. Keeping that full-sized original, though, comes at a price of file size. If you've reduced or masked any of the images, choosing Reduce File Size tells Numbers to get rid of the unused pixels and treat this smaller image as the original. This saves space, but the catch is that Numbers no longer has the larger image should you decide to unmask or otherwise enlarge the picture in your document. The fix in that case is to throw the image out and then insert the original image all over again from your hard disk.

You can reduce the file size for all images in your document or for an individual picture. To shrink all images, choose File → Reduce File Size. To shrink a single image, select it and choose Format → Image → Reduce Image File Size. Either way, Numbers asks if you really want to proceed, as shown in Figure 23-9. When you click Reduce, Numbers applies the squeeze.

Note: Unfortunately this method doesn't do anything to reduce the size of images used as image fills, which includes all images you might have added to table cells. Only images sitting directly in the sheet canvas are affected by the Reduce File Size command.

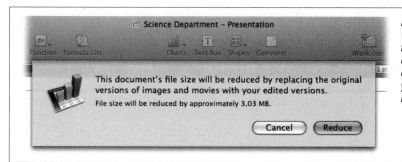

Figure 23-9:
When you choose to reduce the file size, Numbers gives an estimate of how much space it expects to get back and asks if you really want to do it. Click Reduce to proceed.

Choosing File → Reduce File Size also reduces sound or movie files in the document, likewise clipping any unused portions. For details about adding audio and video to your spreadsheet, see page 247.

If you're building your spreadsheet from a template that includes images, Numbers doesn't include those images in your document file, unless you tell it otherwise (or export it to a different file format). This saves disk space and is normally the right thing to do. If you send the document to someone else, after all, they have to have Numbers installed in order to view the file, and that means they have Apple's templates installed, too. This logic falls apart, though, when you're using a custom template that doesn't come standard with Numbers (see Chapter 25 for details about creating your own templates). When that's the case, you can tell Numbers to include the template pictures with your document. Choose File → Save As to save your document from scratch, and click the Advanced Options flippy triangle. Turn on the "Copy template images into document" option, and save.

Adding Movies and Sound

Movies in a spreadsheet? Hey, if accountants can play a starring role at the movie awards, then surely you can award movies a starring role in your accounting.

Video might be useful in a product list, for example, to show a walk-around view of one or more listed gizmos, and a "screencast" movie demonstrating how to use a complex spreadsheet could be a useful training aid. And in the case of the science faculty's expansion proposal, what could be better than an audio interview with superhero Captain Sargasso about how an aquatic studies program will secure Megaville's future.

Adding movies or sound clips to your spreadsheet works just like adding a picture. Click the Media button to open the Media Browser and choose either the Audio or Movies tab. The Audio pane displays your iTunes and Garageband libraries and playlists; the Movies tab shows your videos from iMovie, iTunes, iPhoto, and Photo Booth, as well as files and folders from your Mac's Movies directory. Make a selection and drag it into to the sheet canvas, or choose Insert → Choose and select the file to add. You can also drag a file from the Finder.

Double-click the audio icon or movie image to play the clip, and do the same to stop it. The QuickTime Inspector also offers Play, Pause, Fast-Forward, and Rewind buttons you can use to control playback. The inspector also offers options to limit the clip to a certain passage and how to loop its playback. See page 247 for all the details.

Tip: To trim the file size of the movie and sound clips in your spreadsheet, see the previous section on reducing file size. To limit the shrinking treatment to just one clip, select it and choose Format → Image → Reduce Audio File Size (or Reduce Movie File Size).

Speaking of Hollywood endings, you're no doubt anxious to find out how this chapter's little drama turns out. Does the academy's science faculty get their new departments? The only way to find out, of course, is to float the proposal and send it out there. That's the topic of the next chapter, which tells you how to share your spreadsheet in print and online.

Sharing Your Spreadsheets

You've got a spreadsheet loaded with stunning statistics, artfully crafted formulas, and insightful charts, all wrapped in an elegantly tasteful design. You, dear reader, are an unstoppable number-crunching machine. The only thing that can slow you down, in fact, is keeping all that genius to yourself. When you've got your numbers nailed and your functions formulated, it's time to get your document out there. Whether you're printing the family investment plan for your husband, emailing an Excel file to your boss, or sharing your Little League team's stats online, this chapter covers all the ways Numbers can help slingshot your spreadsheet out of your computer and into the world.

In the next few pages, you'll learn how to print your document, save it in other file formats, share it with other iWork programs, and send it to the far side of the Internet. Let's get to it—the world awaits.

Printing Your Spreadsheet

Like pretty much every other program on the planet, you launch a Numbers print job by choosing File → Print (or pressing ⌘-P). But before you commit your spreadsheet to actual paper sheets, you should do a bit of housekeeping. Select your preferred printer and paper size from the Document Inspector (Figure 24-1); now you're ready to look over your document's layout in Print view.

While you're working on your spreadsheet, Numbers gives you an endless canvas where you can stretch out with your tables, charts, and other design elements. Onscreen, at least, there's no such thing as a page break. When you send those hundreds of columns and thousands of rows to the printer, however, page breaks become a reality. Numbers provides a special Print view that lets you plan your

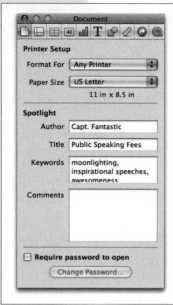

Figure 24-1:
The Document Inspector lets you select the printer you plan to use as well as the paper size for your document. Unlike most programs for your Mac, Numbers doesn't offer the trusty Page Setup dialog box to choose your basic printer options. Those duties are instead shared by the Document Inspector and Numbers' Print view.

hard-copy layout, so you can position page elements and scale the content to arrange your sheets across multiple pages in the best possible way. Chapter 17 provides all the details about using Print view, along with setting margins in the Sheets Inspector, starting on page 574.

When you've got your layout just the way you want it for the sheets you plan to print, you're ready to send it to the printer. If you plan to print just one of your sheets, select it in the Sheets pane. Choose File → Print (or press ⌘-P), and Numbers rolls out the Print dialog box, shown in Figure 24-2.

Tip: If you see only a tiny window with two pop-up menus instead of the full window shown in Figure 24-2, click the blue arrow next to the Printer menu to expand it.

Choose your printer in the Printer pop-up menu if you're sending your spreadsheet to a printer other than the one shown. If you want to print more than one copy, enter a number in the Copies box. If you want to print something less than the whole shebang, enter a page range, like *4* to *8*. This page range applies to what you select in the Print settings, below the Numbers pop-up menu. Choose All Sheets to print the whole document, or Current Sheet to print only the current sheet's pages.

When you turn on the "Include a list of all formulas in the document" checkbox, Numbers tacks the formula list onto the end of your print job. This formula list is the same thing you see when you click the toolbar's Formula List button or choose View → Show Formula List (see page 697). As advertised by the checkbox, the formula list includes formulas from the *entire* document, even when you choose to print only the current sheet.

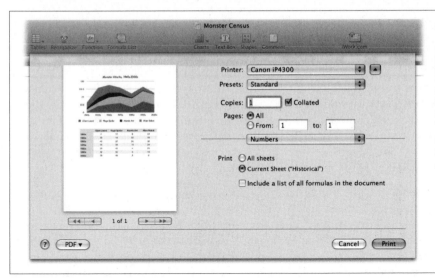

Figure 24-2:
*The Print dialog box gives
you a preview of what
you're about to print on
the left. You can use the
navigation buttons below
the preview image to flip
through your pages.
When you're satisfied
with your print plan, click
the Print button to put
numbers on paper.*

Ready? Click Print to send your spreadsheet to the printer.

Exporting to Other Formats

Paper is all well and good, but chances are that you're going to find yourself sharing your document electronically far more often than you put it on paper. When you're sending your spreadsheet file to friends or coworkers who haven't yet discovered the joys of iWork, Numbers lets you save your document in a handful of other formats to allow even these poor souls to receive the benefit of your labor. You can save your spreadsheet for editing and viewing in Microsoft Excel, Numbers '08, or CSV format. You can also save your document as a read-only PDF file; this is the only option that will always look exactly like your original, but with the obvious drawback that it can't be edited. Each of these choices have their strengths and weaknesses, and this section explains them all.

Note: *Numbers makes it especially easy to export documents as Excel or Numbers '08 files, giving them a privileged spot in the Save dialog box, as you'll see. All your options, however, are available from the Share → Export dialog box.*

Saving an Excel File

The heavyweight champion of the spreadsheet world is, of course, Microsoft Excel. It's far and away the most popular spreadsheet program out there, which means that sooner or later, someone's going to ask for your spreadsheet as an Excel file. Numbers makes it easy to save a copy for Excel: Choose File → Save As, turn on the "Save copy as" checkbox at the bottom of the Save window, choose Excel Document in the pop-up menu next door, and then click Save. (For details on *importing* Excel files, see page 572.)

Tip: If you want to email your spreadsheet, an even faster route is to choose Share → "Send via Mail" → Excel, which hustles the file over to Mail. Numbers exports the file to Excel, launches Mail, and opens a new message with the file already attached.

That part's easy; it's the stuff that comes afterwards that can be tricky. Numbers and Excel have very different ideas about how to lay out documents, and Numbers' export machinery often deals with this in disappointing fashion. The good news is that when you're saving a fairly simple spreadsheet with basic formulas and functions, one table per sheet, the leap to Excel lands gracefully, giving you the results you'd hope for.

But when you've put Numbers through its paces to take advantage of its document-design acumen, the result doesn't translate well to Excel, whose clunky design and formatting features simply can't keep up with Numbers. If your spreadsheet includes more than one table per sheet—one of Numbers' most fundamental features—the tables all get placed on separate worksheets in the exported Excel document. Other objects follow suit, scattering across several Excel worksheets as well. Even a single-sheet Numbers document can morph into many, many worksheets when it contains lots of tables, charts, or design elements. You wind up with a document that doesn't look much like the original.

Note: There are also a range of smaller cosmetic differences. Excel doesn't support custom controls like checkboxes, sliders, and steppers, so those don't make it through to the other side. Subtle design flourishes like shadows may not translate, either.

Exported Excel documents include a cover-page summary saying that the file was exported by Numbers and that its tables now appear on separate sheets (see Figure 24-3). This cover sheet also offers links to the worksheets containing your various tables and objects. The introductory text ends with the less-than-reassuring caveat, "Please be aware that formula calculations may differ in Excel." Alas, these calculation lapses do happen sometimes, especially when you use relatively sophisticated formulas that include lookups (page 744).

Note: Only the most recent vintages of Excel (Excel 2007 or later) know some of the fancier IF functions (like SUMIFS, for example). If your Numbers spreadsheet uses those functions and you open the exported file in an older version of Excel, you'll see the last calculated values of any cells using those formulas, but they'll act like regular numbers, not dynamically updating formulas.

Despite the summary sheet's cautionary message and the occasional slip-up, the exported Excel files are typically usable—your data, formulas, and *most* functions make the trip intact. But the Excel version will almost certainly require some significant reformatting and head-scratching to piece together when you've used Numbers' document-design features to create your spreadsheet. Numbers does its best to let you know about these problems, showing warning messages in the Document Warnings window after the import is complete (see Figure 24-4).

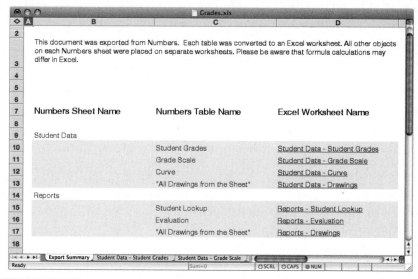

Figure 24-3:
When you export a Numbers document to Excel, the summary worksheet explains that the document came from Numbers and lists links to your tables, charts, and other objects—which are now scattered across several worksheets.

Tip: You can prevent Numbers from adding this summary sheet by exporting the file from the Share → Export window instead of choosing Save As. Choose Share → Export, click the Excel button, and then turn on the "Don't include a summary worksheet" option.

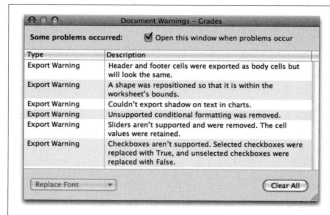

Figure 24-4:
When Numbers runs afoul of compatibility issues while saving your spreadsheet as an Excel document, it details the problems in the Document Warnings window.

So what's the deal? It's not that Numbers' exporter is *bad* so much as the fact that the two programs are simply quite different. Numbers' design-focused perspective doesn't fit well with Excel's workhorse worldview. Unfortunately, the features that make Numbers such a pleasure to use also make it difficult to communicate with Excel. That said, you can ensure that your spreadsheet will look substantially the same in both programs if you stick to one table or object per sheet and use relatively basic formulas. Of course, if you frequently exchange files with Excel users, this puts you in a frustrating position: You have to choose between designing great-looking spreadsheets that only Numbers can build, or hobbling your document to make it look the same in both Numbers and Excel.

If you're sending the spreadsheet to an Excel user for a simple review rather than for editing, then sending a PDF file is a happier alternative. These read-only files are always true to the look of your Numbers document but, alas, you can't edit them.

However you decide to deal with this exchange, it's best to go into it with a game plan. If you know from the start that you'll be sharing your spreadsheet with Excel users, make the decision early on about whether you'll send a PDF or an Excel file. It's important to keep these considerations at the front of mind when you plan to share with Planet Excel. Keep your spreadsheet simple while you're doing the back and forth, saving the high-flying design extravaganza for the very end when you no longer have to cope with the programs' differences.

Note: If you password-protected your Numbers spreadsheet, that protection doesn't apply to the exported Excel version. Numbers warns you about this when you save the file.

Exporting a PDF Document

PDF (Portable Document Format) is the way to go when you don't need—or want—people to edit your spreadsheet. It's also ideal when you want to ensure that anyone can read your document no matter what computer or software they're using—even if they don't even have a spreadsheet program. PDF files are read-only but they pay back this downside with their accuracy—they always look *exactly* like the original document.

To export a copy of your spreadsheet as a PDF, choose Share → Export and then click the PDF button. Numbers shows you the options for exporting to PDF, shown in Figure 24-5.

The Image Quality pop-up menu lets you choose among three levels of image quality, which also affect the file size of the exported document (the better the image quality, the bigger the file). Of course, this option is only important if you actually have pictures in your document. Assuming that you do, here's what the options mean:

- **Good.** Images are reduced to 72 dpi, appropriate for onscreen viewing but not great for printing.

- **Better.** Images are reduced to 150 dpi, fine for printing on an inkjet printer, for example.

- **Best.** No reduction at all. Let 'er rip with the top-quality original images.

The Layout pop-up menu offers a choice between Sheet View and Page View. Sheet View exports the entire sheet as one big page, while Page View chops up the sheets as if you were printing them. In other words, Page View exports the file as it looks in Print view (see page 573).

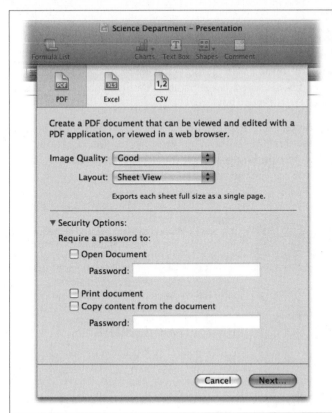

Figure 24-5:
The export window's PDF pane lets you select the image quality, layout, and password options for the exported document. To require a password, turn on the checkboxes for the actions you'd like to protect and then enter your password.

Click the Security Operations flippy triangle to add password protection to the PDF file for any of these three actions:

- **Open document.** The equivalent of putting a "do not pass go" sign in front of the entire file.

- **Print.** Selecting this option also requires you to select the "open document" option and uses the same password.

- **Copy content from the document.** This option has its own password, separate from the open/print option.

Note: If you already password-protected your Numbers document in the Document Inspector (page 570), that protection doesn't apply to the exported PDF. Only the settings you choose in the Share → Export window make their way into the PDF file.

After you've chosen your settings, click Next to specify a name and location for the file, and then click Export.

Exporting a CSV File

CSV stands for "comma-separated values"—the lingua franca of the spreadsheet world. Any spreadsheet can read this plain-text format, but that also means it's the lowest-common-denominator option. No graphics or formatting make its way into the final file, and every table is saved as a separate CSV file; Numbers creates a folder to save all these files.

To export a CSV file, choose Share → Export and click the CSV button. Numbers prompts you to choose the text encoding you want it to use, as shown in Figure 24-6. Unicode (UTF-8) should work with most programs. Click Next to choose a filename and location for the file, and then choose Export.

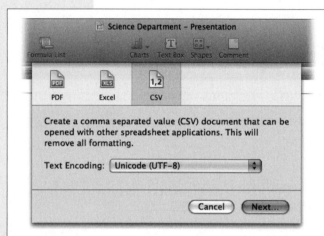

Figure 24-6:
The Share → Export window asks you to choose the text encoding for the exported file. Unicode is typically the way to go, but the menu also includes options for Western (Mac OS Roman) or Western (Windows Latin 1). Only old-school Mac and Windows programs are likely to want those formats, so you should choose those only when you run into problems getting a program to accept the Unicode-formatted file.

Saving Spreadsheets for Numbers '08

When you're sharing your document with friends who haven't gotten around to updating to iWork '09, you can save the document in the iWork '08 format. As you might expect, doing this strips out any features that are new in iWork '09. Here are a few of the features that won't make it through to the Numbers '08 copy of your file:

- Password protection is removed.
- Category rows are removed.
- Mixed charts are converted to image objects instead of editable charts.
- Error bars and trendlines are removed from charts.
- Advanced gradient fills are removed.
- New functions are replaced with calculated values.
- Connection lines are converted to line shapes.
- Custom, duration, and numeral cell formats are removed.

Sharing with Pages and Keynote

One of the best features of iWork is how seamless all the programs feel. They share the same icons, tools, and even features, often making it seem more like you're using a single program than three separate ones. New features in iWork '09 make that bond even stronger by giving Pages and Keynote documents the ability to communicate behind the scenes with your Numbers spreadsheets to fetch chart and mail-merge information.

Using Linked Charts

Numbers provides a much friendlier workspace for making charts than Pages or Keynote, which both rely on the clunky Chart Data Editor to spoon-feed figures to your charts and graphs. If you work with data of any size or update that data frequently, then managing your chart's numbers in your spreadsheet is the way to go, no matter where you want the chart to appear. In iWork '09, Pages and Keynote know how to work with that strategy; when you paste your spreadsheet's chart into a Pages document or Keynote slideshow, iWork forges a link between the two documents. When you update the data in Numbers, you can refresh the chart in Keynote or Pages to display the new data.

For more on this feature, check out the coverage for Pages (page 315) and Keynote (page 449).

Mail Merge with Pages

Pages can use any Numbers spreadsheet as a data source to generate mass-mailings. A typical mail merge plucks address or other contact info from the spreadsheet to address and print letters to individual customers, for example. But the Pages-Numbers mail-merge feature can just as easily use the columns of any Numbers table as data fields.

For more details, read up on mail merge in Pages starting on page 165.

Pasting Tables into Pages or Keynote

You can swap tables back and forth between all the iWork programs, and with only a few caveats, they work just fine anywhere you send them. Pages and Keynote both support formulas and functions, for example, so even sophisticated Numbers calculations make the transition to the other programs with no problem.

What Pages and Keynote can't do, though, is handle references to other tables. When you paste a Numbers table with formulas referencing another table, those formulas get removed and replaced with their calculated values. There are also a few other, relatively minor gotchas to sending your Numbers tables to the other programs:

• Category rows are removed.

• Rows or columns that are hidden in Numbers are removed.

- Comments added to Numbers table cells aren't copied.

- Checkbox, slider, setter, and pop-up controls are removed.

Distributing Your Spreadsheet Online

You might've heard about this thing called the Internet—it's a pretty big deal. The Web and email have of course become essential ways to share documents of all kinds, and Numbers offers a few options for getting your document online and into the mix quickly. Apple's iWork.com service offers a convenient way to review and collaborate on documents with a group, and the Share menu offers a pair of options to quickly catapult your document over to Mail and iWeb for email and website publishing.

Sharing on iWork.com

When you're ready to share a budget plan with a group of colleagues, a team roster with your soccer team, or a census of the city's monsters with interested heroes, iWork.com makes for a convenient online venue. The Web-based service is built right into Numbers and lets your group of invited reviewers check out your spreadsheet online, add comments, or download the document in a variety of formats.

For detailed info about using iWork.com, head back to page 332. For now, here's the executive summary, along with some pointers specific to using iWork.com with Numbers spreadsheets. To send a spreadsheet to iWork.com:

1. **Open the spreadsheet in Numbers and choose Share → "Share via iWork.com".**

   If Numbers prompts you to sign in, enter your Apple ID and password (see page 333).

2. **In the iWork.com invitation window (Figure 24-7), type the names of the people you'd like to view the spreadsheet, and enter the subject and message text for the invitation email.**

3. **If you decide to allow downloads from iWork.com, click Show Advanced to choose the file formats you want to offer.**

   The standard offerings are Numbers '09, Excel, and PDF, but you can choose any combination you like and also add Numbers '08 to the mix.

4. **Click Share, and Numbers sends your document on its way, showing its progress along with the estimated time remaining.**

5. **When it's done, Numbers lets you know and offers to take you to iWork.com. Click the View Document Now button to go there.**

   You can also visit the page any time from the Shared Documents screen at iWork.com: Choose Share → Show Shared Documents.

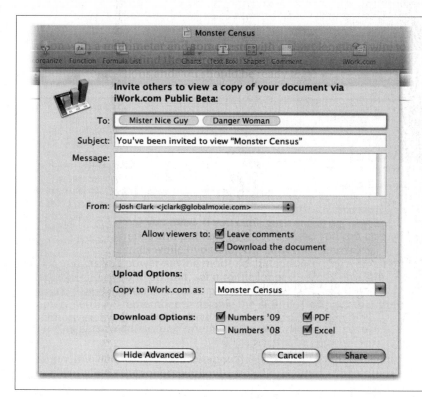

Figure 24-7:
*To invite people to view your
Numbers spreadsheet on
iWork.com, choose Share →
"Share via iWork.com" and
Numbers displays the iWork.
com invitation window. Fill in
your guests' names or email
addresses in the To field, and
Numbers looks up their info
in Address Book for you—just
like typing recipients in an
email message. Type the
subject and message text for
your invite. Then decide
whether to allow visitors to
leave comments or download
the spreadsheet; click Show
Advanced to reveal the
filename and download
options shown here.*

As you can see in Figure 24-8, the iWork.com view of your Numbers spreadsheet offers the same basic layout as it does for Pages and Keynote, with your document displayed in the center pane, sandwiched between the Navigator pane and the info column, which includes notes and publisher info.

The way the document appears on iWork.com is always faithful to your original layout—fonts, charts, and all—and looks just as it would if you were browsing it in Numbers. The layout is always the full Sheet view—there's no such thing as Print view on iWork.com. To see the Print view or otherwise edit the spreadsheet, you have to download the Numbers document from iWork.com and then edit the file in Numbers.

To add a comment about a specific table cell, select that cell and then click Add Comment. A comment bubble appears, tethered to the selected cell. Type your comment and click Post. You can move your comment bubble anywhere you want on the sheet; a yellow line connects cell to bubble no matter where you move it. When you click Add Comment without first selecting a cell, you add a free-floating comment that's not tied to any particular table cell or text. To reply to a comment, click the Reply button in the comment box.

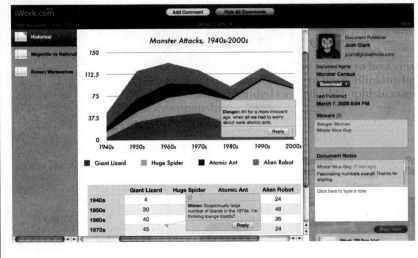

Figure 24-8:
Flip through the sheets of your spreadsheet by clicking the icons in the Navigator pane on the left (click Show Navigator if you don't see it), or by clicking the sheet navigation links at the top of the screen.

Although you can't edit the spreadsheet on iWork.com, you can leave comments. Add a comment to a specific cell by clicking it and then clicking Add Comment, or contribute a free-floating comment by clicking Add Comment without any cells selected. Comments for specific cells are tethered to those cells with a yellow line.

Note: Only the document publisher or the creator of a comment can move or delete a comment bubble on the sheet. Others can temporarily drag the bubble out of the way—to see the text below, for example—but as soon as you release the mouse, the bubble snaps back to position.

Hide a cell comment by clicking the – icon in the comment bubble's top-left corner. When the comment is hidden, its table cell continues to show the orange comment indicator to remind you that there's a comment about it. Hover your cursor over the indicator to reveal the comment temporarily, or click the indicator to make the comment stick around. Just like with Pages and Keynote documents, iWork.com puts an orange comment indicator on icons in the Navigator pane to show that those sheets have comments, hidden or not.

Note: You can't hide free-floating comments; the only way to remove them from view is to delete them permanently by clicking the X icon at the comment's top right.

When you download the spreadsheet in Numbers '09 format, the document includes all the comments added on iWork.com. (Comments aren't included in Excel, PDF, or Numbers '08 documents; they're also not included in the Numbers '09 file if you set the original file to require a password before sending it to iWork.com.)

Emailing Your Spreadsheet

Attach your spreadsheet to an email message directly from Numbers by choosing an option from the Share → "Send via Mail" submenu. Select either Numbers, Excel, or PDF, and Numbers fires up Mail and opens a new message for you with the file already attached. This is especially convenient if you want to send the document as an Excel or PDF file, since it saves you the extra step of exporting the file.

Note: The PDF version gets saved using any options you last used to save a PDF file. Head back to page 820 to review those options.

Adding Spreadsheets to Your iWeb Site

If you use Apple's iWeb program to maintain your website, blog, or podcast, Numbers offers a shortcut to add your spreadsheet in a new page on your site. Choose Share → "Send to iWeb" and select either Numbers or PDF. Numbers passes your document over to iWeb and creates a brand-new page with a thumbnail image of your document. (If you have several sites in iWeb, the program asks which site you want to edit before it creates the page.) On your site, the document appears as an attachment, and visitors can download the document to their computers for viewing.

Note: This feature requires iWeb '08 or later (either iLife '08 or iLife '09).

Creating Custom Numbers Templates

What's that, you don't feel so good? You've got a pain in your spreadsheet? Describe the symptoms: Constant reformatting of table colors and text styles; tedious application of the same familiar formulas; acute boredom with rebuilding the same handful of tables over and over again; accompanied by a throbbing ache at the temples. Friend, I'm afraid you've got a severe case of *time fritteritis,* a condition marked by terrible wastes of attention and mental energy. Happily, the treatment is painless, quickly applied, and features a 100-percent recovery rate: You need a custom template—possibly several.

Custom templates don't have to be complicated for you to feel their soothing effects immediately. Even creating your own custom *blank* template—an empty sheet—can be a huge timesaver when you prestock it with your preferred table styles, favorite object settings, and a savvy selection of reusable tables. Having your very own plain-vanilla starter document in the Template Chooser means you'll no longer have to change colors and text styles *every time* you add a new table or create a new document.

Templates become even more obviously useful when you have forms that you or others fill out all the time: time sheets, invoices, expense reports, worksheets for calculating the odds of acquiring superpowers from ambient gamma rays—you know, the everyday stuff. When you have these go-to documents available in the Template Chooser, you've always got a fresh form at the ready. These templates can be as elaborate as you like—multimedia reports, statements carefully branded with your logo, or complex grade books that you start from scratch every semester. You could even create an order form that fills in product info by doing lookups (page 744) from a catalog on a separate sheet.

This chapter takes you through the elements and techniques of building your own custom templates and adding them to the Template Chooser. You'll also find details about how to find and install third-party templates.

Anatomy of a Numbers Template

The deep, dark secret of Numbers templates is that they have no deep, dark secret. Templates are basically just regular Numbers documents that you happen to stash in the Template Chooser. When you create a template, you build a normal spreadsheet, load it up with tables, sprinkle in your design, and then choose File → "Save as Template". From then on, when you open the Template Chooser, you'll find your new template, along with any others you've created, in the My Templates category.

Your own templates work just like Apple's built-in beauties: Open a document from the Template Chooser and you get a clone of the original, model document as a fresh, untitled file. The spreadsheet is in exactly the same state as when you saved the original template. All the content, formulas, functions, tables, pictures—everything's there as you saved it. Even the window itself is the same—Print view, comments, alignment guides, and rulers come back to life as you left them. Creating a template, in other words, puts your document into suspended animation, ready for you to revive as an entirely new document at any time.

Your custom templates don't need to have any content at all, however: A template can open to a completely empty sheet. This might not seem like much of a time-saver, but even blank templates come loaded with table styles and a bevy of settings to define the look of new objects you add to your document. In fact, it turns out that creating a template like this is the *only* way to save your preferred settings for tables, objects, fonts, page margins, and everything else. Add a set of your own commonly used tables to the toolbar's Tables button, and you're saving some serious time.

Even when you're whipping up a multi-sheet confection of elaborate tables and functions, creating and choosing these background settings for your template is nearly as important as the content itself. Specifically, every template—actually, every Numbers spreadsheet—contains detailed formatting instructions for displaying each and every object. When you create a template, you can choose to leave these attributes in their standard (default) state, or you can modify any or all of them to create your own defaults:

- **Document formatting.** The paper size and orientation (vertical or horizontal), page margins, headers and footers, and page numbering settings.

- **Table styles.** The Styles pane's collection of prefab table formatting, including the default table.

- **Reusable tables.** A collection of table snapshots that you can drop into your document from the toolbar's Tables button.

- **Text boxes, shapes, and connection lines.** Set the standard text style, fill, border, shadow, and so on used for new objects.

- **Charts.** Choose the colors and formatting for every individual type of chart.

- **Pictures and movies.** Configure shadows, reflections, opacity, and outlines applied to new graphics.

Building Your Own Template

Start by opening a spreadsheet—it can be a document you've created in the past or a completely fresh spreadsheet from the template of your choice. Whatever you use, the idea is to start with a document that's already as close as possible to the template you plan to save. This spreadsheet will become the model document that you use as the basis for your template. Choose File → Save As right off the bat to save the file. *Don't* choose "Save as Template" just yet—you're just saving this as a regular Numbers spreadsheet. Give it a name like Gamma Ray Worksheet Model. This way, you can save the file periodically as you work on it, since you won't actually save it as a template file until you've completed your work on this model document.

Start off by getting your document and sheet settings squared away. In the Document Inspector, choose your preferred printer and paper size. Then, for each sheet that you plan to include, go to Print view and set up the headers and footers. Use the Sheets Inspector to set page margins and your page-numbering preferences. Now you're ready to start defining all the styles and standard settings for the document's various elements: table styles, text box styles, shape styles, connection lines, chart styles, image styles, and movie styles.

Adding Table Styles

What's the status of your Styles pane? Does it include any table styles that you never use? Is it missing some that you do? Having the right set of prefab formats always helps, and it's worth taking a few minutes to get this part right. If you need a refresher about the Styles pane and the role of table styles, head back to page 663 for a review.

First, clear out any styles that you don't want. Hover your cursor over the style you want to remove until a triangle appears next to its name. Click the triangle and choose Delete Style. (Numbers won't let you delete a style if it's currently set as the default table style; you can take care of that one later.)

If you already have sample tables in place as working models for the table styles you'd like to add, select them one by one and then click the triangle next to any style in the Styles pane. Choose Create New Style and type a name for your table style.

If you'd like to create additional styles, add a new table to the sheet and format the text, colors, and borders for the table's body cells, header cells, footer cells, and category rows. For each new style, choose Create New Style from one of the table-style menus as described above. When you're done styling the table, delete it.

Finally, choose the default table style for your template. This is the table that Numbers gives you when you add a new sheet, for example. Click the triangle next to the table style you'd like to use, and choose "Set as Default Style for New Tables".

Changing Standard Object Styles

Every time you add a new shape to your spreadsheet, Numbers uses the same graphic styles—the fill, stroke, shadows, and so on. The same goes for all the other objects, too; every spreadsheet has its own settings that determine the standard attributes of text boxes, shapes, pictures, movies, and charts. You can change any of these styles by choosing an object with the exact formatting you want and then telling Numbers to start using that object for its model instead. Going forward, when you add a new object to your spreadsheet, Numbers gives you an object that matches your selected model, with the same background, stroke, font style, and other formatting. These settings don't affect other documents, just the current spreadsheet—until you save it as a template. In that case, all documents based on the template will likewise add objects that match your selected settings.

For example, to set the standard style for a shape:

1. **Insert a shape into your spreadsheet by making a selection from the Shapes pop-up menu (page 241).**

2. **Format the shape with all the styles you want new shapes to have. Choose a fill color, stroke style, shadow, font style, and so on.**

3. **Select the shape and then choose Format → Advanced → Define Default Shape Style.**

You can similarly change the standard settings for every other type of Numbers object—insert the object, format it just so, and then define it as the default style in the Format → Advanced menu. From then on, new objects you add to your document will mimic the formatting of that object.

Note: When you define the standard settings for an object type, all the other objects in the document update to reflect the change. When you change the color of your default shape, for example, all other shapes change color, too, except for any that you *explicitly* set to use a different color. In other words, all shapes still using the original standard settings update to the new standard color.

Defining standard chart styles

Charts offer some complexities—and therefore some extra settings—you don't find in other objects. You can set the chart size, and you can independently choose the styles used by Numbers' various types of charts—kind of. Numbers offers you 19 varieties of charts to choose from, and you're supposed to be able to define a standard style for each type of chart, although in practice it doesn't completely work. In theory, you should format each of the styles the way you want it to look, and then choose Format → Advanced → "Define Default Style for [chart type]".

However, when you define any of the chart styles, it overrides settings you've defined in the other chart styles. Specifically, colors that you define for column, bar, and area charts also apply to their stacked counterparts, so default colors are always the same for both "regular" and stacked charts of each type. With that one exception, all the remaining default settings apply to *all* chart types. So if you set a chart with a certain number of gridlines for one chart type, the remaining chart types also get those same gridlines as their standard setting, no matter what settings you might have given them previously.

This means you should use the "Define Default Style for [chart type]" command to set most default settings for all charts at once, and then set the chart's primary colors one at a time for each chart type.

Adding Reusable Tables

The Tables menu lets you insert precisely preformatted tables, including content, formulas—the whole enchilada. This is insanely useful when you frequently add tables of the same size, or that use the same basic formulas, or even that contain the same complete content (your product catalog, for example, or a schedule of fees). The Tables menu, in other words, lets you prepare blank tables or content-rich grids and include them in your template without actually putting them directly into the template's sheet canvas. This means you always have a cheat sheet at the ready to help you sneak in your favorite tables, no matter how simple or sophisticated.

Create each of the tables you want to include in the Tables menu and, for each one, choose Format → Advanced → Capture Table and give it a name. To remove unwanted tables, choose Format → Advanced → Manage Tables. For more details about capturing reusable tables, see page 667.

Creating the Template Content

With all your background settings in place, you're ready to create the content that will actually appear in the sheet canvas, if you haven't already done so. Unless you're creating a blank template, this is where you polish off your speadsheet's design to make it look the way it should when you or others create a new document from your template.

Add your tables, including all the content, formulas, cell formatting, and placeholder data you want. Add any charts, text boxes, images, shapes, and other content; you can insert them on as many sheets as you like. Go ahead and name the sheets, tables, and charts. Again, *everything* you do here will show up in documents built from your template. Fix it up exactly the way you want it.

If the spreadsheet requires instructions, leave a note for others (or for yourself!) by adding a text box—even better, add a comment to the appropriate cell, or a sticky note to the surface of the sheet. Make sure that comments are visible when you save the template (select View → Show Comments), and your instructions will be visible every time a new document is opened using this template. (See page 600 for more details about comments.)

If you've added pictures or movies to your layout and you'd like to make it easy to replace those with other pictures, turn them into media placeholders. Select the object, and choose Format → Advanced → "Define as Media Placeholder". When you or others drop a picture or movie on the placeholder, Numbers automatically drops it in, replacing the placeholder and formatting the new object to match its size, position, rotation, graphic style, you name it.

When you've got your tables, formulas, and content polished to a high shine, the last step is to make sure the document window is set the way you want it. Select the sheet you want the template to display when it opens. Organize the order of sheets, tables, and charts in the Sheets pane. Turn the rulers on or off. All set? You're ready to save.

Saving and Organizing Your Templates

Now choose File → "Save as Template" and type a name for your new template, just as you'd like it to appear in the Template Chooser. Numbers likes to save your templates in a folder named My Templates. Follow its lead and your template appears, ready for action, in the Template Chooser's My Templates category.

Tip: If you ever want to make changes to your template file, create a new document from the template, make your modifications, and then choose File → "Save as Template" again. Give it the same name as the original to replace the old version.

You don't have to save your template file in the My Templates folder—you can save it anywhere you like—but it'll show up in the Template Chooser only when you save it in that folder, or in a custom Finder folder that you create alongside the My Templates folder. Here are the gory details:

Numbers separates all the templates you've created from its own stock assortment of templates, which it tucks out of harm's way. When you save your templates in the standard location suggested by Numbers, you find them in the My Templates folder by following this path: *[home folder]* → *Library* → *Application Support* → *iWork* → *Numbers* → *Templates* → *My Templates*.

To add a *new* category to the Template Chooser, create a new folder next to My Templates in the Templates folder. Name it for your new category, drag templates from the My Templates folder into it, or choose it when saving new templates. To rename the My Templates category, change the name of its folder here. Drag any templates you no longer need from the My Templates folder to the trash.

And that's it, you're done! No, seriously—you're done. Rest easy: Megaville is a safer place thanks to your heroic document-designing efforts.

Part Four:
Appendix

Appendix A: Installing and Upgrading iWork

4

Installing and Upgrading iWork

Installing iWork '09 on your Mac is a fairly straightforward process—the automated installer that comes with iWork takes care of tucking all the files into their proper locations on your hard drive.

To use iWork '09, you need a Macintosh with a 500 MHz or faster Intel, PowerPC G5, or Power PC G4 processor. Your Mac needs at least 512 MB of RAM (but a more functional minimum is 1 GB—more is always better) and 32 MB of video memory. You also need Mac OS X version 10.4.11 or Mac OS X version 10.5.6 or later, with QuickTime 7.5.5 installed.

Tip: To find out your computer's processor, memory, and Mac OS X version, choose → About This Mac.

The iWork installation consumes 1.2 GB of hard drive space. Be sure your hard drive has room for iWork and still has plenty of extra space left over—not only for the iWork documents you'll be creating, but also because operating a hard drive at near-capacity invites trouble. You should always have at least 5GB of free space on your hard drive.

iWork packages contain a DVD installation disc, so you'll also need a computer with a DVD drive unless you download the trial version from Apple's website and then turn it into the full version by purchasing a serial number from the Apple Store (see page 839).

Finally, to update iWork, use iWork.com, or email documents, you'll also need an Internet connection.

Note: If you have a previous version of iWork on your computer, installing iWork '09 leaves that previous version untouched—your brand-new iWork slides in alongside. You can keep that previous version around if you like, but to avoid confusion you might want to remove it from your Mac after you're satisfied that all is well with your iWork '09 installation. You'll find the old version in your Applications folder with a name like iWork '08 (unless you changed it to something different).

Installing iWork '09

There are two ways to install iWork '09:

- Install from the DVD, if you purchased the retail version of iWork

- Download and install the free 30-day trial version, and then purchase a serial number online

Either way, before installing iWork, make sure you're logged into your computer using an Administrator user account. If you have only one user account on your computer, it's an Administrator account. If you have more than one user account, then at least one of them is an Administrator account. Choose → System Preferences and click Accounts to view a list of user accounts showing who has administrator privileges. (If the administrator is someone other than you, have a little chat with her before installing any software; you'll either need her account password or she'll need to type it in for you during installation.)

If you're installing from the DVD, insert the iWork installation disc in your computer, and the disc's window appears on your screen (Figure A-1). If you're installing the trial version, you first have to download it, which you can do at *www.apple.com/iwork/trial*. Double-click the downloaded file, named *iWork09Trial.dmg*, and a window similar to the one in Figure A-1 opens.

Running the Installer

When you insert the iWork installation disc into your computer, the disc's window appears on your screen, including two icons for "Install iWork '09" and a "Read Before You Install iWork" file (Figure A-1). The Read Before file lists the system requirements, iWork features, and a few installation notes.

When you double-click the "Install iWork '09" icon, the Install iWork window appears, accompanied by a dialog box that reads, "This package contains a program that determines if the software can be installed. Are you sure you want to continue?" Click Continue, and the installer checks your computer's configuration to make sure it's compatible with iWork. Assuming it is, a brief introduction appears to let you know what iWork does. Click Continue, and the Read Me screen appears, displaying the same information as the "Read Before You Install iWork" file you saw earlier. Click continue to move to the next screen: the iWork license agreement that you can enjoy in 15 different languages. Click Continue and then click Agree to affirm you'll be bound by the terms of the license agreement.

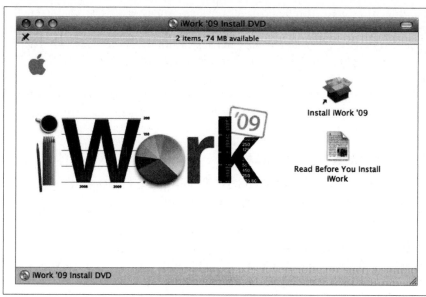

Now that you've satisfied the attorneys, the installer tells you where it plans to do its installing, and it has almost certainly made the correct choice. iWork has to be installed on your startup drive (or partition). If you'd like to choose another location, click Change Install Location and make a different selection. When you've made your choice, click Install, and you're off. The program begins copying files from the installation disc to your hard drive, keeping you up to date on its progress. A couple of minutes later, the "Install Succeeded" message pops up.

The installer deposits a folder named iWork '09 in your Applications directory, with the Keynote, Numbers, and Pages icons inside. Their icons now appear in the Dock, too. Click any of them to fire them up.

If you've just installed from the DVD, you're all done with this stage. Eject the installation disc and skip ahead to the next section.

Note: If you purchased a retail version of iWork '09—that is, you have a physical box and disc for the software—you don't have to enter a serial number. In fact, Apple doesn't even give you one in that case.

When you're running the 30-day trial version of iWork '09, the "Buy or Try" screen appears every time you fire up one of the iWork programs during your trial. Click Try to experiment for free for the first 30 days. When you're ready to purchase a serial number online, click Buy. Follow the instructions at Apple's website, and the company emails you your serial number. Be sure that you're signed in as an administrator when you enter the serial number, and enter it exactly as shown in the email.

If you enter the serial number correctly, when you type its last character, the Continue button becomes active—if it doesn't, go back and proofread your serial number or try entering it again. After you click Continue, iWork takes you back to your selected program, and you're finished with the registration process.

Note: If you use the trial and end up buying the retail version instead of shopping online, you can replace the trial version with the real one simply by installing iWork again, this time from the installation DVD.

Keeping iWork Up to Date

There's one more thing you should do before you start using Pages, Keynote, and Numbers: Make sure your software is up to date. Apple periodically releases updates for all its software. If you're connected to the Internet, you can make sure your new installation of iWork is fully fresh by choosing → Software Update. The Software Update window appears, your computer connects to Apple, and they have a little chat about which versions of Apple software you have on your computer and which updates—if any—are available for that software.

Note: Software Update expects to find Pages, Keynote, and Numbers in only one place: inside the iWork '09 folder, which is nestled inside your Applications folder. Don't rename the programs or the iWork '09 folder—that way, Software Update can find them where it expects to.

The results of this conversation appear in the Software Update window as a list of available updates, each with a checkbox that you can turn on to install that update, or turn off to skip it until another time. If you see updates available for Pages, Keynote, or Numbers, turn on their checkboxes, quit the programs if any of them are running, and then click the Install button (which reads "Install 2 Items" if you turned on two checkboxes, for example). The software updaters present you with their own versions of legal boilerplates, which you have to agree to before proceeding—at which point your computer begins downloading the files. If you have a high-speed Internet connection, this process won't take long at all; if you're connecting via dial-up modem, however, your computer may tie up the phone line for quite some time.

When the updater completes its job, you can launch Pages, Keynote, or Numbers and finally get to work, confident that your programs are absolutely up to date. Software Update periodically checks in with Apple all by itself. If it finds any updates you should know about, its window appears on your screen.

Index

G

Colophon

Rachel Monaghan, Sumita Mukherji, and Adam Witwer provided quality control for *iWork '09: The Missing Manual*.

The cover of this book is based on a series design originally created by David Freedman and modified by Mike Kohnke, Karen Montgomery, and Fitch (*www.fitch.com*). Back cover design, dog illustration, and color selection by Fitch.

David Futato designed the interior layout, based on a series design by Phil Simpson. This book was converted by Abby Fox to FrameMaker 5.5.6. The text font is Adobe Minion; the heading font is Adobe Formata Condensed; and the code font is LucasFont's TheSansMonoCondensed. The illustrations that appear in the book were produced by Robert Romano using Adobe Photoshop CS3.

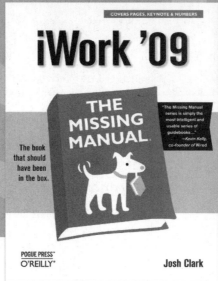